Bedfordshire Historical Record Society

2014

THE BEDFORDSHIRE
HISTORICAL RECORD SOCIETY

Contact details for the Society are on its website
http://www.bedfordshirehrs.org.uk

THE PUBLICATIONS OF THE BEDFORDSHIRE
HISTORICAL RECORD SOCIETY
VOLUME 93

PRIDE OF PEACOCKS

A memoir of a Bedford firm of auctioneers, estate agents and surveyors

Keith Lazenby

Historical introduction
by Professor Richard Moore-Colyer

To Tony & Pauline
with thanks for years of friendship
Keith [illegible] (and Sue)

THE BEDFORDSHIRE HISTORICAL RECORD SOCIETY

THE BOYDELL PRESS

First published 2014

A publication of
Bedfordshire Historical Record Society
published by The Boydell Press
an imprint of Boydell & Brewer Ltd
PO Box 9, Woodbridge, Suffolk IP12 3DF, UK
and of Boydell & Brewer Inc.
668 Mt Hope Avenue, Rochester, NY 14620–2371, USA
website: www.boydellandbrewer.com

ISBN 978–0–85155–080–0

ISSN 0067–4826

The Society is most grateful for financial support from the Simon Whitbread Charitable Trust and other donors who have helped make the publication of this volume possible

Details of previous volumes are available from Boydell and Brewer Ltd

A CIP catalogue record for this book is available from the British Library

Contents

	Page
List of Maps and Illustrations	vii
Foreword *Mark Baker, W. & H. Peacock*	ix
Preface	xi
Acknowledgements	xv
Introduction Auctions and Auction Houses in England: a brief history *Professor Richard Moore-Colyer*	1
Chapter One The Beginning	11
Chapter Two Horne Lane Sale Yards, Bedford	20
Chapter Three 10 Lime Street, Bedford	27
Chapter Four The Sale Rooms, Lime Street, Bedford	37
Chapter Five 6 Dame Alice Street, Bedford	42
Chapter Six 58 St Loyes Street, Bedford	53
Chapter Seven 26 Newnham Street, Bedford	57
Chapter Eight Baldock and the A1 Offices	61
Chapter Nine Property Auction Sales	65
Chapter Ten Surveys	72
Chapter Eleven Lettings and Property Management	76

Chapter Twelve
Advertising and Publicity 84

Chapter Thirteen
Fun and Games 92

Chapter Fourteen
Ministry of Supply Sales, Peacock, Merry and Swaffield 97

Chapter Fifteen
The Egg Packing Station, Bedford 103

Chapter Sixteen
The Rutland Road Store, Bedford 105

Chapter Seventeen
121–123 Midland Road, Bedford, Bartle Potter & Son 106

Chapter Eighteen
The Surveyors 1921 Club 108

Chapter Nineteen
W. & H. Peacock Reborn 111

Appendix 1
Compilation of the Property Auction Records, 1902–1988 113

Appendix 2
Property Auction Records, 1902–1988 115

Works Cited 421

Index of Personal Names 427

Index of Places 437

Subject Index 447

Maps and Illustrations

Cover

Robert Peacock holding the first sale held in the Robert Room, Fenruary 1980. Dudley Peacock is standing to the side of the rostrum.

Photograph: Harry Sedgewick. Courtesy of the *Bedfordshire Times & Citizen*.

Plates are between pages 112 and 113

1 Walter Peacock's first advertisement in the *Bedford Directory 1901*

2 Map of Bedford, *Bedford Directory 1902*

3 Earliest known surviving W. & H. Peacock property auction sale catalogue for properties in Wilden, Colmworth and Blunham, 10 September 1904

4 Instruction Book 1: 1902–December 1904

5 Auctioneers' Handbook, Baldock and Biggleswade, 1937–1963

6 Peacocks' sale yards, c. March 1926

7 Illustrated Property Register, June 1938

8 Plan of the Horne Lane sale yards and Egg Packing Station, c. 1950

9 Jubilee of Messrs W. & H. Peacock, 1951

10 Catalogue of 370 Commercial Motor Vehicles, to be Sold at Auction by W. & H. Peacock, Thursday, 26 March 1953

11 The Peacock family, 1956

Foreword

A former secretary once described W. & H. Peacock as, 'the longest running show in town', and to many a Bedfordian this still holds true.[1] The weekly auction and associated estate agency, established in 1902, quickly became part of the fabric of Bedford and the surrounding area, and over its long history numerous properties have been purchased through, and furnished from, the business.

Keith Lazenby, who worked for Peacocks for nearly sixty years, and was a partner for twenty-four years, has the in-depth knowledge and understanding to be able to give a fascinating insight into the history of the firm. In the following chapters, Keith describes in vivid detail the family atmosphere of working at Peacocks, the characters and the unusual history behind the firm's formation. It was a time when you could lose your job for going to war for Queen and country. Keith recalls memories of working with Mr Walter and Mr Harry Peacock, the founders of the business, and some of the interesting anecdotes of days gone by.

With his immense knowledge of estate agency, Keith also describes the local property history of Bedford and the surrounding villages, and gives an insight into the time when a three-bedroomed town house could be purchased for £1,500.

I have also been privileged to be part of the Peacocks' family, and to work with some of the interesting characters described. As a sixteen-year-old I was fascinated by the formal use of names, for example 'Mr Robert' and 'Mr Dudley'. It was a time, long since gone, when colleagues as well as bosses were referred to by their title.

Like Keith, I also remember fondly the first office I worked in, although possibly through rose-tinted spectacles. It was a two-berth touring caravan, which as each year elapsed, slowly and quietly sunk into the mud of the Horne Lane sale yard. I was also pleased to read that some of the old Peacocks' traditions Keith describes still exist to this day - such as buying cakes on birthdays.

To anyone with an interest in bygone Bedford, or an interest in the thrill of the auction, I thoroughly recommend *Pride of Peacocks*.

Mark Baker, W. & H Peacock
January 2014

1 W. & H. Peacock, and the various names the firm has traded under, has been known colloquially as 'Peacocks'. This convention has been used throughout the text.

Preface

This memoir is of Peacocks, not birds of a feather, but a family firm of auctioneers, estate agents and surveyors. The story spans nearly a hundred years in and around the county town of Bedford, through war and peace, good times and bad times. It tells of some of the characters, principals, staff and clients, as seen through the eyes and memories of the author and others, including former employees, clients and customers. This book is intended to reflect the period from 1901 to 1988 when the business was privately owned, but as the partners and many loyal staff continued association with their new masters, some references to more recent Wilson Peacock years have been included.

Peacocks has touched the life of Bedfordians over several generations through varied activities, some of which may come as a surprise to the reader. The business also extended far beyond the boundaries of Bedfordshire, into the surrounding counties of Buckinghamshire, Cambridgeshire, Hertfordshire, Huntingdonshire and Northamptonshire as well as into many other parts of the country. Peacocks has acted for clients throughout the world, in some cases for generations of the same families.

Contacts with Peacocks may have been associated with one or more aspects of the business, including: sale or purchase of residential, agricultural or commercial property, at auction or by private treaty; letting or leasing of property as a landlord or tenant; valuation of real estate or chattels for probate, sale or letting; land and building surveys; sale or purchase by public auction of furniture, antiques, general chattels, produce, poultry and other livestock, vehicles and other items; acting as insurance agents; storage of furniture and household goods; the Egg Packing Station; the conducting of charity auctions and other charity events; assistance with various local organisations.

Known simply as Peacocks to many people throughout its history, the firm has traded under various names during its development including: Walter M. Peacock, 1901; W. & H. Peacock, from 1902 to 1969; W. & H. Peacock Western & Co., from 1970 to 1975; Peacock, from 1976 to 1988.

By the 1980s many insurance companies, building societies and banks were competing with each other to acquire estate agency businesses, and approaches to the partnership were strongly resisted. Eventually, the changing nature of the property market, rising interest rates and other factors led the partners to agree to sell the business to the Trustee Savings Bank to become part of TSB Property Services Ltd. The partners all agreed to stay on with the business; Dudley Peacock and the author became directors of a subsidiary company, Wilson Smith Howkins Ltd.[1] In

1 The partners at the time were David Clifton, Jonathan Knights, Dudley Peacock, Alan Porter and Keith Lazenby. Wilson Peacock was a uniting of the Peacocks' business (with offices in Bedford, Sandy, Biggleswade, Hitchin and Baldock) and Wilson Smith Howkins of Kettering, another TSB acquisition, with seven offices, *The Bedfordshire Times*, 30 June 1988, p. 3. John Wilson founded the firm of J.

1988, after much deliberation about the goodwill associated with the Peacocks' name in Bedfordshire, the trading name of Wilson Peacock was adopted for all the old offices.

In 1995 the TSB Bank amalgamated with Lloyds Bank to form Lloyds TSB, when Wilson Peacock became part of the chain of Black Horse Agencies. Further changes followed in 1998 when Black Horse Agencies were sold to Bradford and Bingley Building Society, and the trading name became Bradford and Bingley Wilson Peacock. In 2004, the estate agency business changed ownership again to become part of the Countrywide Group.

On the 29 September 2000, a management buy-out of the auction centre sector of the business was effected. This was coupled with the very well-received change back to the original trading name of W. & H. Peacock for the Bedford-based part of the business.[2]

Since the formation of the business by Mr Walter Molesworth Peacock in 1901, shortly to be joined in partnership by his brother, Mr Henry 'Harry' Lionel Peacock, four generations of the Peacock family have served the firm and the community.[3] Mr Harry remained active in the business until he died on his way to the office in 1952, at the age of seventy-six.[4] Mr Walter continued his interest in the business until he passed away in 1957.[5] Mr Robert Molesworth Peacock joined the firm in 1921, succeeding his father Walter Peacock as senior partner in 1957. He continued in that role until relinquishing the honour to his son, Mr Edward Dudley Molesworth Peacock, in 1980.[6] From 1988, when the business became part of TSB Property Services, Mr Dudley Peacock continued to serve as a director of the company trading as Wilson Peacock. Mr Robert Peacock died in 1989.[7] Mr Dudley Peacock died in 2000.[8]

Francis G. M. Peacock, nephew of Mr Walter and Mr Harry and cousin of Mr Robert Peacock, having already qualified as a Chartered Auctioneer and Estate Agent, joined the staff as a furniture auctioneer and valuer in 1953, continuing until his retirement due to ill health in 1992. He died in 2011, aged 81.

Mr Dudley's youngest daughter, Susan, began as a Saturday assistant at the Horne Lane sale yards while still at Bedford High School. After gaining a degree in estate management, Susan qualified as a Chartered Surveyor after joining the

L. Wilson AAI in 1933 and the original office opened in Rushden. Later the firm became known as Wilson Smith & Partners. Howkins Sons & Fatt opened their first office in Northampton in 1932. The firm subsequently changed its name to Howkins & Co. In 1987 Wilson Smith & Partners merged with Howkins & Co. to form Wilson Smith Howkins, Wilson Peacock, *A New Name on the High Street* (1988), p. 1, pamphlet.

2 *The Bedfordshire Times*, 13 October 2000, p. 35 and *Bedfordshire on Sunday*, 5 November 2000, p. 31.

3 The first advertisement for the newly formed W. & H. Peacock was in *The Bedfordshire Times and Independent,* 27 March 1903, p. 1, on the previous week, 20 March 1903 p. 1, the firm had advertised as Walter M. Peacock.

4 Died 17 May 1952, Members of Bedford Modern School, eds, 'Harry Lionel Peacock', *The Eagle; a Magazine edited by Members of Bedford Modern School,* vol. 28, no. 6 (1952), p. 542.

5 Died 8 February in his eightieth year, Members of Bedford Modern School, eds, 'Walter Molesworth Peacock', *The Eagle,* vol. 31, no. 2 (Bedford, 1957), p. 145.

6 Hereafter referred to as Dudley Peacock as this is how he was known to both staff and clients.

7 Born 16 May 1903, died 25 January 1989, Members of Bedford School, eds, 'Robert Molesworth Peacock OBE, JP, FRICS, FAI', *The Ousel*, vol. 92, no. 931 (March 1989), p. 120.

8 Born 26 February 1929, died 1 February 2000, Members of Bedford School, eds, 'Edward Dudley Molesworth Peacock', *The Ousel*, no. 964 (March 2000), pp. 79–80.

St Loyes office as a professionally qualified assistant. By then Mrs Harry Fowler, Susan became an associate partner in 1987.

Clair Peacock, Mr Dudley's eldest daughter, also began as a Saturday assistant at Horne Lane while at school. After university and qualification as a Chartered Surveyor, Clair chose to specialise in the commercial field, working for large corporate companies dealing with their property portfolios.

Apart from members of the Peacock family, the partnership included a few non-family members, all of whom contributed significantly to the success of the various aspects of the business.

Mr Herbert J. Parrott, who joined the firm in 1908 as a book-keeper and accountant, became an auctioneer and was responsible for the Egg Packing Station. Mr George T. F. Robinson, who joined the firm in 1910, went on to become the partner in charge of the estate agency offices at 6 Dame Alice Street until his retirement on 31 December 1963. Following many years on the staff, Frank A. Jeffery, Jonathan M. Knights and the author were taken into the partnership from 1 January 1964, coinciding with the opening of the new estate agency offices at 58 St Loyes Street. Alan B. Porter, Brian S. Porter and Horace S. Dilley joined the partnership from 1 January 1970, when the businesses of W. & H. Peacock and F. W. Western & Co. amalgamated to form W. & H. Peacock Western & Co. David W. Clifton joined the Peacocks' partnership in 1984. In 1987, Christopher J. Horler and Anthony Shemilt became associate partners.

Peacocks could not have succeeded without a loyal and dedicated staff. Many people played a part in the progress of the business, often for all, or most, of their working life. Many staff did this with pride and affection, regarding themselves as members of a very special family. This included the young people who first experienced work by acting as part-time helpers at the Saturday market or, in later years, at Bedford Auction Centre.

Sadly, Mr Dudley Peacock collapsed and died on 1 February 2000 while at work on Wilson Peacock business, attending a site meeting with a client. It was only four weeks before he was due to retire on what would have been his seventy-first birthday. The high esteem and regard in which he was held was reflected by the fact that more than 420 people packed into St Peter De Merton Church, Bedford, for his memorial service.[9]

It was a privilege to have known Mr Dudley Peacock as a friend, employer and then a business partner for over fifty years. I was also fortunate to have known and worked with Mr Walter, Mr Harry and Mr Robert Peacock, together with all the other partners and many of the staff in almost every aspect of the business. At this point it seems appropriate to explain how I was introduced to Peacocks.

I was born in Bedford in 1932, the youngest son of Joseph 'Joe' and Evelyn Lazenby. My mother, a member of the Page family, was a Bedford girl with maternal links to the Summerlin family who were blacksmiths in Biddenham, Stagsden and Wootton. My father came to Bedford in 1917 to work for W. H. Allen Sons & Company Ltd as a draughtsman, and remained with the engineering company throughout his working life.

9 *The Bedfordshire Times and Citizen*, 25 February 2000, p. 7. The memorial service took place on 3 March 2000.

I started school at Elstow village school before attending Bedford Modern School from 1941 to 1944. Father's appointment as Allen's technical representative for the western counties meant a family move to Bristol, when I transferred to Bristol Grammar School to complete my education.

It was during an after-school duty as a librarian, when I listened to a career talk by a prominent Bristol auctioneer and estate agent, that I realised what I wished to do for my career. In 1947, my father was promoted to manage the pump contracts department back in Bedford, and in February 1948 I had to leave school when we moved again.

My father knew both Mr Robert and Mr Harry Peacock, and they kindly agreed to accept me as an articled clerk for three years. Formal articles were duly exchanged binding me to Mr Robert, which led me on to the remainder of my career of over fifty-nine years with Peacocks.

My book would be incomplete without expressing special thanks and appreciation to two people to whom I owe a great debt of gratitude. The late Frank Jeffery took me out on my first day at work on 8 March 1948, fired my enthusiasm for the job and shared his considerable wisdom throughout our time as employees and later as partners. His premature death in 1970 was a huge loss.

Very particular thanks are also due to the late George Robinson, then partner in charge of the Dame Alice Street office, who took me under his wing, taught me so much about all aspects of estate agency and introduced me to many established clients. Under his critical eye, I was given a desk in the office and much responsibility at an early age. George Robinson's long experience led to my learning many stories of interest about various events during the period from 1910 to 1948 that have been incorporated into this memoir.

Each day at Peacocks was different, offering new experiences, meeting new people and playing some small part in their lives. We always did our best to serve our clients, many of whom became friends. George Robinson always reminded the staff that our duty was to our clients who paid us!

Keith Lazenby
March 2014

Acknowledgements

This book would not have been possible without the contributions and continuing interest of many old friends and colleagues at Peacocks. Many are mentioned by name, but it has not been possible to include everyone in the text. Their recollections from the years before 1948 have been particularly valuable, together with various photographs and other memorabilia that have been generously loaned or given to me.

I offer very particular thanks to the editor, Mrs Nicola Avery, who has done so much to convert my efforts into the finished article. Nicola's enthusiasm, enquiring mind, eye to detail and ability to identify the many references has been immensely valuable.

I also wish to gratefully acknowledge Professor Richard Moore-Colyer for writing the informative introduction and Richard Wildman for his encouragement after reading the draft volume. I would also like to thank Richard for his help with sources relating to some of the principals mentioned in the memoir. For his assistance with proof-reading the text, I would like to thank Stuart Antrobus, and for her newspaper research, Mrs Margaret Avery.

This volume would not have been possible without access to the collections and the support of the staff at Bedford Central Library and Bedfordshire and Luton Archives and Records Service.

For helping with enquiries I would like to thank: John Scott, Acting Reeve, Fen Reeves of Biggleswade Common, for information on past and present office holders; Nicholas Bond, Press Officer of the Royal Agricultural Benevolent Institution for information on the Peacock family's work with that organisation; and Kate O'Brien, Archives Researcher, BBC Written Archives Centre, for information on Cecil Clarabut.

Finally, I must acknowledge Mark Baker and Sally Lewis of W. & H. Peacock for their ongoing help and encouragement and generous promotion of the book to their extensive clientele.

Introduction
Auctions and Auction Houses in England: a brief history

When Roman emperors, generals and grandees employed auction procedures to dispose of booty acquired by conquest or plunder, they were pursuing a method of sale already of great antiquity. Moreover, as they bid excitedly at the periodic slave sales in the Forum, wealthy citizens may not have realised that half a millennium earlier their Babylonian forbears were enabled to buy girls of marriageable age via a form of carefully-regulated auction. Again, long after Rome and her empire had become a rather hazy memory, the authorities in far-away China used auction methods to sell off the belongings of deceased monks.[1]

The subsequent history of the auction system in medieval and early modern Europe is rather obscure and while there are hints that auction methods were in use in England in the late fourteen hundreds, there is little hard evidence for the practice before the close of the seventeenth century. By this time, both notices of auctions and details of conditions of sale began to appear, with no less a luminary than Samuel Pepys recording that on 6 November 1660 two ships were sold in London 'by an inch of candle'. Here we have an early mention of the so-called 'English Method' whereby an inch of candle was lit and the person offering the final bid before the candle burned to its base and the guttering flame petered out became the purchaser of the item under auction. This exciting, if slow procedure became for generations the principal means of auction in England. Alternatively, the 'Dutch Method' was available. In this scenario the auctioneer would put up a particular lot at a high price, which he would progressively reduce until a buyer emerged who was prepared to purchase at the latest reduced price. This arrangement remained popular for centuries and continues to be employed from time-to-time today. The leisurely 'English Method', however, has long given way to the process of selling by successively increasing bids which became the predominant means whereby the auctioneer plied his craft.

The auction was to become a major mode of disposal of goods of every description, from the great landed estate to the accumulated bric-a-brac of a suburban attic; from the renowned Old Master painting to a deceased uncle's stamp collection; from the thoroughbred racehorse to the broken-down hunter. Anything and everything could change ownership through the medium of the auction room. This being the case, the premises of the early auctioneers became the haunt of those eighteenth century connoisseurs and collectors hoping to benefit from the discomfiture of the great magnates and merchant princes whose profligacy or family misfortunes obliged them to part with some or all of their art treasures.

1 B. Learmount, *A History of the Auction* (Iver, 1985), pp. 6–11.

With the growth of overseas trade, the settling and exploitation of colonial territories and the consequent expansion of national and personal wealth, there arose an ever-increasing demand for fine furniture and works of art from both the established aristocracy and the burgeoning merchant and professional classes. By the early decades of the eighteenth century demand could no longer be satisfied by the productions of home-bred artists and craftsmen with the result that London-based dealers/auctioneers began to travel to the European continent to seek out treasures for sale to their wealthy clientele. So much was this the case that between 1722 and 1760 no less than 18,000 foreign paintings (many of them from the southern Netherlands) arrived in Britain, and British auction rooms became among the most active in Europe.[2]

Many of the early sales of fine art, books and furniture initially took place in the London taverns and coffee houses, with Garraway's Coffee House in Cornhill being among the more important venues.[3] By the 1730s, however, the principal auctioneers had begun to establish their own salerooms. Typically, the shrewd Christopher Cock, who cleverly exploited newspapers and periodicals to advertise his activities, set up premises in Covent Garden where he sold land, furniture, artworks and bankrupt stock of all descriptions. Meanwhile, the bookseller Samuel Baker auctioned the contents of Sir John Stanley's library in 1744, the year his nephew and heir John Sotheby succeeded to the business and went on to found the great international auction house.[4] Two decades later James Christie held a sale in his Pall Mall premises, the rather unpromising list of goods on offer including two chamber pots, a pair of sheets and four irons. But from such beginnings great events are grown and in 1778 Christies sold Sir Robert Walpole's celebrated collection of pictures, achieving another coup in 1795 with the successful five-day sale of the contents of the studio of Sir Joshua Reynolds.[5] Sotheby's were subsequently to auction such choice collections as Napoleon's St Helena library, while Henry Phillips, who had worked for James Christie before setting up his own business in 1797, had the good fortune to sell the fabulous contents of Fonthill Abbey, home of the author, collector and eccentric, William Beckford. Together with Christies, Sotheby's, Phillips' and Bonham's (established in Leicester Street by Charles Bonham and George Jones in 1793) there were more than sixty London-based auctioneers by the close of the eighteenth century.[6] As these firms grew London became a major international centre and world leader in the fine art market. When the eighteenth century gave way to the nineteenth, direct aristocratic patronage began to wane, and as English artists began to find commissions harder to come by many turned to the auction house as a means of disposing of their works. Concurrently the auction houses became a lifeline for landowners crippled by mortgages, taxes and annuity payments who were desperate to raise ready cash by the sale of works of art and library contents.[7]

2 C. Gould and S. Mesplede, *Marketing Art in the British Isles: 1700 to the Present* (Farnham, 2012), pp. 5–22.
3 Learmount, *A History of the Auction*, p. 47.
4 www.sothebys.com (accessed October 2013).
5 www.christies.com (accessed October 2013).
6 Learmount, *A History of the Auction*, p. 48.
7 S. Kelly, '"This Dangerous Game": Rousseau, Diaz and the Issues of the Auction in the Marketing

If London became the centre of the art trade, the craving of the expanding middle classes for goods and chattels to reflect their rising status was mirrored by a growth in the market for luxury goods in the provinces and a consequent expansion in the number of local auctioneers and auction houses. It is difficult to establish precise numbers of professional auctioneers before the nineteenth century, but evidence from newspapers and contemporary accounts testifies to their local importance. When the household goods of the late Leonard Ayray of Kendal in Westmorland were sold off in December 1690 and January 1691, the event was a major spectacle.[8] To this and kindred local sales were attracted genuine purchasers along with a wide assortment of sensation-seekers, gossips, neighbours and ne'er-do-wells. Many of these saw the occasion as an opportunity to socialise, while those with a taste for *schadenfreude* probably enjoyed speculating on the nature of the misfortune which had enforced the sale. Others yet may have attended and participated out of a sense of sympathy and charity for a popular individual fallen on hard times.

In the case of major country house dispersals, sales tended to be held on the premises, the house and its contents being open for viewing several days before the auction itself. The magnificent Kirby Hall to the east of Corby in Northamptonshire was built by Sir Christopher Hatton, Lord Chancellor to Elizabeth I, and had remained for almost two centuries the centre of one of the county's foremost estates. Upon the death of Edward Finch-Hatton in 1772 a major sale of the contents of the house took place under the auspices of the auctioneers Langford and Sons. This was the prelude to three sales in which the whole contents of the vast mansion were dispersed as the Finch-Hatton family concentrated their resources on their other properties. The sales included paintings by Rubens, Van Dyck, Rembrandt and Ruysdael along with such humble items as chicken coops, old oak furniture and earthenware pottery. With 'an old viol de gambo (sic)', 'an old door' and '6 old tables' in the august company of the Old Masters listed in the 1772 catalogue, the sale provided something for everyone's taste and pocket.[9] Langford's would hold other sales at Kirby Hall early in the next century until the great Elizabethan/Jacobean palace was emptied and began to decline towards the forlorn abandoned state in which it remained until recent years.

The fate of Kirby Hall reflected that of many great country houses from the mid nineteenth to the mid twentieth century. Profligacy and economic indiscipline combined with the declining political significance of landownership and, by the late 1800s, a growing burden of taxation, were among the many reasons leading to the disposal, or at least downsizing of many country properties. Since one man's misfortune is so often another man's opportunity, local auctioneers thrived as estates went into decline. Typically, the firm of Peter Francis of Carmarthen, founded in the early 1890s, was able to benefit from the widespread sales of Welsh estates and the contents of country houses throughout the years of agricultural depression preceding

of Landscapes' in F. Fowle and R. Thomson, eds, *Soil and Stone: Impressionism, Urbanism and Environment* (Aldershot, 2003), pp. 42–45.

8 Sara Pennell, 'All but the Kitchen Sink: Household Sales and the Circulation of Second-hand Goods in Early Modern England' in J. Stobart and I. Van Damme, eds, *Modernity and the Second Hand Trade: European Consumption, Cultures and Practices, 1700–1900* (Basingstoke, 2010), passim.

9 Jon Stobart and R. McArthur, 'Going for a Song? Country House Sales in Georgian England' in J. Stobart and I. Van Damme, *Modernity and the Second Hand Trade*, p. 178.

the Great War.[10] In the year of Peter Francis' foundation there were in the region of eleven thousand auctioneers in England and Wales, some eight thousand more than had existed in 1841. So rapid was the growth of demand for the auctioneers' services and so rich the pickings to be gleaned from the business, that numbers of practising auctioneers had reached more than seventeen and a half thousand by the outbreak of the First World War. Among these, the east midland firm of Henry Spencer and Sons grew from modest beginnings in the 1840s to become a major player in the increasingly competitive market for the sale of country houses and their contents.[11] Frequently, contents would include scholars' or gentlemen's libraries, both eagerly sought after by individual collectors or academic institutions.

If specialist book auctioneers had evolved by the mid nineteenth century, firms and individuals concentrating on the sale of postage stamps were virtually unknown outside London until after the Second World War. But when the Derby-based dealer Geoffrey Manton established his Cavendish Auctions in 1952 he set into motion a flourishing business which would eventually become internationally-celebrated for its specialist expertise. Together with the important Plymouth Philatelic Auctions, Manton's company came to dominate the world of stamp auctions for more than a decade.[12]

The quantum increase in the number of professional auctioneers from the accession of Queen Victoria until the outbreak of the First World War is a direct reflection of the growth in spending power of the burgeoning middle class in Britain. The seemingly inexorable expansion of the Empire coupled with the development of international trade offered opportunities for energetic and entrepreneurial individuals, irrespective of their social origins, to achieve a degree of prosperity undreamt of by their forbears. In this world of economic liberalism and social mobility, moreover, there was every chance for the intelligent, dynamic and go-ahead working man to better himself. By exertion, imagination and the readiness to take risks he could, with a bit of luck, exchange the confines of the slum for the refinements of the suburban villa. And as his income increased, he and his fellow-villa dwellers and those who had been able to distance themselves from the sources of their wealth by purchasing agreeable country properties, sought to underpin their new-found status by way of conspicuous consumption. A desirable house, after all, deserved to be filled with desirable contents. There were now plenty of emporia selling the mahogany furniture, oleographs, prints and assembled bric-a-bric cramming the later Victorian household, yet attendance at auction sales lent an element of *frisson* to accumulating these pieces.

As it was with furniture, art objects and other household *desiderata* so it was with food. Growth in status and spending power would be translated into expanded demand for those staples of the farm, beef, mutton and pork. By 1851 Britain had become an industrial colossus half of whose population of seventeen millions lived in towns where they produced most of the world's coal and steel and a massive and diverse range of industrial products. These towns were focal points of a dynamic

10 R. J. Moore-Colyer, 'The Landed Gentry of Cardiganshire' in G. H. Jenkins and I. G. Jones, eds, *Cardiganshire County History: Volume 3, Cardiganshire in Modern Times* (Cardiff, 1998), pp. 72–75.

11 R. Spencer, *Drama at the Sale* (Retford, nd), p. 23.

12 D. G. Manton, *Something Funny Happened on My Way to the Rostrum* (Derby, 2001), p. 29.

Benthamite urban world wherein enormous wealth coexisted with crushing poverty and creativity and inventiveness with ignorance and obscurantism.

If the growing towns had sucked in country people in countless droves, millions remained in the countryside producing the food needed to sustain industrial productivity. Although early Victorian agriculture remained essentially an animal and man-powered activity, the development of effective horse-drawn and steam-operated machinery began to ease the farm labourer's physical (if not his economic) lot as the Queen's reign wore on. In addition, careful attention to animal breeding had significantly improved the nation's pool of livestock and thereby the potential for butcher's meat production for which demand increased as commercial prosperity trickled down the social ranks in the form of increased wages.

For centuries most dealers and butchers had bought their animals either directly from farmers or at the local periodic fairs, hundreds of which were held up and down the country at different times of the agricultural year. Concurrently, flock-masters would sell wool to merchants at specialist wool fairs, while professional 'jockeys' tended to deal in horses. Throughout the pre-railway period cattle and sheep drovers from Scotland, Wales and the livestock rearing areas of England sold 'store' animals to the graziers of the Midlands and others in the eastern counties who would finish beasts for the market. From Newcastle to Northleach, Welshpool to Wolverhampton and Kendal to Kettering, the roads and byways echoed to the sound of drovers and their charges.[13] The great cattle and sheep fairs were noisy and rumbustuos occasions where old friendships were renewed and fresh ones formed, where gentlemen rubbed shoulders with cutpurses and where money was made and lost. As the days went by and the drink went down so the knife and the knuckle-duster made their appearances and many a man returned home both bruised and bloodied. All manner of licence prevailed at these times in the farming year when the world was turned upside down. So it was that, after drinking deeply at Weyhill Fair, Thomas Hardy's character Michael Henchard sells off his wife to the highest bidder, thereby striking out on a path which would lead firstly to wealth and local celebrity, but ultimately to bitterness and tragedy.[14]

Besides generating much local excitement, the livestock fair, held either in the streets of the town or on its periphery, generated a great deal of muck, mess and inconvenience to the townsfolk. Inns and taverns might benefit from increased trade and the local corporation from tolls on sales, yet the presence of hundreds of cattle and sheep, to say nothing of their drovers, was not to the taste of the more genteel residents of town or borough. To these people it came as something of a relief when the railway pushed its tentacles into the deep countryside and the periodic livestock fairs declined in importance. After the 1850s long-distance droving would become a thing of the past as rail transport proved to be a means not only of getting animals to market in a more timely and efficient manner, but of significantly reducing marketing costs.

This in part was facilitated by the development of urban livestock markets either hard by the railway or in quite close proximity. So it was that Slough Cattle Market opened alongside the Great Western Railway in 1850, Yeovil in the later 1850s and

13 R. J. Moore Colyer, *The Welsh Cattle Drovers,* 2nd ed. (Ashbourne, 2002), pp. 153–54.
14 Thomas Hardy, *The Mayor of Casterbridge* (London, 1984), passim.

Chester in 1870. The Ashford Cattle Market Company, meanwhile, was established in 1856 on a site close to the South Eastern Railway.[15] Elsewhere the process took a little longer so that in Crewe the seasonal cattle fairs, with all their associated muck and pollution, continued to be held in the streets of the town into the 1880s. Early in the decade, however, a new market, complete with sale rings, lairage and a slaughter house, was built on land close to the railway station and this would eventually become the largest livestock auction market in England.[16] As the cattle market became overwhelmingly the most important point of sale for commercial types of livestock, so expanded the need for auctioneers with a specialist understanding of both farmers and their animals. When two Northamptonshire farmers, John and Edward Berry, began to advise their fellows on matters of tenant right and the vagaries of livestock marketing in the closing years of the nineteenth century, they unwittingly laid the foundations of Berry's, among the most influential firms of land agents, valuers and auctioneers in the English midlands.[17] The Berrys would probably have been acquainted with the small group of men who founded the company of Harry H. Bletsoe in the 1870s. Based in Thrapston, Bletsoe's would serve the agricultural community for many generations as agents and valuers and as prominent auctioneers in both Thrapston and Kettering Cattle Markets.[18]

From the outset, the weekly cattle market became a venue for business, gossip and social exchange. But above all it became a safe and secure means of selling livestock. Farmers who had previously (and often with some reluctance) relied upon the credit-worthiness of butchers, dealers and drovers, were now sure of their money which had to be handed over by a purchaser on the day, at the fall of the hammer.[19] To this extent, the availability of a livestock market and its attendant auctioneers was a major stimulus to livestock farming in the second half of the nineteenth century. Besides, it generated a wealth of casual employment, and eventually, with the development of motor transport, considerable opportunities for hauliers and those who maintained and serviced their vehicles.

While many of the weekly markets would eventually come under the aegis of the local authority, others remained in the hands of their founders and successors in title who originated from a variety of social and economic backgrounds. The landowner William Gifford Palmer, for example, was responsible for the foundation of Yeovil Market, while Thomas Buckland, a tenant farmer-cum-land agent from Wraysbury near Windsor, opened Slough Cattle Market a few years earlier.[20] Many miles to the north, Ripon Market became the property of John Francis Bowers (1890 - 1984), a celebrated local farmer, foxhunter, land agent and auctioneer who combined his professional skills with a healthy taste for hard liquor and compliant ladies.[21] Not so,

15 www.hobbsparker.co.uk (accessed October 2013).

16 B. Pennington, *The Fall of the Hammer: Sixty Years in Cattle Markets and the History of Wright-Manley from 1860* (Hargrave, 2002), p. 18.

17 www.berrybros.com (accessed October 2013).

18 www.bletsoe.co.uk (accessed October 2013).

19 Richard Perren, 'The Marketing of Agricultural Products: Farm Gate to Retail Store' in E. J. T. Collins, ed., *The Agrarian History of England and Wales: Volume 7, 1850–1914* (Cambridge, 2000), p. 980.

20 By the 1990s Yeovil would become the base for Premier Livestock Auctions Ltd., one of the strongest livestock marketing organisations in Britain, R. W. Martin, *Paulmers Market* (Yeovil, 1995), pp. 7–8.

21 J. Hurste, *The Intemperate Auctioneer* (Sussex, 2002), passim.

one imagines, the lessees of Crewe Market, Messrs Etches and Manley, of whom the latter was the son of a wheelwright who had also served as village postmaster and chemist.[22] Somewhat earlier, in 1790, the Lincolnshire tenant farmer and thatcher Richard Walter had set up a local auctioneering concern. By 1851 his son Joseph was farming 550 acres of land near Horncastle and selling livestock, thoroughbred horses, furniture and real estate and establishing the foundations of what, within fifty years, would become Lincolnshire's principal auction house.[23] These regional and local auctioneers offered a sterling service to the farming community and, it has been argued, provided a barometer to the livestock trade comparable to that provided by the Stock Exchange in the City of London.[24]

For the majority of regional and local auctioneers in the later nineteenth and earlier twentieth centuries selling livestock was the principal business. From the outset, though, some firms, like that set up by William Hussey of Honiton in Devon, were also involved in land transactions. Before the nineteenth century, land sales had largely been a matter of personal contact between vendor and purchaser, a procedure facilitated by the *Estates Gazette* which, in 1857, provided a medium specifically designed to bring together potential purchasers and those anxious to sell. Even so, a significant proportion of land transactions proceeded via the auction house.[25] Indeed, the growth in demand for land in the second half of the eighteenth century, stimulated by the possibilities offered by the Parliamentary enclosures, formed the market base for the expansion of several of the London-based auctioneering houses.[26] But if the larger estates fell into the hands of the metropolitan auctioneer, smaller properties and their associated goods and chattels and fixtures and fittings were frequently handled by the provincial houses. Aided by the advertising potential of the rapidly expanding local press and the provision of accurate catalogues and inventories, local auctioneers were enabled to attract buyers from a wide catchment area. In this respect the auctioneer closely served the interests of property owners, be they great magnates disposing of real estate to discharge mortgages or other obligations, or modest yeomen selling their pewter to meet outstanding debts.

As he stood above the sale ring disposing of a group of steers or a mob of ageing ewes the auctioneer may have seemed little more than a dispassionate automaton to watching farmers. But when it came to the valuation and sale of long-held family property or treasured heirlooms he became much more than a mere go-between executing a purely mechanical function. In this context he served as a confidant whose discretion and expertise raised him above the status of a simple salesman and placed him in a position of trust with the property-owning classes whose business he undertook. With the establishment of the Auctioneers' Institute in 1886 the profession achieved a degree of respectability on a par with that of the land surveyor, the doctor and the lawyer, and like these people the auctioneer came to enjoy considerable prominence in local society. As his fortune and social status expanded with his

22 Pennington, *The Fall of the Hammer*, p. 7.

23 L. Elvin, *Gab and Gavel: 200 Years of a Family Firm* (Lincoln, 1990), p. 17.

24 Pennington, *The Fall of the Hammer,* pp. 1–2.

25 J. V. Beckett, 'Landownership and Estate Management' in G. E. Mingay, ed., *The Agrarian History of England and Wales: Volume 6, 1750–1850* (Cambridge, 1989), pp. 556–57.

26 J. A. Chartres, 'Country Trades, Crafts and Professions' in G. E. Mingay, ed., *The Agrarian History of England and Wales*, pp. 416–19.

business he was often able to pursue a style and standard of life akin to that enjoyed by those whom he served.

With almost a third of the agricultural land of England and Wales coming under the hammer between the 1880s and 1920s and the auction method dominating the livestock market, the auction houses waxed fat. But their good fortune was not to last and the inter-war period ushered in a lengthy period of depression in the agricultural, land and fine art markets. The latter remained in the doldrums until some years after the Second World War and some auctioneers specialising in this area had difficulty in maintaining the viability of their operations. Their unease was shared by the livestock auctioneers whose business largely disappeared in March 1940 when the government decreed the closure of all fatstock auction sales and their replacement by a policy of centralised purchasing of all meat animals. This restriction was not lifted until 1954 when food rationing came to an end and freedom of marketing was once again permitted. That the livestock auctioneering profession survived at all was in some measure due to the compensation offered from a central fund made available by the Livestock Auctioneers Pool Committee, a body which would eventually evolve into The Livestock Auctioneers Association.[27]

If the fine art market took many years to recover after the war and the demand for land remained desultory until the 1960s, the sale of surplus military equipment provided a timely bonanza for auctioneers the length and breadth of the country. When the war finally ended the Ministry of Defence was charged with the task of offloading unused military and air force equipment valued at billions of pounds. Boots, blankets and bedsteads; lorries, vans and aircraft parts; Nissen huts, tank tracks and radio components; battledress, belts and knickers; anything and everything was up for sale and there was something for everyone. Army surplus sales enabled many a farmer to secure a van, lorry or track-laying vehicle at a knock down price, while all manner of entrepreneurs, scrap dealers and merchants founded profitable businesses on the basis of prudent purchases made on these occasions. The dispersal sales provided a lifeline to many local auction houses whose viability was for the time being assured.[28]

Since the last quarter of the eighteenth century officialdom had taken some interest in the activities of auctioneers, mainly to secure the payment to the Exchequer of all chargeable duties on goods sold. With the singular exception of sales held on a farm, auctioneers were required by law to present the Office of Excise with a clear account of each and every sale they conducted, along with the necessary duties levied, usually on paintings and furniture.[29] Under the Auctioneers Act of 1845, however, this particular burden was removed although the Act specifically reinforced the basic principle that all practising auctioneers be licensed.[30] The issue of monitoring auctioneering businesses was regularly debated throughout the nineteenth century, particularly with regard to ensuring that tolls and rates required by local and national statute were paid as appropriate. In 1813 the woollen and linen

27 http://www.laa.co.uk (accessed October 2013).

28 Learmount, *A History of the Auction*, p. 144.

29 Learmount, *A History of the Auction*, p. 48.

30 The 1845 Act was eventually repealed by the Finance Act of 1949 which removed the obligation for licencing.

drapers of Tewkesbury and the shopkeepers of Bath despatched petitions to the House of Commons complaining of the numerous 'itinerant auctioneers' who were holding sales without paying parochial rates. A bill was debated in the chamber but eventually, largely on the basis of objections from the Lord Mayor and aldermen of the City of London, the matter was quietly dropped. Presumably the 'itinerant auctioneers' had been locally persuaded to mend their ways.[31]

The auctioneering business seems to have avoided further investigation until 1888, two years after the foundation of the Auctioneers' Institute, when a question regarding the licensing issue in Ireland was raised in the House of Commons. To the surprise of many it turned out that under the law virtually anyone could become an auctioneer and that neither the Board of Inland Revenue nor the Board of Agriculture had the power to refuse the grant of an auctioneer's license or to revoke a license already granted.[32] Full registration was closely discussed in 1914 and action taken in 1927 to prohibit the holding of 'mock auctions' and to prevent misrepresentation.[33] A decade later licencing restrictions were widely debated along with the establishment of a fund to guard the public against default and malpractice. These discussions ultimately resulted in the Auctions (Bidding Agreements) Act of 1969.[34]

Behind the various efforts to regulate the conduct of auctions lay the fundamental principle that competition via bidding should be open and transparent and that all those attending the sale should have an equal opportunity to purchase at a price they deemed appropriate. This, in effect, implied the absolute need to eliminate the dealers' ring whose activities could effectively reduce fair competition and thus the price realised by the goods under offer. Despite the provisions of the Auctions (Bidding Agreements) Act of 1927, rings continued to flourish and for decades exercised considerable influence on the outcome of many a country sale. Efforts to prosecute under the Act were persistently frustrated by the difficulty of accumulating compelling evidence against well-organised rings. In fact, so ineffectual was the legislation that it resulted in a single prosecution over a period of forty-three years. When the Act was amended in 1969 and tougher penalties introduced it was fondly hoped that the ring would become a thing of the past, especially after the conviction of nine members of a Carmarthen dealers' ring some eleven years later.[35] Nevertheless many auctioneers today would agree that carefully, quietly and covertly, rings continue to operate. How widespread they may be and how influential on the sale price of items of various categories it is difficult, if not impossible, to estimate.

The distinguished Bedfordshire firm of W. & H. Peacock has, for more than a century, continued to maintain the high traditions of the auctioneering profession. As a company engaged with surveying, auctioneering, valuing and property management, it became and remains, an integral element in the economic and social life both of the town of Bedford and the surrounding countryside. From relatively modest beginnings the company weathered all manner of 'alarums and excursions'

31 HC Deb 27 April 1813 First Ser., vol. 25, cols 1085–7, ProQuest (accessed October 2013).
32 HC Deb 3 July 1888 Third ser., vol. 328, cols 192–3, ProQuest (accessed October 2013).
33 Great Britain, Auctions (Bidding Agreements) Act 1927: George VI, Chapter 12 (1927), http://www.legislation.gov.uk/ (accessed May 2014).
34 Great Britain, Auctions (Bidding Agreements) Act 1969: Elizabeth II, Chapter 56 (1969), http://www.legislation.gov.uk/ (accessed May 2014).
35 Learmount, *A History of the Auction*, pp. 184–87.

and technological changes to emerge as one of the leading players among the auctioneering businesses of the East Midlands. The firm's history is one of ready responsiveness to social, cultural and economic change in both town and county, in large measure facilitated by the loyalty and dedication of its staff. That many staff were regularly prepared to contribute beyond the call of duty reflects the humane and professional manner by which they were treated by management. Moreover, the success of many of Peacocks' pupils who were to move on to other organisations is a testament to the quality of the theoretical and practical training they received under the guidance of senior colleagues. Employers and employed apparently enjoyed convivial relations in an atmosphere characterised by mutual respect and unanimity of purpose. To work for Peacocks was to work within a social and professional framework which engendered a spirit of cooperation and trust. It was, above all, a happy company.

After a century of changes in ownership and name, the auction business was acquired by a former employee in the year 2000 and once again designated W. & H. Peacock. Within a year the firm was commissioned to conduct a landmark sale of furniture, textiles and jewellery on behalf of the Bedford-based Panacea Society whose members promulgated the ideas and prognostications of the eccentric visionary, seer and prophetess Joanna Southcott (1750–1814). Joanna had prophesied that the Day of Judgement would arrive in 2004, a fact which may have given pause for thought to the auctioneers. But poor Joanna turns out to have been wrong and both Bedfordians and W. & H. Peacock have survived to tell the tale. Long may they prosper!

Richard Moore-Colyer,
St George's Day, 2014

Chapter One

The Beginning

Establishment of Walter M. Peacock, auctioneer

Walter Molesworth Peacock was one of four sons of a yeoman farmer, Henry John Peacock, who, during the late nineteenth century, farmed at Grove Farm, Biddenham, which formed part of the Wingfield Estate.[1] Henry John Peacock had previously farmed at Wilstead, on part of the Whitbread Estate.[2]

In 1894, Walter attended a farm sale at Stanford in the parish of Southill for the estate of his late grandfather, John Smith Peacock, and for part of the sale he took the clerk's place. Mr R. B. Stafford was the auctioneer.[3] In November 1894, Walter joined the staff of a long-established firm of local auctioneers and estate agents, Stafford and Rogers Ltd of 83 High Street, Bedford (a site now occupied by National Westminster Bank).[4] He attended all the Saturday livestock auction sales for the next six years.[5] On 29 September 1899, Walter attended the sale at Grove Farm, Biddenham, held for his father.[6]

At this time Great Britain was at war with the Boers, and after attending Stafford and Rogers' Christmas Fat Stock Sale in 1899, Walter became the first man to volunteer to serve in the 28th (Bedfordshire) Company, Imperial Yeomanry, popularly known as Compton's Horse.[7] Compton's Horse was a cavalry unit raised from

1 Henry John Peacock was born at Stanford in the parish of Southill on 1 April 1840. He married Miss Louisa Caroline Edwards and was father to four sons and two daughters, *The Bedfordshire Times and Independent*, 27 November 1931, p. 7.

2 *The Bedfordshire Times and Independent*, 27 November 1931, p. 7. The Wingfields were the largest landowners in Biddenham during the latter part of the nineteenth century. They continued to be so until the immediate post First World War period when their farms, including Grove Farm, were sold, Katherine Fricker, Mary McKeown and Diana Toyn, eds, *The Village of Biddenham through the Ages* (Biddenham, 2012), p. 126. The Whitbread family has been established in Bedfordshire from at least 1314 and is associated with Cardington and Southill. Samuel Whitbread (1720–1796) founded the well-known brewery and his son, another Samuel, extended the estate to include land in Wilstead, http://www.bedfordshire.gov.uk/CommunityAndLiving/ArchivesAndRecordOffice/CommunityArchives/Southill/TheWhitbreadFamily.aspx (accessed February 2014).

3 W. & H. Peacock, *1901–1951: The Partners and Staff Dine on the Occasion of the Firm's Golden Jubilee* (Bedford, 1951), pamphlet.

4 Stafford and Rogers was formed in 1834 by Charles Stafford and John Rogers. They were joined by Arthur W. Merry in 1915 and became Stafford, Rogers and Merry, Stafford and Rogers, *Stafford and Rogers 1834–1951* (Bedford, 1951), pamphlet.

5 W. & H. Peacock, *1901–1964* (Bedford, 1964), pamphlet.

6 The sale was announced in *The Bedfordshire Mercury* 15 September 1899, p. 4 by Stafford and Rogers. It included 322 Oxfordshire Down sheep and lambs, 50 well-bred shorthorns, 16 young and valuable shire horses, 3 nag horses, 38 pigs, 200 head of well-bred poultry and a large assortment of agricultural implements. Henry John Peacock died in 1931, aged 91, *The Bedfordshire Times and Independent*, 27 November 1931, p. 7.

7 Major Lord Alwyne Compton DSO, MP, late of the 10th Hussars, was authorised to raise a corps of mounted troops for service in South Africa by the War Office. Names and addresses of volunteers residing in the county of Bedfordshire were sent to the HQ of the 3rd Volunteer Battalion, Bedfordshire

yeoman farmers and their sons, following an appeal for volunteers, by Major Lord Alwyne Compton, DSO, MP. Together with his brother, Charles Nassau Peacock (later to become a highly regarded dental surgeon in Bedford) Walter went to South Africa, taking his horse Charlie with him from the farm. At Bloemfontein his regiment joined Lord Roberts' column, and he was made bodyguard to Lord Roberts and later to Lord Kitchener.[8]

Returning to England in 1901, Walter, Charles and others, who had served in Compton's Horse, were granted Honorary Freedom of the Borough of Bedford in recognition of their service.[9] Later, in 1904, the South African War Memorial was dedicated at an impressive ceremony in the forecourt of the Swan Hotel, Bedford, where it is still to be seen.[10]

Demobilised in 1901, Walter Peacock returned home to ask for his job back with Stafford and Rogers Ltd, but was refused re-employment as he had not been asked to join the army. Faced with this unhappy news Walter is alleged to have said: 'Well b***** you then – I will set up on my own!'[11]

Thus it was that, in September 1901, Walter Peacock opened his first office as an auctioneer, house agent and valuer on the first floor of 72 High Street, Bedford, almost opposite the Stafford and Rogers Ltd offices. An advertisement for the new business was published in *The Bedfordshire Mercury* newspaper on Friday 20 September 1901 as follows:

'72, HIGH STREET, BEDFORD
September, 1901.
Mr. Walter M. Peacock
Begs to announce that he is opening the above
Offices as HOUSE & ESTATE
AGENT, AUCTIONEER & VALUER.
Having benefitted by six years' experience with
the well-known firm of MESSRS. STAFFORD & ROGERS
of this Borough, he will esteem it an honour to be
favoured with a SHARE of YOUR PATRONAGE,
which shall receive his prompt and best attention.
Private Address:- BIDDENHAM, BEDFORD' [12]

A similar advertisement was published in *The Bedfordshire Times and Independent*

Regiment, 46 Gwyn Street, Bedford, *The Times Digital Archive*, 26 December 1899, p. 9. A farewell was held in Bedford on Saturday 27 January at the George Hotel, *The Bedfordshire Times and Independent*, 2 February 1900, p. 8. The Yeomanry embarked from Albert Docks on 7 February 1900, *The Times Digital Archive*, 8 February 1900, p. 10.

8 *The Eagle,* vol. 31, no. 2, p. 145.

9 *The Bedfordshire Times and Independent,* 1 November 1901, p. 6. The ceremony was led by the Mayor, Ald. H. Burridge, and was attended by various guests including Walter's father. Walter Peacock gave a short reply of thanks to 'all the gentlemen for the honour they had done them', and called for three cheers for the Mayor, three for the Corporation, three for all the others and one for themselves.

10 The statue was unveiled on 2 June 1904 by Lady Cowper, wife of Earl Cowper who was indisposed, H. G. Tibbutt, 'Going to Table Bay', *Bedfordshire Magazine*, vol. 14, no. 109 (Summer, 1974), pp. 189–92.

11 Personal communication to the author by Robert Peacock and George Robinson. Robert Peacock recalled his father's language as follows, 'Those of you who heard my father selling horses after the First World War knew they had an entertainer. He had a flow of language which could stop a horse in mid-air.' *The Bedfordshire Times*, 7 January 1977, p. 5.

12 *The Bedfordshire Mercury*, 20 September 1901, p. 4.

on the same date.[13] The following week, Walter Peacock advertised again in *The Bedfordshire Mercury* and *The Bedfordshire Times and Independent* announcing his first services: furnished and unfurnished houses to let; properties for sale; agricultural matters undertaken.[14]

Bedford's property market in the early 1900s

In 1901, the population of Bedford was 35,144.[15] The street map of Bedford in 1901 shows that the town was relatively compact despite expansion during the housing booms of the late nineteenth century, with homes for both the working and middle classes.[16] New estates were being developed, and Queen's Park to the west of Bedford was an area especially attractive to railwaymen and employees of the relatively new factory of W. H. Allen Sons and Company Limited (known as the Queen's Engineering Works).[17]

On the east side of town there were new streets off Castle Road, where many houses were built by local developers, mostly for letting. This area included the streets between Howbury Street and George Street, all of which led down to the new Russell Park, with the riverside beyond.[18] To the north, behind the Black Tom area of small cottages off Tavistock Street, the district now often referred to as Prime Ministers was in the course of development.[19] In the south there was new development in the areas off Ampthill Road and Elstow Road, a short distance from St John's Station on the London and North Western Railway linking Bedford to Cambridge and, via Bletchley, to Oxford.

The majority of the population in urban areas lived in accommodation rented from private landlords. There was a wide choice of property available to let in all sectors of the market, and rents were freely negotiated. Rents varied from about 3s per week for a small town cottage, to around £1 per week for a larger house in the Saints area of Bedford.[20] A large nine bedroom house, with good servants' quarters and two tennis courts, was available to rent for only £120 per annum.[21]

13 *The Bedfordshire Times and Independent,*20 September 1901, p. 5.

14 *The Bedfordshire Mercury,* 27 September 1901 p. 4 and *The Bedfordshire Times and Independent,* 27 September 1901, p. 5.

15 Kelly's Directories Ltd, *Kelly's Directory of Bedfordshire, Huntingdonshire and Northamptonshire 1903* (London, 1903), p. 22.

16 Between 1871 and 1911 the population of Bedford more than doubled (1871: 16,850; 1911: 39,183). Joyce Godber, *The Story of Bedford* (Luton, 1978), p. 115.

17 In 1894 W. H. Allen, who was searching for a site for an engineering works, saw from the train at Bedford that a thirteen acre site near the railway was for sale; he alighted from the train and purchased the site at Ford End Road, Joyce Godber, *History of Bedfordshire, 1066–1888* (Bedford, 1969), p. 552.

18 Russell Park was opened in 1898, *Kelly's Directory 1903*, p. 22.

19 The Black Tom area comprised roads around the junction of Union Street, Tavistock Street, Roff Avenue (formerly Park Road East) and Clapham Road. The Prime Ministers area included Clarendon Street, Stanley Street, Salisbury Street, Hartington Street, Gladstone Street, Garfield Street (the martyred United States President), Beaconsfield Street, Palmerston Street. Stanley was the family name of Lord Derby; Clarendon and Hartington did not become prime ministers. Some say Black Tom was co-terminous with the Prime Ministers area.

20 The Saints area comprised a number of roads built west of Kimbolton Road including: St Andrew's Road; St Augustine's Road; St Michael's Road and St George's Road. 9 St Andrew's Road, Bedford, was let for £55 per annum by Staffords in April 1903, W. & H. Peacock, *Instruction Book 1: 1902–December 1904*, entry 268.

21 Roseleigh, Shakespeare Road, Bedford, was available to rent at £120 per annum or to buy at £2,250, W. & H. Peacock, *Instruction Book 1*, entry 1128.

The new houses built to let to working class people may have had a small front garden, though many earlier houses opened straight off the street. A small hall, in front of the staircase, led into a front parlour, behind which was the living room and kitchen. Upstairs were two or three bedrooms. There was a coal store outside and a water closet. A small rear garden was usually accessible from a passageway used in common with neighbouring houses. Some homes also had a scullery and a fourth bedroom, or a bathroom. Where there was a bathroom it often had a bath with just a cold water tap.

The old Peacocks' Instruction Books show that it was not uncommon for a house to be available for some months before a tenant was found. The Instruction Books were large bound volumes into which a brief record of the property was entered showing accommodation, price or rent and name of the owner. These continued to be used by Peacocks until about 1964. In villages and country areas most of the houses and cottages still formed part of the large landed estates; these were let through the estate's own agents.

Services, as we know them today, were very limited. Main water and drainage were connected in the town, but such luxuries did not exist in many country areas where water often came from a well.[22] The toilet was to be found in a small shed in the garden, usually an earth closet, comprising a wooden seat with one or sometimes two holes over a pit dug into the ground. Some houses had a hand pump to draw soft water from an underground water tank fed from the roof.

Lighting was often by gas downstairs, with candles or oil lamps upstairs.[23] Cooking was done on a coal-burning range or on a gas stove. Open fires provided heating. A coal-fired copper served to heat water for bathing and wash days when household linen was boiled to get it clean. Gas was not available except in a few villages and towns.[24]

Information from *Instruction Book 1* and the rent collection books of the same period (the latter now sadly lost) showed that houses built for working class people in Dudley Street, Bedford, near Russell Park, were let at 3s 9d per week.[25] In Stafford Road, off Kempston Road, similar houses were let at 4s 3d per week, and could be purchased freehold, either let or with vacant possession, for £185 each.[26]

In 1901, many of the 'posh' houses were in the area near to the Midland Road railway station including Ashburnham Road, Bromham Road and Shakespeare Road. Further large detached houses were being built in the newer area of De Parys Avenue, Park Avenue and Pemberley Avenue, all conveniently near to the then new locations of Bedford Grammar School and Bedford High School.[27] Here rents varied

22 The first water works were erected in Clapham Road, Bedford, in 1866, Godber, *Bedfordshire*, p. 488. Examples of properties with a well as the main water supply can be found in the appendix of property auction sales, e.g. the sale of four cottages in Thurleigh on 1 March 1920.

23 Gas came to Bedford in 1832 under the auspices of the Bedford Gas Company in Greyfriars Walk. At first there was some nervousness about the use of gas in the home, but by 1864 usage had so increased that new, larger works became necessary and the utility was transferred to Ford End Road, Godber, *Bedford,* p. 118.

24 In 1903, gas companies are recorded in Ampthill, Aspley Guise, Biggleswade, Dunstable, Kempston, Leighton Buzzard, Luton, Potton, Sandy, Shefford, Turvey and Woburn, *Kelly's Directory 1903*, p. 221.

25 W. & H. Peacock, *Instruction Book 1,* entry 1210, taken off 10 November 1904.

26 W. & H. Peacock, *Instruction Book 1*, entry 1118, taken off 17 November 1904.

27 Bedford Grammar School was founded in 1552. The school's new premises off De Parys Avenue

from £90 to £120 per annum, and freeholds could be bought for between £1,500 and £3,000.[28]

A typical large house was built on a quarter to half acre plot with ground floor accommodation including an entrance hall, three reception rooms, butler's pantry, kitchen, scullery, larder and store. On the first floor there were often four or five bedrooms, a dressing room, bathroom and water closet. There were attic bedrooms on the second floor where the domestic staff, then employed by most middle class families, were accommodated. Some of the best houses had coach houses and stabling. In 1901, garages and parking provision were things of the future.

With horse transport still in regular use, it was possible to rent stabling and coach houses in the town, and there were livery stables too. Stabling for two horses in Tavistock Street was available to let at £10 per annum. In De Parys Avenue stabling for three horses was on offer at £20 per annum. [29]

As for amenities in larger houses, electric lighting was relatively new, and most were lit by gas.[30] A coal fired range was still used for most cooking and for water heating; a gas stove probably provided secondary cooking. Most living rooms and bedrooms had an open fireplace, though in some bedrooms there might be a fitted gas fire, which also contained a concealed gas ring. Water heating may have been by a solid fuel boiler supplying a hot water system, or by a gas geyser. The latter was potentially very dangerous with a risk of explosion, or even death by carbon monoxide poisoning.

Domestic staff could be summoned by a complex system of mechanical bells from bell pulls around the house.

Very few houses had a telephone connected to the exchange located in St Loyes Street at the corner of Dane Street. The telephone manager was appropriately named Mr R. W. Bell![31]

Many families, attracted to Bedford by the Harpur Trust public schools, found accommodation in three-storey, semi-detached houses in the Saints area and Poets Corner.[32] Most of these houses had been speculatively built and were let at rents between £45 and £65 per annum.[33] It was not uncommon for the landlord to have a house completely redecorated to attract a new tenant, with a £5 per annum reduction in rent for a three year term.

were opened formally on 29 October 1891, Michael De-la-Noy, *Bedford School: A History 1552–2002* (Bedford, 1999), p. 64. Bedford High School opened on 8 May 1882, Joyce Godber and Isabel Hutchins, eds, *A Century of Challenge: Bedford High School 1882 to 1982* (Bedford, 1982), p. 23. Both schools were part of the Harpur Trust, founded in 1566 by Sir William Harpur, a former Lord Mayor of London and Master of the Merchant Taylors' Company.

28 26 St Andrew's Road, Bedford, a detached house with three reception rooms, eight bedrooms, a bathroom 'with hot and cold' was available to let at £85 per annum or to purchase at £1,500. It was let by McConnells in March 1905, W. & H. Peacock, *Instruction Book 1*, entry 271.

29 W. & H. Peacock, *Instruction Book 1*, entry 1007.

30 The provision of electricity to the town started in 1894 from a power station in Prebend Street, Bedford, Arthur Jones, *For the Record Bedford 1945–1974: Land Use and Financial Planning* (Bedford, 1981), p. 27.

31 Telephones were first introduced to Bedford in 1896, Godber, *Bedford*, p. 140.

32 Poets Corner included roads to the west of Shakespeare Road including Chaucer Road, Spencer Road, Milton Road, Sydney Road and Cowper Road.

33 2 Milton Road, Bedford, was available to let at £45 per annum or to buy at £770, W. & H. Peacock, *Instruction Book 1*, entry 1163.

Out of town, larger country houses were also available to let or for sale. In 1903 Turvey Abbey, including stabling and other buildings and seven acres of gardens and grounds, was available to let for 350 guineas per annum.[34]

Also in 1903 Crossland Fosse, Box End, Kempston, a mansion with twelve bedrooms, servants' quarters, gardeners' and coachman's lodges, stabling, a coach house, croquet and tennis lawns, plus fifteen acres of land, and overlooking the river Great Ouse, was to available to let.[35] It was again available in 1907 at £250 per annum unfurnished, £300 per annum furnished, or for sale at £7,000.[36] In 1935 Crossland Fosse was again for sale–at only £8,000.[37]

Bedford's schools and amenities in the early 1900s

The attraction of Bedford's public schools is illustrated by reference to the affordable school fees.[38] For boys there was the Bedford Grammar School, now Bedford School, under the headmastership of J. Surtees Phillpotts MA BCL, with an entrance fee of £2 and tuition fees for those over thirteen years old of £4 per term. There were similar fees for girls at Bedford High School, under headmistress Miss Susan Collie.[39]

Mr C. W. Kaye MA was headmaster of the Boys' Modern School, with fees for boys under sixteen at £1 6s 8d per term. This fee scale also applied to the Girls' Modern School, later Dame Alice Harpur School, under headmistress Miss C. E. Dolby.[40]

Various private schools included: Crescent House School, Linden Road 'for daughters of gentlemen'; Froebel House, 81 Goldington Avenue, a preparatory and kindergarten school; Howard College, Bromham Road, a boarding and day school for young ladies and children; St Andrew's School, Kimbolton Road, a day and boarding school for girls.[41]

Bedford was well provided with free schools run by the recently-formed, but soon to be abolished, School Board of the Borough of Bedford.[42] The Board Schools were in: Ampthill Road, with separate schools for girls, boys and infants; Clapham Road; Goldington Road; Queen's Park; and Priory Street. In addition, there was a cookery and manual instruction centre in Bromham Road behind Priory Terrace.

34 W. & H. Peacock, *Instruction Book 1*, entry 1675. Turvey Abbey was available to let again in January1906 at £380 per annum, W. H. Peacock, *Instruction Book 2: December1904–December 1907*, entry 3051. It was let by Hamptons in May 1907. Turvey Abbey was not a religious foundation but took its name from land that was owned by the Benedictine Abbey of Bec in Normandy. The Manor of Turvey and the Abbey land had been owned by the Mordaunt family from the Norman Conquest; in 1786 the estate was sold to Mr Charles Higgins, a former grocer and Sheriff of London, Turvey Appraisal Committee, *Turvey Now: The 1980s and Beyond* (Turvey, 1981), pp. 3–4.

35 W. & H. Peacock, *Instruction Book 1*, entry 1372.

36 W. & H. Peacock, *Instruction Book 2*, entry 3811.

37 W. & H. Peacock, *Instruction Book*, now lost. Crossland Fosse was erected in 1889, BLARS, PK 1/4/120.

38 The low fees were particularly beneficial to families serving oversees in the forces or in administration, Godber, *Bedford*, p. 135. *Kelly's Directory* mentions other beneficiaries as retired officers, widows of clergymen and professional men, *Kelly's Directory 1903,* p. 22.

39 Bedford Publishing Company, *Bedford Directory 1901* (Bedford, 1901), pp. 2–3.

40 *Bedford Directory 1901*, p. 2.

41 *Bedford Directory 1901,* passim.

42 The Bedford School Board was set up in 1897 and abolished in 1902 following changes in legislation that gave responsibility to Town Councils, Godber, *Bedford*, p. 135.

Elementary schools were to be found in Harpur Street for boys, and in Midland Road for girls and infants. In Bedford, the development of the School Board was a relatively late occurrence as the Governors of the Harpur Trust had almost entirely provided all elementary education in the town, setting up a school for poor boys as early as 1815, and building further schools in 1875 and 1893.[43]

Communication was principally by post, with local same-day deliveries a norm and up to four deliveries a day. There were also deliveries on Sundays. A postcard cost only a halfpenny to post. Urgent messages were sent by telegram, delivered by a boy on a bicycle who would wait to take back a reply.

The horse was the principal means of local transport, but the bicycle was very popular too. Many people simply walked.[44] Village carriers, over one hundred of whom are listed in the 1901 local *Bedford Directory*, transported goods and people from villages on the market days of Saturday and Wednesday, arriving at various local inns during the morning and leaving again around 4.00pm.

Trains were available from Bedford Midland Road station for journeys to London and the north and to Northampton and Hitchin, also serving many village stations and halts along the routes. Trains to Oxford and Cambridge ran from St John's station. Connections were therefore available to the whole railway network.

Most businesses in the town were family run, with the owners occasionally living over the shop.[45] Of the High Street businesses in 1901, only Goldings the iron-mongers remain in their long-standing premises today, although John Bull & Co., jewellers, has relocated elsewhere in the town.[46] Local tradesmen would readily deliver goods to order on credit. Dairymen delivered twice a day and bakers also delivered daily.

Local newspapers included *The Bedfordshire Times and Independent*, *The Bedfordshire Standard* and *The Bedfordshire Mercury*, all published on Fridays, and *The Bedford and County Record* published on Fridays, for Saturday.

The competition for Walter Peacock's new business included other firms of estate agents in the town: Anderson & Co. and William Stafford, with offices in Midland Road; Alexander McConnell and Harry Ball in Mill Street; G. C. Walker and J. R. Eve in St Paul's Square; and Stafford and Rogers Ltd in the High Street.[47] Of these businesses, by 2000, only Wilson Peacock still retained a direct family connection through Dudley Peacock the founder's grandson.

Stafford and Rogers Ltd was to become Stafford, Rogers and Merry Ltd before becoming part of William H. Brown, whose agency activities in Bedford ended in 1992. J. R. Eve & Son, who later took over Harry Ball & Co., both became part of Black Horse Agencies until 1997 by which time their business activity locally had merged with that of Wilson Peacock.

43 Godber, *Bedfordshire*, p. 543.

44 Godber, *Bedford*, p. 132. The first driving licence in Bedford was issued in 1904.

45 Godber, *Bedford*, p. 133.

46 Golding and Grant was established in 1867 and took over the premises of Day & Son, ironmongers at 107 High Street, Bedford, in 1894. It is the longest surviving High Street business, Richard Wildman, *Bedford,* (Stroud, 2001), Britain in Old Photographs, p. 73. John Bull's jewellery shop was founded by a man of that name from Kimbolton in 1829. The 49 High Street premises were sold in February 1964 and the business moved to St. Peter's Street, Stuart Antrobus, *John Bull–Bedford's Oldest Jewellery Firm* (Bedford, 2011), pamphlet.

47 *Bedford Directory 1901* and *Kelly's Directory 1903*, passim.

The early growth of W. & H. Peacock

In April 1902, Harry Peacock joined his brother to form W. & H. Peacock.[48] The new business developed, and by 1903 Peacocks had taken over furniture sale rooms in Lime Street. During 1905, the offices at 72 High Street were closed and the main office moved to 84 High Street, where it continued until 1925 when all departments were transferred to 10 Lime Street.[49] In 1928 the estate agency activities were transferred to 6 Dame Alice Street.[50] The office at 10 Lime Street had been opened in 1906 and became the home for the Bedfordshire Chamber of Agriculture. Walter Peacock was appointed as Honorary Secretary, an office he held for the next twelve years.[51] A store was acquired in Rutland Road for use as a furniture store in the same year.[52]

In 1908 Herbert J. Parrott, who was to serve the firm for over fifty years, joined as a cashier. He had worked for a Bedford solicitor, Theed Pearse, since leaving school. He later served with the Forage Corps, who were responsible for providing forage for horses during the First World War, and subsequently went on to qualify in accountancy. In addition to being chief cashier, Herbert Parrott was skilled in farm accounts and managed the Egg Packing Station. He was made a partner in 1937.

George Robinson, known to the staff as 'GR', joined Peacocks in 1910 straight from school. He trained in all aspects of the business, but developed a particular interest in estate agency.[53] He was also destined to become a partner, and was responsible for the offices at 6 Dame Alice Street until their closure at the end of 1963.[54] George had joined the army during the First World War, and was gassed on the last day of hostilities in 1918.

William 'Bill' Clark, who joined the firm in 1913, worked loyally for Peacocks for fifty-one years in the Lime Street offices as a cashier and bookkeeper, and rose to become manager of the Egg Packing Station until its closure in 1962.[55]

With the outbreak of war in 1914, the Cattle Market in Commercial Road was requisitioned for use by the Highland Division.[56] Peacocks had been holding auction sales here from December 1901.[57] The firm therefore transferred the weekly sales to what was to become known as the 'back yard' of the Horne Lane sale yards. This

48 *The Bedfordshire Times and Bedfordshire Standard*, 5 October 1951, p. 8. He had previously worked for Messrs T. and H. Green, timber importers in Bedford, *Bedfordshire Times and Standard*, 22 May 1952, p. 7.

49 *The Bedfordshire Times and Independent*, 30 June 1905, p. 4 and *The Bedfordshire Times and Independent,* 13 November 1925, p. 8.

50 *The Bedfordshire Times and Independent*, 27 April 1928, p. 1.

51 1906–1918, *The Eagle*, vol. 31, no. 2, p. 145.

52 W. & H. Peacock, *1901–1951.*

53 W. & H. Peacock, *1901–1951.*

54 *The Bedfordshire Times and Bedfordshire Standard*, 30 December 1963, p. 3.

55 *Bedfordshire Times and Bedfordshire Standard*, 19 April 1963, p. 19.

56 From August 1914 to May 1915 Bedford's population suddenly increased with the billeting of 16,000–20,000 part-time Territorial Force soldiers of the Highland Division (later to become the 51st Highland Division) originally formed for defence of the UK. Bedford was an ideal location as the troops could easily be deployed to the south and east coasts in case of enemy invasion. Church halls, public spaces and parks were all made available to help with their training needs, *The Bedfordshire Times and Independent*, 21 August 1914, p. 5 and *The Bedfordshire Times and Bedfordshire Standard*, 5 October 1951, p. 8.

57 *Bedfordshire Times and Independent*, 13 December 1901, p. 5.

was accessible off Gravel Lane, a narrow lane between Midland Road and Horne Lane.

During 1915, Walter and Harry Peacock became honorary joint secretaries of the British Farmers' Red Cross Sales, which were held at the Horne Lane sale yards over the following five years. The purpose of the fund was to raise £100,000, £20,000 for provision of hospitals in Serbia, and the remainder for Red Cross work at home.[58]

Activity at Horne Lane increased, and in 1916 the front yard and poultry yard were opened. Army horse sales also began that year. The first sale was of fifty army horses on 12 February, followed by a second sale of draught horses in June.[59]

In 1916, Ronald Craig became a member of staff. Ronald Craig became a very well-known character as an auctioneer, and went on to serve the firm for over fifty years in the auction department.[60]

The year 1918 heralded the first Christmas Hospital Turkey Draw, a charitable event for the benefit of Bedford Hospital that continued to be held each year for over thirty-five years, and raised significant sums for that worthy cause.[61]

By 1919, the Lime Street office had opened for farm accounts, and the business grew further. Two years later the centre yard cottages at Horne Lane were altered to create the egg salerooms.[62] After the First World War, Peacocks undertook a number of sales to dispose of unwanted war-time equipment.[63]

After 1921, when Robert Peacock joined the firm, there was more development at the Horne Lane sale yards and elsewhere as the business expanded. New estate agency offices at 6 Dame Alice Street and offices at Biggleswade and Baldock were opened in the period before the Second World War. The first of a long-running series of listings for the business appeared in *The Times* newspaper in 1921, in the Auctioneers and Estate Agents Directory. The firm continued to be listed at intervals until 1945.[64]

The Peacocks' story is more fully related in the following chapters dedicated to the different offices and activities.

58 *The Times Digital Archive*, 28 January 1915, p. 11. Records of the progress of this fund were reported in *The Times*. Walter Peacock's contributions are recorded on a number of occasions: £49 3s (second instalment) 31 May 1915, p. 4; £53 15s (third instalment) 5 July 1915, p. 9; eighth instalment (no amount recorded) 18 November 1915, p. 4. In addition, Walter Peacock held agricultural jumble sales in support of the fund. These raised considerable sums, £533 3d and £300 in December 1915, *The Times Digital Archive*, 31 December 1915, p. 2. A photograph of Harry Peacock presiding at one of these auctions can be seen in Richard Wildman, *Bedford: A Pictorial History* (Chichester, 1991), illustration no. 165.

59 *The Bedfordshire Times and Independent*, 4 February 1916, p. 4 and 25 June 1916, p. 4. Peacocks had sold military horses in the past; in 1906 and 1907 they auctioned horses from the Yeomanry Camp at Shorecliffe, *The Bedfordshire Times and Independent*, 1 June 1906, p. 4 and 24 May 1907, p. 4.

60 W. & H. Peacock, *1901–1951*.

61 The fund was set up by Harry Peacock with the aid of his brother. By 1951 they had raised £1,623 for Bedford General Hospital to provide Christmas dinners, *The Eagle*, vol. 28, no. 6, p. 542.

62 *The Bedfordshire Times and Bedfordshire Standard*, 22 May 1952, p. 7.

63 Contents of air-raid shelters were disposed of by instruction of the Mayor of Bedford, *The Bedfordshire Times and Independent*, 7 February 1919, p.4. The Duchess of Bedford ordered an auction of items removed from The Special Military Hospital, Woburn Abbey. These were sold at the Territorial Barracks, Ashburnham Road, Bedford, *The Bedfordshire Times and Independent*, 19 November 1920, p. 6.

64 *The Times Digital Archive*, 18 January 1921, p. 20.

Chapter Two

Horne Lane Sale Yards, Bedford

The early years

For over sixty years, until purchased by North Bedfordshire Borough Council for redevelopment in the 1970s, the sale yard in Horne Lane, Bedford, known to most local people as Peacocks' market, was the venue for regular weekly auction sales of an amazing variety of live and deadstock.[1]

The sale yard was located opposite the Harpur Arms public house and Charles Wells' brewery, on the site where the offices of the Pilgrim Housing Association are now, and only a short walk from St Paul's Square. Initially rented in parts, and later purchased from a Mr Frederick Reeve, the site had a long frontage to the north side of Horne Lane, and on the west side, a return frontage with access from Gravel Lane, a narrow lane that led through to Midland Road. [2] The area originally included: livery stables; cottages, known as Tudor Court cottages; a house, known as The Market House; a wool store; and other buildings. There were Harpur Trust school premises to the north and east respectively occupied by Bedford Modern School and the Elementary, or Harpur Central, School.

The first sales were held in the back yard off Gravel Lane when the cattle market in Commercial Road was requisitioned at the outset of the First World War. By 1916, activity increased when sales commenced in the front yard and poultry sheds. During 1921 to 1922 the middle buildings were converted to an egg saleroom, and by 1923 sales were being held in the furniture yard and chick shed.[3] An ancient wool shed, later known as the Tudor Rooms, was converted for use as a furniture sale room in 1926. The Horne Lane sale yards began to operate as one unit in 1933.[4]

The front yard

The front yard was where larger items were sold including: horses; farm carts; machinery; cars and other vehicles; sheds and poultry houses; builders' equipment; and materials such as baths, sinks, boilers and fireplaces. For many years the front yard sales were conducted by Walter Peacock. Walter was sure of a good company

1 Peacocks opened their new auction centre in Newnham Street following the closure of the Horne Lane sale yards in 1977, *The Bedfordshire Times*, 7 January 1977, p. 5.

2 Personal communication to author by Mr Frederick Reeve, 28 Kimbolton Road, Bedford. Mr Reeve informed the author that he had been present when Peacocks had purchased the site from his father, also called Frederick Reeve.

3 *The Bedfordshire Times and Bedfordshire Standard*, 22 May 1952, p. 7.

4 *The Bedfordshire Times and Bedfordshire Standard*, 5 October 1951, p. 8.

as his sales were usually most entertaining thanks to his quick wit, somewhat forthright vocabulary and forceful personality.[5]

From 1947, when Richard 'Dick' Arnold was granted his first auctioneer's licence, his cheery personality soon established him as another great character as Walter's assistant and eventual successor. Dick Arnold became a familiar front yard character, usually accompanied by the stocky figure of his clerk, Arthur Wilkins. Arthur's job included taking cash and deposits for various lots while the sale progressed; in due course he also became an auctioneer. In the mid-1950s, Dick Arnold left the firm to become a partner in W. S. Johnson & Co., auctioneers and estate agents of Bletchley, where he worked for over forty years. Arthur Wilkins left to work as an estate agent with Bedfordshire Property Sales.

From the mid-1950s front yard sales were taken over by Dudley Peacock as the principal auctioneer, a role that he was to maintain until closure of the yard. In fair weather or foul, Dudley could be found, with board and pencil in hand, cheerfully moving from lot to lot as the sale progressed around the yard. The only shelter from the elements in winter or summer was a large green brolly. Strong shoes or wellies were essential equipment to cope with the mud, puddles and snow of winter.

From 1933 until his retirement in the late 1960s, the front yard porter was a wonderful, down to earth, weather-beaten character, George Henson. George had joined the firm after being thrown out of work by the collapse of the Howard Engineering Works (Britannia Ironworks) as a result of the 1930s depression.[6] His loyalty to Peacocks was beyond reproach. In summer or winter, George would be found in the front yard or in the market office receiving items for sale, sorting, lotting up, and hopefully, remembering the names of the various vendors. If George was missing, he could usually be found refreshing himself at the Harpur Arms with the other porters and customers. On sale days, the porters played a useful role by executing commissions to buy goods for customers unable to be present at the sale in person. Following George Henson's retirement, his role was taken over by Colin Park, who had worked for several years as a van driver and sale porter.

Poultry, small animal sales and the chick sheds

A large area near the middle of the sale yards was occupied by the poultry sheds, which were first constructed in 1921. Poultry was sold from the early days of the sale yards and continued until the closure of the Horne Lane site. These buildings contained long rows of wire cages, in several tiers, to accommodate the many hundred head of poultry of all types, rabbits, guinea pigs and other small animals that were sold every week. Ferrets were usually left in their carrying cages as they were apt to nip any finger that was allowed to stray too near. Each week there was a variety of pullets, old hens, cockerels, ducks and geese. On occasions more exotic birds such as guinea fowl or golden pheasants were entered for sale.

5 A description of a Bedfordshire Farmers' Red Cross Sale of 1916 reported that Mr Walter Peacock's contribution was offered, 'with characteristic humour which kept the crowd in merry mood', *The Bedfordshire Times and Independent*, 1 December 1916, p. 5.

6 The Britannia Ironworks were opened in 1859 by James and Frederick Howard following the success of their father's plough (John Howard). Shown at the Royal Agricultural Society's show in 1839 and at the Great Exhibition in 1851 it became known as the champion plough of England, Godber, *Bedford*, p. 119. The company finally closed in 1932.

The demand for poultry varied from those, mostly local, people seeking a fat cockerel or boiling fowl for the table, to those requiring laying pullets. Poultry dealers were also regular buyers and their vehicles, laden with many crates of birds, could be seen leaving Bedford each Saturday. In the author's time some purchases were made by the local carriers on behalf of their customers such as: James Frederick Felce, a farmer from Riseley; Frederick Lambert Bailey from Turvey; and Harry Eaton, a haulage contractor, from Wollaston.[7]

The large influx to the area of immigrants from many countries, particularly Italy and Asia, increased trade in poultry and rabbits considerably.[8] For many years poultry had been taken away live, sometimes to be kept tied up in a house until required for the pot. In the 1950s, new regulations were introduced that required poultry to be killed under the supervision of the local RSPCA inspector. The inspector attended each week to ensure that all livestock was fit for sale and poultry was slaughtered humanely. Religious rites requiring ritual killing of birds were accommodated by the creation of a special slaughterhouse in one of the old Tower Court cottages.

Rabbits and guinea pigs attracted customers varying from children in search of a pet and local breeders to those seeking rabbits for the table, and the all-important dealers. Many children would indulge in young enterprise by buying and selling rabbits and guinea pigs to boost their pocket money. It was not uncommon for some buyers to find that within a short time their purchase had produced a litter of young.

The poultry sale was Harry Peacock's favourite domain on a Saturday.[9] On warm, sunny days he would be resplendent in his straw boater and linen jacket. Robert Peacock also frequently sold poultry, at lightning speed as he was so familiar with the regular buyers. Poultry was normally sold at a price per head, leaving the sale clerks to work out the price for each lot.

With the influx to the area of people of different nationalities, many with unfamiliar names and accents to Peacocks' staff, it became necessary to devise a simple system to try to reduce mistakes. Buyers' numbers were therefore introduced. Prospective buyers had to pay a deposit to obtain a numbered disc to display to the auctioneer when buying. At the end of the sale, the deposit was deducted from the total of any purchases or refunded if nothing had been bought. This system also helped to minimise the occasions when a buyer decided he had bid too high a price to secure a lot and would leave without paying. As there was no provision for keeping livestock at Horne Lane after the sale, every animal or bird had to be sold. From time to time, the poultry yard would have to be shut due to an outbreak

7 Kelly's Directories Ltd, *Kelly's Directory of Bedfordshire, Huntingdonshire and Northamptonshire 1940* (London, 1940), pp. 169, 192 and 362.

8 People from Italy, India, Pakistan, Poland and the West Indies all came to Bedford from 1947, and continued to do so throughout the 1950s and 1960s; the local brick industry in the Marston Vale was the prime mover, John Brown, *The Un-melting Pot: An English Town and its Immigrants* (London, 1970), pp. 147–48.

9 Harry Peacock was not just an auctioneer of poultry but also a speaker on the subject. *The Bedfordshire Times and Independent* reported his address in 1937 to a meeting of the Bedfordshire Poultry Society on the decline of the local industry. In the previous year twenty farms with 8,000 birds had been sold up and production of eggs was down by two million. The meeting resolved to put the case to the Ministry of Agriculture, the Board of Trade and local MPs, *The Bedfordshire Times and Independent*, 26 March 1937, p. 6.

of fowl pest in the area, resulting in a ban on movement of poultry that could last for several weeks.

The chick shed, in which sales started in 1923, was a scene of much activity each Saturday for many years when thousands of day-old chicks, some ducklings, and occasionally goslings, would be sold. It was a favourite visiting place for small children, including the daughter of Jim Brooks. Jim was the sale porter from 1926 to 1966. Like many others, Jim's daughter loved to be allowed to look inside the boxes of cheeping, fluffy, yellow chicks. The baby ducklings were particularly popular, and sometimes, as a special treat, a child might be allowed to hold one.

The chicks were mostly sent by rail from hatcheries to either Bedford Midland Road or St John's stations for collection by Peacocks' van first thing in the morning. Trade was mostly in pullet chicks to supply local farmers and home poultry keepers. Cockerel chicks could be fattened for the table, but were less favoured, except as Christmas approached. On a bad day as many as 500 cockerel chicks might be bought for only 5s.

In the 1940s and 1950s the chick sales were conducted by one of the partners, Herbert Parrott. Unfortunately, as Herbert's eyesight failed it so adversely affected his writing that on occasions he could not read the names of the vendors to whom he had sold the chicks. Fortunately, thanks to his good memory, Jim Brooks could often come to the rescue by giving the right name for a buyer.

One big advantage for the clerks running the chick sale was that the sale could always be quickly balanced to the penny. Any error in a balance could easily be corrected by a few unexplained casualties, at least on paper, as each week a number of chicks would die anyway of natural causes. The actual casualties provided a feast for Harry Peacock's ferrets. Eventually problems associated with fowl pest in the 1950s, and other controls, led to closure of the chick sale and the area was taken over for furniture sales.[10]

The furniture yard and Tudor Rooms

The furniture yard and Tudor Rooms were usually filled every week with less valuable furniture and antiques, the best items having been taken to the Lime Street sale rooms. The better items were sold in the Tudor Rooms, whilst the remainder was placed under the cover of open sided sheds or even left out in the open. When necessary an overflow of goods would be placed under part of the poultry sheds. If it rained, the goods outside just got wet! The regular auctioneers for the furniture sales were Harry Peacock, Ronald Craig or Francis Peacock.

The furniture sales were the place to find a bargain for restoration, and there were probably few homes in the Bedford area without at least one or two items bought from Peacocks. An old battered chest of drawers could soon be transformed with a new coat of paint and new handles, or might be stripped down to reveal the original pine. Many items bought for a few shillings in the 1940s and 1950s may now be

10 Fowl pest was virtually unknown in Britain until 1947 but soon became a serious problem. *The Times* newspaper reported regularly on outbreaks throughout the 1950s and 1960s. In January 1955 all entrances to Whipsnade Zoo were sealed and visitors required to walk over an antiseptic pad in an effort to stop the disease spreading to rare birds in the collection as it had been found on farms only one mile away, *The Times Digital Archive*, 11 January 1955, p. 5.

worth many hundreds of pounds. Often old furniture was discarded in favour of contemporary furniture that has itself long since needed replacement. On numerous occasions Peacocks' staff or porters had to rescue items of value that were about to be put on a bonfire, while other modern items were being put aside for sale. Just how many lovely items of Victorian or Edwardian furniture were destroyed because they were simply too large for modern houses beggars belief.

The tool shed

Behind the market office was the tool shed, the sale room for smaller articles including hand tools, electrical goods, collectables and other items. Sometimes nicknamed 'the bazaar' this sale was run by Jonathan Knights from the 1960s until the closure of the sale yards. It was here that sales of surplus or bankrupt stock would be held, when items such as Cadbury's Milk Tray chocolates and Heinz baby food were sold at above the retail price. One particularly enterprising articled pupil, Christopher H. Bletsoe, discovered that he could simply buy tools at Woolworth's, enter them in the tool shed sale and make a profit after paying commission week after week.

The tool shed was also utilised as the sale room for pre-Christmas sales of dressed poultry, when a good choice of birds was usually available. Prices normally held up well for the best birds, but as Christmas Day got nearer there were bargains to be had, especially for those prepared to wait until the end of the sale.

The back yard sales

The last, but not the least, of the sale areas was the back yard where bicycles and motorcycles were sold after the completion of the furniture sale. The back yard also held large quantities of salvaged building materials that commanded a steady trade, especially during post-war years when new materials were only obtainable on licence. Materials included large amounts of timber, doors, windows, corrugated iron and asbestos, steel girders and many other items. There were probably numerous garden and allotment sheds in the local area that were built with materials bought from Peacocks.

Tower Court Cottages

At the rear of the sale yards was a terrace of old cottages known as Tower Court. Some of the cottages, although condemned as unfit, remained in occupation until at least the 1950s. These two-up and two-down cottages were eventually converted for other use. The cottage at the east end was converted into a cafe, open on Saturdays, and run by Mrs Wingrave. This provided very welcome sustenance for visitors to the market and for those members of staff who did not relish the option of Mrs 'Lizzie' Vivers' culinary delights offered by the official canteen in the Market House. The other old Tower Court cottages and outbuildings were utilised for storage of 'For Sale' and 'Sold' boards used by the estate agency offices. Part of one of the cottages, as has already been mentioned, was converted to become a ritual slaughter house for poultry.

Virtually all the first floor of the Tower Court cottages was utilised to store old file records of sales and other matters from the various offices, dating back for many years. It was possible to trace a file in a matter of a few minutes. Unfortunately, during the 1960s, the storage areas suffered disruption from a break-in, and many old records were so disturbed as to make it impractical to try to restore them to proper order. Fortunately, however, a quantity of material of interest was saved to be taken into safekeeping by the Bedfordshire County Record Office.[11]

The market office and sale yard staff

The market office was located near the centre of the yard, facing the front yard. It was fitted with a range of large sloping-top clerks' desks with lift-up lids placed along two sides of the room. To work at the desks, staff stood or perched themselves on tall chairs. In winter it was necessary to wrap up well in woollens and overcoats as the only source of warmth came from a couple of inadequate electric fires. The sale clerks ran the files of buyers' accounts and collected payment, mostly in cash, while the paying out clerks completed accounts for the various vendors, who could collect the net proceeds in cash after the sales were over.

The market staff on a Saturday comprised most of the staff from the 10 Lime Street office supplemented by a number of regular part-time assistants. Some part-timers worked for many years in their roles, and further staff were provided by young people seeking a Saturday job to earn pocket money. The young people included children of partners, staff and friends who rapidly caught the spirit of market days and could be relied upon for regular attendance. Their first job was usually as a 'runner', collecting the sale sheets from the different auctioneers and generally running messages. They would then progress to the various clerking jobs, eventually taking in or paying out money. Employment at the market offered a wonderful opportunity for the youngsters to meet and learn how to deal with a wide cross section of the public and to cope with, the thankfully few, troublesome customers.

In the late 1940s and 1950s the market office was supervised by Reginald Damon, the cashier and book-keeper at 10 Lime Street, who had joined the firm after leaving school in 1935. After the Saturday sales he had to ensure that each sale was balanced and the cash checked before the office closed. Reginald Damon progressed to become an auctioneer before leaving to become an accommodation officer at Chicksands USAAF Base and later to run his own estate agency firm.[12]

The regular weekly auctioneers, each responsible for their individual sale, were fully able to deal with any of the different sales if required. The advantage of dealing with the same sale on a regular basis was in knowing the names and faces of the usual buyers and the type of lot that might be of interest to them. Various other auctioneers within Peacocks were trained in the skills of the market or visited as guest auctioneers when help was needed through illness or holidays. These included Keith Brown, Clive Childs, Reginald Damon, Frank Jeffery, Alan Porter, Brian Porter, Arthur Wilkins and the author, to name but a few.

11 Now Bedfordshire and Luton Archives and Records Service, the Peacock archive (reference PK) contains business records, instruction books, property particulars, sale particulars, stocktaking valuations, agency and management files, correspondence and personal papers.

12 In 1936 the Osborne family sold their Chicksands estate to the Crown and in 1939 the RAF moved in. The RAF remained until the 1970s, but in November 1950 American forces also began to arrive. The last squadron stationed at the base was the 774th Air Base Group. They left on 25 April 1995, Anne Allsopp, 'Farewell to Little America', *Bedfordshire Magazine*, vol. 25, no. 194 (Autumn 1995), pp. 47–50.

The Market House

The Market House, adjacent to the Tudor Rooms, was a three-storey property occupied by Mrs Vivers, who acted as caretaker for the market. She was a small lady, but a seemingly fearless character, and woe betide anyone who crossed her! Mrs Vivers provided refreshments for the partners and staff as well as some of the carriers who visited the market. In addition to providing lunches, countless cups of tea were made each Saturday using a large teapot that bubbled away on a gas stove for rather too long between brews. Mrs Vivers worked for the firm from 1927 until her well-deserved retirement in 1963, when she moved to one of the Christie Charity Almshouse flats on Bedford's Embankment.

Change and closure of the sale yards

For a long period sales were also held on Wednesdays, the mid-week market day for the town. The Wednesday sales included market garden produce and fruit, according to season, and eggs. These sales were particularly popular during the post-war austerity years as quantities of locally-grown vegetables and fruit could be bought for bottling in re-usable Kilner jars or for jam making. Eggs could be preserved in water-glass solution in pottery egg crocks. Eventually the Wednesday sales declined in popularity as supplies of fresh produce improved and frozen and imported vegetables started to become available.

Peacocks' market was virtually a club, where friends from town and country would meet, week after week, to exchange news and gossip and to buy or sell goods or livestock. In addition to the various carriers who brought in and took away a variety of goods and produce for their customers, there were also general dealers who both bought and sold on a regular basis. The dealers were interesting characters who were always ready to pick up a bargain one week, only to resell the item another week.

The Horne Lane sale yards closed on Christmas Eve 1976, when the last lot, a turkey, was sold for £11 by Susan Peacock, the fourth generation of the Peacock family to sell at the market over its sixty years' history.[13] The great-granddaughter of Walter Peacock, Susan was watched by her sister Clair; her father, Dudley Peacock; and grandfather, Robert Peacock.

The weekly sales activity, apart from live poultry sales, which were discontinued, was transferred to the new Auction Centre at 26 Newnham Street, Bedford, where sales are still held every Saturday. The quality, variety of goods and the prices are much improved, but there are still many bargains to be found.

13 *The Bedfordshire Times,* 7 January 1977, p. 5.

Chapter Three
10 Lime Street, Bedford

Opening the office

The office at 10 Lime Street, Bedford, was opened in 1906, initially to deal with farming accounts and as the office for Bedfordshire Chamber of Agriculture.[1] Walter Peacock was Secretary of the Bedfordshire Chamber of Agriculture from 1906 to 1918, and was followed by his brother, Francis 'Frank' J. Peacock from 1918 to 1924.[2] The premises were originally leased from Mr F. R. Hockliffe, who owned a large bookshop at 86 and 88 High Street, on the corner with Lime Street.[3] Hockliffe's also ran a second-hand bookshop at 8 Lime Street, largely supported as a source of books needed by pupils at the Harpur Trust schools. The various other agricultural and auction office activities were transferred to Lime Street when the 84 High Street office closed in 1925.[4]

Mr Walter and Mr Harry Peacock at Lime Street

Walter and Harry Peacock had adjoining offices, on the first floor, separated by a wooden partition. For a long period, they enjoyed the use of a single telephone passed from office to office through a sliding hatch in the wall as necessary.

Two more different personalities than Walter and Harry might be difficult to find. Walter was a rather rumbustious character with a most colourful vocabulary, perhaps reflecting his former army service, and ideally suited to dealing with the farmers and horse dealers. It was quite an experience to be taken out by him on a job; he did not suffer fools gladly. Until his pupils came to know him better, he could seem quite scary. In contrast, Harry was very quiet and gentle and never known to use strong language.[5] Harry Peacock was much liked by the staff as he was very kind and had a lovely sense of humour, but he was very careful with money. He was wonderful at placating irate clients who came with any complaints. Harry had a high reputation as an auctioneer and valuer of antique and modern furniture, and

1 The Bedfordshire Chamber of Agriculture and Farmers' Club was established in 1897 under the Presidency of the Duke of Bedford. The objects of the Chamber were to watch over all measures affecting agricultural interests both in and out of Parliament and to discuss any subject whether of a local or general nature bearing on agriculture. Walter and Harry's father was a member of the Society and was reported as being present at a meeting on 11 December 1897, BLARS, SFM 3/348–252.

2 *The Eagle,* vol. 31, no. 2, p. 145.

3 F. R. Hockliffe was Mayor of Bedford for 1915, 1916 and 1918, Godber, *Bedford*, p. 150. His father, also F. R. Hockliffe, started the bookshop (in St Loyes' Street) c. 1880.

4 Peacocks announced the transfer of all their offices to 10 Lime Street in the local press, *The Bedfordshire Times and Independent*, 13 November 1925, p. 8.

5 Commander W. J. A. Willis MVO, OBE, CGM, DL, RN, the Chief Constable of Bedfordshire said of him: 'He was a man of great qualities, wise in his ways, but young in his heart, and a loyal representative of his County. He was a man of natural courtesy and a kind heart, with a great knowledge of his County …' *Bedfordshire Times and Standard*, 22 May 1952, p. 7.

maintained an interest in the activities of the estate agency side of the business. The partnership between Walter and Harry relied upon complete mutual trust and there was no written agreement through over fifty years as partners together.

Robert Peacock joined the firm at Lime Street on 27 September 1921 after completing his professional training with Symonds, Ingamells and Young of Boston, Lincolnshire.[6] He achieved a Gold Medal in Agricultural Valuations from the Chartered Auctioneers' and Estate Agents' Institute, and was very highly regarded as a specialist, acting as arbitrator in various agricultural disputes.[7]

Walter Peacock always retained a strong interest in farming and horses, and maintained farms including College Farm, Oakley.[8] When driving, he sometimes seemed more interested in looking sideways at the passing farms than in looking at the road ahead. For some thirty-eight years he was Honorary Secretary of the Bedfordshire Shire Horse Society providing stallions for stud which, accompanied by a groom, travelled from farm to farm to serve the mares. He was presented with a silver salver in recognition for his long association with the society in 1946.[9] His father, Henry Peacock, had been one of the founders of the Bedfordshire Shire Horse Society in 1890.[10] The society eventually closed in March 1952 due to the decline in heavy horse breeding. Members agreed to allocate part of the £180 surplus to purchase a challenge cup for the heavy turn-out classes at the annual Bedfordshire Agricultural Society shows. The cup was called the 'Walter M. Peacock' to perpetuate recognition of his work with the society since 1908.[11] Walter's other agricultural posts included Chairman of Bedfordshire Light Horse Breeding Society and Chairman of Bedfordshire Agricultural Society.

Serving as a County Councillor from 1935 to 1952, Walter Peacock's interest in helping small farmers was evinced by his membership of the Agricultural Committee, the Smallholdings and Allotments Sub-Committee and the Horse Breeding Sub-Committee of Bedfordshire County Council.[12] Walter also undertook many other civic duties over the years.[13]

The Lime Street office was also used as an administration centre for various charitable purposes. As a member of the Rotary Club of Bedford, Harry Peacock acted as Secretary to the club's Christmas Cheer Fund, later re-named 'The Harry

6 W. & H. Peacock Western & Co., *Staff Dinner to Celebrate Mr Robert's Golden Jubilee with the Firm 1921–1971, 27 September 1971* (Bedford, 1971), pamphlet.

7 *The Bedfordshire Times and Bedfordshire Standard*, 5 October 1951, p. 8.

8 Stocktaking valuations of College Farm, Oakley, and Dungee Farm, Harrold, for W. M. Peacock, 1920–1931, BLARS, PK 3/2/32.

9 *The Bedfordshire Times and Bedfordshire Standard*, 8 February 1946, p. 6.

10 *The Bedfordshire Times and Independent*, 27 November 1931, p. 7.

11 *The Bedfordshire Times and Bedfordshire Standard*, 28 March 1952, p. 5.

12 His election followed a vacancy that had arisen from the elevation of W. Robert Whitworth to aldermanic rank in 1935. His official letter of appointment is part of the Peacock archive, PK 8/4/16. In addition to these agriculturally-themed committees, Walter Peacock also served, at various times, as a member of the County Planning, County Records, Highways and Bridges, Local Government and Standing Joint Committees as well as on the Registration Sub Committee, BLARS, CCY 1936–CCY 1952.

13 He served his village as Chairman of Bromham Parish Council from 1935 to 1951, and was also a member of the Boards of Bromham House and the Three Counties Hospital (he joined the management committee in 1948). Other charitable appointments included trustee to the Dame Ursula Taylor Charity from 1944 to 1952 and the Bromham Coal Charity (1920s to 1942), BLARS PK 8/7/3, PK 9/3, PK 9/4.

Peacock Christmas Cheer Fund' to honour his memory.[14] The fund drew donations from many businesses and individuals and was used to provide one hundredweight of coal every Christmas for poor and needy persons in Bedford, thus giving much needed warmth and comfort during hard times. The office staff, and especially the pupils, were used to assist with administration. It was not uncommon to receive a visit at the office from a disgruntled but needy person to complain that they had not had a bag of coal when their neighbour, or a friend, had received a delivery.[15]

Walter Peacock and Mr Cyril P. Lilley were the joint Honorary Secretaries of the annual Oakley Hunt point to point race meeting, which for many years was administered from 10 Lime Street. Walter served from 1924 for eighteen years. Cyril Lilley was a long-standing manager of The London & Lancashire Insurance Co. Ltd with offices at 7 St Paul's Square, Bedford.

The office was also used for the administration of the County Ball, an important annual event in the social calendar. The ball was held in aid of the Royal Agricultural Benevolent Institution and was initially organised by Walter Peacock, and latterly by Dudley Peacock. Many thousands of pounds were raised for that worthy cause.[16]

Training and progression in the profession

For a long period, until university education became the more favoured means of education for the professions, the accepted way of entry was to serve a period, normally three years, as an indentured articled clerk or pupil to a suitably qualified Chartered Auctioneer and Estate Agent or Chartered Surveyor in an established firm. Until the Second World War, it was normal to pay a premium for that privilege; the payment was then often returned to the pupil as pocket money. Many of the pupils at Peacocks were articled to Robert Peacock, who was highly regarded in the profession.

The pupils were there to learn and therefore accompanied Robert or one of the other partners on a regular basis, especially when meeting clients. In addition, the pupils were required to act as sale clerks and generally assist in the preparation and administration of sales. The pupils were also taught how to carry out linear surveys, calculate areas of land and prepare plans as well as many other tasks undertaken by the business.

14 The Christmas Cheer Fund was set up in 1931. Harry Peacock also began an egg collection for Dr Barnado's Home as well as the previously-mentioned Christmas Hospital Turkey Draw for Bedford General Hospital, *The Eagle*, vol. 28, no. 6, p. 542. In 1939, 2,000 eggs were given for the appeal, *The Bedfordshire Times and Bedfordshire Standard*, 22 March 1940, p. 6.

15 The fund was often oversubscribed. In 1938, 800 names had been entered for the fund but only 600 were able to receive gifts, *The Bedfordshire Times and Independent*, 16 December 1938, p. 7.

16 The Royal Agricultural Benevolent Institution (RABI) was set up in 1860 to support members of the farming community in distress; the charity is still extant. RABI have records of donations, ranging from £42 to £150, for 'Bedfordshire County Ball; per Walter M Peacock', dating from 1935 to 1962 and '... per Dudley Peacock', from 1963 to 1966. In 1925, Walter Peacock was one of several RABI Honorary Local Secretaries in Bedfordshire. These were people of some standing in the local community who volunteered to recruit supporters and collect donations. In 1933, Walter became Secretary to the Bedfordshire RABI committee and was listed as such until 1957, RABI, personal communication to author.

The accepted method of professional study was by correspondence course through the College of Estate Management or similar organisations.[17] The pupils were expected to take advantage of any free time in the office to keep up to date with their study, especially in preparing the various written papers that were needed to progress with the courses. The study courses led to the professional examinations of the Chartered Auctioneers' and Estate Agents' Institute and the Royal Institution of Chartered Surveyors.[18] Many of the subjects were similar and most pupils sat for both sets of examinations. Membership of either organisation was generally considered an acceptable qualification and often both were obtained. The two professional institutions amalgamated in 1970 as the Royal Institution of Chartered Surveyors. In due course, the designation as a Chartered Auctioneer and Estate Agent, considered by some more appropriate to a general practice firm such as Peacocks, was dropped and all became known as Chartered Surveyors.

Pupils who had passed the matriculation examination were encouraged by Robert Peacock to study for a Bachelor of Science degree in estate management as this gained exemption from most of the other professional exams, although this was a much harder method for those studying by correspondence course.

In addition to those pupils who subsequently become partners in Peacocks, a number of former pupils became prominent in the profession through their own businesses or other organisations. These included: Robert L. Harding (started at Peacocks in 1937), Fenn Wright, Colchester; Richard Arnold (started 1938), W. S. Johnson & Co, Bletchley; Jan Church (started 1939), chief surveyor to the Zambian Building Society; Peter W. Moreton (started 1946), chief surveyor, Anglia Building Society; Brian C. Crozier (started 1948), Norris & Duval, Hertford; Christopher Bletsoe (started 1952), Henry Bletsoe & Son, Thrapston; Ronald Salvesen (started 1952), N. A. C. Salvesen & Co, Harpenden; Christopher J. Perks (started 1966), J. R. Eve & Son, Hitchin. Other former pupils or trainees have included Richard 'Dick' Hollands (started 1946) and Nicholas Elsley (started 1973) who went on to join District Valuers' offices.

Wilfred Noel 'Sonnie' Harraway Silkstone, who started as an articled clerk with Peacocks in 1931, became a partner in McConnells.[19] He then took over as the proprietor of Harry Ball, Bedford, in 1947 to become a competitor both in estate agency and auction sales.[20] Harry Ball was originally established in Bedford in 1889.[21]

17 The College of Estate Management was founded in 1919 under the auspices of the Chartered Auctioneers' and Estate Agents' Institute. Distance learning courses were offered from early in the college's history; by 1939 they had 3,774 postal students, http://www.cem.ac.uk/about-us/our-history.aspx (accessed January 2014).

18 The Royal Institution of Chartered Surveyors was created in 1868 and received a Royal Charter in 1881, http://www.rics.org/uk/about-rics/who-we-are/history-and-mandate/history/ (accessed January 2014).

19 Alexander McConnell established his estate agency at 20 Mill Street c. 1903, in 1908 the name was changed to McConnell and Co. and by 1910 it was known as McConnells. The company stayed at the same address for many years; it was still at Mill Street in 1958 when the company name changed yet again to Connells, *Bedfordshire Times and Bedfordshire Standard*, 7 March 1958, p. 11.

20 In April 1947 the proprietor was listed as W. E. Parish FAI, *The Bedfordshire Times and Bedfordshire Standard*, 18 April 1947 p. 4. In June 1947 the proprietor is listed as N. H. Silkstone AALPA, *The Bedfordshire Times and Bedfordshire Standard*, 13 June 1947, p. 4.

21 *Bedfordshire Past and Present*, a special supplement issued with *The Bedfordshire Times* and *The Biggleswade Chronicle*, October 1981, p. 11.

C. E. 'Jim' Heritage, who kindly provided the author with much valuable information about his time with Peacocks in the 1930s, became a successful auctioneer in Spalding, Lincolnshire. He started as a trainee in August 1931, and became an assistant to Walter Peacock in 1937.[22]

Geoffrey Millman started work as a trainee in 1953, but then went on to play cricket for Nottinghamshire and England before taking over the family jewellery business in Bedford.[23]

David R. Taylor started work as an office junior at 10 Lime Street in 1964 before moving to the St Loyes Office to learn about estate agency. David Taylor left to become a partner with C. R. Kilroy in an estate agency business before moving to the south of England to deal with development prospects.[24] As a talented negotiator, and expert in the field of development land acquisition and new homes, David Taylor eventually created the very successful agency in Bedford trading as Compass.[25]

John Wickstead, who started as an articled clerk in 1968, became a senior surveyor with the Woolwich Building Society.

Russell Beard started in the auction department in 1982 before joining the estate agency office at 58 St Loyes Street. He left in 1986 to become a partner in a newly formed agency, Cooper Beard, which has since become well established in the area.[26]

The articled pupils – official and unofficial duties!

Boys will be boys, and in the late 1940s and early 1950s it was not uncommon for pupils' 'studying' to take the form of a game of billiards at the billiard hall in Silver Street or a quiet afternoon at the cinema. When Brian Crozier was a pupil in the late 1940s, a regular port of call for morning coffee was Milo's Cafe, at 70B High Street. One attraction may have been the girls from the Physical Education College who also met at Milo's. Brian was a popular visitor; a popularity that may have been enhanced by the fact that he owned a car, a smart little Standard 8 Tourer, rare for a young man at that time. The Dujon Cafe on the first floor of 34 and 36 High Street, now occupied by Lloyds TSB Bank, was another regular venue, where many of the other up-and-coming surveyors, estate agents and solicitors regularly assembled for morning coffee.

Life for pupils was interesting and very varied as, in addition to regular duties dealing with various weekly auction sales at Horne Lane or in the auction rooms, there were also outside sales. Pupils would assist in the preparation of the sale including lotting up, cataloguing and preparing and arranging advertising schedules. On sale days, the pupils dealt with the sale files and general administration while the principals conducted the actual sale.

22 C. E. Heritage, *W. & H. Peacock: Reminiscences of C. E. Heritage*, typescript.

23 Geoffrey Millman, who died in 2005, aged 70, played for England from 1961 to 1963. He developed his wicket-keeping skills while at Bedford Modern School, *Bedfordshire on Sunday* 10 April 2005, pp. 13, 20 and 93.

24 Kilroys Estate Agency was founded in 1964, the company merged with Bairstow Eves in 1985, *Bedford and Kempston Express*, 27 March 1985, p. 1.

25 Compass was formed in 1995 and initially dealt with land sales and acquisition for building and development companies. It has since expanded to include residential sales, executive homes, new homes, lettings and auctions, http://compasspropertygroup.co.uk/ (accessed March 2014).

26 http://www.cooperbeard.co.uk/ (accessed February 2014).

Pupils might be taken out to assist Robert Peacock with a farm stocktaking valuation. He would stride across ploughed fields at a rapid pace while going around the farm to inspect crops or livestock, the pupil at his heels. When back at the office, the pupil's job entailed checking all the calculations and ensuring that the typed valuation was correct.

Pupils were also taken out to attend arbitrations, either when Robert Peacock was acting for one of the parties or when he was the arbitrator. Arbitration was a means of settling disputes when, for example, a landlord and tenant farmer were unable to agree to a new rent or where there was an outstanding claim for dilapidations. After hearing evidence from both parties, either verbally or from written submissions, an award would be made by the arbitrator. Apart from doing so 'on principle', it was sometimes difficult to understand why some clients would go to arbitration rather than reach a compromise and agree, thus saving significant costs and hassle.

Harry Peacock did not drive and would cycle into the office riding a tall 'sit-up-and-beg' machine. In the summer he was a striking figure, dressed in a jacket and wearing a straw boater. When a car was needed, a pupil was detailed to cycle out to his house, Oakdene, in Days Lane, Biddenham, to collect his Austin 12 car and to drive him around. This job fell to Jan Church during his time as a pupil.

Harry's favourite pastime was to spend Thursday afternoons ferreting – catching rabbits by using ferrets. He would invite one of the pupils or another member of staff to join him on his expeditions. Jan Church recalled how this meant being driver and ferret 'puller-outer'. If a ferret killed a rabbit in a burrow it would stay down the hole. Jan's job would then be to reach down into the burrow to pull out the ferret or, when the ferret was out of reach, to dig down to find it. Jan's fingers were never the same again.

Another of Jan's duties was to drive Harry Peacock and Mrs Peacock to Felixstowe each year for their annual holiday at a boarding house. If Jan exceeded thirty miles an hour he was told to slow down. Arriving one year on a boiling hot day, Mrs Peacock said Jan must be feeling very hot and asked if he would like a drink. She went off and returned with a glass of water; not quite what Jan had hoped for. Harry would give Jan £1 to get back from Felixstowe to Bedford by train, and ask for the change when he got back to the office.

Harry would sometimes invite a pupil to tea on early closing day. On arrival it was not unusual to find him in the garden and in need of assistance with the task in hand. Word soon got around to be busy on those afternoons.

One Christmas time in the early 1950s, when Dick Arnold and Arthur Wilkins were due to collect a dressed turkey from Carlton as the prize for the annual Hospital Draw, Harry Peacock asked that a sack of corn, for his chickens, be dropped off at his house in Biddenham. Dick and Arthur carried the sack between them to the back door and rang the bell. Mrs Peacock opened the door and with surprise said, 'Oh! Arnold, there are two of you. You'd better share this apple.'[27]

In the months before Harry Peacock died he would still try to cycle to the office, much to the concern of the partners and staff. By then there was a shared office car so one of the author's jobs was to run out to Oakdene to collect him before

27 The author was present on this occasion, sitting in the back of the car.

he had time to get out his bike. It was a bit like a game and the prize was to be rewarded with an apple from the apple loft. On the day Harry Peacock died he was being driven by Mrs Peacock, in his car, to the office. They had stopped for petrol at Langley's Garage in Bromham Road, Bedford, when he collapsed. The author would normally have collected him that day but had a rare weekend off.

Until 1969, the large scale Ordnance Survey Maps available for rural areas in Bedfordshire dated mostly from 1901. Although some urban area maps had been revised in 1926, any subsequent boundary changes or later buildings did not show. With photocopiers a thing of the future, whenever a plan of a farm was needed it had to be drawn from scratch after a site survey, or traced onto tracing linen from an Ordnance Survey map. Either way, it was a laborious task that took quite a lot of a pupil's time. If a mistake was made, the whole plan might have to be redrawn.

Once a tracing was completed, copies could be produced on the Arclight plan printer. This comprised a large, cylindrical, glass screen with a canvas cover to sandwich the tracing and a sheet of sensitised paper against the glass. A very bright arc lamp, with the speed controlled by an adjustable fan, then traversed the length of the cylinder to expose the print. It was then necessary to remove the exposed sheet and treat it with an ammonia developing solution. Staff had to be careful to get a correct exposure to obtain a satisfactory print so several attempts could be required.

Another job for the pupils was 'brusseling'. This involved visiting a farm to measure and calculate the area of a growing crop of Brussels sprouts, which were sold as standing to be harvested by the purchaser. Measuring was done with a sixty-six feet long Gunter's steel chain, which seemed to have a remarkable ability to collect mud as it was drawn along the ground. Even on an apparently dry day, Brussels sprouts seemed to retain water in the top of the leaves, just ready to be tipped down the top of Wellington boots. At the end of the survey it was necessary to carefully check that all the ranging rods and survey pins had been safely collected together. It was a great nuisance to be sent back to collect anything left behind. On return to the office there were boots to clean and the chain had to be washed and oiled to prevent it going rusty. On such outings when Dick Arnold was in charge his dog Sam would come along too, and would be exercised by letting him run alongside the car.

Dick Arnold's cars deserve particular mention. For some time Dick owned a Morris Eight Tourer dating from about 1936, which was becoming rather the worse for wear. When the ignition switch eventually gave up, the method of stopping the engine was for Dick to leap out, open the bonnet and lever the lead off the battery. Dick next owned a wonderful car, a Morris Cunard Special. This very attractive, twelve horsepower, open tourer was built with an aluminium clad wooden body. Painted black, the car was upholstered in red leather and had a canvas hood. There were wire spoked wheels and large headlights with wire grills. It was a most exciting car to drive and the first car the author drove at over sixty miles an hour.

On Saturdays the Lime Street staff and pupils all had duties at the sale yards dealing with the different sales. The staff had a half-day off on Thursday, early closing day for shops in Bedford.

It was a tradition to buy cakes for the office on birthdays. The nearby Victory Cake Shop in Lime Street made lovely sugar-cream buns, iced buns and doughnuts. They were not only bought for birthdays.

For many years, the caretakers and cleaners for 10 Lime Street and the auction rooms were members of the Whitehead family, who lived in an old cottage at 7 Lime Street. Mrs Whitehead and her husband had a business as umbrella makers and repairers. Mrs Whitehead's son, Ted, was an expert cabinet maker and furniture restorer, and worked for many auction room clients.

Turner's Fire, 1952

One particular event affecting 10 Lime Street was the epic Turner's fire. The premises of James Turner & Sons, house furnishers and furniture removers, extended from Lime Street to the Arcade, and were located next door to the office, separated by a driveway. On the night of Sunday 16 March 1952, Turner's premises caught fire and the building was completely gutted.[28] At the height of the fire the roof collapsed in a spectacular shower of flame and sparks, leaving just a shell by the time the fire was extinguished. There was considerable risk of the fire spreading to 10 Lime Street, which was thankfully averted by the expertise of the firemen. The following day there was great concern that the high brick side wall might collapse onto the office, so the premises had to be kept empty. Eventually, there was great relief when the wall was safely demolished.

James Turner & Sons (Bedford) Limited was one of Mr C. A. E. C. Howard's companies. C. A. E. C. Howard was a former Mayor of Bedford, Alderman and prominent businessman of vision.[29] Mr Howard's initiative ensured that the burned-out building was replaced with remarkable speed with a new shop constructed like an aircraft hanger. The site was subsequently redeveloped for the Bedford branch of the Trustee Savings Bank, later a branch of Lloyds TSB Bank, with offices above. It later became the China Palace restaurant, which closed in 2013.

External sales

In addition to dealing with the day to day administration of the auction sale rooms and the Horne Lane sale yards, the office dealt with the organisation of all other outside sales. These involved the sale of a huge variety of goods and other items of all descriptions on site at houses, farms, factories or other premises. Many sales took place on the instructions of a receiver in bankruptcy under court order, or were simply due to closure of a business following retirement or relocation. Some sales involved relatively few items, but larger sales could take place over several days. These required a great deal of preliminary work: identifying the different lots; preparing and printing sale catalogues; advertising; security; decisions about the conduct of the sale. Such sales offered a considerable challenge to the skill and versatility of the auctioneers and staff, who may have been called upon to take action at very short notice.

28 The damage was unofficially estimated at £100,000, *The Bedfordshire Times and Bedfordshire Standard*, 21 March 1952, p. 5.

29 C. A. E. C. Howard started a coal, coke and gravel business following redundancy from W. H. Allen Sons and Co. Ltd in the 1930s. From here he branched out into engineering, light-weight concrete factories, road transport and warehousing. In 1979 his Bedford firm employed 650 people. He played for Bedford Rugby Club in 1921 and 1922 and was later Captain of the East Midlands. As Alderman and Mayor he represented Bedford Borough at the Queen's Coronation. He died in 1979, *Bedfordshire Times*, 26 January 1979, p. 2.

Of the very many sales that have been conducted by the firm the majority have been without particular incident, but a few tales may prove of interest. Originally related to the author by George Robinson, they have been confirmed by C. E. Heritage.

During 1932 to 1933 there was a national swindle when investors were conned into the purchase of individual Cox's Orange Pippin apple trees in orchards at Cockayne Hatley, near Potton, with promised huge returns each year after harvest.[30] Bankruptcy of the company resulted in instructions for Peacocks to sell the bankrupt stock.[31] Harry Peacock went, with an assistant, to prepare for the sale, but was chased off the premises at the point of a loaded shotgun. They had to return to the premises later the same day to prepare the catalogue accompanied by a large escort of police.[32]

In 1937, the firm was instructed by Lady E. Randall to sell the contents of Wilby Castle, near Wellingborough.[33] Lady Randall had moved in some fifteen years previously. The contents of a much larger house had been deposited in the castle and nothing had been touched as her ladyship lived in just two small rooms. Despite the fact that several other firms of auctioneers had been sacked by Lady Randall after incurring her displeasure, Harry Peacock managed to keep her sweet. It took about six weeks to sort out and catalogue everything for the sale. In addition to furniture and pictures, this involved opening successive tea chests full of silverware, miniature portraits, china and glassware and even empty fish paste jars. The weights for some eight long-case clocks all had to be matched to the correct clock. The highest priced lot in the sale proved to be a walnut secretaire bookcase that had been found in an outhouse covered in several inches of bird droppings. The eventual sale occupied five days.[34]

Often, when selling a property by auction on site, the sale of the house was immediately followed by sale of the surplus contents. This was a convenient method of giving the purchaser of the property the opportunity to buy any items required, and also saved the costs of removal. [35]

At an on site sale of contents of a house in De Parys Avenue, Bedford, a local worthy purchased some bottles of wine. When he went to collect them the following

30 For more information see Anthony Crossley, *Apple Years at Cockayne Hatley (1929–1946): The History of Coxes Orange Pippin Orchards (Copo) at Cockayne Hatley and its Creator Mr Alexander Whitehead* (Cockayne Hatley, 1996).

31 BLARS, PK 1/4/102 Catalogue of nursery stock of 17,000 fruit trees to be sold by auction by W. & H. Peacock on 14 November 1933 by order of the High Court (Chancery Division) by direction of S.G. Hillier Esq. FCA, the Receiver of Chepco Ltd.

32 C. E. Heritage, *W. & H. Peacock: Reminiscences of C. E. Heritage.*

33 The sale was announced in *The Times*, 27 October 1937, p. 28. It took place from Monday 1 November. Items advertised included antique and modern furniture, Queen Anne specimens, Georgian period sideboards and book cases, Chippendale chairs, French furniture, bracket clocks, dower chests, oil paintings, sporting pictures, silver, decorative china, old cut glass, pewter and Persian carpets and richly decorated rugs.

34 C. E. Heritage, *W. & H. Peacock: Reminiscences of C. E. Heritage.*

35 Peacocks advertised these sales in the local press. For example, the sale of the property Holmdale in Turvey was advertised in the *The Bedfordshire Times and Independent*, 11 April 1924. This sale, under the instruction of Dr Gifford Nash, was to be immediately followed by the household contents including furniture, a grandfather clock, mahogany dining table and writing table, Axminster and Brussels carpets, curios and an art copper gong with beater. Dr Gifford Nash FRCS was the Honorary Surgeon of the County Hospital for thirty-seven years, *The Bedfordshire Times and Independent*, 9 August 1935, p. 8.

day he was disgruntled to learn that after the sale he and some friends (helped, it was believed, by Peacocks' sale porters) had guzzled the lot, to such an effect that he had no recollection of it the next day. On that occasion, Harry Peacock, a strict teetotaller, strictly enforced the sale condition that goods are 'at the purchaser's responsibility at the fall of the hammer.'[36]

There was great interest when the contents of the Nite Spot night club, the last occupier of the former Plaza Cinema on the Embankment, were sold in 1980 prior to the demolition of the building. On that occasion ordinary drinking glasses achieved higher prices than similar new glasses could have been purchased for.[37]

Over the years, the agricultural community was greatly attracted by on site farm sales, usually held on retirement or demise of a farmer, when a good company would attend. Such sales involved a lot of work for the firm's sales staff prior to the actual sale date as it was necessary to identify, assemble and suitably lot up the various items of deadstock as well as the livestock. The deadstock included not only tractors and machinery but also many smaller items such as hand tools. Farmers enjoyed the opportunity to meet their colleagues and the chance to secure a bargain or two. For larger sales, the firm would often arrange for a refreshment caravan to be on site for the well-being of the assembled company. An appropriate Peacocks' marquee would also be erected. Examples of two of many such sales include the following.

On 25 September 1933 there was a sale of farming stock at West End Farm, Kempston, when the sale included: 65 cattle; 8 horses; 107 sheep; 32 pigs; 200 poultry; implements; machinery and sundry other items that achieved a total of £1,260.[38]

In May 1947, following the retirement from farming of Mr F. P. Tinsley, a sale of livestock and deadstock from Park and College Farms at Clapham attracted a large crowd. The sale commenced with the deadstock, which comprised nearly 200 lots varying from troughs and poultry houses to a large selection of implements and machinery, tractors, trailers and other vehicles. The livestock included: over 140 various cattle in fifty-six lots; 14 horses; 115 sheep with lambs and 20 other sheep; 10 pens of pigs including numerous piglets; and 30 head of poultry.[39]

Throughout the firm's history, the auctioneers have also been regularly called upon to conduct auctions for charity fund raising including village flower shows and harvest festivals, thus helping to raise many thousands of pounds for worthy causes. [40]

The Lime Street office remained in operation until after the opening of the Auction Centre in 1977, and then became a ladies hairdresser. For many years the black vitrolite fascia remained, and it was still possible to make out the shadow of the name W. & H. Peacock.

36 C. E. Heritage, *W. & H. Peacock: Reminiscences of C. E. Heritage.*
37 *The Bedfordshire Times*, 9 May 1980, p. 3. The Nite Spot closed its doors on 28 April 1980. It was renowned at the time for having the longest bar in Bedford.
38 *Bedfordshire Times and Independent*, 22 September 1933, p. 8.
39 *Bedfordshire Times and Bedfordshire Standard*, 23 May 1947, p. 4.
40 One of the many charitable sales included a day shoot for ten guns in January 1941 offered by Mr Vic Davison and Mr Mark Young in aid of the Spitfire Fund for Bedfordshire, *The Bedfordshire Times and Bedfordshire Standard,* 24 January 1941, p. 6.

Chapter Four

The Sale Rooms, Lime Street, Bedford

The first sale at Lime Street

Peacocks took over sale rooms in Lime Street, Bedford, for regular weekly sales of antique and modern furniture in 1903. The premises had previously been occupied as an auction sale room by Mr Herbert J. Rayment.

Following an advertisement in *The Bedfordshire Times and Independent* on 23 March 1903, the first sale was held on 3 April 1903. Furniture had been removed from 'Goldington Avenue, Waterloo Road and other residences in Bedford'. The 'Splendid Household Furniture' included:

> A handsome French Dining Room Suite comprising large sideboard, dinner wagon, 10ft. dining table and 6 chairs. Cottage pianoforte in rosewood frame, pine writing table, bamboo, mahogany and other occasional tables, brass kerbs and fire implements, coal hods, Persian rugs, Brussels and Axminster carpets, Indian matting, linoleum and stair carpeting, oak bookcase, carved oak, cane seat, wicker and other occasional chairs; a quantity of books and ornaments; Bedroom appointments consisting of brass rail and iron bedsteads and French spring mattresses, wool mattresses and excellent bedding; mahogany, pine and painted chests of drawers, cane seat chairs, pitch pine wardrobes with plate glass doors, large linen chest, box ottoman, toilet glasses, marble top washstands and commodes; tapestry, plush and other curtains, and numerous effects.[1]

Management and organisation of the sales

Sales were held on Fridays with the exception of Good Friday and Christmas Day, Boxing Day or New Year's Day, when these occurred on a Friday. The sale room was approached down a wide passageway, which opened out into the main room where a broad table stood in the centre with the auctioneer's rostrum at the rear. A staircase led up to the first floor sale room. Furniture for sale was placed all-round the sides of the room and passageway with further items upstairs. Glassware, china, silver plate and silver were displayed on the large table, which would be surrounded by dining chairs for sale.

The building became a hive of activity on Mondays and Tuesdays as furniture and other items were brought in. Only the better items were accepted for sale at Lime Street, the remainder being sent down to the Horne Lane sale yard for the Saturday sale. By Wednesday morning chaos was turned into order; the items for sale were duly lotted up and numbered ready for the catalogue. The hand-written draft of the catalogue was collected for typesetting by the printers, and by late afternoon the proof had been approved and the catalogue printed.

1 *The Bedfordshire Times and Independent*, 23 March 1903, p. 1.

Thursday was view day when, in addition to the general buying public, dealers would arrive to try and discover any items of special interest. It was amazing just how quickly the 'bush telegraph' would work when there were particularly interesting antiques for sale, and potential buyers would come from far and wide.

On busy sale days, the company would crowd into the passageway and saleroom, overflowing up the staircase. The chairs around the central table were usually occupied by ladies who seemed to stake their claim each week, but rarely actually bid for anything. Some would even bring along their knitting or crochet. Depending on the number of lots, the sale would last until two or three o'clock in the afternoon. Except for a few regular buyers who were allowed credit, all purchasers were required to pay for items bought on the sale day. No goods could be removed before they were paid for.

During the many years before the availability of electronic aids the duties of the auctioneer's clerk included writing the draft catalogue as goods were lotted up and ensuring that the correct names of the vendors were recorded. On Thursday morning, the paying out slips had to be prepared with particulars of the lots being sold by each vendor to enable vendors to be paid the net proceeds as soon as possible after the sale. Although Thursday was half-day closing for the office, the sale rooms remained open for viewing. Viewing continued on Friday mornings before commencement of the sale at 10.45am. The clerk sat on the rostrum with the auctioneer to prepare sale bills and accept payment as the sale progressed. From the mid-1950s this practice was discontinued, and all payments were dealt with at the office in 10 Lime Street.

By Saturday lunchtime the majority of the goods would be cleared, and entries for the next sale would start to arrive, often brought in by a village carrier on a market day trip. Peacocks' furniture van, first introduced in the 1920s, was used for both furniture and egg collections. It was available to assist with deliveries on Mondays and Tuesdays, and also collected items for the next sale. On occasion goods would be taken to the firm's furniture repository in Rutland Road, Bedford, for temporary storage. After adoption of a logo in the 1970s, the dark blue van with the white peacock on the sides became a familiar sight in the area and served as a useful advertisement.

One of the major attractions of Peacocks' furniture sales was that the vast majority of articles offered for sale had been removed from households within the district. Often the complete contents of a house were sold following a death or when a family moved overseas. Relatively few items were sold on behalf of dealers. Throughout the difficult times of the inter-war years, however, Ronald Craig would visit sales held in London held by W. B. Hallett, Fox and White to buy furniture that was then brought to Bedford for re-sale.

Lime Street auctioneers and staff

The principal furniture auctioneer was Harry Peacock, later to be assisted by Ronald Craig, who had been employed since leaving school in 1916. Harry was a very gentle man with the humour and personality to maintain the right atmosphere as the sale progressed. He commenced the sale each week, and usually handed over the rostrum to Ronald Craig for sale of the items upstairs.

Ronald Craig took over as principal furniture auctioneer and valuer following the death of Harry Peacock, continuing until his retirement in 1966, after fifty years of service. This achievement was marked by the presentation of a gold watch at a celebration dinner held in his honour at the Embankment Hotel, Bedford. A great character, easily recognised by his shiny bald head, Ronald's quick wit could be relied upon to keep the attention of the company when he was selling on the rostrum. A short visit to the nearby Bear Inn prior to a sale always seemed to enhance the level of his performance.

In 1953, Francis Peacock joined the sale room team as a furniture auctioneer and valuer. A nephew of Walter and Harry Peacock, and cousin of Robert Peacock, Francis had trained and qualified as a Chartered Auctioneer and Estate Agent in Lincoln. Following Ronald Craig's retirement, Francis became the principal furniture auctioneer and valuer, and continued in this important role until early retirement due to ill health. Clive Childs acted as an assistant auctioneer for a number of years in addition to duties in other aspects of the auction department.

The important job of sale room porter was undertaken by a number of loyal employees who served the firm for long periods. In 1949, when the author's training included several months acting as the auctioneer's rostrum clerk, the portly, grey-haired figure of John Vintner held this office. John Vintner had joined Peacocks before the Second World War, and retired in 1950. His successors included Laurie Slater, Jim Brooks and John Day, each a character in his own right. They developed a wide knowledge of furniture and became firm friends with both vendors and purchasers during their period of office. The job involved much physical effort each week as chaos was turned into order ready for each sale.

Furniture fashions

In the post-war years of the 1940s and 1950s there was little demand for large Victorian and Edwardian furniture as larger houses were unpopular. Smaller modern houses were fashionable with demand being for furniture of the 1930s and 1940s. This meant that huge multiple wardrobes, sideboards and dining tables could be bought for only a few pounds. Often, a grandfather clock, too tall for modern houses, could be purchased for as little as £5. Upright pianos attracted very little interest except from Young Farmers' Clubs who ran a series of piano-breaking competitions. These pianos, bought for about 10s, were smashed with sledgehammers into pieces small enough to pass through a potato riddle.

This was to change, however, with the influence of television programmes such as 'The Antiques Road Show', which started in the late 1970s and helped make the public more aware of the potential value of older furniture and household items. Victorian and Edwardian furniture, now antique, became increasingly collectable. In part this was also associated with the revival of interest in Victorian and Edwardian town houses with their larger rooms, coupled with the sad fact that so much had been destroyed when such furniture was unfashionable.

Auction myths and pitfalls

There is a great attraction to auction sales as, except when there is a reserve price, goods must be sold to the highest bidder. This inevitably means that there are some terrific bargains from time to time, but equally some purchases can prove to be very expensive. Bargains arise when there is no serious competition for the lot on offer, but when two or more people want the same item anything can happen, and it is not uncommon to achieve a price above the normal retail price in shops.

Myths about auction sales abound, and it is interesting how some newcomers to the auction scene stand rigidly afraid of even twitching. In reality, the only time a visitor to the sale rooms is likely to end up with an unwanted purchase is by bidding for the wrong lot! Many prospective buyers for a particular lot seem to emit an aura that a skilled auctioneer can identify, enabling him to sense the likelihood of extracting another bid, or even a first bid from that person among a large company. It is rather akin to the customs officer who spots a smuggler who is trying too hard to look innocent.

Methods of bidding vary considerably, a bid may be signalled by a hand, nod, wink or other gesture, or simply by calling out. Waving to a friend during a sale is, of course, unwise, although the auctioneer will usually see that the person is not really paying attention and will question a bid if in doubt. The auctioneer is responsible for calling the bids, and decides on the amount of uplift he will accept from bid to bid, the uplift usually increasing as the bidding increases. Once the hammer falls the highest bidder is legally committed to the purchase and to payment for the lot before removing the items, in accordance with the advertised conditions of sale. Normally a purchase is at the buyer's risk from the fall of the hammer. Any defaulting buyer can be liable to be sued for non-payment, and the auctioneer has the right to resell any items not paid for, if necessary recovering any shortfall from the defaulter.

For many years, surplus goods would often be sent to Peacocks rather than otherwise disposed of, in the hope that they might attract a buyer. Many vendors were surprised and delighted when something unexpectedly sold for a good price, but others were disappointed when they found that the cost of commission and carriage exceeded the sale proceeds. It was not always understood that if there was no reserve price items simply had to be sold to the highest bidder, however low that bid might have been.

Valuation and probate

Peacocks professional assistance in dealing with the estate of a deceased person played an important part in helping executors deal with the estate. In addition to valuation and sale of freehold property, Peacocks' valuers were able to provide valuations for probate purposes and to assist with the clearance and sale of furniture and effects. The prospect of having to clear saleable items did not daunt the porters, but in a number of cases what they discovered, in addition to many antiques, was unusual.

On attending a large detached house in Bromham Road, it was found that the family had apparently never thrown anything away. The large rooms had gradually filled up as newspapers and other rubbish accumulated, leaving a small cell-like area in the middle. A piano and other furniture recovered from the basement showed tide marks caused by flooding. At a house that was cleared in Bushmead Avenue, a bath was found in the ground floor pantry; it had fallen through the ceiling from the bathroom above because of dry rot in the floor.

Other sales and closure

In addition to the regular furniture sales, specialist sales were held from time to time. In particular, a number of successful coin and silver sales were held during the 1960s. The coin sales included a variety of collectable coins of differing age and origin, often sets of special coin issues and gold coins.[2]

From 1941 until 1964 the Lime Street sale rooms were used as a regular venue for property auction sales held at 6.00pm on a Friday evening, following the regular furniture sale. The sale rooms finally closed in 1978, the year after the opening of the new Auction Centre at 26 Newnham Street, Bedford.

2 The first announcement for these specialised sales appeared in *The Bedfordshire Times*, 12 March 1965, p. 27. It followed the success of a more generally advertised sale of antique and modern furnishings, antique and silver plate, *The Bedfordshire Times*, 5 March 1965, p. 13. Amongst other things the first sale included: 1887 Golden Jubilee set of eleven coins; two early Victorian tea services; George III silver teapot; Gold Franc, 1873; Gold Rouble, 1898; Kruger Sovereign, 1894; and Victorian campaign medals.

Chapter Five

6 Dame Alice Street, Bedford

A new estate agency office

The office at 6 Dame Alice Street, Bedford, was opened in 1928. It remained at the heart of the estate agency activities until January 1964, when the present office at 58 St Loyes Street opened.[1] Conveniently located in a prominent position, a short distance from the High Street and near the General Post Office, 6 Dame Alice Street was the centre for house sales and lettings, valuations, surveys, rent collection, property management, insurance and arrangement of residential property auctions. The premises were formerly a public house, the Anchor Inn, and later became the Rosery Tea Rooms. The three-storey building was timber-framed with part stucco exterior and was probably of eighteenth century or earlier origin.

The property was owned by the late Cecil Clarabut, whose own business occupied the adjoining premises. Cecil Clarabut ran a very successful radio and electrical business, and as an expert in early radio had experience of working with the British Broadcasting Company.[2] His extensive premises included a large shop and a recording studio at the rear. His outside broadcasting equipment provided audio services for most important local events such as the Bedford Regatta, Elstow May Festival and the sports days held by large local companies for employees and their families.

With the opening of 6 Dame Alice Street, Harry Peacock maintained a close interest in the estate agency activities, though his own office remained at 10 Lime Street. The Dame Alice Street office was first managed by Walter George Riddy, who is said to have been a hard taskmaster. His assistant was George Robinson who later became manager, and was subsequently a partner in the firm until his retirement at the end of 1963. Frank Jeffery joined the staff in 1935 as an assistant and sales negotiator.

Bedford's property market in the 1920s and 1930s

Between 1928 and the outbreak of the Second World War in 1939, the office dealt with a wide variety of properties for sale or to let by private treaty. Due to the

1 The opening of the offices was announced in *The Bedfordshire Times and Independent*, 27 April 1928, p. 1; the closure in *The Bedfordshire Times and Bedfordshire Standard* on 30 December 1963, p. 1.

2 Cecil Clarabut was a founder member of the Association of Public Address Engineers. He was Chairman for many years and President in 1963. The association has had various name changes and is now known as The Institute of Sound & Communications Engineers, http://www.isce.org.uk/wp-content/uploads/2012/08/ISCE-How-Things-Began.pdf (accessed March 2014). He performed with the BBC in its early days as a baritone on the radio on 8 January, 26 February and 27 December 1926, twice with the Radio Quartet and once with Sydney Bowman's Trio, personal communication to author from BBC. The Clarabut premises can be glimpsed in R. Wildman and A. Crawley, *Bedford Then & Now* (Stroud, 2011), p. 67.

depression, and the threat of war, the property market was slow. There was very little demand for the various large country houses, which remained on the market for several years. A number of large houses were eventually sold for demolition and redevelopment, a fate that resulted in the loss of Cranfield Court and Kempston Hoo.[3] The materials were sold for salvage.

Larger town houses could also prove difficult to sell. Correspondence between W. and H. Peacock and The Midland Bank Executor and Trustee Co. regarding the sale of a property in Park Avenue, Bedford, in 1935, states that: 'we find it very difficult in this neighbourhood to dispose of properties of this type … as the domestic problem is very acute in this part, people will not go in for this type of house.'[4]

In the later 1930s, many builders and developers were building houses for sale with vacant possession or for investment as there was no difference in value.[5] The effect of the Rent Restrictions Acts after the outbreak of war in 1939 led to an increasing reduction in the value of leased property when compared to that of vacant houses.

Peacocks regularly published an Illustrated Property Register, which was distributed from house to house throughout Bedford, as well as being circulated to applicants on mailing lists.[6] The registers included: lists of properties for sale; a series of photographs of local views; advertisements by local shops; a map of Bedford; notes about Bedford and the schools.

The author begins his career

It was to Dame Alice Street that the author, then aged just sixteen, reported at 9.00am on Monday 8 March 1948, little knowing that it was a step that would result in working with the firm, under different business names, for over fifty-nine years. As a new, very young, member of staff, the author was one of the first articled clerks to be attached to the estate agency office without payment of a premium to the firm.

In 1948, the office front had a wide shop window with baize-covered display boards bearing auction posters. The recessed front door opened into a rather dingy

3 Cranfield Court was originally built by the Rev. George Gardner Harter. Work started in 1862 to the design of Thomas Hine of Nottingham in the French Gothic style. It was purchased by a builder in 1934 after a period of uncertainty and abandonment and demolished with the exception of the servants' quarters, Stephen Coleman, *Cranfield* (Bedford, 1986) Bedfordshire Parish Surveys Historic Landscape and Archaeology, p. 47. W. and H. Peacock sold the building materials including a carved oak staircase, stone garden ornaments, fireplaces and a set of six tapestry panels by auction on site on 27 November 1934, BLARS, PK1/4/112/1. A second sale followed on 26 March 1935 by order of the demolition contractor, BLARS, PK 1/4/112/2. Kempston Hoo originally stood in a well wooded park of about thirty acres, and was built in the early 1840s by Mrs Thomas John Green of Bedford. In 1849 the property was purchased by Mr Talbot Barnard, a member of the Bedford banking family. The last tenant was Lt Col. Oscar Eugster before the estate was sold and the house demolished c. 1932, John Wood, *Kempston* (Bedford, 1984), Bedfordshire Parish Surveys Historic Landscape and Archaeology, p. 20 and Victoria Walker, *Old Kempston* (Ochiltree, 2001), p. 34.

4 BLARS, PK 7/4/19 Correspondence dealing with the sale and purchase price of the late A. C. Clark's freehold residence, 3 Park Avenue, Bedford.

5 A new two or three bedroom house on the Queen's Park Estate, Old Ford End Road, Bedford, could, in 1938, be purchased from £500, *The Bedford Record*, 10 May 1938, p. 8. At the same time Peacocks were realising £370–£410 at auction for older terraced properties in Bedford with sitting tenants.

6 These property registers were compiled from at least 1908. An advert appears in the *Bedford Directory 1910* offering the guide 'post free', Bedfordshire Publishing Company, *Bedford Directory 1910* (Bedford, 1910), p. 380.

front office, separated from a middle office by a partly glazed partition. A side door led out to a small yard with a store and WC. At the back was George Robinson's office. A separate entrance door at the front led upstairs to the first floor front room occupied by the book-keeper, and to a kitchen where old records were stored in envelopes set out on shelving. The file relating to any sale or valuation, dating back to the opening of the office in 1928, was easy to find in a matter of minutes. The second floor attic rooms were sub-let to local accountants, Messrs McPherson Timmins and Ednie, as an audit office.

The office safe was kept in a cupboard under the stairs, and although the safe was locked at night the keys were always left in a filing cabinet drawer in the office. Heating was provided by gas fires. These were so inadequate that in cold weather it was necessary to wear an overcoat as well as the usual layers of indoor clothes to try and stay warm.

The telephone was in the middle office, with a single extension through to George Robinson's office. This meant that a member of staff had to rush to the middle office to answer any outside call. The ensuing chaos, in trying to find the required person for whom the call was meant, created an air of activity. For many years there was just one telephone line. The number Bedford 2333 remained, with later prefixes, that of the county homes department at the St Loyes Street office.

In addition to George Robinson, partner in charge, the male staff comprised Frank Jeffery, who was by then studying for the direct final examination of the Chartered Auctioneers' and Estate Agents' Institute, and Jack Alley, a general clerk and assistant. They had both returned to the office after wartime military service. The remainder of the staff included: a cashier/typist/receptionist, Miss Joan Westgarth (later Mrs Joan Beardsmore); George Robinson's secretary, Miss Muriel Smith; Mrs Elizabeth Miller, the bookkeeper; and Miss Sylvia Circuit, the office junior.

Office equipment consisted of two pre-war Royal manual typewriters, an Imperial typewriter, a Roneo duplicator and a large, ancient adding machine, generally known as 'the mangle'. When instructions were received for a property sale, brief details of the property were written into the Instruction Book, a large, leather-bound volume, several inches thick, resembling - and affectionately known as – 'the bible'. Sale particulars were typed onto a stencil to enable copies to be produced on a duplicator. This was a very messy process from which good copies were difficult to achieve; many were unsuitable for distribution. It was almost impossible to use the duplicator without getting ink on the operator's hands.

George Robinson used his car for the office, and occasionally Frank Jeffery was allowed to use it too. Unless travelling with George Robinson, most journeys around the town were on foot or by bicycle. It was not until 1951 that an office car was acquired for general use, a Morris Oxford, which had to be returned to a garage in Kimbolton Road at the end of the working day.

During 1948, Frank Jeffery left the Dame Alice Street office to take over as manager of Bartle Potter & Son, an estate agency purchased by Peacocks, with offices above Hebblethwaite's toy and cycle shop at 121 and 123 Midland Road. Bartle Potter and Son continued to trade under that name and moved to 104 Bromham Road before closing in 1953. Frank Jeffrey then moved back to the Dame Alice Street offices.

George Robinson had been away from the office due to illness during early

1948 and needed an assistant on his return. As a result, the author was taken under his wing. Due to the close working relationship, the author soon met most of the office's clients.

George Robinson had joined Peacocks in 1910, and had a most extensive practical knowledge of all aspects of the business. He was a skilled negotiator, and acted as valuer for several building societies. In the office his word had to be obeyed, right or wrong.

Bedford in 1948

The Bedford of 1948 still had the atmosphere of a provincial market town as affected by post-war austerity, when food, clothes, sweets, coal and petrol were all still rationed. Many other un-rationed items were also in very short supply.

There was two-way traffic in the High Street, and the top end of Harpur Street not only carried two-way traffic, but parking was allowed in the centre of the road. There were some buses, with the bus station located in The Broadway, opposite St Peter's Church. Although some villages enjoyed regular bus services this often meant only a very limited daily service, or in some cases, a bus or two on Wednesday and on Saturday, the market days. Local bus services were provided by the Eastern National Omnibus Company, and Birch Bros buses ran a service through Bedford between Rushden and London, via Hitchin and Hatfield.

In the pre-Beeching era of 1948, railways remained a principal means of local and long-distance travel. Most of the country could be reached from Bedford Midland Road station, travelling south through London via St Pancras or north to Scotland. There were still stations at Ampthill, Oakley and Sharnbrook on the main lines. A branch line served Hitchin via Cardington, Southill, Shefford and Henlow. A further branch line led to Northampton, via Turvey and Olney.[7]

The train services from Bedford St John's station extended to Oxford in the west, linking with the former London Midland & Scottish Railway main line from Euston at Bletchley, and passing through Kempston Hardwick, Stewartby, Lidlington, Ridgmont and Woburn Sands. To the east the line ran via Willington and Blunham to Sandy, crossing the former London and North Eastern Railway main line from King's Cross, through to Potton and Cambridge.

With the pedal cycle still a favourite means of transport, Bedford was often described as a town on wheels. Literally hundreds of bicycles would emerge from the major factories when closing time came each day.

Motor cars were in short supply, and petrol was strictly rationed. Anyone lucky enough to buy a new car could have resold it at a significant premium above the new price.

The larger stores included: Woolworth's, Marks and Spencer and Greens (now British Home Stores) in Midland Road; Braggins, incorporating school outfitting departments called 'Our Boys' and 'Our Girls'; and E. P. Rose & Son in Silver Street.

7 Peacocks later auctioned a number of railway stations by order of British Railways from September 1967 to February 1968. These were Cardington, Oakley, Olney and Southill Stations. See auction records for more information.

Various grocery stores that would deliver weekly orders included: Grimbly Hughes at the corner of High Street and Mill Street; J. Clarke & Son in Harpur Street; and Consumers Tea Company, with a High Street shop and five other branches. Sainsbury's had a shop in Midland Road, and Dudeney & Johnston had a large grocery shop in the High Street and six other branches in the town. There were many butchers and bakers and several dairies, most of whom would deliver orders on request.

Dedicated men's outfitters included: J. A. Beagley and Co. Ltd; J. T. Clayton; H. W. Clifton & Sons; and Harry Hills. At the present day only Clayton's survives, though on a different site.[8]

Furniture stores included: F. Gamman & Son; Harrison & Rowley; Longhurst & Skinner; and Wells & Co.

The principal ironmongers and builders' merchants were Henry Bacchus in the High Street, Randall's in St Mary's Street and Goldings. Henry Bacchus and Randall's have now gone. Goldings, the ironmongers shop in the High Street, was a veritable Aladdin's cave where one could find those odd things that no one else appeared to stock. This shop is still doing well in the town, in the same location.

For entertainment, the Royal County Theatre in Midland Road was the venue for music hall, repertory and amateur operatic productions. Cinemas included: the luxurious, air-conditioned Granada Theatre, complete with a theatre organ that would rise up from the depths; The Plaza, on The Embankment; The Picturedrome, on the south side of the river; and The Empire, in Midland Road.

Bedford Corn Exchange was a popular venue for Saturday night dances, concerts and stage productions. It was also favoured for a number of balls that were highlights of the social season, particularly the Mayor's Ball, the Rotary Ball, the Police Ball, the Farmers' Ball and the County Ball. Seasonal fairs were held in the 'fairground' off Commercial Road, adjacent to the Cattle Market.

In addition to its use for rowing as a sport, the River Great Ouse was used for public boating. Punts, rowing boats and canoes were available for hire from Chetham's Boathouse (now Bedford Rowing Club), Bryant's, or from Foster's in Queens Park. It was possible to go upstream as far as Kempston Mill, or downstream to Cardington Mill. Electric launches provided boat trips.

Bedford Regatta in July was a highlight of the summer season when the river banks would be lined with moored boats and there would be large crowds along The Embankment to watch the races.[9] There was always great rivalry between Bedford School and Bedford Modern School, especially when their first eights clashed during the heats or in the final race.

The river was also used for swimming. Newnham Baths and the Commercial Baths had open air pools that were fed by the river, but swimming also took place in various other parts. There was an annual Long Swim, organised by Bedford

[8] J. T. Clayton was established in 1905 and was originally sited at 3 The Arcade, Bedfordshire Times Publishing Company, *Bedford Directory 1906* (Bedford, 1906), p. 86. In 2009, Claytons moved to their current location within the furnishing store, Hatters, at 532 Goldington Road.

[9] Bedford Regatta was first held on 25 August 1853 although aquatic sports had been held on the river two years prior to this. The first regatta had eight events, one a four-oared race, and the others for sculls, pairs and rhandans. Bedfordshire Times, *Bedford Amateur Regatta July 17th 1913, Diamond Jubilee 1853–1913 Official Programme* (Bedford, 1913), p. 1. The Regatta is still held in the town.

Swimming Club, from the Town Bridge to the Suspension Bridge, over a distance of about half a mile, which drew entries from a wide area. Bedford Modern School also ran a Long Swim, open to pupils.

There remained a significant military presence in the area as many young men, due to embark on their period of compulsory National Service, passed through to report at Kempston Barracks or Cardington Camp.[10] United States Army Air Force personnel were stationed at Chicksands and various other bases in the area. A number of large country properties and some town properties remained requisitioned by the government.

Small businesses could be found in many areas. In addition to corner grocery shops, there were local dairymen, bakers and butchers. Many small builders, decorators, carpenters and plumbers operated from their homes where they also had a workshop. As for estate agents, Peacocks' principal competitors were Stafford, Rogers and Merry Ltd, McConnells, Harry Ball & Co., Douglas Stratford & Co. and Robinson & Hall.

Local building societies, with their own offices, included the Bedfordshire Building Society, the Bedford Permanent Building Society and the Bedford Crown Permanent Building Society. The Halifax also had an office. Other societies were represented through local agencies with either solicitors or estate agents.

Bedford's property market in the 1940s

By 1948, the central housing areas of the town, once highly-favoured residential areas, had become run down.[11] Many of the larger houses in Ashburnham Road, Poets Corner and the Saints area were let as rooms. Many of the small terraced houses between Bromham Road and Midland Road, and in the Queen Street area north of Tavistock Street, were in very poor condition. They lacked bathrooms or other amenities, and were occupied by some of the poorest families. After the war accommodation was in short supply, and there remained a risk that an empty house could be requisitioned.[12]

With so few houses for sale it was unnecessary to prepare a list as it was easy to remember what, if anything, was on offer. This was due, in part, to the fact that all building was under strict government control. Priority for new building was given to places where the war had been hardest felt; Bedford did not suffer greatly

10 Kempston Barracks was built from1874 to 1876. It was associated with the 16th Regiment of Foot, later the Bedfordshire Regiment. Occupying some twenty-three acres it was wound down in 1958. Threatened with demolition in the 1970s the impressive entrance block was retained for alternative uses including a Territorial Army Centre, *The Kempston Souvenir Programme to Commemorate the Queen's Silver Jubilee: Flood-lit Tattoo September 23 1977* (Bedford, 1977), p. 9. Cardington Camp was chosen by the Admiralty in 1916 for airship construction. In the 1920s it was developed with the intention of making it an 'Imperial Air Route Terminus' but this ceased following the R101 airship disaster in 1930. From 1936 to 1953 it was used by the RAF for recruitment and training and later as a de-mob centre. In the 1950s and 1960s it continued as a reception centre for recruits, John Wood, *Cardington and Eastcotts* (Bedford, 1985), Bedfordshire Parish Surveys Historic Landscape and Archaeology, p. 92.

11 A survey undertaken in 1950 by Bedford Borough Council showed that there were 472 houses classed as unfit for habitation and 1,400 of low standard, Jones, *For the Record*, p. 23.

12 The power to requisition rooms and houses was given by the Ministry of Health to local authorities in 1943. Attempts to requisition were not successful in Bedford; requisition notices were served on twenty-two houses and withdrawn on all but two after objections were received, Jones, *For the Record*, p. 21.

from enemy action.[13] Few new houses had been built since the war as a licence was required due to the shortage of building materials, especially bricks, timber and plumbing materials.

It was virtually unheard of to have any unfurnished flats or houses to let due to the effect of the Rent Restrictions Acts and the automatic right to security of tenure granted on occupation. This security extended, not only for the lifetime of the tenant, but for the spouse and near relatives too, for up to two further lifetimes. Furnished properties were available, although subject to certain conditions, and were not restricted. With so few properties for sale in those times of general austerity, there were occasions when, on being told that a particular house was for sale, a prospective purchaser was known to say, 'I'll have it! How much is it?'

Once a sale was agreed, it was normal for a deposit of ten per cent of the agreed price to be paid to the agent subject to contract. Solicitors were advised and the sale was usually completed within four weeks. The exchange of contracts, today so essential, was virtually a formality due to the mutual trust that prevailed. It was almost unheard of, and thought shocking, that a vendor or purchaser withdraw following a handshake on reaching agreement. Bridging loans were usually readily available, and interest rates were very low by later standards.

In 1948 and for some years later, the agreed purchase price was usually just for the house. Any fixtures and fittings, particularly such items as curtain tracks, linoleum or cookers, would be purchased at valuation. Fully fitted carpets were rare, and most curtains and curtain tracks would be removed for use elsewhere; even light bulbs would be taken out. Plants, rose bushes, trees and shrubs might well have been taken from the garden. Sheds or greenhouses were frequently also removed, since new ones were not readily available.

Bedford was still contained within its pre-war boundaries. To the north, houses were scattered along Kimbolton Road, whilst Putnoe Lane ended as an un-adopted gravelled track and bridleway leading to Putnoe Woods and the entrance to Putnoe Farm, then farmed by the Hartop family.[14] The huge area of Laxton's Nurseries extended from behind the lower part of Putnoe Lane across to Goldington Road and was adjoined by a large area of private allotments off Caves Lane.[15] The area north of Bedford Cemetery, now known as Brickhill, extending west towards Clapham was farmland.[16]

Kempston, a large urban district in its own right, was largely regarded as a separate town. It was less favoured for residential purposes due to the effect of fumes from the many brickworks in the Marston Valley.[17]

Within the town, the most favoured areas by house buyers for modern semi-

13 The number of dwellings built in Bedford during the twenty year inter-war period was 3,312 of which 1,037 were local authority houses. In May 1946 there were 2,300 applicants for Bedford Borough's housing list, Jones, *For the Record*, p. 19.

14 Bedford Borough Council started to acquire land in the early 1950s in Putnoe and Goldington, and by April 1952 the Council owned 250 acres in the area, Jones, *For the Record*, p. 44.

15 Laxton Brothers were a well-known firm of Bedford nurserymen, seedsmen and florists founded by Thomas Laxton in 1879. Laxton's sold their 140 acre estate to the Goldington Estate Company for housing development, and closed in 1957, Richard Wildman, 'Laxton of Bedford: the family and the firm', *Bedfordshire Magazine*, vol. 23, no 182 (Autumn, 1992), pp. 244–47.

16 This land was acquired by Bedford Borough Council in October 1954, Jones, *For the Record*, p. 71.

17 Brickmaking in Bedfordshire expanded in scale after the advent of the railways. By 1936, The

detached houses (i.e. late 1930s) included Putnoe Lane, Wendover Drive, Risborough Road, Newnham Avenue, Phillpotts Avenue, Greenshields Road and the eastern end of Castle Road. Houses along the service roads off Elstow Road and Goldington Road were also very popular. The prices of houses in these areas were usually between £2,500 and £3,000.[18] Smaller houses built in the late 1930s around Elstow Road, Mile Road and London Road, and in the western area of Queen's Park, could be purchased from about £1,500 to £2,500.[19] Detached 'modern' three and four-bedroom houses would be in the price range of £3,000 to £4,500.[20] Victorian terraced houses might be bought for around £1,000 without a bathroom, or £1,500 with a bathroom. These were mostly in the Castle Road, Queen's Park, Ampthill Road and Stanley Street areas of the town.[21] The large semi-detached Victorian and Edwardian houses found in the Saints area off Kimbolton Road, and in Poets Corner off Bromham Road, could be bought for less than £2,000, and £3,000 was enough to buy a large detached three-storey house in need of improvement.[22]

To try to put the above into perspective, it is important to remember that the post-war era of 1948 was a period of serious austerity. Many properties remained in need of repair, and there was a general shortage of almost all materials; it was also necessary to obtain a licence to purchase some items for repairs, particularly timber.

Large Victorian houses with big rooms, lofty ceilings and draughty windows and doors, which were difficult to keep warm when supplies of fuel were rationed, became less favoured for purchase as a family home. Many were converted into flats.

Most houses had a limited number of electric power sockets, often only one in a room. Numbers of smaller, older houses still had gas lighting on the ground floor and used candles or oil lamps upstairs. Hot water might be provided by a solid fuel Ideal boiler, a gas geyser or Ascot gas water heater. Some houses, usually those built in the 1930s, had an electric water heater. Open coal fires, slow combustion stoves or gas fires still provided most heating. Fireplaces in bedrooms were rarely used so it was quite common on a winter's morning to find ice on the inside of bedroom windows. What was then grandly called central heating often consisted of a radiator in the hall, one in the lounge and a heated towel rail in the bathroom.

Kitchen appliances were mostly limited to a gas or electric cooker, a copper for boiling laundry and a mangle for wringing the washing. Very few houses had a

London Brick Company had taken over all the smaller companies, and was set to become the largest brick making company in the world, Godber, *Bedfordshire*, p. 554.

18 An advert by Peacocks for a modern semi-detached house in the Castle Road area with two reception rooms, a kitchenette, three bedrooms, garden, garage and Ideal boiler in *The Bedfordshire Times and Bedfordshire Standard*, 1 January 1948, p.1, had an asking price of £2,750.

19 An advert by Peacocks for a modern semi-detached house in the London Road area with two reception rooms, a kitchenette and three bedrooms in *The Bedfordshire Times and Bedfordshire Standard*, 16 April 1948, p. 1, had an asking price of £2,350.

20 An advert by Peacocks for a modern detached house in the Goldington Road area with a lounge, dining room, breakfast room, kitchen, four bedrooms, garden, garage and workshop in *The Bedfordshire Times and Bedfordshire Standard*, 1 January 1948, p. 1, had an asking price of £4,000.

21 An advert by Peacocks for a brick and slate villa residence in the Queen's Park area with six rooms in *The Bedfordshire Times and Bedfordshire Standard*, 27 August 1948, p. 1, had an asking price of £900.

22 An advert by Peacocks for a semi-detached residence 'convenient for Bedford School' with three reception rooms, six bedrooms, domestic quarters and a site for a garage in *The Bedfordshire Times and Bedfordshire Standard*, 11 June 1948, p. 1, had an asking price of £1,600.

refrigerator or washing machine. Many houses still had a cast-iron, coal-fired range to cook on in rural areas.

In country areas and villages, many houses and cottages had no mains water supply and still relied on a well for water, or water was collected in buckets from a standpipe in the road. Main sewerage systems had not reached villages so most of the better properties that had a bathroom relied on a septic tank drainage system that could work satisfactorily for a number of years or, alternatively, a cesspool that required emptying when full. Sanitation for other properties consisted of a shed somewhere in the garden housing a bucket lavatory emptied by the local council, or a simple earth closet, which was just a deep hole in the ground under a wooden seat. A few properties even had a two-seater earth closet!

Post-war de-requisitioning

As the Dame Alice Street office embraced all the estate agency activities of the firm there was a great deal of variety in the work and a lot to learn. This encompassed not only sales and lettings, but also valuations, surveys, rent collection, property management and other tasks. The de-requisitioning of properties that had been taken over for a variety of government purposes during and immediately after the war created a lot of work. This involved the checking of a schedule of condition, mostly having been prepared by Peacocks when the property was first requisitioned, and preparing and agreeing any claims for necessary repairs and redecoration to the property, outbuildings and grounds.

Larger de-requisitioned houses dealt with included: Harrold Hall; Cobb Hall, Sharnbrook; Milton Ernest Grange; and Goldington Hall, Bedford.

Harrold Hall, which had been used by Italian prisoners of war, was delightfully located by the river Great Ouse. It was demolished in the early 1960s, and replaced by an estate of new houses now known as Hall Close. The separate range of stabling, coach house and coachman's cottage was later converted into attractive dwellings.[23] Cobb Hall, previously occupied by the United States Army Air Forces, and later as a billet for nearby Ordnance Depot staff, was also demolished.[24] While Peacocks' staff were working at Milton Ernest Grange, which had been used to house British Military Police and possibly prisoners of war, there were rumours of a ghost.[25] The house was always carefully locked up at the end of each day, but was found to be open again the following morning.

23 The house was originally built in 1608 and much enlarged in 1816, Dick and Pat Mills, eds, *Harrold at the Millennium* (Harrold, 2000), p. 17. On 14 April 1945 No. 611 Italian Working Party was based in the grounds, Stephen Risby, *Prisoners of War in Bedfordshire* (Stroud, 2011), p. 28.

24 Cobb Hall served as a hostel for workers at the Sharnbrook Ordnance Depot, which was used as a bomb and ammunition store from 1942. It primarily supplied bases of the 1st Air Division of the US 8th Air Force. After the war it was used as a National Service Hostels Corporation hostel. http://www.airfieldinformationexchange.org/community/showthread.php?1692-Melchbourne-Park-Sharnbrook-Risely (accessed February 2014). A plan of the hostel made in February 1947 shows sleeping huts, lavatories, a sick bay, shop, theatre, tea bar and lounge, BLARS X660/44–46.

25 Milton Ernest Grange was situated only a few hundred yards away from Milton Ernest Hall that was thought to be used as a Special Operations Executive base early in the war. It was later used by the United States Army Air Force for their 8th Advanced Air Service Command, David Newman, *The Importance of Milton Ernest: Village History and Heritage Trail* (Milton Ernest, 2006), p. 110.

Bedford's property market in the 1950s – Putnoe and Brickhill

With post-war restrictions still applying to building, and the need to obtain a licence for new houses, development was curtailed; this continued until easing of restrictions in 1952.[26] By that time, Bedford Borough Council had acquired Putnoe Farm for development.[27]

As a residential estate, Putnoe was planned with: a variety of council housing; houses built on behalf of the council for sale to buyers without the normal deposit; plots for individual houses; and areas allocated for speculative development by builders who had been active in the district. Within the development, provision was made for parks, schools, shops and other amenities. Development of The Graylings, off Queens Drive, by Luton builders, H. C. Janes Ltd, included some of the first of many hundreds of houses to be built by that company as the new area of Putnoe was developed, to be followed in later years by Brickhill and North Brickhill.[28] It was possible to buy a new Janes' 'G type' semi-detached, three-bedroom house, with living room, kitchen and downstairs bathroom for only £1,800. Larger three-bedroom, semi-detached houses with an upstairs bathroom and separate lounge and dining room cost around £2,150.[29] Other speculatively-built houses on the new developments were built by well-known local builders including: Besbuilt Ltd, Harpur Street, Bedford; T. R. Donnelly, Harrowden Road, Bedford; Gambriel & Sugars, Dane Lane, Wilstead; Holts (Bedford) Ltd, The Crescent, and others.[30]

Office expansion 1950–1964

In about 1951 the premises at 4 Dame Alice Street, previously occupied by the Bedford Division Conservative & Unionist Association, became vacant and were taken over by Peacocks. This added two further ground floor offices, and more first and second floor accommodation extending over a covered gateway. Though the upper space was of little value, except for storage, the extra frontage enabled the firm to install a new office front and fascia with window display boards. The joinery was in polished mahogany with a deep black vitrolite fascia carrying in bold

26 In December 1952, it was announced that there would be a virtual removal of local authority licensing control over private house-building, apart from the size of the house and the quantity of softwood used. Previously, the emphasis had been on local authority building with restrictions on the private share, at one point this had been in a ratio of one private house to nine local authority houses, *The Times Digital Archive*, 17 December 1952, p. 6.

27 Building began in 1953 and by March 1954 the first of the planned 2,000 homes were ready on the Putnoe estate, *The Bedfordshire Times and Bedfordshire Standard*, 12 March 1954, p. 3. By 1957, 1,507 houses had been built and the work on the estate was finally completed in 1960, *The Bedfordshire Times and Bedfordshire Standard*, 12 July 1957, p. 8 and *The Bedfordshire Times and Bedfordshire Standard*, special supplement , 12 February 1960, p. xi.

28 In October 1953, Bedford Borough Housing Committee allocated 136 plots in the Putnoe and Goldington areas to be released for sale to local building companies. The one exception was Messrs H. C. Janes Ltd of Luton, which was included because of the amount of work they had undertaken in the Borough in recent years, Jones, *For the Record*, p. 41.

29 Houses by H. C. Janes Ltd in Queens Drive were advertised from £2,150, and bungalows from £2,240, *The Bedfordshire Times and Bedfordshire Standard*, 21 January 1954, p. 8. In 1956, houses were advertised from £1,800, *The Bedfordshire Times and Bedfordshire Standard*, 4 May 1956, p. 4.

30 Adverts for these properties can be seen in the *The Bedfordshire Times and Bedfordshire Standard*: T. R. Donnelly, 25 June 1954, p. 11 (adjoining Queens Drive) and 1 June 1956, p. 8 (Mount Drive and The Ridgeway); Messrs Holts (Bedford) Ltd, 27 July 1956, p. 6 (Putnoe Street) and 3 August 1956, p. 6 (Heathfield); Redman (Builders) Ltd, 5 November 1954, p. 6 (Braeside).

lettering the name W. & H. Peacock. Inside the office, a smart new front counter was installed. The work was carried out by Mr R. S. Wells, a skilled local cabinet maker and shop-fitter.

During the period between 1950 and 1963 business activities increased. Frank Jeffery qualified as a Chartered Auctioneer and Estate Agent in 1949. The author qualified in 1953, before being called up for National Service in the Royal Engineers, and commissioned as an Officer. A long embarkation leave allowed the author to return to the office for several weeks in 1954 to negotiate the sale of many tenanted houses in Cranfield to sitting tenants. These belonged to a property company that had purchased the houses, subject to the existing protected tenancies, after they had been unsold at the Cranfield estate property auction held by Peacocks in November 1943.[31] In 1953, after graduating in rural estate management from St Catherine's College, Cambridge, Dudley Peacock came to the Dame Alice Street office to gain experience in estate agency activities until the author returned from overseas.[32] Under George Robinson, the fully-qualified office team covered various professional aspects of the business in addition to their substantial input into sales and property management.

At different times a number of property sales negotiators were employed, not least a colourful character, Captain Stanley Plumb. Stanley Plumb was a former Bedford police officer and detective before serving with the Allied Control Council in Berlin. He seemed to know almost everyone in the town and was a mine of information. What he did not know he could usually guess or discover from one of his many former contacts, and he would often find a coin or two for the local tramps who passed on news. A most effective salesman, Stanley Plumb's patience was sorely tried one year when he was sent to a cottage in Water Lane, Kempston, to take particulars for sale. He was not told the client's name, and it was not until he had finished writing down all the particulars of the accommodation that the owner's name was revealed as a former colleague, and the significance of the date was pointed out - it was 1 April. Stanley Plumb always checked the client's name after that day.

By 1962, the lease of the Dame Alice Street office was due to expire. The owner, Mr Cecil Clarabut, was not prepared to negotiate terms that were agreeable to Peacocks for renewal of the lease, nor sell the freehold. This led the partners to look elsewhere, eventually to 58 St Loyes Street, Bedford. The new office was due to open on 1 January 1964, and the Dame Alice Street office closed a few weeks later. The vacated premises were to stand unoccupied for several years before the site was eventually redeveloped with shops and offices. The Post Office was re-located to St Loyes Street, and Dame Alice Street became a one-way street as the traffic routes in Bedford were altered.

With the closing of 6 Dame Alice Street, George Robinson retired after over fifty years' service to the firm. A new partnership was formed from 1 January 1964 between Robert Peacock, Dudley Peacock, Frank Jeffery, Jonathan Knights and the author.

31 *The Bedfordshire Times and Bedfordshire Standard*, 1 October 1943, p. 6.
32 While at Cambridge, Dudley Peacock was a member of the College First Boat and later elected as a member of the Leander Club, *The Ousel,* no. 964 (March 2000), pp. 79–80.

Chapter Six

58 St Loyes Street, Bedford

Development of improved estate agency premises

By 1962, as all attempts to secure the future for the office at 6 Dame Alice Street had proved unsuccessful, the partners were left with little alternative but to find a new site for the increasingly busy estate agency activities.

It was thought important that any new premises should be easy to find, close to the town centre, but not in a prime retail location. With the increasing use and availability of the motor car, car parking was also becoming an important consideration. With three office cars used at Dame Alice Street, it had been calculated that the equivalent of one day per week was being wasted in fetching cars and finding parking spaces. It was apparent that the problem would become worse, as has since been proved.

The redevelopment then taking place in the central area of Bedford, north of Midland Road, including the possibility of a new river bridge at Batts' Ford to link Kingsway and Greyfriars, led the partners to look at 58 St Loyes Street. Plans for a Batts' Ford bridge were later abandoned, but have been periodically revisited.[1]

The St Loyes Street premises had been occupied by The Imperial Cycle and Motor Company as a motorcycle showroom with workshops behind. The owner, Miss Queenie Symonds, an old friend and client of the Peacock family, was very pleased at the prospect of granting a lease to the partners.

Most of the original building was too old and unsuitable for use as offices, so local architect Bernard West RIBA was engaged to design new premises.[2] The brief was to retain the skeleton of the building frontage and to rebuild the remainder, incorporating a garage with access from Brace Street behind the premises. The site was relatively deep but narrow. The original design included offices on the first floor of the new rear extension. The first floor rear offices were ultimately omitted on the grounds of cost as the space was not immediately needed, though provision was made for future extension.

The contract for the building work was awarded to E. W. Harris & Co. Ltd of Kempston. Work commenced in 1963, but various problems were encountered. The

1 The original plan for a bridge at Batts Ford was contained in a 1952 report by C. Max Lock called *Bedford by the River*. The scheme was reviewed again in 1968 but later shelved, *The Bedford Record*, 19 October 1976, p. 3.

2 Bernard West (1926–2006) was a well-known local architect, illustrator and naturalist. He started drawing for *The Bedfordshire Times* while still at Bedford Modern School and contributed sketches and comments to *The Bedfordshire Magazine* for over fifty years, see Gordon Vowles, ed., *Bernard West's Bedfordshire: A Selection of his Sketch-books from the Bedfordshire Magazine 1947–98* (Dunstable, 2007) and Members of Bedford Modern School, eds, 'Obituary of Bernard West', *Eagle News: Old Bedford Modern Club Magazine* (May 2006), p. 92.

position of an important structural column supporting the first floor of the retained part of the building proved to have been incorrectly plotted with the result that the staircase would not fit as originally designed, and the omission of the first floor accommodation at the rear left the building without a kitchen. Fortunately, the problem was solved by creating a kitchen out of part of the garage area.

Constant delays by the contractors, who not long afterwards went into insolvency, caused considerable frustration, not least to the three new partners elect. The Electricity Board failed to connect the new electricity main on time and that alone caused several weeks of delay and irritation. Eventually, the decision was made to open the new office on 1 January 1964, whether or not the work was finished. Thus it was that the author, with office junior, David Ayers, and a secretary, Janice Coles, opened the office on the appointed day, leaving the remainder of the staff at Dame Alice Street for several more weeks.

The suitability of the location had been questioned by many people who, at the time, thought it was a mistake. How wrong they were! Right from the start the office, then the day-to-day responsibility of new partners Frank Jeffery and the author, proved to be a success, virtually doubling the turnover in the first year. Within three years the business developed further, the staff increased, and it became evident that more space would soon be required.

Changes in the 1970s

The amalgamation of W. & H. Peacock with F. W. Western & Co. took place on 1 January 1970. This event was greeted with great enthusiasm, only to be shattered by the very untimely, sudden death of Frank Jeffery on 4 January. The partners and staff were stunned, and there came the realisation that plans for future development of the new, larger partnership could no longer be quite the same. It was a particular blow for the author who had been taken out by Frank Jeffery on the day he first started work, and who had worked closely with him for over twenty years.

As the older and most experienced estate agency partner, 'Jeff' would always question plans for promotional ideas or expansion by the younger partners or staff, as apparently new ideas may have been tried many years before. This usually resulted in the adoption of the best ideas, while others were discarded after further thought. It was the constant aim of the partners to be forward thinking, improving presentation and market share, while at all times retaining a strictly professional approach to the business.

The staffs' working relationship with Frank Jeffery was always close, and almost every report, valuation or property for sale would be discussed with him to ensure that the client received the best advice. Throughout his career of some thirty-five years with Peacocks, both as an employee and partner, Frank Jeffery made a considerable contribution to the firm and was held in high regard by local solicitors, other professionals and his many clients. To this day he is still remembered with great affection. Following Frank Jeffery's death, Dudley Peacock moved his office to St Loyes Street, bringing his secretary, Ann Collins.

In the early 1970s the opportunity arose to secure a lease of the adjacent premises, 60 St Loyes Street, together with an option to purchase the freehold. The ground floor premises had been a china shop, Modern Tableware, run for many years by Mrs Robinson's family, with living accommodation above.

With the prospect of Thurleigh as a possible location for the Third London Airport, it seemed obvious that there might be a need to expand the business rapidly, even though there was no immediate need for use of the whole building.[3] Alterations were therefore made to combine the first floor of 60 St Loyes Street with 58 St Loyes Street. The ground floor shop was temporarily let to Bedfordshire County Council Trading Standards Department as a Consumer Advice Centre, and later to the Save the Children Fund as a charity shop.

Frank Jeffery's death had created a need for more professional assistance with valuations, surveys and property management, and Geoffrey Harrison, a Chartered Surveyor, was employed in that role.

In 1972 it was decided to further develop property management as a separate department under a newly appointed manager, Antony Rowlerson. This, and the need to provide more accommodation for the residential estate agency activities, created further pressure on space.

Further expansion – and a near collapse – in the 1980s and 1990s

By 1981, it was necessary to take over the whole of 60 St Loyes Street. Eddie Shrive and Associates of 63 Harpur Street, Bedford, were commissioned to design a new office front and fascia as part of the overall alterations. This provided a wide display window with a single doorway and a larger sales area. The work was carried out by local builder J. R. H. McPherson of 70 The Grove, Bedford.

The new layout enabled the property management department to take over the ground floor area of 60 St Loyes Street, leaving number 58 for the sales and professional staff. The cost of those alterations was more than the original cost of reconstructing the building back in 1964.

The premises at 62 St Loyes Street, which had been occupied by house furnishers, F. R. Mathison, became vacant during 1981. In due course, they were purchased by Ekins Estate Agents to expand their activities in Bedford. The buildings were old and in poor condition so a total re-development of the site was planned and approved. S. & S. Builders of Woburn Sands were appointed contractors, and work commenced on demolition of the old buildings in April 1982.

One morning, after the demolition work had started, Dudley Peacock received an urgent call at Bedford Magistrates Court, where he was carrying out his weekly duty as a magistrate, asking him to return to the office immediately. The wall and floor of his office were moving and in danger of collapse as the adjacent wall had been demolished. It was then discovered that the side wall of 60 St Loyes Street was not the usual nine inches thick, but only half that thickness. Part of the building was evacuated, and emergency shores were swiftly erected under the supervision of the local building control officer. Bedford architect, Martin Piggott, was duly instructed to carry out an investigation and design the necessary remedial works to prevent the collapse of the building, and it was eventually repaired and restored to use. The author was away celebrating his silver wedding anniversary while this was

3 Thurleigh was one of four shortlisted sites suggested by the Commission on the Third London Airport chaired by Mr Justice Roskill from 1968 to 1971. A local opposition group was formed as the airport would have subsumed most of Thurleigh as well as Keysoe and Bletsoe, Judy Stanton and Lilian Wildman, eds, *Thurleigh through the Years* (Sandy, n.d.), pp. 106–107.

happening, and returned to find the whole office front shored up. Perhaps he could be forgiven for suggesting that he knew the place would collapse in his absence.

Following the sale to TSB Bank in July 1988, Peacocks was held within a subsidiary company, Wilson Smith Howkins Ltd, which encompassed businesses with offices in Northampton, Rushden, Wellingborough, Kettering and Corby in addition to the various Peacock offices. To create a more appropriate title to embrace all the offices, the trading name of Peacock was changed to Wilson Peacock, and new logos and colour schemes were introduced. Alterations to the office interior followed, and the public areas were redecorated and refurbished. A bright new illuminated fascia was installed together with attractive illuminated display panels. An unexpected effect of the new displays was the increase in heat produced by the lighting, making the office too hot for comfort until air conditioning was installed in 1991.

Despite the recession in the property market during the early 1990s, the activities of the various departments in St Loyes Street continued to develop and, yet again, more space was needed. After much deliberation it was decided that a first floor extension should be built over the rear of number 58 St Loyes Street.

The original plans were no longer appropriate as recent building regulations necessitated additional structural works to the existing building. Peter Lloyd and Associates were instructed to prepare the design to provide mostly open plan offices. The contract was awarded to the well-known local builders, C. A. White, who completed the works with relatively little disruption to daily activities, and the office came into use in November 1992.

Although originally intended for the commercial and professional department, the extra offices enabled the residential sales activities to be expanded by introduction of the successful County Homes department on 28 October 1991. This department specialised in quality homes in addition to the general residential sales department.[4]

The amalgamation of TSB Bank with Lloyds Bank resulted in the office becoming part of the Black Horse Agencies, which in turn was acquired by the Bradford and Bingley Building Society in 1998. The offices were again redecorated, refurnished and rebadged in the Bradford and Bingley colours with the familiar bowler hat logo.

The St Loyes Street office played a very significant part in the fortunes and development of the firm, still thought of as Peacocks by many people. The move to St Loyes Street proved to be very successful, and the desirability of the location is perhaps confirmed by the number of other estate agents who later moved to the vicinity.

Several of the former, very loyal, Peacocks' staff remained with Wilson Peacock to continue to work in the best interests of clients under the leadership of Derek Black as manager, maintaining the high level of professionalism that had been the hallmark of Peacocks' success. More recently, as part of Countrywide Agencies, the Wilson Peacock office in St Loyes Street continues to play a significant role as a Bedford estate agency.

4 The County Homes department was announced in *The Bedford Citizen Property Plus* supplement, 31 October 1991. Properties offered through this department had distinctive brochures and 'For Sale' boards and were advertised through three centres based in Market Harborough, Northampton and Bedford.

Chapter Seven

26 Newnham Street, Bedford

A new sale yard in the heart of Bedford

The prospect of closure of the Horne Lane sale yards owing to the forthcoming redevelopment of the area made it a necessity to identify and acquire suitable alternative premises for the weekly auction sales. The partners decided that, while an out-of-town site might offer advantages, the whole essence and character of Peacocks' sales related to the ability of regular visitors to call in when in Bedford for other purposes. The partners were highly conscious of the institution of Peacocks' market that had been created and developed by Saturday sales over sixty years. For many people, a weekly visit to Peacocks was a regular part of their routine, and it was decided to continue to offer that facility if at all possible.[1]

One day, in the spring of 1973, Jonathan Knights had occasion to visit the former Castle Press printing works premises at 26 Newnham Street, Bedford. These were vacant following the collapse of the printing company, and had been for sale for many months through London agents. The sheer size of the premises, not apparent from the street, immediately alerted him to the possibilities for conversion to an auction centre. The property was large enough to replace the Horne Lane sale yards, to absorb the Lime Street sale room activities and accommodate the auction offices as well.

With a prominent, modern, two-floor office block at the front and single-storey buildings behind, the property extended to a floor area of over 20,000 square feet. Loading facilities were restricted, but were capable of improvement by demolition of a boiler house and toilet block. The location was almost ideal, only a relatively short walk from the town centre and Lurke Street multi-storey car park and with on-street parking nearby.

Jonathan Knights quickly arranged for the other partners to view, and having first ascertained that planning permission for change of use was likely to be granted the decision was made to purchase. The partners' offer was accepted on the understanding that contracts would be exchanged quickly, with an early completion, and the deal was done.

As it was not necessary to move in immediately, part of the premises was temporarily let for storage. The remainder was let to Survey Design and Construction Ltd (now well-known as SDC Ltd and still a Bedford-based company) for use as stores for their expanding construction business.

1 The Saturday sales were only very rarely disrupted. One notable exception occurred as a result of the public funeral of the victims of the R101 airship disaster when the usual Saturday sale was held on a Friday, *The Bedfordshire Times and Independent*, 10 October 1930, p. 8.

The first sale

The first sale at Newnham Street was held on Saturday 1 January 1977, when Robert Peacock auctioned the first lot for fifty-six pounds.[2] This comprised an old, two wheeled, wooden barrow laden to overflowing with vegetables. The barrow had long been used to transport goods to and from the Horne Lane sale yards. In post-war times, the barrow was frequently used by a character known as 'Titch' Broughton. Titch was not renowned for his physique, and people wondered how he ever gained enough strength to push the barrow when empty, let alone when fully loaded. Titch was usually dressed in an oversized overcoat for most of the year.

The barrow was bought by the author, and served as a flower barrow in his garden after restoration. Ravages of exposure due to weather subsequently led to a collapse of the wheels; the barrow has now been returned to Peacocks for eventual renovation. The newspaper report of the sale resulted in a letter from a Mrs V. Moore of Bedford, who believed that the barrow had been made by her father, Mr Mark Holmes, for a Mr Richards of Tower Court, at a cost of five pounds.[3] Mark Holmes died on 9 February 1911, so the barrow was probably at least sixty-five years old when sold.

Sale yard life

For a while after the opening, SDC Ltd continued to use the rear of the premises, but it was not long before the whole of the property was needed as sale entries increased. The Newnham Street premises divided conveniently into different sales areas so as to allow as many as four different sales to be conducted at the same time on a Saturday, but with a variety of starting times.

At first some of the regular buyers complained that the new venue had lost the atmosphere of Horne Lane. These were mostly the people who had been looking for the ultimate bargain, to be bought on cold wet days, when there was little or no competition. With all items, except some motor vehicles, now being kept dry and under cover, it soon became evident that the improved premises were resulting in better prices. Some old buyers gave up, but they were soon replaced by a host of new buyers as news of the Bedford Auction Centre spread; every week seemed to produce new visitors from Bedford or much further away.

With the opening of the Auction Centre there was a need to make the most effective use of space, and the problem of being overwhelmed with un-saleable rubbish caused some difficulty. The increasing cost and hassle of removing unsold items to the tip soon made it apparent that the standard of goods accepted for sale had to be improved. Stricter control of the quality of items accepted, aided by increasing laws and regulations affecting items for sale (including upholstery and electrical goods) coupled with the introduction of minimum commission charges had the desired effect.

Goods for sale started to arrive at the Auction Centre on a Monday morning as items sold on the previous Saturday were collected. It was not uncommon for the sales areas to be filled up by Tuesday, leaving space only for small items.

2 The sale was attended by three generations of the Peacock family, Robert, Dudley and Susan Peacock. A plaque to commemorate the opening was unveiled by Robert Peacock, *The Bedfordshire Times*, 7 January 1977, p. 5.

3 Letter to Peacocks from Mrs V. Moore, now lost.

From its opening in 1977 to the present day the Auction Centre has remained open for pre-sale viewing until 8.00pm on Friday evenings, when a facility is provided for prospective buyers to leave written instructions for bids to be made on their behalf.

Each Saturday the Auction Centre started to buzz with activity shortly after opening and a throng of buyers, vendors and the simply curious filled the building. The café, named 'Lot 77', the registration number of Dudley Peacock's car, did a steady trade to keep the company sustained throughout the day, while the local fish and chip shop and the Three Cups and The Castle pubs provided further refreshment.

The sheer volume and variety of goods sold seemed endless. With the exception of livestock, almost everything turned up for sale at some time. There could be: goods removed for sale to clear a deceased person's estate; surplus household goods and furniture; carpets; clothing; electrical goods and appliances; builders' materials and plant; office equipment; the contents of a closed-down shop or factory; garden machinery and equipment; plants and shrubs; bulbs; eggs; bicycles, cars, commercial vehicles and boats.

The sale of a penny farthing bicycle is worthy of mention. It was found by Dudley Peacock during a probate valuation at a property in Kempston in the 1970s. Having been told there was nothing of value in the garage he decided to look anyway, only to find a rusty penny farthing hanging on the wall, which was duly brought into the Auction Centre for sale. As it was thought worthy of some publicity, a phone call to one of the local newspapers resulted in a call back from a reporter who said: 'I hear you have a penny farthing for sale. Do you often have coin sales?'

An amusing sale took place in November 1977 when an artificial leg, found by an eighty-four year old pensioner called Raymond Bull, was put up for auction. Francis Peacock commented: 'I've worked here for twenty-four years and this is the first artificial leg I have ever auctioned … It would be the obvious choice for someone thinking about a pessimistic future.' The leg raised £2.[4]

In 1989, in common with many other auction houses, a buyer's premium was introduced. This was a charge of ten per cent on the bid price of every lot purchased, except for motor vehicles, where the premium was two per cent.

Security at the Auction Centre was inevitably a problem, not only out of hours but also when open to the public. Every effort was taken to prevent theft, but some items were vulnerable and the audacity of some thieves seemed to have no bounds.

Each week the disposal of large quantities of goods progressed through the sale of between two to four thousand separate lots as the Bedford Auction sales became increasingly well-known.

The Robert Room

Sales at the Lime Street sale rooms continued until a first floor sale room, at Newnham Street, known as the Robert Room in honour of Robert Peacock, was opened in 1980. Before the first lot was sold, Robert Peacock surprised all present, not least the partners, by announcing his retirement as senior partner in favour of

4 *The Bedford Record*, 18 October 1977, p. 3.

Dudley Peacock. It was typical of him to make the announcement in this manner to ensure that there was no possibility of dissension by the partners at his decision.

The opening of the Robert Room heralded regular monthly sales of selected antiques and collectors' items held on the first Friday of each month. The sale, for which a printed catalogue was produced and widely circulated, was normally conducted by Francis Peacock. As in the old Lime Street sale rooms, inclusion of items of particular interest drew potential buyers from far and wide. Following Francis Peacock's retirement in 1992, Robert Room sales were taken over by Jonathan Knights, Mark Baker and Simon Rowell. The Robert Room also provided an excellent venue for property auction sales when required. After the retirement of Jonathan Knights, management of the Auction Centre fell to Mark Baker. The regular auctioneers included Simon Rowell, Chris Armstrong, Stuart Good and others, assisted by a loyal band of full and part-time office staff and porters.

On 29 September 2000 the Auction Centre business was acquired from the Bradford & Bingley Building Society, by way of a management buy-out led by Mark Baker, with Ian Fearnley, Simon Rowell and others in support. The trading name of the company reverted to W. & H. Peacock and the business continues to thrive.

Chapter Eight

Baldock and the A1 Offices

Acquisition of business in Baldock and Biggleswade, 1937

The estate agency office at 8 High Street, Baldock, together with an office in the Market House, Biggleswade, was acquired by Robert Peacock in 1937, following the death of Charles Sidney Knowles PASI who had founded the practice. Charles Knowles had also run a small cattle market in the Market Square at Baldock, but that had ceased trading before Robert Peacock took over the business.[1]

The Baldock office building was prominently located at the end of a terrace close to the Market Square. There was a frontage to the Great North Road, the A1. This brought the main road traffic through Baldock until the opening of the A1(M) bypassed the town. The three-storey building, which also had a cellar, had originally been a cobbler's shop. The premises were rented at the princely sum of just £1 per week – plus rates – and for a period of years the first floor was sublet to a chiropodist at 30s per week.

The work of the Baldock office was typical of a general estate agency practice and embraced sales, valuations, surveys and property management. A number of successful property auctions were held in the area, and Peacocks was prominent in the town and surrounding villages.

The first property auction carried out by Peacocks as successor to the late Charles Knowles was held at the Swan Hotel, Biggleswade, on the 18 June 1937.[2] Four lots were offered but only one sold, which comprised four cottages in Cheyney Street, Steeple Morden, Cambridgeshire. The cottages fetched £155. The remaining three lots were sold after the auction. The most notable was of these was 27 - 31 Shortmead Street, Biggleswade, which consisted of a business premises and two cottages with a site of over an acre and a half, bought by Bryants Cycle Merchants of Biggleswade.[3]

An important sale was held on 29 October 1949 at The Sun Hotel, Hitchin, when as joint auctioneers with Drysdale Nurse & Co. of London W1, the Bygrave Manor Estate near Baldock was offered.[4] The estate comprised a farm bailiff's house, a modern residence, farm buildings, fifteen farm-workers' cottages and some 1,030

1 Mr C. S. Knowles was listed as a chartered surveyor, auctioneer, valuer and estate agent at 15 High Street, Biggleswade, and at Baldock and Buntingford, Hertfordshire, Kelly's Directories Ltd, *Kelly's Directory of Bedfordshire 1936* (London, 1936), p. 79.

2 *The Bedfordshire Times and Independent*, 11 June 1937, p. 8.

3 W. & H. Peacock, *Property Auction Book, No. 1: Baldock and Biggleswade, 18 June 1937–15 October 1963*.

4 *The Times Digital Archive*, 3 October 1949, p. 10. A copy of the original sale particulars is held by Hertfordshire Archives and Local Studies Service, D/Z96/2/26.

acres. The farm was sold, with vacant possession, to Mr G. Brookbanks.[5] In addition there was an estate of thirty-six houses, seven of which were sold to the sitting tenants. The remainder were unsold on the day, but later sold to a London property dealer, who subsequently instructed Peacocks to act as managing agents.

Although the Baldock and Biggleswade offices traded in the name of W. & H. Peacock, the business was solely owned by Robert Peacock until 1 January 1970 when it was incorporated into the new partnership trading as W. & H. Peacock Western & Co. The Peacocks' office in Biggleswade had closed in 1940 due to wartime requisition, quite soon after its acquisition.[6] It was not until 1970, with the new partnership, that Peacocks would have a presence in the town again.

John R. A. Williams, who had been articled to Robert Peacock, was appointed as the first manager of Baldock and his wife also worked in the office as secretary and book-keeper. They left the business in 1948 when Jan Church was appointed. The Church family were bakers and corn merchants with premises at 10 St Loyes Street, Bedford.

Jan Church had left Bedford Modern School during the war to join the Royal Marines where he was to experience many exploits, details of which did not become generally known until after his death in 2006, at the age of 84.[7] After demobilisation in 1946 he was articled to Robert Peacock. To quote Jan's own words when talking of his appointment to the Baldock office: 'The salary of six pounds a week seemed to be wealth beyond comprehension, especially as there was a 1936 Morris 8 car to go with the job!'[8]

Following purchase of the freehold by Robert Peacock, considerable improvement was carried out to the building, including the installation of a new shop front, internal modernisation and filling in of the cellar. During the late 1950s, the first floor was converted into a small flat where Jan lived for two or three years.

Jan Church continued as manager until 1968, when he was lured to Africa to take up an appointment as surveyor to the Zambian Building Society. This offered him the opportunity to satisfy an ambition to pursue his interest in big game and wildlife as a volunteer game warden. After Jan later returned to Baldock, he set up in business as an independent Chartered Surveyor, but remained a good friend of his former Peacocks' colleagues. He was a great character who made many friends in Baldock, and continued to play a large part in the life of the town throughout the remainder of his life.

The next manager was Terrance Manson, a Chartered Surveyor, who remained in office until he was replaced by Alan Porter in the early 1970s. Alan was a partner in the extended firm whose experience and enthusiasm considerably enhanced the fortunes of the business at Baldock; he remained in charge until 1981.

5 W. & H. Peacock, *Property Auction Book No. 1: Baldock and Biggleswade*.

6 Peacocks last advert including the Biggleswade office was in the *The Bedfordshire Times and Bedfordshire Standard*, 9 August 1940, p. 4. W. & H. Peacock, *1901–1951*.

7 Jan Church took part in the landings in Sicily and at Salerno. He had other adventures behind enemy lines and was wounded. After returning to the UK he volunteered for a secret operation, involving Marines and Royal Engineers, destroying a German radar installation, Members of Bedford Modern School, eds, 'Obituary of Jan Church', *Eagle News* (May 2007), pp. 201–202.

8 Personal communication to author.

The manager appointed to follow Alan Porter was Christopher J. Horler, who joined the firm after an earlier career in Nottinghamshire. Christopher Horler brought with him considerable experience in rating together with skills as a surveyor.

A small satellite office to Baldock, opened in 1961, was at 138 London Road, Knebworth, Hertfordshire. It was not open daily and was staffed by part-time employees. The office was not really successful and was closed after a few years.[9]

Acquisition of business in Biggleswade and Sandy, 1970

The creation of the new W. & H. Peacock Western & Co. partnership by amalgamation of W. & H. Peacock and F. W. Western & Co. enlarged the scope of the business to include established offices in Biggleswade and Sandy. This reflected the link created by the A1 trunk road corridor. The new partnership consolidated the long and happy relationship that had stemmed from Brian Porter's training with Peacocks, as an articled clerk to Walter Peacock in the 1930s.

The business of F. W. Western & Co. had originated in Sandy in 1897, with offices at 18 St Neots Road. Other offices were situated at 1 Market Square, Biggleswade, where a cattle market was held in Hitchin Street and there were furniture sale rooms.[10] After qualifying as a Chartered Auctioneer and Estate Agent in 1936, Brian S. Porter was taken into partnership by Frederick William Western JP. Frederick Western was also a rate collector, a member of Biggleswade Urban District Council from 1925 to 1939 and clerk to Sandy Parish Council from 1896 to 1939, continuing in post when the town was granted urban status.[11]

During the war years of 1939 to 1945 the business continued on a low key, and the Sandy office closed. When military leave allowed, Brian Porter was known to have been seen selling cattle, sheep and pigs by auction while dressed in army uniform and armed with a revolver. The cattle market was later taken control of by the government following meat rationing and livestock controls.

Frederick Western died in 1939. By that time, Brian Porter had been commissioned into the Royal Artillery, but he was able to secure compassionate leave to restructure the business before returning to serve with the British Expeditionary Force in Europe. He was evacuated from Dunkirk but returned to France shortly after 'D' Day and continued to serve under General Montgomery until the surrender of Germany in 1945. He was demobilised with the rank of Major and, as soon as was allowed, returned to the business.[12]

By 1969, the F. W. Western & Co. partnership included Brian Porter and his long-standing colleague Horace S. Dilley, who had joined the business in 1933, at the office of 1 Market Square, Biggleswade. Horace was made a partner in 1961.[13]

9 W. & H. Peacock, *1901–1964*. This office first appears in an advert in *The Bedfordshire Times and Bedfordshire Standard,* 3 January 1964, p. 7, and is last mentioned in an advert in *The Bedfordshire Times*, 16 July 1971, p. 27.

10 Frederick W. Western established F. W. Western & Co. and Maddison and Western in 1897, the latter firm running the weekly Biggleswade cattle market, *The Bedfordshire Times and Bedfordshire Standard*, 8 December 1939, p. 4.

11 Frederick Western was also a Fellow of the Auctioneers Institute, mainspring of the Sandy Horticultural Society, Honorary Secretary to Crufts dog show and a notable judge of many livestock shows in this country and on the continent, *The Bedfordshire Times and Bedfordshire Standard*, 8 December 1939, p. 4.

12 *The Bedfordshire Times*, 17 June 1977, p. 7.

13 He started as an office boy on 15s a week, *The Biggleswade Chronicle,* 26 August 1983, p. 3.

During the war, Horace had been called up to serve with the Eighth Army in Africa, then in Sicily and Italy.[14]

Alan Porter, Brian Porter's son, joined the partnership in 1962, and became a partner in 1965.[15] He established a new office at 27 Market Square, Sandy, on 28 July 1966, out of an empty shell in a newly built parade of shops.[16] Alan Porter had served his articles as a pupil with Peacocks' auctioneer, Dick Arnold.

Brian Porter played a large part in the local community, serving as a Councillor of the Biggleswade Urban District Council from 1949 to 1955. He was elected as an Independent Member of Bedfordshire County Council in 1955 and a County Alderman in 1961, serving until 1972. He was chairman of the Finance Committee in 1958 and was elected Vice Chairman in 1969. In 1971, Brian Porter was appointed High Sherriff of Bedfordshire - the first from Biggleswade since 1864.[17]

Both Brian Porter and Horace Dilley were involved with many local organisations and were extremely well regarded for their various activities. They both played an important role in the Fen Reeves, who oversee the rights of the commoners of Biggleswade Common.[18] Brian Porter served as a Fen Reeve for many years and was Head Reeve from 1955 until his death in 1977. Horace Dilley was appointed Acting Reeve (effectively Clerk or Secretary of the Fen Reeves) and served in that office for nearly sixty years until his death in 2009. Alan Porter has been Head Reeve since 2010.

The Sandy Show was a big event in East Bedfordshire and involved much work for Brian Porter who was Show Secretary from 1946 to 1952. Horace Dilley was also heavily involved in that organisation.

Opening of the Hitchin and Letchworth Offices, 1980s

Hitchin was identified as a site for a new estate agency office in 1983, and opened with Derek Black as manager.[19] The office was subsequently taken over by Christopher Horler for the commercial and survey departments. The booming property market then led to the acquisition of a further office in Letchworth in 1987.[20]

Following the sale of Peacocks to TSB Property Services in 1988 there was a severe recession in the property market associated with very high mortgage interest rates and many repossessions. By 1994, the Baldock, Hitchin and Letchworth offices had been closed by Peacocks reflecting the depressed property market.

14 *The Biggleswade Chronicle*, 28 January 1994, p. 8.

15 *The Biggleswade Chronicle*, 26 August 1983, p. 3.

16 The first reference to the new office was in *The Biggleswade Chronicle*, 5 August 1966, p. 3.

17 *The Bedfordshire Times*, 17 June 1977, p. 7.

18 Biggleswade Common is the largest area of common land in Bedfordshire – over 300 acres – and dates back to 1200 AD, http://www.letsgo.org.uk/walk/BiggleswadeCommon.aspx (accessed March 2014).

19 The office, at 43 Hermitage Road, was first advertised in *The Biggleswade Chronicle*, 6 January 1984, p. 18.

20 The office was first advertised in *The Biggleswade Chronicle*, 28 October 1988, p. 30 under the Wilson Peacock brand.

Chapter Nine

Property Auction Sales

A tried and tested method of sale

Throughout the history of Peacocks, property auction sales have formed an important part of business activities, especially when market conditions have been appropriate for this well-tried method of sale. It can be claimed that a property sold by public auction has achieved the best price obtainable in the open market. While this statement may attract some criticism and debate, not least at times when the availability of short term bridging loans has been restricted, it has certainly proved effective in the past, as the Peacocks' auction records reveal.

Public auction has long been accepted as the method of sale to adopt when a forced sale has to take place, as evidenced following the repossession and disposal of properties on behalf of mortgagees after borrowers have defaulted. Auction is also especially effective for: sale of properties of unusual type and character where accurate valuation is exceptionally difficult; where there are several keen prospective buyers; and in cases where the parties interested in the proceeds of the sale cannot agree.

Auction sales provide security for both the vendor and the purchaser as a legal contract is created on the fall of the hammer, thus avoiding the uncertainty associated with sale by private treaty, where there are often long delays prior to formal commitment. The vendor has the satisfaction of knowing the resulting price, and the purchaser knows he is certain of the purchase. There can be no gazumping, and any disappointed prospective buyer at least knows that a price has been paid above his own best bid.

There is little doubt that in the atmosphere of a crowded auction room, the competition of the bidding can result in a higher price being achieved than might have been secured by private treaty negotiation. The success of an auction relies on an inherent characteristic whereby the desire to have something is enhanced by the knowledge that someone else wants the same thing. Conversely, an auction is doomed to failure when there is only one potential purchaser present, or if there is no one prepared to bid at all.

Some early sales

Walter Peacock held his first property auction sale at five o'clock on Tuesday 18 November 1902, at the Cock Inn, North Crawley, when two freehold cottages with half an acre of gardens, situated in Little Crawley, were sold for £80, to a Mr E. T. Bailey of Milton Bryan. The cottages were both let and produced an income of £8 per annum.[1]

1 *The Bedfordshire Times and Independent*, 7 November 1902, p. 1.

Walter then went to the Swan Inn at Cranfield, where, commencing at six o'clock, he sold twelve freehold and copyhold cottages at Cranfield, all subject to tenancies and producing £58 1s per annum. These were sold in four lots and achieved a total price of £702 10s.[2] This first Cranfield sale of twelve properties saw the beginning of a long, happy and on-going relationship with solicitors Messrs Sharman and Trethewy of Bedford (now Sharman Law).[3] In the same sale were three freehold cottages at Church Road, Cranfield, let at £7 8s per annum, bought by Messrs Newland and Nash Ltd, the Bedford brewers, for only £32 10s.[4] The cottages in Church Road were sold on behalf of trustees for whom the solicitors were Messrs Chapman and Chaundler of Biggleswade. There is no record of how Walter travelled to the sales that day - perhaps he rode on horseback as he did not have a car.

The next sale, held at the Lion Hotel, 55 High Street, Bedford, on 23 January 1903, heralded the first of just over one hundred sales to be held in the hotel over a period of thirty-eight years, until 16 May 1941. This first sale proved to be a disaster as all four lots were withdrawn, unsold. These included: Woodlands, Battenberg Road (later renamed Marne Street) Kempston; 30 and 32 Ford End Road, Bedford; 5 Sidney Road, Bedford; and a building site, of almost a quarter of an acre, at the corner of Kimbolton Road and Pemberley Crescent (now Pemberley Avenue).[5] The last-named did not attract a single bid.

Three further sales during 1903 proved successful and saw the start of another lasting co-operation with a Bedford firm of solicitors, Conquest & Clare, later known as Conquest, Clare & Binns, with offices at 30a Mill Street, Bedford, a connection that continued until 1994.[6] The practice is now amalgamated with Woodfine Batcheldors of 16 St Cuthbert's Street, Bedford.

The first property auction sale to be advertised by the newly formed partnership of Walter and Harry Peacock took place at the King William IV Inn at Kempston on 10 July 1903, when stabling, other buildings and a yard in High Street, Kempston, were sold for £150.[7]

The sale of Milton Mill, Milton Ernest, was the first of many Peacocks' property auctions, often of farms or business premises, to be held at the Swan Hotel, Bedford.[8] The sale achieved the excellent price of £3,500. Bedford solicitors C. C.

2 *The Bedfordshire Times and Independent,* 7 November 1902, p. 1.

3 Sharman and Trethewy originated in a firm established by Francis John Budd in Bedford in 1809. He had practised briefly at Olney, Buckinghamshire, before coming to the town. The firm was then taken over by Alexander Sharman and a Sharman family connection was maintained from 1831 to 1918. Alexander Sharman was Mayor of Bedford in 1846 and actively political as a Whig. Alfred Tresawna Trethewy practised with the firm during the early 1900s and was the only person of that name to be associated with it, *Bedfordshire on Sunday*, 9 March 1997, p. 8.

4 *The Bedfordshire Times and Independent*, 7 November 1902, p. 1.

5 *The Bedfordshire Times and Independent*, 16 January 1903, p. 1.

6 Conquest & Clare were another well-established local firm of solicitors. They appear in an 1877 local directory with premises in Mill Street and Duke Street, Bedford, and Shortmead Street, Biggleswade, E. R. Kelly, ed., *Post Office Directory of the Counties of Bedford, Huntingdon, Northampton, Berks, Buckingham and Oxford 1877* (London, 1877), p. 148. They had previously been known as Conquest & Stimson, E. R. Kelly, ed., *Post Office Directory of the Counties of Northamptonshire, Huntingdonshire, Bedfordshire, Buckinghamshire, Berkshire and Oxfordshire 1869* (London 1869), p. 326.

7 *The Bedfordshire Times and Independent*, 3 July 1903, p. 1.

8 *The Bedfordshire Times and Independent*, 21 and 28 August 1903, p. 1.

Bell, then with offices at 2 Howard Street (now 48 Harpur Street, Bedford) bid for the buyer, a Mr H. Curtis.

In the first three years of property auctions Peacocks held nine sales at which forty-nine properties were sold. In 1902 seventeen properties were sold and in 1903 nine properties were sold. During 1904 a total of twenty-three properties were successfully sold, including various cottages in Wilden, Colmworth and Blunham, and 23 Ashburnham Road, Bedford. The sale of 23 Ashburnham Road on the 16 March 1904 also included ten £30 'old shares' in the Temperance Permanent Building Society, which were bought by Mr J. F. Reeve for £342 10s.[9]

In 1905, Peacocks sold a house in Bushmead Avenue on instruction of the executors of the will of Mrs Cranfield, this sale also included ten £1 shares in the Bedford Steam Laundry that were sold for £8 10s per share.[10] By 1922, when thirty-five similar £1 shares were sold, the price at auction had increased to £12 15s each.[11] The laundry site, in Goldington Road, Bedford, was more recently occupied by Marshalls Garage, but was redeveloped as Appledore Road in 2005.

The year 1905 also saw the first sale by Peacocks to be held out of the county, when Brunswick House, Clee Hill, Cainham, near Ludlow, Shropshire, failed to reach the reserve at auction, but was sold the next day.[12] The property included a grocer's shop, with living accommodation and various outbuildings, and was sold as a going concern, including the goodwill of the business. It is not known why the firm was instructed to sell a property so far away from Bedford.

The popularity of property auctions waned between 1906 and 1909, when there was little activity, but then, from 1911 to 1918, twenty-four sales were held at various venues, with a good rate of success.

The first property auction instruction to be received from Bedfordshire County Council came in 1914, when Claridge's Farm House, Eggington, was sold at the Swan Hotel, Leighton Buzzard, for £350.[13] Described as an 'Old World Residence', the house contained two reception rooms and five bedrooms. There were pretty ornamental gardens, a greenhouse and conservatory, finely timbered grounds with an orchard, nuttery and wooded moat; the whole area was two acres, one rood, and eighteen poles.

In 1917, the Rushey Ford Estate at Box End, Kempston was sold for £3,260 to Mr F. Ray. The estate included a picturesque gabled farmhouse (now a grade II listed building and known as Rushey Ford House) stabling, a coach and motor house, and a modern farmhouse with ninety-two acres of land.[14]

A notable sale in 1918 was held at the Bull Hotel, Olney, when the Stoke Park Estate at Stoke Goldington, Buckinghamshire was sold for £6,050. This estate included Stoke Park and Church Farm with 214 acres and the 159 acre Stoke Park Wood.[15] It was one of the first of the larger country estates to be sold by Peacocks.

9 *The Bedfordshire Times and Independent*, 19 February 1904, p. 1.
10 BLARS, PK1/4/6. The sale also included The Lilacs, a house in Bushmead Avenue, Bedford.
11 *The Bedfordshire Times and Independent,* 28 April 1922, p. 6.
12 *Auctioneers' Handbook*, now lost.
13 *The Bedfordshire Times and Independent,* 17 July 1914, p. 6.
14 *The Bedfordshire Times and Independent,* 20 July 1917, p. 4.
15 This was a joint sale with the auctioneers P. C. Gambell, *The Bedfordshire Times and Independent,* 21 June 1918, p. 4.

There was little interest in shops and business premises during the period of the First World War. The sale of 105, 107, 109 and 111 Midland Road, Bedford, in May 1914 and of 36 and 38 St Loyes Street, 52 Tavistock Street and prominent corner premises, Harpur House, 44 The Broadway, Bedford, in November 1917 all proved abortive.

A host of venues

It is interesting to review the various venues used for property auction sales in Bedford. After a few sales at the George Hotel, the Lion Hotel (or Red Lion Hotel as it was sometimes known) became the established venue for most sales of houses and cottages, either as investments or with vacant possession. The Lion Hotel was located on the east side of the High Street, between Mill Street and the Market Square. Having closed as an hotel, the building was replaced by shops and offices behind the preserved façade in 1972.[16] Peacocks' property auction sales at the Lion Hotel ended abruptly in 1941, possibly due to some wartime decree, and were transferred to the Lime Street sale rooms, where the first property sale was held on 25 July 1941.[17]

Use of the Lime Street sale rooms continued on a regular basis for a series of ninety-three sales until April 1959, when the Georgian Room at the Swan Hotel, Bedford, became the favoured venue. The last two property sales at Lime Street were held in November 1964.[18]

Several other Bedford venues were used at various times. The Tudor Rooms sale room at Horne Lane was used for a number of sales, the most notable of which was a disastrous failure. This was the sale of properties on the Cranfield Estate in 1943, comprising forty-four houses and bungalows and five building plots.[19] The dwellings had been built in the 1930s and were all let on controlled tenancies. Only three houses and two building plots sold. The plots fetched only £25 each. Peacocks subsequently took over the management and rent collections until the properties became vacant and were sold. In 1954, a number of the sitting tenants, then paying around £1 per week rent, took the opportunity to buy for about £500, subject to their own tenancy. Several refused that chance to buy, even though one hundred per cent mortgages were offered to them. The last of these tenanted houses was not vacated until 1988, when it was sold with vacant possession for £45,000. By that time the rent had increased to the fair rent as registered by the rent officer and was in the region of £600 per annum.

The Town Hall, Bedford, was used in May 1944 for the sale of the Francklin Estate, when five freehold farms, totalling about 890 acres, in the parishes of Bolnhurst, Ravensden and Wilden were auctioned.[20] The estate sold for £17,000, an

16 The Lion Hotel was an old coaching inn. A photograph of the inn with its re-fronted façade of c. 1830 can be seen in Richard Wildman, *Bedford: A Pictorial History*, illustration no. 43. It was associated with the supposed original of Samuel Butler's Hudibras. He was Sir Samuel Luke, the great Bedfordshire parliamentarian of the Civil War period. The Red Lion was the 'Parliamentary' inn, Richard Keverne, *Tales of Old Inns*, 5th ed. (London, 1952), p. 135.

17 *The Bedfordshire Times and Bedfordshire Standard*, 27 June 1941, p. 6.

18 *The Bedfordshire Times and Bedfordshire Standard,* 9 October 1964, p. 10.

19 *The Bedfordshire Times and Bedfordshire Standard*, 1 October 1943, p. 6.

20 Originally yeomen, the Francklin family purchased Glyntils manor in Bolnhurst in 1546, by 1566 they were bearing arms and at the end of the 1500s George Francklin had built up a modest estate in

average price of only £19 2s per acre. The land was mostly heavy clay and difficult to cultivate with the machinery then available.

The new County Hotel (now the Park Inn) was successfully used for three sales during 1972, but there then followed a slump in the property market and auction sales fell out of favour until 1976 when the De Parys Hotel was used.

Sales began at the Newnham Street Auction Centre in April 1977. The Robert Room, opened three years later, provided an excellent venue. On a number of occasions the Robert Room was packed with an eager company, even crowding back on to the landing area. This helped to create a great air of excitement and expectancy, and a long run of highly successful property sales took place.

The De Parys Hotel was the setting for a sale held on 26 March 1987, when Grange Farm, Willington, was sold on behalf of the trustees of the Francis Coles Charitable Foundation. The property comprised a farmyard and buildings covering a site of 2.72 acres with planning permission for eleven new houses and bungalows and for conversion of existing buildings into a further seven dwellings. In the then rapidly escalating property market, the forthcoming sale attracted considerable interest and the sale room was full. Bidding opened at £500,000 and eventually rose to £800,000 before the hammer finally fell. The result far exceeded expectations and resulted in a welcome boost to the foundation, which used the funds to provide grants to needy parishes for the repair of historic country churches.[21]

For many sales of individual properties in country locations, and sometimes in the town, the sale would be conducted on site, to be followed by a sale of the contents. These sales usually attracted considerable interest from bargain-hunters. They also offered the buyer of the property an opportunity to buy carpets, curtains and furniture if required. Such sales were particularly popular in the period before the Second World War, when transporting house contents to Bedford for sale was relatively difficult and expensive in relation to the potential proceeds.

The village pub was another popular location for sales of country property and there is an impressive list of pubs where, at some time, Peacocks have held an auction. As this was usually held in the bar, the presence of the regular customers, as well as curious villagers, helped to ensure a company. Not quite 'rent a crowd' but most useful to help create the right atmosphere for a sale.

Harrold Village Institute was the chosen sale room on various occasions, most notably in December 1959, when tenanted properties forming part of the estate of the Harrold personality, the late Edgar Clayson, were sold.[22] Edgar Clayson was the proprietor of the Harrold building firm C. Clayson and Sons, and undertook many civic responsibilities. These included: Justice of the Peace; Assistant Special Head Constable; member of Bedford Rural District Council; governor of Harrold

North Bedfordshire, Godber, *Bedfordshire*, p. 210. At the time of the sale the vendors had held estate for nearly four hundred years, BLARS, PK 1/4/150.

21 *Auctioneers' Handbook*, now lost

22 The Harrold Park Estate was one of Bedfordshire's oldest estates; it was held by only three owners through six centuries. From 1278 to 1918 the estate was owned by the De Grey family; it then passed to Mr James Day and subsequently to Mr Edgar Clayson. A record of Peacocks' sale of the estate was published in *The Bedfordshire Times and Bedfordshire Standard*, 16 June 1961, p. 10.

Secondary Modern School; magistrate on the Sharnbrook bench; and Committee Member of the Harrold Institute.[23].

Possibly the loveliest setting for a sale was the Saloon at Kimbolton Castle where, in July 1980, Peacocks were privileged to hold a sale of surplus properties from the Kimbolton Estate on behalf of the trustees of His Grace the Duke of Manchester, whose family had formerly owned the historic castle, by then owned and occupied by Kimbolton School.[24]

Following the amalgamation of W. & H. Peacock with F. W. Western & Co., a number of sales were held in Biggleswade, mostly in the St Andrew's Rooms.

Auction ups and downs

Over the years there have been many exciting and interesting sales because the outcome was always unknown until the fall of the hammer. On occasions the reserve price was far exceeded, and there were sale days when even low reserves proved too high. With an auction, the atmosphere in the sale room can rapidly become electric when a further bid is made just as the auctioneer has called a bid for the third and last time and the hammer is about to fall. It is then that the price can spiral up as the bidders battle to buy. The converse occurs, thankfully only rarely, when there is just a single potential purchaser present and no one else. This happened to Robert Peacock at a sale at the Sun Hotel, Hitchin, when the author was attending as his clerk. The vendor's solicitor was present and just one other person. Robert was left with no choice but to simply try to agree a sale at the reserve price, but he failed.[25]

The elation of a successful bidder and the disappointment of the under-bidder often manifests itself. At one sale, to the delight of the auctioneer, Dudley Peacock, and the assembled company, a young engaged couple sitting in the front row celebrated their successful purchase with an enthusiastic hug and kiss as the hammer fell. It was not unknown for a disappointed bidder to leave the room in tears.

The procedure at a property auction sale is simple. Immediately following the sale, the purchaser is required to sign the contract or memorandum of the sale and to pay a deposit of ten per cent of the purchase price. In law, the auctioneer is deemed to be the buyer's agent for the purpose of signing the memorandum in the event that the buyer refuses to do so. There is no record of a Peacocks' auctioneer having to exercise this duty. On a few occasions, when the buyer regretted the purchase, it was possible to transfer the property to the under-bidder without loss.

Mr C. E. Heritage, who was employed as an assistant at 10 Lime Street during the 1930s, recalled an incident from a sale in 1933. When Harry Peacock suggested an opening price for one lot, he was surprised to receive an immediate assenting bid of the amount from an elderly lady, who was well known as a small time dealer. This proved to be the only bid and the lot was duly knocked down to the lady, whereupon she sprang up in a very agitated manner saying: 'Oh, Mr Peacock, I don't want to buy it, I was only trying to give you a start!' Harry agreed to re-offer the property.[26]

23 *The Bedfordshire Times and Bedfordshire Standard,* 9 October 1959, p. 8.

24 *The Bedfordshire Times*, 6 June 1980, p. 27.

25 This was the sale of Bevereley House in Arlesey, which took place on 12 July 1949, *The Bedfordshire Times and Bedfordshire Standard* 2 June 1949, p. 4 and *The Times Digital Archive* 22 June 1949, p. 10.

26 C. E. Heritage, *W. & H. Peacock: Reminiscences of C. E. Heritage.*

Examination of the original auctioneers' handbooks showed that this also happened during a sale at the Red Lion Hotel, Bedford, on 21 July 1933.[27] Lot seven comprised two cottages, 4 and 6 Little Thurlow Street, Bedford, being sold subject to tenancies. The first buyer proved to be a Mrs Norcott, who had bid £220. The auctioneer's book is marked 'No deposit' and the lot was then sold to another person for £210. Little Thurlow Street was in the area close to Allhallows Lane, which was cleared of houses and redeveloped during the 1960s.

One unfortunate event happened at the sale of a property in Bedford in the late 1970s that was being sold subject to a protected tenancy when, to everyone's surprise, the bidding far exceeded the reserve price. After the sale, the purchaser duly signed the contract, but had no cash or cheque with him to pay the deposit. Although the buyer satisfied the vendor's solicitors of his intention to take the deposit to their office the following day he failed to do so. It subsequently transpired that the buyer had no funds and the sale to him was never completed.

Prospective buyers have been known to attend a sale without having inspected any of the properties on offer and bought 'on spec'. On one such occasion a buyer, who had not even seen the outside of an old derelict cottage at Old Harrowden, paid in full, in cash, on the night of the sale.[28] The cottage had no water or drainage and was sold on behalf of the Whitbread Estate. The purchaser had just successfully sold an old car at auction and thought the cottage sounded cheap.

Wielding the gavel

The role of property auctioneer was carried out by several of the partners over the years. In the early days, the auctioneers were either Walter or Harry Peacock. Robert Peacock assumed the role for the first time on 31 August 1926 for a sale at the Swan with Two Nicks Inn, Sharnbrook, when four cottages at Barleycroft, Sharnbrook, were sold for £145 on behalf of a Mr Frank Turner.[29] The purchaser was a Mr Robert Turner of Radwell. It is not known if the parties were related to each other.

Until his death in 1952, Harry Peacock conducted most of the property sales held at the Lime Street sale rooms. The duties were then variously undertaken by Robert Peacock, Dudley Peacock or George Robinson until 1963. From 1964 until 1970, Frank Jeffery officiated at several of the sales. After 1970, the rostrum duties at Bedford property auctions were mostly conducted by Dudley Peacock and the author. Following the formation of W. & H. Peacock Western & Co., property auction sales at Biggleswade were conducted by Dudley Peacock, Brian Porter or Alan Porter.

The auction sale appendix gives details of the sale dates, venues, addresses and prices (where recorded) of all the known Peacock sales based on information taken from various sources including: the original auctioneers' handbooks; local and national newspapers; and sale catalogues held by the Bedfordshire and Luton Archives and Records Service. They offer a valuable historical insight into the changing patterns of sales and prices over the years.

27 *The Bedfordshire Times and Independent*, 23 June 1933, p. 8.
28 The sale took place on 5 November 1976, *The Bedfordshire Times*, 1 October 1986, p. 18.
29 *The Bedfordshire Times and Independent*, 20 August 1926, p. 6.

Chapter Ten

Surveys

Agricultural and land surveys

As a general practice of auctioneers and estate agents, surveyors and valuers, Peacocks was instructed to undertake a variety of surveys. This word may mean different things to people from various walks of life. For Peacocks' agricultural and rural clients, however, surveys usually related to straightforward linear measurement of land and buildings prior to preparation of plans for sale, or for calculating areas to re-define boundaries.

For a surveyor, being instructed by one of the parties in a boundary dispute can be problematic, and is sometimes undertaken with reluctance. The outcome of such a dispute is rarely a happy one for either party, especially when the bills for legal costs and surveyor's fees arrive. The area in dispute might be minimal and the likely effect on the use and enjoyment of the property or its value insignificant. Sadly, the matter of 'principle' can enter the scene to cloud the judgement of the parties. A seemingly trivial matter to others can take on enormous proportions as first solicitors and then surveyors are called in.

Despite man's ability to determine the distance to the moon down to a few millimetres, the precise position of a boundary between two properties is almost impossible to exactly determine at every point along its length. What is shown on a plan as an apparently straight line may waver considerably, and surveyors may have to consider many aspects when working in the field. For example, where is the exact centre of an old hedge that has been growing for over a hundred years? Where, precisely, is the edge of a ditch that has become overgrown? Whose fence or wall is it anyway? Was the fence originally built exactly on the boundary line? Even if measurements are shown on a plan, where precisely do they run from and to? The thickness of a line on a small plan may scale up to be at least twelve inches or more wide. The only parties who 'win' from a dispute are usually the solicitors and surveyors whose fees are paid.

For parties to a boundary dispute, the personal trauma can adversely affect health for many years to come. If the parties can compromise by inviting a solicitor or surveyor to act as an arbitrator, and accept the finding in the award, much cost and worry can be saved. Sadly, if the matter of principle colours the land-owner's opinion and subsequent will to pursue a dispute, it can be taken through to the appropriately-named bitter end.

In one case, when a client was, in the author's opinion, mistaken, the argument related to the position of a fence along a boundary between two driveways that was a maximum of two inches adrift at one end, tapering to about half an inch at the other. Apart from a purely nominal value, the value of the client's property was not adversely affected by the position of the fence, wherever the 'correct' line ran.

There was an on-going civil action involving solicitors and surveyors on both sides, which after some two and a half years, eventually reached a court hearing - only to be settled virtually at the door of the court. Just a few weeks later, the neighbours' dispute blew up again resulting in a fist fight, which in turn led to a Magistrates' Court appearance. Both parties were bound over by the magistrates to keep the peace.

One special boundary case, dealt with by Robert Peacock in the 1950s, was to divide a Bedfordshire farm in half. The farm had been bequeathed to two brothers who could not agree. Whilst most beneficiaries would have been likely to agree to an appropriate division of the fields, perhaps with one field being divided to make equal areas, the brothers took the view that half each meant just that! Robert was required to set out a new straight line boundary to cut the farm exactly in half. A chain link fence was then duly erected along the line that went up and down hill following the contours of the land.

Property surveys

To most potential house buyers, 'survey' relates to an inspection of a property to report on its condition. The author often found that a survey report was seen as a useful tool to try to re-negotiate the purchase price when the list of defects appeared to have painted a worse picture of the property; this re-negotiation often took place sometime after first agreeing the deal. There is little doubt that everyday defects, likely to be found in almost any property, sound so much worse when listed.

Vendors were often concerned a surveyor would spot defects they hoped the buyer had missed. The surveyor's ability to go directly to just the place where there was an issue such as dampness, woodworm infestation, or rotten woodwork, frequently came as a surprise to the house owner. This information was, however, valuable to buyers in highlighting problems, existing or potential, and in assisting their plans for future expenditure.

The author also found that it was important to accept that the standards expected by individuals varied considerably. A purchaser could not reasonably expect any older property to be in 'as new' condition, and character in a property is often created by uneven floors, distorted walls and doorways, or other imperfections.

While working as a surveyor for Peacocks the author took care to point out to purchasers that many defects were likely to be similar to those found in most properties and that they did not significantly affect normal use. Some were attributable to wear and tear and could be remedied with a normal programme of maintenance and redecoration. Proper external maintenance was, however, always important, particularly to roofs and rain water goods, to prevent costly damage. A neglected leaking gutter or downpipe, or a running overflow, could soon lead to dampness and create conditions when timber decay would result.

There is, of course, a limit to the depth of inspection the surveyor can reasonably undertake when looking at a property for a potential buyer. Inspection of concealed areas was so much easier before the era of fitted wall-to-wall carpets or sheet flooring. It is not difficult to imagine a vendor's reaction if confronted by a request to turn back every fitted carpet in the house. The surveyor has to rely largely on finding clues and assessing symptoms of possible trouble.

The potential traps and hazards for the unwary surveyor were many and varied and the author rapidly learnt to take nothing for granted. Even when a vendor made assurances that all was well, it was important to look anyway. Sash windows all needed to be opened, keeping fingers clear, in case the sash cords were broken. Casement windows could be found to have broken hinges. Care was needed when opening doors, in case there was a step the other side. At least one member of Peacocks' staff found that water standing in a flooded cellar is virtually invisible, but still awfully wet! It was funny for all, except the victim. Decayed woodwork had to be readily discovered without causing damage to paint surfaces or making unsightly holes.

During her student days, prior to qualifying as a Chartered Surveyor, Clair Peacock accompanied the author on a survey inspection in Shefford. Imagine the confusion when the author could not see the house chimneys through the binoculars – only to discover that the lens caps were still in place. Clair had omitted to inform him of this fact; after that it seemed only fair to send her to inspect the cellar, spiders and all.

Dampness, a nightmare for many home owners, can cause numerous problems and may often be associated with the effects of condensation and lack of ventilation. Without adequate ventilation, humidity levels can rapidly increase to such an extent that condensation occurs over extensive areas, the first sign of which may be mould growth that rapidly spreads. Cooking, washing and simply breathing create large volumes of moisture vapour in any household. If the moisture cannot escape, condensation will be inevitable.

At one time, the use of paraffin or bottled gas heaters in inadequately ventilated conditions was a notorious source of damp problems. Few people would believe that burning a gallon of paraffin generates more than a gallon of water in vapour form; imagine the effect of spraying a gallon of water around a room.

A visit to one tenanted property in Beatrice Street, Kempston, in the 1950s, to investigate complaints of excessive dampness and mould growth, revealed that the tenant was using an open gas oven and paraffin heaters for heating the house. The resulting moisture vapour was condensing upstairs where the bedding, soft furnishings and clothes were all going black with mould. No windows were opened for ventilation and it was possible to feel the dense humidity. The tenant could not be persuaded that the problem was largely self-inflicted.

Some lessons are learned the hard way. Very early in the author's career, after touching a rust spot on a hot water cylinder, in the days when the cylinders were made of galvanised steel, he was left standing with a finger on the hole until the system was drained down. Despite this, the owner was not really convinced that it was leaking.

Woodworm and wet rot decay can catch the unwary. In an empty house in Pearcey Road, Bedford, the author walked to the middle of the living room floor - the boards gave way due to woodworm and he descended through the floor to his knees. Surveyors find that there are very few older properties where no evidence of woodworm is to be found, though it may have been treated. Often such infestation has been brought in with furniture. Although wooden windows or doors may be affected by wet rot decay, they can remain serviceable for many years before replacement becomes essential.

The dangers of dry rot were amply illustrated when a burglar broke into an unoccupied house in Waterloo Road, Bedford. The garden was overgrown and the property badly neglected, but the house had been lived in. The burglar forced open the front living room window and jumped through. The next thing he knew the floor collapsed into the cellar; he fell through and broke his ankle. The burglar then noticed a piano pointing towards him teetering on what remained of the then steeply sloping floor and froze not daring to move. The burglar had to call for help, was duly arrested, and convicted for his trouble. That floor had one of the most spectacular outbreaks of dry rot decay that the author has ever seen.

A survey of an old house in Aspley Guise revealed a totally unexpected infestation affecting the timbers – house longhorn beetle. The infestation extended through the roof and into the timber framing of partition walls. The larvae of this beetle leave an oval exit hole in the outside of a timber, and they are capable of leaving timber totally devoid of strength and ready to collapse. Dealing with this pest would have been potentially a very costly replacement exercise for the would-be purchaser.

The nature of the shrinkable clay sub-soil in many parts of the Bedford area, can give rise to problems associated with subsidence or heave. Since such damage became an insurable risk, owners or purchasers have become very much more aware of both the problems and costs associated with any necessary underpinning and reinstatement work. The author found that the number of properties where subsidence had been so bad as to necessitate demolition and reconstruction were relatively few, but a large number of properties were affected to a greater or lesser degree. Often cracks appeared during a period of drought and then closed again when ground moisture levels returned to normal; it was impossible, in these circumstances, to predict precisely when major damage might occur. Problems could be much greater where there were large trees nearby as the removal of a tree could subsequently result in heave when normal moisture levels returned, a process that could take several years. Movement could affect a property that had been built for many years, and it was simply impossible to give a guarantee that future movement would not occur. The author found that most older properties, especially those of timber frame construction, had been affected by structural movement at some time in their life. Few were in serious danger of collapse, though floors and walls might well have been uneven or out of square – part of the 'character'.

The surveyor was, and is, rarely a qualified electrician, plumber or heating engineer, but is trained to use careful observation to identify defects that reveal likely problems or the necessity to consider replacement of all or part of an installation. For the author, the most important task was always to alert the buyer to those items that might have been costly to remedy.

Chapter Eleven

Lettings and Property Management

The rented property market and the Rent Restrictions Acts

Lettings, rent collection and property management were always very important to the general estate agency activities of the business from its foundation in 1901, but, from 1972, property management was developed as a specialist department. Peacocks' first advertisement of a property to let appeared in *The Bedfordshire Times and Independent* on 20 September 1901, when 15 Whitbread Avenue, Bedford, was offered to let at a rent of one pound per month.[1]

In the period before the First World War it was more common to rent than purchase, especially for the working class but also for many middle class people too.[2] Wages were low and jobs insecure, and very few working class people could contemplate a purchase. Many properties were bought for investment purposes and there was virtually no difference between the value of a property with vacant possession or when let. Indeed, some properties would be more likely to attract a buyer if already satisfactorily let. It was a free market with no rent control or security of tenure, and a tenancy could be ended by a landlord simply by serving a notice to quit. A landlord could distrain on a tenant's goods to recover arrears of rent.[3]

In Bedford, following the building booms of the late nineteenth century and early twentieth century, there was a surplus of larger houses in the Poets Corner and Saints areas that attracted interest from families drawn to Bedford by the Harpur Trust schools. A landlord would happily redecorate a house throughout if a tenant could be found for a three-year term at a rent of fifty to sixty pounds a year. A number of country houses were also available.

The First World War brought much change. The arrival of the 51st Highland Division in Bedford created a huge demand for accommodation. In addition to billeting soldiers with families, empty houses were requisitioned by the military authorities and owners were paid on the basis of 'per head, per night' for those accommodated. Many of the soldiers were unaccustomed to flushing toilets and running water from indoor taps in the bathrooms they found in Bedford. A number of the properties suffered badly from damage during the military occupation, but owners were compensated for dilapidations when properties were derequisitioned

1 *The Bedfordshire Times and Independent*, 20 September 1901, p. 4.

2 John Burnett, *A Social History of Housing 1815–1970* (Newton Abbott, 1978), p. 145.

3 Peacocks advertised a number of these sales over the years, for example, in 1935, 'Under distraint for rent. Removed from De Pary's Avenue Bedford: The contents of an exceptionally well-furnished house; most of the furniture has been recently purchased', *The Bedfordshire Times and Independent*, 4 October 1935, p. 8.

after the war.[4] During the war rented housing became difficult to obtain and rents were raised.

In consequence of the shortage of housing, the government of the day introduced the first of the Rent Restrictions Acts. Originally intended as a temporary measure during the war, this first Act and other subsequent legislation continued to affect some properties by restricting rents and providing security of tenure.

The first Act was the Increase of Rent and Mortgage Interest (War Restrictions) Act 1915. The object of the Act was to: control rents on smaller, unfurnished, 'working-class' dwellings; protect tenants from eviction; restrict the rates of interest on mortgages; and prevent the calling in of mortgages. Suffice it to say that this legislation, and that which shortly followed it, subsequently had a significantly detrimental effect on the availability of dwellings to let in the private sector of the market, and resulted in a wide differential opening up between the value of a property with vacant possession and a similar property subject to a tenancy protected by the rent legislation.[5]

Some relaxation did occur between 1923 and 1939 when a number of properties were decontrolled.[6] Then, in 1939, the Rent and Mortgage Interest (Restrictions) Act 1939 brought every property into control where the rateable value did not exceed one hundred pounds in London, ninety pounds in Scotland and seventy-five pounds elsewhere.[7] Thus most rents were frozen at September 1939 levels, and the majority of tenants had almost total security of tenure until 1958 when the provisions of the Rent Act 1957 began to take effect.[8]

The considerable amount of new development in the Bedford area during the 1930s, coupled with some relaxation of control, led to a relatively free market where the value either let or with vacant possession more or less equated. Houses were let at rents that showed a return of about ten per cent per annum based on the market price of the house. For example, a house in Phillpotts Avenue or the Castle

4 The Bedford Property Owners' Protection Society, of which H. L. Peacock was Honorary Secretary, was formed to deal with issues between the military authorities and property owners following the billeting of soldiers in the town. A selection of correspondence and other papers can be found in BLARS, PK 5/1/1.

5 The Rent and Mortgage Interest (War Restrictions) Act 1915 became politically difficult to repeal and meant that few, if any, speculative builders would build low cost houses at uneconomic rents. This helped fuel the post-war housing shortage, particularly amongst lower paid workers, Burnett, *A Social History of Housing,* p. 217. Amendments to the 1915 Act were made in 1917, 1918, 1919 and 1920. The Increase of Rent and Mortgage Interest (Restrictions) Act 1919 extended the 1915 Act to cover larger properties by doubling the rent limits, and prolonged the operation of the Act until 1921. The Increase of Rent and Mortgage Interest (Restrictions) Act 1920 extended the duration of rent control and raised rentable value limits so that almost all properties were within scope, Great Britain, House of Commons Library, *The Historical Context of Rent Control in the Private Rented Sector* (2013), Standard Note SN/SP/6737, pp. 2–3, http://www.parliament.uk/business/publications/research/briefing-papers/SN06747/the-historical-context-of-rent-control-in-the-private-rented-sector (accessed May 2014).

6 Decontrol started with the Rent and Mortgage Interest Restrictions Act 1923, which provided for decontrol on properties with vacant possession.

7 Like the 1915 Act, the 1939 Act was also only meant to be in place for six months, but the legislation remained in place until 1968, Great Britain, House of Commons Library, *The Historical Context of Rent Control,* pp. 3–5.

8 The Rent Act 1957 decontrolled more valuable properties as well as all new tenancies after a landlord had secured vacant possession, Great Britain, House of Commons Library, *The Historical Context of Rent Control,* p. 6.

Road area in Bedford could be rented for approximately sixty pounds per annum or purchased for about six hundred pounds.[9]

As the decade closed, however, the threat of another war had an effect on the house sales market. Furthermore, with the depression of the 1930s still in their minds, many people were afraid that house purchase might put a millstone around their neck; something that did not in fact actually happen until the collapse of the property market in the 1990s, when negative equity reared its ugly head to cause great distress.

Throughout the Second World War, any unfurnished rented property that became vacant could only legally be re-let at the controlled rent and very little of that type of accommodation was therefore available. Furnished letting had, to this point, avoided control, provided that the furniture was sufficient to live with, without taking in additional items. Because landlords had started to furnish houses in order to avoid control, the Furnished Houses (Rent Control) Act 1946 was enacted.[10]

After so many years with fixed rents, some relief for landlords came with the Rent Act 1957, when a rent limit was created, based on the 1956 gross value of property for rating purposes. In most cases the new rent limit became twice the 1956 gross value. There was, however, a sting in the tail for landlords who had failed to keep their property in good repair. In such cases the tenant could apply to the local authority for a certificate of disrepair, which if granted reduced the rent. Some landlords misunderstood the regulations and were reluctant to increase the rent, in fear of being faced with large repair bills, which they could not afford to pay. Such landlords suffered significant loss as a result since, in many cases, any repairs required would soon have been paid for by the increase in rent. For a typical three-bedroom terrace house in Bedford where the controlled rent included general and water rates, the rent was 12s 11d per week. The new rent limit increased the inclusive payment to 15s 7d per week. In most cases, the rent limit continued to be effective for some eight more years.

After the Rent Act 1957, a weekly rent that included the general and water rates was charged by the local authority. The rating year started on 1 April so, whenever there was an increase, it was necessary to re-calculate the total payable by each tenant. A formal notice to each tenant was required showing the new amount payable accurate to the nearest halfpenny. Such increases were never well received by the tenants and involved a lot of work for the office staff.

The Rent Act 1965 introduced regulated tenancies (with long-term security of tenure) and a system of 'fair rents', on all lettings of unfurnished property, which if a landlord and tenant were unable to agree a rent, were assessed by the local rent officer. The Act provided for appeal to a Rent Assessment Committee if either party disagreed with the rent officer's assessment. Rent increases had to be phased, and a fresh application for review could be submitted every three years. This was a considerable step forward, but the fair rent, as defined, still fell significantly below

9 5 Denmark Street in the Castle Road area of Bedford was available for sale in January 1932 for £625. The property had two reception rooms, four bedrooms, scullery and bathroom, W. & H. Peacock, *Instruction Book 4: May 1916–December 1932*, entry 1954.

10 This Act created a dual system, one for furnished properties and one for unfurnished properties. The two systems were not amalgamated until the Rent Act 1974, Richard Meredith Jackson, *Jackson's Machinery of Justice*, 8th ed. (Cambridge, 1989), p. 134.

open market rental levels as there was a requirement to assume a 'balanced market'. This meant that it was assumed the number of people seeking to become tenants of particular properties was not substantially larger than the number of those properties available.

Various legislation after 1965 allowed further relaxation whereby, provided proper procedures were followed, landlords could let without losing the right to recover possession. New tenancies could be created at an agreed rent. There are, however, still some long standing tenancies which enjoy the protection afforded by security of tenure, including right to succession, and where rents are still restricted to a fair rent, which is below current market levels.

The complications of rent legislation over the years caught out landlords who failed to take, or act upon, advice, or failed to follow the correct procedures and formalities when letting, thus resulting in the creation of a tenancy which gave security of tenure for life, not only to the tenant, but to close relatives too. Once such a tenancy was established, the effect on the market value of the property was to immediately reduce the value between one third and one half of the open market value with vacant possession. Due largely to the potential pitfalls for the uninformed, not least the risk of accidentally creating a protected tenancy with a disastrous effect on value, few of the local firms of estate agents had any serious interest in undertaking property management until the availability of properties to let increased and more recent legislation made recovery of possession more straightforward.

In addition to the requirements of private tenants, there was a strong demand in the post-war years from British service personnel and their families stationed at one of the army or air force establishments in the area, particularly Grange Camp and the Barracks in Kempston, and RAF Cardington and RAF Henlow.[11] Many properties were taken over as official hirings, which ensured security of payment and appropriate settlement of any claim for dilapidations at the end of the tenancy, often several years later. There was the added advantage of being able to regain possession when required, without risk. Many American servicemen and their families, mostly stationed at Chicksands, Chelveston (Northamptonshire) or Alconbury (Cambridgeshire) bases were also accommodated in the area.

The effect of the collapse of the residential property market in the early 1990s and, more recently, further relaxation of rent controls led to a substantial increase in the availability of houses and flats to let, and created a free market in rents. Demand was sustained for rented properties from various sources including previous home-owners who had lost their property through forced sale or repossession and who were unlikely to venture into purchase again. People needing to move at frequent

11 Grange Camp, Kempston, was constructed in 1939 and was originally used as a Second World War training camp. Later uses included a convalescent depot and emergency evacuation unit. In 1967 it became a base for volunteer reservists of the Royal Corps of Transport, H. A. Carnell, T. Booth, H. G. Tibbutt, eds, *Eight Thousand Years: A Kempston History* (Kempston, 1966), p. 76. The site at Henlow was originally selected by Major-General Trenchard, then commander of the Royal Flying Corps in France, for a repair depot in 1916. It was used to train men in the rapid repair of aircraft and aero-engines. It is famously associated with Frank Whittle, the inventor of the jet engine, who was based at the camp from 1932 to 1934. During the Second World War, Henlow was one of the largest maintenance units in the country. The camp is still operational today, Royal Air Force, *Royal Air Force Henlow at 90: The First Ninety Years 1917–2007,* 6th ed. (Henlow, 2007), pp. 8–29.

intervals to improve career prospects also realised that it was not always easy to do so at times when the property market was slow.

The rapid growth in popularity of 'buy to let' as a form of investment subsequently led to the creation of many other letting agencies in Bedford and elsewhere, which had to become familiar with the complex legislation relating to rented property.

Rent collection and property management

In pre and post-Second World War days, Peacocks employed a rent collector to visit houses and cottages either every week, four-weekly, monthly, or quarterly, to collect rents due in cash. There were rounds to follow each Monday, Tuesday and Wednesday in Bedford and Kempston, extending out as far as Bromham and Harrowden in the Fields. There were further rents to collect in Cranfield every Saturday.

When the author started training in 1948, there was a vacancy for a rent collector waiting to be filled so what better way to learn that part of the job? Whatever the weather, the rent collector set off on a bicycle with a satchel for the money, five pounds worth of change and the rent book. The rent rounds covered many streets that have long since disappeared, though some street names survive in the names of blocks of flats built as part of redevelopment schemes. Between Midland Road and Bromham Road east of Greyfriars there were slum areas that included Gwyn Street, Hassett Street, Greyfriars Walk, Allhallows Lane, Thurlow Street, Beckett Street and Greenhill Street.[12] The Black Tom area included Peel Street, Derby Street, Princes Street, Cobden Street and Albert Street. Some cottages in these areas were dirty and in very poor repair with tenants living in absolute squalor, whilst the next door cottage was kept in pristine condition by very house-proud tenants. It was not uncommon for the rent collector to be offered a cup of tea or coffee, but he needed to pick and choose when to accept.

Most of these properties had just a cold tap over the sink in the kitchen, no bathroom and an outside WC. Many still had gas lighting and cooked on a coal range. For some tenants even a rent of 7s 6d per week was hard to find. Despite the hardship in these areas, tenants who had to be out when the rent collector called would happily leave their door unlocked with the rent book and the money on the table knowing it would be quite safe.

The weekday rounds included visits to all the older areas of the town. Some houses particularly stick in the mind, like one in Howbury Street where the tenant, a regular customer at the Lime Street Sale Rooms, collected clocks, which struck or chimed at different times.

For any new rent collector the first time on the round took much longer than later visits, as the tenants would take the opportunity to complain about any disrepair, sometimes with justification. 'The landlord never spends anything on this house' was a common cry however much had been done. The collector had to take due note and report any complaints on his return to the office.

Visits to Harrowden in the Fields were along unmade tracks to a tiny hamlet of

12 A photograph of the slum properties in Allhallows Lane and the corner of Thurlow Street c. 1933 can be found in Richard Wildman, *Bedford: A Pictorial History*, illustration no. 62.

very run-down cottages, where some of the tenants were persistently in arrears, and it often proved difficult to catch anyone at home. In summer, the route by bicycle to collect rents in Bromham crossed the river and, if the author was quick enough, there was just time enough to divert to have a quick swim on a sunny day.

The Saturday visit to Cranfield usually meant a journey by bus coupled with careful timing; the houses were in two areas about a mile apart. In summertime it was possible to take a public footpath across the fields as a short cut, but in winter it was best to keep to the roads. Dawdling was not advised as, if the mid-morning bus was missed, there was a long wait for the next. One lovely tenant, a Mrs Rollison, from Harter Avenue, would always have a cup of hot coffee, together with a slice of her homemade sponge cake ready for the rent collector every week.

Once back in the office, the rent collector needed to reconcile the cash with the entries in his book. This was not always easy if he had been given the wrong change or forgotten to write down who had paid what. It was also the time to recover from the vagaries of the weather; the author recalls a time when it poured with rain each Saturday for several weeks in succession and he ended up soaking wet and having to try to dry soggy clothes on a gas radiator in the office.

The role of rent collector was usually occupied by a semi-retired man, who enjoyed the exercise and meeting people. Some well-remembered collectors include Reginald Taylor, Arthur Fitt and Mr Wareing, each of whom held the office for a number of years.

Eventually, in the late 1960s, as the number of weekly tenancies fell due to redevelopment and properties falling vacant, house to house collections ceased and all tenants were required to pay at the office.

One of the potential nightmares for a managing agent when a property was empty in the winter was burst pipes, and it was important to ensure that water systems were turned off and drained out. In the days before copper piping and modern central heating, the old lead pipes would bulge if frozen and then begin to leak as the ice thawed out, usually with devastating results. Many older properties in a terrace would be served by one lead pipe with only one stop cock. If that was turned off, all the houses were left without water. Houses with an outside WC were at particular risk of becoming frozen-up, and frost could also break the WC pans unless the tenant provided a heater. Often there was no electricity supply in the property.

Ernest Hardwick, an experienced local plumber and locksmith who lived in Adelaide Square, told the story of being called to a house in St Augustine's Road, Bedford . The family went away during a particularly cold Christmas and returned home to find that a pipe had burst upstairs. The leaking water had frozen as it ran down the staircase to form a waterfall of ice!

Another Ernest Hardwick tale related to two old, absent-minded, spinster ladies from Bromham Road, Bedford. Their gas geyser water heater would not work so they wrote to Ernest, who did not respond directly. The ladies wrote several more letters and sent an urgent telegram. When Ernest eventually went along, he simply put a shilling in the gas meter and the geyser worked immediately. His charge was 7s 6d, rather a lot when the ladies could so easily have just inserted one shilling in the meter themselves.

For all private furnished lettings there were strict procedures to follow. References had to be taken up, usually from a previous landlord and from bankers or employers. The correct form of tenancy agreement had to be prepared and signed by the tenant and the first rent and deposit paid before they were given possession. An inventory and schedule of condition was prepared prior to occupation as this served to protect both landlord and tenant when, at the end of the tenancy, dilapidations had to be assessed and charged for.

Before the days of pocket Dictaphones, the task of taking an inventory could be very tedious, especially if a shorthand secretary was unavailable. The record would have to be written in longhand, noting the condition of all decorations, fixtures and fittings, with a description of every item in the house and a note of any defects. In winter, when the house was unheated, this was a very cold job indeed, which could easily take a whole day to complete. The handwritten record then had to be typed. Checking the inventory again at the end of the tenancy could also be a thankless task, especially when the tenant had moved items from one area to another and had not bothered to replace them in their original rooms.

Although acting as the landlord's agents, it was always necessary to try to act impartially when assessing dilapidations, especially when making allowance for fair wear and tear to which the tenant was entitled. Without the proper record provided by the inventory, a landlord returning home after several years might have an inaccurate memory of the condition and cleanliness of their property, recalling a much rosier picture than had actually existed and forgetting to take account of the inevitable wear that will have taken place in the intermediate period. Equally, the tenant might try to assert that the damage existed prior to occupation. Some tenants were past masters at trying to hide damage they had caused, hoping that the agent would miss finding the evidence. Staining of bedding and carpets were often the cause of dispute, and cleanliness too, particularly when the cooker had been left in very dirty condition. Damaged items were sometimes reassembled in the hope that they would go undetected, but would collapse if touched.

Office management and new technology

Prior to the establishment of the separate property management department, the day to day running of property management activity was shared between the partners, professional staff and secretaries. Frank Jeffery and the author looked after individual landlord clients, and after George Robinson retired at the end of 1963, also took over responsibility for his former clients. The death of Frank Jeffery in 1970 left a void which needed to be filled regarding the work load of property management matters and a professional assistant, Geoffrey Harrison, a Chartered Surveyor, was appointed specifically to deal with property management and survey work.

By 1972, after Geoffery Harrison had left the firm, it became evident that a full-time residential property manager was needed. Dudley Peacock interviewed various candidates before appointing Tony Rowlerson to the new position. Tony had a broad base of managerial experience in various fields and had served in the RAF. Under him the department grew and further staff were dedicated to property management. Mrs Olive Weedon, who as Olive Franklin had joined the firm as an office junior before becoming secretary to George Robinson and then Frank Jeffery, became senior property management secretary, and with her knowledge of clients was a valuable aide to Tony Rowlerson.

In February 1980, Keith Brown was appointed as assistant property manager, a post he was to hold until being appointed manager of the department when Tony Rowlerson retired in 1986.[13] Keith Brown had joined the auction department as an office junior in 1972 and become an auctioneer in 1974, before being invited to transfer to property management. In line with the partners' policy for promotion from within the organisation, Graeme Leech, who had previously been a junior assistant in the estate agency department, was promoted to assistant property manager

After his promotion, Keith Brown continued to serve as an auctioneer whenever help was required. He remained as residential property manager until being promoted to another property management appointment with TSB Property Services in Oxfordshire.

The role of cashier and receptionist at the front counter, aiding all departments, but in particular dealing with rent payments and enquiries, was undertaken by a number of ladies who developed friendly relationships with the many callers at the office. The longest-serving cashiers included Mrs E. 'Mac', Maclean , Mrs Frances Roberts and Miss Jean Campouser.

Property management accounts were in the most capable hands of Mrs Elizabeth 'Jig' Miller, who had maintained the books meticulously since 1946. Jig became a virtual mother figure to the staff. As Elizabeth Wilding, she joined the firm at 6 Dame Alice Street in 1944, and continued working for Peacocks until her retirement in 1982. The nickname 'Jig' stemmed from her habit of saying 'oh, jigger it' when making any mistake. During her long reign as book-keeper, Jig was assisted by various staff, not least Mrs Joyce Merryweather, Mrs Joan Beardsmore and Mrs Elaine Peel, who all returned to work part-time in the department after having their children.

Following Jig's retirement, Geoffrey Tucker briefly took over as book-keeper until, in November 1982, the accounts came under the care of Mrs Carol Sallows, who undertook the unenviable task of converting Peacocks from the traditional manual book-keeping system to computerised accounts. To say that introduction of the new computer accounting system caused headaches would be a total understatement but, with the increased number of accounts to be serviced each month, computerisation had become necessary. Much patience and dedication by Carol Sallows and her staff, input from the partnership secretary Ian Fearnley and computer specialists, to say nothing of the patience and understanding of our landlord clients, proved necessary as the computer operation left much to be desired in terms of presentation of accurate and understandable information. Eventually, three systems later, and once all the gremlins had been removed, the system became very effective, enabling the department to produce meaningful information quickly and accurately, something simply not possible with the old system of manual bookkeeping.

[13] *Peacock Property Scene*, *The Biggleswade Chronicle*, 25 April 1986, p. 27.

Chapter Twelve

Advertising and Publicity

Early advertising in local newspapers

The importance and value of advertising and publicity to any business should not be underestimated; it is, however, particularly important to auctioneers and estate agents. Peacocks have enjoyed a continuous relationship with the local press in Bedford throughout the firm's history, especially with the Bedfordshire Times newspaper series. The first advertisement placed by Peacocks appeared in *The Bedfordshire Times and Independent* on 20 September 1901, regarding the aforementioned house to let in Whitbread Avenue. The following week, a house with: '8 bedrooms, bath h & c. first class servants' offices, in the highest part of Bedford. Repainted and decorated throughout …' was advertised to let at sixty pounds per annum.[1] In the same paper the business also advertised a furnished thirteen bedroom mansion within three miles of Bedford aimed at, 'HUNTING MEN & OTHERS'.[2] The property has not been identified although it is possible that it was Howbury Hall, Renhold, as this property was later recorded in 1919 in *Instruction Book 4* and the accommodation is strikingly similar.[3]

On 13 December 1901, Peacocks advertised the intention to hold monthly sales of: 'HORSES, HARNESS and VEHICLES, IMPLEMENTS, BICYCLES & c. Next Sale, SATURDAY, DEC 21, 1901, at Two o'clock sharp', at Bedford Cattle Market.[4] The advertisement of the 20 December 1901 listed the items for sale on the following day as:

> CHESTNUT Cob, 8 years, 14 hands, the property of Messrs H and W Quenby Kempston; Chestnut yearling COLT by 'Kendall'. Bay Yearling FILLY by 'Janisary' dam by a Derby Winner bred by Jas. E. Platt Esq., Howbury Hall. Bay COB, rising 3 years, 11 hands, quiet to ride and drive, the property of Bedford Tradesmen. Turnout comprising Bay PONY, new light Pony TRAP and set of Brown Harness. Bay MARE, 8 years, 15 hands, quiet to ride and drive; a 2 wheel Lorry, Pony Chaise, 2 Tradesmen's and Luggage Carts, and several sets of Harness, also a number of Pneumatic and Cushion Bicycles, nearly new.[5]

A rival newspaper to *The Bedfordshire Times and Independent* was *The Bedfordshire Standard*, with offices at 61 High Street, Bedford. This paper, and others, was also regularly used by Peacocks to run adverts for auctions, for example, *The*

1 *The Bedfordshire Times and Independent*, 27 September 1901, p. 4.
2 *The Bedfordshire Times and Independent*, 27 September 1901, p. 5.
3 W. & H. Peacock, *Instruction Book 4*, entry 9274.
4 *The Bedfordshire Times and Independent*, 13 December 1901, p. 5.
5 *The Bedfordshire Times and Independent*, 20 December 1901, p. 5

Bedfordshire Standard was used on 3 July 1903 to advertise a sale to be held at the King William IV Inn, Kempston, on 10 July 1903.[6]

The Bedford and District Circular, published by The County Press (Bedford) Limited for a halfpenny, also carried more of the firm's advertising. The issue of Saturday 4 November 1922 included an advertisement for household furniture to be sold at the auction rooms on 10 November 1922. In the same edition, a six-bedroom detached house in Bushmead Avenue, Bedford, was for sale at £1,300.[7]

Peacocks' advertisement in *The Bedford and District Circular* of 22 May 1930 offered a detached six bedroom house in Rothsay Road, Bedford, for sale at £1,850 and a five-bedroom house in St Michael's Road, Bedford, for sale at £1,000.[8] A less terrestrial advertisement in that issue was for flights from Race Meadow, Ampthill Road, Bedford, 'in the latest National Flying Services Saloon Air Taxi' from 5s. On a similar theme, the airship R100 was reported to be at the mooring mast (at Cardington Hangars) again. For those favouring a more traditional form of transport, the Birch Bros coach service to London cost 5s for a day return fare.

Changes in newspaper advertising

Estate agents' advertisements have always been carefully studied by readers; this includes the simply curious as well as potential buyers. In addition, vendors look carefully to see if their property has been listed. For estate agents, there is always most pressure to advertise in periods when there is a buyers' market; advertisements appear to placate anxious vendors. Although it may sometimes seem, at least to vendors, that advertisements have not been read, it only needs a small error in the advertisement to generate a reaction. An estate agent always dreads any mistake or omission – even if the newspaper is at fault – such as the mix up of photographs and descriptions.

The cost of newspaper advertising was a major expense, and for many years a few local newspaper publishers effectively held a monopoly. Their charges were considered exorbitant by the estate agents, who made an informal agreement to restrict the style of their advertisements to single column width, semi-display only. This format, in use from the early 1900s and before, was unfortunately rather uninteresting. With limited numbers of property to sell in the post-war years, however, this style of advertising continued well into the late 1960s. When more property became available, it became important to establish a more prominent image to attract buyers and vendors, so the agreement was abandoned.[9]

Peacocks, Connells and Whitmore & Co. of Harpur Street, Bedford, were the first estate agents to move away from the format of column advertising and employ feature advertising in April 1968.[10]

For a long time, the cost of advertising with a photograph was a relatively

6 *The Bedfordshire Standard*, 3 July 1903, newspaper cutting.

7 *The Bedford and District Circular*, 4 November 1922, newspaper cutting.

8 *The Bedford and District Circular*, 22 May 1930, newspaper cutting.

9 There was still limited use of single column advertising by estate agents until 1969 in *The Bedfordshire Times,* although by this point the advertising had been reduced to one column as the estate agents had moved increasingly to feature advertising. Even at this period, however, the majority of the estate agents only used text in their advertisements.

10 *The Bedfordshire Times*, 12 April 1968, p. 21.

expensive exercise. In addition to taking the original photograph, this involved the production of a special etched copper printing plate. The preparation of the plate took time and the production costs were in addition to the charge for space taken in the newspaper. The appearance of photographs in advertisements was therefore an exceptional occurance and not the rule as it is today.[11]

As changes in printing techniques were developed in the late 1960s, Peacocks discovered, in common with Keith Fletcher, who then worked for rival estate agents, Connells, that it had become possible for the newspaper to reproduce photographs differently. The whole process had been simplified to the extent that *The Bedfordshire Times* no longer needed to make a separate charge for plates, and would only charge for the advertising space taken. This revolution enabled Peacocks to proceed with an advertising campaign using photographs for better quality properties, which proved highly successful, and increased the effectiveness of advertisements immensely. In common with Connells, with whom Peacocks had shared the idea, the rate of success became the envy of other agents, though they thought it very extravagant to use so many pictures. The two companies' joint success lasted for many months, but eventually the edge on the market was reduced when the newspaper advertising representatives realised how effective the photographs were and started to sell the idea to other agents.[12]

The local monopoly of The Bedfordshire Times Publishing Company Limited, which also published *The Bedford Record*, *The Ampthill News*, *The Biggleswade Chronicle* and *The Woburn Reporter*, was to be affected by the publication of the first of a series of free weekly papers in 1964.[13] As time passed, these free papers were to have a major impact on the advertising scene.

It was the publication of *The Bedfordshire Journal* in 1972 that first offered an opportunity to the estate agents to break *The Bedfordshire Times* price monopoly. By that time, the Bedford and District Estate Agents' Association had been formed to provide a united voice in negotiations.[14] Peacocks was one of the leading member firms of the association and, as a major advertiser, strongly supported the proposal to negotiate jointly.

The Bedfordshire Journal was anxious to attract the majority of the estate agents' advertising so as to improve the general readership of the paper and began to offer attractive, lower rates for regular advertising. The introduction of a new, free newspaper was greeted with much scepticism at a time when *The Bedfordshire Times* was the dominant well-read, paid-for local paper. This was an important factor in Peacocks' considerations regarding the placement of adverts, but there was equally a strong need to reduce costs.

11 The first estate agency photographs appear in *The Bedfordshire Times* in 1967 for feature properties. Bedford-based estate agents that made early use of photographs were David Graham & Co. of The Broadway, Connells and Peacocks.

12 The growth of the use of photographs and feature advertising increased gradually from 1967 to 1970; it was not until mid to late 1970 that photographs regularly started to appear in estate agency advertisements.

13 These included *The Bedford and District Weekly Advertiser* (1964 - unknown), *The Bedfordshire Journal* (1972–1986) later continued as *The Bedford Herald* (1986–1998), *The Weekly Advertiser* (1977–1979) and *Bedford* (later *Bedfordshire*) *on Sunday* (1977 to date).

14 The association was formed officially in 1970 and disbanded in 1988. The list of presidents and the president's badge are in the author's collection.

The Estate Agents' Association held various meetings to discuss strategy, and the idea of a special pull-out supplement containing just the advertisements of member firms in the association evolved and was put to *The Bedfordshire Times*. At first this proposal was resisted by the newspaper who claimed it was not possible to produce a supplement for, what was then, a broadsheet newspaper. Eventually, *The Bedfordshire Times* conceded that such a supplement could be produced, perhaps encouraged by the fact that *The Bedfordshire Journal*, a tabloid paper, was prepared to do so. The reduced rates offered by *The Bedfordshire Journal* enabled the association's negotiators to persuade *The Bedfordshire Times* that unless their rates were reduced to a satisfactory level, the bulk of the association members' advertising would be lost.[15]

Negotiations continued back and forth, and although the majority of estate agents were reluctant to leave *The Bedfordshire Times,* and the paper's representatives believed they would retain the business, the paper's rates remained the highest. After a final ultimatum to match the rates offered by *The Bedfordshire Journal* was refused, the association members entered into a contract with *The Bedfordshire Journal*, to the utter disbelief of *The Bedfordshire Times*. The result was that the majority of estate agents' advertising was lost by *The Bedfordshire Times* in June 1979.[16]

Whilst supporting the Bedford and District Estate Agents' Association, Peacocks advertising schedules needed to cover the auction aspects of the business as well, and it had always been made clear that some advertising in *The Bedfordshire Times* would continue on a regular basis, so that a wider readership could be covered each week.

In subsequent years, the battle by the newspapers to retain, or regain, the estate agents' advertising was to continue each time the contract period drew to a close. Changes in law in the 1980s eventually made it illegal for the estate agents to negotiate as a group, and changes in the ownership of estate agency businesses as the large corporate organisations acquired the larger offices led to a weakening of the advantages gained. In due course, the Bedford and District Association of Estate Agents ceased to be effective and was disbanded.

Special newspaper supplements

The *Peacock Property Gazette* was a special supplement published with *The Bedfordshire Journal* in spring 1976 to advertise the extent of services offered by the business through the various offices. The supplement was used to give advance notice of the impending closure of the Horne Lane sale yards and the move to the new Bedford Auction Centre at 26 Newnham Street, planned for early 1977.

Peacock Property Scene, published in six editions from 1986 by *The Bedfordshire Times*, was a further promotional programme to reflect the comprehensive

15 *The Bedfordshire Times* started to produce a supplement from January 1975 under a banner heading of the Bedford and District Estate Agents Association. Member firms at this date included: Allott and Barnard; Amos Horsburgh & Co.; Brown and Merry; Cheffins, Grain & Chalk; Colley Sampson; Connells; Harry Ball; J. R. Eve and Son; Kilroy; Miles; Peacocks; Robinson and Hall; Stonebanks; Stratford.

16 Peacocks continued to place the very occasional, but much reduced, property advert for particular sales.

services offered by the firm, which were more extensive than those offered by other firms within the area, backed as it was by professionally qualified Chartered Surveyors among both the partners and staff.[17] At that time, most local estate agencies only dealt with house sales. Peacocks, however, was able to deal with a broad spectrum of business including: the sale, valuation or letting of all types of real estate; property management and rent collections; valuations for probate or sale; surveys for prospective purchasers, planning applications, linear surveys, preparation of plans; and auction sales of property of all types from landed property to plant and machinery and all chattels.

Various local newspapers have come and gone as the ownership of the publishing companies has changed. *The Bedfordshire Times* moved to a tabloid format on 30 April 1987, and became *The Bedfordshire Times and Citizen* in 1995 on merging with the tabloid *Bedford Citizen*, which had replaced *The Bedford Record. The Bedfordshire Journal* (1972–1986) was discontinued and followed by *The Bedford Herald* (1986–1989), *The Bedford Herald and Post* (1989–1993), and finally *The Herald* (1993–1998) that then ceased publication. *Bedford on Sunday* (later *Bedfordshire on Sunday*) emerged in 1977, as compulsory reading to see what scandals had been revealed each week.

Despite these changes, and the changes in advertising, Peacocks have remained major local advertisers. There are currently property supplements published weekly by both *The Bedfordshire Times and Citizen* and *Bedfordshire on Sunday*, both carrying extensive advertising with full colour photographs.

Local street directories

For many years local street directories were a valuable source of information and now make fascinating reading. In addition to a wealth of local information of general interest, they contain, street by street, details of addresses, occupiers' names, and often, residents' occupations. Some also have an alphabetical A-Z list of individual names and addresses. Pages of advertisements give an interesting insight into the variety of goods and services available. By comparing the maps in different editions of the directories it is possible to see how much a town has expanded from year to year as more streets and estates were built. It is so easy to forget, in the case of Bedford for example, that areas such as Queens Park were the new estates of the early 1900s. Peacocks understood the value of these directories as an advertising medium and used them regularly throughout the firm's history.

The *Bedford Directory 1903* included the first Peacocks' advertisement, and the business continued to advertise in nearly all the subsequent issues.[18] These directories were printed and published by the Bedfordshire Times Publishing Company Limited until 1930. By 1932 the *Bedford Directory*, which also included Kempston,

17 The content of the supplement was varied. Issue one (February 1986) contained an article on the community charge, a brief history of Peacocks, an update on staff training, news about the sale of an oil painting 'Cattle and sheep in a river landscape' by F. R. Lee RA and T. Sidney Cooper and three pages of property adverts. Issue three (April 1986) concentrated on staff news and included the formal and full retirement of Horace Dilley, the award of an associate partnership to Chris Horler at the Baldock office, the retirement of Tony Rowlerson as Property Manager and resultant promotion of Keith Brown.

18 Bedfordshire Publishing Company, *Bedford Directory1903* (Bedford, 1903), p. 8. This advertisement was for Walter M. Peacock and predated his brother joining him in partnership.

was printed by the Sidney Press Limited, a subsidiary company of the Bedfordshire Times, which continued as publishers until 1939.

Kelly's Directories of Bedfordshire were published from 1847 until 1940. Kelly's published their first street directory of *Bedford and Neighbourhood* in 1947 and continued to produce these directories periodically until 1976. The first *Kelly's Directory* advertisement, in the name of Walter M. Peacock, appeared in 1903, when the offices were on the first floor at 72 High Street, Bedford. The telephone number was 205Y3.[19] The 1904 directory included the first Peacocks' advertisement and the firm continued to advertise using various layouts in nearly all the directories published until 1970.

The Illustrated Property Register

By 1908, the scope of services being advertised had increased extensively and the firm was publishing an Illustrated Property Register, sent post free. An advert for the register in the *Bedford Directory 1910* provides details of its contents: lists of unfurnished and furnished houses to let in town and country; properties for sale; shops; stabling; tennis lawns; particulars of schools; and twenty five local views.[20]

Unfortunately, none of the earlier registers are known to have survived intact. Later registers, published in the 1930s, in the author's collection indicate that numbers of larger country houses remained available on the market for some months.[21]

Property sale particulars

The relatively recent availability of high quality electronic copiers and desktop publishing programmes has revolutionised the preparation and presentation of sale particulars, particularly in relation to the rather poor quality particulars that could be produced by early duplicating machines. Prior to that, the alternative was to have items professionally printed.

Local printers were regularly used to produce sale particulars for property auctions, special properties and auction catalogues. Posters were also regularly produced for auction sales to be displayed around the town and county. For many of the early years of Peacocks' history, printing work was carried out by C. F. Timaeus whose print shop was conveniently located in Lime Street. The printing works was situated behind Timaeus's shop at 90 High Street.[22] Much other printing was carried out by Henry Burt & Son, another excellent local company, with a printing works initially in Mill Street, Bedford, and then from 1967 in College Street, Kempston.

19 *Kelly's Directory 1903*, p. 66.

20 *Bedford Directory 1910*, p. 380.

21 A comparison between the registers of November 1937 and June 1938 reveals that a significant proportion of the 'country properties' were available in both. These included Harrold Hall, at £4,500, with fourteen bedrooms and twenty-eight acres of ground and Shortmead House, Biggleswade, at £3,000, with seven bedrooms and four acres of ground. W. & H. Peacock, *An Illustrated Property Register and Housefinder's Guide of the Residential Town of Bedford, November 1937* (Bedford, 1937) and W. & H. Peacock, *An Illustrated Property Register and Housefinder's Guide of the Residential Town of Bedford*, June 1938 (Bedford, 1938).

22 The earliest surviving auction sale catalogue advertises a sale on 10 September 1904 in Wilden, Colmworth and Blunham, and was printed by C. F. Timaeus, BLARS, PK 1/4/3. C. F. Timaeus, founded in 1827, continued to work for Peacocks until the mid-1930s. Timaeus was Bedford's leading printer and bookseller, and publisher of *The Bedfordshire Times and Independent* from 1859 to 1872. The firm finally closed in 1952, *The Bedfordshire Times and Bedfordshire Standard,* 11 July 1952, p. 8.

Henry Burt & Son offered considerable skill and expertise in producing artwork, and were responsible for the printing of countless brochures and catalogues from the 1920s to the 1980s.[23]

While C. F. Timaeus and Henry Burt and Son undertook the majority of printing work, from time to time other printers were used including: W. J. Robinson, 3 Silver Street, Bedford (6 May 1914 sale catalogue of six Bedford properties); Spong and Sons Ltd, Biggleswade (29 April 1938 sale catalogue of a villa in Upper Caldecote); and Tomson and Lendrum Ltd, St Neots (19 July 1950 sale catalogue of a bungalow in Eaton Socon).

Peacocks' logo

From 1972, Peacocks introduced a logo of a peacock silhouette, and this was used on as much of the stationery and advertising material as possible. It appeared on the firm's premises, van, posters, boards, sale particulars and in newspaper advertisements. Leaflets with the logo were prepared for the different departments to illustrate the extent of professional services available. The logo first appeared in the context of a newspaper advertisement in *The Bedfordshire Times* of 1 December 1972.[24]

This was not, however, the first peacock logo to appear in *The Bedfordshire Times;* a Peacocks' estate agency advertisement on 25 August 1972 used a different peacock image that was rather more ornate in design than the silhouette.[25] This logo had been used occasionally from at least the 1950s when it appears on the front of the sale catalogue of the Road Haulage Executive sale of 26 March 1953.[26]

Starting out as a fun idea, the business also introduced, in the 1970s, a navy blue firm's tie decorated with multiple white peacock logos, which cost only fifty pence. The ties became an instant success as a talking point at any meeting or party. They were a great reminder to people who could not remember where or when they had previously met a member of Peacocks' staff. All the male employees were encouraged to wear the tie. When one negotiator complained that blue did not suit his colour scheme, the tie was redesigned with a single, larger, woven peacock logo, of which versions were made in blue, brown, green, maroon and silver-grey.

Estate agency boards

The use of boards has always been an important advertising tool. The early flag boards used by the 84 High Street office were made of vitreous enamel, framed with wood, with a wooden post. These were durable and almost self-cleaning, but very heavy. Local sign writers were also used to prepare and paint special boards to

23 The company was founded by Henry Burt in 1863. An article celebrating its centenary in *The Bedfordshire Times and Standard*, notes the work undertaken for Peacocks. This started when Walter Peacock returned from the Boer War and asked Mr Burt to print a weekly sales catalogue for the furniture sales at Lime Street, *The Bedfordshire Times and Standard*, 22 March 1963, p. 21. Following a merger with the Newnorth group of companies founded by Paul Hooley, the company was renamed Newnorth Burt in 1983.

24 *The Bedfordshire Times*, 1 December 1972, p. 32.

25 *The Bedfordshire Times*, 25 August 1972, p. 23.

26 W. & H. Peacock, *British Road Services Depot, Meadowgate, Bourne, Lincolnshire: Catalogue of 370 Commercial Motor Vehicles, to be Sold at Auction by W. & H. Peacock, Thursday, 26 March 1953*, pamphlet.

order. These were larger than the usual flag boards and contained more information about the property for sale. More recently modern materials have enabled lighter, safer boards to be made.

Nowadays, when the number of properties for sale is much greater than in the past, a board contractor will provide an erection service for a number of agents. Before these services were available, however, the boards were delivered and erected by using the firm's van and sale porters. In the post-war period a part-time porter, 'Titch' Broughton, wheeled the boards about the town on the hand cart that was eventually sold as lot one at the opening of the Auction Centre. Peacocks also employed Mr Sharman, a pensioner, to erect boards in the 1950s. Mr Sharman would tie the boards to his bicycle before wheeling them around the town to their destination.

'For Sale' or 'Sold' boards have always tended to be a target for pranksters who would frequently remove them to another property, not for sale, or simply pull the boards down. An irate owner would quickly contact the office to demand removal in those circumstances. Occasionally a board would be erected at the wrong property by mistake, resulting in profuse apologies by the Peacocks' staff. From time to time a specially painted signboard would disappear, only to be found later being used as a board for mixing cement by builders working nearby.

Auction posters

Auction sales were usually advertised with the use of specially-printed posters displayed at the property and on advertising hoardings throughout the area. The early posters tended to be printed in black, on white paper, with as much information as possible packed into the space, making them quite hard to read. By 1950 a new style of poster was designed by the author, which was printed in two colours and aimed to simply convey the important information of 'what', 'where' and 'when'. The names of any solicitors acting in the sale were also included, at a time when solicitors were not permitted to advertise.[27]

27 It was not until December 1986 that the Law Society relaxed its rules on advertising by solicitors, although it rejected a proposal to allow solicitors to make arrangements with estate agents, banks or building societies to introduce clients, *The Times Digital Archive*, 12 December 1986, p. 7.

Chapter Thirteen

Fun and Games

The annual cricket match

One of the author's early recollections, as a young pupil at Peacocks, was the great enthusiasm for enjoyment shown by the partners and staff. This took various forms including the annual cricket match against F. W. Western & Co. of Biggleswade. This was the highlight of the summer, and one Thursday afternoon in 1948, the author was instructed to be at the Igranic sports field in Kempston (at the corner of High Street and Cemetery Road) in order to take part.[1]

The F. W. Western side was captained by Brian Porter and the team included his elderly father and a number of guest players from the Sandy solicitors E. T. Leeds Smith & Co., who were also keen cricketers. The author cannot remember who won the game, but has recollections of a very generous tea, followed by the players and supporters retiring to the King William IV pub for further refreshment. Cricket matches against F. W. Western were annual events for a number of years, and were greatly enjoyed by both sides.

The Peacocks' archive contains some letters about an earlier, pre-war, friendly cricket match arranged between Robert Peacock and Brian Porter in 1938. The correspondence includes a list of rules agreed by the two teams; one of the rules was that ladies would not be put under restrictions as to bowling as it was felt by the participants that they could be 'quite reasonable about that'. There are also letters relating to the return challenge match held on Thursday 15 June 1939, which Peacocks lost by seventy runs.[2]

There were also cricket matches against Stafford, Rogers & Merry, for which a coveted trophy – a silver coated china chamber pot - had been purchased at an auction. The celebratory beer after the matches was, however, only drunk from tankards!

Research for this book revealed an amusing poetic description by John Williams of a Peacocks' cricket match held at Bromham Park on 27 June 1935. The author is indebted to David Henson, George Henson's son, for the text. The poem, between 'town' and 'county' sides, mentions many of the members of staff involved including Ronald Craig and Robert Peacock (the respective captains), Bill Clarke, Jim Brooks, Reginald Damon and George Robinson. It was obviously a happy and sociable event and the poem ends:

1 The ground, now known as Kempston Hammers Sports and Social Club (Cutler Hammer), is still in use today.

2 BLARS, PK 11/2/1.

In conclusion need I say
We thoroughly enjoyed the day
Our thanks are due as you all know
To our Guvnors for the Show[3]

In later years, as the business grew larger, many more cricket matches took place between Peacocks' offices and against other firms. Football and rounders matches were also played.

Fun on the river

An Old English Fair was held in Mill Meadows, Bedford, in 1936, followed by a procession of illuminated boats on the river in the evening.[4] One of the porters, Ernie Bryant, kindly provided punts for the Peacocks' entry, which included an illuminated 'For Sale' sign that would change to 'SOLD – PEACOCK'.

To celebrate the Festival of Britain in 1951, Bedford held another illuminated procession of boats, which took place on Friday 7 and Saturday 8 September.[5] After due deliberation, it was decided that Peacocks would enter the competition with 'Sawbones 1851', a medical theme that had been successfully used fifteen years before at the Old English Fair. Bedford Hospital entered an impressive nursing tableau, which was near to Peacocks entry in the procession. Students from W. H. Allen built a superb pirate ship, complete with cannons using fireworks and flour bags as ammunition, and there were numerous other excellent entries.

Peacocks again managed to borrow two punts from Ernie Bryant, which were lashed together. An old cast iron bed was 'borrowed' from the sale yards and an operating theatre was created. The lighting was from car batteries and old car headlights. Robert Peacock and D. Pruden, a part-time assistant, paddled; Ronald Craig was in charge of the lights and refreshments, as well as a store of fireworks. Graham Rook, a trainee at 10 Lime Street, lay in bed as the patient. Arthur Wilkins and the author were the surgeons, and Mary Wilkins the nurse. The plan was to anaesthetize the patient with a large mallet before sawing off a leg, which was thrown into the river. The leg had to be attached to a string so that it could be recovered in time for the next operation!

The procession had to pass from St Mary's Gardens, under the Town Bridge, to the Suspension Bridge and then return. There were huge crowds watching the event and they seemed to enjoy the performance, so when the float approached the Town Bridge on the return trip it was suggested that the patient should suddenly wake up and knock the surgeon into the river – which he did. The author swam to the shore and emerged dripping wet to go up the steps to The Embankment to be greeted with the question, 'Are you wet?' He then had to walk back to the sale yards in Horne Lane. By the second performance on the following night, when the Peacocks' float returned towards the bridge the crowd was already yelling 'Knock him in!' so they were duly obliged. The whole event was huge fun, and Peacocks was delighted to

3 John R. A. Williams, *Peacocks Cricket Match (Played at Bromham Park, 27th June, 1935), Nota Bene*, typescript.

4 The Peacocks' entry was called the 'Patients Nightmare' and was a comic reconstruction of an operating theatre, *The Bedfordshire Times and Independent*, 7 August 1936, p. 7. The fair was organised by the Bedford Rotary Club on behalf of the County Hospital new ward fund.

5 *The Bedfordshire Times and Standard*, 14 September 1951, p. 7.

receive third prize. This was a silver-framed perpetual calendar that remained on Ronald Craig's desk in the Lime Street office for many years.

Outings, dinners and parties

For the Whitsun bank holiday in 1950 an outing to Great Yarmouth was arranged by Ronald Craig. This was a particularly notable event as, when the coach arrived at the hotel where lunch had been arranged, it was found to be a Temperance Hotel where no alcohol was served. It took Ronald many years to live that down. A lot of enjoyment was later had, however, on the roller-coaster and other rides at the big fun fair although several of the party came off looking somewhat green.

Another memorable outing took place in 1957 when there was an excursion by a large party of the partners, staff and wives to see the Crazy Gang at the Victoria Palace Theatre in London. Everyone was very amused when a 'Bill Clarke' was mentioned during one of the sketches as this was also the name of the manager of Peacocks' Egg Packing Station.

The partners were generous in arranging celebratory dinners, and a significant number were held over the years. Many of the staff were invited to these occasions from early in the business's history, as witnessed by a surviving recitation given by John Williams at a dinner in 1935, which reveals the names of many of the attendees.[6]

Another celebration dinner for staff was held at the Dujon Restaurant in 1947 to celebrate the return of those who had come back to the firm after their time away on war service.

On 27 September 1951 there was a celebration dinner at the Dujon Rooms, High Street, Bedford, to mark the Golden Jubilee of the firm. Walter and Harry Peacock were present as guests of honour, together with Robert Peacock and the other partners, George Robinson and Herbert Parrott. The celebration also marked the occasion of Dudley Peacock being made a partner. At that time Dudley was still studying for his degree in rural estate management. Virtually the whole of the staff from the offices at Bedford and Baldock was present for the occasion. The toast to 'The two Governors' was proposed by Frank Jeffery, supported by Ronald Craig and Jim Brooks.[7]

A dinner was held in 1964 to mark the opening of the new estate agency office at 58 St Loyes Street, Bedford, and to celebrate the formation of the new partnership when Robert Peacock and Dudley Peacock were joined by Frank Jeffery, Jonathan Knights and the author.

Ronald Craig's fifty years' service with the firm was marked in 1966 by a special dinner held in his honour at The Embankment Hotel, Bedford, when a presentation of a gold watch was made.

The amalgamation of Peacocks with F. W. Western & Co. on 1 January 1970 was celebrated with another staff dinner. By then the partners and staff numbers had increased to forty-nine.

On 27 September 1971, the staff assembled for a dinner to celebrate Robert Peacock's Golden Jubilee with the firm. This was yet another great evening of

6 John R. A. Williams, *Staff Dinner 1935: W. & H. Peacock's Staff in Verse*, typescript.
7 *The Bedfordshire Times and Bedfordshire Standard*, 5 October 1951, p. 8.

reminiscences of the good old days. There was much to celebrate in both Robert Peacock's professional and civic life. He had been: Honorary Secretary to Bedfordshire Chamber of Agriculture in 1924, continuing in that role for twenty-three years; President of the Hertfordshire, Bedfordshire and Buckinghamshire Agricultural Valuers' Association, 1944; President of the Central Association of Agricultural Valuers, 1947; President of the Central Association of Agricultural Valuers, 1949; Chairman of the Bedfordshire and Hertfordshire Branch of the Royal Institution of Chartered Surveyors, 1952; Chairman of the Council of Bedfordshire Agricultural Society in 1958, continuing in that role for ten years; Chairman of the Bedfordshire, Hertfordshire and Huntingdonshire Branch of the Auctioneers' Institute and Provincial Meeting, 1961; and Vice President of the East of England Show, 1969. This list excludes the work he undertook for the Surveyors 21 Club detailed in a later chapter. A year later, in 1972, he was awarded the OBE for his work on the Committee of the Agricultural Holdings Act that dealt with the landlord and tenant farmer relationship.[8]

He had also made time for various other duties including: Chairman to Kempston Urban District Council, 1942; Lieutenant in the Home Guard, 1945; Justice of the Peace from 1956; and Chairman to Ampthill Magistrates Court, 1971.[9]

In 1994, staff gathered to celebrate Dudley Peacock's sixty-fifth birthday. Like his father before him there was much to celebrate. He had been: Chairman of the Chartered Auctioneers and Estate Agents Institute, Bedfordshire, Hertfordshire and Huntingdonshire branch, from 1968 to 1969; President of the Cambridge and Isle of Ely Agricultural Valuers' Association, from 1969 to 1970; President of the Hertfordshire, Bedfordshire and Buckinghamshire Agricultural Valuers' Association, 1971; President of the Midland Counties Agricultural Valuers' Association, 1982.[10] In addition he had also made time for many civic and social duties including: High Sheriff of Bedfordshire, from 1978 to 1979; Chairman of the Bedford Magistrates Bench, from 1985 to 1989; and Deputy Lieutenant for the County of Bedfordshire, 1990.[11]

In common with many businesses, Christmas celebrations at Peacocks were notable occasions for the partners and staff. Every member of staff received a most welcome Christmas bonus in cash. The married members of staff were each presented with a specially ordered, fresh, oven-ready turkey. The Christmas parties in the individual offices were highly enjoyable events and there were many high jinks, perhaps best passed over in this record! Many parties took place after the offices closed on Christmas Eve. In the case of Dame Alice Street, that meant being allowed to close 'early' at five o'clock instead of six o'clock.

Following the expansion of the business to include offices in Biggleswade and Sandy, it became customary to hold a combined party at a suitable venue, to which all the partners and staff were invited as guests. There was always a tasty Christmas dinner accompanied by adequate liquid refreshment. Coaches were laid on so that the guests could all enjoy themselves without the need to drive home afterwards.

8 Her Majesty's Stationery Office, *Supplement to the London Gazette of Tuesday, 23 May 1972*, no. 45678 (1972), p. 6265, http://www.london-gazette.co.uk/issues/45678/supplements/6255 (accessed February 2014).

9 W. & H. Peacock Western & Co, *Staff Dinner to Celebrate Mr Robert's Golden Jubilee with the Firm.*

10 Wilson Peacock, *Mr Dudley's 65th Birthday Party* (Bedford, 1994), pamphlet.

11 *The Bedfordshire Times*, 31 March 1978, p. 5.

The fancy dress parties probably caused most hilarity, and did much to cement friendships between the different offices. There were some headaches the following day and a few red faces too!

Over the years there were numerous romances between members of staff, several of which resulted in marriage. This served to further enhance the strong feeling of 'family' among so many of the staff that worked for Peacocks throughout its period as a privately-owned business.

Chapter Fourteen

Ministry of Supply Sales, Peacock, Merry and Swaffield

Ministry of Supply sales, 1947–1952

Many people will have largely forgotten, or may never have known, the shortages that persisted in the early years following the Second World War. Food, clothing, furniture and petrol were rationed. Materials for manufacturing and building were subject to strict regulations and many prices were controlled. This environment meant that there was considerable interest in the post-war Ministry of Supply sales undertaken by Peacock, Merry and Swaffield.

Throughout the British Isles there were vast quantities of surplus military vehicles, equipment and other items stored in depots, awaiting disposal. One such, Elstow Storage Depot, was sited some four miles south of Bedford, off the A6 trunk road, close to approaches to the village of Wilstead.[1] Now developed as The Wixams, this huge depot and the adjacent munitions factory once extended as far as Ampthill Road at Kempston Hardwick.[2]

The task of disposal lay with the Ministry of Supply which, assisted by the Chartered Auctioneers' and Estate Agents' Institute, selected a panel of auctioneers to sell the items for disposal by public auction, without reserve. Following a meeting in London attended by Robert Peacock, the best-known chattel auctioneer in Bedford, Peacocks were appointed to the panel. The first sale to take place at Elstow Storage Depot was held on 10 and 11 March 1947, when some 350 motor vehicles, 60 factory trucks and miscellaneous equipment including electric motors, cine equipment, 800 stereoscopes and gun sighting telescopes came under the hammer.[3]

The prospect of Peacocks enjoying sole local control of these attractive sales led Jack Merry of Stafford, Rogers and Merry Ltd, the Bedford auctioneers, to make representations to share the work. Arising from these representations a special partnership trading as Peacock and Merry was formed for the second sale at Elstow, which lasted for four days from 30 June 1947.[4]

1 Elstow Storage Depot was opened in 1942 by the Ministry of Supply as a bomb and shell making factory. It was a completely self-contained complex with its own roads, railway, post office, chemist and power plants, Muriel M. Hart, *Portrait of Elstow, Bedfordshire*, (Bedford, 2000), p. 13.

2 The Wixams was identified as a site for strategic development in the Bedfordshire Structure Plan, 1991. The site is now within the administrative boundaries of Bedford Borough Council and Central Bedfordshire Council.

3 *The Bedfordshire Times and Bedfordshire Standard*, 14 February 1947, p. 6 and *The Times Digital Archive,* 17 February 1947, p. 8.

4 *The Bedfordshire Times and Bedfordshire Standard*, 27 June 1947, p. 4.

The Peacock and Merry partnership had conducted just two sales before Norman Foster made persistent overtures on behalf of Swaffield & Son, the old-established Ampthill auctioneers, to participate in the work.[5] Thus it was that a consortium trading as Peacock, Merry and Swaffield was established, and held its first sale at Elstow for three days from 4 November 1947.[6] This partnership continued for thirty-eight sales until the final three day sale from 9 September 1952.[7] Several sales included items located at other depots, some as near as Little Staughton or Woolwich, with others as far afield as Guernsey and Northern Ireland.

The total value of goods sold through the Elstow sales was over £3,000,000 – a vast sum at the time. There had been a total of some 130 sale days. The sales had included a staggering array of items, including approximately 31,000 motor vehicles, over 3,600 motorcycles, nearly 1,000 factory trucks and about 8,000 pedal cycles. Also sold were: thousands of pairs of binoculars; aircraft cameras; cinema projector equipment; various other optical equipment; electric motors; cables; wireless parts; surveying equipment; and quantities of spares of various types.

Motor vehicles included cars, utilities, vans and lorries from 15 hundredweight to 10 ton capacity. There were prime movers and trailers, tippers, half-tracks, armoured cars, amphibious vehicles, jeeps, fire engines, heavy recovery vehicles, mobile cranes, radio vans, command vehicles, petrol tankers, tank transporters, a mobile cinema and many others. Manufacturers, both British and American, included Albion, AEC, Alvis, Austin, Bedford, Chevrolet, Commer, Dennis, Dodge, Ford, Guy, GEC, Hillman, Humber, Karrier, Leyland, MG, Morris, Rolls Royce, Scammell, Standard and Thorneycroft.

Whilst many vehicles had been well used and were dilapidated, many were fully serviceable and merely needed a freshly-charged battery and fuel to be started and driven away. Some trucks, bought for as little as fifty pounds, were driven away to be used for many years. With new cars in very short supply, there was a strong demand for Austin 16 saloon cars that had been returned for sale after use by the Allied Control Council in Germany. Mileages were unknown, but demand was strong and prices were high, in some cases significantly above the list price for a new car. Hundreds of potential buyers came from all parts of the country, and included a variety of people from all walks of life, but they were principally farmers, motor traders and general dealers. Camden Motors Ltd and Pride and Clark Ltd of London bought many vehicles and motorcycles at Elstow, and the Flitwick motor haulage firm of L. W. Vass were regular buyers too. The eventual destination of many of the vehicles was overseas countries, especially the half-tracks, amphibious vehicles and armoured cars.

Of the thirty-eight sales held at Elstow Storage Depot, thirty-one consisted mostly of vehicles. Seven sales were mainly of surplus plant, equipment and stores, which included a vast variety of goods, varying from nails and nuts and bolts, to parachutes, uniforms, boots and shoes. There was electrical equipment, all sorts of

5 Swaffied & Son were established in 1849. In 1947 the partners were Henry Swaffield, Norman B. Foster and Leslie J. Swaffield, *The Bedfordshire Times and Bedfordshire Standard*, 3 January 1947, p. 6.

6 *The Bedfordshire Times and Bedfordshire Standard*, 31 October 1947, p. 4.

7 This sale advertised approximately 800 motor vehicles, including 150 saloon cars, 75 light vans and utilities, 63 tank transporters, 80 jeeps, 80 amphibious carriers, 63 tank transporters and 2 mobile cinemas, *The Bedfordshire Times and Bedfordshire Standard*, 5 September 1952, p. 6.

tools and tons of cycle spares. Some domestic items were sold in small lots, though the majority of lots were of large quantities.

Thorneycroft-Coles mobile cranes and road rollers always commanded serious interest. At least one narrow gauge locomotive was sold as well as a number of diesel locomotives. Large quantities of 4711 eau-de-Cologne, described as 'of German origin' also came under the hammer. Scrap metal was sold too. The variety seemed almost endless.

With so many official regulations affecting the purchase or resale of many items, it is perhaps interesting to look at notices published in the catalogues. This list taken from the catalogue for the fifth sale, held on 14 March 1951, provides some examples of the regulations of the time:[8]

> **1. Wooden Containers**. If any containers purchased at this Sale are broken up by the Purchaser for the recovery of timber, a licence to consume must be obtained from the local Timber Control Area Officer, and a copy of the Sale contract should be sent to him
> **2. Price Control Regulations.** (i) The attention of Buyers purchasing goods (including second-hand goods) for re-sale in the course of their business is directed to the Goods and Services (Price Control) Acts, 1939 to 1943, as amended by the Defence (Price Control) Regulations, 1945, and Defence Regulations 55AB and the
> Orders made under them.[9]
> (ii) The attention of persons bidding who are second-hand goods dealers is directed to the fact that the prices at which they may sell second-hand price-controlled goods are controlled by the Second-hand Goods (Maximum Prices and Records) Order 1949 (S.I.1949 No.1784), and Amending Orders made by the Board of Trade …
> **5. Bedding.** Used or soiled bedding is sold on condition that before re-use the fillings must be processed to conform to the standard of cleanliness required by the draft specification drawn by the British Standards Institution.
> **6. Jute or Hessian Piece Goods.** Unrestricted sale is not permitted by Jute Control, whose Certificate of Approval must be obtained before any re-sale takes place …
> **8. Clothing.** All crested buttons, insignia and badges must be removed before resale; the buttons and insignia must be mutilated and disposed of as scrap …'

Dick Arnold, who had been articled to Peacocks before the war and returned after service as a Captain in the Bedfordshire Yeomanry, was allocated the job of managing the sales. This included careful preparation of the sale catalogues, advertising to approved schedules including in *The Bedfordshire Times and Bedfordshire Standard* and various national newspapers, and arranging view-days and the sale-day operations.

The work of cataloguing, mostly carried out by Dick Arnold and his assistant Arthur Wilkins, involved much more than merely listing the items to be sold in each lot. Every vehicle carried a long serial number as well as a registration number that

8 W. & H. Peacock, Merry and Swaffield, *Catalogue of Surplus Plant Equipment and Stores: Wednesday 14th March 1951* (1951), p. 6, pamphlet.

9 Soon after the start of the Second World War legislation was passed to give the Board of Trade the ability to specify maximum prices and profit margins in order to stabilise the cost of living and provide some assurance of quality (for example the 'utility mark' for clothing). Many of the regulations (albeit with amendments) were still in force for a considerable period after the war. Buyers at auction who intended to re-sell their purchases were still, in 1951, subject to price controls.

had to be recorded and verified against the sale inventory and the sale catalogue. The job of checking numbers mostly fell to the articled clerks, including the author, and was fun on warm and sunny days. In wintertime, in rain or snow, the task meant wading through deep mud and water. Sometimes the water was deep enough to go over the top of Wellington boots, making it necessary to jump from vehicle to vehicle to check the numbers in the draft catalogue. In such conditions the clerks got very cold and it became difficult to write.

Overall management of the sales continued under Dick Arnold, and the Peacocks' office at 10 Lime Street, Bedford, acted as the pre-sale headquarters. The staff were kept busy despatching the printed sale catalogues during the advertising period. Catalogues were six pence each and would admit one person on sale days or two on view days. On sale days auctioneers and general staffing were provided by the various firms on a rota basis, usually with additional help from Peacocks' staff.

The sales were conducted in one of the big Romney huts, warehouse sheds, which could hold a large company. The auctioneer's rostrum stood on a platform at one end with the office adjoining, separated from the public by a glass screen. Here the sale clerks handled the files containing the sale bills for each buyer, made up as the sale progressed. The auctioneer sat with a clerk who helped to spot bids from the large company and who recorded the price and buyers in the auctioneer's sale book. Buyers were required to pay in cash by deposited pre-payments (five days had to be allowed for cheque clearance before the sale), by banker's draft or by cheque, after credit had been established with Westminster Bank for the duration of the sale.

At the end of each day of the earlier sales, the cash was put into linen bank bags and taken back to Bedford by car to be paid in to the bank. Westminster Bank later assisted on sale days by providing an on-site service to verify cheques and accepting responsibility for the very large amounts of cash. The bank's representative, from the Bedford High Street branch, was usually Douglas Catlin, who worked at the branch for many years and was a well-known character in the town. A local taxi served to transport the cash to the bank at the close of day.

Security was in the hands of the friendly Wilstead village bobby, who would duly arrive on his bicycle - a nice break from his daily routine. The policeman was PC 73 Ernest Jacquest, who served at Wilstead from 1947 until his retirement in 1953. PC Jacquest had joined the Bedfordshire Constabulary in March 1926, following seven years in the army, and spent most of his service in local villages.

At sales run by Peacocks, the principal auctioneers were Robert Peacock and Dick Arnold. When Harry Peacock attended he carefully kept a separate record of prices as the sale proceeded as a check in case of dispute. Harry, economical as ever, always used a pencil so that the figures could be erased after the sale to allow the sheets to be ready for re-use.

The auctioneers at 'Merry' sales were normally John I. Scott and Jack Merry. At the sales run by Swaffield & Son, Norman Foster and Leslie Swaffield sold, usually assisted by Dick Arnold.

A 25% deposit was payable for each lot at a desk on the side of the platform. Most deposits were made in cash, with bundles of pound notes or the larger, white, five-pound notes. It was necessary to count the cash very carefully, for it was not uncommon for a note to be missing from a bundle allegedly 'just as collected from the bank', though it would miraculously emerge from the customer's pocket when challenged. Another trick was to carefully fold a note over double and put it in the middle of a bundle, in the hope that it might be counted twice. Sometimes bundles of notes, smelling strongly of mothballs, would be brought out from a shopping basket covered with newspaper.

Buyers were required to pay for each lot before it could be taken from the depot, and although much care was taken to avoid accidental removal of the wrong lot, it happened occasionally, usually with the small items. As any loss of this nature, or shortfall from a bounced cheque, was the auctioneers' responsibility a great deal of care was needed.

The sales at Elstow were always extremely popular among the Peacocks' staff and it was all hands to the pumps apart from those who had to remain in Bedford to deal with the normal weekly sales. Excellent refreshments were supplied by Dudeney & Johnston, then one of Bedford's leading grocers and caterers. As food was still rationed, the superb ham sandwiches, cakes and jam tarts were particularly popular. Articled clerk, Peter Moreton, claimed the record for eating no fewer than thirteen jam tarts in one day, a feast he was never allowed to forget. The generous bonus paid to staff after each sale was also especially appreciated.

On Peacocks' sale days, the office was usually supervised by the cashier, Reginald Damon, while Bill Clarke dealt with transfer of cash and cheques to the bank. The rest of the team who took deposits and ran the sale files included: Marjory Ainsworth; Irene Brooks; Jan Church; Frank Jeffery; Joy Merryweather; and Arthur Wilkins, together with the articled clerks, Peter Moreton, Brian Crozier and the author.

As usual with any auction sale, there were many bargains, but some buyers were carried away by enthusiasm and paid too much. Some dealers, who were regular buyers, would deliberately run up the price of a lot if they perceived other buyers to be in their way, hoping to make the other bidder pay dearly. This was especially the case when a number of dealers established a buyers' ring to try to keep down prices. Though against the law, such rings were notoriously difficult to break. On one particular occasion, Robert Peacock stopped selling and steadfastly refused to carry on because a ring of buyers for optical equipment caused noisy interruptions when a lot was knocked down to a buyer known to be outside the ring.

Road Haulage Executive sales, 1947–1953

The sales at Elstow were not the only surplus sales to be conducted on behalf of government departments. Following nationalisation of the road haulage industry as a result of The Transport Act 1947, Peacocks were appointed by the Road Haulage Executive to hold a series of seven sales of surplus vehicles and equipment at the British Road Services Depot at Meadowgate, Bourne, Lincolnshire.[10] These sales involved the disposal of hundreds of commercial vehicles of different types and makes. The majority of the vehicles were six-ton, four-wheel, dropside trucks, and whilst many were manufactured during the 1940s, a number were made in the 1930s. Manufacturers included some lesser known names, in addition to the most common makers. The list embraced: AEC; Austin; Albion; Bedford; Brockhouse; Commer;

10 W. & H. Peacock, *Catalogue of 370 Commercial Motor Vehicles, to be Sold at Auction by W. H Peacock*.

Dennis; Dodge; Dyson; ERF; Foden; Fordson; Ford; GMC; Humber; Leyland; Maudsley; Morris; Scammell; Seddon; Thorneycroft; and Vulcan. In addition to the vehicles, many lots of vehicle spare parts, engine units and chassis frames were also sold in convenient lots. Organisation of these sales continued to be in the hands of Dick Arnold and followed the well tried methods adopted for the sales at Elstow.

Government surplus sale, 1950

A sale of surplus government hutting and building materials was held at Peak Hill Farm, Clapham on 18 April 1950.[11] This sale, held at a time when such materials were very scarce, included some 700 lots, varying from complete sectional huts, through to such items as sinks and baths, stoves, plasterboard, windows, steel girders, water tanks, roof trusses, telegraph poles, asbestos sheets etc.

Plant and commercial sales, Peacocks and Walker, Walton and Hanson

In the 1960s and 1970s, a number of collective sales of plant and commercial vehicles were held in conjunction with the Nottingham auctioneers and valuers, Walker, Walton & Hanson.[12] These sales were first held at Cranfield Airfield, by arrangement with the College of Aeronautics, before transferring to the western end of the former wartime ammunition factory at Kempston Hardwick, on land leased from London Brick Company Limited.[13] The sales generated significant interest and frequently included various types of cranes and other heavy moving equipment.

There is an amusing incident arising from one of these sales that was told by the late Brian Howard and is recounted with his kind permission. Brian's father, C. A. E. C. Howard, was a frequent visitor to Peacocks' sales. He foresaw the future of transport in utilising tractor vehicles with interchangeable trailers. At one of the war surplus sales, he purchased a sixty-feet-long 'Queen Mary' trailer, as used for carrying aircraft both during and after the war, intending to add a second trailer to develop his idea. For years the second trailer never materialised and the original trailer remained unused. Eventually Brian decided to dispose of the trailer while his father was away on holiday and it was entered into a Kempston Hardwick sale.

C. A. E. C. Howard returned from holiday and went about his business. He told Brian Howard that he had, at last, found a second trailer 'better than the other'. It had been bought at the Kempston Hardwick sale! The entry against that lot in the auctioneers' handbook read, 'Vendor: Mr Brian Howard; Buyer: Mr C. A. E. C. Howard'. Auctioneers do not often get paid commission for selling people their own goods.

11 *The Bedfordshire Times and Bedfordshire Standard*, 7 April 1950, p. 6.

12 Walker, Walton and Hanson were well-known for their long-standing series of auctions at Ruddington Depot, five miles south of Nottingham, dating back to the 1940s, where they disposed of surplus war-time equipment and vehicles on behalf of the Ministry of Supply, *The Times Digital Archive*, 10 June 1946, p. 8 et al.

13 The first sale was held on the 28 April 1965, *The Bedfordshire Times*, 19 March 1965, p. 15. The sale included 500 lots of civil engineering equipment, quarry mining plant, motor vehicle spares, trailers, machine tools, machinery, implements and aircraft. Cranfield Airfield was opened in 1937 as an Operational Training Unit under Fighter Command's 12 Group. After the war it was used briefly as an Empire Test Pilots' School. In 1945 the College of Aeronautics was founded by government sponsorship, Eunice Wilson, 'Cranfield Airfield', *Bedfordshire County Life Magazine*, Issue 5 (Summer, 1999), pp. 35–43.

Chapter Fifteen

The Egg Packing Station, Bedford

The Peacocks' Egg Packing Station occupied an L-shaped block of a former stabling and coach house adjacent to the market office at Horne Lane. As it was run as a separate entity, most employees in other departments knew little about this part of the business.

The sales of eggs at Horne Lane commenced in 1921 to 1922 when cottages near the centre of the yard were converted to an egg sale room. This was followed in 1929 by the development of an Egg Packing Station, accredited by the Ministry of Agriculture.[1] The Egg Packing Station was regularly referred to in Peacocks' newspaper adverts until July 1935 after which there is no significant mention until September 1940. An advert in *The Bedfordshire Times and Bedfordshire Standard* of 6 September 1940 announced the approval of Egg Packing Station number 128 by the Ministry of Food as a result of the new Maximum Prices Order.[2]

The development of egg packing stations was initially in response to national concerns regarding imported eggs and their effect on home egg producers. The Agricultural Produce (Grading and Marking) Act 1928 gave the Ministry powers to prescribe quality marks for British produce and license dealers (such as Peacocks) to use a 'National Mark' on commodities in an effort to boost the purchase of local produce. The 'National Mark' was suspended at the outbreak of the Second World War.[3]

The war brought new controls in an effort to deal with the problems of egg distribution, particularly to large towns, where the shortages were worst.[4] Problems also existed in more rural areas; Peacocks received an anonymous letter dated 13 January 1944 naming a person guilty of buying and then re-selling eggs at inflated prices in Marston Moretaine.[5] Due to these strict war-time and post-war regulations, all eggs were required to be tested, graded and stamped with the egg packing station number.

In 1957 the Egg Marketing Board introduced the 'Lion Mark', which was imprinted on all eggs as well as the packing station number, to enable faulty eggs to be traced back by retailers.

The work of the Egg Packing Station staff varied little over the years. All eggs

1 The opening of the Egg Packing Station was announced in the *Bedfordshire Times and Independent*, 5 April 1929, p. 8.

2 *Bedfordshire Times and Bedfordshire Standard*, 6 September 1940, p. 4. The Home Produced Eggs (Maximum Prices) Orders prescribed the maximum prices at which eggs could be sold by wholesalers to retailers and by retailers to consumers.

3 R. J. Hammond, *Food and Agriculture in Britain 1939–45; Aspects of Wartime Control* (Oxford, 1954), p. 58.

4 Martin Brayley, *The British Home Front 1939–45* (Oxford, 2005), p. 19.

5 BLARS, PK 8/5/8.

delivered to the Egg Packing Station were fed onto a conveyor to be taken to women who 'candled' each egg by holding it in front of a light, to check that it was infertile. The staff were experts and quickly detected any faulty eggs, which had to be discarded because they were fertilised. Double-yolked eggs were also rejected. Every week, thousands of eggs were brought in or were collected by the firm's vans from a large number of farms throughout an allotted area. The drivers would take the appropriate payment to producers on their round.

The Peacocks' archive contains a letter from the Ministry of Food dated 6 June 1947 inviting the business to send suitable candidates on a candlers refresher course. Peacocks decided to nominate Miss G. R. Woodward and Mrs Carter. They were tested on candling thirty dozen boxes of eggs from incoming supplies, which they were able to achieve in eleven and fourteen minutes respectively. They were also tested on candling ten dozen boxes of eggs for faults, and had to take a written exam. Both candidates passed the course that took place at Banbury Egg Packing Station from 8–19 September 1947.[6]

The packing station was first managed by Mr Herbert Parrott until he was succeeded, in 1941, by William Clarke. The packing station team also included porters and a bevy of ladies. Mr Clarke joined Peacocks in 1913 after having served with the Royal Flying Corps from 1917 to 1918. During the Second World War he joined the Home Guard. He was presented with a gold watch for his fifty years of service to Peacocks in 1963.[7]

There was little excitement associated with the activities of the Egg Packing Station apart from an occasion in the 1950s when the huge steel door to the strong room was blown open by burglars. The strong room door was removed to be re-fitted to the newly built strong room at the estate agency office at 58 St Loyes Street, Bedford.

The egg packing business was sold in 1962, the equipment removed, and the buildings used for storage.[8]

6 BLARS, PK 8/5/15.
7 *The Bedfordshire Times and Bedfordshire Standard*, 19 April 1963, p. 19.
8 W. & H. Peacock, *1901–1964*.

Chapter Sixteen

The Rutland Road Store, Bedford

In 1906, Peacocks opened a furniture repository located off Midland Road, Bedford, just to the rear of the corner premises then occupied by Cooper's Seed Merchants and still known by many local people as 'Cooper's Corner'.[1] The premises had previously been occupied as a workshop by George Harrison, a builder.

The building had two floors and contained a simple goods lift. The premises were useful as they enabled the firm to store furniture and household effects for clients going abroad. Perhaps more importantly, the firm could accommodate large quantities of furniture or other goods destined for sale until space was available at the Lime Street sale rooms or at Horne Lane.

During the Second World War, the premises were requisitioned and used for government storage purposes. After de-requisitioning, their usefulness diminished as fewer clients required long-term storage.

In 1955 the building was eventually sold to the Melbreck Furnishing Company who owned the adjoining shop premises at 119a Midland Road.[2]

1 George Cooper founded the seed company, later known as George Cooper & Son, in 1877 in Hertford. In 1882 or 1883 he moved to Bedford and opened a shop in St Paul's Square. In 1890 he bought the freehold of land in Midland Road and had his own shop built for £2,000. The company celebrated its centenary in 1977, *The Bedford Record*, 1 March 1977, pp. 16–17.

2 W. & H. Peacock, *1901–1964*.

Chapter Seventeen

121–123 Midland Road, Bedford, Bartle Potter & Son

In 1948, the partners acquired the business of Messrs Bartle Potter & Son, then practising as auctioneers, valuers and estate agents at 121–123 Midland Road, Bedford.[1] The company occupied the first floor offices above Hebblethwaite's toy and cycle shop, which today forms part of an amusement complex in the area of Midland Road formerly known as Cooper's Corner. Bartle Potter & Son had established a good reputation in the area, though they dealt with many fewer sales than Peacocks. After the acquisition, the company continued to trade under its original name.

Frank Jeffery was appointed manager, Mrs Norah 'Mack' Williams, secretary and Richard Hollands, assistant. Richard Hollands was an articled pupil who had recently returned to complete his training after National Service.

In addition to sales and valuation work, Frank Jeffery dealt with many claims on behalf of clients for loss of the development value of their land arising from the provisions of the Town and Country Planning Act 1947. This Act gave the state a monopoly on the right to develop land; its aim, at the time, was to end land speculation, free up land for use and ensure that increased land values accrued to the community. In brief, the Act deprived landowners of the additional value that would accrue on their land if planning permission was granted for some form of development. A sum of £300 million was made available to land owners who could claim hardship because they had been refused this right. The work of the office therefore involved investigation to identify land with development potential, where a claim could be established.

With the lease of the Midland Road office due to expire, the business was relocated in August 1951 to ground floor premises at 104 Bromham Road, Bedford, continuing there until 1953.[2] At this point, the partners decided to close the Bartle Potter & Son business. Frank Jeffery, by then a Fellow of the Chartered Auctioneers' and Estate Agents' Institute, returned to the office at 6 Dame Alice Street to become the senior professional assistant under George Robinson, the partner in charge of that office. Norah Williams left to become a secretary at H. G. Langley & Co, solici-

1 Bartle Potter & Son, of 5 Bedford Road, WC1, had been practicing in Bedford from at least 1946. The first advert for the local office appeared in *The Bedfordshire Times and Bedfordshire Standard*, 14 June 1946, p. 6. After 8 October 1948 reference to the London address is omitted, *The Bedfordshire Times and Bedfordshire Standard*, 8 October 1948, p. 4.

2 The new address was announced in *The Bedfordshire Times and Bedfordshire Standard*, 17 August 1951, p. 4. The last advert in *The Bedfordshire Times and Bedfordshire Standard* for Bartle Potter & Son was on the 28 March 1953, p. 6.

tors, which later amalgamated with C. C. Bell & Son, for whom she then worked until her retirement. Dick Hollands, having qualified as a Chartered Surveyor, left the firm to join the Valuation Office of the Inland Revenue, where he worked as a qualified valuer for the rest of his professional career.

Chapter Eighteen

The Surveyors 1921 Club

No book about Peacocks would be complete without reference to the Surveyors 1921 Club. This club has had close associations with the firm since its formation in 1921, when the founder members were A. W. Foll, N. B. Foster, E. E. Geeves, H. L. Peacock, W. M. Peacock, H. E. Perks (who was elected as the first president) and J. C. E. Robinson.[1]

> 'The Club was really founded on the Midland Railway, midnight train, from London, after a Valuers' Meeting. The Seven Founders, led by H. E. Perks and whipped in by E. E. Geeves, decided to form a Club to provide an informal Bedford discussion group. The primary object being the elucidation of the then Agricultural Holdings Act 1920, later the 1923 Act. The first meeting was held at the Auctioneers' Institute in Russell Square, London on 15th July 1921, followed by the first dinner at the Russell Hotel.'[2]

As noted above, the decision to form the Surveyors 1921 Club arose from a desire to understand new legislation that followed the First World War, in particular the Agriculture Act 1920.[3] The club then developed to provide opportunities for regular meetings and discussions of professional interest, coupled with meetings of a more social nature.[4] The club has, and still retains, a strong emphasis on encouragement of younger members by enabling them to meet and gain knowledge from the older or more experienced members.

Membership of the club is still largely restricted to Chartered Surveyors and younger persons in the course of training, though a percentage of the membership is now drawn from allied professions. The broad range of members is taken from surveyors in private practice, in corporate employment, from local government, and from the Valuation Office Agency, together with a number of solicitors and architects. Membership, steady at round sixty members for many years, grew steadily to

1 Arthur Wallace Foll PASI was the auctioneer of Foll and Bawden, Woburn Sands. Norman B. Foster was a partner in Swaffield & Son, auctioneers and estate agents, Ampthill. Ernest E. Geeves FAI FIARB was architect and surveyor of Old Post Office, Cheapside, Luton. H. E. Perks was a partner in J. R. Eve and Son, chartered surveyors, land agents and auctioneers, 2 St Paul's Square, Bedford. James Charles Evitt Robinson was a partner in Robinson and Hall, 15a St Paul's Square, Bedford and Chief Executive Officer of Bedford Agricultural Executive Committee, 87 High Street, Bedford.

2 The Surveyors 21 Club, *The Golden Jubilee Book for the members of the Surveyors 1921 Club 1971* (Bedford, 1971), p. 9.

3 The Agriculture Act 1920, amongst other provisions, guaranteed minimum prices for wheat and barley and minimum wages for farm workers. It was not wholly successful, however, and these important sections were repealed in 1921, Edith H. Whetham, 'The Agriculture Act, 1920 and its repeal – the "Great Betrayal"', *British Agricultural History Review*, vol. 22 (1974), pp. 36–49.

4 Outings included a visit by twenty members in June 1961 to woodlands on the Woburn estate, *The Bedfordshire Times and Bedfordshire Standard*, 9 June 1961, p. 10 and to the Marston Moretaine brickworks in May 1968, *The Bedfordshire Times*, 24 May 1968, p. 15.

over 120 by 1971, and peaked at over 140 by 1995. The current membership is around ninety. Membership is kept 'live' by a rule demanding a minimum level of attendance each year.

The requirement for all Chartered Surveyors to undertake continued professional development has enabled the club to offer members a useful bonus by arranging meetings on topics that qualify for that purpose. The highlight of the club year is usually the annual dinner, when members have an opportunity to entertain their professional colleagues and business associates at an informal, but very enjoyable occasion.

The roll of past presidents of the Surveyors 1921 Club contains the names of most leaders of the profession from the local area. These have included J. D. Trustram Eve who was President of the Royal Institution of Chartered Surveyors from 1960 to 1961 and L. H. E. Perks who was President of the Chartered Auctioneers' and Estate Agents' Institute from 1969 to 1970, immediately prior to the amalgamation with the Royal Institution of Chartered Surveyors.[5] Professor Sir Albert Richardson FRIBA of Ampthill, a past President of the Royal Academy, was an Honorary Member of the club.[6]

In addition to Peacocks, strong supporters of the club have included J. R. Eve & Son, Robinson & Hall and Stafford, Rogers and Merry from Bedford, together with Swaffield & Son of Ampthill and Ekins Dilley & Handley of St Neots. Only Robinson & Hall remains in practice under that name, as the other firms have all been absorbed by various corporate take-overs.

The very strong association between Peacocks and the Surveyors 1921 Club has been demonstrated by the long line of former articled pupils and professional assistants who have been, or still are, members of the club, many of whom have progressed within the profession. Almost the first thing any new pupil or professional assistant needed to do on joining Peacocks was to apply to join the club. Countless hours of secretarial and general office administrative assistance were freely provided by Peacocks.

Walter Peacock was the second President from 1926 to 1927 and Harry Peacock served as president from 1929 to 1930. Robert Peacock was to be President three times, from 1931 to1932, 1945 to 1946, and again in the Golden Jubilee year of 1971 to 1972. In addition, Robert served as Honorary Secretary from 1930 to 1931 and from 1932 to 1945. Dudley Peacock was Honorary Secretary of the Surveyors 1921 Club from 1958 to 1963 and served as President from 1963 to 1964.

5 L. H. E. Perks and J. D. Trustram Eve were both partners in the firm of J. R. Eve & Son. J. D. Trustrum Eve was the son of Sir Herbert and Lady Trustrum Eve. He served in France from 1914 to 1918, and in 1939 to 1948 held army staff appointments with the rank of Major. The firm of J. R. Eve and Son had been founded in Hitchin by his grandfather John Richard Eve nearly a century before. He was the first President of the Royal Institution of Chartered Surveyors with Bedfordshire connections since its foundation, *The Bedfordshire Times and Bedfordshire Standard*, 17 June 1960, p. 7.

6 Sir Albert Edward Richardson (1880–1964) was well-known for his interest in Georgian architecture. His obituary in *The Times* said: 'When all his professional distinction is taken into account – his scholarship and his ability as a writer; his gifts as a teacher; his talent as an architect; and his zeal as a preservationist – it is probable that Richardson will still most generally be remembered as the complete Georgian. He had an enthusiasm for all that belonged to the period that brought him into the glorious company of the English – or Irish – eccentrics.' *The Times Digital Archive*, 4 February 1964, p. 15.

Frank Jeffery was President from 1967 to 1968. The author was Honorary Secretary from 1963 to 1964, president from 1973 to 1974 and resumed the role of Secretary from 1992 to 1994, to be followed by Christopher Horler from 1994 to 2000.

Brian Porter, a former Peacock pupil and by then principal of F. W. Western & Co., was President from 1948 to 1949. Richard Arnold, also a former Peacocks' pupil, by then a partner in W. S. Johnson & Co. of Bletchley was President from 1960 to 1961 and again in 1991 to 1992. Francis Peacock served as Honorary Auditor for some thirty years prior to his retirement.

The great contribution to the club by Jonathan Knights demands special mention as Jonathan served as Honorary Secretary for twenty-five years from 1967 to 1992, and as President from 1993 to 1994.

A landmark in the life of the club was reached when Mrs Susan Fowler, Walter Peacock's great grand-daughter, was elected as the first female President from 1999 to 2000.

The Surveyors 1921 Club has long provided a friendly forum that has helped to engender relationships of great benefit to the members in their professional role with the exchange of knowledge and information, but without prejudicing their professionalism when meeting on opposite sides to resolve a case in their clients' best interest.

Chapter Nineteen

W. & H. Peacock Reborn

On 29 September 2000, the various auction businesses, by then owned by the Bradford and Bingley Building Society, were acquired by Mark Baker. Mark, who had started as a clerk at Peacocks in 1975, was at this time managing Peacocks' Bedford and St Neots Auction Centres, and the new business acquired both these divisions plus the Locke & England and Ambrose auction businesses.

The trading name of the businesses at Bedford and St Neots was immediately re-designated as W. & H. Peacock whilst the businesses trading as Locke & England in Leamington Spa and Ambrose in Loughton, Essex, retained their local trading styles.[1] It was particularly fitting to see the Peacocks' brand back in existence in Bedford nearly one hundred years after the business was formed in September 1901.

A major asset of the new business was the existing team of loyal and competent staff who helped to make the transfer of business back to the Peacocks' brand a seamless transaction.

The first major sale by the new Peacocks was held in Bedford for the Panacea Society. This landmark sale was held in a marquee at the Panacea Society site in Albany Road, and comprised antique furniture, collectables, ceramics, textiles and jewellery. It was held over five days from 17 July 2001. *The Times* described the auction, of over 3,000 lots, as, 'the biggest auction to take place in England this year, and probably for many years to come'.[2] Bedford was the world-wide headquarters of the society, which had been formed in c. 1913 by a group of women who shared an interest in the writings of the prophecies of Joanna Southcott (1750–1814). Led by Mable Baltrope, the society campaigned to have Joanna's sealed box of prophecies opened by a meeting of the Bishops of the Church of England. By the 1930s there were over seventy members living in the Albany Road area of Bedford.[3]

Since the re-launch of Peacocks the auction business has moved to keep track with the changing fashions in furniture and the ways in which customers wish to buy. A new website was launched, and more importance placed on providing the entire service from valuation and collection through to sale.

The business has developed a high reputation over a wide area with a dedicated team of experts. The Auction Centre at Bedford has been enlarged to incorporate an additional ground floor saleroom used for regular monthly sales including

1 *The Bedfordshire Times*, 13 October 2000, p. 35 and *Bedfordshire on Sunday*, 5 November 2000, p. 31.

2 *The Times Digital Archive*, 16 July 2001, p. 4. See also W. & H. Peacock, Locke & England and Ambrose, *A Review* (2001). This pamphlet details other notable sales of 2001 such as the estate of Mrs Charles Kneller of Shepherds Hay, Rugby. The auction included a collection of paintings, ceramics and objects d'art.

3 http://panaceatrust.org/ (accessed January 2014).

antique furniture and collectors' items, jewellery, watches, silver and plate, ceramics and glass, books, maps and ephemera, for which fully illustrated catalogues are published. Many auctions are now held live on the Internet through the sale-room.com and i-bidder, allowing buyers to bid from anywhere in the world, just as though they were sitting in the saleroom. The business is still keen, however, to offer the customer the thrill of attending a traditional auction, and all sales are still held in the age-old way with an auctioneer controlling the lively atmosphere of the saleroom.

Specialist sales are held throughout the year at the Bedford Auction Centre including: toys and childhood memorabilia; twentieth century design; rock, pop, film and TV memorabilia. Sporting gun sales were introduced in 2008 in association with Southams of Oundle, a firm of auctioneers, valuers and estate agents.

While introducing different sales and modern methods of bidding, Peacocks have still continued with the very popular Saturday auctions that include an amazing array of around 3,000 lots including: collectors' items; electrical equipment; furniture; office furniture; building and engineering equipment; tools; timber; cycles; plants; vehicles; bankruptcy stock; and other goods.

The business offers all associated auction services including valuation and collection. As well as in-house sales, auctions are often held on business premises and can include assets such as plant and machinery and farm equipment.

The Internet has opened up the opportunity to market services to a far wider audience and now items are regularly purchased from all over the globe. In 2005, Peacocks introduced a client registration system giving customers a unique reference number with which to buy and sell, and currently the company's client database extends to over 65,000 individuals and businesses.

Marketing of sales is now undertaken by the company including website and catalogue design, using its own in-house design studio.

So in 2014, Peacocks is still going strong undertaking auctions and valuations throughout the region. At the Bedford auction every Saturday, Peacocks continues to be a unique and fascinating venue attracting large numbers of auction-goers from far and wide – a lasting legacy to Walter, Harry and the Peacock family.

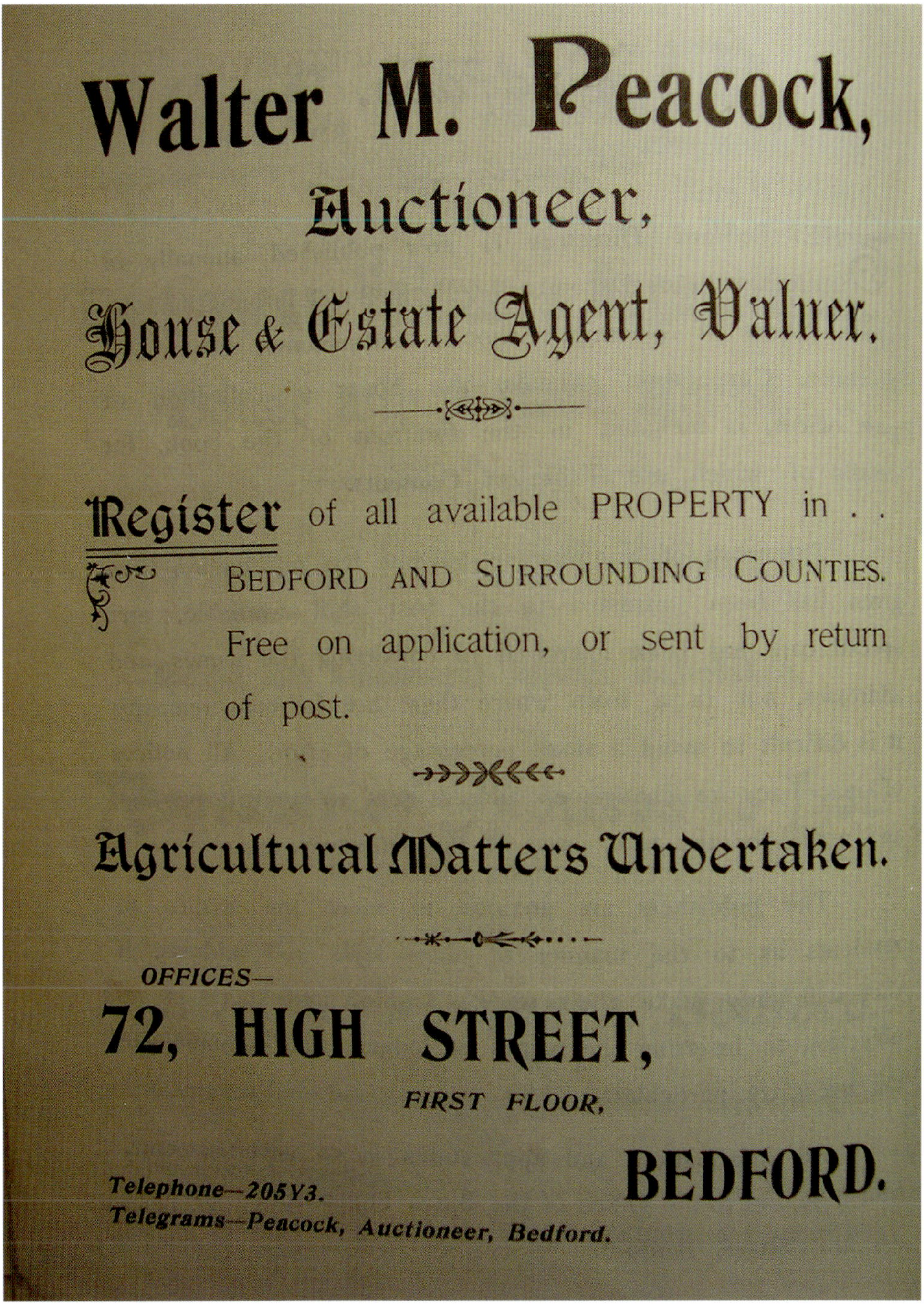

Plate 1. Walter Peacock's first advertisement in the *Bedford Directory 1901*. His brother, Harry Peacock, joined the firm in April 1902 (author's collection).

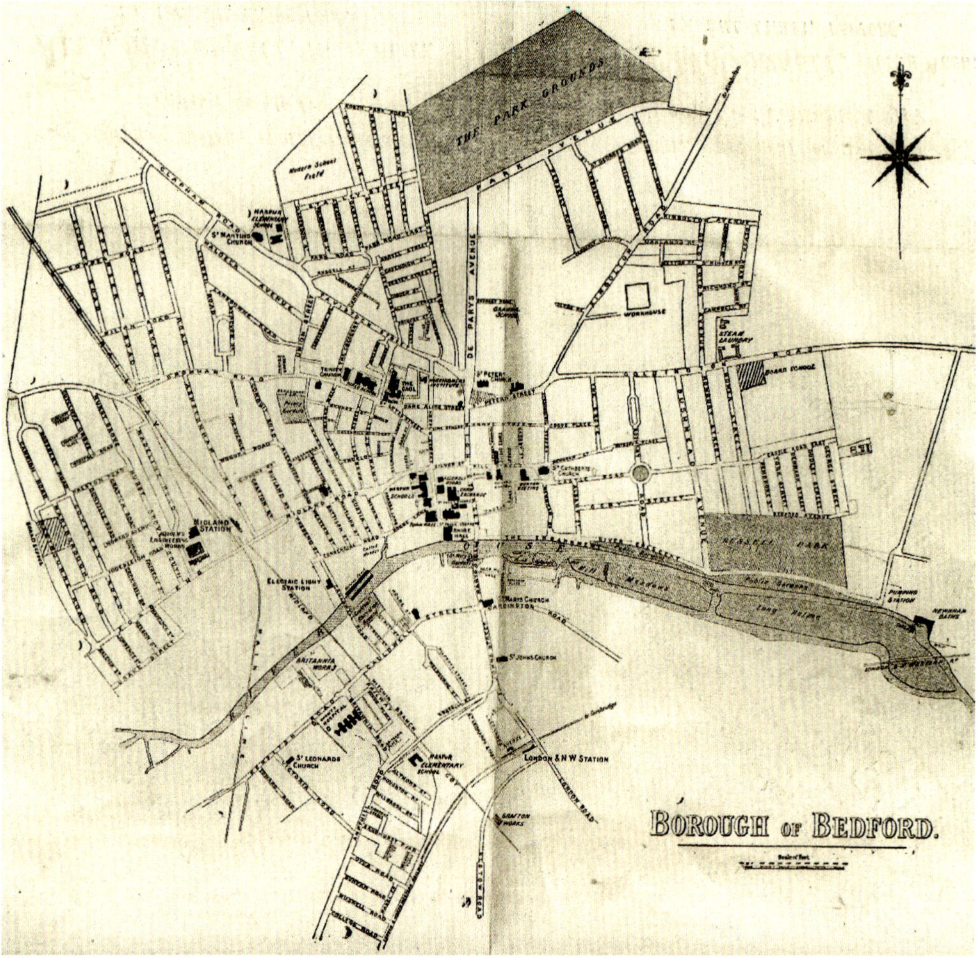

Plate 2. Map of Bedford, *Bedford Directory 1902* (author's collection).

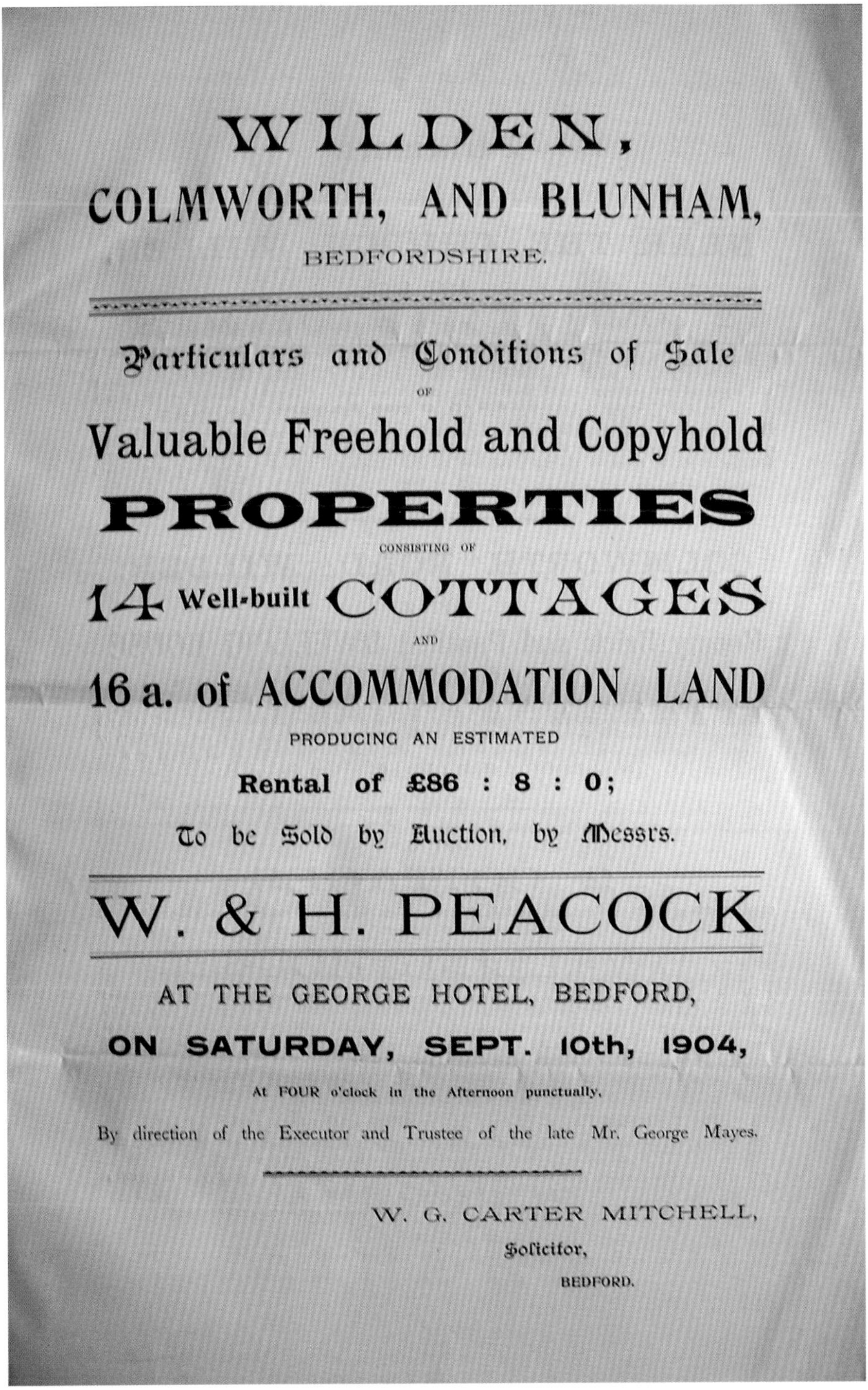

WILDEN,

COLMWORTH, AND BLUNHAM,

BEDFORDSHIRE.

Particulars and Conditions of Sale

OF

Valuable Freehold and Copyhold

PROPERTIES

CONSISTING OF

14 Well-built COTTAGES

AND

16 a. of ACCOMMODATION LAND

PRODUCING AN ESTIMATED

Rental of £86 : 8 : 0;

To be Sold by Auction, by Messrs.

W. & H. PEACOCK

AT THE GEORGE HOTEL, BEDFORD,

ON SATURDAY, SEPT. 10th, 1904,

At FOUR o'clock in the Afternoon punctually,

By direction of the Executor and Trustee of the late Mr. George Mayes.

W. G. CARTER MITCHELL,

Solicitor,

BEDFORD.

Plate 3. Earliest known surviving W. & H. Peacock property auction sale catalogue for properties in Wilden, Colmworth and Blunham, 10 September 1904 (author's collection).

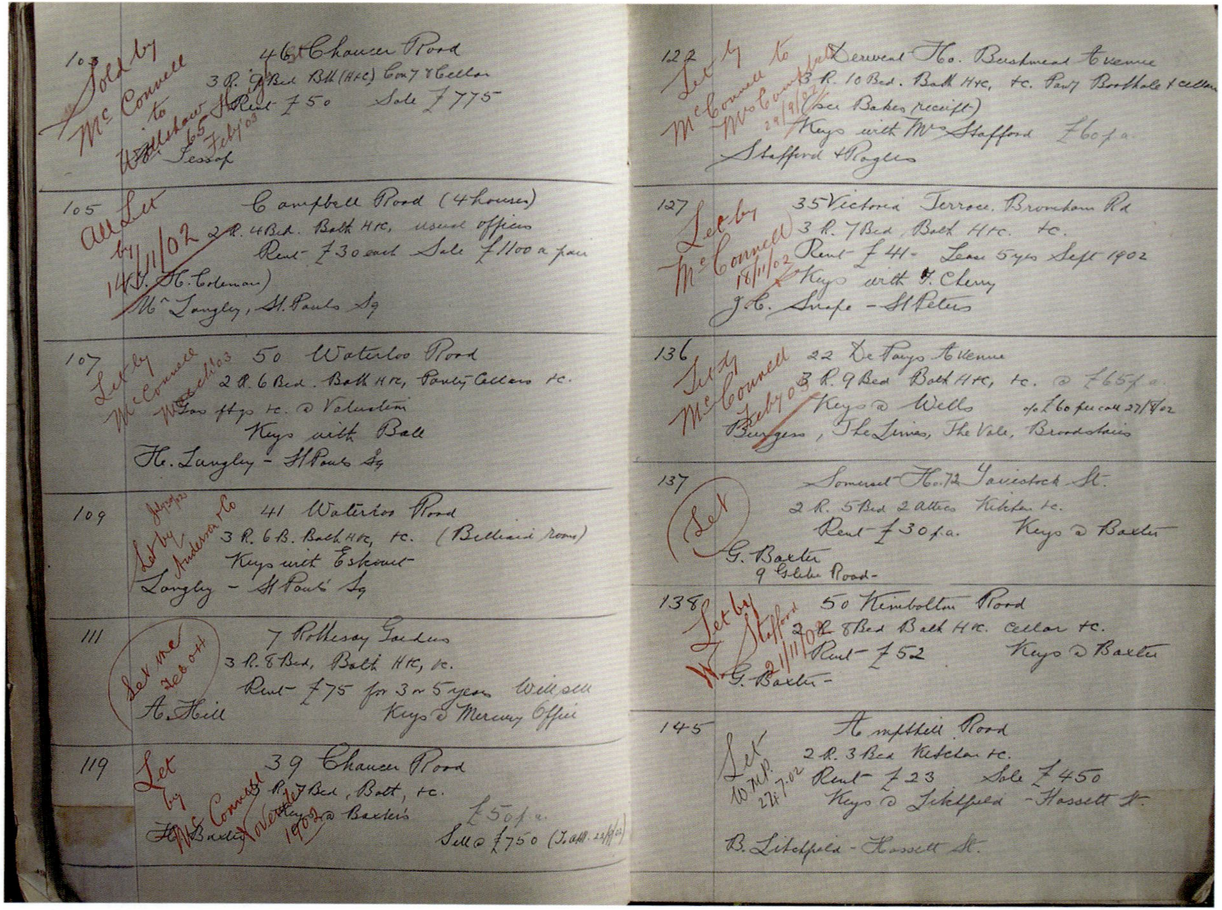

Plate 4. Instruction Book 1: 1902–December 1904. The first entry (number 103) is for 46 Chaucer Road, Bedford, for sale at £775 or for rent at £50 per annum. The property, with three reception rooms, nine bedrooms and a bathroom with hot and cold water was subsequently sold by McConnell in February 1903 (author's collection).

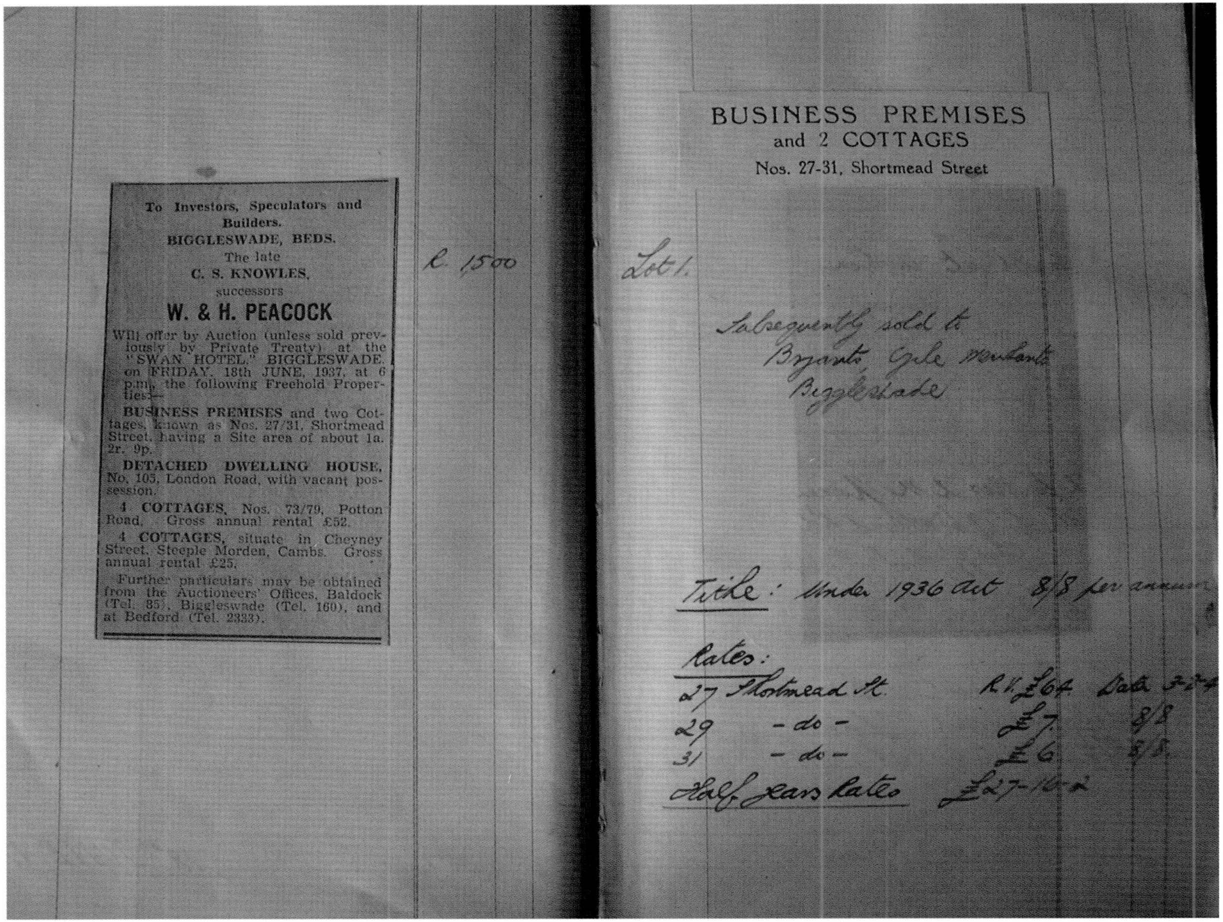

Plate 5. Auctioneers' Handbook, Baldock and Biggleswade, 1937–1963. This is the first entry in the handbook for a sale of properties at the Swan Hotel, Biggleswade, following Robert Peacock's acquisition of Charles S. Knowles' business. It illustrates the additional notes made by the auctioneers for property sales in the handbooks (author's collection).

Plate 6. Peacocks' sale yards, c. March 1926 by G. A. Gearey (courtesy of BLARS, X373/157). In 1948, when the author started work at the sale yards, the building on the right was in somewhat better repair.

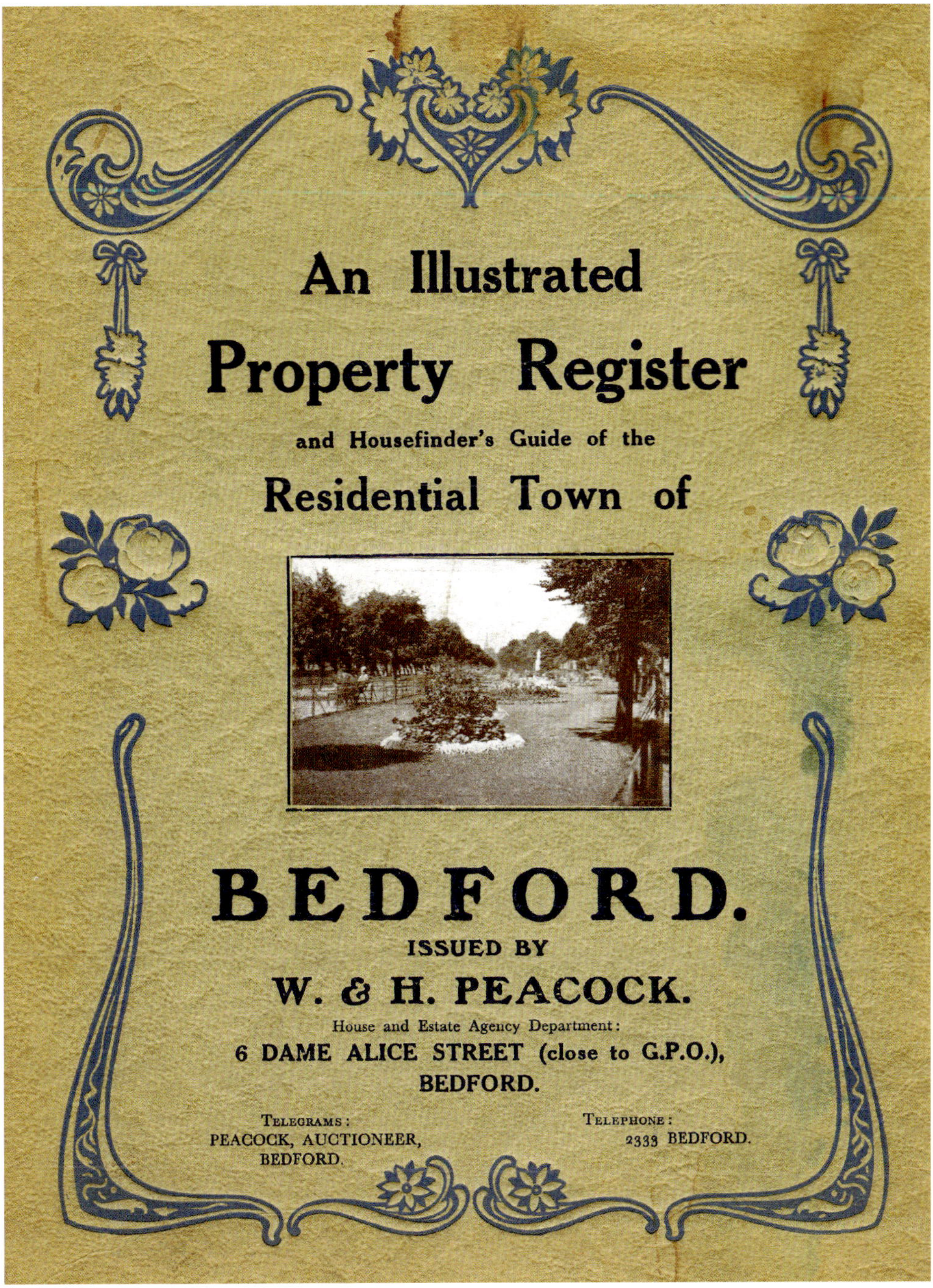

Plate 7. Illustrated Property Register, June 1938. Although produced as ephemera, these property lists were very handsomely presented. Printed by Rush and Warwick (Bedford) Ltd (author's collection).

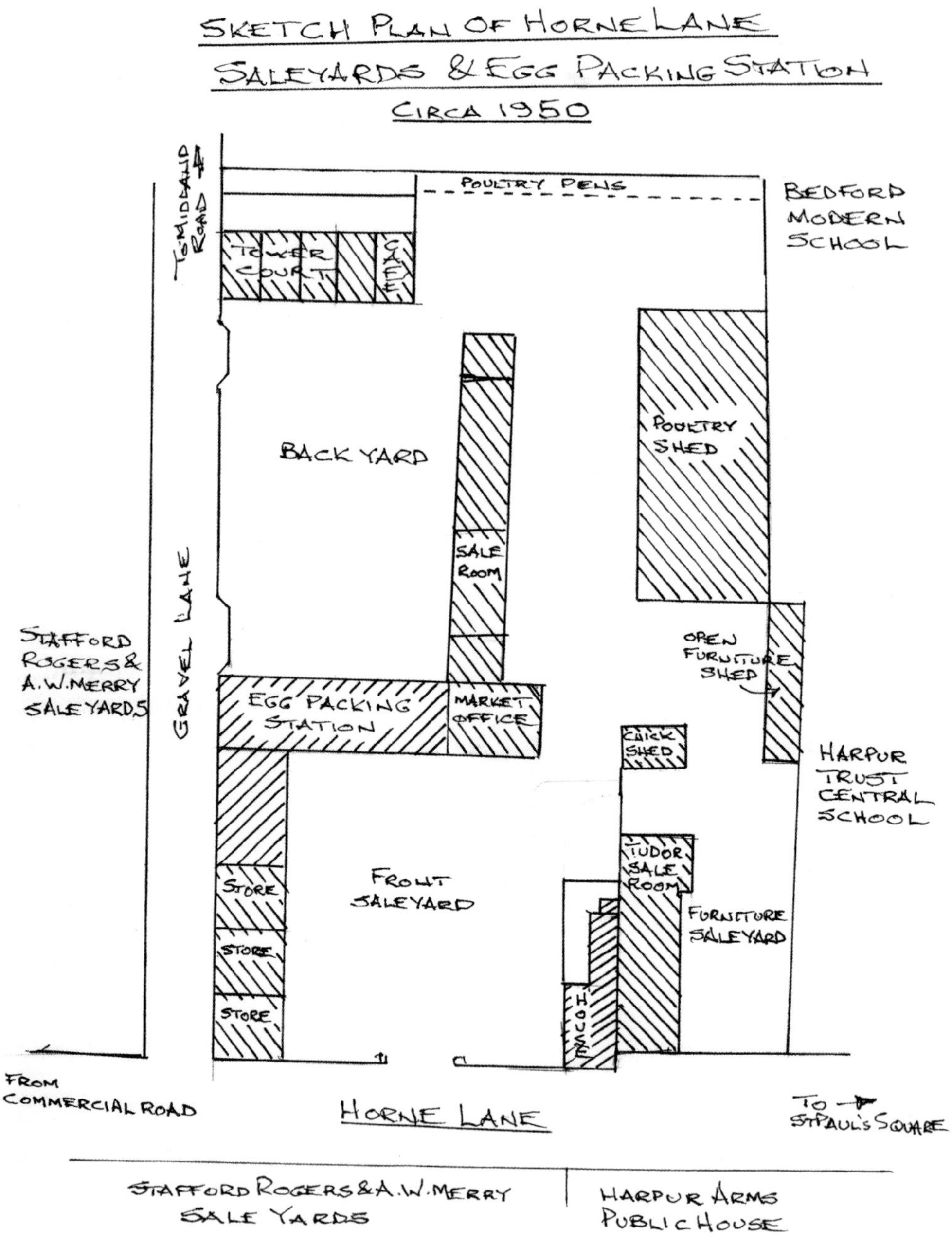

Plate 8. Plan of the Horne Lane sale yards and Egg Packing Station c. 1950, the site extended to some 7,700 square meters (drawn by the author).

Plate 9. Jubilee of Messrs W. & H. Peacock, 1951. Newspaper illustration from *The Bedfordshire Times and Bedfordshire Standard*, 5 October 1951 p. 8. From left to right: Robert Peacock; G. T. F. Robinson; Walter Peacock: Harry Peacock: H. J. Parrott (courtesy of BLARS, Bedfordshire Press Collection, BTNegX547/6).

SIXTH IMPORTANT SALE WITHOUT RESERVE

BY ORDER OF THE ROAD HAULAGE EXECUTIVE

BRITISH ROAD SERVICES DEPOT

MEADOWGATE

BOURNE, LINCOLNSHIRE

Catalogue of

370 COMMERCIAL MOTOR VEHICLES

INCLUDING

4 and 6 WHEELED DROPSIDE TRUCKS
HYDRAULIC TIPPERS, VANS, TRAILERS Etc.
some DIESEL ENGINED VEHICLES

AND

SPARE ENGINE UNITS AND PARTS

TO BE SOLD BY AUCTION BY

W. & H. PEACOCK

THURSDAY, 26th MARCH 1953

at 10.30 a.m.

SOME LOTS WILL BE SOLD AT BOURNE AS LYING AT B.R.S. DEPOT, POINTON, Nr. BOURNE, LINCS.

ON VIEW—24th and 25th March 1953 - - - 9 a.m. to 5 p.m.
SALE DAY - - - - - 9 a.m. to 10.30 a.m.

CATALOGUE: Price 6d. (Admit 1 Person on Sale Day. 2 Persons on View Day).

Auctioneers' Offices
10 LIME STREET, BEDFORD (Phone 66366)
and HIGH STREET, BALDOCK (Phone 85)

Henry Burt & Son Ltd., Mill Street, Bedford

Plate 10. Catalogue of 370 Commercial Motor Vehicles, to be Sold at Auction by W. & H. Peacock, Thursday, 26 March 1953. Peacocks were appointed by the Road Haulage Executive to hold a series of sales from 1947 to 1953 (author's collection).

Plate 11. The Peacock family, 1956. This is one of a series of photographs taken by *The Bedfordshire Times and Bedfordshire Standard* to celebrate four generations of the family. This photograph was unused for the article published in the paper on 14 September 1956, p. 9. Back row from left to right: Robert Peacock; Mrs Margaret Isobel Peacock (wife of Robert); Dudley Peacock; Mrs Harriet Sarah Peacock (second wife of Walter). Front Row from left to right: Mrs Moyra Clair Peacock (wife of Dudley) holding baby Clair Margaret Peacock; Walter Peacock (courtesy of BLARS, Bedfordshire Press Collection, BTNeg5595/10).

Appendix 1
Compilation of the Property Auction Records, 1902–1988

The list of auction records that follows has been compiled from three sources, auctioneers' handbooks, newspaper adverts and sale catalogues.

The lists give, where possible, the date of the auction, the sale venue, a description of the property, the auction price, newspaper references to the auction and references to auction sale catalogues held by the Bedfordshire and Luton Archives and Records Service. Some additional information such as the name of the person responsible for the instruction to Peacocks to undertake the auction, the names of tenants and the rental value of the property is also provided where known.

The amount of information regarding the description of the auctions varies according to the sources available, and the amount of detail provided by those sources. In some cases it has only been possible to construct quite general descriptions. The convention for the order of descriptions is: name of town or village (places outside Bedfordshire have the county in brackets following the place name); name of property; address or description of location; other descriptive details such as type of property; size of property.

As the auctioneers' handbooks listed the price at auction for each lot, which could be made up of more than one item of property, the auction records have generally been recorded to mirror the lots not individual properties.

Auctioneers' handbooks

The auctioneers' handbooks were transcribed by the author over a period of a year between 2000 and 2001. At that time the handbooks were located at the Wilson Peacock offices at 58 St Loyes Street, Bedford, where they had been stored in the strong room since the office opened in 1964. The collection was added to until 1988. By 2014 the handbooks were no longer to be found at the offices, and as no trace of their whereabouts is known, they are now considered to be lost.

The early handbooks included a variety of hard-covered notebooks into which were pasted advertisements or auction catalogues identifying the individual lots to be sold. Additional handwritten notes including the sale price and, where known, the purchaser's name were added by the auctioneer at the time of the sale. In later years the auction handbooks were formulated in Twinlock loose-leaf binders which, in addition to the particulars of the properties, also included details of the special conditions of sale, which in earlier years would have been read out by the vendor's solicitor prior to the sale.

The only remaining auctioneers' handbook known to have survived is the Baldock and Biggleswade office handbook currently in the author's collection. The handbook covers auctions from 18 June 1937 to 4 December 1961. The handbook contains handwritten entries as well as newspaper articles, extracts from auction catalogues and typescript notes pasted onto individual pages of the lined 'Oxford' series notebook. The price obtained at auction for each lot is noted in pencil on the pages with, in some instances, the purchaser's name. Occasional additional notes are also included such as tithe and rateable values.

Newspaper adverts

Peacocks advertised extensively in local newspapers, particularly *The Bedfordshire Times* newspaper series. The transcribed list constructed from the auctioneers' handbooks was later supplemented by reference to these adverts.

A substantial number of additional auction records were found that had not been listed in the original handbooks. This accounts for many of the auction records that do not have a note of the price at auction. Conversely, some auction records were only to be found in the auctioneers' handbooks and not in the newspaper adverts and therefore do not have a newspaper reference.

In the interests of brevity not every advertisement relating to a particular auction has been referenced; only the major references have been included.

It should be noted that Peacocks also advertised in newspapers other than those published in Bedfordshire. References to newspapers in other counties have not been included in the appendix. References from *The Times* of London have, however, been included.

Sale catalogues

Detailed sale catalogues were produced by Peacocks for all their property auction sales. The Bedfordshire and Luton Archives and Records Service has a large collection of these sale catalogues as part of the Peacocks' archive.

Where a sale catalogue still exists for a property the BLARS reference is provided. Those listed as PK un-catalogued have yet to receive BLARS references but will be found in the collection.

The sale catalogues often provide considerable additional information, which could not be recorded as part of the auction record lists in this volume. It is recommended that the sale catalogues are consulted, where possible, for the fullest description of a property. This may include detailed descriptions of rooms, decorations, gardens and grounds. In some cases the sale catalogues include photographs and plans.

Appendix 2
Property Auction Records, 1902–1988

Abbreviations used in the tables

Measurements
a acre
p pole
r rood

Newspaper titles
BC *The Biggleswade Chronicle*
BJ *The Bedfordshire Journal*
BKE *The Bedford and Kempston Express*
BT *The Bedfordshire Times*
BTI *The Bedfordshire Times and Independent*
BTS *The Bedfordshire Times and Bedfordshire Standard*
TDA *The Times Digital Archive*

Other
BLARS Bedfordshire and Luton Archives and Records Service
PK Peacock Archive, Bedfordshire and Luton Archives and Record Office
pa per annum

Property Auction Records 1902–1909

Auction date	Venue	Description	Price	Newspaper references	BLARS references
18 November 1902	North Crawley, The Cock Inn	North Crawley (Bucks), two freehold cottages, gardens, 0.5a	£80	BTI 7 November 1902 p. 1. Total rental £8 pa	-
18 November 1902	Cranfield, The Swan	Cranfield, twelve freehold and copyhold cottages	£702 10s	BTI 7 November 1902 p. 1. Total rental £58 1s pa	-
18 November 1902	Cranfield, The Swan	Cranfield, Church Road, three freehold cottages	£32 10s	BTI 7 November 1902 p. 1. Total rental £7 8s pa	-
23 January 1903	Bedford, The Lion Hotel	Kempston, Woodlands, Battenburg Road, house, offices, building plot	Unsold	BTI 9, 16 January 1903 p. 1	-
23 January 1903	Bedford, The Lion Hotel	Bedford, 30 and 32 Ford End Road, two houses	Unsold	BTI 16 January 1903 p. 1. Occupied by Mrs Waden and Mr H. Cooper. Total rental £31 pa	-
23 January 1903	Bedford, The Lion Hotel	Bedford, 5 Sydney Road, detached residence	Unsold	BTI 9, 16 January 1903 p.1. Occupied by Mrs Rowsell. Rental £30 pa	-
23 January 1903	Bedford, The Lion Hotel	Bedford, Kimbolton Road, corner of Pemberley Crescent, building plot, 10,600 sq ft	Unsold	BTI 9, 16 January 1903 p. 1	-
10 July 1903	Kempston, The King William IV	Kempston, High Street, stabling, buildings, yard	£150	BTI 3 July 1903 p. 1. Bounded on north and west by property of Mrs Kitchener and on east by property of Mr M. Tory	-

Auction date	Venue	Description	Price	Newspaper references	BLARS references
19 September 1903	Bedford, The Swan Hotel	Milton Ernest, Milton Ernest Mill Estate, flour mill, residence, 105a	£3,500	BTI 21, 28 August 1903 p. 1; 18 September p. 1. Tithe free, six pairs of stones	-
15 October 1903	Milton Ernest, The Swan Inn	Milton Ernest, frontage to Town Street, freehold dwelling house, bakehouse, cottage with large garden, stables, other out-buildings	£405	BTI 2 October 1903 p. 1. For many years occupied by Mr G. C. Newell. Rental £35 pa. Premises capable of about twenty sacks of flour a week	-
16 March 1904	Bedford, The Lion Hotel	Bedford, Harrold Villas, 23 Ashburnham Road, freehold semi-detached residence	£495	BTI 19, 26 February 1904 p. 1; 4, 11 March p. 1. On instruction of representatives of Mr Thomas Poole	-
10 September 1904	Bedford, The George Hotel	Wilden, near the church, two freehold cottages	£115	BTI 19, 26 August 1904 p. 1; 2, 9 September p. 1. On instruction of executors of Mr George Mayes	PK 1/4/3. Occupied by Messrs Frank and Johnson. Total rental £9 5s pa. Bounded on west by property belonging to Mr W. Green and on north and east by property of Rev. H. S. Budge
10 September 1904	Bedford, The George Hotel	Wilden, Carlton Cottage, Colmworth Road, freehold dwelling house, arable land, 5a	£320	BTI 19, 26 August 1904 p. 1; 2, 9 September p. 1. On instruction of executors of Mr George Mayes	PK 1/4/3. Occupied by Joseph Franks. Rental £12 10s pa. Bounded on south by property of Mrs Burt, on east by property of T. H. Barnard Esq. and on north by Messrs Jarvis and Co. and the Glebe Land

Auction date	Venue	Description	Price	Newspaper references	BLARS references
10 September 1904	Bedford, The George Hotel	Wilden, Colmworth Road corner, two brick-built cottages, dwelling house, other buildings including a summer house, 3a	£250	BTI 19, 26 August 1904 p. 1; 2, 9 September p. 1. On instruction of executors of Mr George Mayes	PK 1/4/3. Cottages occupied by Messrs Cope and Carter. Summer house occupied by W. King. Total rental £20 18s pa. Bounded by the property of Wilden Charity on the south-east, by that of Mr Slinsby on north and east and that of Mr John Peet on the west
10 September 1904	Bedford, The George Hotel	Colmworth, near The Wheatsheaf, two roomy cottages, garden ground, 1a 2r	£125	BTI 19, 26 August 1904 p. 1; 2, 9 September p. 1. On instruction of executors of Mr George Mayes	PK 1/4/3. Occupied by Messrs Infield and Peet. Total rental £9 pa. Bounded on east by the Medland Estate, on south and west by property of Rev. Allen and on the north-west by property of Mr Ivett
10 September 1904	Bedford, The George Hotel	Colmworth, The City, roomy cottage, garden ground, 3r	£50	BTI 19, 26 August 1904 p. 1; 2, 9 September p. 1. On instruction of executors of Mr George Mayes	PK 1/4/3. Occupied by George Cook. Rental £5 15s pa. Facing City Lane on north, bounded by property of Norris Estate on east and south and property of Messrs Loxley and Wade Gery on west
10 September 1904	Bedford, The George Hotel	Colmworth, The Dean, Channel End, two brick-built cottages with well	£260	BTI 19, 26 August 1904 p. 1; 2, 9 September p. 1. On instruction of executors of Mr George Mayes	PK 1/4/3. Occupied by Messrs Abrahams and Mawby. Total rental £14 pa. Bounded by property of Mr Nixon on west and north and property of Mr Wagstaff on east

Auction date	Venue	Description	Price	Newspaper references	BLARS references
10 September 1904	Bedford, The George Hotel	Blunham, White Horse Lane, three cottages	£265	BTI 19, 26 August 1904 p. 1; 2, 9 September p. 1. On instruction of executors of Mr George Mayes. Occupied by Messrs Little, Battle and Bone. Total rental £15 pa	PK 1/4/3. Copyhold of the Manor of Blunham. Bounded on south by property of Mr F. King, on east by property of Earl Cowper and on the north by Mr Judd and the Chapel Representatives
29 November 1904	North Crawley, The Cock Inn	North Crawley (Bucks), four freehold cottages	£112	BTI 25 November 1904 p. 1. Under the will of Mr George Sutton	-
29 November 1904	North Crawley, The Cock Inn	Little Crawley (Bucks), four cottages, 3r	£85	BTI 25 November 1904 p. 1. Under the will of Mr George Sutton. Total rental £20 pa	-
17 June 1905	Bedford, The Swan Hotel	Wootton, The Elms, country house, freehold property, two well-stocked orchards, stabling for three horses, other buildings, 2a	Unsold	BTI 2, 9, 16 June 1905 p. 4. Occupied by George Waldy Esq. Rental £60 pa	PK 1/4/7. By order of mortgagee
17 June 1905	Bedford, The Swan Hotel	Wootton, The Farm Homestead, adjoining above, large barn, outbuildings, pasture, 24a 1r 9p	Unsold	BTI 2, 9, 16 June 1904 p. 4	PK 1/4/7. By order of mortgagee. Occupied by William Nicholls
24 November 1905	Bedford, The Lion Hotel	Bedford, The Lilacs, 9 Bushmead Avenue	£600	BTI 3, 10, 17 November 1905 p. 4. Together with ten £1 shares in the Bedford Steam Laundry Company	PK 1/4/6. On instruction of executors of Mrs Cranfield

Auction date	Venue	Description	Price	Newspaper references	BLARS references
7 December 1905	Clee Hill, The Golden Cross Inn	Cainham (Shrops), Brunswick House, Clee Hill, business premises	Unsold	-	-
28 August 1906	On site	Kempston, Box End, brick and slate dwelling house	£260 For both lots	BTI 17, 24 August 1906 p. 4. On instruction of the trustee of will of Thomas Summerlin. Occupied by Mrs Summerlin	-
28 August 1906	On site	Kempston, Box End, brick and slate dwelling house	£260 For both lots	BTI 17, 24 August 1906 p. 4. On instruction of the trustee of will of Thomas Summerlin. Occupied by Albert Hart	-
11 October 1907	Shefford, The Black Swan	Shefford, Clifton Fields, eight freehold building sites. Four plots on main road from Shefford to Arlesey. Four plots in Pedley's Lane on the Shefford and Clifton Road	£220	BTI 4 October 1907 p. 4. Each plot has an area of 1r and a frontage of 37ft	PK1/4/8. On instruction of John Redman
19 June 1908	Bedford, The George Hotel	Bedford, 13 and 15 Spencer Road, residences	£535	BTI 29 May 1908 p. 6; 12, 19 June p. 4. Occupied by Mr J. W. Hinchley and Mrs Low. Total rental £37 pa	-
23 July 1909	Bedford, The George Hotel	Houghton Conquest, Bedford Road, baker's premises, bakehouse, buildings	£330	BTI 2, 16 July 1909 p. 6	PK 1/4/9. Occupied by Mr F. Juffs. Includes right to use (in common) a well of drinking water
23 July 1909	Bedford, The George Hotel	Houghton Conquest, paddock of old pasture adjoining the above, suitable for building purposes, 5r	-	BTI 2, 16 July 1909 p. 6	PK1/4/9

Auction date	Venue	Description	Price	Newspaper references	BLARS references
23 July 1909	Bedford, The George Hotel	Bedford, St Gatien, 6 Rutland Road, freehold residence, stabling, motor garage	Unsold	BTI 16 July 1909 p. 6	PK 1/4/9
23 July 1909	Bedford, The George Hotel	Bedford, 11 Western Street, freehold detached residence	£290	BTI 2, 16 July 1909 p. 6. Rental £18 pa	PK 1/4/9. Occupied by Mr J. T. Letts

Property Auction Records 1910–1919

Auction date	Venue	Description	Price	Newspaper references	BLARS references
28 June 1910	Milton Ernest, The Swan Inn	Milton Ernest, three modern stone-built cottages	£400	BTI 10, 17 June 1910 p. 6. On instruction of executors of Mrs Scrivener. Occupied by G. Marsh, Wiles and Musgrove	-
28 June 1910	Milton Ernest, The Swan Inn	Milton Ernest, four freehold cottages	-	BTI 10, 17 June 1910 p. 6. On instruction of executors of Mrs Scrivener. Occupied by Petit, Robinson, Baker and Mrs Salsbury	-
28 June 1910	Milton Ernest, The Swan Inn	Radwell, pasture land, intersected by Midland Railway, 19a 3r 20p	Unsold	BTI 10, 17 June 1910 p. 6. Occupied by Mr W. L. Peck. Rental £35 14s pa	-
28 June 1910	Milton Ernest, The Swan Inn	Radwell, three freehold stone-built cottages, plot of garden land opposite	£165	BTI 24 June 1910 p. 6. On instruction of Mr J. E. Prince Evans. Occupied by Messrs Payne, Harrison and Mrs Hood. Total rental £15 pa	-
15 September 1910	Blunham, The Old Horseshoes	Blunham, Westlea, freehold double-fronted residence	£320	BTI 19 August 1910 p. 4; 9 September p. 4. On instruction of Miss Dixon	-

Auction date	Venue	Description	Price	Newspaper references	BLARS references
16 September 1910	Bedford, The George Hotel	Bedford, 21 Lansdowne Road, double-fronted residence	Unsold	BTI 19 August 1910 p. 4; 9 September p. 4	PK un-catalogued. On instruction of Mrs Fuller
16 September 1910	Bedford, The George Hotel	Bedford, 58 Bushmead Avenue, double-fronted residence	Unsold	BTI 29 July 1910 p. 6; 19 August 1910 p. 4; 9 September p. 4	PK un-catalogued. Estimated rental £80 pa. Part of London College.
26 June 1911	-	Biggleswade, Stratton Street, freehold business premises	Unsold	-	-
1 September 1911	Thurleigh, The Red Lion	Thurleigh, Park End, freehold cottage, 29p	Unsold	BTI 25 August 1911 p. 4. On instruction of mortgagee	-
16 February 1912	Bedford, The Swan Hotel	Bedford, 8 Gibbons Road, freehold residence	£300	BTI 29 January 1912 p. 6; 2, 9 February p. 6. On instruction of executors of Mr Charles Trustram. Occupied by Mr E. A. King. Rental £21 pa	-
16 February 1912	Bedford, The Swan Hotel	Bedford, 9 Gibbons Road, freehold residence	£350	BTI 29 January 1912 p. 6; 2, 9 February p. 6. On instruction of executors of Mr Charles Trustram. Occupied by Mr F. Martin. Rental £25 pa	-
16 February 1912	Bedford, The Swan Hotel	Bedford, 6 and 8 Hurst Grove, freehold residences	£510	BTI 26 January 1912 p. 6; 2, 9 February p. 6. On instruction of executors of Mr Charles Trustram. Occupied by Mr B. Letts and Mr G. J. Tucker. Total rental £30 pa	-
16 May 1912	Kempston, The Bedford Arms	Kempston, Beulah Home, Bunyan Road, range of outbuildings	£180	BTI 3, 10 May 1912 p. 6. On instruction of executors of Amos Barker	-

Auction date	Venue	Description	Price	Newspaper references	BLARS references
28 June 1912	Bedford, The Lion Hotel	Bedford, 29, 31 and 33 Grosvenor Street, three freehold villas	£595	BTI 21 June 1912 p. 6. On instruction of Mrs L. Brittin. Occupied by Mr J. Bennett, Mrs C. Raynor and Mr T. W. Turner. Total rental £42 10s pa	PK un-catalogued
4 October 1912	Great Barford, The Cross	Great Barford, Green End Cottage, house, paddock, building	£300	BTI 20, 27 September 1912 p. 6. Occupied by the Misses Magnus	-
9 November 1912	Bedford, The Swan Hotel	Pavenham, Hill Cottage, freehold residence, valuable arable field, orchard of fruit and walnut trees, 5a 4p	£500	BTI 18 October 1912 p. 6; 1 November p. 6. On instruction of Mr H. W. Litchfield	PK un-catalogued. Bounded on the east by property of Rev. J. E. Linnell and Mr J. Firbank and on the south by property of Mr J. Church
9 November 1912	Bedford, The Swan Hotel	Pavenham, accommodation field, 6a 3r 10p	£405	BTI 18 October 1912 p. 6; 1 November p. 6. On instruction of Mr H. W. Litchfield	PK un-catalogued
21 February 1913	Bedford, The Swan Hotel	Bedford, 31 Albany Road	£505	BTI 7, 14 February 1913 p. 6. On instruction of executors of Mr James Davies. Vacant possession	-
5 June 1913	Ampthill, The White Hart Hotel	Greenfield, agricultural properties, market gardens, rich accommodation pastures, farm house, buildings, 75a	£720 Joint auction with Douglas Stratford & Co.	BTI 16, 23 May 1913 p. 6	-
6 May 1914	Bedford, The Lion Hotel	Bedford, 105 Midland Road, shop	Unsold	BTI 17, 24 April 1914 p. 6; 1 May p. 6. On instruction of executors of Mr John Nicholson	PK/1/4/11. Occupied by T. S. Carpenter
6 May 1914	Bedford, The Lion Hotel	Bedford, 107 Midland Road, shop	Unsold	BTI 17, 24 April 1914 p. 6; 1 May p. 6. On instruction of executors of Mr John Nicholson	PK/1/4/11. Occupied by H. Barfoot

Auction date	Venue	Description	Price	Newspaper references	BLARS references
6 May 1914	Bedford, The Lion Hotel	Bedford, 109 Midland Road, shop, warehouse	Unsold	BTI 17, 24 April 1914 p. 6; 1 May p. 6. On instruction of executors of Mr John Nicholson	PK/1/4/11. Occupied by A. John Ashton
6 May 1914	Bedford, The Lion Hotel	Bedford, 111 Midland Road, Post Office	Unsold	BTI 17, 24 April 1914 p. 6; 1 May p. 6. On instruction of executors of Mr John Nicholson	PK/1/4/11. Occupied by R. Herniman
6 May 1914	Bedford, The Lion Hotel	Bedford, 6 and 8 Waterloo Road	£495 Number 8 withdrawn from auction	BTI 17, 24 April 1914 p. 6; 1 May p. 6. Number 6, rental £28 pa	PK/1/4/11. Occupied by Miss Bell and James Wilkinson
6 May 1914	Bedford, The Lion Hotel	Bedford, 2 Woburn Road, detached residence	Unsold	BTI 17, 24 April 1914 p. 6; 1 May p. 6. On instruction of executors of Mr John Nicholson	PK/1/4/11. Occupied by W. C. Cookson
6 May 1914	Bedford, The Lion Hotel	Bedford, Shellgate, 39 Offa Road, freehold house	Unsold	BTI 24 April 1914 p. 6; 1 May p. 6. Occupied by Mr James King	-
6 May 1914	Bedford, The Lion Hotel	Bedford, Stonehouse, 1 Mabel Road	Unsold	BTI 24 April 1914 p. 6; 1 May p. 6. Occupied by Mr F. Taylor	-
28 July 1914	Leighton Buzzard, The Swan Hotel	Eggington, Claridges Farm House, old-world residence, nuttery, wooded moat, 2a 1r 18p	£350	BTI 17, 24 July 1914 p. 6. On instruction of Bedfordshire County Council	-
31 July 1914	Harrold, The Wheatsheaf Inn	Harrold, frontages to main road from Harrold to Bedford and to the village High Street, fifteen plots of freehold building land	-	BTI 24 July 1914 p. 6. On instruction of Cecil Beck Esq. MP	PK un-catalogued
31 July 1914	Harrold, The Wheatsheaf Inn	Harrold, The Holt, red-brick and tile dwelling house	-	BTI 24 July 1914 p. 6. On instruction of Cecil Beck Esq. MP. Occupied by Captain Johnson. Rental £16 pa	PK un-catalogued. Bounded on the east and south by other property of the vendor, on the west by property of Mrs French Somerville and on north-west by property of Miss Betts

Auction date	Venue	Description	Price	Newspaper references	BLARS references
2 December 1914	Cranfield, The Swan	Cranfield, freehold cottage	£377	BTI 20 November 1914 p. 4. Rental £5 4s pa	-
10 November 1915	Wilstead, The Black Hat	Wilstead, adjoining the Church, farm house, buildings, accommodation pasture, 6a	Unsold	BTI 29 October 1915 p. 6; 5 November p. 4. On instruction of Miss Woodward	-
14 June 1916	Wellingborough, The Hind Hotel	Grendon (Northants), three freehold enclosures of pasture land, 55a	£3,364 Joint auction with J. Pendred & Son	-	PK un-catalogued. On instruction of executors of H. H. Green Esq.
22 July 1916	Bedford, The Swan Hotel	Felmersham and Bedford: Felmersham, Grays Field, Brook Farm Road, smallholding; (near) Felmersham, Knight's Lot, arable field, 19a 1r 15p; Felmersham, grass paddock, two modern cottages; Felmersham, Four Acres, fronting road to Pavenham, arable field, 3a 3r 30p; Bedford, Hope House, 48 Clarendon Street	£1,764	BTI 23, 30 June 1916 p. 4; 7, 14, 21 July p. 4. Hope House rental £36 pa	PK 1/4/15. On instruction of executors of H. M. Green, F. A. Green and others. Grays Field occupied by Mr Bowyer. Grass paddock and two modern cottages occupied by Alfred Roberts. Hope House occupied by Mrs Wylie
2 September 1916	Bedford, The Swan Hotel	Radwell, Radwell Hall Farm, farmhouse, buildings, pasture, arable land, 62a 1r 6p	£2,400	BTI 11, 16, 25 August 1916 p. 4; 1 September p. 4. On instruction of Mr J. C. Hodge. Vacant possession	PK 2/5/2/14

Auction date	Venue	Description	Price	Newspaper references	BLARS references
25 May 1917	Shefford, The White Hart Hotel	Clifton, Pedley's Lane, seven brick and slate dwelling houses	£215	BTI 4, 11, 18 May p. 4. On instruction of executors of Mr Izzard. Total rental £61 12s pa	-
11 August 1917	Bedford, The Swan Hotel	Kempston, Rusheyford House, Box End, freehold agricultural estate, hunting, stabling, two well-built cottages, 92a 1r 20p	£3,260	BTI 20, 27 July 1917 p. 4; 3, 10 August p. 4. On instruction of Messrs A. B. Chibnall and Son	-
7 November 1917	Bedford, The Lion Hotel	Bedford, 36 and 38 St Loyes Street, business premises, cottage	Unsold	BTI 28 September 1917 p. 4; 19, 26 October p. 4. Occupied by Messrs Garlick and Cantwell	-
7 November 1917	Bedford, The Lion Hotel	Bedford, 59 Allhallows Lane	Unsold	BTI 19, 26 October 1917 p. 4	-
7 November 1917	Bedford, The Lion Hotel	Bedford, Harpur House, 44 The Broadway, corner site, two large shops	Unsold	BTI 28 September 1917 p. 4; 19, 26 October p. 4. On instruction of Mr W. W. Beck. Occupied by Mr Davis	-
7 November 1917	Bedford, The Lion Hotel	Bedford, 52 Tavistock Street, shop, dwelling house	Unsold	BTI 28 September 1917 p. 4; 26 October p. 4. Estimated rental £45 pa	-
7 November 1917	Bedford, The Lion Hotel	Bedford, 9 Balsall Street, cottage	£155	BTI 19, 26 October 1917 p. 4. Occupied by Mrs Smith. Rental £11 pa	-
7 November 1917	Bedford, The Lion Hotel	Goldington, 7–11 Alexandra Road, three well-built cottages	Unsold	BTI 28 September 1917 p. 4; 19, 26 October p. 4	-

Auction date	Venue	Description	Price	Newspaper references	BLARS references
17 April 1918	On site	Barton, freehold brick and tiled cottage, 60p	-	BTI 5 April 1918 p. 4. On instruction of Mr Pollard	-
10 May 1918	Bedford, The Swan Hotel	Pavenham, The Elms, freehold modern residence, 6a	£1,310	BTI 19, 26 April 1918 p. 4; 3 May p. 4. Occupied by Mr Edgar Litchfield	-
10 May 1918	Bedford, The Swan Hotel	Haynes, brick and tile cottage, 35p	£300	BTI 19, 26 April 1918 p. 4; 3 May p. 4. On instruction of executors of Mrs Ann Bray. Vacant possession	-
10 May 1918	Bedford, The Swan Hotel	Haynes, Shefford Road, four freehold cottages	£260	BTI 19, 26 April 1918 p. 4; 3 May p. 4. On instruction of executors of Mrs Ann Bray. Occupied by Mrs Roberts, Miss Mabbitt, Mrs Barber and Mr B. Green. Total rental £26 pa	-
10 May 1918	Bedford, The Swan Hotel	Bedford, 182 and 192 Castle Road, well-built residences	Unsold	BTI 19, 26 April 1918 p. 4; 3 May p. 4. On instruction of Mr S. Constant. Number 182 rental £22 pa. 192 rental £28 pa	-
10 May 1918	Bedford, The Swan Hotel	Bedford, Southfields,71 York Street, freehold residence	Unsold	BTI 3 May 1918 p. 4. Occupied by Mrs Blue. Rental £24 pa	-

Auction date	Venue	Description	Price	Newspaper references	BLARS references
15 May 1918	Lidlington, The Green Man Inn	Lidlington, Church Street, two well-built cottages	£150	BTI 19, 26 April 1918 p. 4; 3 May p. 4. Occupied by Messrs Frank Beal and John Wright. Total rental £11 pa	-
18 July 1918	Olney, The Bull Hotel	Stoke Goldington (Bucks), Stoke Park Estate, Church Farm, Stoke Park woodlands, accommodation land, cottages, 392a	£6,050 Joint auction with P. C. Gambell	BTI 14, 21, 28 June 1918 p. 4; 5, 12 July p. 4	-
8 November 1918	Shefford, The White Hart	Shefford, Ivel House, freehold residence, stabling	£640	BTI 18, 25 October 1918 p. 4; 1 November p. 4. On instruction of Mr Thomas T. Sewell. Vacant possession	-
15 November 1918	Bedford, The Lion Hotel	Bedford, Althorpe Terrace, 2–10 Ampthill Road, freehold cottages	£1,295	BTI 18 October 1918 p. 4; 1 November p. 4. On instruction of J. L. Anthony Esq. Occupied by Mrs Pullen and Messrs E. Sibthorpe, E. Harrington, Mr. J Pruden and E. Two. Total rental £77 pa	PK un-catalogued. Number 4 occupied by Mr E. Sibthorpe as draper's shop
15 November 1918	Bedford, The Lion Hotel	Bedford, 37 and 39 Althorpe Street, two brick and slate cottages	Unsold	BTI 25 October 1918 p. 4; 1 November p. 4. On instruction of Miss Pass. Occupied by Messrs F. Inskip and G. Horn. Total rental £22 16s pa	-
15 November 1918	Bedford, The Lion Hotel	Bedford, 6 Bushmead Avenue, freehold residence	Unsold	BTI 18, 25 October 1918 p. 4; 1 November p. 4. On instruction of Mr R. Blott. Occupied by Mrs Willett. Rental £48 pa	PK 1/4/17
15 November 1918	Bedford, The Lion Hotel	Bedford, 5–9 Denmark Street, well-built villas	Unsold	BTI 1 November 1918 p. 4. Total rental £45 pa	-

Auction date	Venue	Description	Price	Newspaper references	BLARS references
15 November 1918	Bedford, The Lion Hotel	Bedford, 74–82 Greyfriars Walk, cottages	£540	BTI 11 October 1918 p. 4; 1 November p. 4. On instruction of trustees of will of Mrs M. J. Edwards. Occupied by H. Clarke, Mrs Edwards, T. Towns, E. Daniels and W. Eaton. Total rental £55 5s pa	PK un-catalogued
15 November 1918	Bedford, The Lion Hotel	Bedford, 27–33 Union Street, cottages	£545	BTI 11 October 1918 p. 4; 1 November p. 4. On instruction of trustees of will of Mrs M. J. Edwards. Occupied by Mrs Johnson, F. P. Orpin, E. H. Jones and J. Hulatt. Total rental £50 7s pa	PK un-catalogued
15 November 1918	Bedford, The Lion Hotel	Bedford, 2–8 Russell Street, cottages	£300	BTI 11 October 1918 p. 4; 1 November p. 4. On instruction of trustees of will of Mrs M. J. Edwards. Occupied by S. Simmons, J. Millard, T. Marshall and E. Leach. Total rental £39 pa	PK un-catalogued
15 November 1918	Bedford, The Lion Hotel	Bedford, 47–51 Russell Street, cottages	£375	BTI 11 October 1918 p. 4; 1 November p. 4. On instruction of trustees of will of Mrs M. J. Edwards. Occupied by G. Woods, W. Mills and C. Tansley. Total rental £36 8s pa	PK un-catalogued
15 November 1918	Bedford, The Lion Hotel	Kempston, 4–8 Woburn Road, cottages	£305	BTI 11 October 1918 p. 4; 1 November p. 4. On instruction of trustees of will of Mrs M. J. Edwards. Occupied by A. Mobbs, G. Mobbs and Mrs Walker. Total rental £31 17s pa	PK un-catalogued

Auction date	Venue	Description	Price	Newspaper references	BLARS references
23 April 1919	Bedford, The Lion Hotel	Bedford, 34–40 Southville Road, four cottages	Unsold	BTI 21 March 1919 p. 4; 18 April p. 4. Total rental £67 12s pa	PK2/5/1/1
23 April 1919	Bedford, The Lion Hotel	Bedford, 42 and 44 Southville Road, two cottages	£500	BTI 21 March 1919 p. 4; 18 April p. 4. Total rental £34 9s pa	PK2/5/1/1
23 April 1919	Bedford, The Lion Hotel	Bedford, 46 Southville Road, cottage	£280	BTI 21 March 1919 p. 4; 18 April p. 4. Rental £18 pa	PK2/5/1/1
23 April 1919	Bedford, The Lion Hotel	Bedford, 50 Southville Road, cottage	£260	BTI 21 March 1919 p. 4; 18 April p. 4. Rental £18 4s pa	PK2/5/1/1
23 April 1919	Bedford, The Lion Hotel	Bedford, 54 and 56 Southville Road, two cottages	Unsold	BTI 21 March 1919 p. 4; 18 April p. 4. Total rental £31 8s	PK2/5/1/1
23 April 1919	Bedford, The Lion Hotel	Bedford, 60 Southville Road, cottage	£275	BTI 21 March 1919 p. 4; 18 April p. 4. Rental £18 4s	PK2/5/1/1
27 May 1919	Haynes, The Greyhound Inn	Haynes, Silver Lane: brick and slate cottage; four red-brick cottages; two brick and rough cast cottages; plot of garden land next to the Chapel; allotment ground of 2a	£505	BTI 16, 23 May 1919 p. 4. Brick and slate cottage occupied by Mr F. Green. Rental £6 14s pa. Four red-brick cottages occupied by Messrs Woodcraft senior, Woodcraft junior, John Street and Mrs Aubrey. Total rental £15 6s pa. Two cottages occupied by Messrs Mayes and Aubrey. Total rental £9 4s pa. Plot of garden land, rental 10s pa. Allotment ground of 2a occupied by tenants of cottages, rental £4 10s pa	-

Auction date	Venue	Description	Price	Newspaper references	BLARS references
25 June 1919	Bedford, The Lion Hotel	Wootton, Potters Cross, cottages	£80	BTI 6, 13, 20 June 1919 p. 4. Total rental £4 4s pa	PK 1/4/19. On instruction of C. E. Frossell. Occupied by George Burraway
25 June 1919	Bedford, The Lion Hotel	Wootton, Potters Cross, three cottages	£110	BTI 6, 13, 20 June 1919 p. 4. Total rental £10 8s pa	PK 1/4/19. On instruction of C. E. Frossell. Occupied by Caleb Redman, H.V. Haddow and Charles Moore
25 June 1919	Bedford, The Lion Hotel	Wootton, Keeley Lane, two cottages	£90	BTI 6, 13, 20 June 1919 p. 4. Total rental £10 8s pa	PK 1/4/19. On instruction of C. E. Frossell. Occupied by George Parrott and John Billing
25 June 1919	Bedford, The Lion Hotel	Bedford, Ashburnham House, 21 Ashburnham Road, freehold double-fronted residence	£650	BTI 6, 13, 20 June 1919 p. 4. On instruction of executors of Mrs Louisa Edwards. Vacant possession	PK un-catalogued
25 June 1919	Bedford, The Lion Hotel	Bedford, rear of 21 Ashburnham Road, frontage to Grafton Road, three building plots	£250	BTI 6, 13, 20 June 1919 p. 4. On instruction of executors of Mrs Louisa Edwards	PK un-catalogued
24 October 1919	Kempston, The King William IV	Kempston, 63 and 65 Bunyan Road, two cottages	£135	BTI 10, 17, 24 October 1919 p. 4. Occupied by Messrs Ellis and Bailey. Total rental £13 pa	-
24 October 1919	Kempston, The King William IV	Wootton, Keeley Lane, two cottages	£90	BTI 10, 17, 24 October 1919 p. 4. Occupied by Dr Clark and Arthur Peters. Total rental £8 8s pa	-
31 October 1919	Harrold, Harrold Institute	Harrold, Churchwardens Cottage	£108	BTI 24, 31 October 1919 p. 4. On instruction of the Charity Commissioners. Occupied by Mr J. Knight	-

Auction date	Venue	Description	Price	Newspaper references	BLARS references
31 October 1919	Harrold, Harrold Institute	Harrold, The Green, three almshouses	£45	BTI 24, 31 October 1919 p. 4. On instruction of the Charity Commissioners	-
7 November 1919	On site	Wilden, Barford Road, two cottages, small area of orchard	£87	BTI 31 October 1919 p. 4. On instruction of executors of Mrs Favell. Occupied by W. Whitmore. One vacant possession. Monthly tenancy of 7s per month	-
8 December 1919	Wootton, The Cock Inn	Wootton, thirteen cottages	£1,550	BTI 28 November 1919 p. 4; 5 December p. 6. On instruction of executors of Mr T. H. Keep. Two detached houses occupied by Messrs Frederick Addington and John Caves. Total rental £74 15s. pa. Four freehold cottages occupied by Messrs Samuel Wadsworth, Charles Wadsworth, William Ashpole and John Gilbert. Total rental £319 10s pa. Five freehold cottages occupied by Messrs Percy Moors, Frederick Ashpole, Thomes Moore, William Loft and Mrs Huckle. Total rental £26 pa. Two cottages occupied by James Stafferton and Mrs Goff. Total rental £8 9s pa	-

Property Auction Records 1920–1929

Auction date	Venue	Description	Price	Newspaper references	BLARS references
1 March 1920	Keysoe, The Chequers Inn	Keysoe, Brook End, three freehold cottages, outbuildings, gardens, 2r 8p	£175	BTI 20, 27 February 1920 p. 6	-
1 March 1920	Thurleigh, The Red Lion	Thurleigh, Cross End, four room cottage, outbuildings, garden	£110	BTI 13, 20 February 1920 p. 6. On instruction of Mrs Eliza Osborn. Vacant possession. Water well	-
14 April 1920	Bedford, The Lion Hotel	Bedford, 1 Lansdowne Road, detached house	Unsold	BTI 19, 26 March 1920 p. 6; 2, 9 April p. 4. Vacant possession	PK un-catalogued. Formerly occupied by the War Department
14 April 1920	Bedford, The Lion Hotel	Bedford, 1 and 3 St Andrews Road, two semi-detached houses	£1,100	BTI 19, 26 March p. 6; 2, 9 April p. 4	PK 1/4/22. Number 1 formerly occupied by the War Department. 3 occupied by Mrs Martin. Rental £50 pa
14 April 1920	Bedford, The Red Lion Hotel	Bedford, 7 Dynevor Road, detached six-bedroom house	£1,350	BTI 2, 9 April 1920 p. 4. Vacant possession	-
26 May 1920	Bedford, The Swan Hotel	Bedford, Aldwick, 77 Castle Road, freehold house	Unsold	BTI 14, 21 May 1920 p. 6	PK 1/4/23. Vacant possession
26 May 1920	Bedford, The Swan Hotel	Elstow, seven freehold cottages	£1,320	BTI 7, 14, 21 May 1920 p. 6. Occupied by Charles Harper, Mr F. G. Baldrey, Mr A. Berwick, Mr George Gooding, Mr Arthur Robinson, Mr F. Curtis, Mr John Wells	-

Auction date	Venue	Description	Price	Newspaper references	BLARS references
26 June 1920	Bedford, The Swan Hotel	Renhold: near Newlands farm, four cottages; fronting main road, two lots of land, 1r 30p and 20p; The Green, thatched cottage; building land 15p; The Green, six cottages; three cottages; four plots of building land; two cottages; two thatched cottages; four lots of building or allotment land; Salph End, two oak timbered cottages; Ravensden Hill, three lots of allotments	£2,055 Only seven lots sold	BTI 28 May 1920 p.6; 4 June p. 4; 11, 18, 25 June p. 6. Several cottages with vacant possession. Thatched cottage on The Green, water supply from tap on The Green	PK1/4/25. Four cottages near Newlands Farm occupied by W. A. Godwin, Mrs E. Constant and W. Clark. Thatched cottage, The Green, occupied by James Pope. Six cottages, The Green, occupied by Mrs Laughton, J. J. Shorley, W. Curtis and Mrs Harlow. Four plots of building land occupied by J. Marsden and A. J. Tompkins. Two cottages occupied by John Gurney and S. Curtis. Two thatched cottages occupied by J. W. Wootton and O. Thompkins. Two oak timbered cottages, Salph End, occupied by Mr Cox
29 June 1920	Guilden Morden, The Six Bells Inn	Steeple Morden (Cambs), frontage to High Road, market garden allotment field	-	-	PK un-catalogued. Occupied by Messrs Kirbyshire, G. and D. Potton, Grayling, Williams, Savage, Miller, Scott and Griffin. Total rental £14 8s pa
29 June 1920	Guilden Morden, The Six Bells Inn	Guilden Morden (Cambs),Tadlow Bridge Field, Little Green, fertile arable field, 5a 1r 14p	-	-	PK un-catalogued. Occupied by Mr James Winders. With two derelict houses and artesian well
29 June 1920	Guilden Morden, The Six Bells Inn	Guilden Morden (Cambs), adjoining Cobbs Lane, 7a 1r 33p	-	-	PK un-catalogued. Occupied by Mr James Winders
29 June 1920	Guilden Morden, The Six Bells Inn	Guilden Morden (Cambs), two brick and flint plaster and slate cottages	-	-	PK un-catalogued. Occupied by David Thompson and Percy Worboys. Total rental £8 8s pa

Auction date	Venue	Description	Price	Newspaper references	BLARS references
14 July 1920	Cranfield, The Swan Inn	Cranfield, Ivy Hall Farm, 58a 0r 38p	£1,500	BTI 28 May 1920 p. 6; 4, 18 June p. 4; 25 June p. 6; 2, 9 July p. 6. On instruction of executors of Mr B. Wells. Occupied by Mr A. J. Wells. Rental £58 pa. Surrounded by moat	-
14 July 1920	Cranfield, The Swan Inn	Cranfield, property formerly known as The Crow Inn, 2a 2r 13p	£330	BTI 18, 25 June 1920 p. 6; 2, 9 July p. 6. On instruction of executors of H. Whitbread	-
14 July 1920	Cranfield, The Swan Inn	Cranfield, three lots of land: 4a 1r 32p; 1r 17p; 22p	£335	BTI 18, 25 June 1920 p. 6; 2, 9 July p. 6. On instruction of executors of H. Whitbread	-
31 July 1920	Bedford, The Swan Hotel	Bedford, Goldington Road, four cottages, corner shop, bakehouse	£645	BTI 16, 23, 30 July p. 6. On instruction of Mr W. Goodwin	-
31 July 1920	Bedford, The Swan Hotel	Bedford, Oakfield, Goldington Road, freehold cottage	-	BTI 16, 23, 30 July p. 6. On instruction of Mr W. Goodwin	-
31 July 1920	Bedford, The Swan Hotel	Bedford, Winton Villa, Goldington Road, freehold villa	-	BTI 16, 23, 30 July p. 6. On instruction of Mr W. Goodwin	-
31 July 1920	Bedford, The Swan Hotel	Bedford, Caradoc, Goldington Road, freehold house	-	BTI 16, 23, 30 July 1920 p. 6. On instruction of Mr W. Goodwin	-
31 July 1920	Bedford, The Swan Hotel	Bedford, Marple House, Goldington Road, freehold house	-	BTI 16, 23, 30 July 1920 p. 6. On instruction of Mr W. Goodwin	-

Auction date	Venue	Description	Price	Newspaper references	BLARS references
31 July 1920	Bedford, The Swan Hotel	Bedford, Goldington Road, freehold corner shop, bakehouse, outbuildings	-	BTI 16, 23, 30 July 1920 p. 6. On instruction of Mr W. Goodwin	-
21 December 1920	-	Carlton, Woodfield, sporting residence, 2a	-	BTI 17 December 1920 p. 6. On instruction of Captain H. Randall. Vacant possession	-
9 February 1921	Bedford, The Red Lion Hotel	Bedford, 76 Howbury Street	£275	BTI 14, 21, 28 January 1921 p. 6; 4 February p. 6	PK 1/4/26. Occupied by Charles Phypers. Rental £15 12s pa
9 February 1921	Bedford, The Red Lion Hotel	Bedford, 78 Howbury Street	£675 for 78, 84 and 86 Howbury Street	BTI 14, 21, 28 January 1921 p. 6; 4 February p. 6	PK 1/4/26. Occupied by C. C. Harlow. Rental £16 6s pa
9 February 1921	Bedford, The Red Lion Hotel	Bedford, 80 Howbury Street	-	BTI 14, 21, 28 January 1921 p. 6; 4 February p. 6	PK 1/4/26. Occupied by Mrs Rachel Rogers. Rental £16 6s pa
9 February 1921	Bedford, The Red Lion Hotel	Bedford, 82 Howbury Street	-	BTI 14, 21, 28 January 1921 p. 6; 4 February p. 6	PK 1/4/26. Occupied by Charles Barratt. Rental £16 6s pa
9 February 1921	Bedford, The Red Lion Hotel	Bedford, 84 Howbury Street	£675 for 78, 84 and 86 Howbury Street	BTI 14, 21, 28 January 1921 p. 6; 4 February p. 6	PK 1/4/26. Occupied by H. C. Hobbs. Rental £16 6s pa
9 February 1921	Bedford, The Red Lion Hotel	Bedford, 86 Howbury Street	£675 for 78, 84 and 86 Howbury Street	BTI 14, 21, 28 January 1921 p. 6; 4 February p. 6	PK 1/4/26. Occupied by George Pope. Rental £16 6s pa

Auction date	Venue	Description	Price	Newspaper references	BLARS references
9 February 1921	Bedford, The Red Lion Hotel	Bedford, 88 Howbury Street	-	BTI 14, 21, 28 January 1921 p. 6; 4 February p. 6	PK 1/4/26. Occupied by Albert Baston. Rental £16 6s pa
9 February 1921	Bedford, The Red Lion Hotel	Bedford, 90 Howbury Street	-	BTI 14, 21, 28 January 1921 p. 6; 4 February p. 6	PK 1/4/26. Occupied by J. Hermon senior. Rental £16 6s pa
9 February 1921	Bedford, The Red Lion Hotel	Bedford, 24 and 26 Bunyan Road, cottages	-	BTI 14 January 1921 p. 6.	PK 1/4/26. Occupied by Miss Larman and Mrs Kingston. Total rental £32 2s pa
9 February 1921	Bedford, The Red Lion Hotel	Bedford, 5 and 7 Argyll Street	-	BTI 14 January 1921 p. 6	PK 1/4/26. Occupied by Messrs A. H. Hall and R. T. Footer. Rental on each property £17 17s pa
9 February 1921	Bedford, The Red Lion Hotel	Bedford, Holt Row, Cauldwell Street, six cottages	-	BTI 4 February 1921 p. 6. Cottages 1 and 2 occupied by representatives of Mrs Gazeley and Mrs Davill. 3 and 4 occupied by Mrs E. Litchfield and Mrs Piggott. 5 and 6 occupied by Mr B. Litchfield and Mr C. Litchfield. Total rental £61 19s 4d pa	-
4 May 1921	Bedford, The Red Lion Hotel	Bedford, 52 St Michael's Road, house	£700	BTI 8, 15, 22, 29 April 1921 p. 6. Occupied by Arthur Curtois Esq. Rental £46 pa	-
4 May 1921	Bedford, The Red Lion Hotel	Renhold, near Newlands Farm, thatched cottage, 7p	£70	BTI 22, 29 April 1921 p. 6	PK 1/4/28. Occupied by W. Clark. Water laid on
4 May 1921	Bedford, The Red Lion Hotel	Renhold, near Newlands Farm, thatched cottage, 19p	£65	BTI 22, 29 April 1921 p. 6	PK 1/4/28. Vacant possession. Water laid on
4 May 1921	Bedford, The Red Lion Hotel	Renhold, near Newlands Farm, kitchen garden, 20p	£20	BTI 22, 29 April 1921 p. 6	PK 1/4/28

Auction date	Venue	Description	Price	Newspaper references	BLARS references
4 May 1921	Bedford, The Red Lion Hotel	Renhold, The Green, thatched cottage, 15p	£100	BTI 22, 29 April 1921 p. 6	PK 1/4/28. Occupied by James Pope
4 May 1921	Bedford, The Red Lion Hotel	Renhold, The Green, pasture paddock, 1a 3r 29p	£100	BTI 22, 29 April 1921 p. 6	PK 1/4/28. Vacant possession
4 May 1921	Bedford, The Red Lion Hotel	Renhold, The Green, pasture paddock, 1a 3r 26p	£110	BTI 22, 29 April 1921 p. 6	PK 1/4/28. Vacant possession
4 May 1921	Bedford, The Red Lion Hotel	Renhold, south side of Ravensden Hill, arable field, 14a 1r 4p	£142	BTI 22, 29 April 1921 p. 6	PK 1/4/28. Vacant possession
4 May 1921	Bedford, The Red Lion Hotel	Bedford, 7 and 7a Roise Street, house, bakehouse	Unsold	BTI 8, 15, 22, 29 April 1921 p. 6. Occupied by Mr A. G. Kent and Ernest Sharpe. Total rental £32 pa	-
4 May 1921	Bedford, The Red Lion Hotel	Bedford, 8 Maitland Street, house	£230	BTI 8, 15, 22, 29 April 1921 p. 6. Occupied by Mrs Banks. Rental £16 4s pa	-
4 May 1921	Bedford, The Red Lion Hotel	Bedford, 5 Battison Street	£200	BTI 15, 22, 29 April 1921 p. 6. Occupied by Mrs Berrill. Rental £12 pa	-
18 May 1921	Thurleigh, The Red Lion Inn	Thurleigh, two freehold cottages	Unsold	BTI 6, 13 May 1921 p. 6. Occupied by Mrs Barnes and Mrs Lyon. Total rental £6 10s pa	-
18 May 1921	Thurleigh, The Red Lion Inn	Ravensden, plot	£35	-	-
20 June 1921	Harrold, Timber Yard	Harrold, Lavendon Road, twenty-two building plots	£551 Joint auction with J. R. Eve and Son	-	PK un-catalogued

Auction date	Venue	Description	Price	Newspaper references	BLARS references
20 June 1921	Harrold, Timber Yard	Harrold, Brook Lane, brick and slate cottage	£124	-	PK un-catalogued. Occupied by H. Pettit. Rental £7 16s pa
20 June 1921	Harrold, Timber Yard	Harrold, Orchard Lane, house, outbuildings, 33p	£360	BTI 27 May 1921 p. 6; 3, 10, 17 June p. 6. By order of Mr A. Bradshaw	-
16 July 1921	Bedford, The Swan Hotel	Wootton, Gadfly Farm, house, 65.587a	£1,200	BTI 10, 17 June 1921 p. 6; 1, 8, 15 July p. 6. On instruction of S. Palgrave Page. Occupied by Mr Joseph Moulden	-
16 July 1921	Bedford, The Swan Hotel	Wootton, Whitworths Farm, house, 825.98a	£900	BTI 10, 17 June 1921 p. 6; 1, 8, 15 July p. 6. On instruction of S. Palgrave Page. Occupied by Mr Joseph Moulden	-
16 July 1921	Bedford, The Swan Hotel	Wootton, Wood End, garden plot, old brickyard	£80	-	-
16 July 1921	Bedford, The Swan Hotel	Bedford, 7–11 Alexandra Road, cottages	-	BTI 24 June 1921 p. 6; 1, 8, 15 July p. 6. Occupied by Messrs Odell, Reynolds and Bithrey. Rentals £15 8s 9d, £16 18s, £14 16s 10d pa respectively	-
27 July 1921	Bedford, The Red Lion Hotel	Bedford 13–23 Dunville Road, six houses	Unsold	BTI 8, 15, 22 July 1921 p. 6. Rental on each property £16 5s pa	-
27 July 1921	Bedford, The Red Lion Hotel	Bedford, 42–46 Dunville Road	£520	BTI 8, 15, 22 July 1921 p. 6. Total rental £50 8s pa	-
31 August 1921	Wootton, The Cock Inn	Wootton, Chapel End, four cottages	£180	BTI 12, 19, 26 August 1921 p. 4. By order of Registrar of Bedford County Court. Occupied by Messrs Folkes, Lovell, Trimmings and Burraway. Total rental £19 15s 4d pa	-

Auction date	Venue	Description	Price	Newspaper references	BLARS references
31 August 1921	Wootton, The Cock Inn	Wootton, Keeley Lane, two cottages	£100	BTI 12, 19, 26 August 1921 p. 4. By order of Registrar of Bedford County Court. Occupied by Messrs Cooper and Ashpole. Total rental £11 12s pa	-
2 September 1921	Haynes, The Greyhound Inn	Haynes, Silver Lane, two cottages	£70	BTI 12, 19, 26 August 1921 p. 4. By order of Registrar of Bedford County Court. Occupied by Messrs Mayes and Aubrey. Total rental £8 4s pa	-
16 September 1921	Bedford, The Red Lion Hotel	Bedford, 49 and 51 Argyll Street, two freehold cottages	£255	BTI 12, 19, 26 August 1921 p. 4; 9, 16 September p. 4. By order of Registrar of Bedford County Court. Occupied by S. W. Facey and John Whitlock. Total rental £34 4s pa	-
5 October 1921	Bedford, The Swan Hotel	Bedford, The Moat House, Woburn Road, large moat, pleasure gardens, 1a 37p	-	BTI 2, 9, September 1921 p. 4; 16, 23, 30 September p. 6. By order of trustees of the late Wynn Williams. Vacant possession. Originally forming part of the Priory of the Greyfriars	-
25 October 1921	Ravensden, The Red Lion Inn	Ravensden, Kimbolton Road, four freehold cottages	£80	BTI 14, 21 October 1921 p. 6. On instruction of Mrs Bancroft. Occupied by Messrs Stanton, Scott, Gurney and Lee. Total rental £20 10s 6d pa	-
25 October 1921	Goldington, The Swan Inn	Goldington, The Green, west side adjoining the vicarage, four thatched cottages	£160	BTI 14, 21 October 1921 p. 6. Occupied on monthly tenancies by Messrs Spavins, Young, Mrs Marshall and Miss Walker. Total rental £29 8s pa	-

Auction date	Venue	Description	Price	Newspaper references	BLARS references
4 November 1921	Bedford, The Red Lion Hotel	Bedford, 32 Rutland Road, freehold residence	£1,025	BTI 14, 21, 28 October 1921 p. 6; 4 November p. 6. Vacant possession	-
24 November 1921	On site	Bedford, 20 Adelaide Square, double-fronted residence	£700	BTI 4, 11, 18 November 1921 p. 6. On instruction of Mrs Potts. Vacant possession	PK 1/4/30
10 January 1922	-	Renhold, Renhold Wood, 5a of underwood	-	BTI 6 January 1922 p. 6	-
10 February 1922	Bedford, The Red Lion Hotel	Bedford, 160 Fosterhill Road, house	£645	BTI 6, 13, 20, 27 January 1922 p. 6; 3, 10 February p. 6	-
10 February 1922	Bedford, The Red Lion Hotel	Bedford, 162 and 164 Fosterhill Road, two houses	Unsold	BTI 6, 13, 20, 27 January 1922 p. 6; 3, 10 February p. 6	-
10 February 1922	Bedford, The Red Lion Hotel	Bedford, 166 Fosterhill Road, house	£600	BTI 6, 13, 20, 27 January 1922 p. 6; 3, 10 February p. 6	-
10 February 1922	Bedford, The Red Lion Hotel	Bedford, 106 Fosterhill Road, freehold residence	£575	BTI 27 January 1922 p. 6; 3 February p. 6. Vacant possession	-
10 February 1922	Bedford, The Red Lion Hotel	Bedford, 8 Alexandra Place, residence	£450	BTI 27 January 1922 p. 6; 3, 10 February p. 6. Vacant possession	-
10 March 1922	Bedford, The Red Lion Hotel	Bedford, 20 Fairfax Road, semi-detached freehold house	£250	BTI 24 February 1922 p. 6; 3, 10 March p. 6. Occupied by Mr Riseley and Mrs Rust. Total rental £28 16s pa	-
10 March 1922	Bedford, The Red Lion Hotel	Bedford, 22 Fairfax Road, freehold semi-detached house	£270	BTI 24 February 1922 p. 6; 3, 10 March p. 6. Occupied by Mr Riseley and Mrs Rust. Total rental £28 16s pa	-

Auction date	Venue	Description	Price	Newspaper references	BLARS references
15 April 1922	Bedford, The Swan Hotel	Bolnhurst, The Manor Farm, farmhouse, three cottages, 313a 2r 34p	-	BTI 24, 31 March 1922 p. 6; 7 April p. 6. Occupied by Mr H. J. Topham. Rental £330 pa	-
5 May 1922	Bedford, The Red Lion Hotel	Bedford, 100 Castle Road, freehold house	£680	BTI 7, 14, 21, 28 April 1922 p. 6; 5 May p. 6. Vacant possession	PK un-catalogued. Also thirty fully paid £5 shares and forty £5 shares in the Bedford Steam Laundry
5 May 1922	Bedford, The Red Lion Hotel	Bedford, 57 Spencer Road, freehold house	£455	BTI 7, 14, 21, 28 April 1922 p. 6; 5 May p. 6. Occupied by Mr F. Golding. Rental £30 pa	-
5 May 1922	Bedford, The Red Lion Hotel	Bedford, 59 Spencer Road, freehold house	£460	BTI 7, 14, 21, 28 April 1922 p. 6; 5 May p. 6. Occupied by Mr H. W. Bowman. Rental £32 10s pa	-
5 May 1922	Bedford, The Red Lion Hotel	Bedford, 3 Park Road North, house	-	BTI 7, 14 April 1922 p. 6. Vacant possession	-
5 May 1922	Bedford, The Red Lion Hotel	Bedford, George Street, garage, garden	-	BTI 7, 14 April 1922 p. 6	-
1 July 1922	Bedford, The Swan Hotel	Kempston, 130 Bedford Road, detached residence	£940	BTI 23, 30 June 1922 p. 6. On instruction of executors of Mr Edward Skevington	-
1 July 1922	Bedford, The Swan Hotel	Kempston, High Street, freehold site used as garden ground with granary, 1r 28p	£300	BTI 23, 30 June 1922 p. 6. On instruction of trustees of the late Mrs Dudley. Occupied by Messrs Quenby	-
1 July 1922	Bedford, The Swan Hotel	Astwood (Bucks), junction of Cranfield Road and Main Road, shop, bakehouse, cottage	Unsold	BTI 23, 30 June 1922 p. 6. Cottages occupied by Messrs E. Hobbs, A. W. Hobbs, the Club and H. Wilding. Total rental £37 12s pa	-

Auction date	Venue	Description	Price	Newspaper references	BLARS references
4 July 1922	Ampthill, The White Hart	Ampthill, Ampthill Knoll Estate, six sites at corner of Station Road and Ashburnham Roads	£150	BTI 23, 30 June 1922 p. 6. On instruction of Claude Pym Esq.	-
6 September 1922	Blunham, The Three Horseshoes	Great Barford, The Gardens, four stud and thatched cottages	-	BTI 25 August 1922 p. 4; 1 September p. 6. On instruction of trustees of Mrs Dudley. Occupied by Messrs Simms, Croft and Wootton. Total rental £16 pa	-
6 September 1922	Blunham, The Three Horseshoes	Great Barford, The Gardens, three brick and tile cottages	-	BTI 25 August 1922 p. 4; 1 September p. 6. On instruction of trustees of Mrs Dudley. Occupied by Mrs Baldrey and Messrs Robinson, Abbott and Norman. Total rental £14 pa	-
6 September 1922	Blunham, The Three Horseshoes	Blunham, Grange Road, two brick and thatch cottages	-	BTI 25 August 1922 p. 4. On instruction of executors of C. T. Woodward. Occupied by Charles Cullip and Mrs Sawford	-
6 September 1922	Blunham, The Three Horseshoes	Blunham, Grange Road, three brick cottages, 1a 0r 2p	£540	BTI 25 August 1922 p. 4. On instruction of executors of C. T. Woodward. Occupied by Mr Joseph Wheatley. Total rental £8 pa	-
3 November 1922	Bedford, The Red Lion Hotel	Bedford, 1 River Street, business premises, blacksmith's shop	-	BTI 20, 27 October 1922 p. 6	-
25 January 1923	Stagsden, The White Horse Inn	Stagsden, two cottages, 30p	-	BTI 19 January 1923 p. 6. Total rental £15 12s pa	-

Auction date	Venue	Description	Price	Newspaper references	BLARS references
16 June 1923	Bedford, The Swan Hotel	Stevington, Duck End Farm and Turvey, Boons Farm, 211a	-	BTI 18, 25 May 1923 p. 6; 1, 8, 15 June p. 6	PK un-catalogued. Vacant possession at Michaelmas 1923
16 June 1923	Bedford, The Swan Hotel	Stevington and Turvey, near the Chapel, accommodation grass, 5.775a	-	BTI 8, 15 June 1923 p. 6	PK un-catalogued. Occupied by Mr Mackness. Rental £12 pa
16 June 1923	Bedford, The Swan Hotel	Stevington and Turvey, frontage to Silver Street, field of rich old pasture, 9.514a	-	BTI 8, 15 June 1923 p. 6	PK un-catalogued. Vacant possession at Michaelmas 1923
16 June 1923	Bedford, The Swan Hotel	Stevington and Turvey, frontage to Silver Lane, grass field, 3.528a	-	BTI 8, 15 June 1923 p. 6	PK un-catalogued. Occupied by Mr W. Sanders. Rental £11 pa
16 June 1923	Bedford, The Swan Hotel	Bedford, 1 River Street, house, business premises	£800	BTI 1, 8, 15 June 1923 p. 6	-
16 June 1923	Bedford, The Swan Hotel	Bedford, 45 Dudley Street, residence	Unsold	BTI 1, 8, 15 June 1923 p. 6	-
16 June 1923	Bedford, The Swan Hotel	Renhold, five room cottage	£65	BTI 1, 8, 15 June 1923 p. 6. Occupied by Mr James Pope	-
31 August 1923	Sharnbrook, The Coffee Tavern Rooms	Sharnbrook, Kennel Hill and High Street West, ten freehold cottages	Unsold	BTI 17, 24, 31 August 1923 p. 6. On instruction of Mr G. C. Lamb. Total rental £77 10s pa	-
28 September 1923	Bedford, The Red Lion Hotel	Bedford,12–22 Derby Street, eleven freehold cottages	£1,190	BTI 14, 21 September 1923 p. 6. Numbers 12 and 14 occupied by E. Croft and Emma Buck. Total rental £30 11s pa. 16 and 18 occupied by Mrs Hart and Mrs Cox. Total rental £30 11s pa. 20 and 22 occupied by Charles Wootton and Edward Garlick. Total rental £30 11s pa	-

Auction date	Venue	Description	Price	Newspaper references	BLARS references
19 October 1923	Bedford, The Red Lion Hotel	Bedford, 34 Rutland Road, family residence	Unsold	BTI 5, 12 October 1923 p. 8. Vacant possession	-
19 October 1923	Bedford, The Red Lion Hotel	Bedford, 2 Grove Place, villa	£500	BTI 28 September 1923 p. 6; 5, 12 October p. 8	-
19 October 1923	Bedford, The Red Lion Hotel	Kempston, 30 High Street, shop, residence, 1a	Unsold	BTI 5, 12 October 1923 p. 8. On instruction of Messrs H. and W. Quenby. Used as a corn merchants	-
7 March 1924	Bedford, The Red Lion Hotel	Bedford, 93 Tavistock Street, shop, residence, three cottages	£375	BTI 15, 22 February 1923 p. 6; 29 February p. 8. Occupied by Mr Neale, Miss Hunt and Miss Panter. Total rental £38 10s pa	-
7 March 1924	Bedford, The Red Lion Hotel	Bedford, 105 Tavistock Street, shop, residence, slaughter house	£1,125	BTI 15, 22 February 1923 p. 6; 29 February p. 8. With goodwill of butcher's business	-
7 March 1924	Bedford, The Red Lion Hotel	Bedford, 2–12 Alexandra Road and 8–16 New Fenlake	-	BTI 15, 22 February 1923 p. 6; 29 February p. 8. Numbers 2 and 4 occupied by Messrs Groom and Sharpe. Total rental £29 5s pa. 6 and 8 occupied by Messrs Bartlett and Noble. Total rental £28 8s 6d pa. 8–16 New Fenlake occupied by Messrs Deane, Loft, Shreaves, Bowler and Horn respectively	-
7 March 1924	Bedford, The Red Lion Hotel	Bedford, 10–14 Chandos Street, three cottages	Unsold	-	-
7 March 1924	Bedford, The Red Lion Hotel	Bedford, 2 and 4 Alexandra Road, two cottages	£315	-	-
7 March 1924	Bedford, The Red Lion Hotel	Bedford, 4–10 Alexandra Road, four cottages	£725	-	-

Auction date	Venue	Description	Price	Newspaper references	BLARS references
7 March 1924	Bedford, The Red Lion Hotel	Bedford, 8–16 New Fenlake, five cottages	£600	-	-
1 April 1924	Bedford, The Red Lion Hotel	Bedford, 25 Clarendon Street, residence	£605	BTI 14, 21, 28 March 1924 p. 8. Vacant possession	-
1 April 1924	Bedford, The Red Lion Hotel	Kempston, 42 and 44 St John's Street, two cottages	£300	BTI 21, 28 March 1924 p. 8. Occupied by George Cox and Mrs Jones. Total rental £31 4s pa	-
1 April 1924	Bedford, The Red Lion Hotel	Bedford, 62–66 Russell Street, three brick and slate cottages	Unsold	BTI 14, 21, 28 March 1924 p. 8. Occupied by Messrs Fuller, Whitemore and Tucker. Total rental £42 18s pa	-
1 April 1924	Bedford, The Red Lion Hotel	Kempston, 33 Bunyan Road, villa	£575	BTI 14, 21, 28 March 1924 p. 8	-
4 April 1924	Shefford, The White Hart Hotel	Shefford, main road to Ampthill, Shefford laundry, adjoining house and double-fronted house	Unsold	BTI 21, 28 March 1924 p. 8. Laundry premises occupied by Mr Louis Gerald Blanc. Rental £100 pa	PK un-catalogued
11 April 1924	Bedford, The Red Lion Hotel	Bedford, 8 St John's Street, business premises	Unsold	BTI 28 March 1924 p. 8; 4 April p. 8. Occupied by Mr A. D. Whittamore. Rental £26 10s pa	-
11 April 1924	Bedford, The Red Lion Hotel	Bedford, 10 St John's Street, business premises	Unsold	BTI 28 March 1924 p. 8; 4 April p. 8. Occupied by Mr A. E. Limmer. Rental of £29 13s 8d pa	-
11 April 1924	Bedford, The Red Lion Hotel	Bedford, 2 Bower Street, villa residence	£400	BTI 28 March 1924 p. 8; 4 April p. 8. Vacant possession	-
11 April 1924	Bedford, The Red Lion Hotel	Bedford, 19 Victoria Road, villa residence	Unsold	BTI 28 March 1924 p. 8; 4 April p. 8. Vacant possession	-

Auction date	Venue	Description	Price	Newspaper references	BLARS references
11 April 1924	Bedford, The Red Lion Hotel	Bedford, 31 Houghton Road, villa	£255	BTI 28 March 1924 p. 8; 4 April p. 8. Occupied by Mr F. H. Wiggle. Rental £18 4s pa	-
11 April 1924	Bedford, The Red Lion Hotel	Bedford, 12 Ridgmont Street, villa	£250	BTI 28 March 1924 p. 8; 4 April p. 8. Occupied by Mr G. W. Townhill. Rental £17 17s pa	-
11 April 1924	Bedford, The Red Lion Hotel	Bedford, Bedesman's Lane behind Kings Arms, stabling, buildings, land	£460	BTI 28 March 1924 p. 8; 4 April p. 8. Occupied by Mr Frederick Carr. Rental £19 pa	-
11 April 1924	Bedford, The Red Lion Hotel	Kempston, Spring Road, building plot	£50	BTI 28 March 1924 p. 8; 4 April p. 8. Occupied by Mrs Mary Hillyer	-
11 April 1924	Bedford, The Red Lion Hotel	Bedford, next to 41 The Embankment, valuable building plot	Unsold	BTI 28 March 1924 p. 8; 4 April p. 8	-
11 April 1924	Bedford, The Red Lion Hotel	Bedford, Tennyson Road, opposite number 18, valuable building plot, 2,640 sq ft	Unsold	BTI 28 March 1924 p. 8; 4 April p. 8	-
15 April 1924	Daventry, The Wheatsheaf Hotel	Daventry (Northants), eleven cottages	£800	-	-
29 April 1924	On site	Turvey, Holmdale, May Road, detached three bedroom house	£800	BTI 4, 11, 18 April p. 8; 25 April p. 6. On instruction of Dr Gifford Nash. Vacant possession	-
1 May 1924	Olney, The Bull Hotel	Olney (Bucks), High Street and East Street, site for business or factory premises	£315	BTI 25 April 1924 p. 6	-

Auction date	Venue	Description	Price	Newspaper references	BLARS references
1 May 1924	Olney, The Bull Hotel	Olney (Bucks), East Street, grass paddock, 3a 0r 26p	£390	BTI 25 April 1924 p. 6	-
9 May 1924	Bedford, The Red Lion Hotel	Bedford, 16 Kimbolton Road, semi-detached house	£750	BTI 25 April 1924 p. 6; 2 May p. 8. Vacant possession	-
9 May 1924	Bedford, The Red Lion Hotel	Bedford, 25 Ampthill Road, semi-detached six bedroom house	£850	BTI 25 April 1924 p. 6; 2 May p. 8. Vacant possession	-
30 May 1924	Bedford, The Red Lion Hotel	Bedford, 24 The Embankment, semi-detached seven bedroom house	£1,300	BTI 16, 23 May 1924 p. 8	-
30 May 1924	Bedford, The Red Lion Hotel	Bedford, 2–12 Nelson Street, six houses	Numbers 2–10 unsold, 12 sold at £265	BTI 16, 23 May 1924 p. 8. Total rental £144 6s pa	-
30 May 1924	Bedford, The Red Lion Hotel	Bedford,13–17 Offa Road, three houses	£625	BTI 16, 23 May 1924 p. 8. Total rental £54 1s pa	-
30 May 1924	Bedford, The Red Lion Hotel	Kempston, 109, 111 and 115 Spring Road	£475	BTI 16, 23 May 1924 p. 8. Total rental £66 12s pa	-
30 May 1924	Bedford, The Red Lion Hotel	Clapham, The Poplars, on main road, detached cottage	£132	BTI 16, 23 May 1924 p. 8. Rental £20 2s 8d pa	-
18 July 1924	Bedford, The Red Lion Hotel	Biddenham, Muree Cottage, detached old-world cottage	£1,300	BTI 4 July 1924 p. 8; 11 July p. 6. Vacant possession	-
19 September 1924	Bedford, The Red Lion Hotel	Lidlington, brick and asbestos tiled bungalow, 3a 2r 14p	£900	BTI 5, 12 September 1924 p. 6	-
19 September 1924	Bedford, The Red Lion Hotel	Lidlington, paddock, 4a 1r 3p	£260	BTI 5, 12 September 1924 p. 6	-

Auction date	Venue	Description	Price	Newspaper references	BLARS references
19 September 1924	Bedford, The Red Lion Hotel	Lidlington, five building plots	Unsold	BTI 5, 12 September 1924 p. 6	-
19 September 1924	Bedford, The Red Lion Hotel	Bedford, 77 Pilcroft Street, three bedroom cottage	£170	BTI 5, 12 September 1924 p. 6	-
19 September 1924	Bedford, The Red Lion Hotel	Colmworth, Top Roxton, Channels End, freehold pasture, 13a 3r 36p	£180	BTI 5, 12 September 1924 p. 6	-
4 November 1924	On site	Riseley, High Street, two cottages, barn, 2r 14p	£550	BTI 24, 31 October 1924 p. 8. Vacant possession	-
14 November 1924	Bedford, The Red Lion Hotel	Bedford, 9–17 Old Ford End Road, five cottages	£920	BTI 7 November 1924 p. 6. Occupied by Messrs Glidewell, Robinson, Blunt, Westerman and Markham. Total rental £71 10s pa	-
14 November 1924	Bedford, The Red Lion Hotel	Bedford, 2–8 Nelson Street, four houses	£865	BTI 7 November 1924 p. 6. Occupied by Messrs Pilsbury, Stewart, Lovell and Hardwick. Total rental £98 7s 3d pa	-
14 November 1924	Bedford, The Red Lion Hotel	Pavenham, country residence, formerly two freehold cottages	-	BTI 31 October 1924 p. 8. Vacant possession	-
3 February 1925	On site	Bedford, 15 Clarendon Street, three bedroom house	£580	BTI 23, 30 January 1925 p. 8. Vacant possession	-
13 February 1925	Bedford, The Red Lion Hotel	Kempston, 1 Woburn Road, detached house, paddock	£780	BTI 30 January 1925 p. 8; 6 February p. 6. On instruction of executor of J. Garner. Vacant possession	-

Auction date	Venue	Description	Price	Newspaper references	BLARS references
13 February 1925	Bedford, The Red Lion Hotel	Kempston, land adjoining 1 Woburn Road	£70	-	-
13 February 1925	Bedford, The Red Lion Hotel	Kempston, 3–9 Woburn Road, four cottages	£290	BTI 30 January 1925 p. 8; 6 February p. 6. On instruction of executor of J. Garner. Total rental £31 4s pa	-
13 February 1925	Bedford, The Red Lion Hotel	Kempston, 80 and 82 St John's Street, two cottages	£160	BTI 30 January 1925 p. 8; 6 February p. 6. On instruction of executor of J. Garner. Total rental £18 17s pa	-
13 February 1925	Bedford, The Red Lion Hotel	Kempston, St John's Street, garden land, 2a 1r 33p	£225	BTI 30 January 1925 p. 8; 6 February p. 6. On instruction of executor of J. Garner. Rental £14 9s 9d pa	-
13 February 1925	Bedford, The Red Lion Hotel	Kempston, pasture land, 1a 0r 29p	£160	BTI 30 January 1925 p. 8; 6 February p. 6. On instruction of executor of J. Garner. Occupied by Mr Jones. Rental £8 10s pa	-
13 February 1925	Bedford, The Red Lion Hotel	Bedford, 5–9 Ford End Road	£585 Number 9 withdrawn from auction	BTI 30 January 1925 p. 8. Occupied by Messrs Munday, Reid and Owen. Total rental £42 pa	-
13 February 1925	Bedford, The Red Lion Hotel	Bedford, 1–5 Hurst Grove, three houses	£750	BTI 30 January 1925 p. 8; 6 February p. 6. Occupied by Messrs, Taylor, Page and Noble. Total rental £39 pa	-

Auction date	Venue	Description	Price	Newspaper references	BLARS references
13 February 1925	Bedford, The Red Lion Hotel	Bedford, land between Bromham Road and Cutcliffe Grove, building site	£450	BTI 30 January 1925 p. 8; 6 February p. 6	-
10 March 1925	Bedford, The Red Lion Hotel	Cranfield, Brook Farm, farmhouse, approx. 70a	£1,800	BTI 27 February 1925 p. 8. On instruction of administration of estate of Mr George Cox	-
10 March 1925	Bedford, The Red Lion Hotel	Cranfield, Bourne End, school house	£175	-	-
29 May 1925	Bedford, The Red Lion Hotel	Bedford, 89 Hurst Grove, three bedroom house	£410	BTI 8, 15, 22 May 1925 p. 8. Rental £25 pa	-
29 May 1925	Bedford, The Red Lion Hotel	Bedford, 6 Sandhurst Road, three bedroom house	£220	BTI 8, 15, 22 May 1925 p. 8. Rental £16 5s pa	-
29 May 1925	Bedford, The Red Lion Hotel	Cranfield, Commerce House, next to Post Office, showroom, shop, living accommodation	£650	BTI 8, 15, 22 May 1925 p. 8	-
29 May 1925	Bedford, The Red Lion Hotel	Bromham, Top Lodge Cottage, two building plots	£575	BTI 8, 15, 22 May 1925 p. 8	-
13 June 1925	Bedford, The Swan Hotel	Clapham, Mount Pleasant Farm, farm buildings, pasture, gardening land, 65.596a	Unsold	BTI 15, 22 May 1925 p. 8; 5, 12 June p. 6. On instruction of trustees of Mr Thomas Clark. Vacant possession	PK 1/4/36, PK 2/5/2/6
13 June 1925	Bedford, The Swan Hotel	Clapham, building land, 18.355a	-	-	PK 1/4/36. Probable gravel deposits under land

Auction date	Venue	Description	Price	Newspaper references	BLARS references
28 June 1925	Houghton Conquest, The Knife and Cleaver	Houghton Conquest, workshop, two cottages	£285	BTI 5, 12 June 1925 p. 6; 19 June p. 8. On instruction of executors of Mr Thomas Quenby. Workshop occupied by Mr John Cooper and Mr Joseph Gadsden. Rental £4 pa. Cottages with vacant possession	-
18 July 1925	Bedford, The Town Hall	Harrold, The Mansion and Harrold Park Estates, comprising Mansion Farm, Manor Farm, Dungee Farm, Park Farm, ten cottages, Harrold Park woodland, Dungee Wood, stone-built Elizabethan mansion, 1,500a	Unsold	BTI 12 June 1925 p. 6; 19, 26 June p. 8; 3, 10, 18 July p. 8. On instruction of Messrs James Day and O. J. Day	-
18 July 1925	Bedford, The Town Hall	Kempston, The Allotments, Wood End, accommodation land, in four lots, 55a	Unsold	BTI 26 June 1925 p. 8; 3, 10, 17 July p. 8. On instruction of Mr Charles Williamson	-
15 August 1925	Bedford, The Swan Hotel	Haynes, Talbot, Plummers Lane, bungalow	£350 for Talbot and 83 Plummers Lane	BTI 31 July 1925 p. 8; 7 August p. 6. On instruction of Mrs P. F. Nichols. Vacant possession	-
15 August 1925	Bedford, The Swan Hotel	Haynes, 83 Plummers Lane, cottage	£350 for Talbot and 83 Plummers Lane	BTI 31 July 1925 p. 8; 7 August p. 6. On instruction of Mrs P. F. Nichols. Occupied by Mr Alfred Cole. Rental £4 12s pa	-
15 August 1925	Bedford, The Swan Hotel	Haynes, 85 Plummers Lane, cottage	£50	BTI 31 July 1925 p. 8. On instruction of Mrs P. F. Nichols. Occupied by Mr D. Hodge. Rental £3 pa	-

Auction date	Venue	Description	Price	Newspaper references	BLARS references
10 September 1925	-	Bromham, The Nurseries, four large green houses	-	BTI 28 August 1925 p. 6; 4 September p. 6. On instruction of Mr Jesse Witney	-
29 January 1926	Bedford, The Red Lion Hotel	Bedford, 8 St John's Street, shop	£560	BTI 8, 15, 22 January 1926 p. 6	PK 2/5/1/4
29 January 1926	Bedford, The Red Lion Hotel	Clapham, Hillside, bungalow, adjacent land, 2a	Unsold	BTI 8, 15, 22 January 1926 p. 6. Good well of water and pump	PK 2/5/1/4
29 January 1926	Bedford, The Red Lion Hotel	Bromham, near The Swan, land, 4.843a	Unsold	BTI 8, 15, 22 January 1926 p. 6	PK 2/5/1/4
16 July 1926	Bedford, The Red Lion Hotel	Kempston, The Yews, St John's Street, charming well wooded property	£1,000	BTI 25 June 1926 p. 8; 2, 9 July p. 8	-
16 July 1926	Bedford, The Red Lion Hotel	Kempston, St John's Street, building site, 15,730 sq ft	-	BTI 2, 9 July 1926 p. 8	-
16 July 1926	Bedford, The Red Lion Hotel	Kempston, St John's Street, building plot, 9,054 sq ft	-	BTI 2, 9 July 1926 p. 8	-
16 July 1926	Bedford, The Red Lion Hotel	Bedford, 4 Derby Street, cottage	£120	BTI 18 June 1925 p. 6; 25 June p. 8; 2, 9 July p. 8. Occupied by Mrs Elizabeth Mann. Rental £14 19s pa	-
16 July 1926	Bedford, The Red Lion Hotel	Oakley, Southdene, opposite church, bungalow	-	BTI 18 June 1925 p. 6; 25 June p. 8. Vacant possession	-
16 July 1926	Bedford, The Red Lion Hotel	Colmworth, Kimbolton Road, arable land, 15a	-	BTI 18 June 1925 p. 6; 25 June p. 8	-
30 July 1926	-	Sharnbrook, next to Sharnbrook Station, eleven valuable building plots	£240 Five sold	BTI 16 July 1926 p. 8; 27 August p. 6	-

Auction date	Venue	Description	Price	Newspaper references	BLARS references
31 August 1926	Sharnbrook, The Swan with Two Nicks	Sharnbrook, Barleycroft, Sharnbrook to Rushden Road, four freehold cottages	£145	BTI 20, 27 August 1926 p. 6. A good well of water serves the four cottages	-
3 September 1926	Bedford, The Red Lion Hotel	Bedford, 24 The Embankment, riverside property	Unsold	BTI 6, 20, 27 August 1926 p. 6. Vacant possession	-
3 September 1926	Bedford, The Red Lion Hotel	Kempston, 9–13 Thornton Street, three cottages	£655	BTI 6, 27 August 1926 p. 6. Rental £50 14s pa	-
25 September 1926	Bedford, The Swan Hotel	Kempston, Top Farm, Box End: farmhouse and 87.599a; two cottages and accommodation pasture, 9.785a; grazing pasture, 19.189a; two accommodation pastures, 24.045a; accommodation paddock, 4.430a; grazing pasture, 12.530a	£4,300	BTI 3, 10, 17, 24 September 1926 p. 6	PK un-catalogued. On instruction of Mr E. Hitchens. Cottages occupied by Messrs Mason and Ibbott as service tenants
25 October 1926	On site	Ravensden, two freehold cottages, accommodation pasture	£400	BTI 15 October 1926 p. 8; 22, 29 October p. 6. On instruction of executors of Mr Jones. One occupied by Mr Albert Jones. Rental £5 pa. One vacant possession	-
5 November 1926	Bedford, The Red Lion Hotel	Riseley, Ivy House, country residence, brick and tile cottage	£900	BTI 15 October 1926 p. 8; 22, 29 October p. 6. Vacant possession	-
5 November 1926	Bedford, The Red Lion Hotel	Bedford, 17 Winifred Road, semi-detached villa	£550	BTI 15 October 1926 p. 8; 22 October p. 6	-

Auction date	Venue	Description	Price	Newspaper references	BLARS references
8 November 1926	On site	Bedford, 103 Dudley Street, villa	£580	BTI 29 October 1926 p. 8; 5 November p. 8. Vacant possession. Household effects sold following sale of property	-
18 January 1927	Bedford, The Swan Hotel	Bedford, 19 St Michael's Road, residence	£700	BTI 7, 14 January 1927 p. 6. By order of executors of Mrs Layton Lund. Vacant possession. Household furniture sold following sale of property	-
27 January 1927	Harrold, Harrold Institute	Harrold, Brook Lane, three freehold cottages	£110	BTI 7, 14, 21 January 1927 p. 6. On instruction of executrix of Mr J. F. Bird. Total rental £17 pa	PK 1/4/39. Occupied by C. Carter, C. Cockings and Miss Coleman
27 January 1927	Harrold, Harrold Institute	Harrold, Carlton and Chellington, eleven cottages, two valuable pasture enclosures about 3.5a. Pasture land situate at Bridge End in Chellington on road leading to Harrold	£900	BTI 14, 21 January 1927 p. 6. On instruction of executors of W. Rudd. Pasture land occupied by Mr Jarvis. Rental £10 pa	PK 1/4/39. Three cottages at Bridge End, Carlton occupied by H. Simons, J. Risely and H. Odell. Earth closets and drinking well. Total rental £19 14s pa. Two cottages at Bridge End Chellington occupied by G. Burbage and J. Spencer. Earth closets and drinking well. Total rental £12 10s pa. Two adjoining cottages in Bridge End, Chellington occupied by E. Brandon and Mrs Drage. Total rental £27 10s pa. Thatched freehold cottage, adjoining previous, occupied by Mrs Barnett. Earth closet and well. Rental £7 16s pa
16 February 1927	-	Bedford, 118 Tavistock Street, freehold five bedroom property	-	BTI 4 February 1927 p. 6. On instruction of Miss Debenham	-

Auction date	Venue	Description	Price	Newspaper references	BLARS references
13 April 1927	Swineshead, The Three Horseshoes	Swineshead, two detached cottages	Unsold	BTI 1 April 1927 p. 8. On instruction of executors of Samuel Garratt. Rental £10 8s pa and £6 10s pa respectively	-
22 April 1927	Bedford, The Red Lion Hotel	Bedford, 30 Cauldwell Street	Unsold	BTI 8, 15 April 1927 p. 8. Suitable for conversion into shops, flats or private residence	-
22 April 1927	Bedford, The Red Lion Hotel	Kempston, Stuart Street, freehold building land, plots 41, 42 and 43 of the Wyman Estate	£60	BTI 8, 15 April 1927 p. 8	-
22 April 1927	Bedford, The Red Lion Hotel	Renhold, bungalow, pasture, 13a	-	BTI 8, 15 April 1927 p. 8	-
22 April 1927	Bedford, The Red Lion Hotel	Kempston, 11–15 Farrer Street	-	BTI 8 April 1927 p. 8	-
17 May 1927	Northill, The Crown Inn	Ickwell, The Green, four freehold cottages	Unsold	BTI 6, 13 May 1927 p. 8. Occupied by Messrs R. Brunt, C. R. Lowe, J. Clark, one vacant possession. Total rental £16 7s pa	-
27 May 1927	On site	Caxton (Cambs), situate on Bourne Road, pasture field, 10a	Unsold	BTI 27 May 1927 p. 8. Occupied by Mr W. Simons	-
17 June 1927	Bedford, The Red Lion Hotel	Bedford, 60 Bromham Road, shop, premises	£1,850	BTI 20 May 1927 p. 8; 3, 10 June p. 8. Occupied by Mr J. Miller. Rental £70 pa	-
17 June 1927	Bedford, The Red Lion Hotel	Bedford, 49 Conduit Road, residence and School of Art	Unsold	BTI 20 May 1927 p. 8; 3, 10 June p. 8. Occupied by Mr J. Miller. Rental £50 pa	-

Auction date	Venue	Description	Price	Newspaper references	BLARS references
17 June 1927	Bedford, The Red Lion Hotel	Kempston, 11–15 Farrer Street, three cottages	£500	BTI 20 May 1927 p. 8; 3, 10 June p. 8. Occupied by Mrs Burridge, Mr Frederick Mann and Mrs Dunkley. Total rental £55 18s pa	-
17 June 1927	Bedford, The Red Lion Hotel	Bedford, 19 and 20 Beauchamp Road	-	BTI 3, 10 June 1927 p. 8. Total rental £20 2s pa	-
27 July 1927	Bedford, The Red Lion Hotel	Clapham: The Lodge, Clapham Road, residence, grounds, 6.5a; Lodge Cottage, garden; fronting Clapham Road, old pasture, 4.5a; fronting Clapham Road, three choice building plots	£2,500	TDA 23 July 1927 p. 24. BTI 8, 15, 22 July 1927 p. 8. On instruction of executors of late Misses Fitzpatrick. Old pasture occupied by Mr W. W. Grant. Building plots occupied by Mr H. Tysoe.	PK 1/4/42/1, PK 1/4/186
27 July 1927	Bedford, The Red Lion Hotel	Oakley, next to the school, nursery, 2.5a	£400	BTI 15, 22 July 1927 p. 8	-
12 August 1927	Edgeware, The Old George Hotel	Edgeware (London), Oakdene and Vecchia, Garratt Road	£700	-	-
8 September 1927	On site	Hinwick, Fordlands, residence, 5a 1r 6p	-	BTI 19, 26 August 1927 p. 6	-
8 September 1927	On site	Hinwick, Sunshine Cottage	-	BTI 19, 26 August 1927 p. 6	-
10 September 1927	Bedford, The Town Hall	Haynes, West End, farmhouse, two cottages, 242a	£325	BTI 19, 26 August 1927 p. 6. On instruction of executors of T. E. Davies	-
10 September 1927	Bedford, The Town Hall	Kempston, Hillwick House, Wood End, 3.5a, two cottages, bungalow, paddock, 4a	£1,425	BTI 19, 26 August 1927 p. 6. On instruction of Col. Colbeck	PK 1/4/46/1. Hillwick House vacant possession. One cottage let on quarterly tenancy to Bedfordshire Constabulary. Rental £11. Bungalow occupied by R. Beard. Rental £7 4s pa

Auction date	Venue	Description	Price	Newspaper references	BLARS references
10 September 1927	Bedford, The Town Hall	Bromham: facing Vicarage Green on Oakley Road, building or accommodation pasture, 2a 2r 8p; fronting Bromham to Oakley Road, building or accommodation pasture, 9a 2r 35p; fronting the village street, three stone-built cottages; fronting main street, two building plots, 1r 1p and 1r 3p; two orchard plots; garden plot 1r 10p	-	BTI 19, 26 August 1927 p. 6	PK 1/4/46/1, PK 1/4/187. Cottages occupied by V. Hyde, H. Seamarks and the executors of F. Clark. Building plots occupied by H. Seamarks, A. Tysoe and I. Bruty. One orchard plot occupied by W. Tebbutt. One vacant possession. Garden plot occupied by F. Pepper
30 September 1927	On site	Felmersham: Townlot Lane, thatched house, dairy pasture; adjoining pasture, 3r 11p; paddock 1a 2r 23p; corner of Old Church Road and Bakers Lane, arable enclosure, 3a 1r 2p; corner of Collick Lane and Radwell Road to Moor End, paddock, 2a 1r 21p; adjoining enclosure, 3a 3r 33p	£500	BTI 16 September p. 8. On instruction of executors of Mr Henry Turner. Household furniture and effects sold following sale of property	PK 1/4/50. Thatched house vacant possession
11 November 1927	Bedford, The Red Lion Hotel	Bedford, 35 and 37 Offa Road	£455	BTI 21, 28 October 1927 p. 8; 4 November p. 8	PK 1/4/53. By order of the executrix
11 November 1927	Bedford, The Red Lion Hotel	Bedford, Kempston Road, Cauldwell Walk, house, three plots	Unsold	BTI 21, 28 October 1927 p. 8; 4 November p. 8	-
2 February 1928	On site	Bedford, Goldington Road, near Fox and Hounds, smallholding, 1.5a	£200	BTI 27 January 1928 p. 6. On instruction of Mr W. A. Juffs	-

Auction date	Venue	Description	Price	Newspaper references	BLARS references
24 February 1928	Bedford, The Red Lion	Bedford, 8 St Mary's Street, shop premises, rear workshop	£1,750 Sold prior to auction	BTI 10 February 1928 p. 6; 17, 24 February p. 8. On instruction of executors of Alan Prole. Shop occupied by Mr John Hamley. Rental £100 pa. Workshop occupied by Mr Shreeves. Rental £22 10s pa	PK 2/5/1/7
24 February 1928	Bedford, The Red Lion	Bedford, 2a Bunyan Road, building suitable for garage, factory or warehouse	Unsold	BTI 3, 10 February 1928 p. 6; 17 February p. 8	PK 1/4/55, PK 2/5/1/7
24 February 1928	Bedford, The Red Lion	Bedford, 16 and 18 Iddesleigh Road, two cottages	£520	BTI 3, 10 February 1928 p. 6; 17 February p. 8. On instruction of executors of Mrs E. Munday	PK 1/4/55, PK 2/5/1/7. Occupied by P. L. Fenton and George Onan
24 February 1928	Bedford, The Red Lion	Bedford, 39 Chaucer Road, in two self-contained flats	£1,150	BTI 3, 10 February 1928 p. 6; 17 February p. 8. Rental £169 pa	PK 1/4/56, PK 2/5/1/7
24 February 1928	Bedford, The Red Lion	Bedford, Goldington Road, near Fox and Hounds, plot of allotment land, 0.5a	Unsold	BTI 10 February 1928 p. 6; 17 February p. 8	PK 1/4/54, PK 2/5/1/7. On instruction of W. Gill
24 February 1928	Bedford, The Red Lion	Bedford, Polhill's Field, Goldington Road, plot of allotment land, 1r	Unsold	BTI 10 February 1928 p. 6; 17 February p. 8	PK 1/4/54. On instruction of W. Gill
4 May 1928	Bedford, The Red Lion Hotel	Bedford, 26 Grove Place, small villa	£505	BTI 13 April 1928 p. 6; 20, 27 April p. 8. Vacant possession	-
4 May 1928	Bedford, The Red Lion Hotel	Bedford, 36 Chaucer Road, family residence	Unsold	BTI 20, 27 April 1928 p. 8. Vacant possession	-

Auction date	Venue	Description	Price	Newspaper references	BLARS references
4 May 1928	Bedford, The Red Lion Hotel	Bedford, 60 Clapham Road, residence	Unsold	BTI 20, 27 April 1928 p. 8. Vacant possession	PK 1/4/57, PK 1/4/188
26 May 1928	Bedford, The Red Lion Hotel	Colmworth, Channels End, smallholding homestead, pasture in convenient lots, 25.5a	£650	BTI 11, 25 May 1928 p. 8. On instruction of Mr J. F. Soutar	-
20 June 1928	On site	Maulden, Hall End, pasture holding, 12a 3r 4p and four valuable building plots	£765	BTI 8, 15 June 1928 p. 6. On instruction of Mr C. Course	-
20 June 1928	On site	Clophill, freehold pasture with osier bed, 4a 0r 6p	Unsold	BTI 15 June 1928 p. 6. On instruction of Mr F. J. Palmer	-
3 July 1928	Bedford, The Swan Hotel	Bedford, Goldington Road, lower field plot of garden land, 1r	£44	BTI 29 June 1928 p. 8	-
3 July 1928	Bedford, The Swan Hotel	Bedford, Kimbolton Road, plot of land, 1a 1r 16p	£225	BTI 22, 29 June 1928 p. 8. On instruction of Mr H. A. Wren	-
14 July 1928	Bedford, The Swan Hotel	Kempston, Kempston House, freehold country residence, gardeners' cottages, gardens, 4a	Unsold Joint auction with G. C. Walker & Co.	TDA 11 July 1928 p. 29	PK un-catalogued. For many years the residence of Mrs Newland. Cottages occupied by Mr T. Wooding and Mr James Harris
14 July 1928	Bedford, The Swan Hotel	Kempston, Wood End Farm and Green End Farm, dairy farm, farm house, homestead, three service cottages, 156a 3r 31p	Unsold Joint auction with G. C. Walker & Co.	TDA 11 July 1928 p. 29. Occupied by Mr James Frossell. Rental £265 pa	PK un-catalogued. One cottage occupied by Mr H. Burraway

Auction date	Venue	Description	Price	Newspaper references	BLARS references
3 August 1928	Bedford, The Red Lion Hotel	Bedford, 31 and 33 Coventry Road, two villas	£550	BTI 20 July 1928 p. 6. Occupied by Mrs E. H. Cartwright and Mr Walter Horace Buck. Total rental £42 18s pa	PK 1/4/59
18 October 1928	On site	Kempston, near Bromham, mid-way between Box End and Bromham Swan, bungalow, 6a 3r 12p	Unsold	BTI 5 October 1928 p. 8; 12 October p. 8. On instruction of Mr Waghorn. Vacant possession. Good well of water	-
30 November 1928	Bedford, The Red Lion Hotel	Bedford, 56 Ampthill Road, desirable residence	£800	BTI 9, 16, 23 November 1928 p. 8. Vacant possession	PK 1/4/61. With electric light, power and gas
5 April 1929	Bedford, The Red Lion Hotel	Bedford, 49 Howbury Street, shop, residence	£750	BTI 8, 29 March 1929 p. 8. Vacant possession	-
5 April 1929	Bedford, The Red Lion Hotel	Bedford, 4 Muswell Road, dwelling house	£330	BTI 8, 29 March 1929 p. 8. Occupied by Mrs James. Rental £21 pa	-
5 April 1929	Bedford, The Red Lion Hotel	Wootton, on main road, shop, residence, two cottages	£495	BTI 8, 29 March 1929 p. 8. On instruction of Mrs Sinfield who is retiring from business as draper and outfitter. Good water supply from well next to the house. Two cottages total rental £15 pa	-
5 April 1929	Bedford, The Red Lion Hotel	Goldington, Barkers Lane near The Green, three freehold cottages	£1,000	BTI 29 March 1929 p. 6. On instruction of executors of Miss Fanny Flood. Occupied by William Beckwith, Mr J. Matthews and Mr Sydney Letts	-
23 April 1929	On site	Maulden, on main Clophill to Ampthill Road, accommodation grasskeeping, 13a	Unsold	BTI 19 April 1929 p.8. On instruction of Mr E. Course	-

Auction date	Venue	Description	Price	Newspaper references	BLARS references
29 April 1929	On site	Stevington, West End, two cottages, gardens, 1r 36p	£160	BTI 12, 19 April 1929 p. 8. On instruction of representatives of late Mr T. Cox. One cottage occupied by Mr G. Harpin. Rental £10 8s pa. One vacant possession	-
31 May 1929	Bedford, The Red Lion Hotel	Bedford, 52 and 54 Honeyhill Road, two villas	£500	BTI 17 May 1929 p. 4; 24, 31 May p. 8. Occupied by Thomas Mutton and William Scott. Total rental £45 1s 4d pa	-
31 May 1929	Bedford, The Red Lion Hotel	Kempston, Green End, two cottages, 1a 0r 10p	£300	BTI 17 May 1929 p. 4; 24, 31 May p. 8. One cottage occupied by Mr T. Wooding. Rental £6 pa. One vacant possession	-
28 June 1929	Bedford, The Red Lion Hotel	Bedford: Fenlake, Sandy Road, adjoining Manor House, old pasture, 2r 30p; similar site adjoining, 2r 26p; similar site adjoining, 2r 25p; larger site adjoining, 1a 0r 39p; smaller site adjoining, 1r 36p; osier bed (suitable for celery garden) 1a 3r 21p; accommodation pasture adjoining, 1a 3r 6p; garden ground adjoining, 1r 20p; near the Anchor Inn, two cottages	£305 for two cottages	BTI 7, 14, 21 June 1929 p. 8	PK 1/4/65. On instruction of Elias Carter. Cottages occupied by Mrs Jones and Mrs Robinson
9 July 1929	Harold, The Mill House	Harrold, Brook Lane, three cottages	£200	BTI 21 June 1929 p. 8. On instruction of late Mrs J. G. Lang. Occupied by C. Cockings, C. Carter and F. Pettit	PK 1/4/66

Auction date	Venue	Description	Price	Newspaper references	BLARS references
30 July 1929	On site	Riseley, freehold sites, gravel bed, accommodation pasture	£290	BTI 19 July 1929 p. 8; 26 July p. 6	-
10 September 1929	On site	Little Crawley (Bucks), six cottages	Unsold	BTI 16, 30 August 1929 p. 6; 6 September p. 6. On instruction of Mr William C. Gibbs. Household furniture sold following sale of property	-
29 November 1929	Bedford, The Red Lion Hotel	Kempston, Orchardside, Box End, old-world residence, kitchen garden, bungalow with gardens, paddock, two building sites	£1,500	BTI 15 November 1929 p. 6; 22 November p. 8. On instruction of the executors of A. B. Chibnall. Vacant possession	PK 1/4/69, PK 4/4/2. Orchardside has electric light, power and telephone
29 November 1929	Bedford, The Red Lion Hotel	Haynes, Plummers Lane, bungalow	£265	BTI 15 November 1929 p. 6; 22 November p. 8. On instruction of executor of Thomas Parker	-
13 December 1929	Bedford, The Red Lion Hotel	Bedford, The Mill, Duck Mill Lane, containing engine house, chaff house, store place, granary on two floors, stables, cart sheds and fronting river	Unsold	BTI 29 November 1929 p. 8; 6 December p. 6	PK 1/4/70. Site has possibilities for other trades
19 December 1929	On site	Stevington, Court Lane, cottage	£170	BTI 6, 13 December 1929 p. 6. Recently occupied by Mrs Raban	-

Property Auction Records 1930–1939

Auction date	Venue	Description	Price	Newspaper references	BLARS references
7 May 1930	On site	Bedford, timber yards, stables, garages, sawmill, open sheds	-	BTI 2 May 1930 p. 6. On instruction of Messrs English Brothers Ltd	-
16 May 1930	Bedford, The Red Lion	Oakley, six freehold cottages, 2r 37p	Unsold	BTI 25 April 1930 p. 6; 2 May p. 6. Occupied by Walter Cox, I. Hullatt, W. S. Panter, T. Roan, A. Hardwick and W. Parker. Total rental £78 pa	-
16 May 1930	Bedford, The Red Lion	Oakley, The Village Reading Room	-	BTI 25 April 1930 p. 6; 2 May p. 6	-
16 May 1930	Bedford, The Red Lion	Kempston, High Street, shop, dwelling house, accommodation pasture, large yards, buildings, 3r 11p	£745	BTI 25 April 1930 p. 6; 2 May p. 6. On instruction of trustee of late Mr M. J. Tory. Shop occupied by Miss Tory	-
24 June 1930	On site	Bedford, 61 Goldington Road, residence	£630	BTI 6, 20 June 1930 p. 8; 13 June p. 6. On instruction of Mrs Dunnett. Household furniture sold following sale of property	-
15 July 1930	On site	Sharnbrook, Park Lane, pasture field used as poultry farm, 3a 1r 22p	Unsold	BTI 4, 11 July 1930 p. 8. On instruction of Mr F. Rose	-
1 August 1930	Bedford, The Red Lion	Bedford, Wasdale, Goldington Road, semi-detached house	£650	BTI 18, 25 July 1930 p. 8	PK 1/4/73. By direction of mortgagee. Occupied by Ernest Parker

Auction date	Venue	Description	Price	Newspaper references	BLARS references
19 August 1930	On site	Riseley, opposite end of Gold Lane, freehold dwelling house with club room and outbuildings	-	BTI 18 July 1930 p. 8. On instruction of Mr S. N. Stevens. Household effects sold following sale of property	-
30 September 1930	On site	Flitwick, Myrtle Villa, Chapel Road	£500	BTI 19 September 1930 p. 6; 26 September p. 8. Household effects sold following sale of property	-
6 October 1930	Bedford, The Red Lion	Bedford, 33 and 35 Prebend Street, centrally situated premises	£750	BTI 19 September 1930 p. 6; 26 September p. 8. Number 35 occupied by Mrs Howe. Rental £28 9s 10d pa	-
12 December 1930	Bedford, The Red Lion Hotel	Bedford, 20, 22 and 42–48 Cavendish Street, six cottages	£1,170	BTI 21, 28 November 1930 p. 8. Re. Mrs Dulley deceased. Numbers 20 and 22 Cavendish Street occupied by Mr J. W. Ayres and Mrs N. Cox on lunar monthly tenancies. Total rental £41 5s 6d pa. 42–48 occupied by Mrs Cox, Messrs C. Stapleton, C. C. Smith and George Hulatt on lunar monthly tenancies. Total rental £86 19s 11d pa	PK un-catalogued
12 December 1930	Bedford, The Red Lion Hotel	Bedford, 21 and 23 Cobden Street, two cottages	£295	BTI 28 November 1930 p. 8. Occupied by Miss A. H. Boston and Mr W. G. Clements. Total rental £35 19s 4d pa	PK un-catalogued
12 December 1930	Bedford, The Red Lion Hotel	Bedford, 77 Castle Road, residence	£740	BTI 28 November 1930 p. 8. Vacant possession	-
12 December 1930	Bedford, The Red Lion Hotel	Wilstead, near Cross Roads, old-world thatched cottage	£360	BTI 21, 28 November 1930 p. 8. Vacant possession	-

Auction date	Venue	Description	Price	Newspaper references	BLARS references
27 February 1931	Bedford, The Red Lion Hotel	Kempston, fronting Up End, south side of Bunyan Road and other side of St John's Street, two valuable building sites	£300	BTI 30 January 1931 p. 6; 6, 13 February p. 6	PK 1/4/74. Vacant possession
27 February 1931	Bedford, The Red Lion Hotel	Bedford, Ampthill Road, building land, suitable for housing estate, factory or warehouse, 5a	£1,400	BTI 30 January 1931 p. 6; 6, 13 February p. 6	PK 1/4/76
27 February 1931	Bedford, The Red Lion Hotel	Bedford, Mayola, 170 Hurst Grove, double-fronted house	£760	BTI 30 January 1931 p. 6; 6, 13 February p. 6	PK 1/4/75. Vacant possession
24 April 1931	Bedford, The Red Lion Hotel	Goldington, Elmwood, New Road, semi-detached villa	£500	BTI 3, 17 April 1931 p. 8; 10 April p. 6	PK 1/4/78, PK 1/4/79. Vacant possession
24 April 1931	Bedford, The Red Lion Hotel	Bedford, Kempston Road, Cauldwell Walk, valuable site for a manufacturer	Unsold	BTI 3, 17 April 1931 p. 8; 10 April p. 6. On instruction of Mr E. Clark	PK 1/4/80. With a corrugated iron factory
5 May 1931	On site	Bromham, Bromham House Estate, grass keeping, 80a	-	BTI 1 May 1931 p. 8. On instruction of the Bedfordshire and Northamptonshire Joint Board for the Mentally Defective	-
26 June 1931	Bedford, The Red Lion Hotel	Bedford, Alexandra House, 36 Alexandra Road, family residence	Unsold	BTI 29 May 1931 p. 6; 5, 12, 19 June p. 8. Vacant possession	PK un-catalogued
26 June 1931	Bedford, The Red Lion Hotel	Bedford, 26 Castle Road, residence	Unsold	BTI 19 June 1931 p. 8. Vacant possession	-
8 August 1931	Bedford, The Swan Hotel	Riseley, College Farm, Bedford to Riseley Road, house, buildings, 70a	Unsold	BTI 17, 24 July 1931 p. 8; 31 July p. 6. On instruction of Mrs Pitts	PK un-catalogued. A well of water near house

Auction date	Venue	Description	Price	Newspaper references	BLARS references
8 August 1931	Bedford, The Swan Hotel	Riseley, Riseley to Keysoe Road, accommodation pasture, 11.631a	£140	BTI 17, 24 July 1931 p. 8; 31 July p. 6	PK un-catalogued. Opposite the windmill
8 August 1931	Bedford, The Swan Hotel	Flitwick, Hollycroft, situated near the station, freehold country residence, 2a	£1,200	BTI 31 July 1931 p. 6; 7 August p. 6	PK 1/4/81, PK 2/5/2/10. Electric light and power. Vacant possession
18 September 1931	Bedford, The Red Lion Hotel	Bedford, 104 Denmark Street, corner shop, bakehouse, garage, yard	Unsold	BTI 14, 28 August 1931 p. 6	PK 1/4/84, PK 2/5/1/13. Goodwill and business of baker included in the sale. Vacant possession
18 September 1931	Bedford, The Red Lion Hotel	Bedford, 3 Costin Street, villa	£480	BTI 14, 28 August 1931 p. 6	PK 1/4/82, PK 1/4/83. Vacant possession
18 September 1931	Bedford, The Red Lion Hotel	Goldington, 17 King Edward Road, villa	£362	BTI 4 September 1931 p. 6	PK 1/4/82. Vacant possession
18 September 1931	Bedford, The Red Lion Hotel	Bedford, 14 Ashburnham Road, residence	Unsold	BTI 4 September 1931 p. 6	PK 1/4/82. Vacant possession
13 November 1931	Bedford, The Red Lion Hotel	Bedford, 125, 129 and 131 Coventry Road	£935	BTI 30 October 1931 p. 6; 6 November p. 6. On instruction of the executors of Mr and Mrs W. E. Smith. Occupied by Messrs R. Bass, F. Underwood and F. Cheney. Total rental £69 18s pa	-
13 November 1931	Bedford, The Red Lion Hotel	Bedford, 36 Chaucer Road, semi-detached residence	Unsold	BTI 6 November 1931 p. 6. Vacant possession	-
13 November 1931	Bedford, The Red Lion Hotel	Bedford, 140 Fosterhill Road, residence	£570	BTI 30 October 1931 p. 6. Vacant possession	-
13 November 1931	Bedford, The Red Lion Hotel	Bedford, 6 and 6a Gwyn Street, business premises	Unsold	BTI 11 September 1931 p. 6; 30 October p. 6; 6 November p. 6. On instruction of Mrs Mattin. Vacant possession	-

Auction date	Venue	Description	Price	Newspaper references	BLARS references
13 November 1931	Bedford, The Red Lion Hotel	Bedford, 142 Fosterhill Road, residence	£670	BTI 30 October 1931 p. 6; 6 November p. 6. On instruction of executors of Mr and Mrs W. E. Smith. Vacant possession	-
13 November 1931	Bedford, The Red Lion Hotel	Sharnbrook, High Street, house, three cottages	£250	-	-
13 November 1931	Bedford, The Red Lion Hotel	Goldington, Cricket Lane, six cottages	£705	BTI 20 October 1931 p. 6; 6 November p. 6. On instruction of executors of Mr Thomas Haynes. Total rental £43 6s 8d pa	PK 1/4/86. One cottage occupied by S. Denton. Three cottages known as Hawthorn Cottages occupied by S. Harlow, B. Benson and B. Short. Two vacant possession
21 March 1932	On site	Sharnbrook, High Street, four freehold cottages	-	BTI 11 March 1932 p. 8. On instruction of executor of Mr Josiah Farrer. First cottage occupied by the late J. Farrer. Vacant possession. Second occupied by Mrs Gilliat. Rental £4 pa. Third occupied by Miss E. J. Peacock. Rental £4 10s pa. Fourth occupied by Mrs F. Peacock. Rental £4 pa. Furniture and effects sold following sale of property	-
15 April 1932	Bedford, The Red Lion Hotel	Bedford, 13–17 Offa Road, three dwelling houses	£675	BTI 11, 18 March 1932 p. 8; 1 April p. 6. Total rental £52 4s 6d pa	-
15 April 1932	Bedford, The Red Lion Hotel	Bedford, 12 Cutcliffe Place, semi-detached modern residence	Unsold	BTI 11, 18 March 1932 p. 8; 1 April p. 6. Vacant possession	PK 1/4/88, PK 2/5/1/9

Auction date	Venue	Description	Price	Newspaper references	BLARS references
27 May 1932	Bedford, The Red Lion Hotel	Bedford, 50–60 Russell Street, six houses	£1,373	BTI 29 April 1932 p. 6; 6, 13 May p. 8. On instruction of executors of Mrs Caroline Price. Total rental £111 16s pa	PK 2/5/1/11
27 May 1932	Bedford, The Red Lion Hotel	Bedford, 62–74 Wellington Street, six houses	£700	BTI 29 April 1932 p. 6; 6, 13 May p. 8. On instruction of executors of Mrs Caroline Price. Total rental £111 5s 4d pa	PK 2/5/1/11
27 May 1932	Bedford, The Red Lion Hotel	Bedford, 12–18 Costin Street, five houses	£830	BTI 29 April 1932 p. 6; 6, 13 May p. 8. On instruction of executors of Mrs Caroline Price	PK 2/5/1/11
27 May 1932	Bedford, The Red Lion Hotel	Bedford, 13–21 Maitland Street, five houses	£1,265	BTI 29 April 1932 p. 6; 6, 13 May p. 8. On instruction of executors of Mrs Caroline Price. Total rental £125 18s 8d pa	PK 2/5/1/11
27 May 1932	Bedford, The Red Lion Hotel	Oakley, near War Memorial, six cottages, 1a 32p	£640	BTI 29 April 1932 p. 6; 6, 13 May p. 8. Number 70 occupied by E. Parrott. 71 occupied by Mrs Trowbridge. 72 occupied by J. Seamarks. 73 occupied by G. Payne. 74 and 75, the Oakley Post Office and General Store, occupied by A. Bowyer. 76 occupied by Mrs E. Parrott. Total rental £57 10s pa	-
27 May 1932	Bedford, The Red Lion Hotel	Bedford, The Poplars, Newnham Lane, off Goldington Road, double-fronted residence, 0.5a	-	BTI 6, 13 May 1932 p. 8. Vacant possession	-

Auction date	Venue	Description	Price	Newspaper references	BLARS references
28 May 1932	Bedford, The Swan Hotel	Great Barford: freehold farm house, cottage, garage, stabling; fronting Village Road, paddock, 2a 38p; building site of 3r; adjacent to main Bedford Road, gardening land, 10a	-	BTI 6, 13 May 1932 p. 8. Occupied by the late William Mitchell. Vacant possession	-
27 June 1932	On site	Bromham, Main Road, stone dwelling house, 1r 3p	Unsold	BTI 17, 24 June 1932 p. 8. On instruction of trustees of the Church Charity. Vacant possession	-
27 June 1932	On site	Bromham, opposite Bromham Green, behind Post Office, freehold building site, 2r 40p	£219 for four lots	BTI 17, 24 June 1932 p. 8	-
27 June 1932	On site	Bromham, Grange Lane, 30p	£219 for four lots	BTI 17, 24 June 1932 p. 8	-
27 June 1932	On site	Bromham, rear of above lot, roadway to Grange Lane, paddock, 1a 6p	£219 for four lots	BTI 17, 24 June 1932 p. 8	-
27 June 1932	On site	Bromham, Village Street, school allotments situated near the school, 2r 19p	£219 for four lots	BTI 17, 24 June 1932 p. 8. At present occupied by allotment tenants	-
8 July 1932	Bedford, The Red Lion Hotel	Kempston, 8 and 10 Marne Street	£650	BTI 17 June 1932 p. 8; 1 July p. 8	PK 1/4/89/1. Occupied by Florence Wills and Sarah Page. Total rental £39 pa
8 July 1932	Bedford, The Red Lion Hotel	Kempston, 38 and 39 Water Lane, cottages	-	BTI 17 June 1932 p. 8; 1 July p. 8	PK 1/4/90, PK 1/4/89/1. Occupied by Frank Boyle and C. Lack. Total rental £31 4s pa

Auction date	Venue	Description	Price	Newspaper references	BLARS references
8 July 1932	Bedford, The Red Lion Hotel	Bedford, 59 George Street	Sold prior to auction	BTI 17 June 1932 p. 8; 1 July p. 8	-
30 August 1932	On site	Bedford, 16 Shaftesbury Avenue, delightful residence	£1,100	BTI 12, 19, 26 August 1932 p. 6. On instruction of R. Hope Esq. Vacant possession. Household furniture sold following sale of property	-
19 September 1932	On site	Biddenham, Tettenhall, Days Lane, freehold residence, 0.5a	£1,500	BTI 2, 9, 16 September p. 6. On instruction of executor of A. E. Clarabut. Vacant possession. Household furniture sold following sale of property	PK 1/4/91
21 September 1932	On site	Sharnbrook, opposite church, modern bungalow, 1.5a	£300	BTI 16 September 1932 p. 6. Vacant possession	-
11 November 1932	Bedford, The Red Lion Hotel	Bedford, 2–46 Althorpe Street, eleven lots	£2,710	-	-
11 November 1932	Bedford, The Red Lion Hotel	Bedford, 36–40 Ford End Road	£920	-	-
11 November 1932	Bedford, The Red Lion Hotel	Bedford, 74 Pembroke Street	£425	BTI 14, 21 October 1932 p. 8; 28 October p. 6. On instruction of executor of A. Clarabut	PK 1/4/92. Occupied by Mr A. Humphriss and sub-let to C. W. Duckworth. Rental £23 8s pa
11 November 1932	Bedford, The Red Lion Hotel	Bedford, 76 Pembroke Street	£425	BTI 14, 21 October 1932 p. 8; 28 October p. 6. On instruction of executor of A. Clarabut	PK 1/4/92. Occupied by Arthur Drake Sadler. Rental £23 8s pa
11 November 1932	Bedford, The Red Lion Hotel	Bedford, 29 Albany Road, double-fronted residence	£900	BTI 14, 21 October 1932 p. 8; 28 October p. 6. On instruction of executor of A. Clarabut	PK 1/4/92. Occupied by Edward Brown. Rental £55 pa

Auction date	Venue	Description	Price	Newspaper references	BLARS references
11 November 1932	Bedford, The Red Lion Hotel	Bedford, 93 Castle Road, semi-detached villa	£700	BTI 14, 21 October 1932 p. 8; 28 October p. 6. On instruction of executor of A. Clarabut	PK 1/4/92. Occupied by C. W. Hanscombe. Rental £38 pa
11 November 1932	Bedford, The Red Lion Hotel	Bedford, 55 Pembroke Street, semi-detached villa	£450	BTI 14, 21 October 1932 p. 8; 28 October p. 6. On instruction of executor of A. Clarabut	PK 1/4/92. Occupied by Albert George Skerman. Rental £30 pa
11 November 1932	Bedford, The Red Lion Hotel	Bedford, 57 Pembroke Street, semi-detached villa	£425	BTI 14, 21 October 1932 p. 8; 28 October p. 6. On instruction of executor of A. Clarabut	PK 1/4/92. Occupied by Mrs Emily Beeching. Rental £23 8s pa
25 November 1932	Kempston, The King William IV	Kempston, West End, smallholding, farm house, two cottages, 46a 3r 18p	£450	BTI 4, 11, 18 November 1932 p. 6. Farm house vacant possession. Cottages let on weekly tenancies to farm servants at 3s	-
6 December 1932	On site	Kempston, 24 High Street, detached double-fronted residence, double coach house, kitchen garden, paddock with fruit trees, 1a	£870	BTI 25 November 1932 p. 8; 2 December p. 8. Vacant possession. Outside effects sold following sale of property	PK 1/4/94, PK 1/4/95
28 February 1933	On site	Kempston, Box End: orchard of 5a; between Bromham and Box End in the Sudan Field, two building plots of 0.5a	£985	BTI 3, 17 February 1933 p. 6; 3 March p. 8	PK 4/4/4
28 February 1933	On site	Kempston, Box End, near Top Farm, pair of cottages	£335	BTI 17 February 1933 p. 6. On instruction of the mortgagee	-
10 March 1933	Bedford, The Swan Hotel	Bedford, 17 Silver Street, Mac Fisheries business premises	£4,950	BTI 10, 17 February 1933 p. 6; 3 March p. 8	PK 1/4/97, PK 1/4/98. On instruction of executors to close estate. Rental £225 pa

Auction date	Venue	Description	Price	Newspaper references	BLARS references
24 March 1933	Bedford, The Red Lion Hotel	Bedford, 2 Althorpe Street, corner shop	-	BTI 24 February 1933 p. 8; 3, 17 March p. 8; 10 March p. 6. On instruction of executors of John Ball	PK un-catalogued. Corner shop occupied by Mr A. G. Bridgeman. Rental £35 pa
24 March 1933	Bedford, The Red Lion Hotel	Bedford, 4 Althorpe Street	-	BTI 24 February 1933 p. 8; 3, 17 March p. 8; 10 March p. 6. On instruction of executors of John Ball	PK un-catalogued. Occupied by Mr P. G. Robinson. Rental £22 8s pa
24 March 1933	Bedford, The Red Lion Hotel	Bedford, 6 Althorpe Street	-	BTI 24 February 1933 p. 8; 3, 17 March p. 8; 10 March p. 6. On instruction of executors of John Ball	PK un-catalogued. Occupied by Mr J. Taylor. Rental £29 8s pa
24 March 1933	Bedford, The Red Lion Hotel	Bedford, 8–12 Althorpe Street	-	BTI 24 February 1933 p. 8; 3, 17 March p. 8; 10 March p. 6. On instruction of executors of John Ball	PK un-catalogued. Occupied by Mrs Denton, Messrs F. J. Brown and W. G. Beaumont. Total rental £58 19s pa
24 March 1933	Bedford, The Red Lion Hotel	Bedford, 14–18 Althorpe Street	-	BTI 24 February 1933 p. 8; 3, 17 March p. 8; 10 March p. 6. On instruction of executors of John Ball	PK un-catalogued. Occupied by Messrs W. Lowell, F. Scott and H. Huckle. Total rental £57 12s pa
24 March 1933	Bedford, The Red Lion Hotel	Bedford, 26–30 Althorpe Street	-	BTI 24 February 1933 p. 8; 3, 17 March p. 8; 10 March p. 6. On instruction of executors of John Ball	PK uncatalogued. Occupied by Messrs A. Myers, W. Goodwin and A. Millard. Total rental £57 12s pa
24 March 1933	Bedford, The Red Lion Hotel	Bedford, 32–36 Althorpe Street	-	BTI 24 February 1933 p. 8; 3, 17 March p. 8; 10 March p. 6. On instruction of executors of John Ball	PK un-catalogued. Occupied by Messrs C. Farrer, A. Joyce and W. Smith. Total rental £57 12s pa

Auction date	Venue	Description	Price	Newspaper references	BLARS references
24 March 1933	Bedford, The Red Lion Hotel	Bedford, 38 and 40 Althorpe Street	-	BTI 24 February 1933 p. 8; 3, 17 March p. 8; 10 March p. 6. On instruction of executors of John Ball	PK un-catalogued. Occupied by Messrs B. Bygrave and H. Clifton. Total rental £39 6s pa
24 March 1933	Bedford, The Red Lion Hotel	Bedford, 42 and 44 Althorpe Street	-	BTI 24 February 1933 p. 8; 3, 17 March p. 8; 10 March p. 6. On instruction of executors of John Ball	PK un-catalogued. Occupied by Messrs F. Wells and A. Millard. Total rental £39 6s pa
24 March 1933	Bedford, The Red Lion Hotel	Bedford, 46 Althorpe Street	-	BTI 24 February 1933 p. 8; 3, 17 March p. 8; 10 March p. 6. On instruction of executors of John Ball	PK un-catalogued. Occupied by Mr W. G. Carroll, stonemason. Rental £23 10s pa
24 March 1933	Bedford, The Red Lion Hotel	Bedford, 34 Ford End Road, villa residence	-	BT 3, 17 March 1933 p. 8; 10 March p. 6. On instruction of trustees of the late Mrs Emma Bull	PK un-catalogued. Occupied by Mr S. W. Furr. Rental £23 2s pa
24 March 1933	Bedford, The Red Lion Hotel	Bedford, 36 Ford End Road, villa residence	-	BT 3, 17 March 1933 p. 8; 10 March p. 6. On instruction of trustees of the late Mrs Emma Bull	PK un-catalogued. Occupied by Mr Alfred Whiting. Rental £23 10s pa
24 March 1933	Bedford, The Red Lion Hotel	Bedford, 38 and 40 Ford End Road, villa residences	-	BT 3, 17 March 1933 p. 8; 10 March p. 6. On instruction of trustees of the late Mrs Emma Bull	PK un-catalogued. Occupied by Messrs G. Prigmore and J. Tildesley. Total rental £46 4s pa
28 March 1933	On site	Renhold, Church End, semi-detached villa	£450	BT 10 March 1933 p. 6; 17 March p. 8. Vacant possession	-
21 April 1933	Bedford, The Red Lion Hotel	Kempston, 57 Bunyan Road, detached residence	£1,075	BT 24 March 1933 p. 6; 7 April p. 8. Off-beer license attached to this property. Vacant possession	PK 2/5/1/14

Auction date	Venue	Description	Price	Newspaper references	BLARS references
21 April 1933	Bedford, The Red Lion Hotel	Kempston, 59, 61 and 61a Bunyan Road, two villas and shop	Unsold	BT 24 March 1933 p. 6; 7 April p. 8. Occupied by Mr H. T. Jeffrey and Mr T. Church. Total rental £57 4s pa	PK 2/5/1/14
21 April 1933	Bedford, The Red Lion Hotel	Bedford, 10 Alexandra Road, semi-detached residence	£365	BTI 31 March 1933 p. 6; 7 April p. 8. Vacant possession	PK 2/5/1/14
25 April 1933	On site	Renhold, near Post Office, charming old-world cottage and farm buildings	£260	BTI 31 March 1933 p. 6; 14 April p. 6. Vacant possession	-
25 April 1933	On site	Oakley, Grace Dieu, Station Road, detached double-fronted house	Unsold	BTI 7 April 1933 p. 8; 14 April p. 6. Vacant possession	-
25 April 1933	On site	Biddenham, valuable water meadow, 22a	£700	BTI 7 April 1933 p. 8; 14 April p. 6	PK un-catalogued. Suitable for riverside tea garden resort with bathing facilities
25 April 1933	On site	Biddenham, enclosure of upland pasture, 6a	£300	BTI 7 April 1933 p. 8; 14 April p. 6	PK un-catalogued
25 April 1933	On site	Biddenham, enclosure of upland pasture, 6a	£300	BTI 7 April 1933 p. 8; 14 April p. 6	PK un-catalogued
25 April 1933	On site	Biddenham, eight half-acre building plots	5 unsold 1 sold £100 1 sold £90 1 sold £85	-	PK un-catalogued
30 May 1933	On site	Wilstead, Rosemont, freehold residence, valuable frontage plot on main Luton Road, 1r 9p	Unsold	BTI 12, 19 May 1933 p. 6. Household furniture sold following sale of property	PK un-catalogued. Shop (unoccupied) at side. Vacant possession

Auction date	Venue	Description	Price	Newspaper references	BLARS references
7 July 1933	Bedford, The Red Lion Hotel	Biddenham, Barringer, New Road, 1a	Unsold	BTI 16 June 1933 p. 6; 23 June p. 8. The house was reviewed in *Country Life*	PK un-catalogued. Built for the late Henry J. Peacock[1]
7 July 1933	Bedford, The Red Lion Hotel	Bedford, 7 and 9 Silver Street, shops	Unsold	BTI 16 June 1933 p. 6; 23 June p. 8	PK un-catalogued. Number 9 has been in the occupation of Messrs Harry Hills Ltd for nearly forty years. Rental £260 pa
8 July 1933	Bedford, The Swan Hotel	Wilden, Crow Hill Farm, land, 29.756a	Unsold Joint auction with Swaffield & Son	-	PK 1/4/99. Described as for many years occupied by John Draper
8 July 1933	Bedford, The Swan Hotel	Wilden, Top Farm, two building plots, 39.5a	- Joint auction with Swaffield & Son	-	PK 1/4/100/1, PK 1/4/100/2. By direction of Jock Draper
8 July 1933	Bedford, The Swan Hotel	Wilden, Elm Cottages, two cottages	-	-	PK 1/4/99. Occupied by Samuel Rogers and John Harper
21 July 1933	Bedford, The Red Lion Hotel	Bedford, 26–30 George Street, three villas	£765	BTI 23 June 1933 p. 8; 7 July p. 8; 14 July p. 6. Number 26 occupied by Miss S. E. Goodwin. 28 occupied by Mr T. Perkins. 30 occupied by Mr H. Rawlins. Total rental £46 16s pa	PK 2/5/1/15. On instruction of Mrs Elizabeth Townsend, deceased

1 Henry J. Peacock had this house built for him following his retirement from farming at Grove Farm. The house was originally called Three Gables, then Barringer and now 17 Biddenham Turn. It was designed, in the arts and crafts style, by his son-in-law, the well-known architect, G. E. Mallows, Fricker, *The Village of Biddenham*, p. 126.

Auction date	Venue	Description	Price	Newspaper references	BLARS references
21 July 1933	Bedford, The Red Lion Hotel	Bedford, 2 and 4 Sandhurst Place, two villas	£500	BTI 23 June 1933 p. 8; 7 July p. 8; 14 July p. 6. Number 2 occupied by Mr E. Wilkinson. 4 occupied by Mr J. H. King. Total rental £35 2s pa	PK 2/5/1/15. On instruction of Mrs Elizabeth Townsend, deceased
21 July 1933	Bedford, The Red Lion Hotel	Bedford, 6 and 8 Sandhurst Place, villas	£505	BTI 23 June 1933 p. 8; 7 July p. 8; 14 July p. 6. Number 6 occupied by Mrs E. Whiting. 8 occupied by Mr A. Eastwell. Total rental £30 11s pa	PK 2/5/1/15. On instruction of Mrs Elizabeth Townsend, deceased
21 July 1933	Bedford, The Red Lion Hotel	Bedford, 35 and 37 Marlborough Road, two villas	£585	BTI 23 June 1933 p. 8; 7 July p. 8; 14 July p. 6. Number 35 occupied by Mr E. A. Perry. 37 occupied by Mr W. Atkin. Total rental £43 11s pa	PK 2/5/1/15. On instruction of Mrs Elizabeth Townsend, deceased
21 July 1933	Bedford, The Red Lion Hotel	Bedford, 1 and 2 Cross Street, pair of villas	£655	BTI 23 June 1933 p. 8; 7 July p. 8; 14 July p. 6. Number 1 occupied by Miss M. Wise. 2 vacant possession. Total rental £23 8s pa	PK 2/5/1/15. On instruction of Mrs Elizabeth Townsend, deceased
21 July 1933	Bedford, The Red Lion Hotel	Bedford, 1–9 Hassett Street, five cottages	£495	BTI 23 June 1933 p. 8; 7 July p. 8; 14 July p. 6. Number 1 occupied by Miss A. Humphries-Read. 3 occupied by Mr F. Berrington. 5 occupied by Mr W. Brouch. 7 occupied by Mr A. Cambers. 9 occupied by Mrs M Longland. Total rental £66 10s pa	PK 2/5/1/15. On instruction of Mrs Elizabeth Townsend, deceased

Auction date	Venue	Description	Price	Newspaper references	BLARS references
21 July 1933	Bedford, The Red Lion Hotel	Bedford, 4 and 6 Little Thurlow Street, two cottages	£210	BTI 23 June 1933 p. 8; 7 July p. 8; 14 July p. 6. Number 4 occupied by Mr H. Barker. 6 occupied by Mr S. Chandler. Total rental £26 18s 8d pa	PK 2/5/1/15. On instruction of Mrs Elizabeth Townsend, deceased
21 July 1933	Bedford, The Red Lion Hotel	Bedford, 13 and 15 Little Thurlow Street, two cottages	£265	BTI 23 June 1933 p. 8; 7 July p. 8; 14 July p. 6. Number 13 occupied by Mr J. H. Walker. 15 occupied by Mr T. A. Ives. Total rental £30 16s 8d pa	PK 2/5/1/15. On instruction of Mrs Elizabeth Townsend, deceased
21 July 1933	Bedford, The Red Lion Hotel	Bedford, 61 and 63 Greyfriars Walk and 1 Roise Street	-	BTI 23 June 1933 p. 8; 7 July p. 8; 14 July p. 6. Number 61 occupied by Mr A. E. Field. 63 occupied by W. T. Allen. 1 occupied by Mr J. Brown. Total rental £45 pa	PK 2/5/1/15. On instruction of Mrs Elizabeth Townsend, deceased
21 July 1933	Bedford, The Red Lion Hotel	Kempston, 15 and 15a Littledale Street, two villas	£500	BTI 30 June 1933 p. 8; 7 July p. 8; 14 July p. 6. Occupied by A. S. Colgrave and A. W. Wilsher. Total rental £43 15s 4d pa	PK 2/5/2/12
21 July 1933	Bedford, The Red Lion Hotel	Marston Moretaine, 159–169 (no road name given), six cottages	Unsold	BTI 7 July 1933 p. 8. Number 159 occupied by Mr Walter Gillett. 161 occupied by Mr Goswell. 163 occupied by Mr Wilson. 165 occupied by Mr Hyde. 167 occupied by Mr Joseph Cave. 169 occupied by Mr Frederick Wooding	-
2 August 1933	Harrold, Harrold Institute	Harrold, approached from Harrold Wood Road, freehold land, 51.136a	£85	BTI 21 July 1933 p. 8; 28 July p. 6. New pasture occupied by Mr T. G. Eden	-

Auction date	Venue	Description	Price	Newspaper references	BLARS references
2 August 1933	Harrold, Harrold Institute	Harrold, Harold to Lavendon Road, freehold smallholding, 36.693a	Unsold	BTI 21 July 1933 p. 8; 28 July p. 6. Farmed by the late Mr C. Tacchi	-
15 August 1933	On site	Ravensden, Echodene, Cleat Hill, smallholding, 5a 3r 10p, five building sites	£725	BTI 21 July 1933 p. 8; 11 August p. 6. On instruction of Mr E. J. Miller	PK un-catalogued
5 September 1933	On site	Wilden, Valentine's Farm: paddock, 3a 1r 11p; accommodation paddock, 4a 16p; cottage and orchard 3r 7p	Unsold	BTI 18, 25 August 1933 p. 6	PK un-catalogued. On instruction of Mrs L. Daws. Vacant possession
26 September 1933	On site	Blunham, Prospect House, freehold property, 1r	Unsold	BTI 8, 15 September 1933 p. 6. Vacant possession	-
1 December 1933	Bedford, The Red Lion Hotel	Clapham, Sunnyside, Oakley Road, detached double-fronted residence	Unsold	BTI 10, 24 November 1933 p. 8	PK 1/4/103. Vacant possession
27 February 1934	On site	Bedford, St Margaret's, 77 Castle Road, freehold residence	£695	BTI 16, 23 February 1934 p. 8. On instruction of executors of Rev. Joseph Shrimpton. Vacant possession. Household furnishings sold following sale of property	-
2 March 1934	Bedford, The Red Lion Hotel	Bedford, 16 Stanley Street, freehold villa	£450	BTI 9 February 1934 p. 6; 16, 23 February p. 8	PK 1/4/104. Vacant possession
2 March 1934	Bedford, The Red Lion Hotel	Bedford, 38 The Grove, residence	£505	BTI 23 February 1934 p. 8	PK 1/4/104. Vacant possession
2 March 1934	Bedford, The Red Lion Hotel	Bedford, 5 Conduit Road, freehold house	£500	BTI 9 February 1934 p. 6; 16, 23 February p. 8	PK 1/4/105. Occupied by Mrs Lawrence. Rental £45 pa

Auction date	Venue	Description	Price	Newspaper references	BLARS references
15 May 1934	On site	Bromham, overlooking Village Green, pair of cottages	£435	BTI 4, 11 May 1934 p. 8. On instruction of the Church Charity of Bromham. One cottage occupied by Mr A. Tysoe. Rental £6 12s pa. One vacant possession	-
31 May 1934	On site	Bedford, 32 Grafton Road, freehold semi-detached villa	Unsold	BTI 11, 18 May 1934 p. 8; 25 February p. 6. Vacant possession. Household furnishings sold following sale of property	-
12 July 1934	On site	Renhold: Newfield Farm, 9a 1r 21p; five building sites; allotment land, 4.5a	Unsold	BTI 22 June 1934 p. 6	PK 2/5/2/15. Vacant possession
13 July 1934	Bedford, The Red Lion Hotel	Bedford, 21 St Michael's Road, semi-detached residence	£600	BTI 22 June 1934 p. 6; 29 June p. 8	-
13 July 1934	Bedford, The Red Lion Hotel	Bedford, 41–44 Tavistock Place, four freehold cottages	£450	BTI 22 June 1934 p. 6; 29 June p. 8. On instruction of executrix of Thomas Hands. Total rental £70 4s pa	-
20 July 1934	Sandy, The Conservative Hall	Sandy, Bedford Road, next to Conservative Club, brick and slate house	-	BTI 15 June 1934 p. 8; 13 July p. 8	PK 1/4/108. Portions of the late estate of Mr Frank Davison. Occupied by Percy Bennett. Catalogue stamped 'sold to tenant'
20 July 1934	Sandy, The Conservative Hall	Sandy, 17–23 Longfield Road	-	BTI 15 June 1934 p. 8; 13 July p. 8	PK 1/4/108. Portions of the late estate of Mr Frank Davison. Occupied by Mr F. C. Wright, Mr A.W. Savage, Mr C. Butcher and Miss Davison

Auction date	Venue	Description	Price	Newspaper references	BLARS references
20 July 1934	Sandy, The Conservative Hall	Sandy, 140 and 142 Great North Road, adjoining the New Inn, Girtford	-	BTI 15 June 1934 p. 8; 13 July p. 8	PK 1/4/108. Portions of the late estate of Mr Frank Davison. Occupied by Mrs E. Watts and Mr S. Osborn
20 July 1934	Sandy, The Conservative Hall	Beeston, York Villa, Great North Road	-	BTI 15 June 1934 p. 8; 13 July p. 8	PK 1/4/108. Portions of the late estate of Mr Frank Davison. Occupied by A. H. Hawkins. Catalogue stamped 'sold to tenant'
20 July 1934	Sandy, The Conservative Hall	Beeston, Victor Villa, adjoining Great North Road	-	BTI 15 June 1934 p. 8; 13 July p. 8	PK 1/4/108. Portions of the late estate of Mr Frank Davison. Occupied by Mr Ernest Brown. Catalogue stamped 'sold to tenant'
20 July 1934	Sandy, The Conservative Hall	Blunham, Northfield, off Grange Road, freehold garden ground, 4a 0r 5p	Unsold	BTI 15 June 1934 p. 8; 13, 27 July p. 8	PK 1/4/108. Portions of the late estate of Mr Frank Davison. Occupied by Walter Gill
20 July 1934	Sandy, The Conservative Hall	Moggerhanger, Wilson's Field and Ladywood Plantation, arable enclosure, 8a	Unsold	BTI 15 June 1934 p. 8; 13, 27 July p. 8	PK 1/4/108. Portions of the late estate of Mr Frank Davison. Vacant possession
20 July 1934	Sandy, The Conservative Hall	Willington, Scarsdale, residence, 3a 14 19p	Unsold	BTI 15 June 1934 p. 8; 13, 27 July p. 8	PK 1/4/108. Portions of the late estate of Mr Frank Davison. Vacant possession
20 July 1934	Sandy, The Conservative Hall	Cople, situated opposite Cople Toll House, garden land, 12a 2r 35p	Unsold	BTI 15 June 1934 p. 8; 13, 27 July p. 8	PK 1/4/108. Portions of the late estate of Mr Frank Davison. Occupied by E. G. Hart
20 July 1934	Sandy, The Conservative Hall	Willington, Croots Farm, Station Road, buildings, 1r 25p	-	BTI 15 June 1934 p. 8; 13 July p. 8	PK 1/4/108. Portions of the late estate of Mr Frank Davison

Auction date	Venue	Description	Price	Newspaper references	BLARS references
20 July 1934	Sandy, The Conservative Hall	Kempston, West End Farm, Elizabethan farm house, block of three cottages, two further cottages, agricultural estate, 246.636 acres	Unsold	TDA 27 June 1934 p. 29. BTI 15 June 1934 p. 8; 22 June p. 6; 13, 27 July p. 8	PK 1/4/108. Portions of the late estate of Mr Frank Davison. Block of cottages occupied by Mr Ashpole, Mrs Ashpole snr and Mr W. Linger. Two further cottages occupied by Messrs F. and W. Walker. Farmed by the late F. B. Newman and now occupied by Messrs G. W. Mardlin and son. Rental £275 pa
20 July 1934	Sandy, The Conservative Hall	Beeston, Dunghill Roadway, garden land, 2.25a	£75	BTI 6 July 1934 p. 6; 13 July p. 8. Lately occupied by Mr Frederick Darnell	PK 1/4/108
20 July 1934	Sandy, The Conservative Hall	Sandy, Brook End, adjoining The Gardener's Arms, garden land, 5.5a; Sandy, fronting Sandy to Hitchin Road, 5.5a; Moggerhanger, garden land, 4a 0r 7p; Moggerhanger, adjoining land, 4a; Blunham, garden land, 4a 3r 31p; Willington, garden land with further four areas adjoining, 5a	-	BTI 15 June 1934 p. 8	PK 1/4/108. Portions of the late estate of Mr Frank Davison. Land at Willington may be of interest to gravel merchants
12 September 1934	Bedford, The Red Lion Hotel	Bedford, 13 Merton Road, residence	£1,005	BTI 31 August 1934 p. 6; 7 September p. 6. On instruction of executors of Mrs Barford. Vacant possession. Household furnishings sold following sale of property	-

Auction date	Venue	Description	Price	Newspaper references	BLARS references
12 September 1934	Bedford, The Red Lion Hotel	Bedford, 3 and 5 Adelaide Square, pair of villas	£660	BTI 31 August 1934 p. 6; 7 September p. 6. Number 5 occupied by Mrs Williamson. Rental £25 pa	-
12 September 1934	Bedford, The Red Lion Hotel	Bedford, 129 Tavistock Street	£300	BTI 31 August 1934 p. 6; 7 September p. 6. Vacant possession	-
18 September 1934	On site	Renhold, Workhouse End, pair of thatched cottages, 1a 3r 22p	£400	BTI 31 August 1934 p. 6; 7 September p. 6	PK 1/4/109/2. On instruction of executors of Miss A. Halsey. First cottage known as Aldwick with vacant possession. Second cottage occupied by F. Curtis. Rental £9 10s pa
18 September 1934	On site	Renhold, adjoining the above, brick and timber bungalow, 22p	-	BTI 31 August 1934 p. 6; 7 September p. 6	PK 1/4/109/2. On instruction of executors of Miss A. Halsey. Household furniture and live and dead stock sold following sale of property
18 September 1934	On site	Renhold, Brickfield House, Salph End, 4a 0r 4p	Unsold	BTI 31 August 1934 p. 6; 7 September p. 6	PK 1/4/109/1. On instruction of F. Locke
7 December 1934	Bedford, The Red Lion Hotel	Bedford, 52 and 54 Bower Street, two villas	£540	BTI 16, 23 November 1934 p. 8. Re. Charles Aley, deceased. Number 52 occupied by Mr C. Mitchell. Rental £13 5s pa. 54 occupied by Mr J. Wells. Rental £17 19s pa	-
7 December 1934	Bedford, The Red Lion Hotel	Bedford, 41 Bower Street, villa	£405	BTI 16, 23 November 1934 p. 8. Re. Charles Aley, deceased. Occupied by Mr Frank Johnson. Rental £15 12s pa	-

Auction date	Venue	Description	Price	Newspaper references	BLARS references
7 December 1934	Bedford, The Red Lion Hotel	Bedford, Polhill Field, Goldington Road, garden ground, 0.5a	£75	BTI 16, 23 November 1934 p. 8. Re. Charles Aley, deceased	-
7 December 1934	Bedford, The Red Lion Hotel	Bedford, Polhill Field, Goldington Road, garden ground, 0.5a	£70	BTI 16, 23 November 1934 p. 8. Re. Charles Aley, deceased	-
7 December 1934	Bedford, The Red Lion Hotel	Bedford, 1 Houghton Road, six room villa	£390	BTI 16, 23 November 1934 p. 8. Re. Samuel Murdock, deceased	-
22 February 1935	Bedford, The Red Lion Hotel	Bedford, 25 Marlborough Road, semi-detached villa	£240	BTI 8 February 1935 p. 8; 15 February p. 6	PK 1/4/113/1. Occupied by Charles Tysoe. Rental £30 2s
22 February 1935	Bedford, The Red Lion Hotel	Bedford, 30 and 32 Little Butts Street, two cottages	£360	BTI 8 February 1935 p. 8; 15 February p. 6	PK 1/4/113/1. Occupied by Harry Lumbers and William Rowley. Total rental £31 4s pa
22 February 1935	Bedford, The Red Lion Hotel	Bedford, 8 Rutland Road, villa residence	£635	BTI 8 February 1935 p. 8; 15 February p. 6	PK 1/4/113/1, PK 1/4/113/2. Vacant possession
22 February 1935	Bedford, The Red Lion Hotel	Bedford, 25 Western Street, villa	Unsold	BTI 8 February 1935 p. 8; 15 February p. 6	PK 1/4/113/1, PK 1/4/113/2. Vacant possession
1 March 1935	Bedford, The Red Lion Hotel	Bedford, 54 York Street, villa	£455	BTI 15 February p. 6; 22 February p. 8. Vacant possession	-
1 March 1935	Bedford, The Red Lion Hotel	Bedford, 5 Bunyan Road, villa	Unsold	BTI 8 February 1935 p. 8; 22 February p. 8. Vacant possession	-
1 March 1935	Bedford, The Red Lion Hotel	Bedford, 3 Dynevor Road, residence	£1,000	BTI 8, 22 February 1935 p. 8. Re. estate of George E. Langley	-
26 April 1935	Bedford, The Red Lion Hotel	Bedford, 14 Lime Street, freehold business premises, 4667 sq ft	£3,000	BTI 29 March 1935 p. 8; 12 April p. 8; 19 April p. 6	PK un-catalogued. Being the old established china warehouse of Messrs Davis Bros. Vacant possession

Auction date	Venue	Description	Price	Newspaper references	BLARS references
19 July 1935	Sandy, The Conservative Hall	Beeston, on Great North Road, adjoining The Cross public house, garden land, 3a 20p	£600	BTI 5 July 1935 p. 8	PK 1/4/116. On instruction of the late Mr J. C. Underwood. Occupied by Joe Brice
19 July 1935	Sandy, The Conservative Hall	Sandy, Bedford Road, near Girton Bridge, garden ground, 4a 3r 10p	£450	BTI 5 July 1935 p. 8	PK 1/4/116. On instruction of the late Mr J. C. Underwood
19 July 1935	Sandy, The Conservative Hall	Sandy, Wharf Farm, Great North Road, opposite Girtford Manor, residence, buildings	£435	BTI 5 July 1935 p. 8	PK 1/4/116. On instruction of the late Mr J. C. Underwood. Vacant possession
26 July 1935	Bedford, The Red Lion Hotel	Bedford, 84 Clapham Road, residence	£750	BTI 5, 12 July 1935 p. 8	PK un-catalogued. Vacant possession
26 July 1935	Bedford, The Red Lion Hotel	Bedford, 13–16 Beauchamp Row, four cottages	£290	BTI 5, 12 July 1935 p. 8	PK un-catalogued. Occupied by Mr J. Dickinson, Mr F. W. Bushby, Mrs E. Wiffin and Mr F. Myers. Total rental £53 14s 8d pa
26 July 1935	Bedford, The Red Lion Hotel	Bedford, 17 and 18 Beauchamp Row, two cottages	£220	BTI 5, 12 July 1935 p. 8	PK un-catalogued. Occupied by Mr S. Beard and Mr C. Dale. Total rental £26 17s 4d pa
26 July 1935	Bedford, The Red Lion Hotel	Clapham, 14 Green Lane	£560	BTI 5, 12 July 1935 p. 8	PK un-catalogued. Occupied by Mr Foster. Rental £48 pa
26 July 1935	Bedford, The Red Lion Hotel	Bedford, 2 York Street, villa	£490	BTI 19 July 1935 p. 8. Vacant possession	-

Auction date	Venue	Description	Price	Newspaper references	BLARS references
30 July 1935	On site	Stevington, Church Street, house adjoining forge, building site 21p and paddock 1a 1r 4p	£572	BTI 19 July 1935 p. 8; 26 July p. 6	PK 1/4/117. On instruction of the executors of George Ruffhead. Vacant possession
17 September 1935	On site	Colmworth, frontage to Chawston and Wilden Roads, Channels End, pasture field, 14a	£130	BTI 13 September 1935 p. 6. Re. Alfred Nixon, deceased. Vacant possession	-
17 September 1935	On site	Colmworth, Channels End, rich old pasture, 5a	£100	BTI 13 September 1935 p. 6. Re. Alfred Nixon, deceased. Vacant possession	-
18 October 1935	Bedford, The Red Lion Hotel	Bedford, 2a Melbourne Street, residence, factory	£950	BTI 27 September 1935 p. 6; 4 October p. 8. Bottling warehouse and store	PK un-catalogued. On instruction of executors of J. W. Burgess. Vacant possession
18 October 1935	Bedford, The Red Lion Hotel	Bedford, 56 Bromham Road, business premises	£1,200	BTI 4, 11 October 1935 p. 8. Vacant possession	-
15 November 1935	Bedford, The Red Lion Hotel	Bedford, 60 Winifred Road, villa	£550	BTI 18 October 1935 p. 8. On instruction of executors of Augustus Charles Sherman	-
15 November 1935	Bedford, The Red Lion Hotel	Bedford, 132 Hurst Grove, semi-detached residence	£545	BTI 18 October 1935 p. 8. On instruction of executors of Augustus Charles Sherman	-
15 November 1935	Bedford, The Red Lion Hotel	Bedford, 4 Fosterhill Road, decontrolled villa	£405	BTI 18 October 1935 p. 8. On instruction of executors of Augustus Charles Sherman. Occupied by Mr A. Thompson. Rental £41 12s pa	-

Auction date	Venue	Description	Price	Newspaper references	BLARS references
10 March 1936	Thurleigh, The Smithy	Thurleigh: semi-detached cottage, 33p; Bolnhurst Road, freehold building plot, 28p; Gammans Close, accommodation land, 7a 2r 29p; Keysoe Road, Mill Hill and Moat, garden ground, 24p; The Rick Yard, garden ground, 28p	£348	BTI 21, 28 February 1936 p. 6; 6 March p. 8. On instruction of executors of the late J. T. Philpott	PK un-catalogued. Cottage formerly occupied by Mr F. Butcher. Accommodation land occupied by Mr John Wagstaff. Rental £12 pa. Mill Hill and Moat occupied by Mr John Fensome. Rental 9s pa. The Rick Yard occupied by Mrs Barnes and Mr Charles Barnes. Rental 9s pa
17 April 1936	Bedford, The Lion Hotel	Bedford, 3 Park Avenue, residence	£1,000	BTI 12 March 1936 p. 8; 10 April p. 6. Vacant possession	-
17 April 1936	Bedford, The Lion Hotel	Bedford, 79 Goldington Avenue, detached double-fronted residence	Unsold	BTI 12 March 1936 p. 8; 10 April p. 6. Vacant possession	-
7 May 1936	On site	Bedford, 10 Woburn Road, detached double-fronted house	£900	BTI 24 April 1936 p. 8; 1 May 1936. On instruction of executors of Maj-General Sir Alliston Toker. Household furnishing sold following sale of property	PK un-catalogued
12 June 1936	Bedford, The Red Lion Hotel	Bedford, 48 Spenser Road, residence	Unsold Joint auction with Robinson and Hall	BTI 22, 29 May 1936 p. 6	-
12 June 1936	Bedford, The Red Lion Hotel	Bedford, 2 and 4 Western Street, pair of villas	Unsold Auction postponed	BTI 22, 29 May 1936 p. 6; 12 June p. 8	-

Auction date	Venue	Description	Price	Newspaper references	BLARS references
12 June 1936	Bedford, The Red Lion Hotel	Keysoe, Hatch End, accommodation field of pasture, 3a 1r 11p	£55 Joint auction with Robinson & Hall	BTI 22, 29 May 1936 p. 6	-
12 June 1936	Bedford, The Red Lion Hotel	Bedford, 185 London Road, modern villa	£610 Joint auction with Robinson & Hall	BTI 22, 29 May 1936 p. 6. On instruction of executors of Mrs Prole	PK un-catalogued. Occupied by Mr Maurice John Parkin. Rental £52 pa
29 September 1936	On site	Bedford, 23 St Michaels Road, residence	£600	BTI 18, 25 September 1936 p. 8. On instruction of the executors of Major James Tagg. Vacant possession. Household furnishing sold following sale of property	-
9 October 1936	Bedford, The Red Lion Hotel	Great Barford, Thaxted House, residence, paddock, 1a 3r 18p	Unsold	BTI 18, 25 September 1936 p. 8; 2 October p. 8	-
9 October 1936	Bedford, The Red Lion Hotel	Bedford, 61 Ford End Road, shop, house	Unsold	BTI 25 September 1936 p. 8; 2 October p. 8	PK un-catalogued. Vacant possession
9 October 1936	Bedford, The Red Lion Hotel	Bedford, 2 and 4 Western Street, pair of villas	£415 Joint auction with Robinson & Hall	BTI 25 September 1936 p. 8; 2 October p. 8	-
20 November 1936	Bedford, The Red Lion Hotel	Bedford, London Road, building land, 14a	£3,300	BTI 6 November 1936 p. 8; 20 November p. 6	-

Auction date	Venue	Description	Price	Newspaper references	BLARS references
20 November 1936	Bedford, The Red Lion Hotel	Bedford, 162 Bromham Road, detached residence	£900	BTI 6 November 1936 p. 8; 20 November p. 6	-
20 November 1936	Bedford, The Red Lion Hotel	Kempston, Bunyan Road, building site, 1.5a	£190	BTI 6 November 1936 p. 8; 20 November p. 6	-
20 November 1936	Bedford, The Red Lion Hotel	Wootton, 1 Potters Cross, detached cottage, building plot	£120	BTI 6 November 1936 p. 8. Rental £11 pa	-
20 November 1936	Bedford, The Red Lion Hotel	Wootton, 11 Potters Cross, cottage	£200	BTI 6 November 1936 p. 8. Rental £13 pa	-
20 November 1936	Bedford, The Red Lion Hotel	Wootton, 28 Potters Cross, semi-detached cottage	Unsold	BTI 6 November 1936 p. 8. Rental £13 pa	-
20 November 1936	Bedford, The Red Lion Hotel	Wootton, 30 Potters Cross, semi-detached cottage	Unsold	BTI 6 November 1936 p. 8	-
20 November 1936	Bedford, The Red Lion Hotel	Wootton, 6 and 8 Keeley Lane, two cottages	£60	BTI 6 November 1936 p. 8. Rental £14 6s pa	-
20 November 1936	Bedford, The Red Lion Hotel	Wootton, 29 and 31 Keeley Lane, two cottages	£45	BTI 6 November 1936 p. 8. Rental £13 pa	-
2 April 1937	Bedford, The Lion Hotel	Clapham, The Lodge Estate, gentleman's residence together with a paddock of 1a 1r 11p and two pastures of 4a 0r 26p and 3a 2r 19p	£3,000	BTI 26 February 1937 p. 8; 12, 19 March p. 6	PK 1/4/122. By the executors of Kezia Cole. Paddock and pastures occupied by Walter Prentice
2 April 1937	Bedford, The Lion Hotel	Bedford, 63 Bromham Road, central premises	Unsold	BTI 26 February 1937 p. 8; 19 March p. 6. Rental £65 pa	PK 2/5/1/17
2 April 1937	Bedford, The Lion Hotel	Bedford, 18 Allhallows Lane, valuable premises	Unsold	BTI 26 February 1937 p. 8; 19 March p. 6. Vacant possession	PK 2/5/1/17
2 April 1937	Bedford, The Lion Hotel	Bedford, 29 and 31 Westbourne Road	£535	BI 12 March 1937 p. 6; 19 March p. 6. Rental £41 3s 4d pa	PK 2/5/1/17

Auction date	Venue	Description	Price	Newspaper references	BLARS references
2 April 1937	Bedford, The Lion Hotel	Kempston, Berachah, Ridge Road, modern villa	Unsold	BTI 26 February 1937 p. 8; 19 March p. 6	PK 2/5/1/17
2 April 1937	Bedford, The Lion Hotel	Kempston, Ridge Road, pair of villas	Unsold	BTI 26 February 1937 p. 8; 19 March p. 6	-
2 April 1937	Bedford, The Lion Hotel	Kempston, Wood End Lane, pair of modern villas	Unsold	BTI 19 March 1937 p. 6. Rental £78 pa	PK 2/5/1/17
2 April 1937	Bedford, The Lion Hotel	Kempston, High Street, three occupied cottages, four condemned cottages	Unsold	BTI 26 February 1937 p. 8; 19 March p. 6. Rental £21 12s pa	-
2 April 1937	Bedford, The Lion Hotel	Kempston, St John's Street, six condemned cottages	£200	BTI 26 February 1937 p. 8; 19 March p. 6	-
2 April 1937	Bedford, The Lion Hotel	Renhold, Highfield, Salph End, modern detached house	£525	BTI 26 February 1937 p. 8; 19 March p. 6. Vacant possession	PK 2/5/1/17
30 April 1937	On site	Kempston, Crossland Fosse, Box End, residential estate, two lodges, stabling, gardens, pasture land, 28a	Unsold	TDA 24 April 1937 p. 24. BTI 5 March 1937 p. 6; 2, 16 April p. 8. Suitable for a building estate	-
30 April 1937	Bedford, The Lion Hotel	Bedford, 50 and 52 Chaucer Road, commodious residences	- Number 52 withdrawn from auction	BTI 9, 16 April 1937 p. 8; 30 April p. 6. Vacant possession	-
8 June 1937	On site	Souldrop, Cross Weir Farm, Bedford to Kettering Road, freehold property, 31a	- Joint auction with Thake & Paginton	BTI 21, 28 May 1937 p. 8; 4 June p. 8. The estate of Mr Brookes	PK un-catalogued. Live and dead farming stock sold following sale of property. Vacant possession

Auction date	Venue	Description	Price	Newspaper references	BLARS references
18 June 1937	Biggleswade, The Swan Hotel	Biggleswade, 27–31 Shortmead Street, business premises, two cottages, 1a 2r 9p	£1,500 Sold after auction	BTI 11 June 1937 p. 8	-
18 June 1937	Biggleswade, The Swan Hotel	Biggleswade, 105 London Road, detached dwelling house	£665 Sold after auction	BTI 11 June 1937 p. 8	-
18 June 1937	Biggleswade, The Swan Hotel	Biggleswade, 73–79 Potton Road, four cottages	£330 Sold after auction	BTI 11 June 1937 p. 8. Total rental £32 pa	-
18 June 1937	Biggleswade, The Swan Hotel	Steeple Morden, (Cambs), Cheyney Street, four cottages	£155	BTI 11 June 1937 p. 8. Total rental £25	-
15 July 1937	St. Neots, The Cross Keys Hotel	Little Gransden, (Cambs), The Lodge Farm, farmhouse, buildings, including woodland, 445a	Unsold	BTI 18, 25 June 1937 p. 8; 2 July p. 8	PK un-catalogued
17 July 1937	Bedford, The Red Lion Hotel	Wilden, South End Farm, 10a	-	-	PK 1/4/121
16 September 1937	On site	Westoning, Hill Crest Farm, Sampshill Road, two accommodation fields, 10a 2r 8p	-	BTI 10 September 1937 p. 8. On instruction of Mr W. H. Fisher. Vacant possession	PK un-catalogued. Suitable for building development
8 October 1937	Bedford, The Red Lion Hotel	Bedford, 28 Winifred Road, house	£650	BTI 17 September 1937 p. 8. On instruction of executor of George Thomas Smith. Vacant possession	-

Auction date	Venue	Description	Price	Newspaper references	BLARS references
8 October 1937	Bedford, The Red Lion Hotel	Bedford, 45 Althorpe Street, house	£260	BTI 17 September 1937 p. 8; 1 October p. 8. On instruction of executor of George Thomas Smith. Rental £12 3s pa	-
8 October 1937	Bedford, The Red Lion Hotel	Bedford, 42 Prebend Street, shop, dwelling	£525	BTI 17 September 1937 p. 8; 1 October p. 8. On instruction of executor of George Thomas Smith. Rental £42 pa	-
8 October 1937	Bedford, The Red Lion Hotel	Bedford, 44 Prebend Street, house	£405	BTI 17 September 1937 p. 8; 1 October p. 8. On instruction of executor of George Thomas Smith. Rental £32 10s pa	-
8 October 1937	Bedford, The Red Lion Hotel	Bedford, 17 Spenser Road, house	£350	BTI 17 September 1937 p. 8; 1 October p. 8. On instruction of executor of George Thomas Smith. Rental £32 pa	-
8 October 1937	Bedford, The Red Lion Hotel	Bedford, 20 Chaucer Road, detached residence	£600	BTI 17 September 1937 p. 8. On instruction of executor of George Thomas Smith. Rental £52 pa	-
8 October 1937	Bedford, The Red Lion Hotel	Bedford, 40 Chaucer Road, semi-detached residence	£500	BTI 17 September 1937 p. 8. On instruction of executor of George Thomas Smith. Vacant possession	-
20 October 1937	Wilden, The Chequers Inn	Wilden, Chequers Hill, three cottages, accommodation land, 3a	£230	BTI 1, 8 October 1937 p. 8. Re. estate of Samuel White. Rental £21 15s pa	-
20 October 1937	Wilden, The Chequers Inn	Wilden, East End, detached cottage	£210	BTI 1, 8 October 1937 p. 8. Re. estate of Samuel White. Rental £31 pa	-

Auction date	Venue	Description	Price	Newspaper references	BLARS references
20 October 1937	Wilden, The Chequers Inn	Wilden, near Post Office, detached cottage	£50	BTI 1, 8 October 1937 p. 8. Re. estate of Samuel White. On a pre-war rental	-
12 November 1937	Bedford, The Lion Hotel	Bedford, 61 York Street, villa	£550	BTI 22, 29 October 1937 p. 8	-
12 November 1937	Bedford, The Lion Hotel	Bedford, 90 Denmark Street, well-built residence	Withdrawn from auction	BTI 22 October 1937 p. 8	-
12 November 1937	Bedford, The Lion Hotel	Bedford, 44 Bower Street, dwelling house with workshops	£450	BTI 22, 29 October 1937 p. 8	-
12 November 1937	Bedford, The Lion Hotel	Clapham, Freshfield, Milton Hill, superior residence	£500	BTI 22, 29 October 1937 p. 8	-
12 November 1937	Bedford, The Lion Hotel	Kempston, 26–30 Water Lane, Bell End, five cottages	£140	BTI 22, 29 October 1937 p. 8. Total rental £25 8s pa	-
10 December 1937	Bedford, The Lion Hotel	Bedford, Leverington, 88 Kimbolton Road	Unsold	BTI 19, 26 November 1937 p. 8. Of interest to builders and speculators	-
10 December 1937	Bedford, The Lion Hotel	Bedford, 61 Waterloo Road, detached corner residence	Unsold	BTI 19, 26 November 1937 p. 8	-
10 December 1937	Bedford, The Lion Hotel	Bedford, 8 Bushmead Avenue, residence	Unsold	BTI 19, 26 November 1937 p. 8	-
10 December 1937	Bedford, The Lion Hotel	Bedford, 23 Spenser Road, villa	Unsold	BTI 19, 26 November 1937 p. 8	-
10 December 1937	Bedford, The Lion Hotel	Bedford, 90 Denmark Street	Unsold	BTI 19, 26 November 1937 p. 8	-

Auction date	Venue	Description	Price	Newspaper references	BLARS references
10 December 1937	Bedford, The Lion Hotel	Sharnbrook, Park Lane, three stone and thatch cottages	Unsold	BTI 19, 26 November 1937 p. 8	-
16 March 1938	Cranfield, The Swan Inn	Cranfield, 2–8 Church Walk	£150	BTI 25 February 1938 p. 8; 4, 11 March p. 8. Number 2 vacant possession. 4–6 total rental £23 8s pa	-
25 March 1938	Bedford, The Red Lion Hotel	Bedford, 1–8 Balsall Street West, eight cottages	£1,225	BTI 4 March 1938 p. 8	PK un-catalogued. Numbers 1–4, total rental £63 14s pa. 5–8 total rental £83 4s pa
25 March 1938	Bedford, The Red Lion Hotel	Bedford, 67 and 69 Fenlake Road, two modern shops, living accommodation	£1,410	BTI 4 March 1938 p. 8	PK un-catalogued. The whole of the property number 67 and shop portion of number 69, together with use of domestic offices, occupied by Mrs Summerfield. Rental £91 pa
25 March 1938	Bedford, The Red Lion Hotel	Bedford, 104 Fenlake Road, house, large building, building site	£710	BTI 4 March 1938 p. 8	PK un-catalogued. House occupied by Mr W. C. Jones. Rental 10s per week
25 March 1938	Bedford, The Red Lion Hotel	Bedford, 1 Cardington Road, residence, extensive outbuildings	Unsold	BTI 18 February 1938 p. 8; 4 March p. 8	PK un-catalogued. Ideal for business premises. Vacant possession
25 March 1938	Bedford, The Red Lion Hotel	Bedford, 21 Ashburnham Road, detached residence	Unsold	BTI 18 February 1938 p. 8	PK un-catalogued. Vacant possession
25 March 1938	Bedford, The Red Lion Hotel	Bedford, 81 Castle Road, detached villa	Unsold	BTI 11 March 1938 p. 8	PK un-catalogued. Vacant possession
25 March 1938	Bedford, The Red Lion Hotel	Bedford, 48 The Grove, central villa residence	Unsold	BTI 18 March 1938 p. 8	PK un-catalogued. Vacant possession
25 March 1938	Bedford, The Red Lion Hotel	Kempston, Church Walk, plot of land, 1a 6p and Water Lane, 20p	£150	BTI 18 March 1938 p. 8	PK un-catalogued. Vacant possession

Auction date	Venue	Description	Price	Newspaper references	BLARS references
6 April 1938	Baldock, The Rose and Crown Hotel	Baldock, (Herts), 2 Jackson Street, house, building plot	£250	-	-
12 April 1938	On site	Houghton Regis, The Limes, Cumberland Street, house	£420	BTI 25 March 1938 p. 8; 8 April p. 6	PK un-catalogued. On instruction of representatives of W. Single. Vacant possession
12 April 1938	On site	Houghton Regis, frontages to Cumberland Street, Queen Street and Marmsey, building site for three houses, 10,500 ft	£130	BTI 25 March 1938 p. 8; 8 April p. 6.	PK un-catalogued. At present cultivated as a garden with fruit trees and bushes
27 April 1938	On site	Bromham, Village Green, pair of cottages	£230	BTI 25 March 1938 p. 8; 5 April p. 8. On instruction of Bromham Church Charity. Occupied by Mr Purser. Rental £5 pa	-
29 April 1938	Sandy, The Conservative Hall	Moggerhanger, Sandy to Bedford Road, freehold garden land, 7a 2r 20p	£330	BTI 8 April 1938 p. 6. On instruction of representative of W. Single	PK un-catalogued. Occupied by Mr H. Breed. Rental £22 10s pa
29 April 1938	Sandy, The Conservative Hall	Caldecote, Vinegar Hill, garden land, 4a 2r 20p	£140	BTI 8 April 1938 p. 6. On instruction of representative of W. Single	PK un-catalogued. Vacant possession on completion
29 April 1938	Sandy, The Conservative Hall	Caldecote, Two Bush, garden land, 13a	£250	BTI 8 April 1938 p. 6. On instruction of representative of W. Single	PK un-catalogued. 7a occupied by Mr G. H. Dent. Rental £14 pa
29 April 1938	Sandy, The Conservative Hall	Caldecote, Wilmer Hill, garden land, 5a	£80	BTI 8 April 1938 p. 6. On instruction of representative of W. Single	PK un-catalogued. Occupied by Mr H. Breed. Rental £15 pa

Auction date	Venue	Description	Price	Newspaper references	BLARS references
29 April 1938	Sandy, The Conservative Hall	Upper Caldecote, Windy Gap, 82 Hitchin Road, freehold villa	£450	BTI 8 April 1938 p. 6; 15 April p. 8	PK un-catalogued. On instruction of executors of C. S. Knowles. Vacant possession
3 May 1938	Cranfield, The Leathern Bottle	Cranfield, 19–25 Broad Green, three cottages and bungalow	Unsold	BTI 22 April 1938 p. 8	PK 2/5/2/8. Number 19 occupied by W. Bennett. Rental £8 pa. 21 occupied by Mrs Gerrard. Rental £5 10s pa. 23 vacant possession. 25 occupied by George Richardson. Rental £6 pa
3 May 1938	Cranfield, The Leathern Bottle	Cranfield, frontage to Broad Green, allotment land, 3r	-	-	PK 2/5/2/8. Occupied by Mr Edward Billington. Rental £1 8s pa
31 May 1938	On site	Thurleigh, Robin's Folly, smallholding, arable, old pasture, 6.467a	£185	BTI 6 May 1938 p. 8; 13 May p. 6. Occupied by Mr Parker. Rental £15 pa	-
31 May 1938	On site	Thurleigh, Keysoe Road, thatched bungalow, barn	£30	BTI 6 May 1938 p. 8; 13 May p. 6. Occupied by Mr S. Gammans. Rental £5 3s pa	-
31 May 1938	On site	Riseley, Yew Tree Cottage, High Street	£350	BTI 6 May 1938 p. 8; 13 May p. 6. Occupied by Mr Wise. Rental £15 pa	-
17 June 1938	Bedford, The Red Lion Hotel	Bedford, 76 Dudley Street, decontrolled villa	£430	BTI 3 June 1938 p. 8	-
17 June 1938	Bedford, The Red Lion Hotel	Bedford, 23 College Road, freehold villa	£350	BTI 27 May 1938 p. 6; 3 June p. 8. Vacant possession	PK un-catalogued
17 June 1938	Bedford, The Red Lion Hotel	Bedford, 33 Spenser Road, semi-detached villa	£400	BTI 3 June 1938 p. 8	PK un-catalogued. Vacant possession
17 June 1938	Bedford, The Red Lion Hotel	Bedford, 66 Bromham Road	-	BTI 6 May 1938 p. 8	

Auction date	Venue	Description	Price	Newspaper references	BLARS references
17 June 1938	Bedford, The Red Lion Hotel	Bedford, 68 Bromham Road	-	BTI 6 May 1938 p. 8	
17 June 1938	Bedford, The Red Lion Hotel	Bedford, 24 De Parys Avenue, residence	Unsold	BTI 6 May 1938 p. 8; 13 May p. 6; 3 June p. 8	PK un-catalogued. Rental £70 pa
17 June 1938	Bedford, The Red Lion Hotel	Bedford, 26 De Parys Avenue, residence	Unsold	BTI 6 May 1938 p. 8; 13 May p. 6; 3 June p. 8	PK un-catalogued. Vacant possession
17 June 1938	Bedford, The Red Lion Hotel	Bedford, 28 De Parys Avenue, residence	£545	BTI 6 May 1938 p. 8; 13 May p. 6; 3 June p. 8	PK un-catalogued. Vacant possession
17 June 1938	Bedford, The Red Lion Hotel	Bedford, 30 De Parys Avenue, residence	Unsold	BTI 6 May 1938 p. 8; 13 May p. 6; 3 June p. 8	PK un-catalogued. Rental £80 pa
17 June 1938	Bedford, The Red Lion Hotel	Bedford, 43 Warwick Avenue, semi-detached residence	Unsold	BTI 6 May 1938 p. 8; 13 May p. 6; 3 June p. 8	PK un-catalogued. Rental £55 pa
17 June 1938	Bedford, The Red Lion Hotel	Bedford, 45 Warwick Avenue, semi-detached residence	Unsold	BTI 6 May 1938 p. 8; 13 May p. 6; 3 June p. 8	PK un-catalogued. Rental £52 pa
17 June 1938	Bedford, The Red Lion Hotel	Bedford, 47 Warwick Avenue, semi-detached residence	Unsold	BTI 6 May 1938 p. 8; 13 May p. 6; 3 June p. 8	PK un-catalogued. Rental £55 pa
17 June 1938	Bedford, The Red Lion Hotel	Bedford, 77 Hartington Street, villa	£370	BTI 20 May 1938 p. 8; 3 June p. 8	PK un-catalogued. Occupied by Mr J. J. Allen. Rental £24 pa
17 June 1938	Bedford, The Red Lion Hotel	Bedford, 79 Hartington Street, villa	£380	BTI 20 May 1938 p. 8; 3 June p. 8	PK un-catalogued. Occupied by Mr E. Green. Rental £24 pa
17 June 1938	Bedford, The Red Lion Hotel	Bedford, 104 Hartington Street, villa	£355	BTI 20 May 1938 p. 8; 3 June p. 8	PK un-catalogued. Occupied by Mr A. H. Lovell. Rental £25 8s pa
17 June 1938	Bedford, The Red Lion Hotel	Bedford, 21 Park Road West, villa	£315	BTI 20 May 1938 p. 8; 3 June p. 8	PK un-catalogued. Occupied by Mr W. W. Whittemore. Rental £24 pa

Auction date	Venue	Description	Price	Newspaper references	BLARS references
17 June 1938	Bedford, The Red Lion Hotel	Bedford, 169 Bower Street, villa	£410	BTI 20 May 1938 p. 8; 3 June p. 8	PK un-catalogued. Occupied by Mrs Statham. Rental £24 16s pa
1 July 1938	On site	Great Barford, Greenfields Dairy Farm, Green End, set of model buildings, 11.915a	Unsold	BTI 10, 17, 24 June 1938 p. 8; 8 July p. 8	PK 2/5/2/1. Vacant possession
1 July 1938	On site	Great Barford, Birchfields Road, Green End, arable field, 6a 10p	Unsold	BTI 10, 17, 24 June 1938 p. 8	PK 2/5/2/1
26 July 1938	On site	Sharnbrook, 2 and 4 Church Way, formerly two cottages	£225	BTI 8, 22 July 1938 p. 8	-
26 July 1938	On site	Sharnbrook, Park Lane, three old-world cottages	£58	BTI 8, 22 July 1938 p. 8	-
29 July 1938	Sandy, The Red Lion Hotel	Sandy, The Laburnhams, 20 Laburnham Road, house, gardeners' buildings, garden ground, 3r 32p	£515	BTI 18, 22 July 1938 p. 8	PK un-catalogued. Now occupied by Mr George Thomas Stockford. Vacant possession on completion
2 September 1938	Bedford, The Lion Hotel	Bedford, 2 Little Butts Street, cottage	£205	BTI 12, 19 August 1938 p. 6	-
2 September 1938	Bedford, The Lion Hotel	Bedford, 39 Wellington Street, villa	£286	-	-
2 September 1938	Bedford, The Lion Hotel	Bedford, 9 Clarendon Street, detached villa	£610	BTI 12, 19 August 1938 p. 6	-
2 September 1938	Bedford, The Lion Hotel	Bedford, 27 and 29 Gwyn Street, central freehold premises	£750	BTI 12, 19 August 1938 p. 6	-
2 September 1938	Bedford, The Lion Hotel	Kempston, 42 Spring Road, Kempston, detached residence	£700	BTI 12, 19 August 1938 p. 6	-

Auction date	Venue	Description	Price	Newspaper references	BLARS references
2 September 1938	Bedford, The Lion Hotel	Renhold, frontage to road leading to Ravensden church, well-wooded plantation, 5.5 a	Unsold	BTI 19 August 1938 p. 6	-
2 September 1938	Bedford, The Lion Hotel	Colmworth, Roothams Green Farm, homestead, buildings orchard, two pasture paddocks	Unsold	BTI 19 August 1938 p. 6	-
20 September 1938	On site	Riseley, detached cottage	Unsold	BTI 26 August 1938 p. 6; 9 September p. 6. On instruction of Mrs Wyatt	-
20 September 1938	On site	Riseley, two cottages	£165	BTI 26 August 1938 p. 6; 9 September p. 6. On instruction of Mrs Wyatt. Total rental £9 10s	-
20 September 1938	On site	Riseley, two timber and corrugated garages, 1a	-	BTI 26 August 1938 p. 6; 9 September p. 6. On instruction of Mrs Wyatt	-
20 September 1938	On site	Keysoe, windmill, farmhouse, homestead, smallholding around mill of 17a 3r 27p	Unsold	BTI 2, 9 September 1938 p. 6. Vacant possession	PK 1/4/124. Stated to be only working corn mill in the county
27 September 1938	London, Berkeley Square	Shefford, Digswell House, gentleman's residence, twelve bedrooms, two cottages, 12a	- Joint auction with John D. Wood & Co.	TDA 28 June 1938 p. 28. BTI 23 September 1938 p. 8	-
25 October 1938	On site	Goldington, 6 Grange Road, modern residence	£640	BTI 7 October 1938 p. 8; 14, 21 October p. 6. Vacant possession. Household furnishings sold following sale of property	-

Auction date	Venue	Description	Price	Newspaper references	BLARS references
27 January 1939	Bedford, The Lion Hotel	Bedford, 3–7 Maitland Street, three villas	£635	BTI 6 January 1939 p. 6; 13 January p. 8. Total rental £63 1s pa	-
27 January 1939	Bedford, The Lion Hotel	Bedford 50 and 52 Greyfriars Walk, two cottages	Unsold	BTI 6 January 1939 p. 6; 13 January p. 8. Total rental £23 8s 4d pa	-
27 January 1939	Bedford, The Lion Hotel	Bedford, 186 London Road, modern semi-detached house	Unsold	BTI 13 January 1939 p. 8	-
27 January 1939	Bedford, The Lion Hotel	Bedford, 2 Canning Street, central shop, living accommodation	Unsold	BTI 30 December 1938 p. 6; 13 January 1939 p. 8	-
27 January 1939	Bedford, The Lion Hotel	Bedford, 4 Canning Street, cottage	Unsold	BTI 30 December 1938 p. 6; 13 January 1939 p. 8	-
27 January 1939	Bedford, The Lion Hotel	Bedford, 73 Hassett Street, decontrolled cottage	£400	BTI 6 January 1939 p. 6; 13 January p. 8	-
27 January 1939	Bedford, The Lion Hotel	Bedford, 39 Warwick Avenue, detached residence	£400	BTI 30 December 1938 p. 6; 12 January 1939 p. 8. Vacant possession	-
27 January 1939	Bedford, The Lion Hotel	Clapham, 69 High Street, lock-up shop	£350	BTI 30 December 1938 p. 6; 13 January 1939 p. 8. Total rental £30 pa	-
22 March 1939	Potton, The Rose and Crown Hotel	Potton, west of Common Road, garden land, 4a 3r and east of Common Road, opposite Boston Lane, garden land, 5a 1r 39p	£360	BTI 17 March 1939 p. 8. On instruction of Messrs J. W. and S. Lenton	-

Auction date	**Venue**	**Description**	**Price**	**Newspaper references**	**BLARS references**
28 March 1939	On site	Wilstead, Elephant and Castle, Bedford to Luton Road, freehold beer-house and block of three cottages	£975	BTI 10, 17 March 1939 p. 8	PK un-catalogued. Cottages situated on east side of The Elephant and Castle. Cottages occupied by Mrs Ellen Summerfield, Miss Elizabeth Ingersoll and Mrs Whiteman. Water laid on but no electric light, three earth closets
13 April 1939	On site	Gamlingay (Cambs), The Eaves, freehold house and building	£425	BTI 24 March 1939 p. 8; 7 April p. 6. Vacant possession	-
5 May 1939	Bedford, The Lion Hotel	Bedford, 20 Dudley Street, decontrolled villa	£380	BTI 14 April 1939 p. 6; 21 April p. 8; 5 May p. 3	-
5 May 1939	Bedford, The Lion Hotel	Bedford, 44 Mabel Road, decontrolled cottage	£300	BTI 14 April 1939 p. 6; 21 April p. 8; 5 May p. 3	-
5 May 1939	Bedford, The Lion Hotel	Bedford, 16 Gwyn Street	Unsold	BTI 17 March 1939 p. 8; 14 April p. 6; 21 April p. 8; 5 May p. 8	-
5 May 1939	Bedford, The Lion Hotel	Bedford, 19 Hassett Street	Unsold	BTI 17 March 1939 p. 8; 14 April p. 6; 21 April p. 8; 5 May p. 8	-
5 May 1939	Bedford, The Lion Hotel	Bedford, 27 Clarendon Street	£550	BTI 21 April 1939 p. 8; 5 May p. 8	-
5 May 1939	Bedford, The Lion Hotel	Ravensden, frontage to main road, plot of land	Unsold	BTI 21 April 1939 p. 8; 5 May p. 8	-
5 May 1939	Bedford, The Lion Hotel	Bedford, 30 Spenser Road	Unsold	BTI 10, 17 March 1939 p. 8; 14 April p. 6; 21 April p. 8; 5 May p. 8. Rental £52 pa	-
5 May 1939	Bedford, The Lion Hotel	Bedford, 25 Garfield Street	-	BTI 10 March 1939 p. 8	-

Auction date	Venue	Description	Price	Newspaper references	BLARS references
5 May 1939	Bedford, The Lion Hotel	Bedford, 11 Offa Road	£225	BTI 14 April 1939 p. 8; 21 April p. 8; 5 May p. 8. Rental £20 2s pa	-
9 May 1939	Harrold, Harrold Institute	Harrold, freehold double-fronted shop, warehouse store room, old cottage	Unsold	BTI 21 April 1939 p. 8; 5 May p. 8. On instruction of executors of Mrs M. L. Rumsey	PK 1/4/126
19 May 1939	Bedford, The Lion Hotel	Bedford, 46 and 48 Midland Road, business premises, double-fronted shop	£950	BTI 28 April 1939 p. 8; 5 May p. 8. In occupation for many years by Mr Carter. Vacant possession	-
19 May 1939	Bedford, The Lion Hotel	Wilstead, Mayfield, Dane Lane, bungalow, 1a	-	BTI 28 April 1939 p. 8; 5 May p. 8	-
21 June 1939	Biggleswade, The Swan Hotel	Biggleswade, 12 Stratton Street, freehold shop, outbuildings, yard	£740	BTI 16 June 1939 p. 8	PK un-catalogued. On instruction of executors of W. S. Savage. Vacant possession
4 July 1939	On site	Stotfold, Croftways, 103 Church Lane, bungalow	-	BTI 16, 23 June 1939 p. 8. Occupied by Mr T. H. Carpenter. Rental £36 8s pa	-
4 July 1939	On site	Harrold, High Street, stone and tile residence	Unsold	BTI 16, 23 June 1939 p. 8	PK un-catalogued. On instruction of executors of Miss A. M. Underwood. Vacant possession
5 July 1939	Biggleswade, The Swan Hotel	Biggleswade, frontage to Chapel Fields, freehold accommodation land, 32p	£155	-	-
28 July 1939	Shefford, The White Hart	Clifton, fronting main road and Pedley Lane: plot of garden land, 1a 2r 38p; plot of land, 1a 3r 34p; garden land, 6a 3r 12p	-	BTI 7, 14 July 1939 p. 8	PK 1/4/127. On instruction of estate of Mrs L. A. Simms. All occupied by Mr P. Cooper

Auction date	Venue	Description	Price	Newspaper references	BLARS references
28 July 1939	Shefford, The White Hart	Shefford, 2 Victoria Road, house and Clophill, garden land, 9.5a	£1,525	BTI 7, 14 July 1939 p. 8	PK un-catalogued. On instruction of executors of Mr James Bone. House occupied by Mr O. Turner. Rental £20 16s pa. Garden land occupied by Mr A. J. Bone. Rental £24 pa
21 September 1939	On site	Bedford, 183 Hurst Grove, modern residence	£875	BTI 8 September 1939 p. 6; 15 September p. 6. On instruction of executors of Mrs A. Townsend. Vacant possession. Household furniture sold following sale of property.	PK 2/3/1/6
22 September 1939	Bedford, The Lion Hotel	Bedford, 25 Garfield Street, villa	£405	BTI 18 August 1939 p. 8; 1, 8 September p. 6. Rental £29 pa	-
22 September 1939	Bedford, The Lion Hotel	Kempston, 186 Bedford Road, shop, accommodation	Unsold	BTI 18 August 1939 p. 8. Vacant possession	-
22 September 1939	Bedford, The Lion Hotel	Kempston, Woodcote, Wood End, detached bungalow	Unsold	BTI 1, 8 September 1939 p. 6. Vacant possession	-
22 September 1939	Bedford, The Lion Hotel	Kempston, 71–75 High Street, three cottages	£270	BTI 18 August 1939 p. 8; 1, 8 September p. 6. Vacant possession	-
28 November 1939	On site	Bedford, 154 Bromham Road, freehold semi-detached residence	Unsold	BTI 10, 17 November 1939 p. 6. Household furniture sold following sale of property	PK 2/3/1/10. On instruction of the trustees of Mr William Clarke. Vacant possession

Auction date	Venue	Description	Price	Newspaper references	BLARS references
12 March 1940	Wootton, The Cock Inn	Wootton, 100 Bedford Road, cottage, accommodation paddock, 3r 16p, also three accommodation pastures at Cause End adjoining cemetery	£325	BTS 1 March 1940 p. 6. On instruction of executrix of S. J. Farrer	PK un-catalogued. All vacant possession
27 March 1940	Sandy, The Red Lion Hotel	Beeston, Oak Tree Field, roadway from Beeston Green, garden land, 6a 3r 29p	£720	BTS 8, 15, 22 March 1927 p. 8. By order of Mrs E. Crawley. Vacant possession	PK un-catalogued. Approached by a roadway through Mr Claude Banes' homestead
27 March 1940	Sandy, The Red Lion Hotel	Beeston, Gravel Pit Field, situated off Beeston Green, timber and tile cart hovel and stable, 9a 1r 35p	£500	BTS 8, 15, 22 March 1927 p. 8. By order of Mrs E. Crawley. Vacant possession	PK un-catalogued
27 March 1940	Sandy, The Red Lion Hotel	Sandy, New Road, near Gas Works, accommodation pasture, 8a 1r 29p	£170	BTS 8, 15, 22 March 1927 p. 8. By order of Mrs E. Crawley. Vacant possession	PK un-catalogued
27 March 1940	Sandy, The Red Lion Hotel	Blunham, Blunham Fields, off Great North Road, adjoining railway bridge through Pope's Farm, feeding pasture, 16a 4p	£400	BTS 8, 15, 22 March 1940 p. 8. Vacant possession	PK un-catalogued
19 April 1940	Bedford, The Red Lion	Bedford, 122 Ampthill Road, corner residence	£455	BTS 29 March 1940 p. 6; 5 April p. 8; 12 April p. 6. Rental £39 pa	PK 1/4/129
19 April 1940	Bedford, The Red Lion	Bedford, 34 Wellington Street, shop, dwelling	£320	BTS 5 April 1940 p. 8; 12 April p. 6	PK 1/4/129. Vacant possession

Auction date	Venue	Description	Price	Newspaper references	BLARS references
19 April 1940	Bedford, The Red Lion	Bedford, 73 Priory Street, detached double-fronted house	£320	BTS 29 March 1940 p. 6; 5 April p. 8; 12 April p. 6. Rental £60 9s pa	PK 1/4/129
19 April 1940	Bedford, The Red Lion	Bedford, 4 Roise Street, house	£290	BTS 29 March 1940 p. 6; 5 April p. 8; 12 April p. 6. Rental £28 12s pa	PK 1/4/129
19 April 1940	Bedford, The Red Lion	Bedford, 6 Roise Street, double-fronted house	£350	BTS 29 March 1940 p. 6; 5 April p. 8; 12 April p. 6. Rental £39 pa	PK 1/4/129
24 May 1940	Bedford, The Red Lion	Bedford, 4 Cross Street, villa	£250	BTS 26 April 1940 p. 6; 3, 10 May p. 6. By order of public trustee, estate of Mrs A. E. Kinsey. Rental £18 13s 6d pa	PK 1/4/130
24 May 1940	Bedford, The Red Lion	Bedford, 5 Cross Street, villa	£250	BTS 26 April 1940 p. 6; 3, 10 May p. 6. By order of public trustee, estate of Mrs A. E. Kinsey. Rental £21 17s pa	PK 1/4/130
24 May 1940	Bedford, The Red Lion	Bedford, 6 Cross Street, villa	£310	BTS 26 April 1940 p. 6; 3, 10 May p. 6. By order of public trustee, estate of Mrs A. E. Kinsey. Rental £21 17s pa	PK 1/4/130
24 May 1940	Bedford, The Red Lion	Bedford, 10 Rothsay Gardens, detached double-fronted residence	£1,000	BTS 26 April 1940 p. 6; 3, 10 May p. 6. By order of public trustee, estate of Mrs A. E. Kinsey. Vacant possession	PK 1/4/130
30 September 1940	-	Carlton, Monk Road, plot of land with building for pigstyes	-	BTS 27 September 1940 p. 6. Regarding J. D. Brown, deceased	-

Auction date	Venue	Description	Price	Newspaper references	BLARS references
4 October 1940	Bedford, The Red Lion	Bedford, 80 Gladstone Street, villa	£325	BTS 13 September 1940 p. 6; 20, 27 September p. 4	-
4 October 1940	Bedford, The Red Lion	Bedford, 82 Gladstone Street, villa	£355	BTS 13 September 1940 p. 6; 20, 27 September p. 4	-
4 October 1940	Bedford, The Red Lion	Bedford, 46–50 Beaconsfield Street, three cottages	Unsold	BTS 13 September 1940 p. 6; 20, 27 September p. 4	-
4 October 1940	Bedford, The Red Lion	Clapham, 22 and 24 The Warren, two cottages	Unsold	BTS 13 September 1940 p. 6; 20, 27 September p. 4. Occupied by Messrs Lumbis and Shelton	-
21 January 1941	-	Sherington (Bucks), Pearcey Cottage, opposite the Village Green, freehold property, garden plot	-	BTS 3 January 1941 p. 6. Household furniture sold following sale of property. Vacant possession	PK un-catalogued
30 January 1941	On site	Ashwell (Herts), Prospect House, Road to Guilden Morden, Georgian-type house, miniature estate, 6a	£1,800	BTS 10 January 1941 p. 6. Household furniture sold following sale of property	PK un-catalogued. Re. estate of W. A. Appleton. Immediate possession
19 February 1941	On site	Carlton, High Street, old-world detached cottage	£90	BTS 7, 14 February 1941 p. 6. By order of executors of John James Short. Vacant possession	PK un-catalogued. Earth closet, well of water with pump
19 March 1941	Biggleswade, The Swan Hotel	Arlesey, 164–168 High Street, three cottages	Unsold	BTS 7, 14 March 1941 p. 6. Re. R.G. Webb, deceased. Total rental £31 10s pa	-
19 March 1941	Biggleswade, The Swan Hotel	Biggleswade, 28 and 30 Banks Road, two cottages	£450	BTS 7, 14 March 1941 p. 6. Re. W. B. Aubrey, deceased. Total rental £33 9s 6d pa	-

Auction date	Venue	Description	Price	Newspaper references	BLARS references
19 March 1941	Biggleswade, The Swan Hotel	Biggleswade, 67 and 69 Hitchin Street, two cottages	£400	BTS 7, 14 March 1941 p. 6. Re. W. B. Aubrey, deceased. Total rental £39 pa	-
1 April 1941	Hitchin, The Sun Hotel	Campton, Highlands Farm, farmhouse, farm buildings, two cottages, 171a	£5,700	BTS 14 March 1941 p. 6. On instruction of executors of G. W. Cook. Vacant possession	PK un-catalogued. Cottages occupied by Mr T. C. Stafferton on service tenancy and Mr W. Burr. Rental 7s per week
1 April 1941	Hitchin, The Sun Hotel	Cainhoe, Park Wood, 90a	£400	BTS 14 March 1941 p. 6. On instruction of executors of G. W. Cook	PK un-catalogued. Timber is chiefly young oak, sporting facilities are notable
16 May 1941	Bedford, The Lion Hotel	Bedford, 28 Park Road West	£310	BTS 9 May 1941 p. 4. Rental £27 16s pa	-
16 May 1941	Bedford, The Lion Hotel	Kempston, 37–43 Woburn Road, four cottages	£500	BTS 25 April 1941 p. 4; 2, 9 May p. 4. Total rental £58 10s pa	-
16 May 1941	Bedford, The Lion Hotel	Kempston, 72 Eaton Road	£340	BTS 25 April 1941 p. 4; 2, 9 May p. 4. Rental £48 2s pa	-
17 July 1941	Blunham, The Salutation Inn	Blunham, Grange Road, western side, garden land, 5a 3r 24p	£550	BTS 27 June 1941 p. 6	PK un-catalogued
17 July 1941	Blunham, The Salutation Inn	Blunham, Hills Field, Grange Road, situate off Red House Farm, garden land, 5a 1p	£250	BTS 27 June 1941 p. 6	PK un-catalogued
17 July 1941	Blunham, The Salutation Inn	Blunham, Grange Road, opposite The Orchard, pasture enclosure, 5a 1r 31p	£280	BTS 27 June 1941 p. 6	PK un-catalogued
23 July 1941	On site	Wilden, Hill Farm, farmhouse, buildings, 36a	£1,000	BTS 11 July 1941 p. 4; 18 July p. 6	-

Auction date	Venue	Description	Price	Newspaper references	BLARS references
25 July 1941	Bedford, Lime Street, sale rooms	Kempston, 58 High Street, cottage	Unsold	BTS 27 June 1941 p. 6; 4 July p. 4	PK 2/5/1/18
25 July 1941	Bedford, Lime Street, sale rooms	Bedford, 21 and 23 Western Street, two villas	Unsold	BTS 27 June 1941 p. 6; 4 July p. 4. Total rental £119 pa	PK 2/5/1/18
25 July 1941	Bedford, Lime Street, sale rooms	Cranfield, 4 Mill Lane, modern detached house	Unsold	BTS 4 July 1941 p. 4; 18 July p. 6. Rental £26 pa	PK 2/5/1/18
28 July 1941	Campton, The White Hart	Campton, Church Farm, opposite Campton Church, modern residence, farm buildings, 53a 1r 12p including half of river	£3,800	BTS 18 July 1941 p. 6	PK 1/4/133. By order of Mr Leslie Hawkins. Vacant possession
30 July 1941	Biggleswade, The Swan Hotel	Biggleswade, Great North Road, market garden land, frontage 204ft, 4a	- Joint auction with F. W. Western & Co.	BTS 18 July 1941 p. 6	PK un-catalogued. Occupied by Mr W. F. Cole. Michaelmas tenancy, rental £16 1s pa
30 July 1941	Biggleswade, The Swan Hotel	Biggleswade, Furzenhall Road, market garden land, 2a	£1,725 Joint auction with F. W. Western & Co.	BTS 18 July 1941 p. 6	PK un-catalogued. Occupied by Mrs A. Bryant. Rental £9 10s pa
30 July 1941	Biggleswade, The Swan Hotel	Biggleswade, 1–4 Furzenhall Road, four cottages	£1,600 Joint auction with F. W. Western & Co.	BTS 18 July 1941 p. 6	PK un-catalogued. Occupied by Messrs K. Elliman, J. Woodward, C. Lawrence and Mr V. J. Woodward. Total rental £48 8s 8d pa

Auction date	Venue	Description	Price	Newspaper references	BLARS references
30 July 1941	Biggleswade, The Swan Hotel	Biggleswade, 33, 35 and 35a St John's Street, three cottages	£320 Joint auction with F. W. Western & Co.	BTS 18 July 1941 p. 6	PK un-catalogued. Number 33 occupied by Mr Day. Rental 7s per week. 34 occupied by Mr Kingsbury. Rental 8s per week. 35a occupied as two cottages by Biggleswade Urban District Council or their tenants on terms not yet agreed
30 July 1941	Biggleswade, The Swan Hotel	Broom, 37 – 51 High Street, pair of brick cottages, four brick cottages, detached cottage, dwelling house, farmstead	£900 Joint auction with F. W. Western & Co.	BTS 18 July 1941 p. 6	PK un-catalogued. Number 37 occupied by Biggleswade Rural District Council. Rental 4s per week. 39 occupied by Mr E. Bland. Rental 12s 2d per month. 41 – 47 occupied by Mrs E. Fisher, Mr J. S. Redman, Mrs F. Endersby, Mr G. Faulkner. 49 occupied by Mr F. J. Faulkner. Farmstead occupied by Mr E. A. Cowland. Rental £26 pa
30 July 1941	Biggleswade, The Swan Hotel	Biggleswade, freehold common right	£25 Joint auction with F. W. Western & Co.	BTS 18 July 1941 p. 6	PK uncatalogued. Number 40 in the Book of the Biggleswade Fen Reeves
13 August 1941	Royston, The Bull Hotel	Therfield (Herts), Slate Hall Farm, farmhouse, bungalow, 83a	Unsold	-	-
19 August 1941	On site	Sharnbrook, High Street, house, butcher's shop, accommodation paddock, orchard, 1a 2r	£1,000	BTS 25 July p. 4; 8 August p. 4. By order of executors of T. W. Higgins. Vacant possession	PK 2/3/1/36. Sale of shop to be followed by surplus household furniture and butcher's stock-in-trade

Auction date	Venue	Description	Price	Newspaper references	BLARS references
23 September 1941	Bolnhurst, Brook Farm	Keysoe, windmill, standing on circa 40p of pasture	-	BTS 12 September 1941 p. 6. 'Famous landmark'	PK 1/4/134, PK 2/3/1/38. By order of Mr John Filsell. One of the few remaining working mills in the country
26 September 1941	Sandy, The Red Lion Hotel	Seddington, adjoining 'The Buttery', house, farm, buildings, garden land, 5a	£775	BTS 19 September p. 6. On instruction of representatives of C. J. Underwood. Occupied by S. E and R. Richards and M. Jeeves. Rental £35 5s excluding house	-
26 September 1941	Sandy, The Red Lion Hotel	Beeston, Cockings and Matthews Fields, garden land, 4a	£275	BTS 19 September p. 6. On instruction of representatives of C. J. Underwood. Occupied by Mr Claude Bates. Rental £18 pa	-
26 September 1941	Sandy, The Red Lion Hotel	Northill, Vinegar Hill, eastern side of Sandy to Hitchin Road, garden land, 6.5a	£375	BTS 19 September p. 6. On instruction of representatives of C. J. Underwood. Occupied by Mr W. G. Baldwin. Rental £26 pa	-
17 October 1941	Bedford, Lime Street, sale rooms	Bedford, 119 Fenlake Road, villa	£490	BTS 26 September 1941 p. 6; 10 October p. 6. By order of personal representatives of Sarah Saunderson. Rental £26 pa	-
17 October 1941	Bedford, Lime Street, sale rooms	Bedford, 115 and 117 Fenlake Road, two villas	£350	BTS 26 September 1941 p. 6; 10 October p. 6. By order of personal representatives of Sarah Saunderson. Total rental £28 3s 4d pa	-

Auction date	Venue	Description	Price	Newspaper references	BLARS references
17 October 1941	Bedford, Lime Street, sale rooms	Wilstead, Littleworth, six cottages	£510	BTS 26 September 1941 p. 6; 10 October p. 6. By order of personal representatives of Sarah Saunderson. Total rental £49 17s pa	-
17 October 1941	Bedford, Lime Street, sale rooms	Wilstead, Church Road, detached residence	£250	BTS 10 October 1941 p. 6. By order of personal representatives of Sarah Saunderson. Rental £10 pa	-
17 October 1941	Bedford, Lime Street, sale rooms	Elstow, two building plots	£90	BTS 10 October 1941 p. 6. By order of personal representatives of Sarah Saunderson	-
20 January 1942	Harrold, Harrold Institute	Harrold, Church Lane, stone double-fronted house	£450	BTS 9 January 1942 p. 6	PK 1/4/137. On instruction of the estate of the late Miss A. L. L. Ashwell. Occupied by Mrs Dewick
20 January 1942	Harrold, Harrold Institute	Harrold, Church Lane, dwelling, shop	£575	BTS 9 January 1942 p. 6	PK 1/4/137. On instruction of the estate of the late Miss A. L. L. Ashwell. Vacant possession
20 January 1942	Harrold, Harrold Institute	Harrold, on north side of High Street near the Wheatsheaf Inn, stone and thatch cottage	£100	BTS 9 January 1942 p. 6	PK 1/4/137. On instruction of the estate of the late Miss A. L. L. Ashwell. Occupied by H. Hulatt
20 January 1942	Harrold, Harrold Institute	Harrold, Brook Lane, pair of brick, stone and slate cottages	£300	BTS 9 January 1942 p. 6	PK 1/4/137. On instruction of the estate of the late Miss A. L. L. Ashwell. Occupied by Charles Knight and H. G. Gaton
20 January 1942	Harrold, Harrold Institute	Harrold, Brook Lane, five cottages	£300	BTS 9 January 1942 p. 6	PK 1/4/137. On instruction of the estate of the late Miss A. L. L. Ashwell. Occupied by S. Coleman, J. Fry, Miss M. Odell and Mrs F. Odell

Auction date	Venue	Description	Price	Newspaper references	BLARS references
20 January 1942	Harrold, Harrold Institute	Harrold, Orchard Lane, on eastern side of Wood Lane, four enclosures of pasture	£1,650	BTS 9 January 1942 p. 6	PK 1/4/137. On instruction of the estate of the late Miss A. L. L. Ashwell, Occupied by G. H. Eden
21 January 1942	Baldock, The Victoria Inn	Baldock (Herts), 65 and 67 Bygrave Road, two houses	£720	-	-
21 January 1942	Baldock, The Victoria Inn	Baldock (Herts), 2 Jackson Street, house	£400	-	-
21 January 1942	Baldock, The Victoria Inn	Arlesey, 166–168 High Street, three cottages	£70	-	-
21 January 1942	Sandy, The Red Lion Hotel	Sandy, 22–28 Laburnham Road, four cottages	£1,020	BTS 9 January 1942 p. 6. Vacant possession	-
13 February 1942	Bedford, Lime Street, sale rooms	Sharnbrook, Normans Road, modern detached residence	£1,300	BTS 30 January 1942 p. 4; 6 February p. 6	PK 1/4/138. Water by pump
13 February 1942	Bedford, Lime Street, sale rooms	Bedford, 7 Wellington Street, villa	£345	BTS 30 January 1942 p. 4; 6 February p. 6. Rental £38 6d pa	PK 1/4/138. Occupied by Mrs Hart
13 February 1942	Bedford, Lime Street, sale rooms	Bedford, 76 York Street, villa	£500	BTS 30 January 1942 p. 4; 6 February p. 6. Rental £39 pa	PK 1/4/138. Occupied by William Wright
13 February 1942	Bedford, Lime Street, sale rooms	Bedford, 107 Gladstone Street, villa	£450	BTS 30 January 1942 p. 4; 6 February p. 6. Rental £26 pa	PK 1/4/138. Occupied by Mrs Bridger
13 February 1942	Bedford, Lime Street, sale rooms	Bedford, 154 Hurst Grove	£530	BTS 30 January 1942 p. 4; 6 February p. 6. Rental £44 4s pa	PK 1/4/138. Occupied by Mr Hughes

Auction date	Venue	Description	Price	Newspaper references	BLARS references
13 February 1942	Bedford, Lime Street, sale rooms	Bedford, 16 Cornwall Road, in two flats	£650	BTS 30 January 1942 p. 4; 6 February p. 6. Total rental £85 8s pa	PK 1/4/138
15 May 1942	Bedford, Lime Street, sale rooms	Bedford, Pemberley Cottage, Pemberley Lane	£925	BTS 24 April 1942 p. 4; 1 May p. 6	PK un-catalogued. Vacant possession
15 May 1942	Bedford, Lime Street, sale rooms	Bedford, 47 Hazelwood Road, modern house	£640	BTS 1 May 1942 p. 6	PK un-catalogued. Vacant possession
15 May 1942	Bedford, Lime Street, sale rooms	Bedford, 9 and 11 Canning Street, two cottages	£245	BTS 17, 24 April 1942 p. 4; 1 May p. 6.	PK un-catalogued. Number 11 occupied by Mrs Chapman. Rental £18 4s pa. 9 occupied by Mr T. Bleasdale. Rental £20 16s pa
15 May 1942	Bedford, Lime Street, sale rooms	Bedford, 73 and 75 Fosterhill Road, two houses	£1,050	BTS 17, 24 April 1942 p. 4; 1 May p. 6.	PK un-catalogued. Number 73 occupied by Mr L. R. Alderton. Rental £55 pa. 75 occupied by Mrs M. D. Brooks. Rental £59 pa
15 May 1942	Bedford, Lime Street, sale rooms	Kempston, 74 Bedford Road, shop, house	£835	BTS 17, 24 April 1942 p. 4; 1 May p. 6	PK un-catalogued. Vacant possession
15 May 1942	Bedford, Lime Street, sale rooms	Kempston, Allerton, Wootton Road, modern semi-detached house	Unsold	BTS 24 April 1942 p. 4; 1 May p. 6	PK un-catalogued. Occupied by Mrs F. L. Hartridge. Rental £35 2s pa
15 May 1942	Bedford, Lime Street, sale rooms	Kempston, Fairview, Wootton Road, modern semi-detached house	Unsold	BTS 24 April 1942 p. 4; 1 May p. 6	PK un-catalogued. Occupied by Mr J. Hill. Rental £35 2s pa
15 May 1942	Bedford, Lime Street, sale rooms	Kempston, The Rambles, Wootton Road	Unsold	BTS 24 April 1942 p. 4; 1 May p. 6	PK un-catalogued. Occupied by Mr A. F. Walton. Rental £35 2s pa

Auction date	Venue	Description	Price	Newspaper references	BLARS references
9 June 1942	Sandy, The Red Lion Hotel	Sandy, either side of the New Road near the Gas Works, pasture, 11a	£500	BTS 22, 29 May 1942 p. 4. On instruction of late Mrs Elizabeth Baldrey. Occupied by Mr S. H. Harrison. Rental £26 10s pa	-
9 June 1942	Sandy, The Red Lion Hotel	Northill, near Budna and Northill Road junction, 5a	£300	BTS 22, 29 May 1942 p. 4. Occupied by three tenants. Total rental £14 16s pa	-
9 June 1942	Sandy, The Red Lion Hotel	Northill, near Budna and Northill Road junction, 10a	£1,025	BTS 22, 29 May 1942 p. 4. Occupied by Mr C. Willmott. Rental £33 pa	-
9 June 1942	Sandy, The Red Lion Hotel	Sandy, Blunham Roods, off Tempsford to Blunham Road, 2.5a	Unsold	BTS 29 May 1942 p. 4. By order of representatives of the late Frank Mayle. Occupied by Mr H. G. Crawley. Rental £6 pa	-
19 June 1942	Bedford, Lime Street, sale rooms	Bedford, 7 Roise Street, house, business premises	£500	BTS 5 June 1942 p. 6; 19 June p. 4. Rental £26 pa	-
19 June 1942	Bedford, Lime Street, sale rooms	Bedford, 9–13 Roise Street, three cottages	£510	BTS 5 June 1942 p. 6; 19 June p. 4. Total rental £52 10s pa	-
19 June 1942	Bedford, Lime Street, sale rooms	Bedford, 55 Foster Street	£190	BTS 5 June 1942 p. 6; 19 June p. 4. Rental £19 2s pa	-
26 June 1942	Gamlingay, The Cock Inn	Gamlingay (Cambs), Mill Street, freehold brick and slate residence	£750	BTS 5 June 1942 p. 6; 19 June p. 4. On instruction of executors of Miss F. M. A. Plowman. Vacant possession	PK un-catalogued
21 July 1942	On site	Bedford, 18 Clapham Road	£645	BTS 5 June 1942 p. 6; 19 June p. 4. Rental £49 8s pa	-

Auction date	Venue	Description	Price	Newspaper references	BLARS references
24 July 1942	Bedford, Lime Street, sale rooms	Harrold, Lavendon Road, four cottages with barns and gardens	£410	BTS 10, 17 July 1942 p. 4. The estate of the late Charles Orpin. Occupied by Messrs Lyons, Pettit, Croot and Wooding. Total rental £40 6s pa	-
24 July 1942	Bedford, Lime Street, sale rooms	Bedford, corner freehold property fronting Lurke Street and Howard Street, 5,000 sq ft	£9,000	BTS 3, 10 July 1942 p. 4	PK 1/4/142. By order of trustees of John Davis. Two floor building formerly a coach house and stabling now used as workshops
8 September 1942	On site	Clifton, Drift Field, on continuation of Church Street beyond Clifton Bury, garden land, 13a	Unsold	BTS 28 August 1942 p. 4. On instruction of Mr David Street	PK un-catalogued
14 October 1942	Biggleswade, The Sun Hotel	Biggleswade Brooklands Farm, garden holding, 94a	£9,200	BTS 25 September 1942 p. 4; 2 October p. 1. On instruction of executors of Allan Ball	-
14 October 1942	Biggleswade, The Sun Hotel	Biggleswade, Crane's Field, four plots of land, 33a	£2,600	BTS 25 September 1942 p. 4; 2 October p. 1. On instruction of executors of Allan Ball	-
30 October 1942	Bedford, Lime Street, sale rooms	Bedford, 12 Howard Street, central villa	£600	BTS 16, 23 October 1942 p. 1. Vacant possession	-
30 October 1942	Bedford, Lime Street, sale rooms	Bedford, 109 George Street, villa	£570	BTS 23 October 1942 p. 1. Rental £39 pa	-
1 December 1942	On site	Bedford, 81 Beverley Crescent, freehold residence, large garden	£1,700	BTS 20, 27 November 1942 p. 1. On instruction of executors of Mrs Florence Mary Blake. Household effects sold following sale of property	PK un-catalogued

Auction date	Venue	Description	Price	Newspaper references	BLARS references
19 February 1943	On site	Kempston, 20–24 Duncombe Street, three cottages	£510	BTS 22, 29 January 1943 p. 1; 19 February p. 6. Total rental £61 2s pa	-
19 February 1943	Bedford, Lime Street, sale rooms	Harrold, Highfield, detached double-fronted residence	£875	-	-
19 February 1943	Bedford, Lime Street, sale rooms	Sharnbrook, at rear of Ivy House, building site, poultry farm	£420	-	-
19 February 1943	Bedford, Lime Street, sale rooms	Riseley, smallholding, house, buildings, 48a	£1,450	-	-
9 March 1943	Baldock, The Rose and Crown Hotel	Baldock (Herts), southern side of Icknield Way, garden plot, 1r 27p	£190	-	-
10 March 1943	Sandy, The Red Lion Hotel	Sandy, Ivel Road, villa	£520	BTS 19 February 1943 p. 6; 26 February p. 4. On instruction of executors of Mrs M. M. Sharpe and Mr H. Sharpe. Rental £26 pa	-
10 March 1943	Sandy, The Red Lion Hotel	Sandy, 9 and 10 Brickhill Road, two villas	£900	BTS 19 February 1943 p. 6; 26 February p. 4. On instruction of executors of Mrs M. M. Sharpe and Mr H. Sharpe. Total rental £59 pa	-
10 March 1943	Sandy, The Red Lion Hotel	Sandy, 21 Laburnham Road, villa	£420	BTS 19 February 1943 p. 6; 26 February p. 4. On instruction of executors of Mrs M. M. Sharpe and Mr H. Sharpe. Rental £26 pa	-

Auction date	Venue	Description	Price	Newspaper references	BLARS references
10 March 1943	Sandy, The Red Lion Hotel	Sandy, 3–7 Longfield Road, three cottages	£570	BTS 19 February 1943 p. 6; 26 February p. 4. On instruction of executors of Mrs M. M. Sharpe and Mr H. Sharpe. Total rental £48 16s pa	-
10 March 1943	Sandy, The Red Lion Hotel	Sandy, 9–15 Longfield Road, four cottages	£700	BTS 19 February 1943 p. 6; 26 February p. 4. On instruction of executors of Mrs M. M. Sharpe and Mr H. Sharpe. Total rental £66 8s pa	-
10 March 1943	Sandy, The Red Lion Hotel	Sandy, 10–16 Longfield Road, four cottages	£775	BTS 19 February 1943 p. 6; 26 February p. 4. On instruction of executors of Mrs M. M. Sharpe and Mr H. Sharpe. Total rental £75 8s pa	-
10 March 1943	Sandy, The Red Lion Hotel	Blunham, High Street, eight cottages	£820	BTS 19 February 1943 p. 6; 26 February p. 4. On instruction of executors of Mrs M. M. Sharpe and Mr H. Sharpe. Total rental £85 12s 9d pa	-
12 March 1943	Potton, The Rose and Crown Hotel	Potton, Old Mill Lane, garden land, 3a 0r 27p	£105	BTS 26 February 1943 p. 4. On instruction of the Sandy Building Society. Rental £7 10s pa	-
12 March 1943	Potton, The Rose and Crown Hotel	Potton, Pesthouse Lane, garden land, 3a 2r 28p	£130	BTS 26 February 1943 p. 4. On instruction of the Sandy Building Society. Rental £10 pa	-
12 March 1943	Potton, The Rose and Crown Hotel	Potton, 15 Blackbird Street, cottage	£450	BTS 26 February 1943 p. 4. On instruction of the Sandy Building Society. Rental £31 pa	-

Auction date	Venue	Description	Price	Newspaper references	BLARS references
12 March 1943	Potton, The Rose and Crown Hotel	Potton, Everton Road, garden land, 1a	£150	BTS 26 February 1943 p. 4. On instruction of the Sandy Building Society. Vacant possession	-
12 March 1943	Potton, The Rose and Crown Hotel	Potton, Everton Road, garden land, 3r	£100	BTS 26 February 1943 p. 4. On instruction of the Sandy Building Society. Vacant possession	-
12 March 1943	Potton, The Rose and Crown Hotel	Potton, Narrow Lane, near Potton Windmill, 4a 1r 30p	£145	BTS 26 February 1943 p. 4. On instruction of the Sandy Building Society. Vacant possession	-
29 March 1943	Stotfold, The Black Lion Inn	Stotfold, 11 Baldock Road, semi-detached villa	£430	BTS 19 March 1943 p. 6. Occupied by Mr D. Sadler. Rental 13s per week	-
29 March 1943	Stotfold, The Black Lion Inn	Stotfold, 77 High Street, house	£625	BTS 19 March 1943 p. 6. Occupied by Mr P. Smith. Rental £30 pa	-
29 March 1943	On site	Harrold, Highfield, on south side of main street, near village centre, freehold residence	-	BTS 19 March 1943 p. 6. On instruction of executors Miss E. Wells. Household furnishings sold following sale of property	PK un-catalogued
24 May 1943	On site	Sharnbrook, Ivy House Poultry Farm, or building site	-	BTS 7 May 1943 p. 6. By order of executor of C. R. Edmonds	-
29 May 1943	Bedford, The Swan Hotel	Riseley, smallholding, house, buildings, 48a	-	BTS 7 May 1943 p. 6; 28 May p. 4	-
23 June 1943	Potton, The Parish Hall	Potton, 4 Horslow Street, meadow, 1a 0r 14p	£845	BTS 11 June 1943 p. 4; 18 June p. 6. By order of Sandy Building Society re. Mr James Manning. Vacant possession	-

Auction date	Venue	Description	Price	Newspaper references	BLARS references
25 June 1943	On site	Wilden, Hill Farm, western side of Bedford Road, farmhouse, buildings, 36a 1r 35p	£1,360	BTS 11 June 1943 p. 4; 18 June p. 6. Vacant possession	PK 1/4/145. On instruction of R. E. C. Dodwell
2 July 1943	Bedford, Lime Street, sale rooms	Bedford, 3 The Embankment, house, in four flats	£2,650	BTS 11, 18 June 1943 p. 4; 25 June p. 6; 2 July p. 4	PK un-catalogued. Occupied by Mr Cyril Stelfox, Mr F. A. James, Mrs H. Horrocks and Mr A. J. Hopkins. Total rental £312 pa
2 July 1943	Bedford, Lime Street, sale rooms	Bedford, 66 Howbury Street, villa	£620	BTS 11 June 1943 p. 4	-
2 July 1943	Bedford, Lime Street, sale rooms	Bedford, 15 Ellington Street, cottage	£270	BTS 11 June 1943 p. 4; 25 June p. 6. Occupied by Mrs Dean. Rental £31 4s pa	-
2 July 1943	Bedford, Lime Street, sale rooms	Bedford, 88 Tavistock Street, terraced house	£250	BTS 11 June 1943 p. 4; 25 June p. 6. Occupied by Mrs Frost. Rental £39 pa	-
2 July 1943	Bedford, Lime Street, sale rooms	Bedford, 3 Western Street, villa	£360	BTS 11 June 1943 p. 4; 25 June p. 6. Occupied by Mrs Tite. Rental £48 2s pa	-
2 July 1943	Bedford, Lime Street, sale rooms	Bedford, 3 Honey Hill Road	-	BTS 11 June 1943 p. 4	-
2 July 1943	Bedford, Lime Street, sale rooms	Kempston, 3 Home Street, modern semi-detached villa	Unsold	BTS 25 June p. 6. Occupied by Mr C. A. Lee. Rental £43 18s pa	-
10 September 1943	Bedford, Lime Street, sale rooms	Bedford, 176 Fosterhill Road, detached double-fronted house	£1,355	BTS 20 August 1943 p. 4; 27 August p. 6	PK un-catalogued

Auction date	Venue	Description	Price	Newspaper references	BLARS references
10 September 1943	Bedford, Lime Street, sale rooms	Bedford, 12 Western Street, terraced house	£360	BTS 20 August 1943 p. 4; 27 August p. 6	PK un-catalogued. Occupied by Mr John Small. Rental £35 10s 8d pa
10 September 1943	Bedford, Lime Street, sale rooms	Bedford, 3 Winifred Road, detached residence, in two flats	Unsold	BTS 20 August 1943 p. 4; 27 August p. 6	PK un-catalogued. Ground floor flat occupied by Mr F. Hyde. Rental £65 pa. First floor flat occupied by Mr F. Bellman. Rental £62 pa
10 September 1943	Bedford, Lime Street, sale rooms	Bedford, 118 and 120 Ampthill Road, two villas	£630	BTS 20 August 1943 p. 4; 27 August p. 6.	PK un-catalogued. Occupied by Mrs Sharpe and Mrs Joyce. Total rental £52 4s pa
10 September 1943	Bedford, Lime Street, sale rooms	Kempston, Farrer Street, opposite Fire Station, building site currently let as garden plots, 1a 21p	£380	BTS 20 August 1943 p. 4; 3 September p. 6. By orders of executors of Alfred Barker. Rental £8 16s pa	PK un-catalogued. Occupied in portions by National Fire Service, Mr Broughton, Mr Jackson, Mr Bullock, Mr Witty, Mr Hoole, A. W. Barker, Mr Slater, Mr Brightman, Mr Mossop, Mr Cook, Mr Bird, Mr Bradley and Mr Curtis
1 October 1943	On site	Ashwell (Herts), Station Road, building land, 1a	£55	-	-
1 October 1943	On site	Ashwell (Herts), Small Gains Lane, arable enclosure, 5a 2r 29p	£200	-	-
9 October 1943	Bedford, Horne Lane, Tudor Rooms	Goldington, Highfields, Bedford to Kimbolton Road, freehold farmhouse, land, 164.1a	£3,500	BTS 17, 24 September p. 6; 1 October p. 6. By order of Mr Fred Monk who is retiring	PK un-catalogued. Vacant possession
9 October 1943	Bedford, Horne Lane, Tudor Rooms	Bromham, Bowels Wood and field, Grange Lane, 22.897a	£1,200	BTS 17, 24 September p. 6; 1 October p. 6. By order of C. W. Phipps Esq. Vacant possession	-

Auction date	Venue	Description	Price	Newspaper references	BLARS references
9 October 1943	Bedford, Horne Lane, Tudor Rooms	Souldrop, The Old Post Office	£250	BTS 17, 24 September p. 6; 1 October p. 6	-
10 November 1943	On site	Caldecote, Grange Lane, seven cottages	£400	-	-
10 November 1943	On site	Caldecote, Grange Lane, garden land, 3r 26 p	Unsold	-	-
12 November 1943	Bedford, Horne Lane, Tudor Rooms	Cranfield Estate, modern building estate, forty-four freeholds (listed below)	-	BTS 1 October 1943 p. 6	PK 1/4/147
12 November 1943	Bedford, Horne Lane, Tudor Rooms	Cranfield, 2 and 4 Hollywell Road, two villas	Unsold	BTS 1 October 1943 p. 6	PK 1/4/147. Occupied by Messrs Allsworth and Denton. Total rental £57 4s pa
12 November 1943	Bedford, Horne Lane, Tudor Rooms	Cranfield, 2 and 4 Bedford Road, two villas	£850	BTS 1 October 1943 p. 6	PK 1/4/147. Occupied by Messrs Cook and Mack. Total rental £68 18s pa
12 November 1943	Bedford, Horne Lane, Tudor Rooms	Cranfield, 206 High Street, semi-detached villa	£400	BTS 1 October 1943 p. 6	PK 1/4/147. Occupied by Mr Holman. Total rental £33 16s pa
12 November 1943	Bedford, Horne Lane, Tudor Rooms	Cranfield, 208 and 210 High Street, two villas	£900	BTS 1 October 1943 p. 6	PK 1/4/147. Occupied by Messrs Humphreys and Shuker. Total rental £67 12s pa
12 November 1943	Bedford, Horne Lane, Tudor Rooms	Cranfield, 214 High Street, semi-detached villa	Unsold	BTS 1 October 1943 p. 6	PK 1/4/147. Occupied by Mrs Dennahy. Rental £33 16s pa
12 November 1943	Bedford, Horne Lane, Tudor Rooms	Cranfield, 2 and 4 Coronation Road, two villas	Unsold	BTS 1 October 1943 p. 6	PK 1/4/147. Occupied by Messrs Parris and Payne. Total rental £57 4s pa

Auction date	Venue	Description	Price	Newspaper references	BLARS references
12 November 1943	Bedford, Horne Lane, Tudor Rooms	Cranfield, 8 Coronation Road, semi-detached villa	Unsold	BTS 1 October 1943 p. 6	PK 1/4/147. Occupied by Mr Brown. Rental £26 pa
12 November 1943	Bedford, Horne Lane, Tudor Rooms	Cranfield, 10 and 12 Coronation Road, pair of bungalows	Unsold	BTS 1 October 1943 p. 6	PK 1/4/147. Occupied by Messrs Farrell and Farrell. Total rental £52 pa
12 November 1943	Bedford, Horne Lane, Tudor Rooms	Cranfield, 14 Coronation Road, semi-detached villa	Unsold	BTS 1 October 1943 p. 6	PK 1/4/147. Occupied by Mr Wilson. Rental £28 12s pa
12 November 1943	Bedford, Horne Lane, Tudor Rooms	Cranfield, 18 and 20 Coronation Road, pair of bungalows	Unsold	BTS 1 October 1943 p. 6	PK 1/4/147. Occupied by Messrs Turner and Smith. Total rental £52 pa
12 November 1943	Bedford, Horne Lane, Tudor Rooms	Cranfield, 24 Coronation Road, semi-detached villa	Unsold	BTS 1 October 1943 p. 6	PK 1/4/147. Occupied by Mr Grimwood. Rental £28 12s pa
12 November 1943	Bedford, Horne Lane, Tudor Rooms	Cranfield, 21 and 23 Coronation Road, pair of bungalows	Unsold	BTS 1 October 1943 p. 6	PK 1/4/147. Occupied by Messrs Billington and Clifton. Total rental £57 4s pa
12 November 1943	Bedford, Horne Lane, Tudor Rooms	Cranfield, 17 and 19 Coronation Road, pair of villas	Unsold	BTS 1 October 1943 p. 6	PK 1/4/147. Occupied by Messrs Salt and Block. Total rental £57 4s pa
12 November 1943	Bedford, Horne Lane, Tudor Rooms	Cranfield, 13 and 15 Coronation Road, pair of villas	Unsold	BTS 1 October 1943 p. 6	PK 1/4/147. Occupied by Messrs Weller and Sealey. Total rental £57 4s pa
12 November 1943	Bedford, Horne Lane, Tudor Rooms	Cranfield, 9 and 11 Coronation Road, pair of bungalows	Unsold	BTS 1 October 1943 p. 6	PK 1/4/147. Occupied by Messrs Battle and Harkins. Total rental £49 8s pa
12 November 1943	Bedford, Horne Lane, Tudor Rooms	Cranfield, 7 Coronation Road, semi-detached villa	Unsold	BTS 1 October 1943 p. 6	PK 1/4/147. Occupied by Mr Gains. Rental £28 12s pa

Auction date	Venue	Description	Price	Newspaper references	BLARS references
12 November 1943	Bedford, Horne Lane, Tudor Rooms	Cranfield, 1 and 3 Coronation Road, pair of villas	Unsold	BTS 1 October 1943 p. 6	PK 1/4/147. Occupied by Messrs Brendling and Atkinson. Total rental £57 4s pa
12 November 1943	Bedford, Horne Lane, Tudor Rooms	Cranfield, 24 Wood End Road, semi-detached villa	Unsold	BTS 1 October 1943 p. 6	PK 1/4/147. Occupied by Mr Lambert. Rental £36 8s pa
12 November 1943	Bedford, Horne Lane, Tudor Rooms	Cranfield, 28 and 30 Wood End Road, pair of villas	Unsold	BTS 1 October 1943 p. 6	PK 1/4/147. Occupied by Messrs Newsome and Thrussell. Total rental £72 16s pa
12 November 1943	Bedford, Horne Lane, Tudor Rooms	Cranfield, 32 Wood End Road, semi-detached villa	Unsold	BTS 1 October 1943 p. 6	PK 1/4/147. Occupied by Mr Ayre. Rental £33 16s pa
12 November 1943	Bedford, Horne Lane, Tudor Rooms	Cranfield, 36 Wood End Road, semi-detached villa	Unsold	BTS 1 October 1943 p. 6	PK 1/4/147. Occupied by Mr Thompson. Rental £36 8s pa
12 November 1943	Bedford, Horne Lane, Tudor Rooms	Cranfield, 2a and 4a Harter Avenue, pair of villas	Unsold	BTS 1 October 1943 p. 6	PK 1/4/147. Occupied by Messrs Rollinson and Macdonald. Total rental £49 8s pa
12 November 1943	Bedford, Horne Lane, Tudor Rooms	Cranfield, 8 Harter Avenue, semi-detached villa	Unsold	BTS 1 October 1943 p. 6	PK 1/4/147. Occupied by Mr Critchlow. Rental £26 pa
12 November 1943	Bedford, Horne Lane, Tudor Rooms	Cranfield, 13 and 15 Harter Avenue, pair of villas	Unsold	BTS 1 October 1943 p. 6	PK 1/4/147. Occupied by Messrs Hunt and Handsley. Total rental £46 16s pa
12 November 1943	Bedford, Horne Lane, Tudor Rooms	Cranfield, 11 Harter Avenue, semi-detached villa	Unsold	BTS 1 October 1943 p. 6	PK 1/4/147. Occupied by Mr Martin. Rental £23 8s pa
12 November 1943	Bedford, Horne Lane, Tudor Rooms	Cranfield, 3 and 5 Harter Avenue, villa	Unsold	BTS 1 October 1943 p. 6	PK 1/4/147. Occupied by Messrs Plumb and Chambers. Total rental £46 16s pa

Auction date	Venue	Description	Price	Newspaper references	BLARS references
12 November 1943	Bedford, Horne Lane, Tudor Rooms	Cranfield, 1a Harter Avenue, corner shop, residence	Unsold	BTS 1 October 1943 p. 6	PK 1/4/147. Occupied by Mr Proctor. Rental £41 12s pa
12 November 1943	Bedford, Horne Lane, Tudor Rooms	Cranfield, 2 and 4 Hatfield Avenue, pair of villas	Unsold	BTS 1 October 1943 p. 6	PK 1/4/147. Occupied by Messrs McLeod and Keaney. Total rental £52 pa
12 November 1943	Bedford, Horne Lane, Tudor Rooms	Cranfield, five building plots: frontage to Bedford Road and Mill Road; next to 1 Coronation Road; next to 2 Coronation Road; Hollywell Road; end of Coronation Road	£50 Two sold	-	PK un-catalogued. Bedford Road occupied by Mr Hudson. Rental £3 pa. Coronation Road plots all have Council Air Raid Shelters. Hollywell Road used as garden ground
22 November 1943	Harrold, Harrold Institute	Harrold, High Street, double-fronted house	£750	-	PK un-catalogued. On instruction of executors of Miss Miriam Betts. Vacant possession
9 February 1944	On site	Carlton, The Causeway, four cottages	£440	BTS 21 January 1944 p. 6. By order of trustees of John Betts. Total rental £31 18s pa	-
12 February 1944	Bedford, Horne Lane, Tudor Rooms	Ravensden, Old Ways Road, smallholding, 15.5a	-	BTS 21, 28 January 1944 p. 6; 11 February p. 6. By order of the trustees of W. Wagstaff	-
12 February 1944	Bedford, Horne Lane, Tudor Rooms	Thurleigh, Backnoe End Farm, agricultural holding, 15.6a	Unsold	BTS 21, 28 January 1944 p. 6; 11 February p. 6. By order of the trustees of W. Wagstaff	-
12 February 1944	Bedford, Horne Lane, Tudor Rooms	Thurleigh, near Chapel, cottage	£625	BTS 21, 28 January 1944 p. 6; 11 February p. 6. By order of the trustees of W. Wagstaff	-

Auction date	Venue	Description	Price	Newspaper references	BLARS references
12 February 1944	Bedford, Horne Lane, Tudor Rooms	Thurleigh, near Chapel, pair of cottages	£260	BTS 21, 28 January 1944 p. 6; 11 February p. 6. By order of the trustees of W. Wagstaff	-
12 February 1944	Bedford, Horne Lane, Tudor Rooms	Thurleigh, near Chapel, building site	Unsold	BTS 21, 28 January 1944 p. 6; 11 February p.6. By order of the trustees of W. Wagstaff	-
23 March 1944	Cranfield, The Leathern Bottle	Cranfield, 2 Crawley Road, cottage, 1a 3r	£460	BTS 3, 10 March 1944 p. 6	PK un-catalogued. By order of executors of Henry Cox. Household furniture sold following sale of property
5 April 1944	Baldock, The Victoria Inn	Baldock (Herts), 77 Clothall Road, villa	£750	BTS 31 March 1944 p. 6	PK un-catalogued. Occupied by Mr T. T. Beck. Rental 20s per week
5 April 1944	Baldock, The Victoria Inn	Baldock (Herts), 79 Clothall Road, villa	£850	BTS 31 March 1944 p. 6	PK un-catalogued. Occupied by Mr G. Broom. Rental 20s per week
5 April 1944	Baldock, The Victoria Inn	Baldock (Herts), Spring Cottage, 81 Clothall Road, detached villa	£575	BTS 31 March 1944 p. 6	PK un-catalogued. Occupied by Baldock Urban District Council. Rental £32 pa
5 May 1944	Bedford, Lime Street, sale rooms	Bedford, 260 and 262 Ampthill Road	-	BTS 7 April 1944 p. 6	-
5 May 1944	Bedford, Lime Street, sale rooms	Bedford, 2a Melbourne Street	-	BTS 7 April 1944 p. 6	-
5 May 1944	Bedford, Lime Street, sale rooms	Bedford, 2 Barkers Lane	-	BTS 7, 21 April 1944 p. 6. Occupied by Mr Chew. Rental £52 pa	-

Auction date	Venue	Description	Price	Newspaper references	BLARS references
5 May 1944	Bedford, Lime Street, sale rooms	Bedford, 11 St Michaels Road, villa	£660	BTS 7, 21 April 1944 p. 6. Occupied by Mr Spinks. Rental £52 pa	PK 1/4/148
5 May 1944	Bedford, Lime Street, sale rooms	Bedford, 4 Spenser Road, semi-detached residence	£490	BTS 7, 21 April 1944 p. 6. Occupied by Mr Harbinson. Rental £39 pa	PK 1/4/148
5 May 1944	Bedford, Lime Street, sale rooms	Bedford, 30 Spenser Road, semi-detached residence	-	BTS 7, 21 April 1944 p. 6. Occupied by Mr Owens. Rental £52 pa	PK 1/4/148
5 May 1944	Bedford, Lime Street, sale rooms	Bedford, 63 Muswell Road, terraced villa	£340	BTS 7, 21 April 1944 p. 6. Occupied by Mr Smith. Rental £35 2s pa	PK 1/4/148
5 May 1944	Bedford, Lime Street, sale rooms	Bedford, 16 Gadsby Street, cottage	£235	BTS 7, 21 April 1944 p. 6. Occupied by Mr Ashpole. Rental £18 4s pa	PK 1/4/148
5 May 1944	Bedford, Lime Street, sale rooms	Bedford, 3 Beaconsfield Street, cottage	£385	BTS 7, 21 April 1944 p. 6. Occupied by Mr Wright. Rental £37 18s 4d pa	PK 1/4/148
5 May 1944	Bedford, Lime Street, sale rooms	Bedford, 3–9 Gratton Road, four cottages	-	BTS 7, 21 April 1944 p. 6. Occupied by Messrs Robinson, Dalrymple, Blackwell and Coles. Total rental £71 17s 8d pa	PK 1/4/148
5 May 1944	Bedford, Lime Street, sale rooms	Bedford, 17 and 19 Gratton Road, terraced villas	£335	BTS 7, 21 April 1944 p. 6. Occupied by Messrs Gardner, Warren, Grainger and Lumley. Total rental £71 17s 8d pa	PK 1/4/148
5 May 1944	Bedford, Lime Street, sale rooms	Bedford, 13 and 15 Gratton Road, terraced villas	-	BTS 7, 21 April 1944 p. 6. Occupied by Messrs Gardner, Warren, Grainger and Lumley. Total rental £71 17s 8d pa	PK 1/4/148

Auction date	Venue	Description	Price	Newspaper references	BLARS references
5 May 1944	Bedford, Lime Street, sale rooms	Bedford, 23 and 25 Russell Street	£320	BTS 7, 21 April 1944 p. 6. Occupied by Messrs White and Mills. Total rental £36 8s pa	-
5 May 1944	Bedford, Lime Street, sale rooms	Bedford, 55 Iddesleigh Road	£315	BTS 7 April 1944 p. 6	PK 1/4/148
5 May 1944	Bedford, Lime Street, sale rooms	Bedford, 33 Holme Street, terraced villa	£275	BTS 7, 21 April 1944 p. 6. Occupied by Mr Padillo. Rental £39 pa	PK 1/4/148
5 May 1944	Bedford, Lime Street, sale rooms	Bedford, 60 Goldington Avenue	£720	BTS 21 April 1944 p. 6. Requisitioned by War Department. Rental £50 pa	PK 1/4/149
5 May 1944	Bedford, Lime Street, sale rooms	Bedford, 62 Goldington Avenue, requisitioned house	£650	BTS 21 April 1944 p. 6. Occupied by Commander Lawder RN. Rental £55 pa	PK 1/4/149
5 May 1944	Bedford, Lime Street, sale rooms	Bedford, 24 St Andrews Road, requisitioned house	£640	BTS 21 April 1944 p. 6. Occupied by Mr Verby. Rental £52 pa	-
5 May 1944	Bedford, Lime Street, sale rooms	Bedford, 45 Cauldwell Street, shop, flat over	£730	BTS 21 April 1944 p. 6. Rental £88 8s pa	PK 1/4/149
6 May 1944	Bedford, The Town Hall	Francklin Estate, five farms in Bolnhurst, Ravensden and Wilden (listed below)	£17,000	TDA 29 April 1944 p. 10. BTS 7, 14, 28 April 1944 p. 6; 5 May p. 6	PK 1/4/150. By order of The Management and Administration Department re. Mr J. Francklin's settled estate. Vendors had held estate for nearly four hundred years at time of sale. Sporting rights let by US Army Air Force. Rental £10 pa
6 May 1944	Bedford, The Town Hall	Bolnhurst, Crowhill Farm, west of Bedford to Kimbolton Road, 182.747a	-	BTS 7, 14, 28 April 1944 p. 6; 5 May p. 6	PK 1/4/150. Occupied by Mr F. Holley. Rental £110 10s pa

Auction date	Venue	Description	Price	Newspaper references	BLARS references
6 May 1944	Bedford, The Town Hall	Bolnhurst and Ravensden, Mavourn Farm, Bolnhurst to Thurleigh Road, 227.159a	-	BTS 7, 14, 28 April 1944 p. 6; 5 May p. 6	PK 1/4/150. Occupied by Mr R. Ingle. Rental £160 pa
6 May 1944	Bedford, The Town Hall	Bolnhurst and Ravensden, Tilwick Farm, Bedford to Bolnhurst Road, 150.907a	-	BTS 7, 14, 28 April 1944 p. 6; 5 May p. 6	PK 1/4/150. Occupied by Mr E. Holt. Rental £80 pa
6 May 1944	Bedford, The Town Hall	Bolnhurst, Blacklands Farm, Bedford to Bolnhurst Road, 152.708a	-	BTS 7, 14, 28 April 1944 p. 6; 5 May p. 6	PK 1/4/150. Farm occupied by Mr E. Shepherd. Rental £70 pa. Pastures occupied by Mr E. Wildman. Rental £7 pa
6 May 1944	Bedford, The Town Hall	Bolnhurst, Brook Farm, Bedford to Bolnhurst Road, 176.728a	-	BTS 7, 14, 28 April 1944 p. 6; 5 May p. 6	PK 1/4/150. Farm occupied by Bedfordshire War Agricultural Executive Committee. Rental £86 10s pa. Portion of land occupied by Ministry of Works. Rental £4 pa. Portion of land occupied by Mr W. H. Bates. Rental £14 10s pa
27 May 1944	Bedford, The Swan Hotel	Houghton Conquest, Conquestbury Farm, freehold agricultural holding, 170a	Sold prior to auction	BTS 5 May 1944 p. 6; 19 May p. 4. On instruction of Charles Gilbert Esq.	PK un-catalogued. Vacant possession. The homestead was constructed by His Grace the Duke of Bedford in the usual substantial style

Auction date	Venue	Description	Price	Newspaper references	BLARS references
30 May 1944	On site	Harrold, High Street, frontage to the Green, three old-world cottages	£350	BTS 12 May 1944 p. 6; 19 May p. 4	PK 7/4/25. Sold by executors of Mrs J. H. Le Fevre. Occupied by J. Waller, Mr J. Drage and Mr J. R. Waller. Total rental £31 10s 8d pa
30 May 1944	On site	Harrold, High Street, butcher's shop, house, two old-world cottages	£1,700	BTS 12 May 1944 p. 6; 19 May p. 4	PK 7/4/25. Sold by executors of Mrs J. H. Le Fevre. Butcher's shop and house vacant possession. Cottages occupied by Mr E. Clayson and Mr Pointer. Total rental £27 10s pa
30 May 1944	On site	Harrold, High Street, large yard	£330	BTS 12 May 1944 p. 6; 19 May p. 4	PK 7/4/25. Sold by executors of Mrs J. H. Le Fevre. Vacant possession
31 May 1944	Baldock, The Victoria Inn	Baldock (Herts), 15–29 South Road, eight cottages	-	BTS 26 May 1944 p. 6. Total rental £102 3s 2d pa	-
11 July 1944	On site	Riseley, Oakwood, High Street, country residence	£1,450	BTS 23, 30 June 1944 p. 6	PK 1/4/151, PK 2/3/1/78. On instruction of executors of Mrs S. H. Osborne. Household items sold following sale of property
25 September 1944	Ashwell, The Three Tuns	Bedford, 31 St Andrew's Road	Unsold	BTS 8 September 1944 p. 6	-
25 September 1944	Ashwell, The Three Tuns	Ashwell (Herts), Station Road, arable land, 14a	£370	BTS 8 September 1944 p. 6. Occupied by Mr G. Longley. Rental £14 pa	-
25 September 1944	Ashwell, The Three Tuns	Ashwell (Herts), Station Road, garden land, 3.5a	£230	BTS 8 September 1944 p. 6. Occupied by Mr S. Dilley. Rental £5 pa	-

Auction date	Venue	Description	Price	Newspaper references	BLARS references
24 October 1944	On site	Bedford, 31 St Andrew's Road	-	BTS 6, 13 October 1944 p. 6. By order of executors of William Nicholls. Household furniture sold following sale of property	-
7 November 1944	Letchworth, Eastcheap, Icknield Hall	Letchworth (Herts), 54 Leys Avenue, The Music Shop	£2,225 Joint auction with J. G. D. Satchell	BTS 3 November 1944 p. 6	PK un-catalogued. On instruction of executors of J. T. Openshaw. Occupied by Mr E. R. Stevens. Rental £125 pa
7 November 1944	Letchworth, Eastcheap, Icknield Hall	Letchworth (Herts), 81 Spring Road, detached house	£800 Joint auction with J. G. D. Satchell	BTS 3 November 1944 p. 6	PK un-catalogued. Occupied by Mr Ludwick. Verbal monthly tenancy, rental £52 pa
7 November 1944	Letchworth, Eastcheap, Icknield Hall	Letchworth (Herts), 85 Spring Road, semi-detached house	£850 Joint auction with J. G. D. Satchell	BTS 3 November 1944 p. 6	PK un-catalogued. Occupied by Mr F. H. Oliver. Rental £55 pa
7 November 1944	Letchworth, Eastcheap, Icknield Hall	Letchworth (Herts), 14 Sollershott East, semi-detached house	£775 Joint auction with J. G. D. Satchell	BTS 3 November 1944 p. 6	PK un-catalogued. Occupied by Mrs Kempster. Rental £55 pa
14 November 1944	On site	Wilden, Chequers Hill, two thatched cottages with gardens	£200	BTS 3, 10 November 1944 p. 6. One cottage occupied by Mr Samuel Croft. Rental £4 5s pa	-
15 November 1944	On site	Chellington, High Street, pair of freehold cottages	£360	BTS 3, 10 November 1944 p. 6. One cottage occupied by Mr John Spencer. Rental £13 pa	PK 1/4/153. Water by standpipe

Auction date	Venue	Description	Price	Newspaper references	BLARS references
15 December 1944	Bedford, Lime Street, sale rooms	Kempston, 40–48 High Street, five cottages	£1,280	BTS 24 November 1944 p. 6; 1 December p. 6. On instruction of administrator of late C. D. Jenkins. Total rental £88 8s pa. Number 40 occupied by Miss Morris. 42 occupied by A. Ford. 44 occupied by C. W. Mackness. 46 occupied by Mr Washbourne. 48 occupied by Mrs Bird	-
15 December 1944	Bedford, Lime Street, sale rooms	Bedford, 23 Grafton Road	£550	BTS 24 November 1944 p. 6. On instruction of administrator of late C. D. Jenkins. Occupied by Mrs Hayden. Rental £52 pa	-
19 December 1944	Stevington	Stevington, Church Lane, two cottages	£150	BTS 15 December 1944 p. 6	PK 1/4/154. On instruction of Mr T. Burridge. Occupied by Miss Hullatt and John Ingram
19 December 1944	On site	Stevington, stone cottage, outbuildings, paddock, 2.33a	£1,200	BTS 8 December 1944 p. 6	-
19 December 1944	On site	Stevington, Frost Field, adjoining the R. D. C. houses, arable field, 12a	£725	BTS 8 December 1944 p. 6. Occupied by Mr P. Keech. Rental £12 pa	-
20 January 1945	Bedford, Horne Lane, Tudor Rooms	Lidlington, 2–6 High Street, three freehold properties	£800	BTS 5, 12 January 1945 p. 6. On instruction of adminstratrix of Edward Bosworth. Occupied by Mr Young, Mrs Dudley and Mr Needham	PK 2/5/2/13
20 January 1945	Bedford, Horne Lane, Tudor Rooms	Lidlington, 1–11 Church Street	-	BTS 5, 12 January 1945 p. 6. On instruction of adminstratrix of Edward Bosworth. Occupied by Messrs E. Pepper, R. Pepper, E. Pepper, Marshall, Cambers and Snowden	PK 2/5/2/13

Auction date	Venue	Description	Price	Newspaper references	BLARS references
20 January 1945	Bedford, Horne Lane, Tudor Rooms	Lidlington, 13–17 Church Street	-	BTS 5, 12 January 1945 p. 6. On instruction of adminstratrix of Edward Bosworth. Occupied by Mr Garrett, Mr Mole and Mrs Rowe	PK 2/5/2/13
1 March 1945	Stotfold, The Black Lion	Stotfold, 76 and 78 Regent Street, freehold cottages	£1,200	BTS 9, 16 February 1945 p. 6	PK un-catalogued. By order of administrators of Miss S. A. I. Elms. Number 76 vacant possession. 78 occupied by Mrs Bilcock. Rental £18 4s pa
1 March 1945	Stotfold, The Black Lion	Stotfold, Regent Street, building site, smallholders buildings, 2r 15p	£725	BTS 9, 16 February 1945 p. 6	PK un-catalogued. By order of administrators of Miss S. A. I. Elms. Vacant possession
1 March 1945	Stotfold, The Black Lion	Stotfold, Common Road, garden or building land, 4.548a	£500	BTS 9, 16 February 1945 p. 6	PK un-catalogued. Occupied by Mr T. Howard. Michaelmas rental, £18 pa
1 March 1945	Stotfold, The Black Lion	Stotfold, Great North Road, garden land, 33.696a	£2,400	BTS 9, 16 February 1945 p. 6	PK un-catalogued. Occupied by Mr H. E. Howard. Michaelmas rental, £69 12s 6d pa
1 March 1945	Stotfold, The Black Lion	Stotfold, 51 and 53 Arlesey Road, two freehold cottages, rear garden land, 63p	£500	BTS 9, 16 February 1945 p. 6	PK un-catalogued. Number 51 occupied by Mr F. Smith. Rental £7 8s pa. 53 occupied by Mrs Bowie. Rental £13 pa. Rear garden land occupied by Mr F. Smith. Rental £1 pa
1 March 1945	Stotfold, The Black Lion	Stotfold, adjoining 51 and 53 Arlesey Road, freehold garden land	£575	BTS 9, 16 February 1945 p. 6	PK un-catalogued. Occupied by Mr F. Smith. Michaelmas rental, £8 5s pa

Auction date	Venue	Description	Price	Newspaper references	BLARS references
1 March 1945	Stotfold, The Black Lion	Stotfold, 25 Queen Street, cottage	-	BTS 9 February 1945 p. 6. Requisitioned by Biggleswade Rural District Council	-
9 March 1945	Bedford, Lime Street, sale rooms	Bedford, 36a Gwyn Street	£800	BTS 9, 26 February 1945 p. 6; 2 March p. 6	PK un-catalogued Vacant possession
9 March 1945	Bedford, Lime Street, sale rooms	Kempston, 61 Stuart Road, modern house	£690	BTS 9, 23 February 1945 p. 6; 2 March p. 6	PK un-catalogued Occupied by Mr W. H. Picking. Rental £42 18s pa
9 March 1945	Bedford, Lime Street, sale rooms	Kempston, 10 Farrer Street, cottage	£260	BTS 9, 23 February 1945 p. 6; 2 March p. 6	PK un-catalogued Occupied by Mr C. Joyce. Rental £23 8s pa
9 March 1945	Bedford, Lime Street, sale rooms	Kempston, 30 and 32 Littledale Street, two cottages	£540	BTS 9, 23 February 1945 p. 6; 2 March p. 6	PK un-catalogued Occupied by Mrs E. Lincoln and Mrs Foster. Total rental £40 6s pa
9 March 1945	Bedford, Lime Street, sale rooms	Kempston, 8 and 10 Marne Street	-	BTS 16, 23 February 1945 p. 6. Total rental £36 8s pa	-
9 March 1945	Bedford, Lime Street, sale rooms	Kempston, 21 Littledale Street, semi-detached residence	£400	BTS 23 February 1945 p. 6; 2 March p. 6	PK un-catalogued Occupied by Mr Hillson. Rental £26 pa
9 March 1945	Bedford, Lime Street, sale rooms	Bedford, 4 Milton Road, requisitioned house	£700	BTS 9, 23 February 1945 p. 6; 2 March p. 6	PK un-catalogued Requisitioned by War Department. Rental £44 pa
9 March 1945	Bedford, Lime Street, sale rooms	Bedford, 31 Spenser Road, requisitioned house	£540	BTS 9, 23 February 1945 p. 6; 2 March p. 6	PK un-catalogued Requisitioned by War Department. Rental £44 pa
9 March 1945	Bedford, Lime Street, sale rooms	Bedford, 58 Clapham Road, in four flats	£850	BTS 9, 23 February 1945 p. 6; 2 March p. 6	PK un-catalogued Occupied by Mrs Stewart, Mrs Mallabar, Mrs Pearce and Mrs Dewer. Total rental £124 16s pa

Auction date	Venue	Description	Price	Newspaper references	BLARS references
9 March 1945	Bedford, Lime Street, sale rooms	Bedford, 2 Barkers Lane, brick workshop	£750	BTS 9, 23 February 1945 p. 6; 2 March p. 6	PK un-catalogued. Occupied by Mr H. Chew. Rental £49 10s pa
9 March 1945	Bedford, Lime Street, sale rooms	Bedford, St Cuthbert's Square, garden land, shed	£1,175	BTS 9, 23 February 1945 p. 6; 2 March p. 6	PK un-catalogued. Vacant possession
9 March 1945	Bedford, Lime Street, sale rooms	Bedford, 2a Bunyan Road, brick building	£900	BTS 9, 23 February 1945 p. 6; 2 March p. 6	PK un-catalogued. Ground floor vacant possession. First floor let for storage of furniture
9 March 1945	Bedford, Lime Street, sale rooms	Bedford, 18 St Augustines Road, desirable residence	£2,100	BTS 23 February 1945 p. 6; 2 March p. 6	PK un-catalogued. Occupied by Mr A. H. Eggington. Rental £60 pa
9 March 1945	Bedford, Lime Street, sale rooms	Stagsden, The Old White Horse, valuable freehold property	£900	BTS 16, 23 February 1945 p. 6; 2 March p. 6	PK un-catalogued. Vacant possession
9 March 1945	Bedford, Lime Street, sale rooms	Bedford, 2 Merton Road, semi-detached house	£1,650	BTS 23 February 1945 p. 6; 2 March p. 6	PK un-catalogued
20 March 1945	Potton, The Rose and Crown Hotel	Potton, 1 Bull Street, two shops, living accommodation	Unsold	BTS 2, 9 March 1945 p. 6. Small Bull Street shop occupied by Messrs G. T. Mayston and Son. Rental £20 16s pa	-
20 March 1945	Potton, The Rose and Crown Hotel	Potton, 3 and 5 Chapel Street, house, garage and buildings	£900	BTS 16 March 1945 p. 6. Occupied by Biggleswade Rural District Council. Rental £42 pa	-

Auction date	Venue	Description	Price	Newspaper references	BLARS references
27 April 1945	-	Harrold, Hillside, adjoining Little Odell, bungalow	£400	BTS 20, 27 April 1945 p. 6	PK 1/4/155, PK 2/4/1. On behalf of W. H. Adams as executor of Joseph Burgess
4 May 1945	Bedford, Lime Street Salerooms	Bedford, 53 Fenlake Road, semi-detached villa	£450	BTS 13, 20 April 1945 p. 6. By order of trustees of Kate Mason, deceased	PK 1/4/156. Occupied by Mr G. Wilkinson. Lunar monthly tenancy, £24 12s 11d pa
4 May 1945	Bedford, Lime Street, sale rooms	Bedford, 55 Fenlake Road, semi-detached villa	£340	BTS 13, 20 April 1945 p. 6. By order of trustees of Kate Mason, deceased	PK 1/4/156. Occupied by Mr E. Newnham. Lunar monthly tenancy, £26 17s 4d pa
4 May 1945	Bedford, Lime Street, sale rooms	Bedford, 57 Fenlake Road, terraced house	£225	BTS 13, 20 April 1945 p. 6. By order of trustees of Kate Mason, deceased	PK 1/4/156. Occupied by Mr G. Handscombe. Rental £17 11s pa
4 May 1945	Bedford, Lime Street, sale rooms	Bedford, 59 Fenlake Road, terraced house	£235	BTS 13, 20 April 1945 p. 6. By order of trustees of Kate Mason, deceased	PK 1/4/156. Occupied by Mr J. L. Darlow. Rental £18 4s pa
4 May 1945	Bedford, Lime Street, sale rooms	Bedford, 61 Fenlake Road, terraced house	£230	BTS 13, 20 April 1945 p. 6. By order of trustees of Kate Mason, deceased	PK 1/4/156. Occupied by Mr D. W. Green. Rental £21 4s 8d pa
4 May 1945	Bedford, Lime Street, sale rooms	Bedford, 63 Fenlake Road, terraced villa	£220	BTS 13, 20 April 1945 p. 6. By order of trustees of Kate Mason, deceased	PK 1/4/156. Occupied by Mrs E. Kilby. Rental £17 11s pa. No gas or electricity installed
4 May 1945	Bedford, Lime Street, sale rooms	Bedford, 65 Fenlake Road, terraced villa	£210	BTS 13, 20 April 1945 p. 6. By order of trustees of Kate Mason, deceased	PK 1/4/156. Occupied by Mr F. Thompson. Rental £17 11s pa
4 May 1945	Bedford, Lime Street, sale rooms	Bedford, 56–66a Pilcroft Street, block of seven cottages	Unsold	BTS 13, 20 April 1945 p. 6. By order of Mr and Mrs Hart	PK 1/4/156. Occupied by Mr Yoxen, Mr Marriott, Mrs Rabbitt, Mr Ibbett, Mrs Wilson, requisition, Mr Mayes. Total rental £117 7s 6d pa

Auction date	**Venue**	**Description**	**Price**	**Newspaper references**	**BLARS references**
4 May 1945	Bedford, Lime Street, sale rooms	Bedford, Polhill Field, Goldington Road, plot of garden ground, 40p	£225	BTS 20 April 1945 p. 6	PK 1/4/156. Seventy fruit trees, thirty gooseberry and current bushes. Vacant possession
4 May 1945	Bedford, Lime Street, sale rooms	Lidlington, Greenhayes, detached cottage	£640	BTS 20 April 1945 p. 6. By order of trustees of Mr and Mrs Bolt	PK 1/4/156. Vacant possession
11 May 1945	On site	Stotfold, 90 Hitchin Road, villa, building, garden land	£880	BTS 20, 27 April 1945 p. 6. On instruction of executors of Mrs Emily Edwards. Household effects sold following sale of property	-
12 May 1945	Bedford, Horne Lane, Tudor Rooms	Thurleigh, Backnoe End Farm, agricultural holding, 62a	£1,500	BTS 27 April 1945 p. 6; 4 May p. 6. Land requisitioned by Air Ministry. Rental £70 pa	PK 1/4/157. On instruction of the trustees of William Wagstaff. Vacant possession. Part of the land is farmed by Bedfordshire War Agricultural Executive Committee
5 June 1945	On site	Clifton, 74 Broad Street, house, 0.5a	£1,500	BTS 25 May 1945 p. 6; 1 June p. 6. On instruction of Mr R. S. Hughes. Vacant possession	-
19 June 1945	On site	Carlton, The Firs, freehold country house	Unsold	BTS 1, 8 June 1945 p. 6. On instruction of Mr C. E. Matthews	PK un-catalogued. Vacant possession, Household furniture sold following sale of property
20 June 1945	On site	Sandy, 8 St Neots Road, villa	£840	BTS 8 June 1945 p. 6. On instruction of administrators of H. A. Munday	-
22 June 1945	Bedford, Lime Street, sale rooms	Bedford, 64 Kimbolton Road, detached double-fronted house	£1,750	BTS 18 May 1945 p. 4; 8 June p. 6	-

Auction date	Venue	Description	Price	Newspaper references	BLARS references
22 June 1945	Bedford, Lime Street, sale rooms	Bedford, 7 Goldington Road, detached residence	£2,300	BTS 18 May 1945 p. 4; 8 June p. 6	-
22 June 1945	Bedford, Lime Street, sale rooms	Bedford, 10 Newnham Avenue	-	BTS 18 May 1945 p. 4	-
22 June 1945	Bedford, Lime Street, sale rooms	Bedford, 34 Chaucer Road, detached house	£1,700	BTS 18 May 1945 p. 4; 8 June p. 6	-
22 June 1945	Bedford, Lime Street, sale rooms	Bedford, 1 King's Place, detached cottage	-	BTS 8 June 1945 p. 6	-
22 June 1945	Bedford, Lime Street, sale rooms	Bromham, Evenley, Stagsden Road, bungalow, 2.5a	£1,800	BTS 18 May 1945 p. 4; 8 June p. 6	-
22 June 1945	Bedford, Lime Street, sale rooms	Kempston, 14 High Street, cottage	£625	BTS 18 May 1945 p. 4; 8 June p. 6	-
22 June 1945	Bedford, Lime Street, sale rooms	Girtford, Manor Farm, Georgian house	£2,900	BTS 1, 8 June 1945 p. 6	-
22 June 1945	Bedford, Lime Street, sale rooms	Milton Ernest, freehold paddock, 1a 25p	Unsold	BTS 8 June 1945 p. 6. By order of the Oakley Hunt trustees	-
7 July 1945	Bedford, Horne Lane, Tudor Rooms	Wilstead, Manor Farm, farmhouse, buildings, two cottages, 205a	-	BTS 1, 8, 22 June 1945 p. 6; 6 July p. 6	PK 2/5/2/23

Auction date	Venue	Description	Price	Newspaper references	BLARS references
14 July 1945	Bedford, Horne Lane, Tudor Rooms	Thurleigh, Scald Farm, farmhouse, buildings, two cottages, terrace of three cottages, cottage, 166.913a	£5,950	BTS 1, 8, 22 June 1945 p. 6; 6 July p. 6	PK un-catalogued. On instruction of executors of Thomas Wagstaff. Two cottages occupied by Mr A. Holly, rental £7 18s pa, and Mr Osborn, rental £8 pa. Terrace of three cottages occupied by Mr A. Gammons, rental £6 pa, and Miss Wrench, rental £5 pa, one vacant possession
27 July 1945	Bedford, Lime Street, sale rooms	Bedford, 10 St Augustine's Road	Unsold	BTS 29 June 1945 p. 6; 1, 27 July p. 6. Rental £60 pa	-
27 July 1945	Bedford, Lime Street, sale rooms	Bedford, 16 Merton Road, detached house	£775	BTS 29 June 1945 p. 6; 6, 27 July p. 6. Rental £52 pa	-
27 July 1945	Bedford, Lime Street, sale rooms	Bedford, 45 Conduit Road	Sold prior to auction	BTS 6, 20 July 1945 p. 6. Vacant possession	-
21 September 1945	Ashwell, The Three Tuns	Ashwell (Herts), Chauntry House, High Street, fifteenth century old-world residence	£3,300	BTS 27 July 1945 p. 6; 7 September p. 6	PK un-catalogued. Currently occupied by a furnished tenant. Vacant possession on completion
28 September 1945	Bedford, Lime Street, sale rooms	Bedford, 3 The Crescent	£1,750	BTS 7, 21 September 1945 p. 6	PK un-catalogued. Vacant possession
28 September 1945	Bedford, Lime Street, sale rooms	Bedford, 12 Queen Alexandra Road, semi-detached villa	£570	BTS 7, 21 September 1945 p. 6	PK un-catalogued. Occupied by Mrs J. Williams. Rental £36 18s 4d pa

Auction date	Venue	Description	Price	Newspaper references	BLARS references
28 September 1945	Bedford, Lime Street, sale rooms	Bedford, 12 St Paul's Road, semi-detached modern residence	Unsold	BTS 7, 21 September 1945 p. 6	PK un-catalogued. Occupied by Mrs Brittain. Rental £44 4s pa
28 September 1945	Bedford, Lime Street, sale rooms	Thurleigh, south side of Thurleigh main road, two brick and slate cottages	Unsold	BTS 7, 21 September 1945 p. 6. By order of Mr Asplin	PK un-catalogued. East cottage occupied by Mr E. Jefferies. Rental £4 11s pa. West cottage occupied by Mr W. Harlow. Rental £4 11s pa
12 October 1945	Bedford, Lime Street, sale rooms	Renhold, The Bungalow, The Green, 1r	£550	BTS 28 September 1945 p. 6	PK un-catalogued Vacant possession
12 October 1945	Bedford, Lime Street, sale rooms	Bedford, 47 Bushmead Avenue, semi-detached house	£700	BTS 28 September 1945 p. 6	PK un-catalogued Occupied by Mrs Kidson. Rental £45 pa
12 October 1945	Bedford, Lime Street, sale rooms	Bedford, 48 Bushmead Avenue, semi-detached corner house	£950	BTS 28 September 1945 p. 6	PK un-catalogued. Occupied by Mrs Shorley. Rental £48 pa
12 October 1945	Bedford, Lime Street, sale rooms	Bedford, 30 Goldington Avenue, semi-detached house	£730	BTS 28 September 1945 p. 6	PK un-catalogued. Occupied by Mrs Shorley. Rental £52 pa
12 October 1945	Bedford, Lime Street, sale rooms	Bedford, 58 Waterloo Road, semi-detached house	£910	BTS 28 September 1945 p. 6	PK un-catalogued. Occupied by Mrs Binyon. Rental £65 pa
12 October 1945	Bedford, Lime Street, sale rooms	Bedford, 57 Risborough Road, semi-detached house	Unsold	BTS 28 September 1945 p. 6. By order of Mr Stapleton	PK un-catalogued. Occupied by Mr E. J. Edwards. Rental £59 11s 8d pa
12 October 1945	Bedford, Lime Street, sale rooms	Bedford, 27 Commercial Road, terraced house	£360	BTS 28 September 1945 p. 6. By order of Mr Stapleton	PK un-catalogued. Occupied by Mrs Gray. Rental £33 7s 4d pa

Auction date	**Venue**	**Description**	**Price**	**Newspaper references**	**BLARS references**
12 October 1945	Bedford, Lime Street, sale rooms	Bedford, 55 Commercial Road, terraced villa	£360	BTS 28 September 1945 p. 6. By order of Mr Stapleton	PK un-catalogued. Occupied by Mr A. W. Swales. Rental £30 8s pa
12 October 1945	Bedford, Lime Street, sale rooms	Bedford, 47 Salisbury Street, terraced villa	Unsold	BTS 28 September 1945 p. 6. By order of Mr Stapleton	PK un-catalogued. Occupied by Mr Bowrill. Rental £52 pa
12 October 1945	On site	Wilden, Manitoba Poultry Farm, bungalow, 3a	Unsold	BTS 28 September 1945 p. 6; 5 October p. 6. By order of Mr Stapleton	PK 2/5/2/22
19 November 1945	On site	Colmworth, Chapel End, semi-detached cottage	£900	BTS 2, 9 November 1945 p. 6	PK 1/4/160, PK 2/2/1. Vacant possession. Household furniture sold following sale of property
19 November 1945	On site	Bromham, New Road, Thistley Green, corrugated and brick bungalow, garden plot	£50	BTS 16 November 1945 p. 6	-
24 November 1945	On site	Bedford, 29 Albany Road, iron studio	£70	BTS 16 November 1945 p. 6	-
24 November 1945	Lavendon, The George Inn	Lavendon, 12 Castle Road, house, farm buildings, paddock	£1,750	BTS 16 November 1945 p. 6. By order of Mrs Ives	-
12 December 1945	On site	Harrold, The Green, freehold house, outhouses, workshops, gardens	£1,400	BTS 23 November 1945 p. 6	PK un-catalogued. By order of Rootham estate. Miss J. Rootham and Mrs Hay to have occupation of kitchen garden nearest the buildings rent free for life
12 December 1945	Harrold, Harrold Institute	Harrold, The Green, garden plot facing Harrold Mill, 1r 10p	£130	BTS 23 November 1945 p. 6	PK un-catalogued

Auction date	Venue	Description	Price	Newspaper references	BLARS references
21 December 1945	Bedford, Lime Street, sale rooms	Renhold, Woodfield Road, bungalow, 81.25a	£580	BTS 30 November 1945 p. 6	-
21 December 1945	Bedford, Lime Street, sale rooms	Kempston, 36 Margetts Road	Sold prior to auction	BTS 30 November 1945 p. 6; 21 December p. 6. Occupied by Mr G. H. Hawkins. Rental £13 pa	-
14 February 1946	On site	Riseley, Easton Cottage, 74 High Street	-	BTS 25 January 1946 p. 6; 1, 8 February p. 6. Vacant possession	PK 1/4/165. By order of executors of Miss E. S. Whitehead
1 March 1946	Bedford, Lime Street, sale rooms	Bedford, 1–9 Howard Street, five cottages	£1,150	BTS 8 February 1946 p. 6; 1 March p. 6	PK un-catalogued. By order of executors of J. J. Stanton. Occupied by F. Stevens, M. Aylott, W. Roberts, Dorothy Livingstone, H. Lugsden. Total rental £167 9s 8d pa
1 March 1946	Bedford, Lime Street, sale rooms	Bedford, 11–19 Howard Street, five cottages	£1,000	BTS 8 February 1946 p. 6; 1 March p. 6	PK un-catalogued. By order of executors of J. J. Stanton. Occupied by W. Mansfield, H. Chapman, E. Freeman, F. Gray, S. Stafferton. Total rental £136 14s 4d pa
1 March 1946	Bedford, Lime Street, sale rooms	Bedford, 13 and 15 Althorpe Street, two villas	£450	BTS 8 February 1946 p. 6; 1 March p. 6	PK un-catalogued. By order of executors of J. J. Stanton. Occupied by A. Root and J. Nickerson. Total rental £42 2s pa
1 March 1946	Bedford, Lime Street, sale rooms	Bedford, 17 and 19 Althorpe Street, two villas	£550	BTS 8 February 1946 p. 6; 1 March p. 6	PK un-catalogued. By order of executors of J. J. Stanton. Occupied by C. Spencer and A. Linger. Total rental £57 12s 8d pa

Auction date	Venue	Description	Price	Newspaper references	BLARS references
1 March 1946	Bedford, Lime Street, sale rooms	Bedford, 21 and 23 Althorpe Street, two villas	£550	BTS 8 February 1946 p. 6; 1 March p. 6	PK un-catalogued. By order of executors of J. J. Stanton. Occupied by J. Potter and C. E. Richards. Total rental £57 17s 8d pa
1 March 1946	Bedford, Lime Street, sale rooms	Bedford, 47 Althorpe Street, villa	£240	BTS 8 February 1946 p. 6; 1 March p. 6	PK un-catalogued. By order of executors of J. J. Stanton. Occupied by T. Burley. Rental £21 17s 8d pa
1 March 1946	Bedford, Lime Street, sale rooms	Bedford, 26 and 28 Great Butt Street, two villas	£525	BTS 8 February 1946 p. 6; 1 March p. 6	PK un-catalogued. By order of executors of J. J. Stanton. Occupied by Kitty Atkins and N. Field. Total rental £72 16s pa
1 March 1946	Bedford, Lime Street, sale rooms	Bedford, 30 and 32 Great Butt Street, two villas	£500	BTS 8 February 1946 p. 6; 1 March p. 6	PK un-catalogued. By order of executors of J. J. Stanton. Occupied by Lilian Milne and A. Jones. Total rental £56 18s 7d pa
1 March 1946	Bedford, Lime Street, sale rooms	Bedford, 34 and 36 Great Butt Street, two villas	£500	BTS 8 February 1946 p. 6; 1 March p. 6	PK un-catalogued. By order of executors of J. J. Stanton. Occupied by A. Longland and O. Davies. Total rental £59 4s 1d pa
1 March 1946	Bedford, Lime Street, sale rooms	Bedford, 30 and 32 Little Butt Street, two villas	£450	BTS 8 February 1946 p. 6; 1 March p. 6	PK un-catalogued. By order of executors of J. J. Stanton. Occupied by A. Burridge and D. Cox. Total rental £42 9s 4d pa
1 March 1946	Bedford, Lime Street, sale rooms	Bedford, 2–10 Derby Street, five cottages	£625	BTS 8 February 1946 p. 6; 1 March p. 6	PK un-catalogued. By order of executors of J. J. Stanton. Occupied by W. Horner, E. Mann, C. Hartin, F. Allen, W. Carrington. Total rental £106 14s 2d pa

Auction date	Venue	Description	Price	Newspaper references	BLARS references
1 March 1946	Bedford, Lime Street, sale rooms	Bedford, 12 and 14 Derby Street, two cottages	£230	BTS 8 February 1946 p. 6; 1 March p. 6	PK un-catalogued. By order of executors of J. J. Stanton. Occupied by Longstaff and C. Ashpole. Total rental £38 4s 10d pa
1 March 1946	Bedford, Lime Street, sale rooms	Bedford, 15 and 17 Derby street, two cottages	£350	BTS 8 February 1946 p. 6; 1 March p. 6	PK un-catalogued. By order of executors of J. J. Stanton. Occupied by R. Murfitt and A. Wright. Total rental £54 5s 6d pa
1 March 1946	Bedford, Lime Street, sale rooms	Bedford, 19 and 21 Derby Street, two cottages	£350	BTS 8 February 1946 p. 6; 1 March p. 6	PK un-catalogued. By order of executors of J. J. Stanton. Occupied by C. Field and S. G. Headlam. Total rental £54 5s 6d pa
1 March 1946	Bedford, Lime Street, sale rooms	Bedford, 23 and 25 Derby Street, two cottages	£250	BTS 8 February 1946 p. 6; 1 March p. 6	PK un-catalogued. By order of executors of J. J Stanton. Occupied by G. Lawson and W. Ormes. Total rental £37 14s pa
1 March 1946	Bedford, Lime Street, sale rooms	Bedford, 28–38 Queen Street, six cottages	£1,170	BTS 8 February 1946 p. 6; 1 March p. 6	PK un-catalogued. By order of executors of J. J. Stanton. Occupied by T. Coles, T. Warner, D. Breeds, W. Cook, A. Odell, E. MacFarlane and the Telephone Manager. Total rental £162 1s 4d pa
1 March 1946	Bedford, Lime Street, sale rooms	Bedford, 31–35 Canning Street, three cottages	£500	BTS 15 February 1946 p. 6; 1 March p. 6. On instruction of W. and T. C. Hipwell. Occupied by W. Summerfield, Mrs Little and F. Panter. Total rental £68 18s pa	-

Auction date	Venue	Description	Price	Newspaper references	BLARS references
1 March 1946	Bedford, Lime Street, sale rooms	Bedford, 3 Rothsay Road, in six flats	Unsold	BTS 22 February 1946 p. 6; 1 March p. 6	-
5 March 1946	On site	Renhold, Top End Road, freehold country cottage, 0.213a	£700	BTS 15 February 1945 p. 6; 1 March p. 6	PK un-catalogued. On instruction of Mr L. Surtees as administrator of Miss A. S. Surtees. Vacant possession. Household furnishings sold following sale of property
28 March 1946	Baldock, The Victoria Inn	Baldock (Herts), 7 Station Road, semi-detached house	Unsold	BTS 15 March 1946 p. 6	PK un-catalogued. Occupied by Mr C. F. A. Hendricks. Rental £41 12s pa
28 March 1946	Baldock, The Victoria Inn	Baldock (Herts), 30 Church Street, corner shop, living accommodation	£950	BTS 15 March 1946 p. 6	PK un-catalogued. Vacant possession
28 March 1946	Baldock, The Victoria Inn	Baldock (Herts), Hill Cottage, Royston Road, cottage, farmery	£550	BTS 15 March 1946 p. 6	PK un-catalogued. Occupied by Mr A. Plum. Rental £28 9s pa
26 April 1946	Bedford, Lime Street, sale rooms	Bedford, 13 Kimbolton Avenue, corner residence	Unsold	BTS 5 April 1946 p. 6; 12 April p. 6	PK un-catalogued. Vacant possession
26 April 1946	Bedford, Lime Street, sale rooms	Bedford, 15 Cornwall Road, semi-detached house	-	BTS 5 April 1946 p. 6; 12 April p. 6	PK un-catalogued. Occupied by Mrs M. Hawkes. Rental £52 pa
26 April 1946	Bedford, Lime Street, sale rooms	Bedford, 19 Cornwall Road, semi-detached house	Unsold	BTS 5 April 1946 p. 6; 12 April p. 6	PK un-catalogued. Occupied by Mrs C. Moule

Auction date	Venue	Description	Price	Newspaper references	BLARS references
26 April 1946	Bedford, Lime Street, sale rooms	Bedford, 21 Cornwall Road, semi-detached house	Unsold	BTS 5 April 1946 p. 6; 12 April p. 6	PK un-catalogued. Occupied by Mrs C. Moule in conjunction with number 19. Rental £90 pa
26 April 1946	Bedford, Lime Street, sale rooms	Bedford, 23 Cornwall Road, semi-detached house	Unsold	BTS 5 April 1946 p. 6; 12 April p. 6	PK un-catalogued. Occupied by Mr G. P. Allen. Rental £48 pa
26 April 1946	Bedford, Lime Street, sale rooms	Bedford, 81 and 83 Newnham Avenue, two villas	Unsold	BTS 5 April 1946 p. 6; 12 April p. 6	PK un-catalogued. Number 81 occupied by Mr E. T. Thompson. 83 occupied by Mrs Saunders. Total rental £39 12s pa
26 April 1946	Bedford, Lime Street, sale rooms	Bedford, 48 Gwyn Street, shop, villa	Unsold	BTS 5 April 1946 p. 6; 12 April p. 6	PK un-catalogued. Occupied by Messrs Bishop and Brooke Ltd. Rental £45 10s pa
26 April 1946	Bedford, Lime Street, sale rooms	Bedford, 50 Gwyn Street, villa	Unsold	BTS 5 April 1946 p. 6; 12 April p. 6	PK un-catalogued. Occupied by Mr J. W. Wells. Rental £27 1s 8d pa
26 April 1946	Bedford, Lime Street, sale rooms	Bedford, 53 Gwyn Street, villa	Unsold	BTS 5 April 1946 p. 6; 12 April p. 6	PK un-catalogued. Occupied by Mrs Q. M. Spindler. Rental £29 5s pa
26 April 1946	Bedford, Lime Street, sale rooms	Bedford, 20a Greenhill Street, workshop	Unsold	BTS 5 April 1946 p. 6; 12 April p. 6	PK un-catalogued. Occupied by Mr W. A. Pinfold. Rental £18 17s pa
26 April 1946	Bedford, Lime Street, sale rooms	Bedford, 33 Greenhill Street, detached villa	£275	BTS 5 April 1946 p. 6; 12 April p. 6	PK un-catalogued. Occupied by Mrs M. A. Richardson. Rental £25 7s 4d pa
26 April 1946	Bedford, Lime Street, sale rooms	Bedford, 24 Hassett Street, villa	£350	BTS 5 April 1946 p. 6; 12 April p. 6	PK un-catalogued. Occupied by Mrs Webb. Rental £43 8s pa
26 April 1946	Bedford, Lime Street, sale rooms	Bedford, 72 Salisbury Street, villa	Unsold	BTS 5 April 1946 p. 6; 12 April p. 6	PK un-catalogued. Occupied by Mrs F. Berrington. Rental £30 6s pa

Auction date	Venue	Description	Price	Newspaper references	BLARS references
26 April 1946	Bedford, Lime Street, sale rooms	Bedford, 74 Salisbury Street, villa	£500	BTS 5 April 1946 p. 6; 12 April p. 6	PK un-catalogued. Occupied by Mr Best. Rental £27 6s pa
26 April 1946	Bedford, Lime Street, sale rooms	Bedford, 76 Salisbury Street, villa	£500	BTS 5 April 1946 p. 6; 12 April p. 6	PK un-catalogued. Occupied by Mr E. M. Appleby. Rental £30 6s pa
26 April 1946	Bedford, Lime Street, sale rooms	Bedford, 78 Salisbury Street, villa	Unsold	BTS 5 April 1946 p. 6; 12 April p. 6	PK un-catalogued. Occupied by Mrs L. Pask. Rental £29 2s pa
26 April 1946	Bedford, Lime Street, sale rooms	Kempston, Hill Grounds, east side of occupational roadway, garden land, 1.75a	£270	BTS 5 April 1946 p. 6; 12 April p. 6. Vacant possession	-
24 May 1946	Bedford, Lime Street, sale rooms	Bedford, 9 Prebend Street, villa	£350	BTS 10 May 1946 p. 6	PK un-catalogued. To close estate of F. G. Smith. Occupied by Mr W. Breed. Rental £30 pa
24 May 1946	Bedford, Lime Street, sale rooms	Bedford, 11 Prebend Street, villa	£350	BTS 10 May 1946 p. 6	PK un-catalogued. To close estate of F. G. Smith. Occupied by Mr E. Caves. Rental £27 4s pa
24 May 1946	Bedford, Lime Street, sale rooms	Bedford, 3 Battison Street, semi-detached villa	£400	BTS 10 May 1946 p. 6	PK un-catalogued. To close estate of F. G. Smith. Occupied by Mr R. S. Ames. Rental £30 pa
24 May 1946	Bedford, Lime Street, sale rooms	Bedford, 25 Battison Street, semi-detached villa	£415	BTS 10 May 1946 p. 6	PK un-catalogued. To close estate of F. G. Smith. Occupied by Mrs Young. Rental £22 8s pa
24 May 1946	Bedford, Lime Street, sale rooms	Bedford, 25 Denmark Street	£400	BTS 10 May 1946 p. 6	PK un-catalogued. To close estate of F. G. Smith. Occupied by Mr Purser. Rental £26 18s pa

Auction date	Venue	Description	Price	Newspaper references	BLARS references
24 May 1946	Bedford, Lime Street, sale rooms	Bedford, 27 Denmark Street	£375	BTS 10 May 1946 p. 6	PK un-catalogued. To close estate of F. G. Smith. Occupied by Mrs Wray. Rental £21 1s pa
24 May 1946	Bedford, Lime Street, sale rooms	Bedford, 45 George Street, villa	£690	BTS 10 May 1946 p. 6	PK un-catalogued. To close estate of F. G. Smith. Occupied by Mr F. C. Bodsworth. Rental £22 pa
28 May 1946	On site	Biddenham, Windmill Hill, country house, grounds	£7,100	BTS 10 May 1946 p. 6. On instruction of trustees of late Major H. J. Randall. Household furnishings sold following sale of property	-
26 July 1946	Bedford, Lime Street, sale rooms	Bedford, 138 Hurst Grove, freehold semi-detached residence	£780	BTS 12, 19 July 1946 p. 6	PK un-catalogued. By order of executors of H. J. Randall. Occupied as two flats by Miss Hedley. Rental £50 pa
26 July 1946	Bedford, Lime Street, sale rooms	Bedford, 140 Hurst Grove, freehold semi-detached residence	£670	BTS 12, 19 July 1946 p. 6	PK un-catalogued. Occupied by Mrs Hopkinson. Rental £39 14s pa
26 July 1946	Bedford, Lime Street, sale rooms	Bedford, 23 King's Place, cottage	Unsold	BTS 12, 19 July 1946 p. 6	PK un-catalogued. Rental £31 4s pa
26 July 1946	Bedford, Lime Street, sale rooms	Harrold, High Street, double-fronted cottage	£380	BTS 12 July 1946 p. 6. By order of D. P. Somerville-Warren	PK un-catalogued
26 July 1946	Bedford, Lime Street, sale rooms	Harrold, High Street, adjoining cottage	£190	BTS 12 July 1946 p. 6. By order of D. P. Somerville-Warren	PK un-catalogued
20 August 1946	On site	Stevington, Church Lane, blacksmith's premises, yard	Auction postponed	BTS 2, 9 August 1946 p. 6	PK un-catalogued. Vacant possession

Auction date	Venue	Description	Price	Newspaper references	BLARS references
18 September 1946	Ashwell, The Three Tuns	Ashwell (Herts), The Cottage, Gardener’s Lane	Unsold	-	PK un-catalogued. Vacant possession
18 September 1946	Ashwell, The Three Tuns	Ashwell (Herts), Gardener’s Lane, cottage	Unsold	-	PK un-catalogued. Occupied by Miss Emily Evans. Rental £14 6s pa
4 October 1946	Bedford, Lime Street, sale rooms	Bedford, 62 Bromham Road, butcher’s shop, house	Unsold	BTS 20 September 1946 p. 6; 4 October 1946 p. 6. By order of executors of Walter Crisp. Vacant possession	-
4 October 1946	Bedford, Lime Street, sale rooms	Bedford, 154 Bromham Road, semi-detached house	£1,200	BTS 27 September 1946 p. 6; 4 October p. 6. Requisitioned by Ministry of Health. Rental £55 pa	-
10 October 1946	On site	Great Staughton (Cambs), Brent Tor, gentleman’s residence, small paddock, 1a 6p	£2,000	BTS 20, 27 September 1946 p. 6	PK un-catalogued. On instruction of H. A. Jeffery Esq. 1934 bungalow with cement facing. Vacant possession on completion
12 October 1946	Bedford, Horne Lane, sale yards	Stevington, Church Lane, blacksmith’s premises, yard	£260	BTS 4 October 1946 p. 6	-
1 November 1946	Bedford, Lime Street, sale rooms	Kempston, 5 Spring Road, double-fronted residence	Auction postponed	BTS 4, 11, 18 October 1946 p. 6; 1 November p. 6. Re. property of Mrs E. M. Mitchell, deceased	-
1 November 1946	Bedford, Lime Street, sale rooms	Bedford, 12 Brereton Road, villa residence	Unsold	BTS 11, 18 October 1946 p. 6	-
1 November 1946	Bedford, Lime Street, sale rooms	Cople, Oakdale, situate well back from road in a spinney, detached bungalow, 4a	£2,050	BTS 11, 18 October 1946 p. 6	-

Auction date	Venue	Description	Price	Newspaper references	BLARS references
1 November 1946	Bedford, Lime Street, sale rooms	Kempston, Ersanmine, Ridge Road, modern semi-detached house	£1,725	BTS 25 October 1946 p. 6. Vacant possession	-
22 November 1946	Blunham, The Old Horse Shoes	Blunham, The Grange Farmhouse, Grange Road, double-fronted residence, yard, outbuildings	£1,800	BTS 8, 22 November 1946 p. 6. Vacant possession	PK un-catalogued. On instruction of Messrs Millard Bros
22 November 1946	Blunham, The Old Horse Shoes	Blunham, Grange Road, accommodation pasture, 7a 2r	£4,250 for twelve lots of land	BTS 8, 22 November 1946 p. 6	PK un-catalogued. On instruction of Messrs Millard Bros. Land farmed by vendors for past thirty years. Vacant possession
22 November 1946	Blunham, The Old Horse Shoes	Blunham, Grange Road, west of Blunham Grange, valuable garden land, 4a 1r 34p	£4,250 for twelve lots of land	BTS 8, 22 November 1946 p. 6	PK un-catalogued. On instruction of Messrs Millard Bros. Land farmed by vendors for past thirty years. Vacant possession
22 November 1946	Blunham, The Old Horse Shoes	Blunham, Grange Road, valuable garden land, eight lots of 5a	£4,250 for twelve lots of land	BTS 8, 22 November 1946 p. 6	PK un-catalogued. On instruction of Messrs Millard Bros. Land farmed by vendors for past thirty years. Vacant possession
22 November 1946	Blunham, The Old Horse Shoes	Blunham, Grange Road, valuable garden land, 7a 1r 10p	£4,250 for twelve lots of land	BTS 8, 22 November 1946 p. 6	PK un-catalogued. On instruction of Messrs Millard Bros. Land farmed by vendors for past thirty years. Vacant possession

Auction date	Venue	Description	Price	Newspaper references	BLARS references
22 November 1946	Blunham, The Old Horse Shoes	Blunham, Grange Road, valuable garden land, 5a 1r 34p	£4,250 for twelve lots of land	BTS 8, 22 November 1946 p. 6	PK un-catalogued. On instruction of Messrs Millard Bros. Land farmed by vendors for past thirty years. Vacant possession
22 November 1946	Blunham, The Old Horse Shoes	Chalton, southern side of Chalton to Blunham Station Road, plot of garden land, 2a 25p	£600	BTS 8, 22 November 1946 p. 6	PK un-catalogued. On instruction of Messrs Millard Bros. Land farmed by vendors for past thirty years. Building value. Vacant possession
22 November 1946	Blunham, The Old Horse Shoes	Chalton, southern side of Chalton to Blunham Station Road, plot of garden land, 5a	£2,000	BTS 8, 22 November 1946 p. 6	PK un-catalogued. On instruction of Messrs Millard Bros. Land farmed by vendors for past thirty years. Building value. Vacant possession
22 November 1946	Blunham, The Old Horse Shoes	Sandy, western side of Sandy to Everton Road, thatch cottage, yard, buildings, second yard, orchard, garden ground, 3r 15p	£900	BTS 8, 22 November 1946 p. 6	PK un-catalogued. On instruction of Messrs Millard Bros. Occupied by Mr G. J. Millard. Rental £40 pa
31 January 1947	Bedford, Lime Street, sale rooms	Bedford, 21 St Mary's Street, central business premises, double-fronted shop	£6,900	BTS 3, 17 January 1947 p. 6	PK un-catalogued. Suitable for a variety of trades. Vacant possession
31 January 1947	Bedford, Lime Street, sale rooms	Bedford, 17 and 19 Garfield Street, two villas	£875	BTS 3, 17 January 1947 p. 6. Total rental £57 4s pa	-
31 January 1947	Bedford, Lime Street, sale rooms	Bedford, 30 and 32 Bower Street, two villas	£675	BTS 3, 17 January 1947 p. 6. Total rental numbers 30–36 £89 8s pa	-

Auction date	Venue	Description	Price	Newspaper references	BLARS references
31 January 1947	Bedford, Lime Street, sale rooms	Bedford, 34 and 36 Bower Street, two villas	£575	BTS 3, 17 January 1947 p. 6. Total rental numbers 30–36 £89 8s pa	-
31 January 1947	Bedford, Lime Street, sale rooms	Bedford, 35 and 37 Pembroke Street, two villas	£750	BTS 3, 17 January 1947 p. 6. Total rental numbers 35–45 £158 19s pa	-
31 January 1947	Bedford, Lime Street, sale rooms	Bedford, 39 and 41 Pembroke Street, two villas	£700	BTS 3, 17 January 1947 p. 6. Total rental numbers 35–45 £158 19s pa	-
31 January 1947	Bedford, Lime Street, sale rooms	Bedford, 43 and 45 Pembroke Street, two villas	£725	BTS 3, 17 January 1947 p. 6. Total rental numbers 35–45 £158 19s pa	-
31 January 1947	Bedford, Lime Street, sale rooms	Bedford, 50 and 52 Denmark Street, two villas	£725	BTS 3, 17 January 1947 p. 6. Total rental numbers 50–60 £155 2s 8d pa	-
31 January 1947	Bedford, Lime Street, sale rooms	Bedford, 54 and 56 Denmark Street, two villas	£750	BTS 3, 17 January 1947 p. 6. Total rental numbers 50–60 £155 2s 8d pa	-
31 January 1947	Bedford, Lime Street, sale rooms	Bedford, 58 and 60 Denmark Street, two villas	£725	BTS 3, 17 January 1947 p. 6. Total rental numbers 50–60 £155 2s 8d pa	-
31 January 1947	Bedford, Lime Street, sale rooms	Bedford, 5 and 7 Farrer Street, two cottages	£400	BTS 3, 17 January 1947 p. 6. Total rental £42 9s 4d pa	-
31 January 1947	Bedford, Lime Street, sale rooms	Bedford, 11 and 13 Gadsby Street, two villas	£825	BTS 3, 17 January 1947 p. 6. Total rental £52 pa	-
31 January 1947	Bedford, Lime Street, sale rooms	Bedford, 28 George Street, villa	£1,100	BTS 17 January 1947 p. 6	-

Auction date	Venue	Description	Price	Newspaper references	BLARS references
11 April 1947	Bedford, Lime Street, sale rooms	Bedford, 19 Fairfax Road, villa	£1,280	BTS 21 March 1947 p. 4; 4 April p. 4	-
11 April 1947	Bedford, Lime Street, sale rooms	Kempston, 21 and 23 High Street, two cottages	Auction postponed	BTS 4 April 1947 p. 4	-
22 April 1947	Yelden, The Chequers	Yelden, adjoining The Chequers, three cottages, vacant plot of ground	£850	BTS 28 March 1947 p. 6; 4, 11, 18 April p. 4. Total rental £46 16s pa. Joint wash house and earth closet	-
17 May 1947	Bedford, Horne Lane, sale yards	Bromham, Thistley Green, site for campers or poultry farm, 1r 22p	£250	BTS 9, 16 May 1947 p. 4. On instruction of Mr G. Wildgust	-
17 May 1947	Bedford, Horne Lane, sale yards	Bromham, Thistley Green, plot of land, 27p	£130	BTS 9, 16 May 1947 p. 4. By order of executors of Robert Jeakings	-
17 May 1947	Bedford, Newnham Avenue, Garden Hut	Bedford, Newnham Avenue, allotment plot no. 241	£8	BTS 9, 16 May 1947 p. 4	-
13 June 1947	Bedford, Lime Street, sale rooms	Bedford, 27 Warwick Avenue, detached house	£2,675	BTS 16, 23, 30 May 1947 p. 4	-
13 June 1947	Bedford, Lime Street, sale rooms	Wootton, Fields Road, four buildings for demolition, paddock	£405	BTS 16, 23, 30 May 1947 p. 4	-

Auction date	Venue	Description	Price	Newspaper references	BLARS references
13 June 1947	Bedford, Lime Street, sale rooms	Kempston, Chantry Estate, adjoining LMS railway line, valuable land, 25a	Sold prior to auction	BTS 16, 23 May 1947 p. 4	-
13 June 1947	Bedford, Lime Street, sale rooms	Stevington, Park End, two plots of land, 0.246a	£40	BTS 30 May 1947 p. 4	-
13 June 1947	Bedford, Lime Street, sale rooms	Bromham, Thistley Green, garden site, caravan, 28p	£110	BTS 30 May 1947 p. 4	-
13 June 1947	Bedford, Lime Street, sale rooms	Bedford, 19–23 Priory Street, three houses	£900	BTS 6 June 1947 p. 4. Total rental £66 pa	-
17 June 1947	Lavendon, The George Inn	Lavendon (Bucks), 6 Northampton Road, detached cottage	£1,000	BTS 23, 30 May 1947 p. 4	-
17 June 1947	Lavendon, The George Inn	Lavendon (Bucks), 41–47 Castle Road, four stone cottages	£120	BTS 23, 30 May 1947 p. 4. Occupied by Mrs Moore, Mrs Panter, Mr Birdler. Number 47 vacant possession	-
17 June 1947	Lavendon, The George Inn	Lavendon (Bucks), 49–53 Castle Road, three cottages	£270	BTS 23, 30 May 1947 p. 4. Occupied by Mr J. J. Panter, Mrs J. Panter and Mrs Gibbons. Total rental £26 9s 6d pa	-
17 June 1947	Lavendon, The George Inn	Lavendon (Bucks), Castle Road, paddock, 1a 1r 9p	£210	BTS 23, 30 May 1947 p. 4. Vacant possession	-

Auction date	Venue	Description	Price	Newspaper references	BLARS references
11 July 1947	Bedford, Lime Street, sale rooms	Bedford, 16 Gwyn Street, villa, office and Bedford, 19 Hassett Street, double-fronted villa, yard	£2,800 Joint auction with P. C. Gambell	BTS 20, 27 June 1947 p. 4	PK 1/4/172. 16 Gwyn Street, house occupied by Mr Probert. Rental £55 18s pa. Office occupied by Mr Bick. Rental £26 pa. 19 Hassett Street, house occupied by Mr Downing. Rental £52 pa. Yard occupied by Messrs Bonnett and Hazell. Rental £52 pa
11 July 1947	Bedford, Lime Street, sale rooms	Bedford, 37 Cauldwell Street, corner shop, living accommodation	£1,400	BTS 20, 27 June 1947 p. 4	PK un-catalogued. Early possession
11 July 1947	Bedford, Lime Street, sale rooms	Bedford, 3 Newnham Road, gentleman's detached double-fronted residence	£3,600	BTS 20, 27 June 1947 p. 4	PK un-catalogued. Early possession
11 July 1947	Bedford, Lime Street, sale rooms	Bedford, 26 Bushmead Avenue, detached house	£975	BTS 20, 27 June 1947 p. 4	PK un-catalogued. Rental £52 pa
11 July 1947	Bedford, Lime Street, sale rooms	Bedford, 33 Shakespeare Road, residence	Unsold	BTS 27 June 1947 p. 4	PK un-catalogued. Vacant possession
11 July 1947	Bedford, Lime Street, sale rooms	Bedford, 22 Brookfield Road, detached modern house, nursery, 1.5a	£5,000	BTS 20, 27 June 1947 p. 4	PK un-catalogued. Sold as going concern. Vacant possession
26 July 1947	Bedford, Horne Lane, Tudor Rooms	Bromham, New Road, Thistley Green, site for campers	£55	BTS 18, 25 July 1947 p. 4. On instruction of A. A. White	-

Auction date	Venue	Description	Price	Newspaper references	BLARS references
26 July 1947	Bedford, Horne Lane, Tudor Rooms	Bromham, New Road Thistley Green,site for campers	Unsold	BTS 18, 25 July 1947 p. 4. On instruction of A. A. White	-
29 July 1947	On site	Bedford, 22 Russell Avenue, residence	£2,400	BTS 11, 18 July 1947 p. 4.	PK 2/4/11. Vacant possession. Household furniture sold following sale of property
12 August 1947	On site	Souldrop, 9 and 10 High Street, two cottages	£610	BTS 25 July 1947 p. 4; 1 August p. 4. Number 9 vacant possession. 10 rental £16 0s 8d pa	-
5 September 1947	Bedford, Lime Street, sale rooms	Bedford, 20 Merton Road, semi-detached residence	£2,150	BTS 15, 22 August 1947 p. 4	PK un-catalogued. Vacant possession can be arranged
5 September 1947	Bedford, Lime Street, sale rooms	Bedford, 47 Irwin Road, modern semi-detached house	£1,125	BTS 15, 22 August 1947 p. 4	PK un-catalogued. Rental £45 10s pa
5 September 1947	Bedford, Lime Street, sale rooms	Bedford, 2 and 4 Albert Street, two cottages	£300	BTS 15, 22 August 1947 p. 4	PK un-catalogued. Occupied by Messrs Hartley and Jones. Rental £36 3s 8d pa
5 September 1947	Bedford, Lime Street, sale rooms	Bedford, 12 Linden Road, detached residence, in two flats	£3,600	BTS 15, 22 August 1947 p. 4	PK un-catalogued. Ground floor flat occupied by Mr Munton. Rental £99 19s pa. First floor flat vacant possession
5 September 1947	Bedford, Lime Street, sale rooms	Bedford, 10 Spenser Road, semi-detached residence	£950	BTS 22, 29 August 1947 p. 4	PK un-catalogued. Occupied by Mrs Manders. Rental £55 pa
5 September 1947	Bedford, Lime Street, sale rooms	Marston Moretaine, Ashbrook, freehold farm, approached through Roxhill Farm, 77.537a	£2,800	BTS 15, 22 August 1947 p. 4	PK un-catalogued. By order of E. W. Stratford. Vacant possession

Auction date	Venue	Description	Price	Newspaper references	BLARS references
5 September 1947	Bedford, Lime Street, sale rooms	Moggerhanger, 2 and 4 Park Lane, two modern villas	£1,150	BTS 15, 22 August 1947 p. 4	PK un-catalogued. Occupied by Mr E. H. Ashwell and Mrs Rhodes. Total rental £70 4s pa
5 September 1947	Bedford, Lime Street, sale rooms	Rushden (Northants), Rosalind, Avenue Road, detached bungalow	£1,800	BTS 15, 22 August 1947 p. 4	PK un-catalogued
5 September 1947	Bedford, Lime Street, sale rooms	Stagsden, almost opposite Northampton Turn, Thistley Green, semi-detached villa	£860	BTS 22 August 1947 p. 4	PK un-catalogued
5 September 1947	Bedford, Lime Street, sale rooms	Stagsden, Thistley Green, adjoining above, villa	£410	BTS 22 August 1947 p. 4	PK un-catalogued. Occupied by Mrs White. Rental £26 pa
16 September 1947	On site	Willington, The Timbers, sixteenth century house, 0.5a	£4,800	BTS 22 August 1947 p. 4; 5 September p. 4. Household furniture sold following sale of property	PK un-catalogued. By order of the owner N. P. Forward Esq. Vacant possession
15 October 1947	Ashwell, The Three Tuns	Ashwell (Herts), Rest Haven, High Street, freehold detached house, garden, 1r 17p	£2,700	BTS 10 October 1947 p. 4. On instruction of Miss D. M. Sale. Vacant possession	-
16 October 1947	Baldock, The Town Hall	Baldock (Herts), Fairview, 39 Letchworth Road, freehold residence	£2,600 Joint auction with Messrs Simmons	-	-
17 October 1947	Bedford, Lime Street, sale rooms	Bedford, 107 Hurst Grove, semi-detached residence	£820	BTS 26 September 1947 p. 4; 3 October p. 4	PK un-catalogued. Occupied by Mrs Gregson. Rental £45 10s pa

Auction date	Venue	Description	Price	Newspaper references	BLARS references
17 October 1947	Bedford, Lime Street, sale rooms	Bedford, 14 Hassett Street, shop, dwelling	£1,200	BTS 26 September 1947 p. 4; 3 October p. 4	PK un-catalogued. Occupied by Mr Fairmaner. Rental £117 pa
17 October 1947	Bedford, Lime Street, sale rooms	Bedford, 23 St Cuthbert's Street, detached double-fronted residence	£3,000	BTS 26 September 1947 p. 4; 3 October p. 4	PK un-catalogued. Early possession
17 October 1947	Bedford, Lime Street, sale rooms	Bedford, 22 Bedesman's Place, house	£320	BTS 3 October 1947 p. 4	PK un-catalogued. Rental £22 6s pa
17 October 1947	Bedford, Lime Street, sale rooms	Turvey, The Gables, Bedford to Northampton Road, country residence, two grass paddocks of 4.5a, total property 6a	£5,000	BTS 26 September 1947 p. 4; 3 October p. 4	PK un-catalogued. Portion or rear paddock occupied by Mrs Wright. Rental £5 pa. Portion of paddock occupied by Mr Tongue. Rental 4s pa. Remainder vacant possession
21 October 1947	On site	Willington, Northville, Willington Road, farm house, buildings, garden ground, 2a 3r	£2,650	BTS 10 October 1947 p. 4	PK un-catalogued. By order of Mr Arthur C. Cope. Vacant possession. Household furniture sold following sale of property. Garden ground of 1a 26p cropped by Mr T. H. Saunders
28 October 1947	Bedford, The Swan Hotel	Bedford, 28 Shakespeare Road, detached double-fronted residence	£3,500 Joint sale with Swaffield & Son	BTS 10, 24 October 1947 p. 4	PK un-catalogued. Part occupied by Miss Watson. Rental £71 10s pa

Auction date	Venue	Description	Price	Newspaper references	BLARS references
21 November 1947	Bedford, Lime Street, sale rooms	Bromham, New Road, Thistley Green, semi-detached bungalow	£800	BTS 31 October 1947 p. 4; 7, 14 November p. 4	PK un-catalogued. Early possession
21 November 1947	Bedford, Lime Street, sale rooms	Bromham, New Road, Thistley Green, semi-detached bungalow	£440	BTS 31 October 1947 p. 4; 7, 14 November p. 4	PK un-catalogued. Rental £30 19s 8d pa
21 November 1947	Bedford, Lime Street, sale rooms	Bromham, Main Road, Thistley Green, plot of land, 51p	£250	BTS 31 October 1947 p. 4; 7, 14 November p. 4	PK un-catalogued. Vacant possession
21 November 1947	Bedford, Lime Street, sale rooms	Bedford, 41 Shakespeare Road, house, in three flats	£2,500	BTS 7, 14 November 1947 p. 4	PK un-catalogued. Top floor flat rental £44 7s pa. First floor flat £57 8s pa. Ground floor flat early possession
21 November 1947	Bedford, Lime Street, sale rooms	Bedford, 83 Ashburnham Road, semi-detached requisitioned house	Unsold	BTS 31 October 1947 p. 4; 7, 14 November p. 4	PK un-catalogued. Requisitioned by Ministry of Health. Compensational rental £55 pa
12 December 1947	Carlton, The Angel Inn	Carlton, High Street, eight cottages, large stone barn	£1,200	BTS 28 November 1947 p. 4; 5 December p. 4	PK un-catalogued. Occupied by W. Deveraux, Mrs Brandon, R. Chambers, G. Clayton, W. Franklin, S. Jordan, J. Stock, one vacant possession. Total rental, £70 11s 7d pa
20 January 1948	Harrold, Harrold Institute	Harrold, Brook Lane, five cottages	£410	BTS 2, 9, 16 January 1948 p. 4. Estate of W. C. Odell	PK 1/4/176. Occupied by S. Coleman, J. Fry. M.F. Odell and Mrs E. Robinson, one vacant possession. Total rental £27 16s pa

Auction date	Venue	Description	Price	Newspaper references	BLARS references
30 January 1948	Bedford, Lime Street, sale rooms	Bedford, Wellington Street, builder's yard, premises	£1,300	BTS 9, 16, 23 January 1948 p. 4. On instruction of executors of Frank Ebden	PK un-catalogued. Vacant possession
30 January 1948	Bedford, Lime Street, sale rooms	Kempston, Box End, orchard site, 0.75a	£320	BTS 16, 23 January 1948 p. 4. Vacant possession	PK un-catalogued. Vacant possession
21 April 1948	On site	Thurleigh, Scald End, detached double-fronted cottage	£800	BTS 9, 16 April 1948 p. 4. Household effects sold following sale of property	-
30 April 1948	Bedford, Lime Street, sale rooms	Bedford, 21 Russell Avenue, house	£1,300	BTS 9, 16, 23 April 1948 p. 4. Rental £52 pa	-
30 April 1948	Bedford, Lime Street, sale rooms	Bedford, 10–18 Little Butt Street, five cottages	£658	BTS 9, 23 April 1948 p. 4. Rental £89 7s 6d pa	-
30 April 1948	Bedford, Lime Street, sale rooms	Bedford, 42 Gwyn Street, villa	Unsold	BTS 9, 16, 23 April 1948 p. 4. Rental £29 6s 1d pa	-
30 April 1948	Bedford, Lime Street, sale rooms	Clapham, Green Lane, plot of land	-	BTS 9 April 1948 p. 4. Vacant possession	-
28 May 1948	Bedford, Lime Street, sale rooms	Potton, The Limes, Blackbird Street, detached house, 0.5a	Unsold	BTS 7, 14 May 1947 p. 4	PK un-catalogued. Early possession
28 May 1948	Bedford, Lime Street, sale rooms	Bedford, 55 Priory Street, villa	£250	BTS 7, 14 May 1947 p. 4	PK un-catalogued. Rental £31 4s pa
28 May 1948	Bedford, Lime Street, sale rooms	Kempston, 47 Chantry Avenue, modern bungalow	£620	BTS 7, 14 May 1947 p. 4	PK un-catalogued. Rental £45 18s 8d pa

Auction date	**Venue**	**Description**	**Price**	**Newspaper references**	**BLARS references**
2 July 1948	Bedford, Lime Street, sale rooms	Bedford, 106 Miller Road, semi-detached house	£925	BTS 4, 11, 18 June 1948 p. 4. Rental £43 19s pa	-
2 July 1948	Bedford, Lime Street, sale rooms	Bedford, 114 Miller Road, semi-detached house	£925	BTS 4, 11, 18 June 1948 p. 4. Rental £52 2s 8d pa	-
2 July 1948	Bedford, Lime Street, sale rooms	Bedford, 194 Fosterhill Road, detached house	Unsold	BTS 4, 11, 18 June 1948 p. 4. Rental £100 pa	-
2 July 1948	Bedford, Lime Street, sale rooms	Bedford, 14 Putnoe Lane, modern semi-detached house	Unsold	BTS 4, 11, 18 June 1948 p. 4	-
2 July 1948	Bedford, Lime Street, sale rooms	Bedford, 27 Russell Avenue, semi-detached house	Unsold	BTS 25 June 1948 p. 4	-
2 July 1948	Bedford, Lime Street, sale rooms	Bedford, 21 and 23 Western Street, two villas	Unsold	BTS 4, 11, 18 June 1948 p. 4. Number 21 let as three flats. Total rental £120 10s 4d pa	-
2 July 1948	Bedford, Lime Street, sale rooms	Bedford, 47 and 49 Wellington Street, shop, two dwellings, garage, loft	£1,000	BTS 18 June 1948 p. 4. By order of executors of Miss L. Gray. Rental £104 pa	-
2 July 1948	Bedford, Lime Street, sale rooms	Milton Ernest, Thurleigh Road, plot of land, over 0.5a	Unsold	BTS 4, 11, 18 June 1948 p. 4. Vacant possession	-
2 July 1948	Bedford, Lime Street, sale rooms	Stevington, 14 and 16 Silver Street, two cottages	£340	BTS 4, 11, 18 June 1948 p. 4. Number 16 rental £9 2s pa	-
6 July 1948	Cranfield, The Swan Inn	Cranfield, 125–131 High Street, four cottages	£1,200	BTS 18 June 1948 p. 4; 2 July p. 4. One vacant possession. Total rental £52 pa	-

Auction date	Venue	Description	Price	Newspaper references	BLARS references
28 July 1948	Luton, The George Hotel	Barton, Sideways, detached property	£4,400	BTS 9, 16, 23 July 1948 p. 4	-
30 July 1948	Bedford, Lime Street, sale rooms	Bedford, 122 Hurst Grove, semi-detached residence	Sold prior to auction	BTS 2 July 1948 p. 4	-
30 July 1948	On site	Great Barford, Clairville, situate on main road from Great Barford to St Neots, old-world cottage	Unsold	BTS 16, 23 July 1948 p. 4	-
8 October 1948	Bedford, Lime Street, sale rooms	Bedford, 14–20 Beaconsfield Street, four villas	£1,100	BTS 24 September 1948 p. 4. Total rental £95 8s 10d pa	-
8 October 1948	Bedford, Lime Street, sale rooms	Bedford, 48–52 Park Road West, three villas	£850	BTS 24 September 1948 p. 4. Total rental £63 8d pa	-
8 October 1948	Bedford, Lime Street, sale rooms	Bedford, 54–58 Park Road West, three villas	£900	BTS 24 September 1948 p. 4. Total rental £75 1s 6d pa	-
8 October 1948	Bedford, Lime Street, sale rooms	Bedford, 35–39 Palmerston Street, three villas	£925	BTS 24 September 1948 p. 4. Total rental £75 3s 8d pa	-
8 October 1948	Bedford, Lime Street, sale rooms	Bedford, 41–47 Palmerston Street, four villas	£1,500	BTS 24 September 1948 p. 4. Total rental £107 18s pa	-
8 October 1948	Bedford, Lime Street, sale rooms	Bedford, 26 and 28 Little Butt Street, two villas	£400	BTS 24 September 1948 p. 4. Total rental £54 6s 7d pa	-

Auction date	Venue	Description	Price	Newspaper references	BLARS references
8 October 1948	Bedford, Lime Street, sale rooms	Bedford, 38–42 Little Butt Street, three villas	£725	BTS 24 September 1948 p. 4. Total rental £60 2s 6d pa	-
8 October 1948	Bedford, Lime Street, sale rooms	Bedford, 3–11 Cauldwell Place, five cottages	£1,100	BTS 24 September 1948 p. 4. Total rental £108 13s 2d pa	-
8 October 1948	Bedford, Lime Street, sale rooms	Bedford, 4–12 Cauldwell Place, five cottages	£1,100	BTS 24 September 1948 p. 4. Total rental £119 1s 2d pa	-
8 October 1948	Bedford, Lime Street, sale rooms	Bedford, 37 Wellington Street, cottage	£330	BTS 17, 24 September 1948 p. 4. Rental £32 10s pa	-
8 October 1948	Bedford, Lime Street, sale rooms	Bedford, 5 Bedesman's Place, cottage	£300	BTS 17, 24 September 1948 p. 4. Rental £26 10s pa	-
8 October 1948	Bedford, Lime Street, sale rooms	Bedford, 19 King's Place, house	£350	BTS 17, 24 September 1948 p. 4. Rental £31 17s pa	-
8 October 1948	Bedford, Lime Street, sale rooms	Bedford, 9 Stanley Street, villa	Unsold	BTS 17, 24 September 1948 p. 4	-
8 October 1948	Bedford, Lime Street, sale rooms	Bedford, 22 Chaucer Road, house, in three flats	£1,400	BTS 24 September 1948 p. 4	-
19 October 1948	On site	Oakley, 92 Station Road, detached house, 2r 19p	£2,450	BTS 1, 8 October 1948 p. 4. Household furnishings sold following sale of property	-
16 November 1948	On site	Pavenham, Sedrup Cottage, 34 Mill Lane, old-world cottage	£2,325	BTS 22, 29 October 1948 p. 4. Household furnishings sold following sale of property	-

Auction date	Venue	Description	Price	Newspaper references	BLARS references
19 November 1948	Bedford, Lime Street, sale rooms	Bedford, 7 Maitland Street, villa	£570	BTS 29 October 1948 p. 4; 5 November p. 4	PK un-catalogued. Early possession
19 November 1948	Bedford, Lime Street, sale rooms	Bedford, 3 and 5 Maitland Street, two villas	£490	BTS 29 October 1948 p. 4; 5 November p. 4	PK un-catalogued. Total rental £43 13s 2d pa
19 November 1948	Bedford, Lime Street, sale rooms	Bedford, 36 Stanley Street, corner shop, living accommodation	Unsold	BTS 29 October 1948 p. 4; 5 November p. 4	PK un-catalogued. Early possession
19 November 1948	Bedford, Lime Street, sale rooms	Bromham, Minlaton, Village Green, modern residence	£1,200	BTS 29 October 1948 p. 4; 5 November p. 4	PK un-catalogued. Early possession
3 December 1948	Bedford, Lime Street, sale rooms	Bedford, 62 Castle Road, house	Unsold Joint auction with J. D. Hamp & Lowery	BTS 12, 19 November 1948 p. 6	-
2 February 1949	Sharnbrook, The Swan	Sharnbrook, High Street, two cottages, blacksmith's cottage	£1,500	BTS 7, 21 January 1949 p. 4. Re. R. C. Newell, deceased	PK 1/4/179. One cottage occupied by J. Read, greengrocer. Rental £24 14s pa. One occupied by Mrs Mole. Rental £15 10s pa. Blacksmith's cottage occupied by Mr Allen. Rental £24 18s pa
2 February 1949	Sharnbrook, The Swan	Sharnbrook, High Street, smallholding, garden, 1a 1r 6p	£150	BTS 7, 21 January 1949 p. 4. Re. R. C. Newell, deceased	PK 1/4/179. Occupied by Mr J. Read. Rental £5 pa
2 February 1949	Sharnbrook, The Swan	Sharnbrook, Church Lane, three cottages	£200	BTS 7, 21 January 1949 p. 4. Re. R. C. Newell, deceased	PK 1/4/179. Occupied by C. Roast, J. Knell and J. Hulatt. Total rental £41 12s pa

Auction date	Venue	Description	Price	Newspaper references	BLARS references
2 February 1949	Sharnbrook, The Swan	Sharnbrook, Church Lane, cottage	£300	BTS 7, 21 January 1949 p. 4. Re. R. C. Newell, deceased	PK 1/4/179. Occupied by J. Bance. Rental £19 10s pa
2 February 1949	Sharnbrook, The Swan	Sharnbrook, Church Lane, house, cottage	£730	BTS 7, 21 January 1949 p. 4. Re. R. C. Newell, deceased	PK 1/4/179. House occupied by W. Hales. Rental £39 pa. Cottage occupied by Mrs T. Newell. Rental £16 18s pa
2 February 1949	Sharnbrook, The Swan	Bletsoe, approached from main road, riverside plot for bathing and fishing	£100	BTS 7, 21 January 1949 p. 4. Re. R. C. Newell, deceased	PK 1/4/179. Vacant possession
2 February 1949	Sharnbrook, The Swan	Wymington, 21–33 High Street, six cottages	£460	BTS 7, 21 January 1949 p. 4. Re. R. C. Newell, deceased	PK 1/4/179. Total rental £82 2s 4d pa
2 February 1949	Sharnbrook, The Swan	Sharnbrook, Sharnbrook Mill	-	BTS 14, 21 January 1949 p. 4	PK 1/4/179. Mill owners will remove the machinery
4 February 1949	Bedford, Lime Street, sale rooms	Bedford, 3 Winifred Road, house, in two flats	£1,430	BTS 14, 21 January 1949 p. 4. Rental £117 pa	-
4 February 1949	Bedford, Lime Street, sale rooms	Bedford, 27 Ashburnham Road, house	£950	BTS 7, 21 January 1949 p. 4. Rental £52 pa	-
4 February 1949	Bedford, Lime Street, sale rooms	Kempston, 25 King Street, house	£350	BTS 7, 21 January 1949 p. 4. Total rental for numbers 25, 43 and 57, £20 18s 2d pa	-
4 February 1949	Bedford, Lime Street, sale rooms	Kempston, 43 King Street, villa	£500	BTS 7, 21 January 1949 p. 4. Total rental for numbers 25, 43 and 57, £20 18s 2d pa	-
4 February 1949	Bedford, Lime Street, sale rooms	Kempston, 51 King Street, villa	£605	BTS 7, 21 January 1949 p. 4. Rental £32 1s pa	-

Auction date	Venue	Description	Price	Newspaper references	BLARS references
4 February 1949	Bedford, Lime Street, sale rooms	Kempston, 57 King Street, villa	Unsold	BTS 7, 21 January 1949 p. 4. Total rental for numbers 25, 43 and 57, £20 18s 2d pa	-
4 February 1949	Bedford, Lime Street, sale rooms	Kempston, 180 Bedford Road, villa	£410	BTS 7, 21 January 1949 p. 4. Rental £20 18s 2d pa	-
4 February 1949	Bedford, Lime Street, sale rooms	Northill, Ickwell Road, plot of land, caravan, 1r	£150	BTS 21 January 1949 p. 4	-
4 March 1949	Bedford, Lime Street, sale rooms	Bedford, 9 and 10 Derwent Place, two villas	£300 Number 9 sold prior to auction	BTS 28 January 1949 p. 4; 11, 18 February p. 4. Number 9 vacant possession. 10 rental £21 4d pa	-
4 March 1949	Bedford, Lime Street, sale rooms	Bedford, 10–16 Gratton Road, four villas	Unsold	BTS 28 January 1949 p. 4; 11 February p. 4. Total rental £93 16s 4d pa	-
15 March 1949	Shefford, The White Hart Hotel	Campton, Church Farm, garden holding, double-fronted farm house, foreman's house, farm buildings, 84a	£8,500	BTS 25 February 1949 p. 4; 11 March p. 4. On instruction of Messrs E. J. White and Sons	PK un-catalogued. Church Farm vacant possession. Foreman's cottage occupied by Mr J. W. Pontin on service tenancy
15 March 1949	Shefford, The White Hart Hotel	Campton, Shefford Road, accommodation or building paddock, 3r 5p	£150	-	PK un-catalogued. Vacant possession
18 March 1949	Bedford, Lime Street, sale rooms	Bedford, 55 Phillpotts Avenue, semi-detached house	£2,625	BTS 25 February 1949 p. 4; 11 March p. 4	PK un-catalogued. Vacant possession

Auction date	Venue	Description	Price	Newspaper references	BLARS references
18 March 1949	Bedford, Lime Street, sale rooms	Sharnbrook, El Arish, Mill Road, semi-detached house	£1,750	BTS 25 February 1949 p. 4; 11 March p. 4	PK un-catalogued. Vacant possession
18 March 1949	Bedford, Lime Street, sale rooms	Bedford, 17 Commercial Road, terraced villa	£540	BTS 11 March 1949 p. 4	PK un-catalogued. Occupied by Mr Gates. Rental £32 10s pa
18 March 1949	Bedford, Lime Street, sale rooms	Bedford, 10 and 12 Bedesman's Place, cottages	£300	BTS 11 March 1949 p. 4	PK un-catalogued. Number 10 occupied by Mrs Hazel. Rental £19 10s pa. 12 occupied by Mrs Parton. Rental £19 10s pa
18 March 1949	Bedford, Lime Street, sale rooms	Bedford, 36 Houghton Road, semi-detached villa	£620	BTS 11 March 1949 p. 4	PK un-catalogued. Occupied by Mrs G. E. Lewis. Rental £37 14s pa
7 April 1949	-	Bedford, Royal County Theatre and Luton, The Grand Theatre, freehold for sale. Also Bedford, 153 and 155 Midland Road and 2 and 2a Grafton Street	- Joint auction with Knight, Frank and Rutley	TDA 10 March 1949 p. 10; 24 March p. 8. The properties form a corner block and allow for expansion of the Royal County Theatre. BTS 28 January 1949 p. 4	-
29 April 1949	Bedford, Lime Street, sale rooms	Bedford, 39 Bushmead Avenue, semi-detached house	Unsold	BTS 1, 15 April 1949 p. 4	-
29 April 1949	Bedford, Lime Street, sale rooms	Bedford, 19 Cornwall Road, semi-detached house, in two flats	Unsold	BTS 25 March 1949 p. 4; 1 April p. 4. First flat vacant possession. Second flat rental £66 6s pa	-

Auction date	Venue	Description	Price	Newspaper references	BLARS references
29 April 1949	Bedford, Lime Street, sale rooms	Bedford, 16 Myrtle Road, semi-detached house	- Withdrawn from auction	BTS 25 March 1949 p. 4; 1 April p. 4	-
29 April 1949	Bedford, Lime Street, sale rooms	Bedford, 77 Ashburnham Road, house	Unsold	BTS 1, 8 April 1949 p. 4. Rental £91 pa	-
29 April 1949	Bedford, Lime Street, sale rooms	Bedford, 60 Westbourne Road, villa	£1,250	BTS 8, 29 April 1949 p. 4. Vacant possession	-
29 April 1949	Bedford, Lime Street, sale rooms	Stagsden, Grafham, detached house	£2,800 Sold prior to auction	BTS 8, 15 April 1949 p. 4	-
29 April 1949	Bedford, Lime Street, sale rooms	Willington, Sedes Mea, Station Road, old-world cottage	£2,800	BTS 25 March 1949 p. 4; 1, 8 April p. 4	-
20 May 1949	Bedford, Lime Street, sale rooms	Bedford, 15 Richmond Road, house	Unsold	BTS 29 April 1949 p. 4; 6 May p. 4	-
20 May 1949	Bedford, Lime Street, sale rooms	Riseley, 94 High Street, detached cottage	£1,050	BTS 6 May 1949 p. 4; 13 May p. 6	PK 2/5/1/21. Vacant possession
20 May 1949	Bedford, Lime Street, sale rooms	Riseley, The Bungalow, detached house	£3,100	BTS 29 April 1949 p. 4; 13 May p. 6	PK 2/5/1/21. Vacant possession
20 May 1949	Bedford, Lime Street, sale rooms	Riseley, paddocks adjoining The Bungalow, 5.5a	£400	BTS 6 May 1949 p. 4. Occupied by Mr Smith. Rental £6 pa	-

Auction date	Venue	Description	Price	Newspaper references	BLARS references
20 May 1949	Bedford, Lime Street, sale rooms	Houghton Conquest, Greenways, 68 Bedford Road, bungalow,	Unsold	BTS 29 April 1949 p. 4; 6 May p. 4; 13 May p. 6	PK 2/5/1/21. Vacant possession
20 May 1949	Bedford, Lime Street, sale rooms	Bedford, Lindores, 351 Goldington Road, detached bungalow	£3,500	BTS 29 April 1949 p. 4; 6 May p. 4; 13 May p. 6	PK 2/5/1/21. Vacant possession
20 May 1949	Bedford, Lime Street, sale rooms	Bedford, 103 Warwick Avenue, house	Unsold	BTS 6 May 1949 p. 4; 13 May p. 6	PK 2/5/1/21. Vacant possession
1 June 1949	Guilden Morden, Six Bells	Guilden Morden (Cambs), Fox Cottage	£550	BTS 13, 27 May 1949 p. 6	PK un-catalogued. Vacant possession
17 June 1949	Bedford, Lime Street, sale rooms	Bedford, 119 Winchester Road, villa	£980	BTS 20, 27 May 1949 p. 6; 3 June p. 6	PK un-catalogued. Rental £58 10s pa
17 June 1949	Bedford, Lime Street, sale rooms	Bedford, 39 Hurst Grove, semi-detached house	Unsold	BTS 20, 27 May 1949 p. 6; 10 June p. 4	PK un-catalogued. Vacant possession
17 June 1949	Bedford, Lime Street, sale rooms	Bedford, Bunyan Arbour, Elstow Road, detached bungalow	£2,600	BTS 27 May 1949 p. 6; 2, 10 June p. 4	PK un-catalogued. Vacant possession
6 July 1949	Baldock, The Victoria Inn	Baldock (Herts), 16 Pembroke Road, double-fronted villa	£1,100	BTS 17 June 1949 p. 6; 24 June p. 4. Vacant possession	-
12 July 1949	Hitchin, The Sun Hotel	Arlesey, Beverley House, country residence, garden, 1a	Unsold	TDA 22 June 1949 p. 10. BTS 2, 10 June 1949 p. 4; 8 July p. 4	PK un-catalogued. Occupied by Mrs Lawrence

Auction date	Venue	Description	Price	Newspaper references	BLARS references
15 July 1949	Bedford, Lime Street, sale rooms	Wilstead, The Thatched Cottage, Ivy Lane	£1,250	BTS 24 June 1949 p. 4; 1 July p. 6. Vacant possession	-
15 July 1949	Bedford, Lime Street, sale rooms	Bedford, Goodwin's Garage, 175 Goldington Road, corner premises	Unsold	BTS 24 June 1949 p. 4; 1, 8 July p. 6. Vacant possession	-
15 July 1949	Bedford, Lime Street, sale rooms	Bedford, 177 Goldington Road, semi-detached house	Unsold	BTS 24 June 1949 p. 4; 1 July p. 6. Vacant possession	-
15 July 1949	Bedford, Lime Street, sale rooms	Bedford, 20 Wellington Street, villa	£330	BTS 1 July 1949 p. 6. Occupied by Mr Wildman. Rental £24 1s pa	-
15 July 1949	Bedford, Lime Street, sale rooms	Bedford, 12 Kimbolton Road, semi-detached house	£3,100	BTS 24 June 1949 p. 4; 1 July p. 6. By order of the Charity Commissioners. Vacant possession	-
19 July 1949	Cranfield, The Memorial Hall	Cranfield, 10 Bedford Road, detached bungalow, plot of ground adjoining	£840	BTS 24 June 1949 p. 4; 1 July p. 6	-
12 August 1949	Bedford, Lime Street, sale rooms	Swineshead, Green End Farm, freehold thatched farmstead, buildings, paddocks, orchards, arable, 9.5a	£1,800	BTS 15 July 1949 p. 6; 29 July p. 4	-
17 August 1949	Bedford, The Swan Hotel	Harrold, Harrold Hall, fourteen bedrooms, 8a 3r 12p	Unsold	TDA 2 August 1949 p. 10. BTS 22 July 1949 p. 6; 29 July p. 4; 5 August p. 4. Vacant possession	PK un-catalogued

Auction date	Venue	Description	Price	Newspaper references	BLARS references
17 August 1949	Bedford, The Swan Hotel	Harrold, Grovemount, freehold detached residence	Unsold	BTS 22 July 1949 p. 6; 29 July p. 4. Vacant possession	-
17 August 1949	Bedford, The Swan Hotel	Harrold, Dungee Road, two bungalows	Unsold	BTS 22 July 1949 p. 6; 29 July p. 4. Occupied by Messrs Susanne and Cockings. Total rental £33 14s pa	-
17 August 1949	Bedford, The Swan Hotel	Harrold, two enclosures of good arable land, 12a	Unsold	BTS 22 July 1949 p. 6; 29 July p. 4. Occupied by Mr Norman	-
23 September 1949	Bedford, Lime Street, sale rooms	Bedford, 42 Mill Street, freehold double-fronted premises	£4,000	BTS 2 September 1949 p. 4; 9 September p. 6. Vacant possession	-
23 September 1949	Bedford, Lime Street, sale rooms	Bedford, 22 Beverley Crescent, modern residence	£3,000	BTS 2 September 1949 p. 4; 9 September p. 6	-
23 September 1949	Bedford, Lime Street, sale rooms	Bedford, 66 The Grove, residence	£1,900	BTS 2 September 1949 p. 4; 9 September p. 6	-
23 September 1949	Bedford, Lime Street, sale rooms	Bedford, 8 The Grove, villa	Unsold	BTS 2 September 1949 p. 4; 9 September p. 6. Numbers 8 and 10 total rental £58 10s pa	-
23 September 1949	Bedford, Lime Street, sale rooms	Bedford, 10 The Grove, villa	£300	BTS 2 September 1949 p. 4; 9 September p. 6. Numbers 8 and 10 total rental £58 10s pa	-
23 September 1949	Bedford, Lime Street, sale rooms	Bedford, 8 and 10 Argyll Street, two cottages	£700	BTS 2 September 1949 p. 4; 9 September p. 6. Total rental £58 4s 7d pa	-

Auction date	Venue	Description	Price	Newspaper references	BLARS references
23 September 1949	Bedford, Lime Street, sale rooms	Bedford, 14–18 Argyll Street, three cottages	£800	BTS 2 September 1949 p. 4; 9 September p. 6. Total rental £74 12s 10s pa	-
23 September 1949	Bedford, Lime Street, sale rooms	Bedford, 5 Trevor Street, villa	Unsold	BTS 2 September 1949 p. 4; 9 September p. 6. Rental £36 4s 9d pa	-
23 September 1949	Bedford, Lime Street, sale rooms	Bedford, 6 Pattershall Street, villa	Unsold	BTS 2 September 1949 p. 4; 9 September p. 6 Rental £19 7s 10d pa	-
23 September 1949	Bedford, Lime Street, sale rooms	Bedford, 51 and 53 Priory Street, two villas	Unsold	BTS 2 September 1949 p. 4; 9 September p. 6. Total rental £54 12s pa	-
23 September 1949	Bedford, Lime Street, sale rooms	Bedford, 61–65 Priory Street, three cottages	Unsold	BTS 2 September 1949 p. 4; 9 September p. 6. Total rental £72 18s 7d pa	-
23 September 1949	Bedford, Lime Street, sale rooms	Bedford, 29 Queen Street, corner cottage	Unsold	BTS 2 September 1949 p. 4; 9 September p. 6. Rental £320 11s 8d pa	-
23 September 1949	Bedford, Lime Street, sale rooms	Kempston, 6 Farrer Street, cottage	Unsold	BTS 2 September 1949 p. 4; 9 September p. 6. Rental £14 7s 1d pa	-
23 September 1949	Bedford, Lime Street, sale rooms	Kempston, 10 Farrer Street, cottage	Unsold	BTS 2 September 1949 p. 4; 9 September p. 6. Rental £24 3s 2d pa	-
23 September 1949	Bedford, Lime Street, sale rooms	Wilstead, Littleworth, six cottages	Unsold	BTS 2 September 1949 p. 4; 9 September p. 6. Total rental £74 19s 4d pa	-
23 September 1949	Bedford, Lime Street, sale rooms	Carlton, Moor Road, three brick, stone, slate cottages	£250	BTS 2 September 1949 p. 4. Total rental £28 18s 6d pa	-

Auction date	Venue	Description	Price	Newspaper references	BLARS references
25 October 1949	Hitchin, The Sun Hotel	Baldock (Herts), Bygrave Manor Estate (listed below)	Joint auction with Drysdale Nurse and Co.	TDA 3 October 1949 p. 10. Two small residences, fifteen cottages, thirty six dwelling houses. Total rental £2,050 pa, 1,030a	Hertfordshire Archives and Local Studies Service, D/Z96/2/26
25 October 1949	Hitchin, The Sun Hotel	Baldock (Herts), farm house, three sets of buildings, fifteen farm worker's cottages, 995a	£22,500 Joint auction with Drysdale Nurse & Co.	TDA 3 October 1949 p. 10. BTS 30 September 1949 p. 4; 14 October p. 4. By order of mortgagees	Hertfordshire Archives and Local Studies Service, D/Z96/2/26
25 October 1949	Hitchin, The Sun Hotel	Baldock (Herts), 1 Ashwell Road	Unsold	BTS 30 September 1949 p. 4; 14 October p. 4. Occupied by Mr H. Winstone	Hertfordshire Archives and Local Studies Service, D/Z96/2/26
25 October 1949	Hitchin, The Sun Hotel	Baldock (Herts), 4 Ashwell Road	£700	BTS 30 September 1949 p. 4; 14 October p. 4. Occupied by Mr F. Noble	Hertfordshire Archives and Local Studies Service, D/Z96/2/26
25 October 1949	Hitchin, The Sun Hotel	Baldock (Herts), 5 Ashwell Road	£625	BTS 30 September 1949 p. 4; 14 October p. 4. Occupied by Mr S. Clynes	Hertfordshire Archives and Local Studies Service, D/Z96/2/26
25 October 1949	Hitchin, The Sun Hotel	Baldock (Herts), 6 Ashwell Road	Unsold	BTS 30 September 1949 p. 4; 14 October p. 4. Occupied by Mrs Broadella	Hertfordshire Archives and Local Studies Service, D/Z96/2/26
25 October 1949	Hitchin, The Sun Hotel	Baldock (Herts), 7 Ashwell Road	Unsold	BTS 30 September 1949 p. 4; 14 October p. 4. Requisitioned by Hitchin Rural District Council	Hertfordshire Archives and Local Studies Service, D/Z96/2/26

Auction date	Venue	Description	Price	Newspaper references	BLARS references
25 October 1949	Hitchin, The Sun Hotel	Baldock (Herts), 9, 10, 11, 12, 13 Ashwell Road	Unsold	BTS 30 September 1949 p. 4; 14 October p. 4. Number 9 occupied by Mr Allen. 10 occupied by Mr B. Brown. 11 occupied by Mrs Bass. 12 requisitioned by Hitchin Rural District Council. 13 occupied by Mr S. Frost.	Hertfordshire Archives and Local Studies Service, D/Z96/2/26
25 October 1949	Hitchin, The Sun Hotel	Baldock (Herts), 15–17 Ashwell Road, two bungalows, site	Unsold	BTS 30 September 1949 p. 4; 14 October p. 4. Number 15 occupied by Mr J. Ingman. 16 building site. 17 occupied by Mr Brigham	Hertfordshire Archives and Local Studies Service, D/Z96/2/26
25 October 1949	Hitchin, The Sun Hotel	Baldock (Herts), 19, 20, 21, 22, 23 Ashwell Road, five houses	Unsold	BTS 30 September 1949 p. 4; 14 October p. 4. Number 19 requisitioned by Hitchin Rural District Council. 20 occupied by Mrs Webb. 21 requisitioned by Hitchin Rural District Council. 22 occupied by Mr Dyer. 23 occupied by Mr D. W. Hill	Hertfordshire Archives and Local Studies Service, D/Z96/2/26
25 October 1949	Hitchin, The Sun Hotel	Baldock (Herts), 300 Wedon Way, house	£675	BTS 30 September 1949 p. 4; 14 October p. 4. Occupied by Mr G. M. Tompkins	Hertfordshire Archives and Local Studies Service, D/Z96/2/26
25 October 1949	Hitchin, The Sun Hotel	Baldock (Herts), 302 and 303 Wedon Way, house, building site	£675	BTS 30 September 1949 p. 4; 14 October p. 4. Number 302 occupied by Mr Buchanan. 303 building site	Hertfordshire Archives and Local Studies Service, D/Z96/2/26
25 October 1949	Hitchin, The Sun Hotel	Baldock (Herts), 304–306 Wedon Way, two houses, building site	Unsold	BTS 30 September 1949 p. 4; 14 October p. 4. Number 304 building site. 305 occupied by Mrs Lawrence. 306 occupied by Mr J. F. Carlton	Hertfordshire Archives and Local Studies Service, D/Z96/2/26
25 October 1949	Hitchin, The Sun Hotel	Baldock (Herts), 307 and 308 Wedon Way, bungalow, house	Unsold	BTS 30 September 1949 p. 4; 14 October p. 4. Number 307 occupied by Mr A. A. J. Keath. 308 occupied by Mr J. J. H. Hillier	Hertfordshire Archives and Local Studies Service, D/Z96/2/26

Auction date	Venue	Description	Price	Newspaper references	BLARS references
25 October 1949	Hitchin, The Sun Hotel	Baldock (Herts), 309 and 310 Wedon Way, two building sites	Unsold	BTS 30 September 1949 p. 4; 14 October p. 4.	Hertfordshire Archives and Local Studies Service, D/Z96/2/26
25 October 1949	Hitchin, The Sun Hotel	Baldock (Herts), 312 Wedon Way, house	£700	BTS 30 September 1949 p. 4; 14 October p. 4. Occupied by Mr W. Smith	Hertfordshire Archives and Local Studies Service, D/Z96/2/26
25 October 1949	Hitchin, The Sun Hotel	Baldock (Herts), 313–315 Wedon Way, two houses, building site	Unsold	BTS 30 September 1949 p. 4; 14 October p. 4. Number 313 occupied by Mr F. Barnes. 314 building site. 315 requisitioned by Hitchin Rural District Council	Hertfordshire Archives and Local Studies Service, D/Z96/2/26
25 October 1949	Hitchin, The Sun Hotel	Baldock (Herts), 31 Wedon Way, house	£775	BTS 30 September 1949 p. 4; 14 October p. 4. Occupied by H. W. Trappitt	Hertfordshire Archives and Local Studies Service, D/Z96/2/26
25 October 1949	Hitchin, The Sun Hotel	Baldock (Herts), 32, 33, 34 Wedon Way, three houses	Unsold	BTS 30 September 1949 p. 4; 14 October p. 4. Number 34 requisitioned by Hitchin Rural District Council. 33 occupied by Mr P. Barker. 32 occupied by Mr S. V. Dutton	Hertfordshire Archives and Local Studies Service, D/Z96/2/26
25 October 1949	Hitchin, The Sun Hotel	Baldock (Herts), 26, 27, 28, 29, 30 Wedon Way, houses, building site	Unsold	BTS 30 September 1949 p. 4; 14 October p. 4. Number 26 occupied by Mr A. R. Holliers. 27 building site. 28 and 29 requisitioned by Hitchin Rural District Council. 30 occupied by Mr N. A Bishop	Hertfordshire Archives and Local Studies Service, D/Z96/2/26
25 October 1949	Hitchin, The Sun Hotel	Baldock (Herts), 25 Wedon Way, house	£600	BTS 30 September 1949 p. 4; 14 October p. 4. Occupied by G. B. Chapman	Hertfordshire Archives and Local Studies Service, D/Z96/2/26
25 October 1949	Hitchin, The Sun Hotel	Baldock (Herts), 24 Wedon Way, house	Unsold	BTS 30 September 1949 p. 4; 14 October p. 4. Occupied by Mr H. Keech	Hertfordshire Archives and Local Studies Service, D/Z96/2/26

Auction date	Venue	Description	Price	Newspaper references	BLARS references
28 October 1949	Bedford, Lime Street saleroom	Bedford, 17 Campbell Road, house	£1,925	BTS 7 October 1949 p. 6; 21 October p. 6. Vacant possession	-
28 October 1949	Bedford, Lime Street saleroom	Bedford, 62 Adelaide Square	£1,650	BTS 7 October 1949 p. 6; 21 October p. 6	PK un-catalogued. Vacant possession
28 October 1949	Bedford, Lime Street saleroom	Bromham, Hill Cottages, three old-world cottages	Unsold	BTS 7 October 1949 p. 6; 21 October p. 6	PK un-catalogued. Occupied by Mrs Walker, J. Maxey and Mrs Wornest. Total rental £58 10s pa
28 October 1949	Bedford, Lime Street saleroom	Bedford, 76 Castle Road, detached double-fronted residence	Sold prior to auction	BTS 14 October 1949 p. 4; 21 October p. 6. Vacant possession	PK un-catalogued. Vacant possession
28 October 1949	Bedford, Lime Street saleroom	Bedford, 13 Oaklands Road, detached double-fronted residence	Unsold	BTS 7 October 1949 p. 6; 21 October p. 6. Vacant possession	PK un-catalogued. Vacant possession
28 October 1949	Bedford, Lime Street saleroom	Wootton, 25 and 27 Keeley Lane, two cottages	£330	BTS 21 October 1949 p. 6	PK un-catalogued. Total rental £26 8s pa
29 October 1949	Bedford, Lime Street saleroom	Kempston, 86 Eaton Road, semi-detached residence	Withdrawn from auction	BTS 14, 28 October 1949 p. 4; 21 October p. 6	-
9 December 1949	Bedford, Lime Street saleroom	Keysoe, Glebe Cottage, Bedford to Kimbolton Road, old-world detached residence	Unsold	BTS 23 November 1949 p. 4; 2 December p. 6	PK un-catalogued. Vacant possession

Auction date	Venue	Description	Price	Newspaper references	BLARS references
9 December 1949	Bedford, Lime Street saleroom	Bedford, 33 Tennyson Road, modern residence	Unsold	BTS 23 November 1949 p. 4; 2 December p. 6	PK un-catalogued. Vacant possession
9 December 1949	Bedford, Lime Street saleroom	Woburn Sands, Hillside, 36 Station Road, residence	Unsold	BTS 23 November 1949 p. 4; 2 December p. 6	PK un-catalogued. Vacant possession
9 December 1949	Bedford, Lime Street saleroom	Kempston, 86 Eaton Road, modern residence	Unsold	BTS 11 November 1949 p. 4; 2 December p. 6	PK un-catalogued. Vacant possession
9 December 1949	Bedford, Lime Street saleroom	Bedford, 2 Boswell Place	Sold prior to auction	BTS 11 November 1949 p. 4	-

Auction date	Venue	Description	Price	Newspaper references	BLARS references
3 February 1950	Bedford, Lime Street, sale rooms	Biddenham, Alma, Bedford to Northampton Road, freehold residence	Unsold	BTS 12 January 1950 p. 4. Vacant possession	PK un-catalogued
3 February 1950	Bedford, Lime Street, sale rooms	Bedford, 18 Ford End Road, shop, dwelling	Unsold	BTS 12 January 1950 p. 4	PK un-catalogued. Vacant possession
3 February 1950	Bedford, Lime Street, sale rooms	Bedford, 14 and 16 Ford End Road, two shops, dwellings	Sold prior to auction	BTS 12 January 1950 p. 4; 27 January p. 6	PK un-catalogued. Number 14 rental £53 pa. 16 rental £52 pa
3 February 1950	Bedford, Lime Street, sale rooms	Bedford, 20 Ford End Road, villa	Sold prior to auction	BTS 12 January 1950 p. 4; 27 January p. 6	PK un-catalogued. Rental £28 19s pa
3 February 1950	Bedford, Lime Street, sale rooms	Bedford, 22 Ford End Road, villa	£385	BTS 12 January 1950 p. 4	PK un-catalogued. Rental £29 pa
3 February 1950	Bedford, Lime Street, sale rooms	Bedford, 62 Wellington Street, villa	Unsold	BTS 12 January 1950 p. 4	PK un-catalogued. Rental £35 2s pa
3 February 1950	Bedford, Lime Street, sale rooms	Bedford, 64 Wellington Street, villa	£350	BTS 12 January 1950 p. 4	PK un-catalogued. Rental £25 15s 8d pa
3 February 1950	Bedford, Lime Street, sale rooms	Bedford, 68 Wellington Street, villa	£350	BTS 12 January 1950 p. 4	PK un-catalogued. Rental £27 1s 8d pa
3 February 1950	Bedford, Lime Street, sale rooms	Bedford, 13 and 15 Priory Street, two villas	£540	BTS 12 January 1950 p. 4	PK un-catalogued. Total rental £54 3s 4d pa

Auction date	Venue	Description	Price	Newspaper references	BLARS references
3 February 1950	Bedford, Lime Street, sale rooms	Bedford, 57 Hassett Street, villa	£200	BTS 12 January 1950 p. 4	PK un-catalogued. Rental £22 2s pa
3 February 1950	Bedford, Lime Street, sale rooms	Bedford, 13 Maitland Street, villa	Sold prior to auction	BTS 12 January 1950 p. 4; 20 January p. 6	-
3 February 1950	Bedford, Lime Street, sale rooms	Willington, Kelowna, adjoining station, bungalow, compact smallholding, 7.427a	£4,000	BTS 12 January 1950 p. 4	PK un-catalogued. Built for present owner under architect's supervision
10 March 1950	Bedford, Lime Street, sale rooms	Bedford, 18 Rutland Road, semi-detached house	Unsold	BTS 10, 17 February 1950 p. 6. By order of the executors of Sir George Royle CBE	-
10 March 1950	Bedford, Lime Street, sale rooms	Bedford, 20 Rutland Road, semi-detached house	£1,100	BTS 10, 17 February 1950 p. 6. By order of the executors of Sir George Royle CBE. Rental £48 10s pa	-
10 March 1950	Bedford, Lime Street, sale rooms	Bedford, Rutland Road, plot of land, garage	£425	BTS 10 February 1950 p. 6	-
10 March 1950	Bedford, Lime Street, sale rooms	Bedford, 29 Castle Road, detached house	£2,050	BTS 24 February 1950 p. 6; 3, 10 March p. 6. By order of executors of Miss A. Hermitage. Household effects sold following sale of property	-
10 March 1950	Bedford, Lime Street, sale rooms	Bedford, 57 The Grove, house	Unsold	BTS 10, 17 February 1950 p. 6. The residence of the late Rowland Hill	-

Auction date	Venue	Description	Price	Newspaper references	BLARS references
20 April 1950	Harrold, Harrold Institute	Little Odell, 9, 10, 11 and 12 The Folly, cottages, land, buildings	£1,525	BTS 24, 31 March 1950 p. 6. By order of executors of J. Fairey	PK un-catalogued. 9–11 occupied by Messrs Kennedy, Cockings and Swannell. Total rental £52 10s pa. Number 12 together with land and buildings occupied by Mr W. J. Newman. Rental £59 pa.
20 April 1950	Harrold, Harrold Institute	Carlton, 1–6 The Green, cottages	£1,150	BTS 24, 31 March 1950 p. 6. By order of executors of J. Fairey. Total rental £104 14s pa	PK un-catalogued. Number 1 occupied by Mr Dunford. Rental £26 pa. 2 occupied by Mr Boundes. Rental £28 pa. 3 occupied by Miss Hilton. Rental £15 12s pa. 4 occupied by Miss Flute. Rental £6 10s pa. 5 occupied by Mr Jordan. Rental £13 pa. 6 occupied by Mr Handley. Rental £15 12s pa

Auction date	Venue	Description	Price	Newspaper references	BLARS references
20 April 1950	Harrold, Harrold Institute	Harrold, 1–10 Mansion Lane, cottages	£1,650	BTS 24, 31 March 1950 p. 6. By order of executors of J. Fairey. Total rental £158 9s pa	PK un-catalogued. Number 1 occupied by Miss Smith. Rental £5 5s pa. 2 occupied by Miss Woodham. Rental £13 pa. 3 occupied by Mrs Bowers. Rental £15 12s pa. 4 occupied by Mrs Mitton. Rental £19 10s pa. 5 occupied by Mrs Knight. Rental £8 pa. 6 occupied by Mr Ward. Rental £6 2s pa. 7 occupied by Mr Smith. Rental £26 pa. 8 occupied by Mr Ratcliffe. Rental £19 10s pa. 9 occupied by Mr Draper. Rental £26 pa. 10 occupied by Mr Northern. Rental £19 10s pa
20 April 1950	Harrold, Harrold Institute	Carlton, High Street, old-world freehold cottage and attached cottage	£1,850	BTS 24, 31 March 1950 p. 6. By order of executors of Mrs G. S. Howe	PK un-catalogued
12 May 1950	Bedford, Lime Street, sale rooms	Bedford, 350 Goldington Road, bungalow, nursery, large glasshouse	Unsold	BTS 21, 28 April 1950 p. 6; 5 May p. 4. Vacant possession	PK un-catalogued
12 May 1950	Bedford, Lime Street, sale rooms	Bedford, 350 Goldington Road, plot of garden ground	Unsold	BTS 21, 28 April 1950 p. 6	PK un-catalogued. Access over a 10ft wide right of way from Brookfield Road
12 May 1950	Bedford, Lime Street, sale rooms	Bedford, 9 Lawrence Street, villa residence	£670	BTS 21, 28 April 1950 p. 6	PK un-catalogued. Rental £44 4s pa

Auction date	Venue	Description	Price	Newspaper references	BLARS references
12 May 1950	Bedford, Lime Street, sale rooms	Kempston, 45 Spring Road, semi-detached residence	£2,290	BTS 21, 28 April 1950 p. 6	PK un-catalogued. Vacant possession
20 May 1950	Bedford, The Swan Hotel	Sharnbrook House Estate (listed below)	-	BTS 7, 23 April 1950 p. 6; 12 May p. 6	PK 1/4/189
20 May 1950	Bedford, The Swan Hotel	Sharnbrook House, Georgian country house, gardener's cottage in grounds, garage, stabling, dairy, various stores, 10.865a	£4,000 The Mansion and grounds sold prior to auction	BTS 7, 23 April 1950 p. 6; 12, 19 May p. 6	PK 1/4/189. Gardener's cottage rental £18 4s pa. This lot carries with it the ownership of four oak pews in Sharnbrook Church
20 May 1950	Bedford, The Swan Hotel	Sharnbrook, Home Farm, buildings, 42.277a	£1,950	BTS 7, 23 April 1950 p. 6; 12 May p. 6	PK 1/4/189. Occupied by Messrs Marries and Rose. Rental £80 pa
20 May 1950	Bedford, The Swan Hotel	Sharnbrook, village shop, two adjacent buildings	£675	BTS 7, 23 April 1950 p. 6; 12 May p. 6	PK 1/4/189. Formerly used as a social hall. Rental £58 10s pa
20 May 1950	Bedford, The Swan Hotel	Sharnbrook, nursery garden, greenhouses, 0.38a	£400	BTS 7, 23 April 1950 p. 6; 12 May p. 6	PK 1/4/189. Occupied by C. Sanders. Rental £15 pa. Formerly kitchen garden to Sharnbrook House
20 May 1950	Bedford, The Swan Hotel	Sharnbrook, opposite Sharnbrook House, cottage, 2.502a	£590	BTS 7, 23 April 1950 p. 6; 12 May p. 6	PK 1/4/189
16 June 1950	Bedford, Lime Street, sale rooms	Sandy, 87 St Neots Road, house, garage	Unsold	BTS 26 May 1950 p. 6; 2 June p. 4. Vacant possession	-

Auction date	Venue	Description	Price	Newspaper references	BLARS references
16 June 1950	Bedford, Lime Street, sale rooms	Oakley, 68 High Street, villa	£360	BTS 19 May 1950 p. 6; 2 June p. 4. Occupied by Mr G. Smith. Rental £26 pa	-
16 June 1950	Bedford, Lime Street, sale rooms	Haynes, Woodside, West End, freehold poultry farm, two bungalows, 6a	Unsold	BTS 2 June 1950 p. 4	-
16 June 1950	Bedford, Lime Street, sale rooms	Biddenham, Tacolneston, country residence with private drive	Sold prior to auction	BTS 19 May 1950 p. 6; 9 June p. 6	-
19 July 1950	St. Neots, The Cross Keys Hotel	Eaton Socon, Silver Birches, Great North Road, bungalow	Joint auction with S. V. Ekins	-	PK un-catalogued. Vacant possession
21 July 1950	Bedford, Lime Street, sale rooms	Bedford, 27 Pemberley Avenue	Unsold	BTS 23 June 1950 p. 6; 7 July p. 6. Vacant possession	-
21 July 1950	Bedford, Lime Street, sale rooms	Bedford, The Dial House, Park Avenue, corner residence	£5,000	BTS 23 June 1950 p. 6; 7 July p. 6. Architect designed residence	-
21 July 1950	Bedford, Lime Street, sale rooms	Clapham, Riverside, 101 High Street, detached residence	-	BTS 23 June 1950 p. 6; 7 July p. 6	-
24 July 1950	Luton, The George Hotel	Luton, Wigmore Hall Farm, Georgian farmhouse, buildings, 149a	-	BTS 30 June 1950 p. 6. On instruction of executors of William and Benjamin Hartop	-

Auction date	Venue	Description	Price	Newspaper references	BLARS references
1 September 1950	Sharnbrook, The Swan with Two Nicks	Sharnbrook, High Street West, three cottages	£975	BTS 11 August 1950 p. 4. Two cottages occupied by Miss Peacock and Mrs Wintle	-
1 September 1950	Sharnbrook, The Swan with Two Nicks	Sharnbrook, Normans Road, two cottages under demolition order	£80	BTS 11 August 1950 p. 4	-
6 September 1950	-	Renhold, Salph End Farm, 14a	Sold prior to auction. Joint auction with George Trollope and Sons	TDA 29 May 1950 p. 10; 24 July p. 10; 21 August p. 10; 4 September p. 10. Vacant possession. BTS 4 August 1950 p. 4	-
8 September 1950	Bedford, Lime Street, sale rooms	Riseley, 118 High Street, detached cottage, smallholding, 3a 1r 15p	£1,150	BTS 25 August 1950 p. 4; 1 September p. 4	PK un-catalogued. Vacant possession
8 September 1950	Bedford, Lime Street, sale rooms	Bedford, 95 Hartington Street, substantial villa	£510	BTS 1 September 1950 p. 4	PK un-catalogued. Rental £44 17s pa
8 September 1950	Bedford, Lime Street, sale rooms	Bedford, 88 Harrowden Road, modern detached residence	£970	BTS 1 September 1950 p. 4; 8 September p. 6	PK un-catalogued. Rental £71 3s 6d pa
8 September 1950	Bedford, Lime Street, sale rooms	Stevington, 35–39 Park End, three cottages	£610	BTS 1 September 1950 p. 4; 8 September p. 6	PK un-catalogued. Rental £39 pa. Water from well, earth closet

Auction date	Venue	Description	Price	Newspaper references	BLARS references
8 September 1950	Bedford, Lime Street, sale rooms	Kempston, 15 Duncombe Street, cottage	£300	BTS 1 September 1950 p. 4; 8 September p. 6	PK un-catalogued. Rental £24 14s pa
8 September 1950	Bedford, Lime Street, sale rooms	Kempston, 17 Duncombe Street, cottage	£340	BTS 1 September 1950 p. 4	PK un-catalogued. Rental £25 2s 8d pa
8 September 1950	Bedford, Lime Street, sale rooms	Wootton, Fields Road, freehold arable land	£120	BTS 1 September 1950 p. 4; 8 September p. 6	PK un-catalogued. Occupied by Mrs B. Saunders. Rental £5 pa
8 September 1950	Bedford, Lime Street, sale rooms	Bedford, 268 Goldington Road, semi-detached double-fronted residence	£2,500	BTS 18 August 1950 p. 4; 8 September p. 6	PK un-catalogued. Vacant possession
8 September 1950	Bedford, Lime Street, sale rooms	Kempston, 30 King Street, villa	Unsold	BTS 1 September 1950 p. 4; 8 September p. 6	PK un-catalogued. Rental £33 16s pa
8 September 1950	Bedford, Lime Street, sale rooms	Kempston, 204–208 Bedford Road, three cottages	Unsold	BTS 1 September 1950 p. 4; 8 September p. 6	PK un-catalogued. Total rental £79 6s pa
21 September 1950	On site	Wootton, Keeley Lane, cottage, paddock, 2–2.75a	Unsold	BTS 8 September 1950 p. 6; 15 September p. 4. Cottage with vacant possession. Paddock occupied by Mr Boyles. Rental £4 pa. Household effects sold following sale of property	-
28 September 1950	Sharnbrook, The Swan with Two Nicks	Sharnbrook, Rose Cottage, Kendal Hill, old-world cottage	£875	BTS 8, 22, 29 September p. 6; 15 September p. 4; 6 October p. 4. Re. Alfred Payne, deceased. Vacant possession	-

Auction date	Venue	Description	Price	Newspaper references	BLARS references
6 October 1950	Bedford, Lime Street, sale rooms	Bedford, 17 and 17a St John's Street, business premises known as The Bluebird Cafe	Unsold	BTS 8, 22, 29 September 1950 p. 6; 15 September p. 4	PK un-catalogued. Vacant possession
6 October 1950	Bedford, Lime Street, sale rooms	Bedford, 2 Hardwick Road, villa	-	BTS 8 September 1950 p. 6; 15 September p. 4. Vacant possession	-
6 October 1950	Bedford, Lime Street, sale rooms	Kempston, 220 Bedford Road, cottage	-	BTS 8 September 1950 p. 6; 15 September p. 4	-
6 October 1950	Bedford, Lime Street, sale rooms	Kempston, 222 Bedford Road, cottage	-	BTS 8 September 1950 p. 6; 15 September p. 4	-
6 October 1950	Bedford, Lime Street, sale rooms	Kempston, 224 Bedford Road, cottage	£250	BTS 8 September 1950 p. 6; 15 September p. 4	PK un-catalogued. Rental £17 15s 4d pa
6 October 1950	Bedford, Lime Street, sale rooms	Kempston, 226 Bedford Road, cottage	Unsold	BTS 8 September 1950 p. 6; 15 September p. 4	PK un-catalogued. Rental £17 11s pa
6 October 1950	Bedford, Lime Street, sale rooms	Kempston, 232 Bedford Road, cottage	£250	BTS 8 September 1950 p. 6; 15 September p. 4	PK un-catalogued. Rental £18 19s 2d pa
6 October 1950	Bedford, Lime Street, sale rooms	Kempston, 234 Bedford Road, cottage	£250	BTS 8 September 1950 p. 6; 15 September p. 4	PK un-catalogued. Rental £17 13s 2d pa
6 October 1950	Bedford, Lime Street, sale rooms	Kempston, 236 Bedford Road, cottage	-	BTS 8 September 1950 p. 6; 15 September p. 4	-

Auction date	Venue	Description	Price	Newspaper references	BLARS references
6 October 1950	Bedford, Lime Street, sale rooms	Bedford, 42 Melbourne Street, villa	£335	BTS 8, 22 September 1950 p. 6	PK un-catalogued. Rental £24 12s 6d pa
6 October 1950	Bedford, Lime Street, sale rooms	Bedford, 36 Melbourne Street, villa	£250	BTS 8, 22 September 1950 p. 6	PK un-catalogued. Rental £20 14s 6d pa
6 October 1950	Bedford, Lime Street, sale rooms	Bedford, 44 Melbourne Street, villa	£300	BTS 8, 22 September 1950 p. 6	PK un-catalogued. Rental £27 19s pa
6 October 1950	Bedford, Lime Street, sale rooms	Bedford, 46 Melbourne Street, villa	£320	BTS 8, 22 September 1950 p. 6	PK un-catalogued. Rental £27 13s pa
11 October 1950	Baldock, The Victoria Inn	Baldock (Herts), 20–30 Pembroke Road, six cottages	£570	-	-
11 October 1950	Baldock, The Victoria Inn	Baldock (Herts), 31–43 South Road, seven cottages	-	-	-
11 October 1950	Baldock, The Victoria Inn	Baldock (Herts), 83–101 Clothall Road, ten cottages	Unsold	-	-
11 October 1950	Baldock, The Victoria Inn	Baldock (Herts), 1 and 3 Pembroke Road, two villas	£700	-	-
11 October 1950	Baldock, The Victoria Inn	Baldock (Herts), 6 and 8 Royston Road, two cottages	£420	-	-
17 October 1950	Sharnbrook, The Swan with Two Nicks	Sharnbrook, High Street at corner of Normans Road, old-world residence	£1,350	BTS 13 October 1950 p. 4	-

Auction date	Venue	Description	Price	Newspaper references	BLARS references
31 October 1950	Hitchin, The Sun Hotel	Ashwell (Herts), Bewlay, Slip End, detached residence	£5,000	BTS 27 October 1950 p. 4. Vacant possession	-
3 November 1950	Bedford, Lime Street, sale rooms	Bedford, 4 Honey Hill Road, villa	£1,675	BTS 6, 13, 27 October 1950 p. 4	PK un-catalogued. Vacant possession
3 November 1950	Bedford, Lime Street, sale rooms	Kempston, Cottage Farm, 55a	Unsold	BTS 6 October 1950 p. 4; 20, 27 October p. 6	PK un-catalogued. Vacant possession
3 November 1950	Bedford, Lime Street, sale rooms	Kempston,Woburn Road, modern detached house, 0.5a	Unsold	BTS 6 October 1950 p. 4; 20, 27 October p. 6	PK un-catalogued. Vacant possession
30 January 1951	Stotfold, The Black Lion Inn	Stotfold, Borrowdale, 136 Hitchin Road, detached house	£1,700	-	-
30 January 1951	Stotfold, The Black Lion Inn	Stotfold, 107 Hitchin Road, semi-detached house	£900	-	-
2 March 1951	Bedford, Lime Street, sale rooms	Bedford, 94 Hurst Grove, semi-detached villa	£1,500	BTS 9 February 1951 p. 4; 16 February p. 6	PK un-catalogued. Vacant possession
2 March 1951	Bedford, Lime Street, sale rooms	Clapham, Orchard Lea, The Baulk, detached residence	£1,000	BTS 9 February 1951 p. 4	PK un-catalogued. Let to Mr A. G. Mossman. Rental £36 pa
2 March 1951	Bedford, Lime Street, sale rooms	Bedford, 40 Ampthill Road, freehold semi-detached residence	£650	BTS 9 February 1951 p. 4; 16 February p. 6	PK un-catalogued. Let to Miss D. J. Brown. Rental £28 pa

Auction date	Venue	Description	Price	Newspaper references	BLARS references
2 March 1951	Bedford, Lime Street, sale rooms	Bedford, 47 Iddesleigh Road, freehold detached villa, three lock-up garages	£1,900	BTS 26 January 1951 p. 4; 9 February p. 4; 16 February p. 6	PK un-catalogued. Vacant possession
2 March 1951	Bedford, Lime Street, sale rooms	Bedford, 6 The Crescent, semi-detached double-fronted residence	Unsold	BTS 10 January 1951 p. 6; 26 January p. 4; 16 February p. 6. On instruction of W. Dunstall	PK un-catalogued. Vacant possession
2 March 1951	Bedford, Lime Street, sale rooms	Blunham, South Mills, cottage, market garden land, 2.5a	Sold prior to auction	BTS 2 February 1915 p. 6; 9 February p. 4; 16 February p. 6; 2 March p. 4. Rental £12 pa	-
6 April 1951	Bedford, Lime Street, sale rooms	Bedford, 35 and 37 Union Street, two terraced houses	Sold prior to auction	BTS 26 January 1951 p. 4; 9 February p. 4; 9 March p. 6; 6 April p. 6. Total rental £46 3s pa	-
6 April 1951	Bedford, Lime Street, sale rooms	Harrold, 11 and 13 Brook Lane, two cottages	£550	BTS 9 March 1951 p. 6. Occupied by Mr Chambers and Mrs Douglas. Total rental £13 10s pa	-
6 April 1951	Bedford, Lime Street, sale rooms	Harrold, 13 The Green, old stone and thatched cottage	£480	BTS 9 March 1951 p. 6. Vacant possession	-
6 April 1951	Bedford, Lime Street, sale rooms	Blunham, South Mills and Ridgeway Road, two cottages, smallholding, 2.5a	Unsold	BTS 9 March 1951 p. 6. One cottage rental £12 pa	-
6 April 1951	Bedford, Lime Street, sale rooms	Bedford, 6 Beverley Crescent, semi-detached house	£3,600	BTS 9 March 1951 p. 6. Vacant possession	-

Auction date	Venue	Description	Price	Newspaper references	BLARS references
6 April 1951	Bedford, Lime Street, sale rooms	Bedford, 1 Denmark Street, villa	Unsold	BTS 23 March 1951 p. 4. Vacant possession	-
4 May 1951	Bedford, Lime Street, sale rooms	Bedford, 7 Granville Street, semi-detached villa	£1,775	BTS 13 April 1951 p. 6; 4 May p. 4	PK un-catalogued. Vacant possession
4 May 1951	Bedford, Lime Street, sale rooms	Bedford, 90 Salisbury Street, villa	Unsold	BTS 20 April 1951 p. 4; 4 May p. 4. By order of trustees of late F. G. Kemp	PK un-catalogued. Vacant possession
4 May 1951	Bedford, Lime Street, sale rooms	Bedford, 46 Brookfield Road, bungalow	£2,825	BTS 6, 13 April 1951 p. 6; 4 May p. 4	PK un-catalogued. Vacant possession
8 June 1951	Bedford, Lime Street, sale rooms	Bedford, 52 Melbourne Street, villa	Sold prior to auction	BTS 18 May 1951 p. 4; 25 May p. 6. Vacant possession	-
8 June 1951	Bedford, Lime Street, sale rooms	Bedford, 78 Ford End Road, villa	£1,700	BTS 18 May 1951 p. 4; 25 May p. 6	PK un-catalogued. Vacant possession
8 June 1951	Bedford, Lime Street, sale rooms	Bedford, corner of Kimbolton Road and Putnoe Lane, building plot, 8,325 sq ft	£1,225	BTS 11 May 1951 p. 6; 25 May p. 6	PK un-catalogued. By order of the Corporation of Bedford
8 June 1951	Bedford, Lime Street, sale rooms	Thurleigh, The Matchbox, opposite Baptist Chapel, thatched cottage	£920	BTS 11 May 1951 p. 6; 25 May p. 6	PK un-catalogued. Earth closet
8 June 1951	Bedford, Lime Street, sale rooms	Bromham, Hillcrest, The Green, semi-detached house	£2,100	BTS 11 May 1951 p. 6; 25 May p. 6	PK un-catalogued. Vacant possession

Auction date	Venue	Description	Price	Newspaper references	BLARS references
8 June 1951	Bedford, Lime Street, sale rooms	Cranfield, 80 High Street, smallholding, cottage, 3a 32p	£1,000	BTS 18 May 1951 p. 6; 25 May p. 6	PK un-catalogued. Vacant possession
8 June 1951	Bedford, Lime Street, sale rooms	Bedford, 53 Pembroke Street, freehold residence	£2,400	BTS 11 May 1951 p. 6; 25 May p. 6. By order of the Corporation of Bedford	PK un-catalogued. Vacant possession
3 July 1951	On site	Bedford, The Headlands, 50 Beverley Crescent, freehold detached period style residence	£4,000	BTS 1, 15 June 1951 p. 4	PK un-catalogued. Household furnishings sold following sale of property
6 July 1951	Bedford, Lime Street, sale rooms	Bedford, 51 Honeyhill Road, freehold villa	£1,650	BTS 15 June 1951 p. 4; 6 July p. 6	PK un-catalogued. Vacant possession
6 July 1951	Bedford, Lime Street, sale rooms	Bedford, 97 Denmark Street, freehold villa	Unsold	BTS 15 June 1951 p. 4; 6 July p. 6	PK un-catalogued. Vacant possession
6 July 1951	Bedford, Lime Street, sale rooms	Wootton, 79–83 Cause End Road, two cottages, house, orchard, 1a 19p	£1,400	BTS 8 June 1951 p. 6; 22 June p. 4; 6 July p. 6. Previously known as The Star. One cottage rental £6 10s pa	-
20 July 1951	Bedford, Lime Street, sale rooms	Bedford, Windermere, 184 Castle Road, freehold semi-detached residence	£1,800	BTS 29 June 1951 p. 5; 20 July p. 7	PK un-catalogued. By order of the Court of Protection. Vacant possession
20 July 1951	Bedford, Lime Street, sale rooms	Clapham, 22 High Street, freehold residence	£2,250	BTS 29 June 1951 p. 5; 20 July p. 7	-

Auction date	Venue	Description	Price	Newspaper references	BLARS references
18 September 1951	On site	Sharnbrook, Lawn Cottage, High Street, picturesque freehold residence, bungalow at rear	£1,500	BTS 17, 24 August 1951 p. 4	PK un-catalogued. Lawn Cottage vacant possession. Bungalow occupied by Mr F. Baker. Rental £16 18s pa
21 September 1951	Bedford, Lime Street, sale rooms	Bedford, Kimbolton Road, freehold building plot	£1,100	BTS 31 August 1951 p. 6; 7 September p. 4; 21 September p. 6	PK un-catalogued
21 September 1951	Bedford, Lime Street, sale rooms	Bozeat (Northants), 31–39 High Street, five cottages	Unsold	BTS 31 August 1951 p. 6; 7 September p. 4; 21 September p. 6	PK uncatalogued. Number 31 occupied by Mr Tompkins. Rental £16 18s 9d pa. 33 occupied by Mr Coleclough. Rental £11 9s 8d pa. 35 and 37 vacant possession. 39 occupied by Mrs Corby. Rental £11 9s 8d pa. All with earth closets, main water from standpipe, two shared iron wash houses
-	-	Bedford, 136 Goldington Road, old-world residence	-	BTS 14 September 1951 p. 6; 5 October p. 6	-
4 October 1951	Sandy, The Red Lion Hotel	Blunham, Cowyard Farm, east side of High Street in centre of village adjoining School and Baptist Chapel, garden land, 15a 3r 17p	£3,700 for five lots	BTS 14 September 1951 p. 6	PK un-catalogued. Vacant possession

Auction date	Venue	Description	Price	Newspaper references	BLARS references
4 October 1951	Sandy, The Red Lion Hotel	Blunham, south side of the road from Blunham village to the Great North Road, pasture land, 31a 2r 31p	£3,700 for five lots	BTS 14 September 1951 p. 6	PK un-catalogued. Occupied by Mr J. T. Readman. Verbal Michaelmas tenancy, rental £60 pa
4 October 1951	Sandy, The Red Lion Hotel	Blunham, Tuppens Field, west side of Grange Road north of Blunham Grange, garden land, 26a 3r 9p	£3,700 for five lots	BTS 14 September 1951 p. 6	PK un-catalogued. Vacant possession
4 October 1951	Sandy, The Red Lion Hotel	Blunham, Marefield, situate to west of above, garden land, 20a 1r 35p	£3,700 for five lots	BTS 14 September 1951 p. 6	PK un-catalogued. Vacant possession
4 October 1951	Sandy, The Red Lion Hotel	Blunham, Saulsbury's Field, situate to south of above, garden land, 12a 2r 8p	£3,700 for five lots	BTS 14 September 1951 p. 6	PK un-catalogued. Vacant possession
19 October 1951	Bedford, Lime Street, sale rooms	Cranfield, The Bungalow, Wood End Road, 3a	£1,700	BTS 28 September 1951 p. 6; 5 October p. 6	PK un-catalogued. Vacant possession
19 October 1951	Bedford, Lime Street, sale rooms	Cranfield, Wood End Road, orchard, 0.603a	£170	BTS 28 September 1951 p. 6; 5 October p. 6	PK un-catalogued. Orchard of prime fruit trees including plums, damsons and apples
19 October 1951	Bedford, Lime Street, sale rooms	Bedford, 18 Russell Avenue, residence	£2,200	BTS 28 September 1951 p. 6; 5 October p. 6	PK un-catalogued. Vacant possession

Auction date	Venue	Description	Price	Newspaper references	BLARS references
6 November 1951	On site	Harrold, 27 Orchard Lane, detached house	£2,600	BTS 28 September 1951 p. 6; 5, 19 October p. 6	-
9 November 1951	Bedford, Lime Street, sale rooms	Renhold, The Thatched Cottage, The Green	Unsold	BTS 19 October 1951 p. 6. Drainage by cesspool. Vacant possession	-
9 November 1951	Bedford, Lime Street, sale rooms	Haynes, 9 and 11 Northwood End Road, two cottages, 2.25a	£2,000 Joint auction with Hendales	BTS 12, 19, 26 October 1951 p. 6. Number 9 rental £15 12s pa	-
7 December 1951	Bedford, Lime Street, sale rooms	Bedford, 9 Wellington Street, villa	£1,400	BTS 16 November 1951 p. 6; 7 December p. 6. Vacant possession	-
24 January 1952	Stotfold, The Black Lion Inn	Stotfold, 76 Hitchin Road, villa residence	£1,900	-	-
22 February 1952	Bedford, Lime Street, sale rooms	Kempston, 53 Bunyan Road, double-fronted villa	Sold prior to auction	BTS 18 January 1952 p. 6; 8, 15 February p. 4. Vacant possession	-
22 February 1952	Bedford, Lime Street, sale rooms	Kempston, 55 Bunyan Road, semi-detached house	Sold prior to auction	BTS 1 February 1952 p. 6; 8, 15 February p. 4	-
22 February 1952	Bedford, Lime Street, sale rooms	Kempston, 55a Bunyan Road, detached bungalow	Sold prior to auction	BTS 18 January 1952 p. 6; 8, 15 February p. 4. Vacant possession	-
22 February 1952	Bedford, Lime Street, sale rooms	Bedford, 60 Warwick Avenue, semi-detached house	£1,850	BTS 18 January 1952 p. 6; 8, 15 February p. 4. Vacant possession	-
22 February 1952	Bedford, Lime Street, sale rooms	Bedford, 3–9 Gratton Road, villas	Sold prior to auction	BTS 18 January 1952 p. 6. Rental £86 13s 4d pa	-

Auction date	Venue	Description	Price	Newspaper references	BLARS references
22 February 1952	Bedford, Lime Street, sale rooms	Bedford, 51 Beverley Crescent	-	BTS 25 January 1952 p. 4; 8, 15 February p. 4. Vacant possession	-
22 February 1952	Bedford, Lime Street, sale rooms	Bedford, 17 Ombersley Road, villa	Unsold	BTS 1 February 1952 p. 6; 8, 15 February p. 4. Vacant possession	-
22 February 1952	Bedford, Lime Street, sale rooms	Bedford, 17 George Street, semi-detached house	Unsold	BTS 25 January 1952 p. 4; 8, 15 February p. 4. Vacant possession	-
22 February 1952	Bedford, Lime Street, sale rooms	Bedford, 24 Cutcliffe Place, semi-detached house	£3,000	BTS 25 January 1952 p. 4; 8, 15 February p. 4. By order of the official solicitor, Borough of Bedford. Vacant possession. Household contents sold following sale of property by order of the executors of Mrs Sutton	-
22 February 1952	Bedford, Lime Street, sale rooms	Bedford, 238 Ampthill Road, semi-detached house	£2,300	BTS 1 February 1952 p. 6; 8, 15 February p. 4. Household contents sold following sale of property by order of the executors of Mrs Sutton	-
16 April 1952	Baldock, The Victoria Inn	Baldock (Herts), 9–15 Hitchin Street, four freehold cottages	£550	(Advert pasted in *Property Auction Book, No. 1: Baldock and Biggleswade*) Number 9 occupied by Mr F. J. Drover. Rental 13s 8d per week. 11 occupied by Mr R. V. Mellor. Rental 8s 2d per week. 13 occupied by Mr C. Hickford. Rental 6s 6d per week. 15 occupied by Mr D. Wilsher. Rental 7s 8d per week	-
18 April 1952	Bedford, Lime Street, sale rooms	Bedford, 15 Kathie Road, corner business premises	Unsold	BTS 21 March 1952 p. 4. General business embracing grocery, tobacco and greengrocery. Vacant possession	-

Auction date	Venue	Description	Price	Newspaper references	BLARS references
18 April 1952	Bedford, Lime Street, sale rooms	Bedford, 164 Castle Road, semi-detached house	Unsold	BTS 11 April 1952 p. 4. Vacant possession	-
18 April 1952	Bedford, Lime Street, sale rooms	Bedford, 119 Fenlake Road, semi-detached house	£1,400	BTS 21 March 1952 p. 4. Vacant possession	-
18 April 1952	Bedford, Lime Street, sale rooms	Bedford, 28 and 30 Garfield Street, villas	Unsold	BTS 21 March 1952 p. 4. Total rental £22 18s 3d pa	-
9 May 1952	Bedford, Lime Street, sale rooms	Milton Ernest, next to Police House, plot of land where cottages have recently been demolished	£75	BTS 11, 18 April 1952 p. 4	-
9 May 1952	Bedford, Lime Street, sale rooms	Milton Ernest, blacksmith's shop	£275	BTS 11, 18 April 1952 p. 4	-
9 May 1952	Bedford, Lime Street, sale rooms	Harrold, 123 High Street, cottage, plot of land	£285	BTS 11, 18 April 1952 p. 4. Cottage has to be demolished	-
9 May 1952	Bedford, Lime Street, sale rooms	Bedford, 41 Gwyn Street, villa	Sold prior to auction	BTS 18 April 1952 p. 4; 25 April p. 6. Vacant possession	-
9 May 1952	Bedford, Lime Street, sale rooms	Bedford, 103 Hurst Grove, villa	Unsold	BTS 11, 18 April 1952 p. 4	-
9 May 1952	Bedford, Lime Street, sale rooms	Bedford, 34 Cauldwell Street	£2,500	BTS 18 April 1952 p. 4; 25 April p. 6. Vacant possession	-

Auction date	Venue	Description	Price	Newspaper references	BLARS references
9 May 1952	Bedford, Lime Street, sale rooms	Bedford, 22 Stanley Street, house	£2,000	BTS 11, 18 April 1952 p. 4	-
9 May 1952	Bedford, Lime Street, sale rooms	Kempston, 11 Orchard Street, detached bungalow	£2,300	BTS 18 April 1952 p. 4; 25 April p. 6. Vacant possession	-
4 July 1952	Bedford, Lime Street, sale rooms	Bedford, 65 Honey Hill Road, detached double-fronted house	£1,850	BTS 23 May 1952 p. 6; 20, 27 June p. 6. Vacant possession	-
4 July 1952	Bedford, Lime Street, sale rooms	Bedford, Morley Villa, 6 Clarendon Street, semi-detached house	£1,750	BTS 13, 20, 27 June 1952 p. 6	-
4 July 1952	Bedford, Lime Street, sale rooms	Bedford, Cotswold, 19 Kingsley Road, semi-detached house	Unsold	BTS 30 May 1952 p. 4; 20, 27 June p. 6. Vacant possession	-
8 July 1952	On site	Sharnbrook, Barleycroft, Park Lane, modern detached residence	Unsold	BTS 16 May 1952 p. 4; 23 May p. 6; 20, 27 June p. 6. Vacant possession. Surplus household contents sold following sale of property	-
12 September 1952	Bedford, Lime Street, sale rooms	Bedford, 57 and 59 Priory Street, two villas	Unsold	BTS 22 August 1952 p. 4; 5 September p. 6. Number 57 occupied by Mr W. Vernon. Rental £22 10s 8d pa. 59 occupied by Miss Valentine. Rental £24 6s pa	-
12 September 1952	Bedford, Lime Street, sale rooms	Kempston, 26 Park Road, semi-detached villa	£1,575	BTS 22 August 1952 p. 4; 5 September p. 6. By order of the executors of Ellen Worrall. Vacant possession	-
12 September 1952	Bedford, Lime Street, sale rooms	Bedford, 61 Southville Road, general store	£1,400	BTS 22 August 1952 p. 4; 5 September p. 6. Vacant possession	-

Auction date	Venue	Description	Price	Newspaper references	BLARS references
12 September 1952	Bedford, Lime Street, sale rooms	Clophill, 3 and 5 Bedford Road, cottages	Withdrawn from auction	BTS 22 August 1952 p. 4; 5 September p. 6	-
7 November 1952	Bedford, Lime Street, sale rooms	Biggleswade, 56 and 58 Sun Street, two cottages, lock-up cobbler's shop	Unsold	BT 5 September 1952 p. 6; 10, 24 October p. 6. Vacant possession. Number 56 occupied by Mrs Potts. Rental £16 18s pa. Lock-up shop occupied by Mr T. Marlow. Rental £24 14s pa	-
7 November 1952	Bedford, Lime Street, sale rooms	Kempston, 37–41 Bunyan Road, three villas	£240 Number 41 withdrawn from auction	BTS 17 October 1952 p. 6. Total rental £63 14s pa	-
7 November 1952	Bedford, Lime Street, sale rooms	Wilstead, corner of Ivy Lane and Chapel End, old-world detached cottage	Unsold	BTS 17, 24 October 1952 p. 6. Vacant possession	-
7 November 1952	Bedford, Lime Street, sale rooms	Sharnbrook, Western Place, High Street, semi-detached double-fronted house	£1,150	BTS 10, 17 October 1952 p. 6. Vacant possession	-
7 November 1952	Bedford, Lime Street, sale rooms	Bedford, 9 Pemberley Avenue, detached house	Withdrawn from auction	BTS 2, 10, 24 October 1952 p. 6. Vacant possession	-
7 November 1952	Bedford, Lime Street, sale rooms	Clophill, 3 and 5 Bedford Road, two cottages	£160	BTS 5 September 1952 p. 6; 24 October p. 6. By order of the Minister of Transport. Number 3 occupied by Mr Juffs. Rental £7 3s pa. 5 occupied by Mr H. C. Cole. Rental £15 12s pa	-

Auction date	Venue	Description	Price	Newspaper references	BLARS references
12 November 1952	Baldock, The Rose and Crown Hotel	Baldock (Herts), 50 Salisbury Road, freehold semi-detached house	£1,100	-	-
12 November 1952	Baldock, The Rose and Crown Hotel	Baldock (Herts), 52 Salisbury Road, freehold semi-detached house	£1,125	-	-
28 November 1952	Bedford, Lime Street, sale rooms	Blunham, Warwick Villa, detached double-fronted residence	Unsold	BTS 7 November 1952 p. 6	PK un-catalogued. Vacant possession
28 November 1952	Bedford, Lime Street, sale rooms	Blunham, Barford Road, market garden land, 2a	Unsold	BTS 7 November 1952 p. 6	PK un-catalogued. Vacant possession
28 November 1952	Bedford, Lime Street, sale rooms	Blunham, Barford Road, market garden land, 8a 2r 6p	Unsold	BTS 7 November 1952 p. 6	PK un-catalogued. Vacant possession
28 November 1952	Bedford, Lime Street, sale rooms	Kempston, 19 Littledale Street, freehold semi-detached house	£1,450	BTS 7 November 1952 p. 6	PK un-catalogued. Vacant possession
27 February 1953	Bedford, Lime Street, sale rooms	Sharnbrook, Ardlui, High Street, semi-detached residence	£1,300	BTS 16 January 1953 p. 6; 27 February p. 6. By order of executors of Mrs B. A. Pike. Household contents sold following sale of property	-
10 April 1953	Bedford, Lime Street, sale rooms	Carlton, Homelea, smallholding situated on The Moor, 2.5a	£1,925	BTS 20 March 1953 p. 6; 3 April p. 6	-

Auction date	Venue	Description	Price	Newspaper references	BLARS references
10 April 1953	Bedford, Lime Street, sale rooms	Clapham, The Links, bungalow	£4,000	BTS 30 January 1953 p. 6; 3 April p. 6. Vacant possession	-
10 April 1953	Bedford, Lime Street, sale rooms	Biddenham, St Margarets, Days Lane, detached house	Unsold	BTS 27 February 1953 p. 6; 3 April p. 6	-
10 April 1953	Bedford, Lime Street, sale rooms	Bedford, 17 Warwick Avenue, detached house	Unsold	BTS 27 February 1953 p. 6; 3 April p. 6	-
10 April 1953	Bedford, Lime Street, sale rooms	Bedford, 39 Ashburnham Road, detached house, in two flats	Unsold	BTS 20 March 1953 p. 6; 3 April p. 6. Ground floor flat rental £46 6s 10d pa	-
5 May 1953	On site	Bedford, St Cross, 23 Park Avenue, detached house	£4,000	BTS 10 April 1953 p. 6; 1 May p. 6. Architect designed modern house. Vacant possession. Household effects sold following sale of property	-
27 May 1953	On site	Guilden Morden (Cambs), Laburnum Cottage, detached freehold cottage, 5.22a	Unsold	-	-
5 June 1953	Bedford, Lime Street, sale rooms	Bedford, 147 Kimbolton Road, modern semi-detached house	£2,550	BTS 8, 29 May 1953 p. 6. Vacant possession	-
5 June 1953	Bedford, Lime Street, sale rooms	Bedford, 54 Cauldwell Street, business premises	£1,000	BTS 8, 29 May 1953 p. 6. Vacant possession	-

Auction date	Venue	Description	Price	Newspaper references	BLARS references
18 June 1953	Olney, The Bull Hotel	Olney (Bucks), West Street, orchard, garden land, 2.75a	Unsold	BTS 29 May 1953 p. 6; 5, 12 June p. 6. Vacant possession	
18 June 1953	Olney, The Bull Hotel	Olney (Bucks), 35 Midland Road, villa	£1,250	BTS 29 May 1953 p. 6; 5, 12 June p. 6. On instruction of executors of Mrs L. A. Exton. Vacant possession	-
23 June 1953	On site	Bedford, 34 Pemberley Avenue, detached modern house	£4,800	BTS 22, 29 May 1953 p. 6; 5, 19 June p. 6. Vacant possession. Household contents sold following sale of property on instruction of Mrs Turner-Jones	-
30 June 1953	On site	Bromham, Dee-Kay, Stagsden Road, modern house	£2,400	BTS 5, 12, 26 June 1953 p. 6. By order of Sir Holland Goddard. Vacant possession. Household contents sold following sale of property	-
8 July 1953	On site	Seddington, The Buttery, Great North Road, near Sandy, freehold property, 2.43a	Unsold	BTS 12, 26 June 1953 p. 6; 3 July p. 6. Vacant possession	PK un-catalogued. Occupied as a roadhouse with bed and breakfast accommodation
10 July 1953	Bedford, Lime Street, sale rooms	Bedford, 4 Millbrook Road, semi-detached residence	Unsold	BTS 26 June 1953 p. 6; 10 July p. 6	PK un-catalogued. By order of the Court of Protection. Vacant possession
10 July 1953	Bedford, Lime Street, sale rooms	Bedford, 36 Althorpe Street, villa	Unsold	BTS 12, 26 June 1953 p. 6. Vacant possession	PK un-catalogued. Vacant possession
10 July 1953	Bedford, Lime Street, sale rooms	Bedford, 307 Goldington Road, detached residence, adjoining plot	£2,600	BTS 12, 19, 26 June 1953 p. 6	PK un-catalogued. Plot currently used as orchard but would make building plot

Auction date	Venue	Description	Price	Newspaper references	BLARS references
10 July 1953	Bedford, Lime Street, sale rooms	Newton Blossomville (Bucks), The Croft, detached modern house	Unsold	BTS 12, 26 June 1953 p. 6	PK un-catalogued. Vacant possession
31 July 1953	Bedford, Lime Street, sale rooms	Turvey, Alberta, Station Road, semi-detached house	Unsold	BTS 26 June 1953 p. 6; 10, 31 July p. 6	-
31 July 1953	Bedford, Lime Street, sale rooms	Milton Ernest, The Forge, Bedford to Rushden Road	Sold by private treaty	BTS 10 July 1953 p. 6	-
31 July 1953	Bedford, Lime Street, sale rooms	Bedford, 282 Ampthill Road, modern residence	Sold by private treaty	BTS 10 July 1953 p. 6. Vacant possession	-
At early date	-	Bedford, Grove House, Bromham Road, gentleman's residence	-	BTS 3, 10 July 1953 p. 6; 7 August p. 6. On instruction of the executors of W. S. Brocklehurst	-
8 September 1953	On site	Newton Blossomville (Bucks), The Rafters	-	BTS 11 August 1953 p. 6; 4 September p. 6. On instruction of Miss Dorothy Watts	-
29 September 1953	Baldock, The Victoria Inn	Baldock (Herts), 7 Salisbury Road, freehold semi-detached villa	£850	-	-
23 October 1953	Bedford, Lime Street, sale rooms	Bedford, 39 Conduit Road, semi-detached house	Unsold	BTS 2, 23 October 1953 p. 6	PK un-catalogued. Property adjusted as two flats. Vacant possession
23 October 1953	Bedford, Lime Street, sale rooms	Bedford, 41 Conduit Road, semi-detached house	Unsold	BTS 2, 9 October 1953 p. 6. Occupied by Major A. C. Hoare. Rental £60 pa	PK un-catalogued

Auction date	Venue	Description	Price	Newspaper references	BLARS references
23 October 1953	Bedford, Lime Street, sale rooms	Bedford, 19 Firbank Road, villa	£300	BTS 9 October 1953 p. 6; 16 October p. 8. Occupied by Mr A. B. Spencer. Rental £35 8s 6d pa	PK un-catalogued
23 October 1953	Bedford, Lime Street, sale rooms	Bedford, 8 and 10 Great Butts Street, villa residences	Unsold	BTS 2, 9 October 1953 p. 6	PK un-catalogued. Occupied by Mrs Lawford. Rental £35 6s 4d pa
17 November 1953	Sharnbrook, Swan with Two Nicks	Sharnbrook, The Retreat, Park Lane, cottage	£1,230	BTS 30 October 1953 p. 6; 13 November p. 6. On instruction of executors of Mrs B. M. Glasspole. Vacant possession	-
26 January 1954	Hitchin, The Sun Hotel	Holwell (Herts), Ramerick Nurseries, nursery, nine heated glasshouses, bungalow, 5.78a	-	BTS 15, 22 January 1954 p. 6. Vacant possession	-
23 March 1954	On site	Guilden Morden (Bucks), High Street, freehold cottage	Unsold	-	-
7 May 1954	Bedford, Lime Street, sale rooms	Bedford, 74 Kimbolton Road, house	£1,500	BTS 19 March 1954 p. 8; 30 April p. 7; 7 May p. 8. Vacant possession	-
7 May 1954	Bedford, Lime Street, sale rooms	Bedford, 34a Gladstone Street, builder's yard, business premises	Unsold	BTS 26 March 1954 p. 8; 30 April p. 6; 7 May p. 8	-
7 May 1954	Bedford, Lime Street, sale rooms	Bromham, Aberfolyle, modern house with garage	Withdrawn from auction	BTS 26 March 1954 p. 8	-
7 May 1954	Bedford, Lime Street, sale rooms	Bromham, Stagsden Road, two plots	£470	BTS 26 March 1954 p. 8; 30 April p. 6; 7 May p. 8. Planning permission for a pair of houses	-

Auction date	Venue	Description	Price	Newspaper references	BLARS references
7 May 1954	Bedford, Lime Street, sale rooms	Bedford, 19 Old Ford End Road	Withdrawn from auction	BTS 19 March 1954 p. 8	-
7 May 1954	Bedford, Lime Street, sale rooms	Bedford, 21 Old Ford End Road, villa	£295	BTS 19 March 1954 p. 8; 30 April p. 6; 7 May p. 8. Occupied by Mr Ashley. Rental £29 8d pa	-
11 May 1954	Carlton, The Angel	Carlton, The Causeway, two cottages	£250	BTS 16 April 1954 p. 6; 7 May p. 8. On instruction of the executors of C. A. Stewart. Occupied by Messrs Kilpin and Jones. Rental £20 8s pa	-
21 May 1954	On site	Sandy, 10 St Neots Road, residence	Unsold	BTS 7 May 1953 p. 8. Vacant possession	-
25 June 1954	Bedford, Lime Street, sale rooms	Bedford, 5 Bradgate Road, semi-detached house	£2,650	BTS 14 May 1954 p. 6; 4, 25 June p. 6. Vacant possession	-
25 June 1954	Bedford, Lime Street, sale rooms	Bedford, 53 Bromham Road, semi-detached house	£1,650	BTS 28 May 1954 p. 10; 4, 25 June p. 6. Vacant possession	-
-	-	Comberton (Cambs), Old Farm, freehold farm, 55a	Withdrawn from auction	BTS 11, 18, 25 June 1953 p. 6; 2 July p. 6	-
25 August 1954	Lavendon, The George Hotel	Lavendon (Bucks), 8 Northampton Road, detached residence	£1,000	BTS 30 July 1953 p. 6; 13 August p. 6. Vacant possession	-
13 October 1954	Reed, The Cabinet	Reed (Herts), Drage's Farm, freehold cottage, land, buildings	Unsold	-	-
5 November 1954	Bedford, Lime Street, sale rooms	Bedford, 14 Cardington Road, house	£1,400	BTS 8 October 1954 p. 8; 5 November p. 6. Vacant possession	-

Auction date	**Venue**	**Description**	**Price**	**Newspaper references**	**BLARS references**
5 November 1954	Bedford, Lime Street, sale rooms	Bedford, 28 College Road, house	£1,200	BTS 8 October 1954 p. 8; 5 November p. 6. Vacant possession	-
5 November 1954	Bedford, Lime Street, sale rooms	Sharnbrook, Eversleigh, Odell Road, semi-detached house	Unsold	BTS 8 October 1954 p. 8; 5 November p. 6. Vacant possession	-
10 November 1954	Rushden, The Victoria Hotel	Rushden (Northants), Rushden Lodge, house, 20a	£4,100	BTS 15 October 1954 p. 8; 20 October p. 6. Vacant possession	-
3 December 1954	Bedford, Lime Street, sale rooms	Wilstead, Old Manor, detached double-fronted residence	Unsold	BTS 5 November 1954 p. 6; 19 November p. 6; 3 December p. 8	-
20 April 1955	Ashwell, The Three Tuns	Ashwell (Herts), 1–10 Limekiln Lane, ten freehold cottages	£825 Sold following auction	(Advert pasted in *Property Auction Book, No. 1: Baldock and Biggleswade*) Number 1 occupied by Mrs Izzard. 2 occupied by Mrs Bryant. 3 occupied by Mrs Hare. 4 occupied by Mrs Brown. 5 occupied by Mrs Collins. 6 occupied by Mrs Goodchild. 7 occupied by Mrs Waldock. 8 occupied by Mr Haylock. 9 occupied by Mr Anderson. 10 occupied by Mrs Jackson. Total rental £172 18s pa.	-
26 April 1955	Baldock, The Rose and Crown	Baldock (Herts), 39–47 Church Street, five cottages	£625	(Advert pasted in *Property Auction Book, No. 1: Baldock and Biggleswade*) Number 39 occupied by Mr H. Castle. 41 occupied by Mrs H. Jardine. 43 occupied by Mrs A. Castle. 45 occupied by Mr A. M. Beadle. 47 occupied by Mr L. O. Fisher. Total rental £90 2s 8d pa	-

Auction date	Venue	Description	Price	Newspaper references	BLARS references
26 April 1955	Baldock, The Rose and Crown	Rushden (Northants), Daisy Cottage, Southern Green, detached freehold cottage	£1,300	-	-
14 May 1955	Bedford, The Swan Hotel	Clapham, Little Park Farm, house, 154a	£10,600	BTS 25 March 1955 p. 8; 15 April p. 6. On instruction of administrators of late F. P. Tinsley	-
14 May 1955	Bedford, The Swan Hotel	Biddenham, Bridge Meadow, 21.962a	£2,200	BTS 25 March 1955 p. 8; 15 April p. 6. On instruction of administrators of late F. P. Tinsley	-
14 May 1955	Bedford, The Swan Hotel	Bedford, Cardington Road, meadow, 11a	Unsold	BTS 25 March 1955 p. 8; 15 April p. 6. On instruction of administrators of late F. P. Tinsley	-
26 July 1955	On site	Bedford, 26 Clapham Road, seven bedroom semi-detached house	£2,100	BTS 15 April 1955 p. 6; 1, 8, 15 July p. 8. On instruction of executors of Mrs Mary Turnbull. Vacant possession. Household effects sold following sale of property	-
6 September 1955	Offord D'Arcy, The Horseshoe	Offord D'Arcy (Cambs), 23 High Street, detached four bedroom house	Unsold	BTS 12, 19 August 1955 p. 6; 26 August p. 8. Occupied by Mr Aves. Rental £36 8s pa	-
9 September 1955	Bedford, Lime Street, sale rooms	Bedford, 9 De Parys Avenue, detached house	£5,000	BTS 19 August 1955 p. 6; 26 August p. 8	-
9 September 1955	Bedford, Lime Street, sale rooms	Marston Shelton, The Nook, 13 Upper Shelton Road, semi-detached house	Unsold	BTS 12, 19 August 1955 p. 6; 26 August p. 8	-

Auction date	Venue	Description	Price	Newspaper references	BLARS references
18 November 1955	Bedford, Lime Street, sale rooms	Bedford, 126 Bromham Road, old-world house	£3,300	BTS 28 October 1955 p. 8; 18 November p. 8	-
18 November 1955	Bedford, Lime Street, sale rooms	Bedford, 128 Bromham Road, old-world house	£3,050	BTS 28 October 1955 p. 8; 18 November p. 8	-
18 November 1955	Bedford, Lime Street, sale rooms	Bedford, 21 Commercial Road, corner property	£1,475	BTS 28 October 1955 p. 8; 18 November p. 8	-
7 December 1955	Ashwell, The Three Tuns	Ashwell (Herts), High Street, five freehold cottages	£1,150	(Advert pasted in *Property Auction Book, No. 1: Baldock and Biggleswade*) Occupied by Mrs J. Covington, Mr H. Bryant, Mr W. Revel, Mr R. Harris. Total rental £56 18s 8d pa	-
13 December 1955	Baldock, The Rose and Crown	Baldock (Herts), Orchard Road, building plot	£300	-	-
13 December 1955	Baldock, The Rose and Crown	Baldock (Herts), Icknield Way East, building plot	£425	-	-
13 December 1955	Baldock, The Rose and Crown	Baldock (Herts), Icknield Way East, building plot	£425	-	-
13 December 1955	Baldock, The Rose and Crown	Baldock (Herts), Icknield Way East, building plot	£425	-	-
13 December 1955	Baldock, The Rose and Crown	Baldock (Herts), Icknield Way East, building plot	£425	-	-

Auction date	Venue	Description	Price	Newspaper references	BLARS references
21 February 1956	On site	Keysoe, Byways, Keysoe Row, semi-detached cottage	Unsold	BTS 3, 17 February 1956 p. 6. Earth closet, water from standpipe	-
7 March 1956	Bedford, The Swan Hotel	Bedford, 11 High Street, Belfast Linen warehouse, 3,270 sq ft	Unsold	TDA 27 February 1956 p. 14. Vacant possession. BTS 10, 24 February p. 6	-
10 April 1956	Sharnbrook, The Swan with Two Nicks	Sharnbrook, Manorlee, Bedford Road, house	£2,900	BTS 16 March 1956 p. 8; 23 March p. 10; 6 April p. 6	-
11 April 1956	Blunham, The Salutation Inn	Blunham, garden land, 3.019a	£310	BTS 16 March 1956 p. 8; 6 April p. 6. On instruction of executors of C. and T. C. Gurney	-
11 April 1956	Blunham, The Salutation Inn	Blunham, garden land, 3.975a	£430	BTS 16 March 1956 p. 8; 6 April p. 6. On instruction of executors of C. and T. C. Gurney	-
11 April 1956	Blunham, The Salutation Inn	Blunham, garden land, 6.137a	£470	BTS 16 March 1956 p. 8; 6 April p. 6. On instruction of executors of C. and T. C. Gurney	-
11 April 1956	Blunham, The Salutation Inn	Blunham, garden land, 5.206a	£315	BTS 16 March 1956 p. 8; 6 April p. 6. On instruction of executors of C. and T. C. Gurney	-
11 April 1956	Blunham, The Salutation Inn	Blunham, garden land, 5.156a	£315	BTS 16 March 1956 p. 8; 6 April p. 6. On instruction of executors of C. and T. C. Gurney	-

Auction date	Venue	Description	Price	Newspaper references	BLARS references
11 April 1956	Blunham, The Salutation Inn	Blunham, garden land, 6.180a	£780	BTS 16 March 1956 p. 8; 6 April p. 6. On instruction of executors of C. and T. C. Gurney	-
11 April 1956	Blunham, The Salutation Inn	Blunham, 10–18 Great Barford Road, five cottages	£930	BTS 16 March 1956 p. 8; 6 April p. 6. On instruction of executors of C. and T. C. Gurney	-
17 April 1956	On site	Olney (Bucks), Siriol House, Bridge Street, double-fronted house	£1,625	BTS 23 March 1956 p. 10; 13 April p. 8. Household effects sold following sale of property	-
17 April 1956	On site	Olney (Bucks), 26 Bridge Street	£200	BTS 23 March 1956 p. 10; 13 April p. 8. Rental £20 16s pa	-
17 April 1956	-	Olney (Bucks), 78–82 High Street	Withdrawn from auction	BTS 23 March 1956 p. 10	-
9 May 1956	Ashwell, The Three Tuns	Ashwell (Bucks), Jessamine House	Unsold	(Advert pasted in *Property Auction Book, No. 1: Baldock and Biggleswade*) On instruction of executors of Miss D. M. Sale	-
9 May 1956	Ashwell, The Three Tuns	Ashwell (Bucks), The Gables	£3,100	(Advert pasted in *Property Auction Book, No. 1: Baldock and Biggleswade*) On instruction of executors of Miss D. M. Sale	-
15 May 1956	Baldock, The Rose and Crown	Lower Caldecote, 18–22 Grange Lane, market garden land	£400	-	-
15 May 1956	Baldock, The Rose and Crown	Baldock (Herts), The Old Brewery	£2,050	-	-

Auction date	Venue	Description	Price	Newspaper references	BLARS references
15 May 1956	Baldock, The Rose and Crown	Baldock (Herts), 6 Pond Lane	£525	-	-
15 May 1956	Baldock, The Rose and Crown	Baldock (Herts), 23 Church Street	£600	-	-
15 May 1956	Baldock, The Rose and Crown	Baldock (Herts), 21 Church Street	£875	-	-
1 June 1956	Bedford, Lime Street, sale rooms	Bedford, 93 Denmark Street, house	£1,175	BTS 20 April 1956 p. 8; 18, 25 May p. 8	-
-	-	Bedford, 7 Farrer Street	Withdrawn from auction	BTS 20 April 1956 p. 8	-
1 June 1956	Bedford, Lime Street, sale rooms	Bedford, 1 Little Grove Place, end terrace cottage	£900	BTS 11 May 1956 p. 10; 18, 25 May p. 8	-
7 June 1956	Banbury, The White Lion Hotel	Culworth (Northants), Linnell and Ansteys Farm, stone farmhouse, 91a	£5,000	BTS 18, 25 May 1956 p. 8. Vacant possession	-
20 July 1956	Bedford, Lime Street, sale rooms	Bedford, Oakleigh, 55 Victoria Road, semi-detached house	Unsold	BTS 1 June 1956 p. 8; 6, 13 July p. 8	-
20 July 1956	Bedford, Lime Street, sale rooms	Bromham, Doddershall, detached old-world cottage	Unsold	BTS 18 May 1956 p. 8; 6, 13 July p. 8	-
20 July 1956	Bedford, Lime Street, sale rooms	Carlton, 1 Elm Cottages, The Causeway	£500	BTS 4 May 1956 p. 10; 6, 13 July p. 8. Vacant possession	-

Auction date	Venue	Description	Price	Newspaper references	BLARS references
20 July 1956	Bedford, Lime Street, sale rooms	Carlton, 2 Elm Cottages, The Causeway	£260	BTS 4 May 1956 p. 10; 18 May p. 8; 6, 13 July p. 8. Rental £11 14s pa	-
24 July 1956	Aspley Guise, The Bell Hotel	Aspley Guise, 30–32 Mount Pleasant, two cottages, shop	£475	BTS 6, 13 July 1956 p. 8. Number 32 occupied by Mrs Davis. Rental £18 4s pa	-
27 July 1956	Bedford, Lime Street, sale rooms	Bedford, 51 Bushmead Avenue, detached house	Unsold	BTS 6, 13, 20 July 1956 p. 8. On instruction of executors of C. R. Tingey. Household effects sold following sale of property	-
28 August 1956	Turvey, The Three Cranes	Turvey, 1 and 2 Jacks Lane, cottages	-	BTS 17, 24 August 1956 p. 6. Number 1 occupied by Mr G. E. Newton. Rental £10 pa	-
27 September 1956	On site	Olney (Bucks), Courtney House, five bedroom house, cottage	Unsold	BTS 17 August 1956 p. 6; 31 August p. 8; 21 September p. 6. Household effects sold following sale of property	-
29 September 1956	Bedford, The Swan Hotel	Radwell, Underwood Farm, house, 50a	£5,400	BTS 7 September 1956 p. 4; 27 September p. 6	-
2 October 1956	On site	Great Barford , buildings, land, 9.174a	£1,375	BTS 7 September 1956 p. 4; 27 September p. 6. On instruction of Mr W. S. Green	-
2 October 1956	On site	Great Barford, land, 8.75a	Unsold	BTS 7 September 1956 p. 4; 27 September p. 6. On instruction of Mr W. S. Green	-
9 October 1956	On site	Flitwick, 95 Station Road, cottage	Unsold	BTS 28 September 1956 p. 6. Vacant possession	-
12 October 1956	Bedford, Lime Street, sale rooms	Bedford, 73 Bromham Road, detached house	Unsold	BTS 17 August 1956 p. 6; 5 October p. 8	-

Auction date	Venue	Description	Price	Newspaper references	BLARS references
30 October 1956	Stotfold, The Crown	Stotfold, 86 Hitchin Road, semi-detached house	£850	-	-
2 November 1956	Blunham, The Salutation Inn	Blunham, freehold garden holding, house, 9.37a	£850	BTS 12 October 1956 p. 6; 26 October p. 6. On instruction of S. J. Ashwell	-
2 November 1956	On site	Willington, The Nurseries, Barford Road, glasshouse, 9.5a	£2,400	BTS 12, 26 October 1956 p. 6; 19 October p. 8. On instruction of Messrs E. L. Lack and Sons	-
7 November 1956	On site	Clifton, 16 Hitchin Lane, freehold garden holding, house, 11a	£3,000	BTS 19 October 1956 p. 8; 26 October p. 6	-
7 November 1956	On site	Clifton, The Baulk, freehold garden land, 10a	£625	BTS 19 October 1956 p. 8; 26 October p. 6	-
20 November 1956	Baldock, The Rose and Crown	Baldock, 20 Salisbury Road, semi-detached villa	£380	(Advert pasted in *Property Auction Book, No. 1: Baldock and Biggleswade*) Occupied by Mrs E. L. Stratton. Rental £26 pa	-
20 November 1956	Baldock, The Rose and Crown	Baldock (Herts), 26 Salisbury Road, modern freehold detached bungalow	Unsold	-	-
4 December 1956	Bedford, Lime Street, sale rooms	Kempston, Redcliffe, 149 Spring Road, semi-detached house	Unsold	BTS 16, 23 November 1956 p. 9. Vacant possession. Household effects sold following sale of property	-

Auction date	Venue	Description	Price	Newspaper references	BLARS references
19 January 1957	Bedford, The Swan Hotel	Ravensden, Post Office, shop, house, buildings, 7a	£2,200	BTS 21 December 1956 p. 7	-
19 January 1957	Bedford, The Swan Hotel	Ravensden, Cross Roads, land, 62.188a	£3,200	BTS 21 December 1956 p. 7; 11 January p. 9. Rental £51 16s pa	-
19 January 1957	Bedford, The Swan Hotel	Great Barford, Bedford Road, accommodation land, 7a	£700	BTS 21 December 1956 p. 7; 11 January p. 9. Rental £105 pa	-
19 January 1957	Bedford, The Swan Hotel	Great Barford, Roxton Road, garden land, 4.5a	£500	-	-
19 January 1957	Bedford, The Swan Hotel	Great Barford, Roxton Road, garden land, 8.5a	£550	BTS 21 December 1956 p. 7. Vacant possession	-
19 January 1957	Bedford, The Swan Hotel	Great Barford, Roxton Road, garden land, 9a	£425	BTS 21 December 1956 p. 7. Vacant possession	-
19 January 1957	Bedford, The Swan Hotel	Great Barford, Roxton Road, garden land, 2.5a	£200	BTS 21 December 1956 p. 7. Vacant possession	-
19 January 1957	Bedford, The Swan Hotel	Thurleigh, Piggots and Top End Farms, Cross End, 263a	£9,750	BTS 21 December 1956 p. 7; 11 January p. 9. Rental £550 pa	-
19 January 1957	Bedford, The Swan Hotel	Bedford, 26 Rutland Road, house	£575	BTS 21 December 1956 p. 7; 11 January p. 9. Rental £56 pa	-
19 January 1957	Bedford, The Swan Hotel	Bedford, 28 Rutland Road, house	£650	BTS 21 December 1956 p. 7; 11 January p. 9. Rental £45 pa	-

Auction date	Venue	Description	Price	Newspaper references	BLARS references
26 April 1957	Bedford, Lime Street, sale rooms	Kempston, Ampthill Road, adjacent Cow Bridge, industrial land, 1.6a	£1,650	BTS 22 March 1957 p. 9; 19 April p. 9. By order of Bedfordshire County Council. Vacant possession	-
26 April 1957	Bedford, Lime Street, sale rooms	Wootton, 34 Bedford Road, detached house	Unsold	BTS 22 March 1957 p. 9; 19 April p. 9. Re. Thomas George Ayres, deceased	-
1 June 1957	Bedford, The Swan Hotel	Thurleigh, Piggots and Top End Farms, Cross End, 256.99a	Unsold	BTS 10 May 1957 p. 9; 31 May p. 9	-
7 June 1957	Tempsford, The Wheatsheaf Inn	Gamlingay (Cambs), Woodbury Low Farm, house, 250.706a	£7,600	BTS 17 May 1957 p. 9; 31 May p. 9. By direction of the Minister of Agriculture, Fisheries and Food. Occupied by Mr C. E. Schwier. Rental £578 pa	-
23 July 1957	On site	St Neots (Cambs), 9 East Street, business premises	Unsold	BTS 12, 19 July 1957 p. 7. Vacant possession	-
26 July 1957	On site	Harrold, 10 Orchard Lane, freehold old-world cottage	£400	BTS 12, 19 July 1957 p. 7. Vacant possession	-
24 October 1957	Shefford, The Church Hall	Campton, adjoining 5 Mill Lane, building plot	£85 Joint auction with H. C. Kempson & Son	BTS 4 October 1957 p. 9. On instruction of executors of E. H. Taylor JP. With planning permission	-
24 October 1957	Shefford, The Church Hall	Shefford, 22 Ampthill Road, cottage	£100	BTS 4 October 1957 p. 9. On instruction of executors of E. H. Taylor JP	-
24 October 1957	Shefford, The Church Hall	Shefford, 24 Ampthill Road, cottage	£80	BTS 4 October 1957 p. 9. On instruction of executors of E. H. Taylor JP	-

Auction date	Venue	Description	Price	Newspaper references	BLARS references
24 October 1957	Shefford, The Church Hall	Shefford, 28 Ampthill Road, cottage	£65	BTS 4 October 1957 p. 9. On instruction of executors of E. H. Taylor JP	-
24 October 1957	Shefford, The Church Hall	Shefford, 10a Ampthill Road, semi-detached house	£925	BTS 4 October 1957 p. 9. On instruction of executors of E. H. Taylor JP	-
24 October 1957	Shefford, The Church Hall	Shefford, 10b Ampthill Road, semi-detached house	£1,200	BTS 4 October 1957 p. 9. On instruction of executors of E. H. Taylor JP	-
24 October 1957	Shefford, The Church Hall	Shefford, 39 New Street, cottage	£115	BTS 4 October 1957 p. 9. On instruction of executors of E. H. Taylor JP	-
24 October 1957	Shefford, The Church Hall	Shefford, 41 New Street, cottage	£70	BTS 4 October 1957 p. 9. On instruction of executors of E. H. Taylor JP	-
24 October 1957	Shefford, The Church Hall	Shefford, 55 New Street, cottage	£50	BTS 4 October 1957 p. 9. On instruction of executors of E. H. Taylor JP	-
24 October 1957	Shefford, The Church Hall	Shefford, 59 New Street, cottage	£50	BTS 4 October 1957 p. 9. On instruction of executors of E. H. Taylor JP	-
24 October 1957	Shefford, The Church Hall	Shefford, 10 and 12 High Street, butchers shop, hairdresser's	£2,000 for number 10	BTS 4 October 1957 p. 9. On instruction of executors of E. H. Taylor JP. Rental £295 11s 5d pa	-
24 October 1957	Shefford, The Church Hall	Meppershall, 75 Shefford Road, semi-detached house	£1,025	BTS 4 October 1957 p. 9. On instruction of executors of E. H. Taylor JP	-
24 October 1957	Shefford, The Church Hall	Shefford, The Firs, 13 Hitchin Road, detached house	£1,600	BTS 4 October 1957 p. 9. On instruction of executors of E. H. Taylor JP	-
24 October 1957	Shefford, The Church Hall	Shefford, 82 Clifton Road, cottage	£40	BTS 4 October 1957 p. 9. On instruction of executors of E. H. Taylor JP	-

Auction date	Venue	Description	Price	Newspaper references	BLARS references
24 October 1957	Shefford, The Church Hall	Shefford, 84 Clifton Road, cottage	£180	BTS 4 October 1957 p. 9. On instruction of executors of E. H. Taylor JP	-
24 October 1957	Shefford, The Church Hall	Shefford, 165 Clifton Road, cottage	£330	BTS 4 October 1957 p. 9. On instruction of executors of E. H. Taylor JP	-
24 October 1957	Shefford, The Church Hall	Clifton, 59 Pedley Lane, cottage	£65	BTS 4 October 1957 p. 9 On instruction of executors of E. H. Taylor JP	-
24 October 1957	Shefford, The Church Hall	Clifton, 63 Pedley lane, cottage	£55	BTS 4 October 1957 p. 9. On instruction of executors of E. H. Taylor JP	-
24 October 1957	Shefford, The Church Hall	Clifton, 52 Broad Street, cottage	£220	BTS 4 October 1957 p. 9. On instruction of executors of E. H. Taylor JP	-
24 October 1957	Shefford, The Church Hall	Henlow, 2 and 4 Hitchin Road, Henlow Camp, two modern lock-up shops, two flats over	£3,250	BTS 4 October 1957 p. 9. On instruction of executors of E. H. Taylor JP. Rental £293 pa	-
24 October 1957	Shefford, The Church Hall	Henlow, Henlow Camp, modern corner shops, four flats over	£4,500	BTS 4 October 1957 p. 9. On instruction of executors of E. H. Taylor JP. Rental £469 12s 8d pa	-
24 October 1957	Shefford, The Church Hall	Haynes, Sandpit Farmhouse, four bedroom house	Unsold	BTS 4 October 1957 p. 9. On instruction of C. E. L. Taylor Esq. JP	-
24 October 1957	Shefford, The Church Hall	Clophill, The Glen, detached house	Unsold	BTS 11 October 1957 p. 9. Vacant possession	-
24 October 1957	Shefford, The Church Hall	Haynes, 38 and 40 Silver End Road, two cottages	£120	BTS 11 October 1957 p. 9	-

Auction date	Venue	Description	Price	Newspaper references	BLARS references
24 October 1957	Shefford, The Church Hall	Haynes, 42 and 44 Silver End Road, two cottages	£75	BTS 11 October 1957 p. 9	-
24 October 1957	Shefford, The Church Hall	Haynes, adjoining 46 Silver End Road, garden plot	£30	BTS 11 October 1957 p. 9	-
24 October 1957	Shefford, The Church Hall	Clophill, old-world cottage, garden, 1a	Withdrawn from auction	BTS 11 October 1957 p. 9. On instruction of Mrs A. J. Bone	-
15 February 1958	Bedford, The Swan Hotel	Campton, Woodhall Farm, house, 117.945a	£10,500	BTS 13 December 1957 p. 9; 31 January p. 7. On instruction of Mr H. F. Bowley. Vacant possession	-
19 February 1958	Biggleswade, The Masonic Rooms	Biggleswade, Turnpike Farm, house, cottage, 90.186a	£11,250	BTS 10, 31 January 1958 p. 7. On instruction of C. G. Ball. Vacant possession	-
1 March 1958	Bedford, The Swan Hotel	Sandy, Bridge Farm, thatched farmhouse, 90.728a including 30a of rich gravel deposits	£9,700 Joint auction with Swaffield & Son	BTS 14 February 1958 p. 7	-
1 March 1958	Bedford, The Swan Hotel	Kempston, Mill Meadows, grazing land, 40a	Unsold	BTS 14 February 1958 p. 7. On instruction of Bedfordshire County Council. Vacant possession	-
15 April 1958	Gamlingay, The Hardwicke Arms	Gamlingay (Cambs), 6 Green End, de-licensed residential property, formerly The Spotted Cow, 1r 21p	Unsold	BTS 28 March 1958 p. 11; 11 April p. 7. On instruction of Messrs E. K. and H. Fordham Ltd. Vacant possession	-
25 April 1958	Bedford, Lime Street, sale rooms	Bedford, 5 and 7 Lurke Street, houses	£800	BTS 11 April 1958 p. 7; 18 April p. 9. Occupied by Mrs K. E. Two and Mr George Plester. Total rental £78 pa	-

Auction date	Venue	Description	Price	Newspaper references	BLARS references
25 April 1958	Bedford, Lime Street, sale rooms	Bedford, 9 Lurke Street, house	£1,000	BTS 11 April 1958 p. 7; 18 April p. 9. Vacant possession	-
25 April 1958	Bedford, Lime Street, sale rooms	Bedford, 11 Lurke Street, house	£1,000	BTS 11 April 1958 p. 7; 18 April p. 9. Vacant possession	-
25 April 1958	Bedford, Lime Street, sale rooms	Bedford, 40 and 46 Queen Street	Withdrawn from auction	BTS 11 April 1958 p. 7	-
25 April 1958	Bedford, Lime Street, sale rooms	Houghton Conquest, Bedford Road, 1.275a	Unsold	BTS 11 April 1958 p. 7; 18 April p. 9. With planning permission. Vacant possession	-
13 May 1958	On site	Hitchin (Herts), 3 Park Street	£3,900	-	-
6 June 1958	Bedford, Lime Street, sale rooms	Harrold, 119 High Street, semi-detached house	Unsold	BTS 25 April 1958 p. 11; 23 May p. 9. Vacant possession	-
6 June 1958	Bedford, Lime Street, sale rooms	Harrold, 121 High Street, semi-detached house	Unsold	BTS 25 April 1958 p. 11; 23 May p. 9	-
6 June 1958	Bedford, Lime Street, sale rooms	Harrold, plot adjoining 119 High Street	Unsold	BTS 25 April 1958 p. 11; 23 May p. 9	-
6 June 1958	Bedford, Lime Street, sale rooms	Harrold, High Street, paddock	£650	BTS 25 April 1958 p. 11; 23 May p. 9. With planning permission	-
6 June 1958	Bedford, Lime Street, sale rooms	Bedford, Brookfield Road, plot	£430	BTS 9 May 1958 p. 11; 23 May p. 9. With planning permission	-

Auction date	Venue	Description	Price	Newspaper references	BLARS references
5 July 1958	Bedford, The Swan Hotel	Willington, Grange Farm, freehold garden holding, farm house, farm buildings, ten cottages, 390a	Joint auction with Swaffield & Son	BTS 9 May 1958 p. 11; 13 June p. 9. On instruction of the trustees of Mark Young, deceased	-
25 July 1958	Bedford, Lime Street, sale rooms	Felmersham, near Pavenham Road, site	Unsold	BTS 6 June 1958 p. 11; 18 July p. 9. With planning permission	-
25 July 1958	Bedford, Lime Street, sale rooms	Bedford, 59 and 61 Garfield Street, business premises	£1,900	BTS 6 June 1958 p. 11; 20 June p. 9; 18 July p. 9. Vacant possession	-
19 August 1958	Weston, The Red Lion	Weston (Herts), The Cottage, Fore Street	£3,500	-	-
25 September 1958	Bedford, Lime Street, sale rooms	Turvey, Norfolk Road, stabling	Withdrawn from auction	BTS 12, 19 September 1958 p. 9. Vacant possession	-
6 October 1958	Bedford, Lime Street, sale rooms	Bromham, 90–92 Village Road	£3,500	BTS 19 September 1958 p. 9; 10 October p. 11. On instruction of executors of Mrs H. S. Peacock	-
6 October 1958	Bedford, Lime Street, sale rooms	Bromham, Woodstock, Village Road	-	BTS 19 September 1958 p. 9; 10 October p. 11. On instruction of executors of Mrs H. S. Peacock	-
8 October 1958	Biggleswade, The Crown Hotel	Biggleswade, Swanbourne, 110 London Road, 1a	Unsold	BTS 19 September 1958 p. 9; 26 September p. 11. On instruction of A. E. F. Hall	-
24 October 1958	Bedford, Lime Street, sale rooms	Biddenham, Vicar's Close, two building plots	Unsold	BTS 3 October 1958 p. 11; 17 October p. 9. On instruction of administrator of Captain Herbert Haines	-

Auction date	Venue	Description	Price	Newspaper references	BLARS references
18 March 1959	Ashwell, The Three Tuns Hotel	Ashwell (Herts), Edgeley, Station Road, detached modern bungalow	£2,000	-	-
10 April 1959	Bedford, Lime Street, sale rooms	Ampthill, 37 Ampthill Street, in two flats	Withdrawn from auction	BTS 13 March 1959 p. 11; 10 April p. 11. One flat let unfurnished. Rental £129 7s pa	-
10 April 1959	Bedford, Lime Street, sale rooms	Cople, Dog Farm House	£2,400	TDA 20, 26 March 1959 p. 24. Former Dog Inn. With planning permission for non-residential hotel. BTS 27 February 1959 p. 9; 10 April p. 11	-
10 April 1959	Bedford, Lime Street, sale rooms	Cople, petrol filling station site	£1,600	TDA 20, 26 March 1959 p. 24. With outline planning permission. BTS 27 February 1959 p. 9; 10 April p. 11	-
10 April 1959	Bedford, Lime Street, sale rooms	Cople, Dog Farm, market garden, 59.429a	£3,900	TDA 20, 26 March 1959 p. 24. BTS 27 February 1959 p. 9; 10 April p. 11	-
10 April 1959	Bedford, Lime Street, sale rooms	Cople, Dog Farm, arable enclosure, 18.887a	-	TDA 20, 26 March 1959 p. 24. BTS 27 February 1959 p. 9; 10 April p. 11	-
10 April 1959	Bedford, Lime Street, sale rooms	Bromham, 78 Village Road, sub post office	Unsold	BTS 13 March 1959 p. 11; 10 April p. 11. Vacant possession	-
6 May 1959	Baldock, The Rose and Crown	Baldock (Herts), 18 Salisbury Road, freehold modern semi-detached house	-	-	-
22 May 1959	Bedford, Lime Street, sale rooms	Riseley, 28 Gold Street, redevelopment site	-	BTS 24 April 1959 p. 11; 22 May 1959 p. 9	-

Auction date	Venue	Description	Price	Newspaper references	BLARS references
22 May 1959	Bedford, Lime Street, sale rooms	Sharnbrook, The Old Village Bakery, High Street, business premises	Withdrawn from auction	BTS 24 April 1959 p. 11	-
20 June 1959	Bedford, The Swan Hotel	Blunham, Lodge Farm, house, buildings, 56a	-	BTS 15 May 1959 p. 9; 20 May p. 9; 19 June p. 9	-
1 July 1959	Baldock, The Rose and Crown	Rushden (Northants), 3 Southern Green, thatched cottage	-	-	-
22 September 1959	Kimbolton, The White Lion Hotel	Stow Longa (Hunts), Church Farm, house, buildings, 139a	£9,300	BTS 28 August 1959 p. 9; 18 September p. 11	-
5 December 1959	Bedford, The Swan Hotel	Ravensden, Hill Farm, house, buildings, two cottages, 146a	£14,750	BTS 6, 27 November 1959 p. 11. On instruction of trustees of M. B. Sunderland. Vacant possession	-
5 December 1959	Bedford, The Swan Hotel	Radwell, Old Farm, house, 10a	£1,950	BTS 13, 27 November 1959 p. 11. Re. A. J. Bowyer in bankruptcy	-
16 December 1959	Harrold, Harrold Institute	Harrold, 11 Church Walk, semi-detached house	£575	BTS 13, 27 November 1959 p. 11; 4 December p. 13. On instruction of executors of Edgar Clayson. Rental £57 12s 8d pa	-
16 December 1959	Harrold, Harrold Institute	Harrold, 13 Church Walk, semi-detached house	£575	BTS 13, 27 November 1959 p. 11; 4 December p. 13. On instruction of executors of Edgar Clayson. Rental £57 12s 8d pa	-

Auction date	Venue	Description	Price	Newspaper references	BLARS references
16 December 1959	Harrold, Harrold Institute	Harrold, 15 Church Walk, semi-detached house	£575	BTS 13, 27 November 1959 p. 11; 4 December p. 13. On instruction of executors of Edgar Clayson. Rental £57 12s 8d pa	-
16 December 1959	Harrold, Harrold Institute	Harrold, 19b High Street, house	£800	BTS 13, 27 November 1959 p. 11; 4 December p. 13. On instruction of executors of Edgar Clayson. Rental £72 16s pa	-
16 December 1959	Harrold, Harrold Institute	Harrold, 99 High Street, cottage	£200	BTS 13, 27 November 1959 p. 11; 4 December p. 13. On instruction of executors of Edgar Clayson. Rental £36 pa	-
16 December 1959	Harrold, Harrold Institute	Harrold, 103 and 105 High Street	£240	BTS 13, 27 November 1959 p. 11; 4 December p. 13. On instruction of executors of Edgar Clayson. Total rental £32 pa	-
16 December 1959	Harrold, Harrold Institute	Harrold, 166–178 High Street, eight cottages	£875	BTS 13, 27 November 1959 p. 11; 4 December p. 13. On instruction of executors of Edgar Clayson. Total rental £173 19s pa	-
16 December 1959	Harrold, Harrold Institute	Harrold, 33 and 35 Brook Lane	£250	BTS 13, 27 November 1959 p. 11; 4 December p. 13. On instruction of executors of Edgar Clayson. Total rental £14 16s pa	-
16 December 1959	Harrold, Harrold Institute	Harrold, High Street, plot	£350	BTS 13, 27 November 1959 p. 11; 4 December p. 13. On instruction of executors of Edgar Clayson. Vacant possession	-

Auction date	Venue	Description	Price	Newspaper references	BLARS references
16 December 1959	Harrold, Harrold Institute	Harrold, 7 and 9 The Green, two cottages	£340	BTS 13, 27 November 1959 p. 11; 4 December p. 13. On instruction of executors of Edgar Clayson. Total rental £57 12s 8d pa	-
16 December 1959	Harrold, Harrold Institute	Harrold, 11 The Green, cottage	£310	BTS 13, 27 November 1959 p. 11; 4 December p. 13. On instruction of executors of Edgar Clayson. Rental £31 16s pa	-

Auction date	Venue	Description	Price	Newspaper references	BLARS references
1 March 1960	Stotfold, The Crown	Stotfold, 4 Astwick Road, detached villa	-	(Advert pasted in *Property Auction Book, No. 1: Baldock and Biggleswade*) On instruction of executors of Nathan Cooper. Vacant possession	-
1 March 1960	Stotfold, The Crown	Stotfold, 17 Astwick Road, terraced cottage	-	(Advert pasted in *Property Auction Book, No. 1: Baldock and Biggleswade*) On instruction of executors of Nathan Cooper. Occupied by Ernest Gentle. Rental £4 15s pa	-
8 April 1960	On site	Turvey, Chantry Farm, grasskeeping, 150a	£634	BTS 25 March 1960 p. 11; 8 April p. 11	-
19 April 1960	Buckingham, The White Hart Hotel	Twyford (Bucks), Churchview Farm, house, 83a	£10,750	BTS 1 April 1960 p. 13; 15 April p. 9. Vacant possession	-
20 June 1960	-	Downe (Kent), Downe Court, compact residential freehold estate, 325a	Joint auction with Baxter, Payne and Lepper	TDA 17 June 1960 p. 26; BTS 10 June 1960 p. 11	-
22 February 1961	Bedford, The Swan Hotel	Bedford, 32–34 Brereton Road, business premises, office, warehouse, garages, yard	£10,000	BTS 20 January 1961 p. 9; 17 February p. 11. Vacant possession	-
22 February 1961	Bedford, The Swan Hotel	Bedford, 27 St Peter's Street, shop premises	Unsold	BTS 20 January 1961 p. 9; 17 February p. 11. Vacant possession	-

Auction date	Venue	Description	Price	Newspaper references	BLARS references
22 February 1961	Bedford, The Swan Hotel	Clapham, Lodge Estate, High Street, freehold building plot with river frontage	£850	BTS 20 January 1961 p. 9; 17 February p. 11. On instruction of the trustees of Bedford Angling Club	-
3 March 1961	Potton, The Rose and Crown	Potton, 4 Spencer Close, detached bungalow	£1,975	BTS 24 February 1961 p. 11; 3 March p. 11. Vacant possession	-
10 June 1961	Bedford, The Swan Hotel	Harrold, Manor Farm, 528a	£30,000	BTS 5, 19 May 1961 p. 11; 16 June p. 10. Rental £1,840 pa	PK 1/4/190. On instruction of Edgar Clayson. Occupied by Mrs F. E. Brady and Mr A. J. Cony
10 June 1961	Bedford, The Swan Hotel	Harrold, Harrold Park Farm, farm house, two cottages, 151.903a	£11,500	BTS 5, 19 May 1961 p. 11; 16 June p. 10. Vacant possession	PK 1/4/190. On instruction of Edgar Clayson
1 July 1961	Northampton, The Angel Hotel	Stoke Bruerne (Northants), Stoke Gap Farm, gentleman's residence, two bungalows, farm buildings, 248.033a	Unsold Joint auction with Pierce, Thorpe and Marriott	BTS 9, 16 June 1961 p. 11. On instruction of Mr C. R. Brett	-
10 July 1961	Biggleswade, The Conservative Hall	Biggleswade, Broadview, Caldecote Road, farmhouse buildings, market garden land, 24a	£10,000	BTS 5 May 1961 p. 11; 9, 30 June p. 11. On instruction of H. Godfrey Esq.	-

Auction date	Venue	Description	Price	Newspaper references	BLARS references
18 July 1961	Beckenham, Bromley Road, Public Hall	Downe (Kent), Downe Court Estate	Unsold Joint sale with Baxter, Payne and Lepper	-	-
1 December 1961	Bedford, Lime Street, sale rooms	Willington, Belmont, Bedford Road, detached double-fronted residence	£3,100	BTS 10 November p. 11; 1 December p. 11. Vacant possession	-
4 December 1961	Arlesey, The Oak	Arlesey, 70 Church Lane, Church End	Unsold	(Advert pasted in *Property Auction Book, No. 1: Baldock and Biggleswade*) On instruction of W. Whittaker Esq. Vacant possession	-
4 December 1961	Arlesey, The Oak	Arlesey, Ventnor, 21 Stotfold Road	Unsold	(Advert pasted in *Property Auction Book, No. 1: Baldock and Biggleswade*) On instruction of W. Whittaker Esq. Vacant possession	-
4 December 1961	Arlesey, The Oak	Arlesey, freehold building plot	Unsold	(Advert pasted in *Property Auction Book, No. 1: Baldock and Biggleswade*) On instruction of W. Whittaker Esq. Vacant possession	-
31 March 1962	Bedford, The Swan Hotel	Ravensden, Highfields Farm, house, buildings, 207a	£28,000	BTS 2 March 1962 p. 11; 23 March p. 13. On instruction of executor of H. S. Allen. Vacant possession	-
30 April 1962	Blunham, The Salutation Inn	Blunham, 107 High Street, cottage	£1,200	BTS 6 April 1962 p. 13; 27 April p. 9. Vacant possession	-

Auction date	Venue	Description	Price	Newspaper references	BLARS references
29 June 1962	Riseley, The Fox and Hounds	Riseley, 66 High Street, building plot	£530	BTS 15, 29 June 1962 p. 9. Planning permission for two houses. Vacant possession	-
3 July 1962	Wilstead, The Red Lion	Wilstead, Ferndale, 145 Cotton End Road, detached freehold residence	£1,700	BTS 27 April 1962 p. 9; 8 June p. 11; 29 June p. 9. On instruction of the Court of Protection	-
26 July 1962	Clophill, The Flying Horse	Clophill, Hilltop Farm, house, pig and poultry smallholding, 4.49a	Unsold	BTS 6 July 1962 p. 11; 20 July p. 9. Vacant possession	-
24 August 1962	Shefford, The White Hart	Campton, Campton Mill, mill house, gardens, 9a	-	BTS 20 July 1962 p. 9. On instruction of Mr A. R. Boston	-
4 September 1962	On site	Carlton, Rose Villa, Pavenham Road, detached double-fronted house	£2,500	BTS 3 August 1962 p. 7; 31 August p. 9. Household effects sold following sale of property	-
21 September 1962	Bedford, The Swan Hotel	Bedford, 115, 115a and 115b Midland Road and Alexandra Road, corner freehold property, 7,000sq ft	Unsold	BTS 27 April 1962 p. 9; 21 September p. 13	PK un-catalogued. On instruction of the executors of William Warwick. Number 115A vacant possession. 115 occupied by Messrs Morgans chemist. Rental £120 pa. 115B occupied by Messrs Miltons (Wallpapers) Ltd. Rental £80 pa
21 September 1962	Bedford, The Swan Hotel	Harrold, Odell Road building land, 4.723a	Unsold	BTS 22 June 1962 p. 11; 21 September p. 13. On instruction of executors of E. Clayson Esq. JP	-

Auction date	Venue	Description	Price	Newspaper references	BLARS references
21 September 1962	Bedford, The Swan Hotel	Harrold, Carlton Road, building land, 0.449a	Unsold	BTS 22 June 1962 p. 11; 21 September p. 13. On instruction of executors of E. Clayson Esq. JP	-
30 November 1962	Sharnbrook, The Swan with Two Nicks	Sharnbrook, Normans Road, detached double-fronted old-world cottage	£870	BTS 9, 30 November 1962 p. 6. Vacant possession	-
19 June 1963	Bedford, The Swan Hotel	Bedford, 89 and 91 Midland Road	Unsold	BTS 17, 24 May 1962 p. 7; 14 June p. 7	PK un-catalogued. Vacant possession
19 June 1963	Bedford, The Swan Hotel	Bedford, 3–7 Priory Street, freehold corner property, 5500 sq ft	Unsold	BTS 17, 24 May 1962 p. 7; 14 June p. 7	-
10 July 1963	Northampton, The Angel Hotel	Chapel Broughton and Broughton, (Northants), Houghton Mill Farm, cottage, pasture field, grazing land, 83a	Sold prior to auction	BTS 14, 21 June 1963 p. 7. On instruction of C. Hayward Esq.	-
15 July 1963	Winslow, The Bell Hotel	Little Horwood and Mursley (Bucks), Lower Grove Farm and Mursley Farm, adjoining Swanbourne Station, 148a	£24,250	BTS 21 June 1963 p. 7. On instruction of British Railway Board	-
21 September 1963	Bedford, The Swan Hotel	Wootton, Rest Harrow Farm, house, 35.553a	£10,000	BTS 16 August 1963 p. 7; 6 September p. 7. Vacant possession	-

Auction date	Venue	Description	Price	Newspaper references	BLARS references
15 October 1963	Ashwell, The Bushel and Strike	Ashwell (Herts), Little Garth, Mill Street, detached house	Unsold	-	-
16 December 1963	Luton, The George Hotel	Eversholt, Rads End House, 6.5a and a further 19.5a to be offered separately	Sold prior to auction. Joint auction with Knight, Frank & Rutley	TDA 21 November 1963 p. 26, 12 December p. 20. BTS 15 November 1963 p. 8; 6 December p. 8. On instruction of R. J. Godber Esq. Vacant possession	-
7 March 1964	Bedford, The Swan Hotel	Souldrop, Knotting Fox Farm, house, 176a	£28,000	BTS 14, 21 February 1964 p. 9. Vacant possession	-
24 March 1964	Sandy, The Lion Hotel	Sandy, adjacent 27 Bedford Road, building plot	-	BTS 6 March 1964 p. 10. Planning permission for a single dwelling and garage. Vacant possession	-
3 April 1964	Bedford, Lime Street, sale rooms	Kempston, 22 Chantry Road, semi-detached house	£2,700	BTS 13, 20 March 1964 p. 9. Vacant possession	-
3 April 1964	Bedford, Lime Street, sale rooms	Houghton Conquest, Rectory Lane, allotment land, 8.22a	£4,100	BTS 13, 20 March 1964 p. 9	-
27 May 1964	Bedford, The Swan Hotel	Bedford, 10 St Paul's Square, business premises	£16,500 Joint auction with Weatherall, Green & Smith	TDA 11 May 1964 p. 21. BTS 8 May 1964 p. 10. Former Bedford Trustee Savings Bank. Vacant possession	-
13 June 1964	Bedford, Horne Lane, Tudor Rooms	Ampthill, Houghton Park Farm, house, cottage, 276 a	£44,000	BTS 22 May 1964 p. 9; 12 June p. 11. Vacant possession	-

Auction date	Venue	Description	Price	Newspaper references	BLARS references
10 July 1964	Bedford, Lime Street, sale rooms	Bedford, 187 Kimbolton Road, detached house, 1a	£7,300	BTS 5, 12, 19 June 1964 p. 11; 10 July p. 10. Outline planning permission for further detached house. Vacant possession	-
10 July 1964	Bedford, Lime Street, sale rooms	Sharnbrook, Willingdon, Mill Road, semi-detached house	£2,100	BTS 5, 19 June 1964 p. 11; 10 July p. 10. Vacant possession	-
10 July 1964	Bedford, Lime Street, sale rooms	Clophill, Blair Cottage, 6 Mill Lane, detached cottage	£2,900	BTS 12, 19 June 1964 p. 11. Vacant possession	-
10 July 1964	Bedford, Lime Street, sale rooms	Bedford, 41 The Grove, house	£3,900	BTS 26 June 1964 p. 10; 10 July p. 10. Latterly used as three flats. Vacant possession	-
18 September 1964	Turvey, The Manor Room	Turvey, Covington's Yard, two cottages	£1,450	BTS 24 July 1964 p. 9; 21 August p. 9; 28 August p. 10; 18 September p. 10. Vacant possession	-
18 September 1964	Turvey, The Manor Room	Turvey, two parcels of building land, 1.5a and 1a	Auction postponed	BTS 24 July 1964 p. 9; 21 August p. 9	-
19 September 1964	Bedford, Horne Lane, Tudor Rooms	Bromham, Bromham Hospital, pasture land, 47.03a	£8,000	BTS 24 July 1964 p. 9; 28 August p. 10; 18 September p. 10. On instruction of Minister of Health. Vacant possession	-
19 September 1964	Bedford, Horne Lane, Tudor Rooms	Bromham, Bromham Hospital, pasture land, 8.25a	£1,200	BTS 24 July 1964 p. 9; 28 August p. 10; 18 September p. 10. On instruction of Minister of Health. Occupied by Scouts	-
19 September 1964	Bedford, Horne Lane, Tudor Rooms	Bromham, Bromham Hospital, arable land, 28.808a	£5,600	BTS 24 July 1964 p. 9; 28 August p. 10; 18 September p. 10. On instruction of Minister of Health. Rental £155 pa	-

Auction date	Venue	Description	Price	Newspaper references	BLARS references
19 September 1964	Bedford, Horne Lane, Tudor Rooms	Sharnbrook, The Manor, house, 2a	£12,250	BTS 24 July 1964 p. 9; 28 August p. 10; 18 September p. 10	-
19 September 1964	-	Blunham, South Mills Farm, cottages, gravel deposits, alluvial land, 183a	-	TDA 28 August 1964 p. 18. Gravel deposits of 40a. BTS 28 August 1964 p. 10; 18 September p. 10. Cottages let at £1,200 pa	-
6 November 1964	Bedford, Lime Street, sale rooms	Bedford, 14 Bromham Road, freehold shop and premises	Unsold	BTS 2, 9 October 1964 p. 10; 30 October p. 11. Vacant possession	PK un-catalogued.
6 November 1964	Bedford, Lime Street, sale rooms	Bedford, 1 Salisbury Street	-	BTS 9 October 1964 p. 10	-
6 November 1964	Bedford, Lime Street, sale rooms	Bedford, 26 and 30 Argyll Street	-	BTS 9 October 1964 p. 10	-
6 November 1964	Bedford, Lime Street, sale rooms	Eaton Socon, 31–45 Cross Hall Road	-	BTS 9 October 1964 p. 10	-
27 November 1964	Turvey, The Manor Room	Turvey, May Road, building land, 1.5a	£8,200	BTS 13, 27 November 1964 p. 10. On instruction of Mrs P. K. C. Hanbury	PK un-catalogued. Outline planning consent for residential development. Vacant possession
12 March 1965	Bedford, The Swan Hotel	Sutton, Church Farm, 66a	£15,500	BT 19 February 1965 p. 15; 5 March p. 13. Planning permission for a house and buildings. Vacant possession	-
12 March 1965	Bedford, The Swan Hotel	Bedford, adjoining 23 Greenshields Road, building plot	£2,900	BT 19 February 1965 p. 15; 5 March p. 13. Outline planning permission for single dwelling house or bungalow	-

Auction date	Venue	Description	Price	Newspaper references	BLARS references
12 March 1965	Bedford, The Swan Hotel	Bedford, 200 Honeyhill Road, detached modern house	£4,000	BT 19 February 1965 p. 15; 5 March p. 13. Vacant possession	-
12 March 1965	Bedford, The Swan Hotel	Bedford, 70 Ford End Road, semi-detached house	£2,375	BT 19 February 1965 p. 15; 5 March p. 13. Vacant possession	-
11 May 1965	Harrold, Harrold Institute	Harrold, West View House, detached house	£4,500	BT 16 April 1965 p. 11; 7 May p. 15. On instruction of the executors of Mrs A. L. Richardson	-
11 May 1965	Harrold, Harrold Institute	Harrold, High Street, building plot	£650	BT 16 April 1965 p. 11; 7 May p. 15. On instruction of the executors of Mrs A. L. Richardson. Suitable for one detached dwelling	-
11 May 1965	Harrold, Harrold Institute	Harrold, Ouse Lea, 7 Church Walk, cottage	Unsold	BT 16 April 1965 p. 11; 7 May p. 15. On instruction of the executors of Mrs A. L. Richardson	-
11 May 1965	Harrold, Harrold Institute	Harrold, 12–18 Dove Lane, four cottages	£1,300	BT 16 April 1965 p. 11; 7 May p. 15. On instruction of the executors of Mrs A. L. Richardson	-
11 May 1965	Harrold, Harrold Institute	Harrold, 132–138 High Street, four cottages	£1,400	BT 16 April 1965 p. 11; 7 May p. 15. On instruction of the executors of Mrs A. L. Richardson	-
14 May 1965	Bedford, The Swan Hotel	Bedford, 5 Woburn Road, seven bedroom terraced house	£3,800	BT 16 April 1965 p. 11; 7 May p. 15. Vacant possession	-
14 May 1965	Bedford, The Swan Hotel	Bedford, 271 London Road, semi-detached house	£3,700	BT 16 April 1965 p. 11; 7 May p. 15. Vacant possession	-

Auction date	Venue	Description	Price	Newspaper references	BLARS references
14 May 1965	Bedford, The Swan Hotel	Bedford, 187 Kimbolton Road, building plot	£2,400	BT 16 April 1965 p. 11; 7 May p. 15. Vacant possession	-
14 May 1965	Bedford, The Swan Hotel	Wilstead, The Central Garage and 3 Cotton End	£12,000	BT 26 March 1965 p. 15; 9 April p. 15; 23 April p. 13; 7 May p. 15. Vacant possession	-
14 May 1965	Bedford, The Swan Hotel	Great Barford, 13 Silver Street, cottage	Unsold	BT 16 April 1965 p. 11; 7 May p. 15. Vacant possession	-
14 May 1965	Bedford, The Swan Hotel	Great Barford, Silver Street, plot	£1,150	BT 16 April 1965 p. 11; 7 May p. 15	-
6 September 1965	Dunstable, The Halfway House	Haynes, Cottage Farm, West End, arable land, 7.5a	£4,300	BT 13 August 1965 p. 9; 27 August p. 11	-
6 September 1965	Dunstable, The Halfway House	Haynes, Cottage Farm, West End	£2,200	BT 13 August 1965 p. 9; 27 August p. 11	-
6 September 1965	Dunstable, The Halfway House	Toddington, Herne Manor Farm, house, buildings, 117.249a	29,500	BT 13 August 1965 p. 9; 27 August p. 11. Vacant possession	-
6 September 1965	Dunstable, The Halfway House	Pepperstock, Bonner's Farm, Dutch barn, 93a	£22,000	BT 13 August 1965 p. 9; 27 August p. 11	-
6 September 1965	Dunstable, The Halfway House	Pepperstock, Bonner's Farm, detached modern cottage	£3,000	BT 13 August 1965 p. 9; 27 August p. 11	-
6 September 1965	Dunstable, The Halfway House	Pepperstock, accommodation land, 24a	£4,100	BT 13 August 1965 p. 9; 27 August p. 11	-

Auction date	Venue	Description	Price	Newspaper references	BLARS references
24 September 1965	Bedford, The Swan Hotel	Bedford, 93 Ashburnham Road, freehold detached double-fronted house	Unsold	BT 30 July 1965 p. 11; 3 September p. 9	PK un-catalogued. Vacant possession
16 October 1965	Bedford, The Swan Hotel	Cranfield, Leys Farm, house, buildings, 97a	£20,000	BT 24 September 1965 p. 15. Vacant possession	-
3 December 1965	Bedford, The Swan Hotel	Bedford, 30 Kimbolton Road, house	£5,100 Joint auction with Connells	BT 3 December 1965 p. 13	-
3 December 1965	Bedford, The Swan Hotel	Bedford, 30a Kimbolton Road, house	£3,250 Joint auction with Connells	BT 3 December 1965 p. 13	-
3 December 1965	Bedford, The Swan Hotel	Bedford, 30b Kimbolton Road, house	£2,750 Joint auction with Connells	BT 3 December 1965 p. 13	-
10 December 1965	Bedford, The Swan Hotel	Clophill, Northfields Farm, farmhouse, two cottages, 313a	£72,000	TDA 17 November 1965 p. 22. BT 12 November 1965 p. 15	PK 1/4/183
14 December 1965	Harrold, Harrold Institute	Harrold, 43 High Street, freehold residence	£2,300	BT 19 November 1965 p. 15; 10 December p. 15. On instruction of Bedfordshire County Council	-
25 March 1966	Bedford, The Swan Hotel	Bedford, 129 Goldington Road, semi-detached house	£2,300	BT 4, 11, 25 March 1966 p. 15. Rental £150 pa	-
25 March 1966	Bedford, The Swan Hotel	Bedford, 66 George Street, terraced house	£750	BT 4, 11 March 1966 p. 15. Rental £58 pa	-
25 March 1966	Bedford, The Swan Hotel	Bedford, 7 Maryville Road, terraced house	£2,300	BT 4, 11, 25 March 1966 p. 15. Vacant possession	-

Auction date	Venue	Description	Price	Newspaper references	BLARS references
25 March 1966	Bedford, The Swan Hotel	Turvey, High Street, two cottages	£700	BT 4 March 1966 p. 15; 18 March p. 9. On instruction of Turvey House Estate	-
6 May 1966	Baldock, The Rose and Crown Hotel	Ashwell (Herts), Sunnymead Farm, poultry broiler farm	-	BT 22, 29 April 1966 p. 15	-
12 August 1966	Bedford, The Swan Hotel	Biddenham, 114 Bromham Road, detached house	£8,000	BT 1 July 1966 p. 11; 15 July p. 15; 12 August p. 11. On instruction of executors of E. G. Webb. Vacant possession	-
25 November 1966	Bedford, The Swan Hotel	Bedford, 65 Elstow Road, semi-detached house	£4,000	BT 2, 28 October 1966 p. 13; 18 November p. 13. Vacant possession	-
25 November 1966	Bedford, The Swan Hotel	Bedford, 128 Castle Road, detached house	£3,500	BT 21, 28 October 1966 p. 13; 18 November p. 13. Vacant possession	-
25 November 1966	Bedford, The Swan Hotel	Bedford, 122 Bromham Road, detached town house	£7,100	BT 21, 28 October 1966 p. 13; 18 November p. 13. Vacant possession	-
25 November 1966	Bedford, The Swan Hotel	Bedford, 88 Dudley Street, terraced villa	Auction cancelled	BT 28 October 1966 p. 13; 18 November p. 13. Vacant possession	-
7 December 1966	On site	Maulden, Water End Farm, house, buildings, market garden land, 24a	£8,150	BT 18 November 1966 p. 13; 2 December p. 13. On instruction of the trustee in bankruptcy	-
7 December 1966	On site	Maulden, Water End Farm, 6.9a	£1,300	BT 18 November 1966 p. 13; 2 December p. 13. On instruction of the trustee in bankruptcy	-
7 December 1966	On site	Maulden, Water End Farm, 4.905a	£575	BT 18 November 1966 p. 13; 2 December p. 13. On instruction of the trustee in bankruptcy	-

Auction date	Venue	Description	Price	Newspaper references	BLARS references
27 January 1967	Shefford, The White Hart	Campton, 2 The Village Greenway, semi-detached cottage	£700	BT 6 January 1967 p. 9; 20 January p. 11. On instruction of the Secretary of State for Defence	-
10 March 1967	Bedford, The Swan Hotel	Bedford, 2 Bradgate Road, detached house	Unsold	BT 10, 24 February 1967 p. 11. Vacant possession	-
10 March 1967	Bedford, The Swan Hotel	Bedford, adjoining 2 Bradgate Road, building plot with four garages	Unsold	BT 24 February 1967 p. 11. Outline planning permission for detached house. Vacant possession	-
10 March 1967	Bedford, The Swan Hotel	Bedford, 235 London Road, corner house	-	BT 10, 24 February 1967 p. 11. Vacant possession	-
10 March 1967	Bedford, The Swan Hotel	Bedford, 100 Howbury Street, semi-detached villa	£2,000	BT 10, 24 February 1967 p. 11. Vacant possession	-
14 June 1967	Bedford, The Swan Hotel	Bedford, 29–31 St Peter's Street, Conservative Club	£23,500	BT 10 March 1967 p. 13; 21 April p. 15; 9 June p. 13. On instruction of the liquidator. Vacant possession	-
23 June 1967	Bedford, The Swan Hotel	Henlow, Henlow Camp, garden land, 14.5a	£3,800	BT 9 June 1967 p. 13; 23 June p. 13	-
23 June 1967	Bedford, The Swan Hotel	Souldrop, Middle Farm, house, buildings, 182.78a	£44,250	BT 12 May 1967 p. 15; 23 June p. 13. On instruction of Messrs C. D. and A. D. Brookbanks. Including Lordship of the Manor of Colworth. Vacant possession	-
14 July 1967	Bedford, The Swan Hotel	Clapham, 25 Green Lane, semi-detached house	£2,950	BT 9 June 1967 p. 13; 30 June p. 13	-

Auction date	Venue	Description	Price	Newspaper references	BLARS references
14 July 1967	Bedford, The Swan Hotel	Goldington, pasture, 16a	£4,200	BT 9 June 1967 p. 13; 30 June p. 13	-
14 July 1967	Bedford, The Swan Hotel	Bedford, 174 Bromham Road, detached house	Unsold	BT 9 June 1967 p. 13; 30 June p. 13. Outline planning permission for additional house. Vacant possession	-
15 September 1967	Bedford, The Swan Hotel	Cardington, Cardington Station and depot	£1,750	BT 4 August 1967 p. 8; 18 August p. 7. On instruction of British Railways	-
8 December 1967	Bedford, The Swan Hotel	Oakley, Oakley Station and depot, 1,400a	£5,100	BT 20 October 1967 p. 14; 24 November p. 14; 8 December p. 12. On instruction of British Railways. Station house rental £91 4s 4d pa	-
8 December 1967	Bedford, The Swan Hotel	Olney (Bucks), Olney Station and depot	-	BT 20 October 1967 p. 14. On instruction of British Railways	-
23 February 1968	Bedford, The Swan Hotel	Southill, Southill Station House and depot	£4,300	BT 26 January 1968 p. 10; 23 February p. 12	-
23 February 1968	Bedford, The Swan Hotel	Southill, Southill Station, two railway cottages	£1,600	BT 26 January 1968 p. 10; 23 February p. 12	-
26 July 1968	Bedford, The Swan Hotel	Keysoe, Grange Farm, house, two cottages, 431a	£112,000	BT 14 June 1968 p. 14; 5 July p. 14. On instruction of J. Walker Esq. Vacant possession	-
31 July 1968	On site	Budna, Grove Farm, house, buildings, 97.77a	£33,000 Joint auction with Bidwell & Sons	BT 28 June 1968 p. 26. Vacant possession	-
2 August 1968	Bedford, The Swan Hotel	Bletsoe, 9–14 Bletsoe, six old-world cottages	£3,800	BT 12 July 1968 p. 26; 26 July p. 12. On instruction of Bovril Ltd. Five cottages let. Total rental £185 pa	-

Auction date	Venue	Description	Price	Newspaper references	BLARS references
2 August 1968	Bedford, The Swan Hotel	Thurleigh, Keysoe Road, building plot	£1,250	BT 5 July 1968 p. 14. On instruction of the trustees of the Baptist Chapel. Outline planning consent for one dwelling	-
2 August 1968	Bedford, The Swan Hotel	Bedford, 28 Bushmead Avenue, detached house	£3,000	BT 12 July 1968 p. 26; 26 July p. 12. Vacant possession	-
2 August 1968	Bedford, The Swan Hotel	Bedford, 82 Castle Road, business, residential occupation	£2,900	BT 12 July 1968 p. 26; 26 July p. 12. Vacant possession	-
23 October 1968	Turvey, The Three Cranes	Turvey, Little Gains Farm, buildings, 58.659a	£14,000	BT 27 September 1968 p. 10. Planning permission for farmhouse	-
23 October 1968	Turvey, The Three Cranes	Turvey, Little Gains Farm, Bakers Close, river frontage, 16.213a	£3,800	BT 27 September 1968 p. 10. Vacant possession	-
22 November 1968	Bedford, The Swan Hotel	Biddenham, 7 Bromham Road, detached house	£6,800	BT 4, 25 October 1968 p. 10	-
22 November 1968	Bedford, The Swan Hotel	Biddenham, adjoining 7 Bromham Road, building plot	£3,750	BT 4, 25 October 1968 p. 10. Outline planning for single dwelling	-
22 November 1968	Bedford, The Swan Hotel	Bedford, 122 Coventry Road, house	£800	BT 25 October 1968 p. 10. Rental £45 10s pa	-
22 November 1968	Bedford, The Swan Hotel	Kempston, 4 Duncombe Street, house	£360	BT 1 November 1968 p. 10. Rental £46 3s pa	-

Auction date	Venue	Description	Price	Newspaper references	BLARS references
22 November 1968	Bedford, The Swan Hotel	Riseley, 90–92 High Street, old-world cottage	£2,650	BT 4, 25 October 1968 p. 10. Vacant possession	-
22 November 1968	Bedford, The Swan Hotel	Bedford, 75 Bower Street, shop, living accommodation	£4,000	BT 25 October 1968 p. 10. Vacant possession	-
27 November 1968	Biggleswade, The Swan Hotel	Biggleswade, former Territorial Army Centre, office block, drill hall, lorry garage, other useful buildings, adjoining house, occupied as two flats	£29,500	BT 25 October 1968 p. 10. On instruction of the Territorial Auxiliary and Volunteer Association of East Anglia	-
21 February 1969	Bedford, The Swan Hotel	Bedford, 115 Dudley Street, workshop	£1,350	BT 17 January 1969 p. 10; 14 February p. 15. Vacant possession	-
21 February 1969	Bedford, The Swan Hotel	Bedford, 33 Irwin Road, semi-detached house	£3,500	BT 17 January 1969 p. 10; 14 February p. 15. Vacant possession	-
21 February 1969	Bedford, The Swan Hotel	Bedford, 39 St Michael's Road, semi-detached house	£2,850	BT 17 January 1969 p. 10; 14 February p. 15. Vacant possession	-
21 February 1969	Bedford, The Swan Hotel	Willington, situate on A603, building plot	£3,300	BT 17 January 1969 p. 10; 14 February p. 15. Vacant possession	-
21 February 1969	Bedford, The Swan Hotel	Oakley, Rectory Cottage, period cottage with river frontage	£6,400	BT 17 January 1969 p. 10; 14 February p. 15. Vacant possession	-

Auction date	Venue	Description	Price	Newspaper references	BLARS references
2 April 1969	Bedford, The Swan Hotel	Dean, School House, detached house, 2.5a	£2,500	BT 28 February 1969 p. 14; 7 March p. 15	-
29 April 1969	Leighton Buzzard, The Swan Hotel	Leighton Buzzard, Bedford Street, haulage contractors' yard, workshop	-	BT 11 April 1969 p. 14; 25 April p. 8. On instruction of Messrs Roberts Bros in dissolution of partnership	-
27 June 1969	Bedford, The Swan Hotel	Bedford, 14 Western Street, terraced house	£1,650	BT 23 May 1969 p. 8; 6 June p. 15. Vacant possession	-
27 June 1969	Bedford, The Swan Hotel	Bedford, 37 Goldington Road, detached house	£12,200	BT 23 May 1969 p. 8; 6 June p. 15. Vacant possession	-
27 June 1969	Bedford, The Swan Hotel	Bedford, 8 The Avenue	- Withdrawn from auction	BT 23 May 1969 p. 8; 6 June p. 15. Vacant possession.	-
27 June 1969	Bedford, The Swan Hotel	Bedford, 11 Glebe Road, semi-detached house	£3,500	BT 6 June 1969 p. 15. Vacant possession	-
25 July 1969	Bedford, The Swan Hotel	Odell, Horsefair Lane, building plot	£1,000	BT 18 July 1969 p. 14. On instruction of the Rt. Hon. Lord Luke TD, DL, JP	-
25 July 1969	Bedford, The Swan Hotel	Odell, High Street, two building plots	£1,750	BT 18 July 1969 p. 14. On instruction of the Rt. Hon. Lord Luke TD, DL, JP	-
25 July 1969	Bedford, The Swan Hotel	Odell, 1 Church Lane, detached cottage	Unsold	BT 18 July 1969 p. 14. On instruction of the Rt. Hon. Lord Luke TD, DL, JP	-
25 July 1969	Bedford, The Swan Hotel	Wilden, 46 High Street, semi-detached cottage	£800	BT 18 July 1969 p. 14. On instruction of the trustees of Mrs Emma Smith. Occupied by M. T. Peet. Rental £1 per week	-

Auction date	Venue	Description	Price	Newspaper references	BLARS references
25 July 1969	Bedford, The Swan Hotel	Wilden, 48 High Street, semi-detached cottage	£1,850	BT 18 July 1969 p. 14. On instruction of the trustees of Mrs Emma Smith. Occupied by Mrs I. A. Ives. Rental £15s per week	-
25 July 1969	Bedford, The Swan Hotel	Carlton, 83 The Causeway, end terrace cottage	£1,100	BT 18 July 1969 p. 14	-
24 October 1969	Bedford, The Swan Hotel	Bedford, 8 The Avenue, semi-detached seven bedroom house	£3,375	BT 19 September 1969 p. 35	-
24 October 1969	Bedford, The Swan Hotel	Bedford, 25 Trinity Road, house	£1,900	BT 19 September 1969 p. 35; 17 October p. 27	-
24 October 1969	Bedford, The Swan Hotel	Oakley, 51 High Street, detached house	£3,500	BT 19 September 1969 p. 35; 17 October p. 27	-
24 October 1969	Bedford, The Swan Hotel	Oakley, 51 High Street, building plot	£1,600	BT 19 September 1969 p. 35; 17 October p. 27	-
24 October 1969	Bedford, The Swan Hotel	Kempston, 53 Stuart Road, detached house, office	Unsold	BT 19 September 1969 p. 35; 17 October p. 27	-

Property Auction Records 1970–1979

Auction date	Venue	Description	Price	Newspaper references	BLARS references
19 February 1970	St Neots, The Cross Keys	St Neots (Cambs), 35 East Street, semi-detached house	£1,750	BT 30 January 1970 p. 27. Requires improvement	-
18 March 1970	Sandy, The Red Lion Hotel	Seddington, Westholme, detached double-fronted residence	-	BT 20, 27 February 1970 p. 10. On instruction of R. G. Buckle Esq.	-
18 March 1970	Sandy, The Red Lion Hotel	Sandy, Blunham Meadows, market garden land, 12.5a	-	BT 20, 27 February 1970 p. 10. On instruction of R. G. Buckle Esq.	-
1 April 1970	Biggleswade, The Crown Hotel	Biggleswade, Dunton Road, arable land, 14.019a	£5,000	BT 13, 20 March 1970 p. 8; 27 March p. 14. On instruction of Messrs F. D. and T. J. Maynard. Vacant possession	-
1 April 1970	Biggleswade, The Crown Hotel	Biggleswade, Dunton Road, arable land, 27.519a	£8,300	-	-
10 April 1970	Bedford, The Swan Hotel	Swineshead, The Old Rectory, house, 1a	-	BT 13 February 1970 p. 31; 20 February p. 27; 6 March p. 32. On instruction of executor of E. N. Sturgess. Vacant possession	-
10 April 1970	Bedford, The Swan Hotel	Swineshead, building plot adjoining The Old Rectory	-	BT 6 March 1950 p. 32. On instruction of executor of E. N. Sturgess	-
10 April 1970	Bedford, The Swan Hotel	Cranfield, Bedford Road, arable land, 22.810a	£4,800	BT 6 March 1950 p. 32. On instruction of executor of E. N. Sturgess	-
10 April 1970	Bedford, The Swan Hotel	Willington, market garden land, 6.214a	£1,200	BT 6 March 1950 p. 32. On instruction of executor of E. N. Sturgess	-

Auction date	Venue	Description	Price	Newspaper references	BLARS references
10 April 1970	Bedford, The Swan Hotel	Bedford, 63 Commercial Road, house	£500	BT 13 February 1970 p. 31; 6 March p. 32. Rental £52 pa	-
7 May 1970	Bedford, The Swan Hotel	Bedford, 65 Commercial Road, three bedroom end terrace house	£1,300	BT 13 February 1970 p. 31; 6 March p. 32. Vacant possession	-
7 May 1970	Bedford, The Swan Hotel	Bedford, 9 George Street, three bedroom semi-detached house	£4,300	BT 6 March 1950 p. 32. On instruction of the executor	-
10 June 1970	Langford, The Wrestlers	Langford, High Street, freehold building plot, known as The Red House	-	BT 29 May 1970 p. 14	-
17 July 1970	Bedford, The Swan Hotel	Bedford, 16 Prebend Street, house	Unsold	BT 22 May 1970 p. 27; 3 July p. 23; 10 July p. 18. For improvement. Vacant possession	-
17 July 1970	Bedford, The Swan Hotel	Bedford, 33 Spenser Road	-	BT 22 May 1970 p. 27	-
17 July 1970	Bedford, The Swan Hotel	Renhold, 45 Green End Road	-	BT 22 May 1970 p. 27	-
17 July 1970	Bedford, The Swan Hotel	Sharnbrook, Hillcot, Kennel Hill, stone cottage	£800	BT 3 July 1970 p. 23; 10 July p. 18	-
17 July 1970	Bedford, The Swan Hotel	Bedford, 3 and 5 Cobden Street, two houses	£500	BT 5 June 1970 p. 21; BT 3 July p. 23; 10 July p. 18. Rental £76 pa	-
17 July 1970	Bedford, The Swan Hotel	Bedford, 4 Ampthill Road, shop, living accommodation	£5,200	BT 3 July 1970 p. 23; 10 July p. 18	-

Auction date	Venue	Description	Price	Newspaper references	BLARS references
17 July 1970	Bedford, The Swan Hotel	Bedford, 44 Polhill Avenue, detached house	Unsold	BT 3 July 1970 p. 23; 10 July p. 18	-
17 July 1970	Bedford, The Swan Hotel	Bedford, 70a George Street, lock-up garage	£600	BT 3 July 1970 p. 23; 10 July p. 18	-
17 July 1970	Bedford, The Swan Hotel	Wilstead, North End Farm, bungalow, 28.36a	£12,000	BT 29 May 1970 p. 21; 3 July p. 10; 10 July p. 18. Vacant possession	-
23 July 1970	Olney, The Bull Inn	Weston Underwood (Bucks), Appletrees, detached cottage	£3,700	BT 3 July 1970 p. 23; 10 July p. 18	-
23 July 1970	Olney, The Bull Inn	Weston Underwood (Bucks), Chapel Lane Cottage	£3,700	BT 3 July 1970 p. 23; 10 July p. 18	-
31 July 1970	Biggleswade, The Crown Hotel	Biggleswade, The Gentleman's Residence, 55 London Road,	-	BT 3 July 1970 p. 10; 17 July p. 14. By order of executors of F. J. C. Hilton	-
25 September 1970	Biggleswade, The Memorial Hall	Biggleswade, Shortmead Street, building land, 4a 1r 25p	-	BT 21 August 1970 p. 14; 4 September p. 14. On instruction of the Vicar of Biggleswade and St. Alban's Diocesan Board of Finance. Vacant possession	-
6 November 1970	Bedford, The Swan Hotel	Warrington (Bucks), farm pasture, 37a	Unsold	BT 25 September 1970 p. 20; 30 October p. 14. Planning permission for farm house	-
6 November 1970	Bedford, The Swan Hotel	Shefford, 7 and 8 Deadman's Cross	Unsold	BT 28 August 1970 p. 24; 25 September p 20	-
6 November 1970	Bedford, The Swan Hotel	Haynes, Warren Bungalow, woodland, 11a	-	BT 28 August 1970 p. 24	-

Auction date	Venue	Description	Price	Newspaper references	BLARS references
11 November 1970	Potton, The Rose and Crown	Potton, 22 and 24 Horslow Street, freehold houses	-	BT 23 October 1970 p. 8	-
2 December 1970	Stotfold, The Crown	Stotfold, Meadow Way, two building plots	-	BT 13 November 1970 p. 14	-
18 December 1970	Bedford, The Swan Hotel	Bedford, 96 Winchester Road, three bedroom semi-detached house	£3,500	BT 6 November 1970 p. 18; 4 December p. 25	-
18 December 1970	Bedford, The Swan Hotel	Bedford, 39 Spencer Road, six bedroom corner house	£2,850	BT 6 November 1970 p. 18; 4 December p. 25. Used as two flats	-
24 February 1971	Potton, The Rose and Crown Hotel	Potton, Common Road and Gamlingay Road, freehold market garden land, 44a	-	BT 5 February 1971 p. 14. Vacant possession	-
17 March 1971	Sandy, The Red Lion Hotel	Sandy, Bridge Farm, house, outbuildings, 14a	-	BT 19 February 1971 p. 12; 26 February p, 14; 12 March p. 10	-
17 March 1971	Sandy, The Red Lion Hotel	Sandy, Vinegar Hill, Beeston Brook End, freehold market garden land, 24a 1r 8p	-	BT 26 February 1971 p. 14; 12 March p. 10. On instruction of representatives of the late G. A. Cope Esq.	-
23 April 1971	Bedford, The Swan Hotel	Bedford, 42 The Grove, three bedroom town house	£3,300	BT 29 January 1971 p. 13; 23 April p. 19	-
23 April 1971	Bedford, The Swan Hotel	Bedford, 19 Grove Place, house	£6,400	BT 22 January 1971 p. 2; 23 April p. 19. Planning permission for offices	-
23 April 1971	Bedford, The Swan Hotel	Wilstead, building plots	Auction postponed	BT 22 January 1971 p. 21; 23 April p. 19	-

Auction date	Venue	Description	Price	Newspaper references	BLARS references
23 April 1971	Bedford, The Swan Hotel	Keysoe, Rose Cottage, Hatch Lane, 0.75a	£1,100	BT 5 March 1971 p. 19; 23 April p. 19	-
23 April 1971	Bedford, The Swan Hotel	Bromham, 76 Village Road, semi-detached cottage	£2,600	BT 26 March 1971 p. 16; 23 April p. 19	-
28 May 1971	Bedford, The Swan Hotel	Kempston, 51 Stuart Road, light industrial premises	£11,000	BT 7 May 1971 p. 8; 21 May p. 10. On instruction of J. B. Pinnock Esq. FCA as liquidator of E. W. Harris & Co. Suitable for builder's yard. Vacant possession	-
28 May 1971	Bedford, The Swan Hotel	Turvey, Carlton Road, three stone cottages, vehicle depot, workshop	Unsold	BT 7 May 1971 p. 8; 21 May p. 10. On instruction of Messrs F. & C. Bailey who have retired from long established haulage business. Vacant possession	-
28 May 1971	Bedford, The Swan Hotel	Wilden, Bryher Farm, bungalow, buildings, 3a	£7,500	BT 14, 21 May 1971 p. 10	-
25 June 1971	Bedford, The Swan Hotel	Bedford 21–24 Corby Close, four semi-detached houses	Unsold	BT 21 May 1971 p. 23. By order of Bedfordshire and Luton Police Authority. Vacant possession	-
25 June 1971	Bedford, The Swan Hotel	Bedford, 13 Cardington Road, seventeenth century cottage	£3,000	BT 21 May 1971 p. 23; 18 June p. 29. Vacant possession	-
25 June 1971	Bedford, The Swan Hotel	Bletsoe, 18–21, cottages	£6,500	BT 21 May 1971 p. 23; 28 May p. 27. For improvement. Vacant possession	-

Auction date	Venue	Description	Price	Newspaper references	BLARS references
4 August 1971	Langford, The Wrestlers	Langford, East Road, building land, 0.410a	-	BT 16 July 1971 p. 12. On instruction of executors of Mr George Pateman. With benefit of planning permission	-
29 September 1971	Langford, The Wrestlers	Langford, 81 and 83 Cambridge Road, smallholder's homestead, 27a	-	BT 30 July 1971 p. 13; BT 10 September p. 4	-
29 September 1971	Langford, The Wrestlers	Langford, frontage to Gurney's Lane, market garden land, 10a 10p	-	BT 10 September 1971 p. 4	-
29 September 1971	Langford, The Wrestlers	Langford, frontage to Gurney's Lane, market garden, 7a	-	BT 10 September 1971 p. 4	-
14 October 1971	Bedford, The Swan Hotel	Ravensden, Grange Farm, Bedford to Kimbolton Road, five cottages, 400a	£88,000	BT 30 July 1971 p. 13; 27 August p. 13; 10 September p. 4. On instruction of the trustees of M. B. Sunderland. Arable and stock farm	-
11 November 1971	Potton, The Rose and Crown Hotel	Potton, Everton Road, eight building sites	-	BT 15 October 1971 p. 16; 29 October p. 6. On instruction of Ivel Holdings Ltd. With detailed planning permission	-
26 November 1971	Cranfield, The Leathern Bottle	Cranfield, Green's Close, Astwood Road, detached cottage, 8.75a	£10,900	BT 22 October 1971 p. 28; 29 October p. 29; 5 November p. 24; 19 November p. 12. On instruction of Mrs A. E. Wilson	-
3 December 1971	Bedford, The Swan Hotel	Clophill, High Street, building plot	£5,100	BT 22 October 1971 p. 28; 29 October p. 29. Outline planning permission	-
3 December 1971	Bedford, The Swan Hotel	Clophill, High Street, building plot	£4,500	BT 22 October 1971 p. 28; 29 October p. 29. Outline planning permission	-

Auction date	Venue	Description	Price	Newspaper references	BLARS references
3 December 1971	Bedford, The Swan Hotel	Houghton Conquest, The Grove, freehold building plot	£3,650	BT 29 October 1971 p. 29. Outline planning permission	-
3 December 1971	Bedford, The Swan Hotel	Kempston, 34 King Street, semi-detached house	£1,525	BT 12 November 1971 p. 27. Rental £49.92 pa	-
21 January 1972	Bedford, The Swan Hotel	Bedford, 9 Hawkins Road, house	£1,400	BT 17 December 1971 p. 29; 7 January 1972 p. 23. Rental £59.80 pa	-
21 January 1972	Bedford, The Swan Hotel	Bedford, 25 Hawkins Road, house	£1,700	BT 17 December 1971 p. 29; 7 January 1972 p. 23. Rental £164.32 pa	-
21 January 1972	Bedford, The Swan Hotel	Kempston, 3 West End Road, Box End, semi-detached cottage	£5,600	BT 7 January 1972 p. 23	-
21 January 1972	Bedford, The Swan Hotel	Sharnbrook, Barleycroft, Park Lane, bungalow, 4.679a	£8,550	BT 26 November 1971 p. 33; 17 December 1971 p. 29; 7 January 1972 p. 23. Planning permission for one detached dwelling	-
21 January 1972	Bedford, The Swan Hotel	Wilstead, 69–77 Cotton End Road	£6,600	BT 7 January 1972 p. 23. Permission for two dwellings	-
21 January 1972	Bedford, The Swan Hotel	Biddenham, Deep Spinney, Bromham Road, wooded amenity land, 3.2a	£2,500	BT 17 December 1971 p. 29; 7 January 1972 p. 22	-
28 March 1972	Guilden Morden, The Three Tuns	Guilden Morden (Cambs), High Street, freehold building land	-	BT 3 March 1972 p. 4; 24 March p. 25. On instruction of Messrs Greene King & Sons Ltd. Planning permission for four houses	-

Auction date	Venue	Description	Price	Newspaper references	BLARS references
29 March 1972	Biggleswade, The Crown Hotel	Lower Caldecote, Elm Farm, Great North Road, freehold farm buildings, grassland, market garden land	-	BT 3 March 1972 p. 4; 24 March p. 25. On instruction of executors of Mrs Marion Alice Gee	-
7 April 1972	Bedford, The Swan Hotel	Pertenhall, Yew Tree Cottage, detached cottage	£9,500	BT 11 February 1972 p. 25; 25 February p. 23; 24 March p. 25	-
7 April 1972	Bedford, The Swan Hotel	Bromham, Ivydene, 80 Village Road, semi-detached cottage	£4,800	BT 3, 10 March 1972 p. 21; 24 March p. 25	-
7 April 1972	Bedford, The Swan Hotel	Radwell, The Comptons, Felmersham Road, field, 0.9a	£1,700	BT 3 March 1972 p. 21; 24 March p. 25. Planning consent for caravan site	-
7 April 1972	Bedford, The Swan Hotel	Bedford, 5 Fernlea Close, terraced house	£7,000	BT 11 February 1972 p. 25; 25 February p. 23; 24 March p. 25	-
7 April 1972	Bedford, The Swan Hotel	Lower Stondon, 56–58 Bedford Road, Henlow Camp	£7,600	BT 10 March 1972 p. 21; 24 March p. 25. Site for development	-
28 April 1972	Bedford, The Swan Hotel	Keysoe, The Chequers, de-licenced pub	£13,600	BT 14 January 1972 p. 24; 11 February p. 25; 25 February p. 23; 17 March p. 22; 31 March p. 16; 21 April p. 14	-
28 April 1972	Bedford, The Swan Hotel	Keysoe, plot adjoining The Chequers	£4,600	BT 3 March 1972 p. 21; 31 March p. 16; 21 April p. 14. With planning permission	-

Auction date	Venue	Description	Price	Newspaper references	BLARS references
28 April 1972	Bedford, The Swan Hotel	Bedford, 22 Newnham Street, house	£4,600	BT 17 March 1972 p. 22; 31 March p. 16; 7 April p. 21; 21 April p. 14. For improvement	-
28 April 1972	Bedford, The Swan Hotel	Bedford, 3 Glebe Road, semi-detached house	£9,300	BT 31 March 1972 p. 16; 7 April p. 21; 21 April p. 14	-
28 April 1972	Bedford, The Swan Hotel	Bedford, 66 and 68 St Loyes Street, shops, offices, flat	£33,000	BT 21 April 1972 p. 14	-
28 April 1972	Bedford, The Swan Hotel	Bedford, 21 and 23 Lurke Street, freehold site for offices	£78,000	BT 14 April 1972 p. 8; 21 April p. 14. By order of Bedford Corporation	-
19 May 1972	Bedford, The Swan Hotel	Sharnbrook, 24 High Street, cottage	Unsold	BT 28 April 1972 p. 26	-
19 May 1972	Bedford, The Swan Hotel	Sharnbrook, 63 High Street, cottage	£5,500	BT 28 April 1972 p. 26. For improvement	-
19 May 1972	Bedford, The Swan Hotel	Ravensden, The Old School	£7,000	BT 14 April 1972 p. 23; 21 April p. 14; 28 April p. 26	-
19 May 1972	Bedford, The Swan Hotel	Bedford, 27 Stanley Street, semi-detached house	£5,000	BT 12 May 1972 p. 24	-
19 May 1972	Bedford, The Swan Hotel	Bedford, 123 Coventry Road, house, garage	£6,900	BT 14 April 1972 p. 23; 21 April p. 14; 28 April p. 26	-
19 May 1972	Bedford, The Swan Hotel	Bedford, 83 Marlborough Road, terraced house	-	BT 21 April 1972 p. 14; 28 April p. 26	-
19 May 1972	Bedford, The Swan Hotel	Wootton, 1 Potter's Cross, detached cottage	£8,100	BT 14 April 1972 p. 23; 21 April p. 14; 28 April p. 26	-

Auction date	Venue	Description	Price	Newspaper references	BLARS references
19 May 1972	Bedford, The Swan Hotel	Willington, worked out gravel pit, 21a	£21,000	BT 7 April 1972 p. 17; 14 April p. 14	-
19 May 1972	Bedford, The Swan Hotel	Willington, speculative land at edge of village, 51a	-	BT 7 April 1972 p. 17; 14 April p. 14	-
9 June 1972	Bedford, The Swan Hotel	Houghton Conquest, Rose Cottage, Chapel End Road	£7,750	BT 5, 19 May 1972 p. 14; 26 May p. 22. For improvement	-
9 June 1972	Bedford, The Swan Hotel	Bedford, 46 Althorpe Street, detached house	£4,750	BT 12 June 1972 p. 24; 19 May p. 14; 26 May p. 22. For improvement	-
9 June 1972	Bedford, The Swan Hotel	Bedford, 10 Stafford Road, house	£2,600	BT 5, 19 May 1972 p. 14; 26 May p. 22. Controlled tenancy £55.92 pa	-
9 June 1972	Bedford, The Swan Hotel	Carlton, Vine Cottage, 34 High Street, cottage, 1.25a	£11,500	BT 12 May 1972 p. 24; 26 May p. 22	-
9 June 1972	Bedford, The Swan Hotel	Odell, Horsefair Lane, plot with river frontage	£9,500	BT 5, 19 May 1972 p. 14; 26 May p. 22	-
21 June 1972	Langford, The Wrestlers	Langford, 8 Station Road, terraced cottage	-	BT 9 June 1972 p. 20. On instruction of executor of Mr P. J. Whiteman. Vacant possession	-
5 July 1972	Potton, The Rose and Crown	Potton, 2 West End Lane, freehold semi-detached house	-	BT 16 June 1972 p. 8; 30 June p. 14	-
7 July 1972	Bedford, The County Hotel	Bedford, 6 Aspley Road	£7,000	BT 9 June 1972 p. 21; 16 June p. 22	-
7 July 1972	Bedford, The County Hotel	Bedford, 19 Stanley Street, middle terrace house	£5,800	BT 9 June 1972 p. 21; 16 June p. 22	-

Auction date	Venue	Description	Price	Newspaper references	BLARS references
7 July 1972	Bedford, The County Hotel	Bedford, 1 Howbury Street, house	£6,700	BT 9 June 1972 p. 21; 16 June p. 22	-
7 July 1972	Bedford, The County Hotel	Bedford, 25 Brereton Road, terrace house	£4,000	BT 9 June 1972 p. 21; 23 June p. 14	-
7 July 1972	Bedford, The County Hotel	Bedford, 27 Brereton Road, terrace house	£3,800	BT 9 June 1972 p. 21	-
7 July 1972	Bedford, The County Hotel	Bedford, 60 and 60a Harpur Street, corner shop, office	£15,250	BT 9 June 1972 p. 21; 16 July p. 22	-
7 July 1972	Bedford, The County Hotel	Staploe, Old Farm Cottage	£14,500	BT 2 June 1972 p. 20; 9 June p. 21 and 24; 16 June p. 22. For improvement	-
21 July 1972	Ampthill, The White Hart Hotel	Flitwick, 74 Kings Road, detached bungalow	-	BT 14 July 1972 p. 6; 21 July p. 14	-
26 July 1972	Biggleswade, The Crown Hotel	Biggleswade, 1 Claremont Cottages, freehold terraced dwelling house	- Joint auction with Trudgill and Co.	BT 7 July 1972 p. 18	-
28 July 1972	Bedford, The Swan Hotel	Cranfield, Bedford Road, building plot	£6,500	BT 23 July 1972 p. 14. Planning consent for one detached dwelling	-
28 July 1972	Bedford, The Swan Hotel	Bedford, 35 Beverley Crescent, semi-detached house	£8,000	BT 23 July 1972 p. 14. Vacant possession	-
28 July 1972	Bedford, The Swan Hotel	Bedford, 17 Sidney Road, semi-detached house	-	BT 23 July 1972 p. 14. Rental £71.48 pa	-
28 July 1972	Bedford, The Swan Hotel	Pertenhall, The Post Office Cottage, detached period cottage	-	BT 30 June 1972 p. 14. Vacant possession	-

Auction date	Venue	Description	Price	Newspaper references	BLARS references
28 July 1972	Bedford, The Swan Hotel	Blunham, 20 The Hill, detached house, buildings	£10,300	BT 7 July 1972 p. 18; 14 July p. 6. For improvement	-
28 July 1972	Bedford, The Swan Hotel	Moggerhanger, adjoining 34 Blunham Road, building plot	£6,200	BT 30 June 1972 p. 14	-
28 July 1972	Bedford, The Swan Hotel	Sandy, Girtford Bridge, arable land, 4.8a	£2,600	BT 7 July 1972 p. 18; 14 July p. 6	-
6 September 1972	-	Potton, Brook House and Brook Cottage, frontage to Royston Street, building land, 3a	-	BT 21 July 1972 p. 14; 28 July p. 18. On instruction of Biggleswade Rural District Council. Planning permission for residential development	-
15 September 1972	Bedford, The County Hotel	Bletsoe, Old Pear Tree Cottage	Auction postponed	BT 11 August 1972 p. 23; 18 August p. 21	-
15 September 1972	Bedford, The County Hotel	Wilstead, building plot	Auction postponed	BT 11 August 1972 p. 23; 18 August p. 21. Outline planning permission for two dwellings	-
21 September 1972	Sandy, The Red Lion	Sandy, Brickhill Road, freehold single building plot, 0.12a	-	BT 25 August 1972 p. 16; 8 September p. 19. On instruction of Sandy Urban District Council	-
27 September 1972	Sandy, The Conservative Club	Sandy, London Road, residential building land, 0.64a	- Joint auction with J. R. Eve and Son	BT 1 September 1972 p. 6; 15 September p. 14. Outline planning permission for seven dwellings	-
5 October 1972	Bedford, The County Hotel	Biddenham, Bromham Road, horticultural land, 2a	-	BT 25 August 1972 p. 23. The estate of Mrs E. D. Rollins. Rental £143 pa	-

Auction date	Venue	Description	Price	Newspaper references	BLARS references
5 October 1972	Bedford, The County Hotel	Bedford, 99 Denmark Street, in two flats	£5,800	BT 25 August 1972 p. 23. The estate of Mrs E. D. Rollins. Total rental £117 pa	-
5 October 1972	Bedford, The County Hotel	Bedford, 20 Foster Street, terrace house	£1,500	BT 25 August 1972 p. 23. The estate of Mrs E. D. Rollins. Rental £41.79 pa	-
5 October 1972	Bedford, The County Hotel	Bedford, 55 Foster Street, terraced house	£1,500	BT 25 August 1972 p. 23. The estate of Mrs E. D. Rollins. Rental £41.24 pa	-
5 October 1972	Bedford, The County Hotel	Bedford, 47 Salisbury Street, terraced house	£2,700	BT 25 August 1972 p. 23. The estate of Mrs E. D. Rollins. Rental £62.40 pa	-
5 October 1972	Bedford, The County Hotel	Bedford, 55 Salisbury Street, terraced house	£2,700	BT 25 August 1972 p. 23. The estate of Mrs E. D. Rollins. Rental £61.10 pa	-
5 October 1972	Bedford, The County Hotel	Bedford, 48 Winifred Road, semi-detached house	£4,000	BT 25 August 1972 p. 23. The estate of Mrs E. D. Rollins. Rental £78 pa	-
5 October 1972	Bedford, The County Hotel	Bedford, 52 Winifred Road, semi-detached house	£3,800	BT 25 August 1972 p. 23. The estate of Mrs E. D. Rollins. Rental £84 pa	-
5 October 1972	Bedford, The County Hotel	Kempston, 52 Orchard Street, semi-detached house	£3,600	BT 25 August 1972 p. 23. The estate of Mrs E. D. Rollins. Rental £69.74 pa	-
5 October 1972	Bedford, The County Hotel	Kempston, 54 Orchard Street, semi-detached house	£3,800	BT 25 August 1972 p. 23. The estate of Mrs E. D. Rollins. Rental £69.81 pa	-
5 October 1972	Bedford, The County Hotel	Bedford, 31 Beaconsfield Street, terraced house	£5,100	BT 25 August 1972 p. 23. The estate of Mrs E. D. Rollins. For improvement. Vacant possession	-

Auction date	Venue	Description	Price	Newspaper references	BLARS references
5 October 1972	Bedford, The County Hotel	Bedford, 33 Beaconsfield Street, terraced house	£5,100	BT 25 August 1972 p. 23. The estate of Mrs E. D. Rollins. For improvement. Vacant possession	-
5 October 1972	Bedford, The County Hotel	Bedford, 9 Bradgate Road, semi-detached house	£11,000	BT 25 August 1972 p. 23. The estate of Mrs E. D. Rollins. Vacant possession	-
5 October 1972	Bedford, The County Hotel	Bedford, 24 Foster Street, terraced house	£3,800	BT 25 August 1972 p. 23. The estate of Mrs E. D. Rollins. For improvement. Vacant possession	-
5 October 1972	Bedford, The County Hotel	Wilstead, Church Road, two building plots	£10,500	BT 25 August 1972 p. 23	-
5 October 1972	Bedford, The County Hotel	Biddenham, 45 Main Road, semi-detached house	£9,100	BT 25 August 1972 p. 23; 1 September p. 15	-
5 October 1972	Bedford, The County Hotel	Bletsoe, Old Pear Tree Cottage, period cottage	£6,000	BT 25 August 1972 p. 23. Vacant possession	-
5 October 1972	Bedford, The County Hotel	Bedford, 28–30 Fosterhill Road, shop, living accommodation	Unsold	BT 25 August 1972 p. 23	-
5 October 1972	Bedford, The County Hotel	Bedford, 150 Castle Road, terraced house	£6,400	BT 25 August 1972 p. 23	-
5 October 1972	Bedford, The County Hotel	Bedford, 38 St Peter's Street, freehold double-fronted shop, offices	£28,500 Joint auction with Knight, Frank and Rutley	BT 25 August 1972 p. 23; 15 September p. 14. On instruction of Miss Gertrude Davey	-

Auction date	Venue	Description	Price	Newspaper references	BLARS references
11 October 1972	Sandy, The Red Lion	Beeston, 44 High Road, semi-detached house	-	BT 22 September 1972 p. 14. On instruction of Mrs L. M. M. Ball and E. C. Brown	-
11 October 1972	Sandy, The Red Lion	Beeston, 44 High Road, smallholders headquarters, range of outbuildings	-	BT 22 September 1972 p. 14. On instruction of Mrs L. M. M. Ball and E. C. Brown	-
11 October 1972	Sandy, The Red Lion	Budna, Budna Road, woodland, 1r 10p	-	BT 22 September 1972 p. 14. On instruction of Mrs L. M. M. Ball and E. C. Brown	-
25 October 1972	Souldrop, The Bedford Arms	Souldrop, Rose Cottage, 8 High Street	£7,100	BT 6 October 1972 p. 25; 20 October p. 20. For improvement	-
31 October 1972	Langford, The Wrestlers	Henlow, Langford Road, market garden land, 13a 2r	-	BT 6 October 1972 p. 14; 20 October p. 20. On instruction of G. Endersby Esq. Vacant possession	-
30 November 1972	Bedford, The Swan Hotel	Shefford, sawmill, timber yard, 1.5a	-	BT 27 October 1972 p. 8. For redevelopment	-
15 December 1972	Bedford, The County Hotel	Wilstead, 125 Cotton End Road, semi-detached cottage, building plot	£12,200	BT 27 October 1972 p. 30; 24 November p 30; 15 December p. 26	-
15 December 1972	Bedford, The County Hotel	Bedford, 107 Bromham Road, semi-detached corner house	£12,500	BT 27 October 1972 p. 30; 24 November p 30; 15 December p. 26	-
15 December 1972	Bedford, The County Hotel	Bedford, 107 and 113 Marlborough Road	£2,500 Number 107 withdrawn from auction	BT 24 November 1972 p. 30; 15 December p. 26. Number 113 rental £48.10 pa	-

Auction date	Venue	Description	Price	Newspaper references	BLARS references
12 March 1973	Olney, The Bull Hotel	Emberton (Bucks), Prospect House, detached country house, 4.11a	£23,500	BT 19 January 1973 p. 30; 16 February p. 30	-
28 March 1973	Sandy, The Red Lion	Sandy, 24 Bedford Road, semi-detached property	-	BT 9 March 1973 p. 8. Vacant possession	-
25 April 1973	Cranfield, The Leathern Bottle	Cranfield, 176–178 High Street, two cottages	£9,500	BT 30 March 1973 p. 31; 6 April p. 29. For improvement	-
7 June 1973	Biggleswade, The Crown Hotel	Seddington, pasture land known as Longlake and Bailey's Meadow, off A1, 14a 1r 4p	-	BT 11 May 1973 p. 16. Vacant possession	-
13 June 1973	Gamlingay, The Cock	Gamlingay (Cambs), 16 Drove Road, freehold horticultural holding, 3.706a	-	BT 11 May 1973 p. 16. On instruction of R. F. Butler Esq.	-
25 July 1973	Biggleswade, The Crown Hotel	Biggleswade, Furzenhall Road, building land, 0.58a	-	BT 15 June 1973 p. 25; 6 July p. 8. On instruction of Messrs G. Rowlett and Sons Ltd. Outline planning consent for seven houses	-
25 July 1973	Biggleswade, The Crown Hotel	Biggleswade, 60 Drove Road, headquarters of a market gardener, house, market garden buildings	-	BT 29 July 1973 p. 24	-

Auction date	Venue	Description	Price	Newspaper references	BLARS references
26 September 1973	On site	Langford, Church Farm, agricultural land, 106a	-	BT 24 August 1973 p. 23; 14 September p. 12. On instruction of Messrs E. M. Street Ltd	-
18 October 1973	Baldock, The Town Hall	Baldock (Herts), Clothall Road, ten tenanted cottages, single building plot, tenanted agricultural land, 10a	Building plot withdrawn from auction	BT 7 September 1973 p. 24; 28 September p. 16. On instruction of trustees of Wm. Sale, deceased	-
15 March 1974	Biggleswade, The Crown Hotel	Biggleswade, 53 and 55 High Street, commercial premises	-	BT 8 February 1974 p. 14	-
18 April 1974	Bedford, The Swan Hotel	Stevington, Court Lane, building plot	-	BT 22 March 1974 p. 17; 29 March p. 21. On instruction of Stevington Parish Council	-
29 July 1974	Lavendon, The Horseshoe Inn	Lavendon, Turvey Road, accommodation land, 1.253a	£2,950	BT 19 July 1974 p. 25	-
18 February 1975	Shefford, The White Hart	Chicksands, RAF Chicksands, rough pasture, woodland, 17.491a	£8,250	BT 24 January 1975 p. 12. On instruction of the Secretary of State for Defence. Freehold part subject to tenancy	-
17 April 1975	Colmworth, The Village Hall	Colmworth, Wheatsheaf Farm, house, buildings, 3.3a	£17,750	BT 28 March 1975 p. 14. Vacant possession	-
17 April 1975	Colmworth, The Village Hall	Colmworth, Wheatsheaf Farm, arable land, 40.7a	£20.00	BT 28 March 1975 p. 14. Vacant possession	-

Auction date	Venue	Description	Price	Newspaper references	BLARS references
17 April 1975	Colmworth, The Village Hall	Colmworth, Wheatsheaf Farm, arable land, 25.7a	£12,000	BT 28 March 1975 p. 14. Vacant possession	-
4 November 1975	Ampthill, The White Hart	Lidlington, Sheeptick End, detached bungalow, outbuildings, 6a	Unsold	BT 3 October 1975 p. 22	-
3 December 1975	Shefford, The White Hart Hotel	Campton, building land, 0.8a	-	BT 14 November 1975 p. 28. On instruction of Messrs Greene King and Sons. Outline planning permission. Vacant possession	-
10 December 1975	Biggleswade, The Crown Hotel	Biggleswade, Hitchin Street, market gardener's yard, four common rights	-	BT 14 November 1975 p. 28	-
10 December 1975	Biggleswade, The Crown Hotel	Biggleswade, London Road and Hitchmead, market gardening land, 34a	-	BT 14 November 1975 p. 28	-
23 March 1976	Hitchin, The Sun Hotel	Shillington, Bury Road, accommodation land, 9.5a	-	BT 27 February 1976 p. 21. On instruction of G. C. Scannell Esq. and Weyman and Utley Landscapes Ltd. Vacant possession	-
22 April 1976	Bedford, The County Hotel	Cranfield, The Manor House, Bourne End, imposing country house, 1.82a	-	BT 19 March 1976 p. 28; 26 March p. 14; 2 April p. 26	-

Auction date	Venue	Description	Price	Newspaper references	BLARS references
22 April 1976	Bedford, The County Hotel	Cranfield, Washingley Farm, Bourne End, arable land, 143a	-	BT 19 March 1976 p. 28; 26 March p. 14	-
16 July 1976	Bedford, The County Hotel	Turvey, three building plots, 1.5a	-	BT 9 July 1986 p. 23	-
22 September 1976	Willington, The Memorial Hall	Willington, The Limes, house, buildings, market garden land, 4.5a	£28,000	BT 3 September 1976 p. 22	-
30 September 1976	Thurleigh, The Village Hall	Thurleigh, High Street, single building plot	£3,500	BT 6 August 1976 p. 10. On instruction of trustees of Thurleigh Baptist Chapel. Outline permission for one house	-
27 October 1976	Walsworth, Methodist Chapel	Walsworth (Herts), The Methodist Chapel, potential building land	-	BT 8 October 1976 p. 30	-
5 November 1976	Bedford, De Parys Hotel	Bedford, 99 Gladstone Street, former decorator's yard, buildings	£28,000	BT 1 October 1976 p. 18	-
5 November 1976	Bedford, De Parys Hotel	Bedford, 27 Cedar Road, middle terrace house	£3,800	BT 8 October 1976 p. 30. Rental £325 pa	-
5 November 1976	Bedford, De Parys Hotel	Old Harrowden, near The Gate public house, derelict detached cottage	£1,300	BT 1 October 1976 p. 18	-

Auction date	Venue	Description	Price	Newspaper references	BLARS references
5 November 1976	Bedford, De Parys Hotel	Harrold, Pointers Lodge, Church Walk, house, buildings, 0.4a	£13,000	BT 1 October 1976 p. 18	-
5 November 1976	Bedford, De Parys Hotel	Bedford, 2A Lurke Street, former garage, workshop	Withdrawn form auction	BT 1 October 1976 p. 18; 22 October p. 31	-
16 November 1976	Biggleswade, The Crown Hotel	Biggleswade, Furzenhall Road, market garden land, 4.969a	-	BT 29 October 1976 p. 26. Vacant possession	-
17 November 1976	Henlow, The Parachute	Henlow, 37 High Street, detached residence	-	BT 22 October 1976 p. 31; 29 October p. 26	-
11 January 1977	Biggleswade, The Crown Hotel	Biggleswade, Coldharbour, Potton Road, market garden land, 3a	-	BT 10 December 1976 p. 23; 7 January 1977 p. 26. On instruction of H. J. Dean Esq. Vacant possession	-
3 March 1977	Potton, The Rose and Crown	Cockayne Hatley, Church Farm Lodge, Potton Road	-	BT 28 January 1977 p. 12; 4 February p. 24	-
10 March 1977	Langford, The Wrestlers	Langford, Common Farm, Common Road, arable land, 3a	-	BT 4 February 1977 p. 24	-
7 April 1977	Biggleswade, The Crown Hotel	Lower Caldecote, riverside pasture, 41a	-	BT 11 March 1977 p. 17. On instruction of R. L. Capon Esq.	-

Auction date	Venue	Description	Price	Newspaper references	BLARS references
15 April 1977	Bedford, Newnham Street, Auction Centre	Bromham, 72 Village Road, detached house	Unsold	BT 25 April 1977 p. 28; 11 March p. 17; 15 April p. 22. On instruction of Bromham Church Charity	-
17 June 1977	Bedford, Newnham Street, Auction Centre	Bletsoe, The Old School	£5,800	BT 29 April 1977 p. 28; 27 May p. 32. For conversion	-
17 June 1977	Bedford, Newnham Street, Auction Centre	Willington, 31 Chapel Lane, three bedroom house	Unsold	BT 29 April 1977 p. 28; 27 May p. 32	-
17 June 1977	Bedford, Newnham Street, Auction Centre	Haynes, 91 Silver End Road, semi-detached cottage	Unsold	BT 29 April 1977 p. 28; 27 May p. 32	-
29 June 1977	On site	Langford, Church Hall, Church Street, garden	-	BT 22 April 1977 p. 26; 29 April p. 18; 17 June p. 16. Outline planning permission for two dwellings	-
16 September 1977	On site	Podington, good arable land, 28.4a	-	BT 12 August 1977 p. 14	-
26 October 1977	Tempsford, The Anchor Hotel	Sandy, Highfield Farm, house, buildings, 200a	-	BT 7 October 1977 p. 24; 21 October p. 30. On instruction of Mr Peter Howard	-

Auction date	Venue	Description	Price	Newspaper references	BLARS references
17 November 1977	Wrestlingworth, The Ongley Arms	Eyeworth, on Eyeworth to Wrestlingworth Road, arable land, 3a	-	BT 21 October 1977 p. 30. On instruction of trustees of Eyeworth Charity	-
21 December 1977	Biggleswade, St Andrew's Church Hall	Potton, Home Farm, 1.43a	-	BT 11 November 1977 p. 28; 25 November p. 32; 9 December p. 18. On instruction of the Ministry of Agriculture, Fisheries and Food. Consent for seven dwellings	-
20 January 1978	Bedford, Newnham Street, Auction Centre	Biddenham, 20–28 Main Road, four cottages with part possession	£13,500	BT 9 December 1977 p. 18 and 26; 6 January 1978 p. 30	-
20 January 1978	Bedford, Newnham Street, Auction Centre	Bedford, 65 Victoria Road, semi-detached house	£11,000	BT 9 December 1977 p. 18 and 26; 6 January 1978 p. 30	-
20 January 1978	Bedford, Newnham Street, Auction Centre	Shefford, 53a Ampthill Road, bungalow	-	BT 30 December 1977 p. 22; 6 January 1978 p. 30	-
20 January 1978	Bedford, Newnham Street, Auction Centre	Shefford, 69 Ampthill Road, business premises, formerly bakery	-	BT 30 December 1977 p. 22; 30 January 1978 p. 30	-

Auction date	Venue	Description	Price	Newspaper references	BLARS references
15 February 1978	Ampthill, The White Hart	Maulden, 49 Ampthill Road, market garden premises, house, garage, 4.75a	£20,000	BT 13, 27 January 1978 p. 30; 3 February p. 22	-
7 March 1978	Riseley, The Fox and Hounds	Riseley, Keysoe Road, pasture land, 28.158a	£37,250 Joint auction with Messrs Bidwells	BT 17 February 1978 p. 24; 3 March p. 24. By order of the mortgagees	-
19 April 1978	On site	Ashwell (Herts), Ashwell Methodist Church, High Street	-	BT 10 March 1978 p. 22	-
2 May 1978	Biggleswade, St Andrew's Rooms	Biggleswade, 106 Hitchin Street	-	BT 21 April 1978 p. 33. On instruction of Mid Bedfordshire District Council	-
2 May 1978	Biggleswade, St Andrew's Rooms	Biggleswade, 109 Hitchin Street	-	BT 21 April 1978 p. 33. On instruction of Mid Bedfordshire District Council	-
2 May 1978	Biggleswade, St Andrew's Rooms	Biggleswade, 25 Back Street	-	BT 21 April 1978 p. 33. On instruction of Mid Bedfordshire District Council	-
2 May 1978	Biggleswade, St Andrew's Rooms	Arlesey, 23 Hospital Road	-	BT 21 April 1978 p. 33. On instruction of Mid Bedfordshire District Council	-
2 May 1978	Biggleswade, St Andrew's Rooms	Clophill, 11 Mill Lane	-	BT 21 April 1978 p. 33. On instruction of Mid Bedfordshire District Council	-
21 June 1978	Sandy, The Kings Arms	Sandy, 21 and 23 Church Path, pair of cottages	-	BT 12 May 1978 p. 24. On instruction of the Crown Estate Commissioners	-

Auction date	Venue	Description	Price	Newspaper references	BLARS references
30 June 1978	Bedford, Newnham Street, Auction Centre	Bedford, 52 Coventry Road, three bedroom mid-terrace house	£5,300	BT 9 June 1978 p. 22	-
12 July 1978	Biggleswade, St Andrew's Rooms	Henlow, Middlefield Farm, farmhouse, 1.5a	£30,500	BT 16 January 1978 p. 24. Vacant possession	-
12 July 1978	Biggleswade, St Andrew's Rooms	Henlow, Middlefield Farm, 3 Hitchin Road, farm cottage	£12,000	BT 16 January 1978 p. 24. Vacant possession	-
12 July 1978	Biggleswade, St Andrew's Rooms	Henlow, Middlefield Farm, shed, market garden land, 22a	£34,000	BT 16 January 1978 p. 24. Vacant possession	-
12 July 1978	Biggleswade, St Andrew's Rooms	Henlow, Middlefield Farm, market garden land, 1.7a	£3,800	BT 16 January 1978 p. 24. Vacant possession	-
26 July 1978	Sandy, The King's Arms	Sandy, Cartwheel Nursery, on A1	£5,000	BT 30 June 1978 p. 22. On instruction of Mr V. Bywater	-
26 July 1978	Sandy, The King's Arms	Sandy, Cartwheel Nursery, on A1, market garden land, 6.2a	£8,000	BT 30 June 1978 p. 22. On instruction of Mr V. Bywater	-
-	-	Ickwell, Ickwell Green, period cottage	-	BT 14 July 1978 p. 28	-
23 August 1978	Sandy, The King's Arms	Northill, 19 Thorncote Green, cottage, workshop	£18,000	BT 7 July 1978 p. 26; 4 August p. 25	-

Auction date	Venue	Description	Price	Newspaper references	BLARS references
23 August 1978	Sandy, The King's Arms	Sandy, 4 Laburnham Road, house, buildings	£16,200	BT 7 July 1978 p. 26; 4 August p. 25	-
23 August 1978	Sandy, The King's Arms	Sandy, 21–23 Church Path, two cottages	£9,200	BT 7 July 1978 p. 26; 4 August p. 25	-
13 September 1978	Biggleswade, St Andrew's Rooms	Henlow, Town Farm, market garden land, 51.6a	-	BT 11 August 1978 p. 22. On instruction of Mr H. A. Mager	-
13 September 1978	Biggleswade, St Andrew's Rooms	Arlesey, arable land, 4.858a	£7,100	BT 26 August 1978 p. 22. On instruction of Mr R. A. Webb. Vacant possession	-
13 September 1978	Biggleswade, St Andrew's Rooms	Biggleswade, Ivel Mill	-	BT 9 June 1978 p. 22; 30 June p. 22; 7 July p 27; 28 July p. 22. For conversion to six flats and site for seven dwellings	-
20 October 1978	Bedford, Newnham Street, Auction Centre	Bedford, 20 Gratton Road, house	£4,500	BT 25 August 1978 p. 27; 29 September p. 29; 6 October p. 31. For improvement	-
20 October 1978	Bedford, Newnham Street, Auction Centre	Kempston, 52 Thornton Street, house	£6,300	BT 25 August 1978 p. 27; 29 September p. 29. For improvement	-
20 October 1978	Bedford, Newnham Street, Auction Centre	Souldrop, 20 High Street, end terrace cottage	£5,200	BT 4 August 1978 p. 25: 25 August p. 26; 1 September p. 24. For improvement	-

Auction date	Venue	Description	Price	Newspaper references	BLARS references
20 October 1978	Bedford, Newnham Street, Auction Centre	Shefford, 61 and 63 Ampthill Road	-	BT 25 August 1978 p. 27; 6 October p. 31	-
20 October 1978	Bedford, Newnham Street, Auction Centre	Shefford, 6 Campton Road, house	£4,000	BT 25 August 1978 p. 27; 6 October p. 31	-
20 October 1978	Bedford, Newnham Street, Auction Centre	Bedford, 90 Kimbolton Road, detached house	£31,000	BT 25 August 1978 p. 27; 29 September p. 29; 6 October p. 31. On instruction of the Secretary of State for Defence	-
1 November 1978	Biggleswade, The Crown Hotel	Upper Caldecote, 2 The Green, detached house	£19,750	BT 22 September 1978 p. 26; 29 September p. 29; 13 October p. 25. For improvement	-
1 November 1978	Biggleswade, The Crown Hotel	Upper Caldecote, Biggleswade Road, arable land, 3a	£7,000	BT 29 September p. 29. Vacant possession	-
3 November 1978	Bedford, Newnham Street, Auction Centre	Cockayne Hatley, Rose Cottage, 3 Village Road	£21,750	BT 29 September 1978 p. 29; 13 October p. 25. For improvement	-
3 November 1978	Bedford, Newnham Street, Auction Centre	Blunham, The Ovens, 2 High Street	Sold prior to auction	BT 22 September 1978 p. 26; 29 September p. 29; 13 October p. 25	-

Auction date	Venue	Description	Price	Newspaper references	BLARS references
3 November 1978	Bedford, Newnham Street, Auction Centre	Renhold, adjoining 27 Ravensden Road, building plot	£9,700	BT 27 October 1978 p. 30. On instruction of the trustees of Renhold Charity Cottages	-
3 November 1978	Bedford, Newnham Street, Auction Centre	Wilstead, 80 Bedford Road, detached bungalow	£15,500	BT 25 August 1978 p. 27; 29 September p. 29; 3 November p. 31	-
15 December 1978	Little Gransden, The Village Hall	Great Gransden (Cambs), Jakins, cottage, paddock, 1.75a	£40,000	BT 10 November 1978 p. 24; 24 November p. 27	-
15 December 1978	Little Gransden, The Village Hall	Great Gransden (Cambs), paddock, 3.5a	£5,200	BT 10 November 1978 p. 24	-
12 January 1979	Bedford, Newnham Street, Auction Centre	Bedford, 8 Aspley Road, terraced house	£6,500	BT 15 December 1978 p. 21	-
12 January 1979	Bedford, Newnham Street, Auction Centre	Bedford, 34 Aspley Road, terraced house	£6,100	BT 1 December 1978 p. 29; 29 December p. 20	-

Auction date	Venue	Description	Price	Newspaper references	BLARS references
12 January 1979	Bedford, Newnham Street, Auction Centre	Bedford, 10 Dunville Road, terraced house	£3,700	BT 1 December 1978 p. 29. For improvement	-
12 January 1979	Bedford, Newnham Street, Auction Centre	Bedford, 7 Firbank Road, terraced house	£6,000	BT 24 November 1978 p. 27; 8 December p. 25. Vacant possession	-
12 January 1979	Bedford, Newnham Street, Auction Centre	Bedford, 5 Prebend Street	Sold prior to auction	BT 24 November 1978 p. 27. Vacant possession	-
12 January 1979	Bedford, Newnham Street, Auction Centre	Harrold, 18 Orchard Lane, eighteenth century cottage	-	BT 1 December 1978 p. 29; 15 December p. 20; 29 December p. 21. For improvement	-
12 January 1979	Bedford, Newnham Street, Auction Centre	Kempston, 114 High Street	Auction postponed	BT 1 December 1978 p. 29; 15 December p. 20	-
7 March 1979	Biggleswade, St Andrew's Rooms	Sandy, market garden land, 0.825a	-	BT 26 January 1979 p. 22; 23 February p. 24. On instruction of Messrs L. A. Edwards, A. F and H. G. Bygraves, trustees of V. C. M. Cuvelier	-

Auction date	Venue	Description	Price	Newspaper references	BLARS references
7 March 1979	Biggleswade, St Andrew's Rooms	Upper Caldecote, market garden land, 10.575a	£18,000	BT 26 January 1979 p. 22; 23 February p. 24. On instruction of Messrs L. A. Edwards, A. F and H. G. Bygraves, trustees of V. C. M. Cuvelier	-
7 March 1979	Biggleswade, St Andrew's Rooms	Upper Caldecote, market garden land, 6a	£13,500	BT 26 January 1979 p. 22; 23 February p. 24. On instruction of Messrs L. A. Edwards, A. F and H. G. Bygraves, trustees of V. C. M. Cuvelier	-
7 March 1979	Biggleswade, St Andrew's Rooms	Upper Caldecote, market garden land, 6a	£14,000	BT 26 January 1979 p. 22; 23 February p. 24. On instruction of Messrs L. A. Edwards, A. F and H. G. Bygraves, trustees of V. C. M. Cuvelier	-
7 March 1979	Biggleswade, St Andrew's Rooms	Upper Caldecote, market garden land, 6a	£14,000	BT 26 January 1979 p. 22; 23 February p. 24. On instruction of Messrs L. A. Edwards, A. F and H. G. Bygraves, trustees of V. C. M. Cuvelier	-
7 March 1979	Biggleswade, St Andrew's Rooms	Ickwell Green, market garden land, 14.75a, spinney, 1.31a	£38,500	BT 26 January 1979 p. 22; 23 February p. 24. On instruction of Messrs L. A. Edwards, A. F and H. G. Bygraves, trustees of V. C. M. Cuvelier	-
7 March 1979	Biggleswade, St Andrew's Rooms	Northill, market garden land, 14.289a	£22,000	BT 26 January 1979 p. 22; 23 February p. 24. On instruction of Messrs L. A. Edwards, A. F and H. G. Bygraves, trustees of V. C. M. Cuvelier	-
28 March 1979	Podington, The Cricket Pavilion	Podington, 5 Gold Street, four bedroom cottage	£17,500	BT 26 January 1979 p. 26; 9 February p. 27	-

Auction date	Venue	Description	Price	Newspaper references	BLARS references
30 March 1979	Bedford, Newnham Street, Auction Centre	Bedford, 18 George Street, mid-terrace house	£7,500	BT 23 February 1979 p. 30	-
30 March 1979	Bedford, Newnham Street, Auction Centre	Bedford, 23 Westbourne Road, mid-terrace house	£7,600	BT 23 February 1979 p. 30	-
30 March 1979	Bedford, Newnham Street, Auction Centre	Bedford, 35a Garfield Street, workshop, offices	Unsold	BT 2 February 1979 p. 28	-
30 March 1979	Bedford, Newnham Street, Auction Centre	Old Harrowden, 247 and 248, two cottages	£13,250	BT 26 January 1979 p. 26	-
30 March 1979	Bedford, Newnham Street, Auction Centre	Kempston, 114 High Street, cottage	£8,000	BT 26 January 1979 p. 26	-
30 March 1979	Bedford, Newnham Street, Auction Centre	Kempston, High Street, garden land, 0.374a	£1,500	BT 26 January 1979 p. 26	-

Auction date	Venue	Description	Price	Newspaper references	BLARS references
30 March 1979	Bedford, Newnham Street, Auction Centre	Bromham, 4 Millfield, detached bungalow	Unsold	BT 9 February 1979 p. 27; 16 March p. 32	-
30 March 1979	Bedford, Newnham Street, Auction Centre	Great Barford, 80 Roxton Road, house	Unsold	BT 9 February 1979 p. 27; 2 March p. 29. For improvement	-
30 March 1979	Bedford, Newnham Street, Auction Centre	Flitwick, 111 Station Road, cottage	£7,750	BT 26 January 1979 p. 26; 23 February p. 30. For improvement	-
30 March 1979	Bedford, Newnham Street, Auction Centre	Marston Moretaine, 2 Upper Shelton Road, cottage	£4,000	BT 2 March 1979 p. 24. For improvement	-
30 March 1979	Bedford, Newnham Street, Auction Centre	Marston Moretaine, Oakdene, smallholding, 0.716a	£3,000	BT 2 March 1979 p. 24	-
30 March 1979	Bedford, Newnham Street, Auction Centre	Clophill, Church End, pasture land, 2.03a	£3,750	BT 2 March 1979 p. 24	-

Auction date	Venue	Description	Price	Newspaper references	BLARS references
27 April 1979	Bedford, Newnham Street, Auction Centre	Bedford, 40 St Leonard's Street, cottage	£3,900	BT 13 April 1979 p. 27; 20 April p. 25. For improvement	-
27 April 1979	Bedford, Newnham Street, Auction Centre	Bedford, 49 Goldington Avenue, first floor flat	£6,100	BT 30 March 1979 p. 32; 20 April p. 25	-
27 April 1979	Bedford, Newnham Street, Auction Centre	Kempston, 2 Beatrice Street, end terrace house	£5,500	BT 30 March 1979 p. 32; 20 April p. 25. By order of Bedfordshire County Council. For improvement	-
27 April 1979	Bedford, Newnham Street, Auction Centre	Wootton, 136–140 Bedford Road, three cottages, old bakehouse	£12,000	BT 23 March 1979 p. 29; 20 April p. 25	-
27 April 1979	Bedford, Newnham Street, Auction Centre	Northill, 35–39 Thorncote Road, three period cottages	£25,000	BT 30 March 1979 p. 32; 6 April p. 28; 20 April p. 25	-
27 April 1979	Bedford, Newnham Street, Auction Centre	Bromham, Bridge House, 1 Bridge End, with river frontage	£54,500	BT 23 March p. 29; 30 March p. 32; 6 April p. 28; 20 April p. 25	-

Auction date	Venue	Description	Price	Newspaper references	BLARS references
30 May 1979	Biggleswade, St Andrew's Rooms	Ickwell, The Den, 27 The Green, thatched cottage	-	BT 27 April 1979 p. 34	-
27 July 1979	Bedford, Newnham Street, Auction Centre	Harrold, Church Walk, building plot with river frontage, 1a	£32,000	BT 29 June 1979 p. 29	-
27 July 1979	Bedford, Newnham Street, Auction Centre	Pulloxhill, building plot	-	BT 29 June 1979 p. 29	-
29 August 1979	Biggleswade, St Andrew's Rooms	Potton, The Chequers, 8 Brook End	-	BT 10 August 1979 p. 28. On instruction of Messrs Greene King (Biggleswade) Ltd	-
29 August 1979	Biggleswade, St Andrew's Rooms	Henlow, Town Farm Buildings, High Street	-	BT 10 August 1979 p. 28. On instruction of H. A. Mager Esq.	-
30 August 1979	Sandy, The Conservative Club	Potton, 6 Deepdale, detached house	Auction postponed	BT 10 August 1979 p. 28. On instruction of F. E. Neaves Esq.	-
30 August 1979	Sandy, The Conservative Club	Moggerhanger, 6 St John's Road, older type semi-detached house	-	BT 10 August 1979 p. 28. On instruction of trustees of Mr A. A. Lowe	-
30 August 1979	Sandy, The Conservative Club	Moggerhanger, 8 St John's Road, older type semi-detached house	-	BT 10 August 1979 p. 28. On instruction of executor of Mrs Ruth Hall	-

Auction date	Venue	Description	Price	Newspaper references	BLARS references
30 August 1979	Sandy, The Conservative Club	Sandy, 18 Longfield Road	-	BT 10 August 1979 p. 28. On instruction of administrators of Mr L. G. Tice	-
14 September 1979	Bedford, Newnham Street, Auction Centre	Kempston, SSM International Club, 86 Bedford Road	£97,000	BT 3 August 1979 p. 25	-
14 September 1979	Bedford, Newnham Street, Auction Centre	Stagsden, Hadleigh House, 210 Bedford Road, semi-detached house	£27,500	BT 3 August 1979 p. 25	-
19 September 1979	Biggleswade, St Andrew's Rooms	Upper Caldecote, 3 The Green, semi-detached house	-	BT 3 August 1979 p. 25	-
19 September 1979	Biggleswade, St Andrew's Rooms	Potton, 6 Deepdale, detached house	-	BT 10 August 1979 p. 28. On instruction of F. E. Neaves Esq.	-
2 November 1979	Bedford, Newnham Street, Auction Centre	Great Barford, land, with 480 yards of river frontage, 15.3a	£25,000	BT 28 September 1979 p. 28	-
2 November 1979	Bedford, Newnham Street, Auction Centre	Sharnbrook High Street, three building plots, 1.1a	£60,000	BT 28 September 1979 p. 28	-
2 November 1979	Bedford, Newnham Street, Auction Centre	Wilden, High Street, 0.29a	-	BT 28 September 1979 p. 28	-

Auction date	Venue	Description	Price	Newspaper references	BLARS references
18 January 1980	Bedford, Newnham Street, Auction Centre	Bedford, 14 Ouseland Road, detached house	£18,000	BT 30 November 1979 p. 46. For improvement	-
18 January 1980	Bedford, Newnham Street, Auction Centre	Bedford, 12 Ashburnham Road, semi-detached house	Unsold	BT 30 November 1979 p. 46	-
18 January 1980	Bedford, Newnham Street, Auction Centre	Bedford, 26 Newnham Street	-	BT 30 November 1979 p. 46	-
21 March 1980	Woburn, The Bedford Arms Hotel	Aspley Heath, Homewood Cottage, 69 and 69a Church Lane, two houses, garage	£58,000	BT 15 February 1980 p. 27	-
21 March 1980	Woburn, The Bedford Arms Hotel	Little Brickhill (Bucks), Glebe Farm, paddock, 4a	-	BT 15 February 1980 p. 27	-
28 March 1980	Bedford, Newnham Street, Auction Centre	Radwell, Stanilands, Moor End, house, 4a	£47,000	BT 15 February 1980 p. 27	-

Auction date	Venue	Description	Price	Newspaper references	BLARS references
28 March 1980	Bedford, Newnham Street, Auction Centre	Radwell, Moor End, paddock, 3.75a	£8,100	BT 15 February 1980 p. 27	-
28 March 1980	Bedford, Newnham Street, Auction Centre	Bedford, 14 Mabel Road, house	£10,600	BT 22 February 1980 p. 27. For improvement	-
28 March 1980	Bedford, Newnham Street, Auction Centre	Milton Ernest, Marsh Lane, building plot	£12,500	BT 29 February 1980 p. 30. Outline planning permission for detached bungalow	-
28 March 1980	Bedford, Newnham Street, Auction Centre	Bedford, 11 Harrowden Road, semi-detached house	£11,500	BT 22 February 1980 p. 27	-
11 April 1980	Bedford, Newnham Street, Auction Centre	Riseley, 8 Rotten Row, period cottage, two building plots, 0.728a	£32,500	BT 14 March 1980 p. 27. For improvement. Building plots with outline planning permission	-
11 April 1980	Bedford, Newnham Street, Auction Centre	Bedford, 42 St Leonard's Street, two bedroom cottage	Unsold	BT 29 February 1980 p. 30; 7 March p. 29	-

Auction date	Venue	Description	Price	Newspaper references	BLARS references
23 May 1980	Bedford, Newnham Street, Auction Centre	Cople, 25 Willington Road, house	£19,000	BT 25 April 1980 p. 21	-
23 May 1980	Bedford, Newnham Street, Auction Centre	Willington, 35 Church Road, house	£9,000	BT 25 April 1980 p. 21	-
23 May 1980	Bedford, Newnham Street, Auction Centre	Wootton, 10 Cranfield Road, cottage	£7,750	BT 25 April 1980 p. 21. Outline planning permission for replacement dwelling	-
4 July 1980	Bedford, Newnham Street, Auction Centre	Bedford, 84 Ampthill Road, shop, flat	£23,000 Joint auction with Stratfords	BT 6 June 1980 p. 27; 20 June p. 28. Shop vacant	-
4 July 1980	Bedford, Newnham Street, Auction Centre	Bromham, 74 Village Road, cottage	£10,000 Joint auction with Stratfords	BT 20 June 1980 p. 28; 27 June p. 29	-
4 July 1980	Bedford, Newnham Street, Auction Centre	Bedford, Behal Stores, Southville Road	Sold prior to auction	BT 6 June 1980 p. 27; 20 June p. 28 Sold as going concern	-

Auction date	Venue	Description	Price	Newspaper references	BLARS references
4 July 1980	Bedford, Newnham Street, Auction Centre	Old Harrowden, 247 and 248, detached period property	Sold prior to auction	BT 23 May 1980 p. 32; 20 June p. 28	-
4 July 1980	Bedford, Newnham Street, Auction Centre	Bedford, 81 Ford End Road, middle terrace house	Sold prior to auction	BT 23 May 1980 p. 32; 20 June p. 28	-
9 July 1980	Biggleswade, St Andrew's Rooms	Dunton, 10–20 Cambridge Road	-	BT 20 June 1980 p. 28. On instruction of Mid Bedfordshire District Council	-
9 July 1980	Biggleswade, St Andrew's Rooms	Potton, Mill Lane, arable land, 3.747a	-	BT 20 June 1980 p. 28. On instruction of the trustees of Potton Consolidated Charities	-
9 July 1980	Biggleswade, St Andrew's Rooms	Langford, Cambridge Road, arable land, 1a	-	BT 20 June 1980 p. 28. On instruction of S. Pateman	-
9 July 1980	Biggleswade, St Andrew's Rooms	Biggleswade, Furzenhall Road, arable land, 4.243a	-	BT 20 June 1980 p. 28. On instruction of Mrs N. M. Woodhead	-
17 July 1980	Kimbolton School, The Lewis Hall	Kimbolton Estate (Cambs), (listed below)	-	BT 6 June 1980 p. 27; 20 June p. 28; 11 July p. 30	PK un-catalogued. By direction of his Grace the Duke of Manchester, the remaining portions of the estate, let and vacant cottages, buildings for conversion, vacant pastures
17 July 1980	Kimbolton School, The Lewis Hall	Brampton (Cambs), 32 Buckden Road, detached cottage	£7,250	BT 6 June 1980 p. 27; 20 June p. 28; 11 July p. 30. Rental £49.66 pa	PK un-catalogued

Auction date	Venue	Description	Price	Newspaper references	BLARS references
17 July 1980	Kimbolton School, The Lewis Hall	Stonely (Cambs), 23 Park Lane, cottage	£7,500	BT 6 June 1980 p. 27; 20 June p. 28; 11 July p. 30. Rental £38 pa	PK un-catalogued
17 July 1980	Kimbolton School, The Lewis Hall	Stonely (Cambs), 23 and 25 Hatchett Lane	£9,500	BT 6 June 1980 p. 27; 20 June p. 28; 11 July p. 30. Number 23 rental £26 pa. 25 rental £151.32 pa	PK un-catalogued
17 July 1980	Kimbolton School, The Lewis Hall	Stonely (Cambs), Hatchett Lane, allotments, 1.17a	£1,500	BT 6 June 1980 p. 27; 20 June p. 28; 11 July p. 30	PK un-catalogued
17 July 1980	Kimbolton School, The Lewis Hall	Kimbolton (Cambs), Rookery Lane, garden, 0.3a	£850	BT 6 June 1980 p. 27; 20 June p. 28; 11 July p. 30	PK un-catalogued
17 July 1980	Kimbolton School, The Lewis Hall	Kimbolton (Cambs), Rookery Lane, allotments	£2,300	BT 6 June 1980 p. 27; 20 June p. 28; 11 July p. 30	PK un-catalogued
17 July 1980	Kimbolton School, The Lewis Hall	Kimbolton (Cambs), Dukes Row, allotments	£6,000	BT 6 June 1980 p. 27; 20 June p. 28; 11 July p. 30	PK un-catalogued
17 July 1980	Kimbolton School, The Lewis Hall	Kimbolton (Cambs), Dukes Row, pasture, 2.67a	£4,900	BT 6 June 1980 p. 27; 20 June p. 28; 11 July p. 30	PK un-catalogued
17 July 1980	Kimbolton School, The Lewis Hall	Kimbolton (Cambs), The Carnaby, 1.29a	£3,600	BT 6 June 1980 p. 27; 20 June p. 28; 11 July p. 30	PK un-catalogued
17 July 1980	Kimbolton School, The Lewis Hall	Kimbolton (Cambs), The Carnaby, garage, workshop	£2,900	BT 6 June 1980 p. 27; 20 June p. 28; 11 July p. 30	PK un-catalogued
17 July 1980	Kimbolton School, The Lewis Hall	Kimbolton (Cambs), Newtown, 4 Duke's Row, cottage	£8,250	BT 6 June 1980 p. 27; 20 June p. 28; 11 July p. 30	PK un-catalogued

Auction date	Venue	Description	Price	Newspaper references	BLARS references
17 July 1980	Kimbolton School, The Lewis Hall	Stonely (Cambs), 7–11 Brookside	£18,500	BT 6 June 1980 p. 27; 20 June p. 28; 11 July p. 30. Number 7 let. 9 and 11 vacant possession	PK un-catalogued
17 July 1980	Kimbolton School, The Lewis Hall	Stonely (Cambs), 27 Hatchett Lane, cottage	£12,000	BT 6 June 1980 p. 27; 20 June p. 28; 11 July p. 30	PK un-catalogued
17 July 1980	Kimbolton School, The Lewis Hall	Grafham (Cambs), 8 and 10 Church Road, two cottages	£14,500	BT 6 June 1980 p. 27; 20 June p. 28; 11 July p. 30	PK un-catalogued
17 July 1980	Kimbolton School, The Lewis Hall	Kimbolton (Cambs), Grass Yard, school building and office	£14,000	BT 6 June 1980 p. 27; 20 June p. 28; 11 July p. 30	PK un-catalogued
17 July 1980	Kimbolton School, The Lewis Hall	Kimbolton (Cambs), Grass Yard, school building, office	£15,500	BT 6 June 1980 p. 27; 20 June p. 28; 11 July p. 30	PK un-catalogued
17 July 1980	Kimbolton School, The Lewis Hall	Kimbolton (Cambs), Grass Yard, building plot	£16,000	BT 6 June 1980 p. 27; 20 June p. 28; 11 July p. 30	PK un-catalogued
8 August 1980	Bedford, Newnham Street, Auction Centre	Thurleigh, 10 Cross End, detached cottage	£30,000	BT 6 June 1980 p. 27; 20 June p. 28; 11 July p. 30; 18 July p. 26	-
8 August 1980	Bedford, Newnham Street, Auction Centre	Bromham, South Lodge, 6 Village Road, detached cottage	Unsold	BT 4 July 1980 p. 27; 11 July p. 30; 18 July p. 26; 8 August p. 24	-

Auction date	Venue	Description	Price	Newspaper references	BLARS references
8 August 1980	Bedford, Newnham Street, Auction Centre	Old Warden, 147 Tunnel Cottages	Sold prior to auction	BT 4 July 1980 p. 27; 11 July p. 30; 18 July p. 26. For improvement	-
1 October 1980	Biggleswade, St Andrew's Rooms	Sandy, London Road, redevelopment site, formerly All Saints' Church	-	BT 19 September 1980 p. 23. Under instruction of Sandy Parochial Church Council	-
1 October 1980	Biggleswade, St Andrew's Rooms	Arlesey, High Street, building plot, paddock	-	BT 19 September 1980 p. 23. On instruction of the trustees of the Robert Lucas Charity. Outline planning consent	-
7 November 1980	Bedford, Newnham Street, Auction Centre	Bedford, 13 Conduit Road, semi-detached house	£7,250	-	-
26 November 1980	Biggleswade, St Andrew's Rooms	Blunham, The Bungalow, Ridgeway Road	-	BC 31 October 1981 p. 31. On instruction of executors of Miss A. A. Rawlins	-
26 November 1980	Biggleswade, St Andrew's Rooms	Stotfold, 90 Astwick Road, semi-detached house	-	BC 31 October 1981 p. 31. On instruction of executors of Sidney Jack Seymour	-
26 November 1980	Biggleswade, St Andrew's Rooms	Gamlingay (Cambs), Green End, building plot	-	BC 31 October 1981 p. 31. On instruction of M. W. Smith Esq.	-
26 November 1980	Biggleswade, St Andrew's Rooms	Biggleswade, 48–50 The Baulk, two adjoining houses	-	BC 31 October 1981 p. 31. On instruction of Hugh Pollock Esq.	-

Auction date	Venue	Description	Price	Newspaper references	BLARS references
9 January 1981	Bedford, Newnham Street, Auction Centre	Kempston, Marlborough Park, development land, 1.146a	£45,000	-	-
9 January 1981	Bedford, Newnham Street, Auction Centre	Bedford, 25 Campbell Road, semi-detached house	£16,000	-	-
9 January 1981	Bedford, Newnham Street, Auction Centre	Bedford, 166 Hurst Grove, in three flats	£13,500	-	-
9 January 1981	Bedford, Newnham Street, Auction Centre	Pulloxhill, Tyburn Lane, plot, paddock 0.5a	Unsold	-	-
9 January 1981	Bedford, Newnham Street, Auction Centre	Bedford, 34 St Leonards Street, cottage	£7,600	-	-
28 January 1981	Biggleswade, Conservative Club	Sandy, 1 Beeston Green, detached period cottage	-	BC 9 January 1981 p. 24. Re. Mrs E. G. Hereford, deceased	-

Auction date	Venue	Description	Price	Newspaper references	BLARS references
28 January 1981	Biggleswade, Conservative Club	Sandy, London Road, re-development site, 0.6a	-	BC 9 January 1981 p. 24. Under instruction of Sandy Town Council	-
1 May 1981	Bedford, Newnham Street, Auction Centre	Kempston, 54 Thornton Street, house	£7,000	BJ 2 April 1981 p. 25. Rental £286 pa	-
1 May 1981	Bedford, Newnham Street, Auction Centre	Wilstead, adjoining 52 Cotton End Road, accommodation land, 3.33a	£7,200	BJ 2 April 1981 p. 25	-
1 May 1981	Bedford, Newnham Street, Auction Centre	Wilstead, 80 Cotton End Road	£6,000	BJ 2 April 1981 p. 25; 16 April p. 30. Let to tenant	-
1 May 1981	Bedford, Newnham Street, Auction Centre	Wilstead, 82 Cotton End Road, cottage	£8,100	BJ 2 April 1981 p. 25; 16 April p. 30. Let to tenant	-
1 May 1981	Bedford, Newnham Street, Auction Centre	Clapham, 68 and 70 High Street, two cottages	£14,500	BJ 2 April 1981 p. 25	-

Auction date	Venue	Description	Price	Newspaper references	BLARS references
1 May 1981	Bedford, Newnham Street, Auction Centre	Bedford, 5 Preston Road, semi-detached house	£15,800	BJ 2 April 1981 p. 25; 16 April p. 30	-
1 May 1981	Bedford, Newnham Street, Auction Centre	Renhold, 88 Hookhams Lane, detached bungalow, 1.75a	£44,000	BJ 2 April 1981 p. 25	-
1 May 1981	Bedford, Newnham Street, Auction Centre	Wilden, off Johnson's Lane, arable land, 4.55a	£10,000	BJ 2 April 1981 p. 25	-
1 May 1981	Bedford, Newnham Street, Auction Centre	Bromham, Bridge End Dahlia Nursery, 1.75a	£12,500	BJ 2 April 1981 p. 25	-
1 May 1981	Bedford, Newnham Street, Auction Centre	Stevington, Court Lane, building plot 0.7a	£15,000	BJ 2 April 1981 p. 25	-
1 May 1981	Bedford, Newnham Street, Auction Centre	Stevington, Court Lane, building plot, 2a	£19,500	BJ 2 April 1981 p. 25; 16 April p. 30	-

Auction date	Venue	Description	Price	Newspaper references	BLARS references
1 May 1981	Bedford, Newnham Street, Auction Centre	Harrold, Church Walk, building plot, 0.4a	£25,000	BJ 2 April 1981 p. 25	-
13 May 1981	Biggleswade, St Andrew's Rooms	Gamlingay (Cambs), 86 Church Street, semi-detached house	-	BC 10 April 1981 p. 43. On instruction of representatives of Mrs Eunice Dewsbury	-
13 May 1981	Biggleswade, St Andrew's Rooms	Upper Caldecote, 207 Biggleswade Road, semi-detached house	-	BC 10 April 1981 p. 43. On instruction of Mrs V. M. Stokes	-
13 May 1981	Biggleswade, St Andrew's Rooms	Potton, 13 Sandy Road, end of terrace cottage	-	BC 10 April 1981 p. 43. On instruction of Mrs E. M. Sills	-
13 May 1981	Biggleswade, St Andrew's Rooms	Potton, 64 Everton Road, terraced cottage	-	BC 10 April 1981 p. 43. On instruction of executors of Mr F. J. Bennett	-
16 June 1981	Bedford, Newnham Street, Auction Centre	Clophill, Beadlow Top Farm, buildings, grade two arable land, 198a	-	BT 17 April 1981 p. 27; 1 May p. 28. On instruction of Messrs R. and M. Gobey	-
16 June 1981	Bedford, Newnham Street, Auction Centre	Clophill, Shefford Road, grade two arable land, 11a	-	BT 24 April 1981 p. 25; 1 May p. 28; 15 May p. 25. On instruction of Mr A. E. Matthews	-

Auction date	Venue	Description	Price	Newspaper references	BLARS references
3 July 1981	Bedford, Newnham Street, Auction Centre	Biddenham, 20 Church End, semi-detached cottage	£23,000	BT Property Times, 11 June 1981 p. 5	-
3 July 1981	Bedford, Newnham Street, Auction Centre	Old Warden, 141 Warden Road, detached eighteenth century cottage	£28,500	BT Property Times, 11 June 1981 p. 5	-
15 July 1981	Biggleswade, St. Andrew's Rooms	Sutton, part of Standalone Farm, market garden, arable land, 72.6a and 134.8a	Arable land 134.8a withdrawn from auction	BT 15 May 1981 p. 25; 9 July p. 26. Vacant possession	-
4 September 1981	Bedford, Newnham Street, Auction Centre	Bedford, 1 Rosamond Road, semi-detached house	£10,750	-	-
4 September 1981	Bedford, Newnham Street, Auction Centre	Bedford, 3 Rosamond Road, semi-detached house	£9,500	-	-
4 September 1981	Bedford, Newnham Street, Auction Centre	Hitchin (Herts), 66 Bedford Road, detached house	£13,000	-	-

Auction date	Venue	Description	Price	Newspaper references	BLARS references
4 September 1981	Bedford, Newnham Street, Auction Centre	Clapham, 32 The Warren, semi-detached cottage	Unsold	-	-
4 September 1981	Bedford, Newnham Street, Auction Centre	Wilden, 35 High Street, detached house	£19,000	-	-
4 September 1981	Bedford, Newnham Street, Auction Centre	Tilbrook, Trickets Cottage, High Street, period cottage	Unsold	-	-
4 September 1981	Bedford, Newnham Street, Auction Centre	Cranfield, 118 Bedford Road, detached house	Unsold	-	-
9 September 1981	Biggleswade, St Andrew's Rooms	Biggleswade, 2 Laurel View, terraced cottage	-	BC 24 July 1981 p. 39	-
9 September 1981	Biggleswade, St Andrew's Rooms	Langford, 20 Station Road, terraced cottage	-	BC 24 July 1981 p. 39	-
9 September 1981	Biggleswade, St Andrew's Rooms	Biggleswade, 90 The Baulk, end of terrace	-	BC 24 July 1981 p. 39	-

Auction date	Venue	Description	Price	Newspaper references	BLARS references
9 September 1981	Biggleswade, St Andrew's Rooms	Dunton, Baptist Church premises, single storey building	-	BC 31 July 1981 p. 49	-
9 September 1981	Biggleswade, St Andrew's Rooms	Broom, Southill Road, arable land, 1a	-	BC 31 July 1981 p. 49	-
9 September 1981	Biggleswade, St Andrew's Rooms	Biggleswade, 23 Hitchin Street	-	BC 7 August 1981 p. 36	-
14 October 1981	Biggleswade, St Andrew's Rooms	Beeston, The Green, detached bungalow	-	BC 21 August 1981 p. 28. BJ 8 October 1981 p. 26	-
14 October 1981	Biggleswade, St Andrew's Rooms	Langford, 20 Station Road, terraced cottage	-	BC 18 September 1981 p. 26; 9 October p. 32	-
4 November 1981	Aspley Guise, The Holt Hotel	Aspley Heath, Daneswood Convalescent Home, 14,800 sq ft, 4.19a	£240,000	TDA 4 November 1981 p. 23. BJ 8 October 1981 p. 26	-
4 November 1981	Aspley Guise, The Holt Hotel	Aspley Heath, Daneswood bungalow	£30,000	BJ 8 October 1981 p. 26	-
6 November 1981	Bedford, Newnham Street, Auction Centre	Kempston, 18 Chantry Road, detached house	£10,000	BJ 8 October 1981 p. 26	-

Auction date	Venue	Description	Price	Newspaper references	BLARS references
6 November 1981	Bedford, Newnham Street, Auction Centre	Bedford, 74 Denmark Street, house	£13,750	BJ 8 October 1981 p. 26. For improvement	-
8 December 1981	Colmworth, The Village Hall	Colmworth, The Bungalow, Chapel Lane	£44,500	BJ 8 October 1981 p. 26	-
9 December 1981	Biggleswade, St Andrew's Rooms	Potton, 4 West End Lane, semi-detached cottage	-	BC 16 October 1981 p. 31	-
9 December 1981	Biggleswade, St Andrew's Rooms	Biggleswade, 34 Saffron Road, detached house	-	BC 16 October 1981 p. 31	-
9 December 1981	Biggleswade, St Andrew's Rooms	Sandy, 55 Cambridge Road, semi-detached cottage	-	BC 20 November 1981 p. 40	-
16 February 1982	Bedford, Newnham Street, Auction Centre	Kempston, Marlborough Park, two plots	Unsold	-	-
5 March 1982	Bedford, Newnham Street, Auction Centre	Bedford, 72 Kimbolton Road, semi-detached house	£29,000	-	-

Auction date	Venue	Description	Price	Newspaper references	BLARS references
2 April 1982	Bedford, Newnham Street, Auction Centre	Bedford, 19 Balmoral Avenue, building plot	£21,250	-	-
2 April 1982	Bedford, Newnham Street, Auction Centre	Kempston, 60 College Street, house	Unsold	-	-
7 May 1982	Bedford, Newnham Street, Auction Centre	Eaton Socon (Cambs), 80 Great North Road, modernised house	Unsold	-	-
9 June 1982	-	Sandy, 13 Ivel Road, semi-detached cottage	-	BC 8 April 1982 p. 32	-
9 June 1982	-	Potton, Everton Road, building land	-	BC 8 April 1982 p. 32. Outline planning consent	-
9 June 1982	-	Shefford, Bedford Road, building land, 0.6a	-	BC 8 April 1982 p. 32. Outline planning consent	-
2 July 1982	Bedford, Newnham Street, Auction Centre	Turvey, 4 Elmwood, semi-detached house	£26,500	BC 11 June 1982 p. 25	-

Auction date	Venue	Description	Price	Newspaper references	BLARS references
2 July 1982	Bedford, Newnham Street, Auction Centre	Bromham, 62 Village Road, detached bungalow, 0.5a	£36,500	BC 11 June 1982 p. 25	-
2 July 1982	Bedford, Newnham Street, Auction Centre	Kimbolton (Cambs), Newtown, 3 Duke's Row, terraced cottage	Unsold	BC 11 June 1982 p. 25	-
2 July 1982	Bedford, Newnham Street, Auction Centre	Bedford, 31 Iddesleigh Road, terrace cottage	-	BC 11 June 1982 p. 25	-
28 July 1982	At Biggleswade	Wrestlingworth, Church Lane, development land	Unsold	BC 11 June 1982 p. 28; 6 August p. 29. On instruction of executors of Mrs M. C. Warren	-
28 July 1982	At Biggleswade	Shefford, Bedford Road, land	-	BC 11 June 1982 p. 28. On instruction of Baptist Union Corp. Ltd	-
28 July 1982	Biggleswade, St Andrew's Rooms	Biggleswade, 15 Chapel Fields, end terrace cottage	Unsold	BC 18 June 1982 p. 28; 9 July p. 32; 6 August p. 29. On instruction of Mid Bedfordshire District Council	-
28 July 1982	Biggleswade, St Andrew's Rooms	Biggleswade, Hitchmead Road, arable land, 3.75a	-	BC 23 July 1982 p. 28. On instruction of G. C. Kidman Esq.	-
6 August 1982	Bedford, Newnham Street, Auction Centre	Colmworth, Kennell Farm, house, 1.3a	£53,000	BC 16 July 1982 p. 28	-

Auction date	Venue	Description	Price	Newspaper references	BLARS references
6 August 1982	Bedford, Newnham Street, Auction Centre	Sharnbrook, Sharnside, Park Lane, semi-detached period cottage	£21,500	-	-
3 September 1982	Bedford, Newnham Street, Auction Centre	Astwood, Astwood Park Farm, house, 10.53a	£76,000	-	-
8 September 1982	Biggleswade, St Andrew's Rooms	Langford, 92 Church Street, residential property	-	BC 23 July 1982 p. 28. On instruction of trustees of Mr Herbert Clark	-
8 September 1982	Biggleswade, St Andrew's Rooms	Biggleswade, 33 Fairfield Road	-	BC 23 July 1982 p. 28. On instruction of executors of Mr F. J. Bennett	-
10 September 1982	Biggleswade, The Stratton House Hotel	Biggleswade, industrial land, 8.5a	£430,000	-	-
16 September 1982	Fenny Stratford, The Swan Hotel	Whaddon (Bucks), Woodpond Farmhouse	£50,000	-	-
5 November 1982	Bedford, Newnham Street, Auction Centre	Northill, Northill School House	£21,600	-	-
15 December 1982	Biggleswade, St Andrew's Rooms	Wilstead, main A6 road, 5.35a	-	BC 12 November 1982 p. 30. On instruction of Society for Promoting Christian Knowledge	-

Auction date	Venue	Description	Price	Newspaper references	BLARS references
15 December 1982	Biggleswade, St Andrew's Rooms	Northill, west side of Northill to Thorncote Green Road, land, 24.042a	-	BC 12 November 1982 p. 30. On instruction of Mrs Peggy Phillips	-
15 December 1982	Biggleswade, St Andrew's Rooms	Langford, Barnes Road Field, 14.225a	-	BC 12 November 1982 p. 30. On instruction of trustees of Charles Seward	-
15 December 1982	Biggleswade, St Andrew's Rooms	Langford, Henlow Turn Field, on road leading to Henlow, 9.331a	-	BC 12 November 1982 p. 30. On instruction of trustees of Charles Seward	-
15 December 1982	Biggleswade, St Andrew's Rooms	Langford, adjoining New Road, land, 1a	-	BC 10 December 1982 p. 31. On instruction of I. Rowley Esq.	-
15 December 1982	Biggleswade, St Andrew's Rooms	Biggleswade, 156 London Road, detached bungalow	-	BC 12 November 1982 p. 30	-
15 December 1982	Biggleswade, St Andrew's Rooms	Sandy, 17 Stratford Road, semi-detached house	-	BC 12 November 1982 p. 30	-
4 February 1983	Bedford, Newnham Street, Auction Centre	Bedford, 53 Victoria Road, house	£10,000	-	-
4 February 1983	Bedford, Newnham Street, Auction Centre	Bedford, 30 Grosvenor Street, terrace house	£12,800	-	-

Auction date	Venue	Description	Price	Newspaper references	BLARS references
23 February 1983	Biggleswade, St Andrew's Rooms	Biggleswade, 37 London Road, house, orchard	-	BC 14 January 1983 p. 23. On instruction of executor of Mrs W. M. Matthews. Vacant possession	-
23 February 1983	Biggleswade, St Andrew's Rooms	Baldock (Herts), 16 and 26 Icknield Way	-	BC 14 January 1983 p. 23. On instruction of executor of Mrs W. M. Matthews	-
23 February 1983	Biggleswade, St Andrew's Rooms	Langford, 103 High Street	-	BC 14 January 1983 p. 23. On instruction of executor of Mrs W. M. Matthews	-
23 February 1983	Biggleswade, St Andrew's Rooms	Biggleswade, 19 Chapel Fields	-	BC 14 January 1983 p. 23. On instruction of executor of Mrs W. M. Matthews	-
23 February 1983	Biggleswade, St Andrew's Rooms	Biggleswade, 21 St John's Street	-	BC 14 January 1983 p. 23. On instruction of executor of Mrs W. M. Matthews	-
23 February 1983	Biggleswade, St Andrew's Rooms	Biggleswade, 94, 96 and 106 Sun Street	-	BC 14 January 1983 p. 23. On instruction of executor of Mrs W. M. Matthews	-
23 February 1983	Biggleswade, St Andrew's Rooms	Biggleswade, 17 and 25 The Baulk	-	BC 14 January 1983 p. 23. On instruction of executor of Mrs W. M. Matthews	-
2 March 1983	Biggleswade, St Andrew's Rooms	Langford, Glenfield, 97 (formerly 75) Church Street	-	BC 14 January 1982 p. 23; 11 February p. 22. On instruction of executrix of Mr John Clark	-
27 April 1983	Biggleswade, St Andrew's Rooms	Biggleswade, 116 London Road, semi-detached house	-	BC 4 March 1983 p. 25; 18 March p. 26	-
27 April 1983	Biggleswade, St Andrew's Rooms	Biggleswade, 106 Sun Street, terrace house	-	BC 4 March 1983 p. 25; 18 March p. 26	-

Auction date	Venue	Description	Price	Newspaper references	BLARS references
27 April 1983	Biggleswade, St Andrew's Rooms	Wrestlingworth, High Street, building land	-	BC 4 March 1983 p. 25	-
27 April 1983	Biggleswade, St Andrew's Rooms	Langford, approached from Mill Lane adjoining River Ivel, agricultural land, 17a	-	BC 4 March 1983 p. 25	-
3 June 1983	Bedford, Newnham Street, Auction Centre	Sharnbrook, Old Mill House, Kennell Hill	Unsold	BJ Property Journal 29 April 1983 p. 8	-
3 June 1983	Bedford, Newnham Street, Auction Centre	Bromham, Village Road, single building plot, 0.16a	-	BJ Property Journal 29 April 1983 p. 8	-
8 June 1983	Biggleswade, St Andrew's Rooms	Hatch, 7 Brook End, house, buildings	£67,000	BC 6 May 1982 p. 27. On instruction of B. J. Brawn & Sons	-
8 June 1983	Biggleswade, St Andrew's Rooms	Hatch, Brook End, land, 3.64a	£8,000	BC 6 May 1982 p. 27. On instruction of B. J. Brawn & Sons	-
8 June 1983	Biggleswade, St Andrew's Rooms	Beeston, 16 The Green, garden land, 2.58a	Unsold	BC 6 May 1982 p. 27. On instruction of B. J. Brawn & Sons. Water abstraction licence	-
8 June 1983	Biggleswade, St Andrew's Rooms	Beeston, land, 3.95a	£13,000	BC 6 May 1982 p. 27. On instruction of B. J. Brawn & Sons	-

Auction date	Venue	Description	Price	Newspaper references	BLARS references
16 June 1983	Bedford, Newnham Street, Auction Centre	Great Barford, Willoughby Farm, arable land, 194.8a	£360,000	BC 6 May 1982 p. 27. On instruction of J. V. Brown Esq.	-
22 June 1983	-	Shillington, High Road, two single plots, 0.25a	-	BC 13 May 1983 p. 27	-
8 July 1983	Bedford, Newnham Street, Auction Centre	Souldrop, Pools Lane, bungalow, 3.55a	Unsold	BJ Property Journal 29 April 1983 p. 8	-
8 July 1983	Bedford, Newnham Street, Auction Centre	Bedford, 8 The Embankment, semi-detached nine bedroom house	£55,500	BJ Property Journal 29 April 1983 p. 8	-
8 July 1983	Bedford, Newnham Street, Auction Centre	Oakley, The Spinney, Church Lane, detached chalet bungalow	£68,000	BJ Property Journal 24 June 1983 p. 7	-
8 July 1983	Bedford, Newnham Street, Auction Centre	Oakley, Church Lane, adjoining the Spinney, building plot, 0.35a	-	BJ Property Journal 24 June 1983 p. 7	-

Auction date	Venue	Description	Price	Newspaper references	BLARS references
8 July 1983	Bedford, Newnham Street, Auction Centre	Bromham, Village Road, single building plot, 0.16a	£18,500	BJ Property Journal 24 June 1983 p. 7	-
10 August 1983	Eversholt, The Green Man	Westoning, Wood End, arable land, 30.66a	£70,000	-	-
9 September 1983	Bedford, Newnham Street, Auction Centre	Kempston, 15 and 17 High Street, shop, living accommodation	£31,200	BJ Property Journal 22 July 1983 p. 17. For improvement	-
9 September 1983	Bedford, Newnham Street, Auction Centre	Bedford, 13 Conduit Road, house	£8,000	BJ Property Journal 22 July 1983 p. 17. Rental £582 pa	-
21 September 1983	Biggleswade, St Andrew's Rooms	Biggleswade, 99 Potton Road	-	BC 29 July 1983 p. 22. On instruction of Mrs D. M. Warden. Subject to unfurnished tenancy	-
21 September 1983	Biggleswade, St Andrew's Rooms	Wrestlingworth, Eyeworth Road, single building plot, 0.25a	-	BC 29 July 1983 p. 22. On instruction of F. J. Randall	-
30 September 1983	-	Stevington, agricultural land, 138a	-	BJ Property Journal 26 August 1983 p. 9	-
26 October 1983	Biggleswade, St Andrew's Rooms	Clifton, The Linkway, single building plot	-	BC 16 September 1983 p. 33. On instruction of Mr G. S. Brown	-
26 October 1983	Biggleswade, St Andrew's Rooms	Northill, arable land, 1.64a	-	BC 7 October 1983 p. 31. On instruction of Mid Bedfordshire District Council	-
10 November 1983	Fenny Stratford, The Swan Hotel	Whaddon (Bucks), Churchill Farm House, dilapidated farmhouse	£68,000	TDA 5 October 1983 p. 29. BJ Property Journal 7 October 1983 p. 3	-

Auction date	Venue	Description	Price	Newspaper references	BLARS references
11 November 1983	Bedford, Newnham Street, Auction Centre	Bromham, The Briars, Bromham Park, detached house, 1.22a	£70,000	BJ Property Journal 30 September 1983 p.19; 28 October p. 2	-
11 November 1983	Bedford, Newnham Street, Auction Centre	Elstow, adjoining 194 Wilstead Road, building plot	£19,000	BJ Property Journal 30 September 1983 p. 19. Outline planning consent for one dwelling	-
9 December 1983	Bedford, Newnham Street, Auction Centre	Bedford, 50 and 52 Bromham Road, two shops	£86,000	BJ Property Journal 7 October 1983 p. 3. Rental £7,500 pa	-
20 December 1983	Bedford, Newnham Street, Auction Centre	Blunham, Park Farm, five bedroom house, small garden plot, two large building plots (one with outbuildings), pasture of 5a, pasture with river frontage of 17.5a	-	BC 18 November 1983 p. 27; 9 December p. 20. On instruction of Mr and Mrs C. J. Holmes	-
21 December 1983	Biggleswade, St Andrew's Rooms	Sandy, St Neots Road, residential development land, 0.7s	-	BC 18 November 1983 p. 27. On instruction of Court of Protection	-
21 December 1983	Biggleswade, St Andrew's Rooms	Sandy, 132 St Neots Road, detached residence	-	BC 18 November 1983 p. 27. On instruction of Court of Protection	-
21 December 1983	Biggleswade, St Andrew's Rooms	Potton, 26 Sutton Mill Road, terraced cottage	-	BC 18 November 1983 p. 27. On instruction of Court of Protection	-
3 February 1984	Bedford, Newnham Street, Auction Centre	Stagsden, Church Room and St Leonard's Cottage	£28,500	BJ Property Journal 25 November 1983 p. 3. By order of the trustees. For improvement	-
3 February 1984	Bedford, Newnham Street, Auction Centre	Bedford, 6 Nursery Gardens, modern detached house	-	BJ Property Journal 6 January 1984 p. 7	-

Auction date	Venue	Description	Price	Newspaper references	BLARS references
15 February 1984	Biggleswade, St Andrew's Rooms	Tempsford, adjoining A1, arable land, 21a	-	BC 6 January 1984 p. 25. On instruction of Mrs P. D. Cope. BJ Property Journal 10 February 1984 p. 17. Vacant possession	-
24 February 1984	Kimbolton School, The Lewis Hall	Kimbolton (Cambs), Grass Yard, building plot, 0.66a	£38,500	BJ Property Journal 13 January 1984 p. 17	-
29 March 1984	Biggleswade, St Andrew's Rooms	Northill, 13–17 Bedford Road, period cottages	-	BC 10 February 1984 p. 23; 2 March p. 21. Subject to statutory tenancy	-
13 April 1984	Bedford, Newnham Street, Auction Centre	Cranfield, 172 High Street, cottage	£18,000	BC Property Express 1984 p. 3. BJ Property Journal 24 February 1984 p. 18	-
13 April 1984	Bedford, Newnham Street, Auction Centre	Bedford, 106 Castle Road, shop	£23,250	BC 9 March 1984 p. 24. BJ Property Journal 6 January 1984 p. 7. Rental £2,100 pa	-
13 April 1984	Bedford, Newnham Street, Auction Centre	Bedford, 45 St Cuthberts Street, shop	Sold prior to auction	BC 9 March 1984 p. 24. Rental £2,700 pa. BJ Property Journal 6 January 1984 p. 7	-
20 June 1984	Stewkley, The Village Hall	Stewkley (Bucks), 88 High Street, thatched cottage	£57,000	BKE Property Express 23 May 1984 p. 9	-
6 July 1984	Bedford, Newnham Street, Auction Centre	Bedford, 38 Houghton Road, semi-detached house	£22,000	BKE Property Express 2 May 1984 p. 8; 6 June 1984 p. 18. Vacant possession	-
6 July 1984	Bedford, Newnham Street, Auction Centre	Clapham, 26 and 28 The Warren, two cottages	£24,000	BKE Property Express 25 April 1984 p. 5. For improvement	-

Auction date	Venue	Description	Price	Newspaper references	BLARS references
6 July 1984	Bedford, Newnham Street, Auction Centre	Wilden, High Street, building plot	£27,000	BKE Property Express 25 April 1984 p. 5	-
6 July 1984	Bedford, Newnham Street, Auction Centre	Kempston, 50 Bunyan Road, detached house	£18,000	BKE Property Express 25 April 1984 p. 5. Vacant possession	-
6 July 1984	Bedford, Newnham Street, Auction Centre	Kempston, corner of Hill Rise and Durler Avenue, amenity land, 0.15a	£2,800	BKE Property Express 23 May 1984 p. 9	-
6 July 1984	Bedford, Newnham Street, Auction Centre	Bedford, 10 Cutcliffe Place, corner bungalow	£21,000	BKE Property Express 23 May 1984 p. 9; 6 June 1984 p. 18	-
6 July 1984	Bedford, Newnham Street, Auction Centre	Cranfield, Gossards Green, Bourne End, detached cottage	£46,000	BKE Property Express 25 April 1984 p. 5; 6 June 1984 p. 18. For improvement	-
6 July 1984	Bedford, Newnham Street, Auction Centre	Hardmead (Bucks), buildings, arable land, 124.299a	£250,000	BKE Property Express 6 June 1984 p. 18	-

Auction date	Venue	Description	Price	Newspaper references	BLARS references
14 September 1984	Bedford, Newnham Street, Auction Centre	Oakley, High Street, building plot	£30,000	BKE Property Express 6 June 1984 p. 18	-
14 September 1984	Bedford, Newnham Street, Auction Centre	Oakley, High Street, building plot	£30,000	BKE Property Express 6 June 1984 p. 18	-
14 September 1984	Bedford, Newnham Street, Auction Centre	Oakley, High Street, building plot	£34,500	BKE Property Express 6 June 1984 p. 18	-
14 September 1984	Bedford, Newnham Street, Auction Centre	Bedford, Kempston Marina, development site, boatyard, marina on the Great Ouse	Postponed to 2 November 1984	BKE Property Express 4 July 1984 p. 14	-
14 September 1984	Bedford, Newnham Street, Auction Centre	Oakley, 29 Church Lane, adjoining building plot	Sold prior to auction	BKE Property Express 4 July 1984 p. 14	-
14 September 1984	Bedford, Newnham Street, Auction Centre	Kempston, Stonedale Road, building site	-	BKE Property Express 18 July 1984 p. 13. With planning permission for four semi-detached dwellings	-

Auction date	Venue	Description	Price	Newspaper references	BLARS references
14 September 1984	Bedford, Newnham Street, Auction Centre	Biddenham, river meadows, 8.9a	-	BKE Property Express 25 July 1984 p. 4	-
5 October 1984	Bedford, Newnham Street, Auction Centre	Bedford, 50 Sandhurst Road, semi-detached house	Unsold	BKE Property Express 15 August 1984 p. 14	-
5 October 1984	Bedford, Newnham Street, Auction Centre	Cranfield, 94 and 96 High Street, two cottages	Unsold	BKE Property Express 15 August 1984 p. 14. For improvement	-
5 October 1984	Bedford, Newnham Street, Auction Centre	Cople, 23 Willington Road, house	£13,250	BKE Property Express 29 August 1984 p. 15. Rental £570 pa	-
30 October 1984	Sandy, The King's Arms	Gamlingay (Cambs), glasshouse nursery, house, packing shed, 3.69a	Auction cancelled. Joint auction with Robinson and Hall	BC 5 October 1984 p. 29; 26 October p. 39. Vacant possession	-
2 November 1984	Bedford, Newnham Street, Auction Centre	Kempston, Kempston Marina, building site	£50,000	BKE Property Express 4 July 1984 p. 14	-

Auction date	Venue	Description	Price	Newspaper references	BLARS references
2 November 1984	Bedford, Newnham Street, Auction Centre	Kempston, Kempston Marina	£30,000	BKE Property Express 4 July 1984 p. 14	-
29 November 1984	Hitchin, The Sun Hotel	Hitchin (Herts), St Faith's Close, two storey barn, garden	Auction postponed	BC 9 November 1984 p. 27	-
1 February 1985	Bedford, Newnham Street, Auction Centre	Harrold, 144 High Street, detached house	£33,500	-	-
1 February 1985	Bedford, Newnham Street, Auction Centre	Clapham, 144 Milton Road, detached house, 1a	£44,000	-	-
6 March 1985	Biggleswade, The Stratton House Hotel	Biggleswade, Scroups Farm, Langford Road, derelict cottages, 1.4a	-	BC 25 January 1985 p. 21	-
12 April 1985	Bedford, Newnham Street, Auction Centre	Kempston, Stonedale Road, four plots	£50,000	BKE Property Supplement 10 April 1985 p. 12. Outline planning permission for four houses	-

Auction date	Venue	Description	Price	Newspaper references	BLARS references
7 June 1985	Bedford, Newnham Street, Auction Centre	Colmworth, New Road, Kimbolton Road, detached period farm house	£30,000	BKE Property Supplement 10 April 1985 p. 12	-
7 June 1985	Bedford, Newnham Street, Auction Centre	Bedford, 74 Clapham Road, detached house	£30,000	BKE Property Supplement 10 April 1985 p. 12. Poor structure	-
6 September 1985	Bedford, Newnham Street, Auction Centre	Wilden, Shrubbery Farm, period farm house, 19.58a	£120,000	BC 2 August 1985 p. 24. BJ 8 August 1985 p. 26	-
6 September 1985	Bedford, Newnham Street, Auction Centre	Wilden, Shrubbery Farm, arable land, 44.98a	£102,000	BC 2 August 1985 p. 24. BJ 8 August 1985 p. 26	-
6 September 1985	Bedford, Newnham Street, Auction Centre	Wilden, Shrubbery Farm, arable land, 12.79a	£37,000	BC 2 August 1985 p. 24. BJ 8 August 1985 p. 26	-
6 September 1985	Bedford, Newnham Street, Auction Centre	Cardington, Chapel Farm, Chapel End, barns for conversion	£62,000	BC 2 August 1985 p. 24. BJ 8 August 1985 p. 26. By order of S. C. Whitbread Esq.	-

Auction date	Venue	Description	Price	Newspaper references	BLARS references
6 September 1985	Bedford, Newnham Street, Auction Centre	Old Warden, 142 Warden Street, detached period cottage	£40,000	BC 28 June 1985 p. 30. BJ 8 August 1985 p. 26. Vacant possession	-
6 September 1985	Bedford, Newnham Street, Auction Centre	Houghton Conquest, two building plots	£48,000	BC 2 August 1985 p. 24. BJ 8 August 1985 p. 26. Outline planning consent for one detached dwelling with garage	-
6 September 1985	Bedford, Newnham Street, Auction Centre	Stonely (Cambs), 7 Brookside, cottage	Unsold	-	-
1 November 1985	Bedford, Newnham Street, Auction Centre	Lidlington, 27 Church Street, end terrace house	£21,000	-	-
1 November 1985	Bedford, Newnham Street, Auction Centre	Great Barford, 61 High Street, detached period cottage	£70,000	-	-
1 November 1985	Bedford, Newnham Street, Auction Centre	Stagsden, White Horse, High Street, cottage, 2.05a	£70,000	-	-

Auction date	Venue	Description	Price	Newspaper references	BLARS references
6 November 1985	Sandy, The Conservative Club	Sandy, adjoining the Conservative Club, residential building land, 0.98a	-	BC 27 September 1985 p. 23	-
15 January 1986	Biggleswade, St Andrew's Rooms	Biggleswade, 4 Southview, semi-detached house	-	BC 3 January 1986 p. 17. BKE Property Express 11 December 1985 p. iv	-
15 January 1986	Biggleswade, St Andrew's Rooms	Biggleswade, 78 and 81 Shortmead Street	Sold prior to auction	BC 3 January 1986 p. 17. BKE Property Express 11 December 1985 p. iv	-
15 January 1986	Biggleswade, St Andrew's Rooms	Ashwell (Herts), Whittington Farm, farmhouse, buildings, 27.5a	-	BC 10 January 1986 p. 29. BKE Property Express 11 December 1985 p. iv	-
15 January 1986	Biggleswade, St Andrew's Rooms	Great Offley (Herts), Methodist Chapel	£75,000	BC 10 January 1986 p. 29; 21 February 1986 (Peacock's Property Scene no. 1 p. 1). BKE Property Express 11 December 1985 p. iv. Consent to conversion to four units	-
15 January 1986	Biggleswade, St Andrew's Rooms	Biggleswade and Langford, arable land, 92.69a	-	BC 10 January 1986 p. 29. BKE Property Express 11 December 1985 p. iv	-
7 February 1986	Bedford, Newnham Street, Auction Centre	Bedford, 66 Tavistock Street, period property	£51,000	BKE Property Express 11 December 1985 p. iv. For improvement	-

Auction date	Venue	Description	Price	Newspaper references	BLARS references
7 February 1986	Bedford, Newnham Street, Auction Centre	Stevington, 30 Court Lane, detached double-fronted house	£56,000	BKE Property Express 11 December 1985 p. iv	-
7 February 1986	Bedford, Newnham Street, Auction Centre	Kempston, Box End, accommodation land, 3.59 a	£15,000	-	-
7 February 1986	Bedford, Newnham Street, Auction Centre	Kempston, Box End, amenity land, 0.75a	£10,000	-	-
19 March 1986	Sandy, The Conservative Club	Sandy, 3 Ivel Road, period detached house, residential building land, 0.672a	-	BC 31 January 1986 p. 24; 7 March p. 30. BT 13 February 1986 p. 19	-
16 April 1986	Biggleswade, St Andrew's Rooms	Biggleswade, Langford Road, grade one arable land, 24a	-	BC 21 March 1986 p. 30. Vacant possession	-
9 May 1986	Bedford, Newnham Street, Auction Centre	Keysoe, Stapleton's Cottage, Keysoe Row West, detached cottage	£36,500	BC 23 May 1986 p. 27 (Peacock's Property Scene no. 4)	-

Auction date	Venue	Description	Price	Newspaper references	BLARS references
11 July 1986	Bedford, Newnham Street, Auction Centre	Great Barford, The White Hart, High Street, former pub	£70,000	BC 20 June 1986 p. 36 (Peacock's Property Scene no. 5)	-
11 July 1986	Bedford, Newnham Street, Auction Centre	Old Harrowden, 249 High Road, cottage	£40,000	BC 20 June 1986 p. 36 (Peacock's Property Scene no. 5); 25 July p. 27 (Peacock's Property Scene no. 6). For improvement	-
17 July 1986	Bedford, Newnham Street, Auction Centre	Sandy, Stone Axe Farm, Victorian farmhouse, farm buildings, arable land, 14.5a	-	BC 20 June 1986 p. 33 and 36 (Peacock's Property Scene no. 5)	-
20 August 1986	Biggleswade, St Andrew's Rooms	Northill, 10 and 12 Thorncote Road, pair of period cottages	-	BC 20 June 1986 p. 36 (Peacock's Property Scene no. 5); 1 August p. 32; 15 August p. 28	-
24 September 1986	Biggleswade, St Andrew's Rooms	Gamlingay (Cambs), The Green Man, The Cinques, de-licensed public house	-	BC 20 June 1986 p. 36 (Peacock's Property Scene no. 5); 1 August p. 32; 15 August p. 28	-
24 September 1986	Biggleswade, St Andrew's Rooms	Wrestlingworth, 30 High Street, house	Sold prior to auction	BC 20 June 1986 p. 36 (Peacock's Property Scene no. 5); 1 August p. 32; 15 August p. 28; 12 September p. 31	-
24 September 1986	Biggleswade, St Andrew's Rooms	Wrestlingworth, land to rear of 30 and 32 High Street	Sold prior to auction	BC 20 June 1986 p. 36 (Peacock's Property Scene no. 5); 1 August p. 32; 15 August p. 28; 19 September p. 33	-

Auction date	Venue	Description	Price	Newspaper references	BLARS references
24 September 1986	Biggleswade, St Andrew's Rooms	Shefford, 34 and 34a High Street	-	BC 15 August 1986 p. 28	-
24 September 1986	Biggleswade, St Andrew's Rooms	Biggleswade, 1 and 2 Sunderland Hall Farm Cottages	-	BC 15 August 1986 p. 28	-
24 September 1986	Biggleswade, St Andrew's Rooms	Biggleswade, 3 and 4 West Sunderland Hall Farm Cottages	-	BC 15 August 1986 p. 28	-
10 October 1986	Bedford, Newnham Street, Auction Centre	Bedford, 166 George Street	£18,000	-	-
10 October 1986	Bedford, Newnham Street, Auction Centre	Carlton, The Manse, 57 The Causeway, detached house	£75,000	-	-
5 December 1986	Bedford, Newnham Street, Auction Centre	Harrold, 30 and 32 Brook Lane, two cottages and plot	£46,500	-	-
5 December 1986	Bedford, Newnham Street, Auction Centre	Ampthill, Bedford Street, building plot	£38,000	-	-
5 December 1986	Bedford, Newnham Street, Auction Centre	Kempston, Westdale Walk, plot	£22,500	-	-

Auction date	Venue	Description	Price	Newspaper references	BLARS references
5 December 1986	Bedford, Newnham Street, Auction Centre	Stevington, 29 Silver Street, cottage	Unsold	-	-
5 December 1986	Bedford, Newnham Street, Auction Centre	Willington, Grange Farm House Bedford Road	£91,000	-	-
6 February 1987	Bedford, Newnham Street, Auction Centre	Wilstead, 8 Dane Lane, semi-detached house	£52,000	BT Property Supplement 29 January 1987 p. 9	-
6 February 1987	Bedford, Newnham Street, Auction Centre	Steppingley, West House Eversholt Road, detached house	£133,000	BT Property Supplement 29 January 1987 p. 9	-
6 February 1987	Bedford, Newnham Street, Auction Centre	Grafham (Cambs), 4 Buckden Road, model farm cottages	Unsold	BC 28 November 1986 p. 31. BT Property Supplement 29 January 1987 p. 9. For improvement	-
6 February 1987	Bedford, Newnham Street, Auction Centre	Bedford, 76 Howbury Street, house with covered way, three car garage	£54,000	BT Property Supplement 29 January 1987 p. 9. For improvement	-

Auction date	Venue	Description	Price	Newspaper references	BLARS references
25 March 1987	On Site	Rushden (Northants), Queen Victoria Hotel	£250,000	-	-
26 March 1987	Bedford, De Parys Hotel	Willington, Grange Farm, site for residential development	£800,000	-	-
10 April 1987	Bedford, Newnham Street, Auction Centre	Harrold, 10 Mansion Lane, cottage	£30,000	-	-
10 April 1987	Bedford, Newnham Street, Auction Centre	Radwell, Cherry Dene, Moor End, cottage	Unsold	-	-
10 April 1987	Bedford, Newnham Street, Auction Centre	Renhold, Hillcrest, Hookhams Lane, plot 1	£83,000	-	-
10 April 1987	Bedford, Newnham Street, Auction Centre	Renhold, Hillcrest, Hookhams Lane, plot 2	£85,000	-	-

Auction date	Venue	Description	Price	Newspaper references	BLARS references
26 November 1987	Baldock, The Goldcrest Hotel	Stotfold, Brook Street, building land, 1.5a	-	BC 23 October 1987 p. 33. Outline consent for residential development	-
11 December 1987	Bedford, Newnham Street, Auction Centre	Cockayne Hatley, building land, 0.33a	-	BC 13 November 1987 p. 28	-
15 April 1988	Bedford, Newnham Street, Auction Centre	Bedford, 62 The Grove, detached house	£125,000	BT 3 March 1988 p. 29. For improvement	-
15 April 1988	Bedford, Newnham Street, Auction Centre	Renhold, 28 Church End, semi-detached house	£60,500	BT 28 January 1988 p. 30; 3 March p. 29. For improvement	-
6 May 1988	Kimbolton School, The Lewis Hall	Kimbolton (Cambs), Moreto, Grass Yard, period cottage	£75,000	BT 15 March 1988 p. 37; 24 March p. 32	-
10 June 1988	Bedford, Newnham Street, Auction Centre	Bedford, 19 Barkers Lane, semi-detached house	£59,000	BT 31 March 1988 p. 42; 28 April p. 34	-
10 June 1988	Bedford, Newnham Street, Auction Centre	Cople, Willington Road, 0.34a	£76,000	BT 7 April 1988 p. 32. Planning permission for detached dwelling and garage	-
10 June 1988	Bedford, Newnham Street, Auction Centre	Bedford, 1 Dynevor Road, detached house, in six flats	£292,000 Joint auction with Farebrothers	BT 2 June 1988 p. 31. Vacant possession	-
10 June 1988	Bedford, Newnham Street, Auction Centre	Bedford, 26 Newnham Street	Joint auction with Farebrothers	BT 28 April 1988 p. 34	-

Auction date	Venue	Description	Price	Newspaper references	BLARS references
16 June 1988	Biggleswade, The Stratton House Hotel	Potton, 4–8 Chapel Street, period property	-	BC 15 April 1988 p. 25; 3 June p. 26	-
16 June 1988	Biggleswade, The Stratton House Hotel	Biggleswade, 128 Hitchin Street	-	BC 15 April 1988 p. 25	-
8 July 1988	Bedford, Newnham Street, Auction Centre	Bedford, 15 Stafford Road	£48,000	BT 19 May 1988 p. 42. For improvement. Vacant possession	-
8 July 1988	Bedford, Newnham Street, Auction Centre	Cople, 10 Grange Lane, cottage	£61,000	BT 19 May 1988 p. 42. For improvement. Vacant possession	-
8 July 1988	Bedford, Newnham Street, Auction Centre	Bedford, 10 Willow Road, detached house	£98,000	BT 9 June 1988 p. 34. For improvement. Vacant possession	-
14 July 1988	-	Hatch, period semi-detached cottage	-	BC 3 June 1988 p. 26	-
-	-	Stotfold, Wrayfield, agricultural land	-	BC 19 August 1988 p. 47	-
-	Bedford, Newnham Street, Auction Centre	Biggleswade, Lawrence Road, semi-detached house	-	BC 9 September 1988 p. 25. BT 29 September 1988 p. 46	-
-	Bedford, Newnham Street, Auction Centre	Dunton, Biggleswade Road, single building plot	-	BC 16 September 1988 p. 25. BT 29 September 1988 p. 46. Outline planning permission	-
14 October 1988	Bedford, Newnham Street, Auction Centre	Kempston, 28 Beatrice Street, house	£44,500	BT 11 August 1988 p. 41; 25 August p. 45. Outside toilet, plans approved for bathroom extension	-

Auction date	Venue	Description	Price	Newspaper references	BLARS references
14 October 1988	Bedford, Newnham Street, Auction Centre	Bedford, adjoining 91 Brackley Road, building site	£83,000	BT 25 August 1988 p. 45. Planning permission for three flats	-
14 October 1988	Bedford, Newnham Street, Auction Centre	Great Barford, Roxford, 71 Addingtons Road, detached house	Unsold	BT 28 July 1988 p. 39; 4 August p. 34. Vacant possession	-
14 October 1988	Bedford, Newnham Street, Auction Centre	Great Barford, 106 Green End Road, farm house	£80,000	BT 25 August 1988 p. 45. For improvement	-
14 October 1988	Bedford, Newnham Street, Auction Centre	Keysoe, Elm Farm, Keysoe Row East, derelict house, 2.2a	£18,000	BT 25 August 1988 p. 45; 29 September p. 46. Vacant possession	-
14 October 1988	Bedford, Newnham Street, Auction Centre	Keysoe, West View Cottage	£29,000	BT 25 August 1988 p. 45. Rental £60 pa	-
14 October 1988	Bedford, Newnham Street, Auction Centre	Sandy, Thorncote Farm, Thorncote Green, house, orchard, paddock, 2.57a	£259,000	BT 25 August 1988 p. 45; 29 September p. 46	-

Auction date	Venue	Description	Price	Newspaper references	BLARS references
2 December 1988	Bedford, Newnham Street, Auction Centre	Wootton, 54 Church Road, detached bungalow	£102,000	BT 20 October 1988 p. 48. Vacant possession	-
2 December 1988	Bedford, Newnham Street, Auction Centre	Bedford, 15 Clarendon Street, terraced house	£45,000	BT 3 November 1988 p. 40. Vacant possession	-
2 December 1988	Bedford, Newnham Street, Auction Centre	Renhold, Top End Farm Cottage, 1 Top End	£104,000	BT 20 October 1988 p. 48	-
2 December 1988	Bedford, Newnham Street, Auction Centre	Renhold, Top End, plot, 0.7a	£113,000	BT 20 October 1988 p. 48	-
8 December 1988	Biggleswade, The Stratton House Hotel	Beeston, near Sandy, building land, 2.06a	-	BT 10 November 1988 p. 45. Outline planning consent for residential development	-
8 December 1988	Biggleswade, The Stratton House Hotel	Sutton, near Sandy, plot, 0.5a	-	BT 10 November 1988 p. 45. Detailed planning consent for three bungalows	-

Works Cited

Archive services

Bedfordshire and Luton Archives and Records Service (BLARS)
CCY 1936–CCY 1952 Bedfordshire County Council Yearbooks
PK Peacock Archive
SFM 3/348–252 Bedfordshire Chamber of Agriculture and Farmers' Club
X660/44–46 Sharnbrook USAAF Depot

Hertfordshire Archives and Local Studies Service
D/Z96/2/26 Bygrave Manor Estate, Baldock

Newspapers

The Bedford and District Circular
The Bedford and Kempston Express
The Bedford Citizen
The Bedford Record
The Bedfordshire Mercury
Bedfordshire on Sunday
The Bedfordshire Standard
The Bedfordshire Times
The Bedfordshire Times and Bedfordshire Standard
The Bedfordshire Times and Citizen
The Bedfordshire Times and Independent
The Biggleswade Chronicle
The Times Digital Archive

Websites

The Airfield Information Exchange http://www.airfieldinformationexchange.org/community/showthread.php?1692-Melchbourne-Park-Sharnbrook-Risely
Bedfordshire and Luton Archives and Records Service http://www.bedfordshire.gov.uk/CommunityAndLiving/ArchivesAndRecordOffice/Community Archives/Southill/TheWhitbreadFamily.aspx
Berrys
http://www.berrybros.com
Bletsoe's
http://www.bletsoe.co.uk
Christie's
http://www.christies.com
The College of Estate Management
http://www.cem.ac.uk/about-us/our-history.aspx

Compass Land and Property Group
http://compasspropertygroup.co.uk/
Cooper Beard Residential Sales
http://www.cooperbeard.co.uk/
Forest of the Marston Vale, Let's Go: Bedfordshire's Promoted Routes & Sites http://www.letsgo.org.uk/walk/BiggleswadeCommon.aspx
Hobbs Parker Group
http://www.hobbsparker.co.uk
The Institute of Sound & Communications Engineers
http://www.isce.org.uk/wp-content/uploads/2012/08/ISCE-How-Things-Began.pdf
The Livestock Auctioneers Association Limited
http://www.laa.co.uk
The Panacea Charitable Trust and Museum
http://panaceatrust.org/
The Royal Institution of Chartered Surveyors
http://www.rics.org/uk/about-rics/who-we-are/history-and-mandate/history/
Southerby's
http://www.sothebys.com

Primary sources

Heritage, C. E., *W. & H. Peacock: Reminiscences of C. E. Heritage*, typescript, author's collection.

Peacock, W. & H., *Instruction Book 1: 1902–December 1904*, author's collection.

Peacock, W. & H., *Instruction Book 4: May 1916–December 1932*, author's collection.

Peacock, W. & H., *Property Auction Book, No. 1: Baldock and Biggleswade, 18 June 1937–15 October 1963*, author's collection.

Williams, John R. A., *Peacocks' Cricket Match (Played at Bromham Park, 27th June 1935), Nota Bene*, typescript, author's collection.

Williams, John R. A., *Staff Dinner 1935: W. & H. Peacocks' Staff in Verse*, typescript, author's collection.

Secondary sources

Allsopp, Anne, 'Farewell to Little America', *Bedfordshire Magazine*, vol. 25, no. 194 (Autumn 1995), pp. 47–50.

Antrobus, Stuart, *John Bull – Bedford's Oldest Jewellery Firm* (2011), pamphlet, Bedford Central Library, Local Studies Collection

Beckett, J. V., 'Landownership and Estate Management' in G. E. Mingay, ed.,*The Agrarian History of England and Wales: Volume 6, 1750–1850* (Cambridge, 1989), pp. 545–640.

Bedford Publishing Company, *Bedford Directory 1901* (Bedford, 1901).

Bedfordshire Publishing Company, *Bedford Directory 1903* (Bedford, 1903).

Bedfordshire Times, *Bedford Amateur Regatta July 17th 1913, Diamond Jubilee 1853–1913 Official Programme* (Bedford, 1913).

Bedfordshire Times Publishing Company, *Bedford Directory 1906* (Bedford, 1906).

Bedfordshire Times Publishing Company, *Bedford Directory 1910* (Bedford, 1910).

Brayley, Martin, *The British Home Front 1939–45* (Oxford, 2005).

Brown, John, *The Un-melting Pot: An English Town and its Immigrants* (London, 1970).

Burnett, John, *A Social History of Housing 1815–1970* (Newton Abbott, 1978).

Carnell, H. A., T. Booth and H. G. Tibbutt, eds, *Eight Thousand Years: A Kempston History* (Kempston, 1966).

Chartres, J. A., 'Country Trades, Crafts and Professions' in G. E. Mingay, ed., *The Agrarian History of The Agrarian History of England and Wales: Volume 6, 1750–1850* (Cambridge, 1989), pp. 416–466.

Coleman, Stephen, *Cranfield* (Bedford, 1986), Bedfordshire Parish Surveys Historic Landscape and Archaeology.

Crossley, Anthony, *Apple Years at Cockayne Hatley (1929–1946): The History of Coxes Orange Pippin Orchards (Copo) at Cockayne Hatley and its Creator Mr Alexander Whitehead* (Cockayne Hatley, 1996).

De-la-Noy, Michael, *Bedford School: A History 1552–2002* (Bedford, 1999).

Elvin, L., *Gab and Gavel: 200 Years of a Family Firm* (Lincoln, 1990).

Fricker, Katherine, Mary McKeown and Diana Toyn, eds, *The Village of Biddenham through the Ages* (Biddenham, 2012).

Godber, Joyce, *History of Bedfordshire, 1066–1888* (Bedford, 1969).

Godber, Joyce, *The Story of Bedford* (Luton, 1978).

Godber, Joyce and Isabel Hutchins, eds, *A Century of Challenge: Bedford High School 1882 to 1982* (Biggleswade, 1982).

Gould, C. and S. Mesplede, *Marketing Art in the British Isles: 1700 to the Present* (Farnham, 2012).

Great Britain, Auctions (Bidding Agreements) Act 1927: George VI, Chapter 12 (1927), http://www.legislation.gov.uk/.

Great Britain, Auctions (Bidding Agreements) Act 1969: Elizabeth II, Chapter 56 (1969), http://www.legislation.gov.uk/.

Great Britain, House of Commons Library, *The Historical Context of Rent Control in the Private Rented Sector* (2013), Standard Note SN/SP/6737, ttp://www.parliament.uk/business/publications/research/briefing-papers/SN06747/the-historical-context-of-rent-control-in-the-private-rented-sector.

HC Deb 27 April 1813 First Ser., vol. 25, cols 1085–7, ProQuest.

HC Deb 3 July 1888 Third Ser., vol. 328, cols 192–3, ProQuest.

Hammond, R. J., *Food and Agriculture in Britain 1939–45: Aspects of Wartime Control* (Oxford, 1954).

Hardy, Thomas, *The Mayor of Casterbridge* (London, 1984).

Hart, Muriel M., *Portrait of Elstow, Bedfordshire* (Bedford, 2000).

Her Majesty's Stationery Office, *Supplement to the London Gazette of Tuesday, 23 May 1972,* no. 45678 (1972), p. 6265, http://www.london-gazette.co.uk/issues/45678/supplements/6255.

Hurste, J., *The Intemperate Auctioneer* (Sussex, 2002).

Jackson, Richard Meredith, *Jackson's Machinery of Justice*, 8th ed. (Cambridge, 1989).

Jones, Arthur, *For the Record Bedford 1945–1974: Land Use and Financial Planning* (Bedford, 1981).

Kelly, E. R., ed., *Post Office Directory of the Counties of Bedford, Huntingdon, Northampton, Berks, Buckingham and Oxford 1877* (London, 1877).

Kelly, E. R., ed., *Post Office Directory of the Counties of Northamptonshire, Huntingdonshire, Bedfordshire, Buckinghamshire, Berkshire and Oxfordshire 1869* (London 1869).

Kelly, S., '"This Dangerous Game": Rousseau, Diaz and the Issues of the Auction in the Marketing of Landscapes' in F. Fowle and R. Thomson, eds, *Soil and Stone: Impressionism, Urbanism and Environment* (Aldershot, 2003), pp. 33–48.

Kelly's Directories Ltd, *Kelly's Directory of Bedfordshire 1936* (London, 1936).

Kelly's Directories Ltd, *Kelly's Directory of Bedfordshire, Huntingdonshire and Northamptonshire 1903* (London, 1903).

Kelly's Directories Ltd, *Kelly's Directory of Bedfordshire, Huntingdonshire and Northamptonshire 1940* (London, 1940).

The Kempston Souvenir Programme to Commemorate the Queen's Silver Jubilee: Flood-lit Tattoo September 23 1977 (Bedford, 1977), pamphlet, Bedford Central Library, Local Studies Collection.

Keverne, Richard, *Tales of Old Inns*, 5th ed. (London, 1952).

Learmount, Brian, *A History of the Auction* (Iver, 1985).

Manton, D. G., *Something Funny happened on My Way to the Rostrum* (Derby, 2001).

Martin, R. W., *Paulmers Market* (Yeovil, 1995).

Members of Bedford Modern School, eds, 'Harry Lionel Peacock', *The Eagle; A Magazine edited by Members of Bedford Modern School*, vol. 28, no. 6 (1952), p. 542.

Members of Bedford Modern School, eds, 'Walter Molesworth Peacock', *The Eagle; A Magazine edited by Members of Bedford Modern School*, vol. 31, no. 2 (Bedford, 1957), p. 145.

Members of Bedford Modern School, eds, 'Obituary of Bernard West', *Eagle News: Old Bedford Modern Club Magazine* (May 2006), p. 92.

Members of Bedford Modern School, eds, 'Obituary of Jan Church', *Eagle News* (May 2007), pp. 201–202.

Members of Bedford School, eds, 'Edward Dudley Molesworth Peacock', *The Ousel*, no. 964 (March 2000), pp. 79–80.

Members of Bedford School, eds, 'Robert Molesworth Peacock', *The Ousel*, vol. 92, no. 931 (March 1989), p. 120.

Mills, Dick and Pat Mills, eds, *Harrold at the Millennium* (Harrold, 2000).

Moore-Colyer, R. J., 'The Landed Gentry of Cardiganshire' in G. H. Jenkins and I. G. Jones, eds, *Cardiganshire County History: Volume 3, Cardiganshire in Modern Times* (Cardiff, 1998), pp. 51–75.

Moore-Colyer, R. J., *The Welsh Cattle Drovers,* 2nd ed. (Ashbourne, 2002).

Newman, David, *The Importance of Milton Ernest: Village History and Heritage Trail* (Milton Ernest, 2006).

Peacock, W. & H., *1901–1951: The Partners and Staff Dine on the Occasion of the Firm's Golden Jubilee* (Bedford, 1951), pamphlet, author's collection.

Peacock, W. & H., *1901–1964* (Bedford, 1964), pamphlet, author's collection.

Peacock, W. & H., *British Road Services Depot, Meadowgate, Bourne, Lincolnshire: Catalogue of 370 Commercial Motor Vehicles, to be Sold at Auction by W. & H. Peacock, Thursday, 26 March 1953*, pamphlet, author's collection.

Peacock, W. & H., *Catalogue of 370 Commercial Motor Vehicles to be Sold at Auction by W. & H. Peacock Thursday, 26th March 1953* (1953), pamphlet, author's collection.

Peacock, W. & H., *An Illustrated Property Register and Housefinder's Guide of the Residential Town of Bedford, November 1937* (Bedford, 1937), pamphlet, author's collection.

Peacock, W. & H., *An Illustrated Property Register and Housefinder's Guide of the Residential Town of Bedford, June 1938* (Bedford, 1938), pamphlet, author's collection.

Peacock, W. & H., Locke & England and Ambrose, *A Review* (2001), pamphlet, Bedford Central Library, Local Studies Collection.

Peacock, W. & H., Merry and Swaffield, *Catalogue of Surplus Plant Equipment and Stores: Wednesday 14th March 1951* (1951), pamphlet, author's collection.

Peacock, W. & H., Western & Co., *Staff Dinner to Celebrate Mr Robert's Golden Jubilee with the Firm 1921–1971, 27 September 1971* (Bedford, 1971), pamphlet, author's collection.

Pennell, Sara, 'All but the Kitchen Sink: Household Sales and the Circulation of Second-hand Goods in Early Modern England' in J. Stobart and I. Van Damme, eds, *Modernity*

and the Second Hand Trade: European Consumption, Cultures and Practices, 1700–1900 (Basingstoke, 2010), pp. 37–56.
Pennington, B., *The Fall of the Hammer: Sixty Years in Cattle Markets and the History of Wright-Manley from 1860* (Hargrave, 2002).
Perren, Richard, 'The Marketing of Agricultural Products: Farm Gate to Retail Store' in E. J. T. Collins, ed., *The Agrarian History of England and Wales: Volume 7, 1850–1914* (Cambridge, 2000).
Risby, Stephen, *Prisoners of War in Bedfordshire* (Stroud, 2011).
Royal Air Force, *Royal Air Force Henlow at 90: The First Ninety Years 1917–2007*, 6th ed. (Henlow, 2007).
Spencer, R., *Drama at the Sale* (Retford, n.d.).
Stafford and Rogers, *Stafford and Rogers 1834–1951* (Bedford, 1951), pamphlet, Bedford Central Library, Local Studies Collection.
Stanton, Judy and Lilian Wildman, eds, *Thurleigh through the Years* (Sandy, n.d.).
Stobart, Jon and R. McArthur 'Going for a Song? Country House Sales in Georgian England' in J. Stobart and I. Van Damme, eds, *Modernity and the Second Hand Trade: European Consumption, Cultures and Practices, 1700–1900* (Basingstoke, 2010), pp. 175–195.
The Surveyors 21 Club, *The Golden Jubilee Book for the Members of the Surveyors 1921 Club 1971* (Bedford, 1971), author's collection.
Tibbutt, H. G., 'Going to Table Bay', *Bedfordshire Magazine*, vol. 14, no. 109 (Summer, 1974), pp. 189–192.
Turvey Appraisal Committee, *Turvey Now: The 1980s and Beyond* (Turvey, 1981).
Vowles, Gordon, ed., *Bernard West's Bedfordshire: a Selection of his Sketch-books from the Bedfordshire Magazine 1947–98* (Dunstable, 2007).
Walker, Victoria, *Old Kempston* (Ochiltree, 2001).
Whetham, Edith H., 'The Agriculture Act, 1920 and its repeal – the "Great Betrayal"', *British Agricultural History Review*, vol. 22 (1974), pp. 36–49.
Wildman, Richard, *Bedford* (Stroud, 2001), Britain in Old Photographs.
Wildman, Richard, *Bedford: A Pictorial History* (Chichester, 1991).
Wildman, Richard, 'Laxton of Bedford: the Family and the Firm', *Bedfordshire Magazine*, vol. 23, no. 182 (Autumn, 1992), pp. 244–247.
Wildman, Richard and A. Crawley, *Bedford Then & Now* (Stroud, 2011).
Wilson, Eunice, 'Cranfield Airfield', *Bedfordshire County Life Magazine*, Issue 5 (Summer, 1999), pp. 35–43.
Wilson Peacock, *A New Name on the High Street* (1988), pamphlet, author's collection.
Wilson Peacock, *Mr Dudley's 65th Birthday Party* (Bedford, 1994), pamphlet, author's collection.
Wood, John, *Cardington and Eastcotts* (Bedford, 1985), Bedfordshire Parish Surveys Historic Landscape and Archaeology.
Wood, John, *Kempston* (Bedford, 1984), Bedfordshire Parish Surveys Historic Landscape and Archaeology.

Index of Personal Names

A reference may occur more than once on a page.
n after arabic numerals refers to a footnote on that page.

Abbott, Mr 143
Abrahams, Mr 118
Adams, W. H. 235
Addington, Frederick 132
Ainsworth, Marjory 101
Alderton, L. R. 213
Aley, Charles 183, 184
Allen, F. 242; G. P. 245; H. S. 325; J. J. 197; Mr 263, 273; Rev. 118; W. H. 13n.17; W. T. 178
Alley, Jack 44
Allsworth, Mr 221
Ames, R. S. 246
Anderson, Mr 304
Anthony, J. L. 128
Appleby, E. M. 246
Appleton, W. A. 206
Armstrong, Chris 60
Arnold, Richard 21, 30, 32, 33, 64, 99–100, 110
Ashley, Mr 303
Ashpole, C. 243; Frederick 132; Mr 140, 182, 226; Mrs 182; William 132
Ashton, A. John 124
Ashwell, A. L. L. 211, 212; E. H. 256; S. J. 311
Asplin, Mr 239
Atkin, W. 177
Atkins, Kitty 242
Atkinson, Mr 223
Aubrey, Mr 130, 140; Mrs 130; W. B. 206, 207
Aves, Mr 305
Ayers, David 54
Aylott, M. 241
Ayray, Leonard 3
Ayre, Mr 223
Ayres, J. W. 165; Thomas George 313

Bailey, E. T. 65; Frederick Lambert 22; Mr 131, 223
Baker, 121; F. 291; Mark 60, 111; Samuel 2
Baldrey, Elizabeth 214; F. G. 133; Mrs 143
Baldwin, W. G. 210
Ball, Allan 215; C. G. 316; John 173, 174; L. M. M. 355
Baltrope, Mable 111
Bance, J. 264
Bancroft, Mrs 140
Banes, Claude 204
Banks, Mrs 138
Barber, Mrs 127
Barfoot, H. 123
Barford, Mrs 182
Barker, A. W. 220; Alfred 220; Amos 122; H. 178; P. 274
Barnard, T. H. 117; Talbot 43n.3
Barnes, Charles 187; F. 274; Mrs 138, 187
Barnett, Mrs 155
Barratt, Charles 136
Bartlett, Mr 145
Bass, Mrs 273; R. 167
Baston, Albert 137
Bates, Claude 210; W. H. 228
Battle, Mr 119, 222
Beadle, A. M. 304
Beal, Frank 128
Beard, R. 157; Russell 31; S. 185
Beardsmore, Joan *see* Westgarth, Joan
Beaumont, W. G. 173
Beck, Cecil 124; T. T. 225; W.W. 126
Beckford, William 2
Beckwith, William 161
Bedford, Duchess of 19n.63; Duke of 27n.1, 228
Beeching, Emily 172
Bell, Miss 124; R. W. 15
Bellman, F. 220
Bennett, F. J. 385, 392; J. 123; Percy 180; W. 196
Benson, B. 168
Berrill, Mrs 138
Berrington, F. 177, 245
Berry, Edward 6; John 6
Berwick, A. 133
Best, Mr 246
Betts, John 224; Miriam 224; Miss 124
Bick, Mr 254
Bilcock, Mrs 232
Billing, John 131
Billington, Edward 196; Mr 222
Bindler, Mr 253
Binyon, Mrs 239
Bird, J. F. 155; Mr 220; Mrs 231
Bishop, N. A. 274
Bithrey, Mr 139
Black, Derek 56, 64
Blackwell, Mr 226
Blake, Florence Mary 215
Blanc, Louis Gerald 146
Bland, E. 209
Bleasdale, T. 213
Bletsoe, Christopher H. 24, 30
Block, Mr 222
Blott, R. 128
Blue, Mrs 127
Blunt, Mr 149
Bodsworth, F. C. 247
Bolt, Mr 236; Mrs 236

Bonaparte, Napoleon 2
Bone, A. J. 203, 316; James 203; Mr 119
Bonham, Charles 2
Bonnett, Mr 254
Boston, A. H. 165; A. R. 326
Bosworth, Edward 231, 232
Boundes, Mr 279
Bowers, John Francis 6; Mrs 280
Bowie, Mrs 232
Bowler, Mr 145
Bowley, H. F. 316
Bowman, H. W. 142
Bowrill, Mr 240
Bowyer, A. 169; A. J. 320; Mr 125
Boyle, Frank 170
Boyles, Mr 284
Bradley, Mr 220
Bradshaw, A. 139
Brady, F. E. 324
Brandon, E. 155; Mrs 258
Bray, Ann 127
Breed, H. 195; W. 246
Breeds, D. 243
Brendling, Mr 223
Brett, C. R. 324
Brice, Joe 185
Bridgeman, A. G. 173
Bridger, Mrs 212
Brigham, Mr 273
Brightman, Mr 220
Brittain, Mrs 239
Brittin, Mrs 123
Broadella, Mrs 272
Brocklehurst, W. S. 301
Brookbanks, A. D. 335; C. D. 335; G. 62
Brookes, Mr 190
Brooks, Irene 101; Jim 23, 39, 92, 94; M. D. 213
Broom, G. 225
Brouch, W. 177
Broughton, Mr 220; Titch 58, 91
Brown, B. 273; D. J. 287; E. C. 355; Edward 171; Ernest 181; F. J. 173; G. S. 397; J. 178; J. D. 205; J. V. 396; Keith 25, 82–3, 88n.17; Mr 222; Mrs 304
Brunt, R. 156
Bruty, I. 158
Bryant, A. 208; Ernie 93; H. 306; Mrs 304
Buchanan, Mr 273
Buck, Emma 144; Walter Horace 161
Buckland, Thomas 6
Buckle, R. G. 341
Budd, Francis John 66n.3
Budge, *Rev.* H. S. 117
Bull, Emma 174; John 17n.46; Raymond 59
Bullock, Mr 220
Burbage, G. 155
Burgess, J. W. 186; Joseph 235
Burley, T. 242
Burr, W. 207
Burraway, George 131; H. 160; Mr 139
Burridge, A. 242; *Alderman* H. 12n.9; Mrs 157; T. 231
Burt, Henry 90n.23; Mrs 117
Bushby, F. W. 185
Butcher, C. 180; F. 187
Butler, R. F. 356
Bygrave, B. 174
Bygraves, A. F. 368, 369; H. G. 368, 369
Bywater, V. 364

Cambers, A. 177; Mr 231
Campouser, Jean 83
Cantwell, Mr 126
Capon, R. L. 360
Carlton, J. F. 273
Carpenter, T. H. 202; T. S. 123
Carr, Frederick 147
Carrington, W. 242
Carroll, W. G. 174
Carter, C. 155, 162; Elias 162; Mr 118, 202; Mrs 104
Cartwright, E. H. 161
Castle, A. 304; H. 304
Catlin, Douglas 100
Cave, Joseph 178
Caves, E. 246; John 132
Chambers, Mr 223, 288; R. 258
Chandler, S. 178
Chapman, G. B. 274; H. 241; Mrs 213
Cheney, F. 167
Chew, H. 234; Mr 225
Chibnall, A. B. 126
Childs, Clive 25, 39
Christie, James 2
Church, 62; J. 123; Jan 30, 32, 62, 62n.7, 101; T. 175
Circuit, Sylvia 44
Clarabut, A. 171, 172; A. E. 171; Cecil 42, 42n.2, 52
Clark, A. C. 43n.4; Dr 131; E. 166; F. 158; Herbert 392; J. 156; John 394; Thomas 151; W. 134, 137; William 18
Clarke, Bill 92, 94, 101, 104; H. 129; William 203
Clayson, E. 229, 326, 327; Edgar 69, 69n.22, 320, 321, 322, 324
Clayton, G. 258
Clements, W. G. 165
Clifton, David W. xin.1, xiii; H. 174; Mr 222
Clynes, S. 272
Cockings, C. 155, 162; Mr 270, 279
Colbeck, Col. 157
Cole, Alfred 152; H. C. 297; Kezia 189; W. F. 208
Coleclough, Mr 291
Coleman, Miss 155; S. 211, 258
Coles, Janice 54; Mr 226; T. 243
Colgrave, A. S. 178
Collie, Susan 16
Collins, Ann 54; Mrs 304
Compton, *Major Lord* Alwyne 11n.7, 12
Constant, E. 134; S. 127
Cony, A. J. 324

Cook, Christopher 2; G. W. 207; George 118; Mr 220, 221; W. 243
Cookson, W. C. 124
Cooper, George 105n.1; H. 116; John 152; Mr 140: Nathan 323; P. 202; T. Sidney 88n.17
Cope, Arthur C. 257; G. A. 344; Mr 118; P. D. 399
Corby, Mrs 291
Course, C. 160; E. 161
Covington, J. 306
Cowland, E. A. 209
Cowper, Earl 12n.10, 119; Lady 12n.10
Cox, D. 242; George 146, 151; Henry 225; Mr 134; Mrs 144, 165; N. 165; T. 162; Walter 164
Craig, Ronald 19, 23, 38–9, 92, 93–4
Cranfield, Mrs 67, 119
Crawley, E. 204; H. G. 214
Crisp, Walter 248
Critchlow, Mr 223
Croft, E. 144; Mr 143; Samuel 230
Croot, Mr 215
Crozier, Brian C. 30, 31, 101
Cullip, Charles 143
Curtis, F. 133, 183; H. 67; Mr 220; S. 134; W. 134
Curtois, Arthur 137
Cuvelier, V. C. M. 368, 369

Dale, C. 185
Dalrymple, Mr 226
Damon, Reginald 25, 92, 101
Daniels, E. 129
Darlow, J. L. 235
Darnell, Frederick 182
Davey, Gertrude 354
Davies, James 123; O. 242; T. E. 157
Davill, Mrs 137
Davis, John 215; Mr 126; Mrs 310
Davison, Frank 180, 181, 182; Miss 180; Vic 36n.40
Daws, L. 179
Day, James 69n.22, 152; John 39; Mr 209; O. J. 152
De Grey, 69n.22
Dean, H. J. 360; Mrs 219
Deane, Mr 145
Debenham, Miss 155
Dennahy, Mrs 221
Dent, G. H. 195
Denton, Mr 221; Mrs 173; S. 168
Deveraux, W. 258
Dewer, Mrs 233
Dewick, Mrs 211
Dewsbury, Eunice 385
Dickinson, J. 185
Dilley, Horace S. xiii, 63–4, 88n.17; S. 229
Dixon, Miss 121
Dodwell, R. E. C. 219
Dolby, C. E. 16
Douglas, Mrs 288
Downing, Mr 254
Drage, J. 229; Mrs 155
Draper, Jock 176; John 176; Mr 280
Drover, F. J. 294
Duckworth, C. W. 171
Dudley, Mrs 142, 143, 231
Dulley, Mrs 165
Dunford, Mr 279
Dunkley, Mrs 157
Dunnett, Mrs 164
Dunstall, W. 288
Dutton, S. V. 274
Dyer, Mr 273

Eastwell, A. 177
Eaton, Harry 22; W. 129
Ebden, Frank 259
Eden, G. H. 212; T. G. 178
Edmonds, C. R. 218
Edwards, E. J. 239; Emily 236; L. A. 368, 369; Louisa 131; Louisa Caroline 11n.1; M. J. 129; Mrs 129
Eggington, A. H. 234
Elliman, K. 208
Ellis, Mr 131
Elms, S. A. I. 232
Elsley, Nicholas 30
Endersby, F. 209; G. 355
Etches, 7
Eugster, Lt Col. Oscar 43n.3
Evans, Emily 248
Eve, John Richard 109n.5
Exton, L. A. 300

Facey, S. W. 140
Fairey, J. 279, 280
Fairmaner, Mr 257
Farrell, Mr 222
Farrer, C. 173; J. 168; Josiah 168; S. J. 204
Faulkner, F. J. 209; G. 209
Favell, Mrs 132
Fearnley, Ian 60, 83
Felce, James Frederick 22
Fensome, John 187
Fenton, P. L. 159
Field, A. E. 178; C. 243; N. 242
Filsell, John 210
Finch-Hatton, Edward 3
Firbank, J. 123
Fisher, E. 209; L. O. 304; W. H. 191, 192
Fitt, Arthur 81
Fitzpatrick, Misses 157
Fletcher, Keith 86
Flood, Fanny 161
Flute, Miss 279
Folkes, Mr 139
Foll, Arthur Wallace 108, 108n.1
Footer, R. T. 137
Ford, A. 231
Forward, N. P. 256
Foster, Norman B. 98, 98n.5, 100, 108, 108n.1; Mr 185; Mrs 233

Fowler, Mrs Harry *see* Peacock, Susan
Francklin, 68n.20; George 68n.20; J. 227
Frank, Mr 117
Franklin, Olive 82; W. 258
Franks, Joseph 117
Freeman, E. 241
French Somerville, Mrs 124
Frossell, C. E. 131; James 160
Frost, Mrs 219; S. 273
Fry, J. 211, 258
Fuller, Mr 146; Mrs 122
Furr, S. W. 174

Gadsden, Joseph 152
Gains, Mr 222
Gammans, S. 196
Gammons, A. 238
Gardner, Mr 226
Garlick, Edward 144; Mr 126
Garner, J. 149, 150
Garratt, Samuel 156
Garrett, Mr 232
Gates, Mr 266
Gaton, H. G. 211
Gazeley, Mrs 137
Gee, Marion Alice 348
Geeves, Ernest E. 108, 108n.1
Gentle, Ernest 323
Gerrard, Mrs 196
Gibbons, Mrs 253
Gibbs, William C. 163
Gilbert, Charles 228; John 132
Gill, W. 159; Walter 181
Gillett, Walter 178
Gilliat, Mrs 168
Glasspole, B. M. 302
Glidewell, Mr 149
Gobey, M. 385; R. 385
Godber, R. J. 328
Goddard, *Sir* Holland 300
Godfrey, H. 324
Godwin, W. A. 134
Goff, Mrs 132
Golding, F. 142
Good, Stuart 60
Goodchild, Mrs 304
Gooding, George 133
Goodwin, S. E. 176; W. 135, 136, 173
Goswell, Mr 178
Grainger, Mr 226
Grant, W. W. 157
Gray, F. 241; L. 260; Mrs 239
Grayling, Mr 134
Green, B. 127; D. W. 235; E. 197; F. 130; F.A. 125; H. H. 125; H. M. 125; Mrs Thomas John 43n.3; W. 117; W. S. 310
Gregson, Mrs 256
Griffin, Mr 134
Grimwood, Mr 222
Groom, Mr 145
Gurney, C. 307, 308; John 134; Mr 140; T. C. 307, 308

Haddow, H. V. 131
Hailey, James 221
Haines, *Captain* Herbert 318
Hales, W. 264
Hall, A. E. F. 318; A. H. 137; Ruth 373
Halsey, A. 183
Hamley, John 159
Hanbury, P. K. C. 330
Handley, Mr 279
Hands, Thomas 180
Handscombe, C. W. 172; G. 235
Handsley, Mr 223
Harbinson, Mr 226
Harding, Robert L. 30
Hardwick, A. 164; Ernest 81; Mr 149
Hardy, Thomas 5
Hare, Mrs 304
Harkins, Mr 222
Harlow, C. C. 136; Mrs 134; S. 168; W. 239
Harper, Charles 133; John 176
Harpin, G. 162
Harpur, *Sir* William 15n. 27
Harrington, E. 128
Harris, E. W. 345; James 160; R. 306
Harrison, Geoffrey 55, 82; George 105; Mr 121; S. H. 214
Hart, Albert 120; E. G. 181; Mr 235; Mrs 144, 212, 235
Harter, *Rev.* George Gardner 43n.3
Hartin, C. 242
Hartley, Mr 255
Hartop, 48; Benjamin 282; William 282
Hartridge, F. L. 213
Hatton, *Sir* Christopher 3
Hawkes, M. 244
Hawkins, A. H. 181; G. H. 241; Leslie 208
Hay, Mrs 240
Hayden, Mrs 231
Haylock, Mr 304
Haynes, Thomas 168
Hayward, C. 327
Hazel, Mrs 266
Hazell, Mr 254
Headlam, S. G. 243
Hedley, Miss 247
Hendricks, C. F. A. 244
Henson, David 92; George 21, 92
Hereford, E. G. 382
Heritage, C. E. 31, 35, 70
Hermitage, A. 278
Hermon, J. 137
Herniman, R. 124
Hickford, C. 294
Higgins, Charles 16n. 34; T. W. 209
Hill, D. W. 273; J. 213; Rowland 278
Hillier, J. J. H. 273; S. G. 35n.31
Hillson, Mr 233
Hillyer, Mary 147
Hilton, F. J. C. 343; Miss 279
Hinchley, J. W. 120
Hine, Thomas 43n.3
Hipwell, T. C. 243; W. 243

Hitchens, E. 154
Hoare, *Major* A. C. 301
Hobbs, A. W. 142; E. 142; H. C. 136
Hockliffe, F. R. 27, 27n.3
Hodge, D. 152; J. C. 125
Hollands, Richard 30, 106–7
Holley, F. 227
Holliers, A. R. 274
Holly, A. 238
Holman, Mr 221
Holmes, C. J. 398; Mark 58
Holt, E. 228
Hood, Mrs 121
Hoole, Mr 220
Hooley, Paul 90n.23
Hope, R. 171
Hopkins, A. J. 219
Hopkinson, Mrs 247
Horler, Christopher J. xiii, 63, 64, 88n.17, 110
Horn, G. 128; Mr 145
Horner, W. 242
Horrocks, H. 219
Howard, Brian 102; C. A. E. C. 34, 34n.29, 102; Frederick 21n.6; H. E. 232; James 21n.6; John 21n.6; Peter 361; T. 232
Howe, G. S. 280; Mrs 165
Huckle, H. 173; Mrs 132
Hudson, Mr 224
Hughes, Mr 212; R. S. 236
Hulatt, George 165; H. 211; J. 263
Hullatt, I 164; J. 129; Miss 231
Humphreys, Mr 221
Humphries-Read, A. 177
Humphriss, A. 171
Hunt, Miss 145; Mr 223
Hussey, William 7
Hyde, F. 220; Mr 178; V. 158

Ibbett, Mr 235
Ibbott, Mr 154
Infield, Mr 118
Ingersoll, Elizabeth 201
Ingle, R. 228
Ingman, J. 273
Ingram, John 231
Inskip, F. 128
Ives, I. A. 340; Mrs 240; T. A. 178
Ivett, Mr 118
Izzard, Mr 126; Mrs 304

Jackson, Mr 220; Mrs 304
Jacquest, Ernest 100
James, F. A. 219; Mrs 161
Jardine, H. 304
Jarvis, Mr 155
Jeakings, Robert 252
Jeeves, M. 210
Jefferies, E. 239
Jeffery, Frank A. xiii, xiv, 25, 42, 44, 52, 54–5, 71, 82, 101, 106, 110; H. A. 248.
Jeffrey, H. T. 175
Jenkins, C. D. 231
Johnson, Captain 124; Frank 183; Mr 117; Mrs 129
Jones, A. 242; Albert 154; E. H. 129; George 2; Mr 150, 154, 255, 303; Mrs 146; W. C. 194
Jordan, Mr 279; S. 258
Joyce, A. 173; C. 233; Mrs 220
Judd, Mr 119
Juffs, F. 120; Mr 297; W. A. 158

Kaye, C. W. 16
Keaney, Mr 224
Keath, A. A. J. 273
Keech, H. 274; P. 231
Keep, T. H. 132
Kemp, F. G. 289
Kempster, Mrs 230
Kennedy, Mr 279
Kent, A. G. 138
Kidman, G. C. 391
Kidson, Mrs 239
Kilby, E. 235
Kilpin, Mr 303
Kilroy, C. R. 31
King, E. A. 122; F. 119; J. H. 177; James 124; W. 118
Kingsbury, Mr 209
Kingston, Mrs 137
Kinsey, A. E. 205
Kirbyshire, Mr 134
Kitchener, Lord 12; Mrs 116
Knell, J. 263
Kneller, Mrs Charles 111
Knight, Charles 211; J. 131; Mrs 280
Knights, Jonathan M. xin.1, xiii, 24, 52, 57, 60, 94, 110
Knowles, C. S. 196; Charles Sidney 61, 61n.1

Lack, C. 170
Lamb, G. C. 144
Lambert, Mr 223
Lang, J. G. 162
Langley, George E. 184
Larman, Miss 137
Laughton, Mrs 134
Lawder, Commander 227
Lawford, Mrs 302
Lawrence, C. 208; Mrs 179, 268, 273
Lawson, G. 243
Laxton, Thomas 48n.15
Layton Lund, Mrs 155
Lazenby, Evelyn xiii; Joseph xiii; Keith *passim*; xi, xiii–xiv; 43, 52, 110
Le Fevre, J. H. 229
Leach, E. 129
Lee, C. A. 219; F. R. 88n.17; Mr 140
Leech, Graeme 83
Lenton, J. W. 200; S. 200
Letts, B. 122; J. T. 121; Sydney 161
Lewis, G. E. 266
Lilley, Cyril P. 29
Limmer, A. E. 146
Lincoln, E. 233

Linger, A. 241; W. 182
Linnell, *Rev.* J. E. 123
Litchfield, B. 137; C. 137; E. 137; Edgar 127; H. W. 123
Little, Mr 119; Mrs 243
Livingstone, Dorothy 241
Locke, F. 183
Loft, Mr 145; William 132
Longland, A. 242; M. 177
Longley, G. 229
Longstaff, 243
Lovell, A. H. 197; Mr 139, 149
Low, Mrs 120
Lowe, A. A. 373; C. R. 156
Lowell, W. 173
Loxley, Mr 118
Ludwick, Mr 230
Lugsden, H. 241
Luke, Lord 339; *Sir* Samuel 68n.16
Lumbers, Harry 184
Lumbis, Mr 206
Lumley, Mr 226
Lyon, Mrs 138
Lyons, Mr 215

Mabbitt, Miss 127
Macdonald, Mr 223
MacFarlane, E. 243
Mack, Mr 221
Mackness, C. W. 231; Mr 144
Maclean, E. 83
Mager, H. A. 365, 373
Magnus, Misses 123
Mallabar, Mrs 233
Mallows, G. E. 176n.1
Manchester, Duke of 70, 378
Manders, Mrs 255
Manley, 7
Mann, E. 242; Elizabeth 153; Frederick 157
Manning, James 218
Mansfield, W. 241
Manson, Terrance 62
Manton, Geoffrey 4
Mardlin, G. W. 182
Markham, Mr 149
Marlow, T. 297
Marries, Mr 281
Marriott, Mr 235
Marsden, J. 134
Marsh, G. 121
Marshall, Mr 231; Mrs 140; T. 129
Martin, F. 122; Mr 223; Mrs 133
Mason, Kate 235; Mr 154
Matthews, A. E. 385; C. E. 236; J. 161; W. M. 394
Mattin, Mrs 167
Mawby, Mr 118
Maxey, J. 275
Mayes, George 117, 118, 119; Mr 130, 140, 235
Mayle, Frank 214
Maynard, F. D. 341; T. J. 341
McConnell, Alexander 30n.19
McLeod, Mr 224
McPherson, J. R. H. 55
Mellor, R. V. 294
Merry, Arthur W. 11n.4; Jack 97, 100
Merryweather, Joy 101; Joyce 83
Millard, A. 173, 174; G. J. 250; J. 129
Miller, E. J. 179; Elizabeth 44, 83; J. 156; Mr 134
Millman, Geoffrey 31, 31n.23
Mills, Mr 227; W. 129
Milne, Lilian 242
Mitchell, C. 183; E. M. 248; William 170
Mitton, Mrs 280
Mobbs, A. 129; G. 129
Mole, Mr 232; Mrs 263
Monk, Fred 220
Moore, Charles 131; Mrs 253; Thomas 132; V. 58
Moors, Percy 132
Mordaunt, 16n.34
Moreton, Peter W. 30, 101
Morris, Miss 231
Mossman, A. G. 287
Mossop, Mr 220
Moulden, Joseph 139
Moule, C. 244, 245
Munday, E. 159; H. A. 236; Mr 150
Munton, Mr 255
Murdock, Samuel 184
Murfitt, R. 243
Musgrove, 121
Mutton, Thomas 162
Myers, A. 173; F. 185

Nash, Dr Gifford 35n.35, 147
Neale, Mr 145
Neaves, F. E. 373, 374
Needham, Mr 231
Newell, G. C. 117; R. C. 263, 264; T. 264
Newland, Mrs 160
Newman, F. B. 182; W. J. 279
Newnham, E. 235
Newsome, Mr 223
Newton, G. E. 310
Nicholls, William 119, 230
Nichols, P. F. 152
Nicholson, John 123, 124
Nickerson, J. 241
Nixon, Alfred 186; Mr 118
Noble, F. 272; Mr 145, 150
Norcott, Mrs 71
Norman, Mr 143, 270
Northern, Mr 280

Odell, A. 243; F. 211; H. 155; M. 211; M. F. 258; Mr 139; W. C. 258
Oliver, F. H. 230
Onan, George 159
Openshaw, J. T. 230
Ormes, W. 243
Orpin, Charles 215; F. P. 129
Osborn, Eliza 133; Mr 238; S. 181
Osborne, 25n.12; S. H. 229

Owen, Mr 150
Owens, Mr 226

Padillo, Mr 227
Page, Mr 150; Sarah 170
Palgrave Page, S. 139
Palmer, F. J. 160; William Gifford 6
Panter, F. 243; J. 253; J. J. 253; Miss 145; Mrs 253; W. S. 164
Parish, W. E. 30n.20
Park, Colin 21
Parker, Ernest 164; Mr 196; Thomas 163; W. 164
Parkin, Maurice John 188
Parris, Mr 221
Parrott, E. 169; George 131; Herbert J. xiii, 18, 23, 94, 104, Plate 9
Parton, Mrs 266
Pask, L. 246
Pass, Miss 128
Pateman, George 346; S. 378
Payne, Alfred 284; G. 169; Mr 121, 221
Peacock, Charles Nassau 12; Clair xiii, 26, 74, Plate 11; Dudley *see* Peacock, Edward Dudley Molesworth; E. J. 168; Edward Dudley Molesworth xi, xiii, xiii, 17, 21, 26, 29, 52, 54, 55, 58n.2, 59, 60, 70, 71, 82, 94, 95, 109, Plate 11; F. 168; Francis G. M. xii, 23, 39, 59, 60, 110; Francis J. 27; H. S. 318; Harriet Sarah Plate 11; Harry see Peacock, Henry Lionel; Henry John 11, 11n.1, 12n.9, 27n.1, 28, 176n.1; Henry Lionel xii, xiii, xiv, 18, 19, 19n.58, 19n.61, 22, 22n.9, 23, 27–9, 27n.5, 29n.14, 32–3, 35–6, 38–9, 42, 66, 70–1, 94, 100, 108–9, Plate 9; John Smith 11; Margaret Isobel Plate 11; Miss 283; Moyra Clair Plate 11; Robert Molesworth xii, xiii, xiii, xiv, 12n.11, 19, 22, 26, 28, 29–30, 32, 39, 52, 58, 58n.2, 59, 61–2, 70, 71, 73, 92, 93, 94–5, 97, 100–1, 109, Plate 9, Plate 11; Susan xii, xiii, 26, 58n.2, 110; Walter Molesworth xii, xiii, 11–13, 17, 18, 19, 19n.58, 19n.61, 20, 21n.5, 27–9, 28n.12, 28n.13, 29n.16, 31, 63, 65–6, 71, 88n.17, 89, 90n.23, 94, 108–9, Plate 9, Plate 11
Pearce, Mrs 233
Pearcey, Frank 209
Peck, W. L. 121
Peel, Elaine 83
Peet, John 118; M. T. 339; Mr 118
Pepper, E. 231; F. 158; R. 231
Pepys, Samuel 1
Perkins, T. 176
Perks, Christopher J. 30; H. E. 108, 108n.1; L. H. E. 109, 109n.5
Perry, E. A. 177
Peters, Arthur 131
Petit, 121
Pettit, F. 162; H. 139; Mr 215
Phillips, Henry 2; Peggy 393
Phillpotts, J. Surtees 16
Philpott, J. T. 187
Phipps, C. W. 220
Phypers, Charles 136
Picking, W. H. 233
Piggott, Martin 55; Mrs 137
Pike, B. A. 298
Pilsbury, Mr 149
Pinfold, W. A. 245
Pitts, Mrs 166
Platt, Jas. E. 84
Plester, George 316
Plowman, F. M. A. 214
Plum, A. 244
Plumb, Mr 223; *Capt.* Stanley 52
Pointer, Mr 229
Pollard, Mr 127
Pollock, Hugh 381
Pontin, J. W. 265
Poole, Thomas 117
Pope, George 136; James 134, 138, 144
Porter, Alan B. xin.1, xiii, 25, 62–4, 71; Brian S. xiii, 25, 63–4, 71, 92, 110
Potter, J. 242
Potton, D. 134; G. 134
Potts, Mrs 141, 297
Prentice, Walter 189
Price, Caroline 169
Prigmore, G. 174
Prince Evans, J. E. 121
Probert, Mr 254
Proctor, Mr 224
Prole, Alan 159; Mrs 188
Pruden, D. 93; J. 128
Pullen, Mrs 128
Purser, Mr 195, 246
Pym, Claude 143

Quenby, H. 84, 145; Messrs 142; Thomas 152; W. 84, 145

Raban, Mrs 163
Rabbitt, Mrs 235
Randall, *Lady* E. 35; F. J. 397; *Captain* H. 136; H. J. 247; *Major* H. J. 247
Ratcliffe, Mr 280
Rawlins, A. A. 381; H. 176
Ray, F. 67
Rayment, Herbert J. 37
Raynor, C. 123
Read, J. 263
Readman, J. T. 292
Redman, Caleb 131; J. S. 209; John 120
Reeve, Frederick 20, 20n.2; J. F. 67
Reid, Mr 150
Revel, W. 306
Reynolds, *Sir* Joshua 2; Mr 139
Rhodes, Mrs 256
Richards, C. E. 242; Mr 58; R. 210; S. E. 210
Richardson, A. L. 331; *Sir* Albert Edward 109, 109n.6; George 196; M. A. 245
Riddy, Walter George 42
Riseley, Mr 141
Risely, J. 155

Roan, T. 164
Roast, C. 263
Roberts, Alfred 125; Frances 83; Lord 12; Messrs 339; Mrs 127; W. 241
Robinson, 121; Arthur 133; E. 258; George T. F. xiii, xiv, 12n.11, 18, 35, 42, 44–5, 52, 71, 82, 92, 94, 106, Plate 9; James Charles Evitt 108, 108n.1; Mr 143, 149, 226; Mrs 54; P. G. 173
Rogers, John 11n.4; Rachel 136; Samuel 176
Rollins, E. D. 352, 353, 354
Rollinson, Mr 223
Rollison, Mrs 81
Rook, Graham 93
Root, A. 241
Rootham, J. 240
Rose, F. 164; Mr 281
Rowe, Mrs 232
Rowell, Simon 60
Rowlerson, Antony 55, 82–3, 88n.17
Rowley, I. 393; William 184
Rowsell, Mrs 116
Royle, *Sir* George 278
Rudd, W. 155
Ruffhead, George 186
Rumsey, M. L. 202
Rust, Mrs 141

Sadler, Arthur Drake 171; D. 218
Sale, D. M. 255, 308; Wm. 357
Sallows, Carol 83
Salsbury, Mrs 121
Salt, Mr 222
Salvesen, Ronald 30
Sanders, C. 281; W. 144
Saunders, B. 284; Mrs 245; T. H. 257
Saunderson, Sarah 210, 211
Savage, A. W. 180; Mr 134; W. S. 202
Sawford, Mrs 143
Scannell, G. C. 358
Schwier, C. E. 313
Scott, F. 173; John I. 100; Mr 134, 140; William 162
Scrivener, Mrs 121
Sealey, Mr 222
Seamarks, H. 158; J. 169
Seward, Charles 393
Sewell, Thomas T. 128
Seymour, Sidney Jack 381
Sharman, Alexander 66n.3; Mr 91
Sharpe, Ernest 138; H. 216, 217; M. M. 216, 217; Mr 145; Mrs 220
Shelton, Mr 206
Shemilt, Anthony xiii
Shepherd, E. 228
Sherman, Augustus Charles 186
Shorley, J. J. 134; Mrs 239
Short, B. 168; John James 206
Shreaves, Mr 145
Shreeves, Mr 159
Shrimpton, *Rev.* Joseph 179
Shuker, Mr 221
Sibthorpe, E. 128
Silkstone, Wilfred Noel Harraway 30, 30n.20
Sills, E. M. 385
Simmons, S. 129
Simms, L. A. 202; Mr 143
Simons, H. 155; W. 156
Sinfield, Mrs 161
Single, W. 195
Skerman, Albert George 172
Skevington, Edward 142
Slater, Laurie 39; Mr 220
Slinsby, Mr 118
Small, John 220
Smith, C. C. 165; Emma 339, 340; F. 232; F. G. 246, 247; G. 282; George Thomas 191, 192; M. W. 381; Miss 280; Mr 222, 226, 267, 280; Mrs 126; Muriel 44; P. 218; W. 173, 274; W. E. 167, 168
Snowden, Mr 231
Somerville-Warren, D. P. 247
Sotherby, John 2
Soutar, J. F. 160
Southcott, Joanna 10, 111
Spavins, Mr 140
Spencer, A. B. 302; C. 241; J. 155; John 230
Spindler, Q. M. 245
Spinks, Mr 226
Stafferton, James 132; S. 241; T. C. 207
Stafford, Charles 11n.4; R. B. 11
Stanley, *Sir* John 2
Stanton, J. J. 241, 242, 243; Mr 140
Stapleton, C. 165; Mr 239, 240
Statham, Mrs 198
Stelfox, Cyril 219
Stevens, E. R. 230; F. 241; S. N. 165
Stewart, C. A. 303; Mr 149; Mrs 233
Stock, J. 258
Stockford, George Thomas 198
Stokes, V. M. 385
Stratford, E. W. 255
Stratton, E. L. 311
Street, David 215; John 130
Sturgess, E. N. 341
Summerfield, Ellen 201; Mrs 194; W. 243
Summerlin, xiii; Mrs 120; Thomas 120
Sunderland, M. B. 320, 346
Surtees, A. S. 244; L. 244
Susanne, Mr 270
Sutton, George 119; Mrs 294
Swaffield, Henry 98n.5; Leslie J. 98n.5, 100
Swales, A. W. 240
Swannell, Mr 279
Symonds, Queenie 53

Tacchi, C. 179
Tagg, *Major* James 188
Tansley, C. 129
Taylor, C. E. L. 315; David R. 31; E. H. 313, 314, 315; F. 124; J. 173; Mr 150; Reginald 81
Tebbutt, W. 158
Thompkins, O. 134
Thompson, A. 186; David 134; E. T. 245; F. 235; Mr 223

Thrussell, Mr 223
Tice, L. G. 374
Tildesley, J. 174
Timaeus, C. F. 89, 89n.22
Tingey, C. R. 310
Tinsley, F. P. 36, 305
Tite, Mrs 219
Toker, *Maj-General Sir* Alliston 187
Tompkins, A. J. 134; G. M. 273; Mr 291
Tongue, Mr 257
Topham, H. J. 142
Tory, M. 116; M. J. 164; Miss 164
Townhill, G. W. 147
Towns, T. 129
Townsend, A. 203; Elizabeth 176, 177, 178
Trappitt, H. W. 274
Trenchard, Major-General 79n.11
Trethewy, Alfred Tresawna 66n.3
Trimmings, Mr 139
Trowbridge, Mrs 169
Trustram, Charles 122
Trustram Eve, J. D. 109, 109n.5; Lady 109n.5; *Sir* Herbert 109n.5
Tucker, G. J. 122; Geoffrey 83; Mr 146
Turnbull, Mary 305
Turner, Frank 71; Henry 158; Mr 222; O. 203; Robert 71; T. W. 123
Turner-Jones, Mrs 300
Two, E. 128; K. E. 316
Tysoe, A. 158, 180; Charles 184; H. 157

Underwood, A. M. 202; C. J. 210; F. 167; J. C. 185

Valentine, Miss 296
Verby, Mr 227
Vernon, W. 296
Vintner, John 39
Vivers, Lizzie 24, 26

Wade Gery, Mr 118
Waden, Mrs 116
Wadsworth, Charles 132; Samuel 132
Waghorn, Mr 161
Wagstaff, John 187; Mr 118; Thomas 238; W. 224, 225; William 236
Waldock, Mrs 304
Waldy, George 119
Walker, F. 182; J. 336; J. H. 178; Miss 140; Mrs 129, 275; W. 182
Waller, J 229; J. R. 229
Walpole, *Sir* Robert 2
Walter, Joseph 7; Richard 7
Walton, A. F. 213
Ward, Mr 280
Warden, D. M. 397
Wareing, Mr 81
Warner, T. 243
Warren, M. C. 391; Mr 226
Warwick, William 326
Washbourne, Mr 231
Watson, Miss 257
Watts, Dorothy 301; E. 181
Webb, E. G. 334; Mrs 245, 273; R. A. 365; R. G. 206
Weedon, Olive 82
Weller, Mr 222
Wells, A. J. 135; B. 135; E. 218; F. 174; J. 183: J. W. 245; John 133; R. S. 52
West, Bernard 53, 53n.2
Westerman, Mr 149
Western, Frederick William 63, 63n.10, 63n.11
Westgarth, Joan 44, 83
Wheatley, Joseph 143
Whitbread, 11n.2, 7; H. 135; S. C. 404; Samuel 11n.2
White, A. A. 254, 255; Mr 227; Mrs 256; Samuel 192, 193
Whitehead, E. S. 241; Mrs 34; Ted 34
Whiteman, Mrs 201; P. J. 350
Whitemore, Mr 146
Whiting, Alfred 174; E. 177
Whitlock, John 140
Whitmore, W. 132
Whittaker, W. 325
Whittamore, A. D. 146
Whittemore, W. W. 197
Whittle, Frank 79n.11
Whitworth, W. Robert 28n.12
Wickstead, John 31
Wiffin, E. 185
Wiggle, F. H. 147
Wildgust, G. 252
Wilding, Elizabeth *see* Miller, Elizabeth; H. 142
Wildman, E. 228; Mr 269
Wiles, 121
Wilkins, Arthur 21, 25; 32, 93, 99, 101; Mary 93
Wilkinson, E. 177; G. 235; James 124
Willett, Mrs 128
Williams, J. 238; John R. A. 62, 92, 94; Mr 134; Norah 106; Wynn 140
Williamson, Charles 152; Mrs 183
Willis, *Commander* W. J. A. 27n.5
Willmott, C. 214
Wills, Florence 170
Wilsher, A. W. 178; D. 294
Wilson, A. E. 346; John L.xin.1; Mr 178, 222; Mrs 235
Winders, James 134
Wingfield, 11n.2
Wingrave, Mrs 24
Winstone, H. 272
Wintle, Mrs 283
Wise, M. 177; Mr 196
Witney, Jesse 153
Witty, Mr 220
Woodcraft, Messrs 130
Woodham, Miss 280
Woodhead, N. M. 378
Wooding, Frederick 178; Mr 215; T. 160, 162
Woods, G. 129
Woodward, C. T. 143; G. R. 104; J. 208; Miss 125; V. J. 208
Wootton, Charles 144; J. W. 134; Mr 143

Worboys, Percy 134
Wornest, Mrs 275
Worrall, Ellen 296
Wray, Mrs 247
Wren, H. A. 160
Wrench, Miss 238
Wright, A. 243; F. C. 180; John 128; Mr 226; Mrs 257: William 212
Wyatt, Mrs 199
Wylie, Mrs 125

Young, Mark 36n.40, 318; Mr 140, 231; Mrs 246
Yoxen, Mr 235

Index of Places

A reference may occur more than once on a page.
n after arabic numerals refers to a footnote on that page.

Bedford place names have been listed in two sequences, general place names and street names.

County names have been added to place names outside Bedfordshire unless they are major well-known places.

Ampthill, 109; Ampthill Street 319; Ashburnham Road 143; Bedford Street 409; gas company 14n.24; Houghton Park Farm 328; Station 45; Station Road 143; Swaffield & Son 98, 98n.5, 100, 108n.1, 109; White Hart 123, 143, 351, 358, 363
Arlesey, 325, 365; Church End 325; Church Lane 325; High Street 206, 212, 381; Oak 325; Stotfold Road 325; Three Counties Hospital 28n.13
Ashford, Kent, Cattle Market Company 6
Ashwell, Hertfordshire, 308; Bushel and Strike 328; Chauntry House 238; E. K. and H. Fordham Ltd 316; Gardener's Lane 248; High Street 238, 256, 306, 363; Limekiln Lane 304; Methodist Church 363; Mill Street 328; Prospect House 206; Slip End 287; Small Gains Lane 220; Station Road 220, 229, 319; Sunnymead Farm 334; Three Tuns 229, 238, 248, 256, 304, 306, 308, 319; Whittington Farm 406
Aspley Guise, 75; Bell 310; gas company 14n.24; Holt Hotel 388; Mount Pleasant 310
Aspley Heath, 388; Church Lane 375; Daneswood Convalescent Home 388
Astwood, Buckinghamshire, Astwood Park Farm 392; Cranfield Road 142; Main Road 142

Baldock, Hertfordshire, 61, 272, 308; Ashwell Road 272, 273; Bygrave Road 212; C. S Knowles 61; cattle market 61; Church Street 244, 304, 309; Clothall Road 225, 286, 357; Goldcrest Hotel 416; Hitchin Street 294; Icknield Way 216, 394; Icknield Way East 306; Jackson Street 195, 212; Letchworth Road 256; Market Square 61; Orchard Road 306; Peacocks' office, 8 High Street 19, 61–2, 64, 88n.17; Pembroke Road 268, 286; Pond Lane 309; Rose and Crown 195, 216, 298, 304, 305, 306, 308, 309, 311, 319, 320, 334; Royston Road 244, 286; Salisbury Road 298, 301, 311, 319; South Road 229, 286; Station Road 244; Town Hall 256, 357; Victoria 212, 225, 229, 244, 268, 286, 294, 301; Wedon Way 273, 274
Banbury, Oxfordshire, Egg Packing Station 104; White Lion 309
Barton, 127, 261
Bedford, general place names; Alexander McConnell *see* Connells; Allott and Barnard 87n.15; Amos Horsburgh & Co. 87n.15; Ampthill Road Board School 16; Anchor 42, 162; Anderson & Co. 17; Bairstow Eves 31n.24; Bartle Potter & Son 44, 106–7, 106n.1; Batts' Ford 53, 53n.1; Bear 39; Bedford Crown Permanent Building Society 47; Bedford Division Conservative & Unionist Association 51; Bedford Gas Company 14n.23; Bedford Permanent Building Society 47; Bedford School 14, 14n.27, 16, 46, 49n.22; Bedford Steam Laundry Company 67, 119, 142; Bedford Trustee Savings Bank 328; Bedfordshire and Luton Archives and Records Service (formerly Bedfordshire County Record Office) 25, 25n.11, 71, 113–14; Bedfordshire Building Society 47; Bedfordshire Property Sales 21; Bedfordshire Times Publishing Company Ltd 84, 86, 88; Behal Stores 377; Belfast Linen 307; Besbuilt Ltd 51; billiard hall 31; Bishop and Brooke Ltd 245; Black Horse Agencies 17; Black Tom 13, 13n.19, 80; Bluebird Café 285; Braggins 45; Brickhill 48, 51; Britannia Ironworks 21, 21n.6; Brown and Merry 87n.15; Bryant's boathouse 46; C. A. White 56; C. C. Bell 66, 107; C. F. Timaeus 89, 89n.22, 90; Castle (public house) 59; Castle Press printing works 57; Cattle Market 18, 20; Charles Wells' brewery 20; Cheffins 87n.15; Chetham's boathouse 46; China Palace 34; Clapham Road Board School 16; Colley Sampson 87n.15; Commercial Baths 46; Compass 31, 31n.25; Connells (formerly Alexander McConnell, McConnells, McConnell and Co.)17, 30, 30n.19, 85–6, 86n.11, 87n.15; Conquest, Clare & Binns (formerly Conquest & Clare) 66, 66n.6; Conservative Club 335; Consumer Advice Centre 55; Consumers Tea Company 46; cookery and manual instruction

centre 16; Cooper Beard 31; Cooper's Corner 105, 105n.1,106; Cooper's Seed Merchants 105, 105n.1; Corn Exchange 46; County Hotel 69, 350, 351, 352, 353, 354, 355, 358, 359; County Press (Bedford) Ltd 85; Crescent House School 16; Dame Alice Harpur School 16; David Graham & Co. 86n.11; Davis Bros 184; Day & Son 17n.46; De Parys Hotel 69, 359, 360, 411; Douglas Stratford & Co. 47; Dudeney & Johnston 46, 101; Dujon 31, 94; E. P. Rose & Son 45; Eddie Shrive and Associates 55; Ekins Estate Agents 55; electricity station 15n.30; Embankment Hotel 39, 94; Empire 46; English Brothers Ltd 164; F. Gamman & Son 46; F. R. Mathison 55; Fenlake 162; Foster's boathouse 46; Fox and Hounds 158, 159; Froebel House 16; G. C. Walker 17; George Hotel 12n.7, 68, 117, 118, 119, 120, 121, 122; Girls' Modern School *see* Dame Alice Harpur School; Goldings (formerly Golding and Grant) 17, 17n.46, 46; Goldington 51, 336; Goldington Estate Company 48n.15; Goldington Hall 50; Goldington Road Board School 16; Goodwin's Garage 269; Grain & Chalk 87n.15; Grammar School *see* Bedford School; Granada Theatre 46; Greens 45; Grimbly Hughes 46; H. G. Langley & Co 106; H. W. Clifton & Sons 46; Halifax 47; Harpur Arms 20–1; Harpur Street Elementary School 17, 20; Harrison & Rowley 46; Harry Ball & Co. (formerly Harry Ball) 17, 30, 47, 87n.15; Harry Hills Ltd 46, 176; Hebblethwaite's 44, 106; Henry Bacchus 46; Henry Burt & Son 89–90, 90n.23; High School 14, 14n.27, 16; Hockliffe's bookshop 27, 27n.3; Holts (Bedford) Ltd 51, 51n.30; Hospital 19, 19n.61, 93, 93n.4; Howard College 16; Howard Engineering Works 21, 21n.6; Imperial Cycle and Motor Company 53; J. Clarke & Son 46; J. A. Beagley and Co. Ltd 46; J. R. Eve & Son (formerly J. R. Eve) 17, 87n.15, 108n.1, 109; J. R. H. McPherson 55; J. T. Clayton 46, 46n.8; James Turner & Sons (Bedford) Ltd 34; John Bull & Co. 17; Kilroys 31, 87n.15; Kings Arms 147; Langley's Garage 33; Laxton's Nurseries 48, 48n.15; Lion Hotel 66, 68, 71, 116, 117, 119, 123, 124, 126, 128, 129, 131, 133, 136–51 *passim*, 153, 154, 155–80 *passim*, 182–94 *passim*, 196–207 *passim*; Lloyds TSB Bank 31, 34; London & Lancashire Insurance Co. Ltd 29; Longhurst & Skinner 46; Mac Fisheries 172; Marks and Spencer 45; Marshalls Garage 67; McConnells see Connells; McPherson Timmins and Ednie 44; Melbreck Furnishing Company 105; Midland Road Elementary School 17; Midland Road Station 17, 45; Miles 87n.15; Mill 163; Mill Meadows 93; Milo's Café 31; Miltons (Wallpapers) Ltd 326; Modern School 16, 20, 31n.23, 46, 47; Modern Tableware 54; Morgans chemist 326; National Westminster Bank 11, 100; Newland and Nash Ltd 66; Newnham Baths 46; Nite Spot 36, 36n.37; Our Boys 45; Our Girls 45; Ouse (river) 46, 93–4; Park Inn *see* County Hotel; Peacocks' Egg Packing Station xiii, 18, 94, 103–4; Peacocks' Horne Lane sale yards 18–19, 20–6, 34, 37, 57–8, 87, 105, 248, 252, Plate 6, Plate 8; Peacocks' Horne Lane sale yards, back yard 24; Peacocks' Horne Lane sale yards, front yard 20–1; Peacocks' Horne Lane sale yards, Market House 26; Peacocks' Horne Lane sale yards, market office 25; Peacocks' Horne Lane sale yards, poultry and chick sheds 21–3, 103; Peacocks' Horne Lane sale yards, tool shed 24; Peacocks' Horne Lane sale yards, Tower Court Cottages 22, 24, 58; Peacocks' Horne Lane sale yards, Tudor Rooms 20, 23, 68, 220, 221, 223, 224, 225, 231, 232, 236, 237, 238, 254, 255, 328, 329, 330; Peacocks' Lime Street sale rooms 18, 27, 37, 38, 39, 40, 41, 57, 59, 68, 71, 80, 105, 208, 210, 211, 212, 213, 214, 215, 216, 219, 220, 225, 226, 227, 231, 233–71 *passim*, 275, 278, 280–306 *passim*, 309, 310, 311, 313, 316, 317, 318, 319, 320, 325, 328, 329, 330; Peacocks' Newnham Street Auction Centre xiii, 26, 57–60, 69, 87, 91, 111, 112, 361, 362, 364, 365, 366, 367, 368, 370, 371, 372, 373, 374, 375, 376, 377, 378, 380–93 *passim*, 395–419 *passim*; Peacocks' Newnham Street Auction Centre, Robert Room 59–60, 69; Peacocks' office, 6 Dame Alice Street xiii, 18–19, 42–5, 50–4, 95, 106; Peacocks' office, 72 High Street 12, 18, 89; Peacocks' office, 84 High Street 18, 27, 90; Peacocks' office, 10 Lime Street 18, 19, 25–36, 38, 42, 100; Peacocks' office, 58 St Loyes xiii, 31, 42, 44, 52–6, 94, 104, 113; Peacocks' store, Rutland Road 18, 38, 105; Peter Lloyd and Associates 56; Physical Education College 31; Picturedrome 46; Pilgrim Housing Association offices 20; Plaza Cinema 36, 46; Poets Corner 15, 15n.32, 47, 49, 76; Polhill(s) Field 159, 184, 236; Post Office 42, 52, 124; Prime Ministers 13, 13n.19; Priory of Greyfriars 53, 140; Priory Street Board School 16; Putnoe 48n.14, 51, 51n.27, 51n.28; Putnoe Farm 48, 51; Putnoe Woods 48; Queen's Engineering Works 13; Queen's Park 13, 16, 43, 46, 49, 49n.21, 88; Queen's Park Board School 16; Race Meadow 85; Randall's 46; Red Lion Hotel *see* Lion Hotel; Redman (Builders) Ltd 51n.30; Robinson and Hall (formerly Robinson & Hall) 47, 87n.15, 108n.1, 109; Rosery Tea Rooms 42; Royal County Theatre 46, 266; Rugby Club 34n.29; Russell Park 13, 13n.18; Sainsbury's 46; St Andrew's School 16; St John's Station 13, 17, 45; St Mary's Gardens 93; Saints area 13, 13n.20, 15, 47, 49, 76; Save the Children Fund charity shop

55; sawmill 164; School of Art 156; SDC Ltd (formerly Survey Design and Construction Ltd) 57–8; Sharman Law (formerly Sharman and Trethewy) 66, 66n.3; Sidney Press 89; South African War Memorial 12, 12n.10; Stafford, Rogers and Merry (formerly Stafford and Rogers Ltd) 11, 11n.4, 12, 17, 47, 92, 97, 100, 109; Stonebanks 87n.15; Stratford 87n.15; Swan 12, 66, 68, 117, 119, 122, 123, 125, 126, 127, 133, 134, 135, 136, 139, 140, 141, 142, 144, 151, 152, 154, 155, 160, 166, 167, 170, 172, 176, 218, 228, 257, 269, 270, 281, 305, 307, 310, 312, 313, 316, 318, 320, 323, 324, 325, 326, 327, 328, 330–52 *passim*, 355, 357; T. and H. Green 18; T. R. Donnelly 51, 51n.30; telephone exchange 15; Temperance Building Society 67; Territorial Barracks 19n.63; Three Cups 59; timber yard 164; Town Hall 68, 152, 157, 158, 227, 228; Trustee Savings Bank 34; Victory Cake Shop 33; W. H. Allen Sons and Company Ltd xiii, 13, 13n.17, 34n.29, 93; W. J. Robinson 90, water works 14n.22; Wells & Co. 46; Whitmore & Co. 85; William H. Brown 17; William Stafford 17; Woodfine Batcheldors *see* Conquest, Clare & Binns; Woolworth's 45

Bedford, street names; Adelaide Square 81, 141, 183, 275; Albany Road 111, 123, 171, 240; Albert Street 80, 255; Alexandra Place 141; Alexandra Road 126, 139, 145, 166, 175, 326; Allhallows Lane 71, 80, 80n.12, 126, 189; Althorpe Street 128, 171, 173, 174, 192, 241, 242, 300, 350; Ampthill Road 13, 16, 49, 85, 128, 137, 148, 161, 166, 204, 220, 225, 287, 294, 301, 342, 377, 413; Appledore Road 67; Argyll Street 137, 140, 270, 271, 330; Ashburnham Road 14, 19n.63, 47, 66, 117, 131, 167, 194, 258, 264, 267, 299, 333, 375; Aspley Road 350, 367; Avenue, The 339, 340; Balmoral Avenue 390; Balsall Street 126, 194; Barkers Lane 161, 225, 234, 416; Battison Street 138, 246; Beaconsfield Street 13n.19, 206, 226, 261, 353, 354, 413; Beauchamp Road 157; Beauchamp Row 185; Beckett Street 80; Bedesman's Lane 147; Bedesman's Place 257, 262, 266; Beverley Crescent 215, 270, 288, 290, 294, 351; Boswell Place 276; Bower Street 146, 183, 193, 198, 250, 251, 338; Brace Street 53; Brackley Road 418; Bradgate Road 303, 335, 354; Braeside 51n.30; Brereton Road 248, 323, 351; Broadway, The 45, 68, 86n.11, 126; Bromham Road 14, 16, 33, 40, 44, 47, 49, 81, 106, 151, 156, 186, 189, 196, 197, 203, 248, 301, 303, 306, 310, 330, 334, 336, 355, 398; Brookfield Road 254, 289, 317; Bunyan Road 137, 159, 184, 234; Bushmead Avenue 40, 67, 85; 119, 122, 128, 193, 239, 254, 266, 310, 337; Campbell Road 275, 382; Canning Street 200, 213, 243; Cardington Road 194, 303, 305, 345; Castle Road 13, 49, 49n.18, 77, 127, 133, 142, 165, 166, 172, 179, 194, 263, 275, 278, 290, 295, 334, 337, 354, 399; Cauldwell Place 262; Cauldwell Street 137, 156, 227, 254, 295, 299; Cauldwell Walk 158, 166; Cavendish Street 165; Caves Lane 48; Cedar Road 359; Chandos Street 145; Chaucer Road 15n.32, 159, 167, 190, 192, 237, 262; Clapham Road 13n.13, 16, 160, 185, 214, 233, 305, 404; Clarendon Street 13n.19, 125, 146, 149, 198, 201, 296, 419; Cobden Street 80, 165, 342; College Road 196, 304; Commercial Road 18, 20, 46, 239, 240, 266, 306, 342; Conduit Road 156, 179, 238, 301, 381, 397; Corby Close 345; Cornwall Road 213, 244, 245, 266; Costin Street 167, 169; Coventry Road 161, 167, 337, 349, 364; Cowper Road 15n.32; Crescent, The 51, 238, 288; Cricket Lane 168; Cross Street 177, 205; Cutcliffe Grove 150; Cutcliffe Place 168, 294, 400; Dame Alice Street 42, 52; Dane Street 15; De Parys Avenue 14, 14n.27, 15, 35, 76, 197, 305; Denmark Street 78, 128, 167, 193, 246, 247, 251, 289, 290, 309, 353, 389; Derby Street 80, 144, 153, 242, 243; Derwent Place 265; Duck Mill Lane 163; Dudley Street 14, 144, 155, 196, 201, 334, 338; Dunville Road 139, 368; Dynevor Road 133, 184, 416; Ellington Street 219; Elstow Road 13, 49, 268, 334; Embankment 147, 148, 154, 219, 396; Fairfax Road 141, 252; Farrer Street 251, 309; Fenlake Road 194, 210, 235, 295; Fernlea Close 348; Firbank Road 302, 368; Ford End Road 13n.17, 14n.23, 66, 116, 150, 171, 174, 188, 277, 289, 331, 378, 413; Foster Street 214, 353, 354; Fosterhill Road 141, 167, 168, 186, 213, 219, 260, 354; Gadsby Street 226, 251; Garfield Street 13n.19, 201, 202, 250, 295, 318, 370; George Street 13, 142, 171,176, 215, 247, 251, 294, 333, 342, 343, 370, 409; Gibbons Road 16, 122; Gladstone Street 13n.19, 206, 212, 302, 359; Glebe Road 339, 349; Goldington Avenue 16, 37, 187, 227, 239, 372; Goldington Road 48–9, 49n.20, 67, 135, 136, 158, 159, 160, 164, 184, 236, 237, 268, 269, 280, 284, 291, 300, 333, 339; Grafton Road 131, 180, 231, 266; Grange Road 199; Granville Street 289; Gratton Road 226, 265, 293, 365; Gravel Lane 19–20; Graylings, The 51; Great Butt(s) Street 242, 302; Green (Goldington) 140; Greenhill Street 80, 245; Greenshields Road 49, 330; Greyfriars Walk 14n.23, 80, 129, 178, 200; Grosvenor Street 123, 393; Grove, The 55, 179, 194, 270, 278, 329, 344, 416; Grove Place 145, 159, 344; Gwyn Street 12n.7, 80, 167, 198, 201, 233, 245, 254, 259, 295; Hardwick Road 285; Harpur Street 45–6, 51, 55, 85, 351; Harrowden Road 51, 283, 376; Hartington Street 13n.19, 197, 283; Hassett Street 80, 177, 200, 201, 245, 254, 257, 278; Hawkins

Road 347; Hazelwood Road 213; Heathfield 51n.30; High Street 11, 12, 17, 17n.46, 27, 31, 45–6, 66, 68, 84, 89, 307; Highfields 220; Holme Street 227; Honey Hill Road 162, 219, 287, 290, 296, 331; Horne Lane 18–19, 20, 103; Houghton Road 147, 184, 266, 399; Howard Street 66, 215, 241, 412; Howbury Street 13, 80, 136, 137, 161, 219, 335, 351, 410; Hurst Grove 122, 150, 151, 166, 186, 203, 212, 247, 256, 261, 268, 287, 295, 382; Iddesleigh Road 159, 227, 288, 391; Irwin Road 255, 338; Kathie Road 294; Kempston Road 158, 166, 203; Kimbolton Avenue 244; Kimbolton Road 13n.20, 16, 44, 48–9, 116, 148, 160, 193, 236, 269, 289, 291, 299, 302, 329, 332, 333, 366, 389; King Edward Road 167; King's Place 237, 247, 262, 302; Kingsley Road 296; Kingsway 53; Lansdowne Road 122, 133; Lawrence Street 280; Lime Street 27, 34, 89, 184; Linden Road 16, 255; Little Butt(s) Street 184, 198, 242, 259, 261, 262; Little Grove Place 309; Little Thurlow Street 71, 178; London Road 49, 49n.19, 188, 200, 331, 335; Lurke Street 215, 316, 317, 349, 360; Mabel Road 124, 201, 376; Maitland Street 138, 169, 200, 263, 278; Marlborough Road 177, 184, 349, 355; Maryville Road 333; Melbourne Street 186, 225, 286, 289; Merton Road 182, 234, 238, 255; Midland Road 17, 19, 20, 44, 45, 46, 47, 53, 68, 105, 106, 123, 124, 202, 266, 326, 327; Mile Road 49; Mill Street 17, 46, 89, 270; Millbrook Road 300; Miller Road 260; Milton Road 15n.32, 15n.33, 233; Mount Drive 51n.30; Muswell Road 161, 226; Myrtle Road 267; Nelson Street 148, 149; New Fenlake 145, 146; New Road 166; Newnham Avenue 49, 237, 245, 252; Newnham Lane 169; Newnham Road 254; Newnham Street 57–8, 349, 375, 416; Nursery Gardens 398; Oaklands Road 275; Offa Road 124, 148, 158, 168, 202; Old Ford End Road 43, 149, 303; Ombersley Road 294; Ouseland Road 375; Palmerston Street 13n.19, 261; Park Avenue 43, 187, 282, 299; Park Road East 13n.19; Park Road North 142; Park Road West 197, 207, 261; Pattershall Street 271; Peel Street 80; Pemberley Avenue 282, 297, 300; Pemberley Crescent 66, 116 *see also* Pemberley Avenue; Pemberley Lane 213; Pembroke Street 171, 172, 251, 290; Phillpotts Avenue 49, 77, 265; Pilcroft Street 149, 235; Polhill Avenue 343; Poplars, The 169; Prebend Street 15n.30, 165, 192, 246, 342, 368; Preston Road 384, 414; Princes Street 80; Priory Street 16, 205, 253, 259, 271, 277, 296, 327; Priory Terrace 16; Putnoe Lane 48, 49, 260, 289; Putnoe Street 51n.30; Queen Alexandra Road 238; Queen Street 47, 243, 271, 317; Queen's Drive 51, 51n.29, 51n.30; Richmond Road 267; Ridgeway, The 51n.30; Ridgmont Street 147; Risborough Road 49, 239; River Street 143, 144; Roff Avenue 13n.19; Roise Street 138, 178, 205, 214; Rosamond Road 386; Rothsay Gardens 205; Rothsay Road 85, 244; Russell Avenue 255, 259, 260, 292; Russell Street 129, 146, 169, 227; Rutland Road 121, 141, 145, 184, 278, 312; St Andrew's Road 13n.20, 15n.28, 133, 227, 229, 230; St Augustine's Road 13n.20, 81, 234, 238; St Cuthbert's Square 234; St Cuthbert's Street 257, 399; St Georges's Road 13n.20; St John's Street 146, 153, 285; St Leonard's Street 372, 376, 382; St Loyes Street 27n.3, 52, 62, 68, 126, 349; St Mary's Street 46, 159, 250; St Michael's Road 13n.20, 85, 137, 155, 180, 188, 226, 338; St Paul's Road 239; St Paul's Square 17, 20, 29, 328; St Peter's Street 17n.46, 323, 335, 354; Salisbury Street 13n.19, 240, 245, 246, 289, 330, 353; Sandhurst Place 177; Sandhurst Road 151, 402; Sandy Road 162; Shaftesbury Avenue 171, 413; Shakespeare Road 13n.21, 14, 15n.32, 254, 257, 258; Sidney Road 66, 351; Silver Street 31, 45, 90, 172, 176; Southville Road 130, 296, 377; Spencer Road 15n.32, 120, 142, 344, 412; Spenser Road 187, 192, 193, 196, 201, 226, 233, 255, 342; Stafford Road 14, 350, 417; Stanley Street 13n.19, 49, 179, 262, 263, 296, 349, 350; Sydney Road 15n.32, 116; Tavistock Place 180; Tavistock Street 13, 13n.19, 15, 47, 68, 126, 145, 155, 183, 219, 406; Tennyson Road 147, 276; Thurlow Street 80, 80n.12; Trevor Street 271; Trinity Road 340; Union Street 13n.19, 129, 288; Victoria Road 146, 309, 362, 393; Warwick Avenue 197, 200, 252, 268, 293, 299; Waterloo Road 37, 75, 124, 193, 239; Wellington Street 169, 198, 204, 212, 259, 260, 262, 269, 277, 293; Wendover Drive 49; Westbourne Road 189, 267, 370; Western Street 121, 184, 187, 188, 208, 219, 220, 260, 339; Whitbread Avenue 76, 84; Willow Road 417; Winchester Road 268, 344; Winifred Road 154, 186, 191, 220, 264, 353; Woburn Road 124, 140, 187, 331; York Street 127, 184, 185; 193, 212

Beeston, 395, 419; Brook End 344; Cockings Field 210; Dunghill Roadway 182; Gravel Pit Field 204; Great North Road 181,185; Green 204, 388, 395; High Road 355; Matthews Field 210; Oak Tree Field 204

Biddenham, xiii, 11n.2, 148, 175, 282, 402; Bedford to Northampton Road 277; Biddenham Turn 176n.1; Bridge Meadow 305; Bromham Road 334, 337, 347, 352; Church End 386; Days Lane 32, 171, 299; Deep Spinney 347; Grove Farm 11, 11n.2, 176n.1; Main Road 354, 362; New Road 176; Vicar's Close 318; water meadow 175; Windmill Hill 247

Biggleswade, 71, 209, 351, 391, 392, 406, 409, 415; Back Street 363; Banks Road

206; Baulk, The 381, 387, 394; Brooklands Farm 215; Bryants Cycle Merchants 61; C. S. Knowles 61; Caldecote Road 324; cattle market 63, 63n.10; Chapel Fields 202, 391, 394, 415; Chapman and Chaundler 66; Common 64; Conservative Club 382, 383; Conservative Hall 324; Crane's Field 215; Crown 318, 341, 343, 348, 351, 356, 357, 358, 360, 366; Drove Road 356, 413; Dunton Road 341; F. W. Western & Co. xiii, 54, 63, 92, 94, 110 *see also* Biggleswade, Maddison and Western, and Sandy, F. W. Western; Fairfield Road 392; Furzenhall Road 208, 356, 360, 378; gas company 14n.24; Great North Road 208; Greene King (Biggleswade) Ltd (formerly Greene King & Sons Ltd) 347, 358, 373; High Street 209, 357; Hitchin Street 63, 207, 358, 363, 388, 417; Hitchmead (Road) 358, 391, 413; Ivel Mill 365; Langford Road 403, 407; Laurel View 387; Lawrence Road 417; London Road 191, 318, 343, 358, 393, 394; Maddison and Western 63n.10 *see also* F. W. Western; Market Square 63; Masonic Rooms 316; Memorial Hall 343; Peacocks' office, Market House 19, 61–3; Potton Road 191, 360, 397; Saffron Road 389; St Andrew's Church Hall 362; St Andrews's Rooms 70, 363, 365, 368, 369, 373, 374, 378, 381, 388, 389, 392, 393, 394, 395, 397, 398, 399, 406, 407, 408, 409, 415; St John's Street 209, 394; Scroups Farm 403; Shortmead House 89n.21; Shortmead Street 61, 191, 343, 406; Southview 406; Spong and Sons Ltd 90; Stratton House Hotel 392, 403, 417, 419; Stratton Street 122, 202; Sun 215; Sun Street 297, 394; Sunderland Hall Farm 409; Swan 61, 191, 202, 206, 207, 208, 209, 338; Territorial Army Centre 338; Turnpike Farm 316

Bletchley, Buckinghamshire, W. S. Johnson & Co. 21, 30, 110

Bletsoe, 55n.3, 264, 336, 345, 352, 354; Old School 361

Blunham, 67, 89n.22, 121, 179, 182, 288, 292, 298, 307, 308, 311; Barford Road 298; Blunham Fields 204; Cowyard Farm 291; Grange Lane 413; Grange Road 143, 181, 207, 249, 250; Great Barford Road 308; High Street 217, 325, 366; Hill, The 352; Hills Field 207; Lodge Farm 320; Marefield 292; Millard Bros 249, 250; Old Horseshoes 121, 249, 250; Park Farm 398; Ridgeway Road 288, 381; Salutation 207, 307, 308, 311, 325; Saulsbury's Field 292; South Mills 288; South Mills Farm 330; Three Horseshoes 143; Tuppens Field 292; White Horse Lane 119

Bolnhurst, 68; Blacklands Farm 228; Brook Farm 228; Crowhill Farm 227; Manor Farm 142; Mavourn Farm 228; Tilwick Farm 228

Boston, Lincolnshire, Symonds, Ingamells and Young 28

Bourne, Lincolnshire, British Road Services Depot 101–2

Bozeat, Northamptonshire, High Street 291

Brampton, Cambridgeshire, Buckden Road 378

Bromham, 81, 151, 153, 161, 166, 170, 275, 302, 309; Bowels Wood 220; Bridge End 372, 384; Bromham Hospital 329; Bromham House 28n.13, 166; Bromham to Oakley Road 158; College Farm 28; Dahlia Nursery 384; Grange Lane 170, 220; Green 170, 180, 195, 263, 289; Main Road 170, 258; main street 158, 170; Millfield 371; New Road 240, 254, 255, 258; Nurseries 153; Oakley Road 158; Park 92, 398; Post Office 319; Stagsden Road 237, 300, 302; Swan 153, 161; Thistley Green 240, 252, 253, 254, 255, 256, 258; Vicarage Green 158; Village Road 318, 319, 345, 348, 361, 377, 380, 391, 395, 397; Village Street 158, 170

Broom, High Street 209; Southill Road 388

Broughton, Northamptonshire, Houghton Mill Farm 327

Buckingham, White Hart 323

Budna, Budna Road 355; Grove Farm 336

Buntingford, Hertfordshire, C. S. Knowles 61

Cainham, Shropshire, Brunswick House 67, 120; Clee Hill 67, 120; Golden Cross 120

Cainhoe, Park Wood 207

Campton, 358; Church Farm 208, 265; Highlands Farm 207; Mill 326; Mill Lane 313; Shefford Road 265; Village Greenway 335; White Hart 208; Woodhall Farm 316

Cardington, 11n.2; Chapel End 404; Chapel Farm 404; Hangars 85; Mill 46; RAF Camp 47, 47n.10, 79; Station 336

Carlton, 136, 236; Angel 258, 303; Bridge End 155; Causeway, The 224, 303, 309, 310, 340, 409; Firs, The 236; Green 279; High Street 206, 258, 280, 350; Monk Road 205; Moor, The 298; Moor Road 271; Pavenham Road 326

Carmarthen, Carmarthenshire, 9; Peter Francis 3, 4

Caxton, Bourne Road 156

Chalton, 250

Chapel Broughton, Northamptonshire, *see* Broughton

Chellington, Bridge End 155; High Street 230

Chester, Cheshire, cattle market 6

Chicksands, RAF Base 25n.12, 357; USAAF Base 25, 25n.12, 47, 79

Clapham, 48, 148, 151, 153, 189, 299; Baulk, The 287; Clapham Road 157; College Farm 36; Green Lane 185, 259, 335; High Street 200, 282, 290, 324, 383, 414; Little Park Farm 305; Milton Hill 193; Milton Road 403; Mount Pleasant Farm 151; Oakley Road 179; Park Farm 36; Peak Hill Farm 102; Warren, The 206, 387, 399

Clifton, 311; Broad Street 236, 315; Church Street 215; Drift Field 215; Hitchin Lane

311; Linkway, The 397; Pedley(s) Lane 126, 202, 315
Clophill, 160, 203, 315, 316; Beadlow Top Farm 385; Bedford Road 297; Church End 371; Flying Horse 326; High Street 346; Hilltop Farm 326; Mill Lane 329, 363; Northfields Farm 333; Shefford Road 385
Cockayne Hatley, 416; Coxes Orange Pippin Orchards 35; Potton Road 360; Village Road 366
Colchester, Essex, Fenn Wright 30
Colmworth, 67, 89n.22, 118; Channel(s) End 118, 149, 160, 186; Chapel End 240; Chapel Lane 389; Chawston Road 186; City Lane 118; Kennell Farm 391; Kimbolton Road 153, 269, 404; New Road 404; Roothams Green Farm 199; Village Hall 357, 358, 389; Wheatsheaf 118; Wheatsheaf Farm 357, 358; Wilden Road 186
Comberton, Cambridgeshire, Old Farm 303
Cople 181, 248; Dog Farm 319; Dog Inn 319; Grange Lane 417; petrol station 319; Willington Road 377, 402, 416
Corby, Northamptonshire, Kirby Hall 3
Cotton End, Wood Lane 415
Cranfield, 52, 66, 68, 80, 81, 116, 125, 135, 151; Airfield 102, 102n.13; Astwood Road 346; Bedford Road 221, 224, 269, 341, 351, 387; Bourne End 151, 358, 359, 400; Broad Green 196; Brook Farm 151; Church Road 66, 116; Church Walk 194; Commerce House 151; Coronation Road 221, 222, 223, 224; Cranfield Court 43, 43n.3; Crawley Road 225; Crow 135; Green's Close 346; Harter Avenue 81, 223, 224; Hatfield Avenue 224; High Street 221, 260, 290, 356, 399, 402; Hollywell Road 221, 224; Ivy Hall Farm 135; Leathern Bottle 196, 225, 346, 356; Leys Farm 333; Manor House 358; Memorial Hall 269; Mill Lane 208; Mill Road 224; moat 135; school house 151; Swan 66, 116, 125, 135, 194, 260; Washingley Farm 359; Wood End Road 223, 292
Crewe, Cheshire, cattle market 6, 7
Culworth, Northamptonshire, Linnell and Ansteys Farm 309

Daventry, Northamptonshire, 147; Wheatsheaf Hotel 147
Dean, School House 339
Derby, Derbyshire, Cavendish Auctions 4
Downe, Kent, Downe Court 323, 325
Dunstable, gas company 14n.24; Halfway House 332
Dunton, Baptist Church 388; Biggleswade Road 417; Cambridge Road 378

Eaton Socon, Cambridgeshire, 90; Cross Hall Road 330; Great North Road 282, 390
Eggington, Claridge's Farm House 67, 124; moat 124
Elstow, 133, 211; Storage Depot 97–101, 97n.1; Wilstead Road 398; Wixams 97, 97n.2
Emberton, Buckinghamshire, Prospect House 356
Eversholt, Rads End House 328
Eyeworth, Eyeworth to Wrestlingworth Road 362
Felmersham, 125, 412; Bakers Lane 158; Brook Farm Road 125; Collick Lane 158; Four Acres 125; Grays Field 125; Knight's Lot 125; Moor End 158; Old Church Road 158; Pavenham Road 318; Radwell Road 158; Townlot Lane 158
Fenny Stratford, Buckinghamshire, Swan 392, 397
Flitwick, Chapel Road 165; Hollycroft 167; King's Road 351; L. W. Vass 98; Station Road 310, 371
Fonthill Gifford, Wiltshire, Fonthill Abbey 2

Gamlingay, Cambridgeshire, 201, 402; Church Street 385; Cinques, The 408; Cock 214, 356; Drove Road 356; Green End 316, 381; Green Man 408; Hardwicke Arms 316; Mill Street 214; Spotted Cow 316; Woodbury Low Farm 313
Girtford, Manor Farm 237
Goldington, see Bedford
Grafham, Cambridgeshire, Buckden Road 410; Church Road 380
Great Barford, 123, 143, 188, 261, 310, 374, 412; Addingtons Road 418; Bedford Road 170, 312; Birchfields Road 198; Cross 123; Green End 198; Green End Road 418; Greenfields Dairy Farm 198; High Street 405, 408; Roxton Road 312, 371; Silver Street 332; Village Road 170; White Hart 408; Willoughby Farm 396
Great Gransden, Cambridgeshire, 367
Great Offley, Hertfordshire, Methodist Chapel 406
Great Staughton, Cambridgeshire, 248
Greenfield, 123
Grendon, Northamptonshire, 125
Guilden Morden, Cambridgeshire, 134, 268, 299; Cobbs Lane 134; High Street 302, 347; Little Green 134; Six Bells 134; Tadlow Bridge Field 134; Three Tuns 347

Hardmead, Buckinghamshire, 400
Harpenden, Hertfordshire, N. A. C. Salvesen & Co. 30
Harrold, 69n.22, 124, 131, 202, 216, 218, 235, 270, 331; almshouses 132; Brook Lane 139, 155, 162, 211, 258, 288, 321, 409; C. Clayson and Sons 69; Carlton Road 327; Church Lane 211; Church Walk 320, 321, 331, 360, 373, 385; Dove Lane 331; Dungee Farm 28n.8, 152; Dungee Road 270; Dungee Wood 152; Elizabethan mansion 152; Green 132, 240, 288, 322; Hall 50, 50n.23, 89n.21, 269; Hall Close 50; Harrold Park Farm 324; Harrold Park woodland 152; High Street 124, 202, 211, 224, 229, 247, 295, 317, 321, 331,

333, 403; Institute 69, 70, 131, 132, 155, 178, 179, 202, 211, 212, 224, 240, 258, 279, 280, 320, 321, 322, 331, 333; Ivy House Poultry Farm 218; Lavendon Road 138, 179, 215; Manor Farm 152, 324; Mansion Farm 152; Mansion Lane 280, 411; Mill House 162; Odell Road 326; Orchard Lane 139, 212, 292, 313, 368; Park Farm 152; Secondary Modern School 70; Timber Yard 138, 139; Wheatsheaf 124; Wood Lane 212; Wood Road 178
Harrowden in the Fields *see* Old Harrowden
Hatch, 417; Brook End 395
Haynes, 127, 343; Chapel 130; Cottage Farm 332; Greyhound 130, 140; Northwood End Road 293; Plummers Lane 152, 163; Sandpit Farmhouse 315; Shefford Road 127; Silver End Road 315, 316, 361, 415; Silver Lane 130, 140; West End 157, 282
Henlow, High Street 360, 373; Hitchin Road 315, 364; Langford Road 355; Middlefield Farm 364; Parachute 360; RAF Camp 79, 79n.11, 315, 335; Town Farm 365
Hertford, Hertfordshire, Norris & Duval 30
Hinwick, 157
Hitchin, Hertfordshire, Bedford Road 386; Hermitage Road 64; J. R. Eve & Son 30, 109n.5; Park Street 317; Peacocks' office, 19 Hermitage Road 64; St Faith's Close 403; Sun 61, 70, 207, 268, 272, 273, 274, 287, 302, 358, 403
Holwell, Hertfordshire, Ramerick Nurseries 302
Honiton, Devon, William Hussey 7
Horncastle, Lincolnshire, Richard Walter 7
Houghton Conquest, 120, 152, 405; Bedford Road 120, 268, 317; Chapel End Road 350; Conquestbury Farm 228; Grove, The 347; Knife and Cleaver 152; Rectory Lane 328
Houghton Regis, Cumberland Street 195; Marmsey 195; Queen Street 195

Ickwell, Green 156, 364, 369, 373

Kempston, 48, 59, 150, 153, 415; Ampthill Road 313; Barracks 47, 47n.10, 79; Battenburg Road 66, 116 *see also* Marne Street; Beatrice Street 74, 373, 417; Bedford Arms 122; Bedford Road 142, 203, 213, 284, 285, 374; Box End 16, 67, 120, 126, 154, 161, 163, 172, 190, 259, 347, 407; Bunyan Road 122, 131, 146, 166, 174, 175, 189, 293, 297, 400; Chantry Avenue 259; Chantry Estate 253; Chantry Road 328, 388; Church Walk 194; College Street 89, 390; Cottage Farm 287; Crossland Fosse 16, 16n.37, 190; Duncombe Street 216, 284, 337; Durler Avenue 400; E. W. Harris & Co. 53, 345; Eaton Road 207, 275, 276; Farrer Street 156, 157, 220, 233, 271; gas company 14n.24; Grange Camp 79, 79n.11; Green End 162; Green End Farm 160; Harefield Avenue 414; High Street 66, 116, 142, 145,164, 172, 190, 203, 208, 231, 237, 252, 368, 370, 397, 415; Hill Grounds 246; Hill Rise 400; Home Street 219; Igranic sports field 92; Kempston Hoo 43, 43n.3; Kempston House 160; King Street 264, 265, 284, 347; King William IV 66, 85, 116, 131, 172; Littledale Street 178, 233, 298; Margetts Road 241; Marina 401, 402, 403; Marlborough Park 382, 389; Marne Street 66, 170, 233 *see also* Battenburg Road; Mill 46; Mill Meadows 316; Newnorth Burt *see* Bedford, Henry Burt & Son; Orchard Street 296, 353; Park Road 296; Ridge Road 190, 249; Rushey Ford House 67, 126; St John's Street 146, 150, 153, 166, 190; Spring Road 147, 148, 198, 248, 281, 311; SSM International Club 374; Stonedale Road 401, 403; Stuart Road 233, 340, 345; Stuart Street 156; Sudan Field 172; Thornton Street 154, 365, 383; Top Farm 154; Up End 166; Water Lane 52, 170, 193, 194; West End 172; West End Farm 36, 182; West End Road 347; Westdale Walk 409; Woburn Road 129, 149, 150, 207, 287; Wood End 152, 157, 190, 203; Wood End Farm 160; Wootton Road 213
Kempston Hardwick, 102
Kendal, Westmorland, 3
Kettering, Northamptonshire, Berry Brothers 6; Wilson Smith Howkins xi, xin.1
Keysoe, 55n.3, 348, 418; Bedford to Kimbolton Road 275; Brook End 133; Chequers 133, 348; Elm Farm 418; Grange Farm 336; Hatch End 188; Hatch Lane 188, 345; Keysoe Row 307; Keysoe Row East 418; Keysoe Row West 407; windmill 199, 210
Kimbolton, Cambridgeshire, Carnaby, The 379; Dukes Row 379, 391; Grass Yard 380, 399, 416; Rookery Lane 379; School 70, 378, 379, 380, 399, 416; White Lion 320
Knebworth, Hertfordshire, Peacocks' office, 138 London Road 63

Langford, 406, 415; Barnes Road 393; Cambridge Road 346, 378; Church Farm 357; Church Hall 361; Church Street 361, 392, 394; Common Farm 360; Common Road 360; East Road 346; Gurney's Lane 346; Henlow Turn Field 393; High Street 342, 394; Mill Lane 395; New Road 393; Station Road 350, 387, 388; Wrestlers 342, 346, 350, 355, 360
Lavendon, Buckinghamshire, Castle Road 240, 253; George 240, 253, 303; Horseshoe 357; Northampton Road 253, 303; Turvey Road 357
Leighton Buzzard, Bedford Street 339; gas company 14n.24; Robert Bros 339; Swan Hotel 67, 124, 339
Letchworth, Hertfordshire, Icknield Hall 230; Leys Avenue 230; Peacocks' office 64; Sollershott East 230; Spring Road 230
Lidlington, 148, 149, 236; Church Street 128,

231, 232, 405; Green Man 128; High Street 231; Sheeptick End 358
Little Brickhill, Buckinghamshire, Glebe Farm 375
Little Crawley, Buckinghamshire, 65, 119, 163
Little Gransden, Cambridgeshire, Lodge Farm 191; Village Hall 367
Little Horwood, Buckinghamshire, Lower Grove Farm 327
London, 2; Beckenham 325; Berkley Square 199; Bonham's 2; Camden Motors Ltd 98; Christies 2; Christopher Cock 2; Cornhill 2; Covent Garden 2; Edgeware 157; Garratt Road 157; Garraway's Coffee House 2; Leicester Street 2; Old George Hotel 157; Pall Mall 2; Phillips 2; Pride and Clark Ltd 98; Russell Hotel 108; Russell Square 108; Sotherby's 2; Victoria Palace Theatre 94; W. B. Hallett, Fox and White 38
Lower Caldecote, 195, 360; Elm Farm 348; Grange Lane 221, 308; Great North Road 348;
Lower Stondon, Bedford Road 348; Henlow Camp 348
Luton, gas company 14n.24; George 261, 282, 328; Grand Theatre 266; H. C. Janes 51, 51n.28, 51n.29; Old Post Office 108n.1; Wigmore Hall Farm 282

Marston Moretaine 103, 178; Ashbrook Farm 255; London Brick Company 49n.17, 102, 108n.4; Oakdene 371; Upper Shelton Road 305, 371
Marston Shelton, see Marston Moretaine
Maulden, Ampthill Road 363; Clophill to Ampthill Road 161; Hall End 160; Water End Farm 334
Meppershall, Shefford Road 314
Milton Bryan, 65
Milton Ernest, 121, 237, 295; Bedford to Rushden Road 301; Grange 50, 50n.25; Hall 50n.25; Marsh Lane 376; Mill 66, 117; Special Operations Executive base 50n.25; Swan 117, 121; Thurleigh Road 260; Town Street 117
Moggerhanger, 182; Blunham Road 353; Ladywood Plantation 181; Park Lane 256; St John's Road 373; Sandy to Bedford Road 195; Wilson's Field 181
Mursley, Buckinghamshire, Mursley Farm 327

Newton Blossomville, Buckinghamshire, 301
North Crawley, Buckinghamshire, 116, 119; Cock 65, 116, 119
Northampton, Angel Hotel 324, 327
Northill, 214, 369, 397; Bedford Road 399; Crown 156; Ickwell Road 265; School House 392; Thorncote Green 364, 393; Thorncote Road 372, 408; Vinegar Hill 210
Nottingham, Walker, Walton & Hanson 102, 102n.12

Oakley, 153, 157, 164, 169, 338; Church Lane 396, 401; General Store 169; High Street 282, 340, 401; Post Office 169; Station 45, 336; Station Road 175, 262; Village Reading Room 164
Odell, Church Lane 339; High Street 339; Horsefair Lane 339, 350
Offord D'Arcy, Cambridgeshire, High Street 305; Horseshoe 305
Old Harrowden, 71, 80, 359, 370, 378, 412; High Road 408
Old Warden, 381; Warden Road 386; Warden Street 405
Olney, Buckinghamshire, 310; Bridge Street 308; Bull 67, 128, 147, 148, 300, 343, 356; East Street 147, 148; High Street 147, 308; Midland Road 300; Station 336; West Street 300
Oundle, Northamptonshire, Southams 112

Pavenham, 123, 127, 149; Mill Lane 262
Pepperstock, 332; Bonner's Farm 332
Pertenhall, 348, 351
Plymouth, Devon, 4
Podington, 361; Cricket Pavilion 369; Gold Street 369
Potton, Blackbird Street 217, 259; Boston Lane 200; Brook End 373; Bull Street 234; Chapel Street 234, 417; Chequers 373; Common Road 200, 344; Deepdale 373, 374; Everton Road 218, 346, 385, 390; G. T. Mayston and Son 234; Gamlingay Road 344; gas company 14n.24; Home Farm 362; Horslow Street 218, 344; Limes, The 259; Mill Lane 378; Narrow Lane 218; Old Mill Lane 217; Parish Hall 218; Pesthouse Lane 217; Rose and Crown 200, 217, 218, 234, 324, 344, 350, 360; Royston Street 352; Sandy Road 385; Spencer Close 324; Sutton Mill Road 398; West End Lane 350, 389
Pulloxhill, 373; Tyburn Lane 382

Radwell, 71, 121; Felmersham Road 348; Moor End 375, 376, 411; Old Farm 320; Radwell Hall Farm 125; Underwood Farm 310
Ravensden, 68, 138, 154, 201; Church End 414; Cleat Hill 179; Cross Roads 312; Grange Farm 346; Highfields Farm 325; Hill Farm 320; Kimbolton Road 140; Old School 349; Old Ways Road 224; Post Office 312; Ravensden Hill 134, 138; Red Lion 140
Reed, Hertfordshire, Cabinet, The 303, Drage's Farm 303;
Renhold, 134, 144, 156, 175, 199; Church End 174, 416; Green 134, 138, 239, 293; Green End Road 342; Hookhams Lane 384, 411, 412; Howbury Hall 84; Newfield Farm 180; Newlands Farm 134, 137; Ravensden Hill 134; Ravensden Road 367; Salph End 134, 183, 190; Salph End Farm 283; Top End 419; Top End Farm 419; Top End Road 244; Wood 141; Woodfield Road 241; Workhouse End 183

Retford, Nottinghamshire, Henry Spencer and Sons 4
Ripon, Yorkshire, cattle market 6
Riseley, 22, 154, 163, 199, 216, 218, 267; College Farm 166; Fox and Hounds 326, 363; Gold Lane 165, 319; High Street 149, 196, 229, 241, 267, 283, 326, 338; Keysoe Road 363; Riseley to Bedford Road 166; Riseley to Keysoe Road 167; Rotten Row 376
Royston, Hertfordshire, Bull Hotel 209
Rushden, Northamptonshire, 304; Avenue Road 256; Queen Victoria 411; Southern Green 305, 320; Victoria Hotel 304

St Neots, Cambridgeshire, Cross Keys 191, 282, 341; East Street 313, 341; Ekins Dilley & Handley 109; Peacocks' Auction Centre 111; Tomson and Lendrum Ltd 90
Sandy, 63, 368, 406; All Saints' Church 381; Bedford Road 180, 185, 328, 356; Beeston Green 382; Blunham Meadows 341; Blunham Roods 214; Brickhill Road 216, 352; Bridge Farm 316, 344; Brook End 182; Cambridge Road 389; Cartwheel Nursery 364; Church Path 363, 365; Conservative Club 352, 373, 374, 407; Conservative Hall 180, 181, 182, 185, 195, 196; E. T. Leeds Smith & Co. 92; F. W. Western & Co. 63–4 *see also* Biggleswade, F. W. Western & Co.; gas company 14n.24; Girtford Bridge 352; Great North Road 181, 185; Highfield Farm 361; Ivel Holdings Ltd 346; Ivel Road 216, 390, 407; King's Arms 363, 364, 365, 402; Laburnham Road 198, 212, 216, 365; Lion 328; London Road 352, 381, 383; Longfield Road 180, 217, 374; New Road 204, 214; Peacocks' office, 18 St Neots Road 63–4; Red Lion 198, 204, 210, 212, 214, 216, 217, 291, 292, 341, 344, 352, 355; St Neots Road 236, 281, 303, 398; Sandy Building Society 217, 218; Sandy to Everton Road 250; Sandy to Hitchin Road 182; Stone Axe Farm 408; Stratford Road 393; Thorncote Farm 418; Thorncote Green 418; Vinegar Hill 344; Wharf Farm 185
Seddington, 210, 341; Bailey's Meadow 356; Great North Road 300; Longlake 356
Sharnbrook, 71, 171, 216, 281; Bedford Road 307; church 281; Church Lane 263, 264; Church Way 198; Cobb Hall 50, 50n.24; Coffee Tavern Rooms 144; High Street 168, 209, 263, 286, 291, 297, 298, 320, 349, 374; High Street West 144, 283; Home Farm 281; Ivy House Poultry Farm 218; Kendal Hill 284; Kennel(l) Hill 144, 342, 395; Manor House 329; Mill 264, 395; Mill Road 266, 329; National Service Hostels Corporation hostel 50n.24; Normans Road 212, 283, 327; Odell Road 304; Old Mill House 395; Ordnance Depot 50, 50n.24; Park Lane 164, 194, 198, 296, 302, 347, 392; Sharnbrook House 281; Sharnbrook to Rushden Road 154; station 45, 153; Swan 71, 154, 263, 264, 283, 284, 286, 302, 307, 327
Shefford, 74, 128; Ampthill Road 313, 314, 362, 366; Bedford Road 390, 391; Black Swan 120; Campton Road 366; Church Hall 313, 314, 315, 316; Clifton Fields 120; Clifton Road 314, 315; Deadman's Cross 343; Digswell House 199; Firs, The 314; gas company 14n.24; High Street 314, 409; Hitchin Road 314; laundry 146; main road to Ampthill 146; Mill 326; New Street 314; Pedley's Lane 120; sawmill 355; timber yard 355; Victoria Road 203; village shop 281; White Hart 126, 128, 146, 202, 203, 265, 326, 335, 357, 358
Sherington, Buckinghamshire, 206
Shillington, Bury Road 358; Church Street 415; High Road 396
Shorncliffe, Kent, Yeomanry Camp 19n.59
Slough, Berkshire, cattle market 5, 6
Souldrop, 221; Bedford Arms 355; Bedford to Kettering Road 190; Cross Weir Farm 190; High Street 255, 355, 365; Knotting Fox Farm 328; Middle Farm 335; Pools Lane 396
Southill, 11n.2; Station 336
Spalding, Lincolnshire 31
Stagsden, xiii, 143, 256, 267, 398; Bedford Road 374; High Street 405; White Horse 143, 234, 405
Stanford, 11, 11n.1
Staploe, 351
Steeple Morden, Cambridgeshire, Cheyney Street 61, 191; High Road 134
Steppingley, Eversholt Road 410
Stevington, 144, 231, 397, 415; Church Lane 231, 247, 248; Church Street 186; Court Lane 163, 357, 384, 407; Duck End 415; Duck End Farm 144; Frost Field 231; Park End 253, 283; Silver Lane 144; Silver Street 144, 260, 410; West End 162
Stewkley, Buckinghamshire, High Street 399; Village Hall 399
Stoke Bruerne, Northamptonshire, Stoke Gap Farm 324
Stoke Goldington, Buckinghamshire, Church Farm 67, 128; Stoke Park 67, 128; Stoke Park Wood 67, 128
Stonely, Cambridgeshire, Brookside 380, 404; Hatchett Lane 379, 380; Park Lane 379
Stotfold, Arlesey Road 232; Astwick Road 323, 381; Baldock Road 218; Beverley House 268; Black Lion 218, 232, 233, 287, 293; Brook Street 416; Church Lane 202; Common Road 232; Crown 311, 323, 344; Great North Road 232; High Street 218; Hitchin Road 236, 287, 293, 311; Hospital Road 363; Meadow Way 344; Queen Street 233; Regent Street 232; Three Counties Hospital 13; Wrayfield 417
Stow Longa, Huntingdonshire, Church Farm 320
Sutton, 419; Church Farm 330; Standalone Farm 386

136, 138, 142, 167, 320, 362, 372; *see also* shops
Baldock Urban District Council tenant 225
balls (dances) in Bedford 29, 46
bankruptcy auctions by Peacocks 24, 34–5, 112, 320, 334
Baptist Union Corp. Ltd instruct auction 391
barns auctioned by Peacocks 332, 404
Bedford and District Circular (The) adverts by Peacocks 85; *see also* newspapers
Bedford and District Estate Agents' Association 86–7, 87n.15
Bedford Angling Club instruct auction 324
Bedford Borough Council: housing developer 48, 48n.14, 48n.16, 51; instruct auction 294; *see also* Bedford Corporation
Bedford Corporation: grants Freedom of the Borough 12, 12n.9; instruct auction 289, 290, 349; *see also* Bedford Borough Council
Bedford County Court instruct auction 139, 140
Bedford Property Owners' Protection Society 77n.4
Bedford Regatta 46, 46n.9
Bedfordshire Agricultural Society 28, 95
Bedfordshire and Hertfordshire Branch of the Royal Institution of Chartered Surveyors 95
Bedfordshire and Luton Police Authority instruct auction 345; *see also* Bedfordshire Constabulary
Bedfordshire and Northamptonshire Joint Board for the Mentally Defective instruct auction 166
Bedfordshire Chamber of Agriculture 18, 27, 27n.1, 95
Bedfordshire Constabulary 100; tenant 157; *see also* Bedfordshire and Luton Police Authority
Bedfordshire County Council: instruct auction 67, 124, 313, 316, 333, 372; served by Brian Porter 64; served by Walter Peacock 28
Bedfordshire, Hertfordshire and Huntingdonshire Branch of the Auctioneers' Institute and Provincial Meeting 95
Bedfordshire Journal (The): negotiations regarding advertising rates 86–7; *Peacock Property Gazette* 87; *see also* newspapers
Bedfordshire Light Horse Breeding Society 28; *see also* horses
Bedfordshire Mercury (The) adverts by Peacocks 12–13; *see also* newspapers
Bedfordshire Poultry Society 22n.9; *see also* poultry
Bedfordshire Shire Horse Society 28; *see also* horses
Bedfordshire Standard (The) adverts by Peacocks 84–5; *see also* newspapers
Bedfordshire Times (The): negotiations regarding advertising rates 86–7; *Peacock Property Scene* 87; *see also* newspapers
Bedfordshire Times and Independent (The) adverts by Peacocks 12–13, 37, 76, 84; *see also* newspapers
Bedfordshire War Agricultural Executive Committee land farmed by 228, 236
beer houses auctioned by Peacocks 174, 201; *see also* public houses
bicycles: auctioned by Peacocks 24, 84, 98, 112; in Bedford 17, 45; spare parts auctioned by Peacocks 99; *see also* penny farthing
bidding: buyers' numbers introduced by Peacocks 22; dealers' rings 9, 101; failure to meet reserve price at Peacocks 70; failure to provide deposit to Peacocks 70–1; legal commitment to purchase 40, 65, 70; legislation 9; methods 1, 40; reserve price 39–40; *see also* auction sales; Auctions (Bidding Agreements) Act 1927; Auctions (Bidding Agreements) Act 1969
Biggleswade Rural District Council: instruct auction 352; requisitioned property 233; tenant 209, 234
Biggleswade Urban District Council: served by Brian Porter 64; tenant 209
binoculars auctioned by Peacocks 98
blacksmiths' premises auctioned by Peacocks 143, 247, 248, 263, 295
boating in Bedford 46, 93–4; *see also* Bedford Regatta
Boer War *see* South African War
books: auction sales 2, 4; auctioned by Peacocks 112; shops in Bedford 27; *see also* shops
bottling warehouse auctioned by Peacocks 186
boundary disputes *see* land
brewers instruct auction 316, 347, 358, 373
brickyards: auctioned by Peacocks 139; in Marston Moretaine 48, 48n.17
bridges in Bedford 53
British Railway Board instruct auction 327, 336; *see also* railways
Bromham Church Charity instruct auction 170, 180, 195, 361
Bromham Coal Charity 28n.13
Bromham House Estate 166
Bromham Parish Council 28n.13
'brusseling' *see* farms
builders: in Bedfordshire 51, 55, 56, 105; yards auctioned by Peacocks 259, 302, 345
building land auctioned by Peacocks 66, 69, 120, 124, 131, 134, 138, 143, 147, 149, 151, 153, 156, 157, 158, 160, 163, 166, 170, 172, 175, 176, 180, 186, 187, 188, 189, 190, 191, 194, 195, 211, 216, 218, 220, 224, 225, 232, 273, 274, 289, 291, 300, 306, 313, 317, 318, 319, 324, 325, 326, 327, 328, 329, 330, 331, 332, 335, 337, 338, 339, 340, 341, 342, 343, 344, 346, 347, 351, 352, 354, 355, 356, 357, 358, 359, 367, 373, 374, 376, 381, 382, 383, 384, 385, 389, 390, 391, 395, 396, 397, 398, 399, 340, 341, 342, 403, 405, 406, 407, 409, 411, 413, 415, 419; *see also* land
building materials: auctioned by Peacocks 20, 24, 43, 43n.3, 98, 102, 112; shortages 48
building societies: in Bedford 47; instruct auction 217, 218

bus services in Bedfordshire 45, 85
business premises auctioned by Peacocks 61, 68, 120, 122, 126, 144, 146, 147, 167, 172, 184, 186, 191, 194, 294, 299, 313, 318, 323, 328, 337, 357; *see also* garages; offices; shops
butchers: in Bedford 46; shops auctioned by Peacocks 145, 209, 229, 248, 314; *see also* shops; slaughter house
buyer's premium introduced by Peacocks 59
Bygrave Manor Estate 61–2, 272–4

cabinet makers in Bedford 34, 52
cafes: auctioned by Peacocks 285; in Bedford 31, 285; *see also* restaurants
cake shop in Bedford 33; *see also* shops
Cambridge and Isle of Ely Agricultural Valuers' Association 95
camp sites auctioned by Peacocks 252, 254, 255
caravans: auctioned by Peacocks 253, 265; planning permission for caravan site 348
carriers in Bedfordshire 17, 22
cars: auctioned by Peacocks 20, 98; in Bedford 45; owned by Dudley Peacock 59; spare parts auctioned by Peacocks 102n.13; *see also* vehicles
cattle: auctioned by Peacocks 36; fairs 5–6; market in Baldock 63; market in Bedford 18; market in Biggleswade 63, 63n.10; markets 5–6
Central Association of Agricultural Valuers 95
ceramics auctioned by Peacocks 111–12; *see also* china
chapels: auctioned by Peacocks 359, 406; instruct auction 359; *see also* churches
Charities *see* Bromham Church Charity; Bromham Coal Charity; Charity Commissioners; Christmas Cheer Fund; Dame Ursula Taylor Charity; Eyeworth Charity; Francis Cole Charitable Foundation; Potton Consolidated Charities; Renhold Charity; Robert Lucas Charity; Royal Agricultural Benevolent Institution; Society for Promoting Christian Knowledge
Charity Commissioners instruct auction 131, 132, 269
Chartered Auctioneers' and Estate Agents' Institute: 7, 9, 28, 30, 97; Bedfordshire, Hertfordshire and Huntingdonshire branch 95; *see also* Royal Institution of Chartered Surveyors
Chartered Surveyors professional training 30, 108–9
china: auctioned by Peacocks 35, 35n.33, 37; shops in Bedford 54, 184; *see also* ceramics; shops
Christmas Cheer Fund 28–9
churches: auctioned by Peacocks 388; hall auctioned by Peacocks 361; *see also* Baptist Union Corp. Ltd; chapels; Diocese of St Albans; pews; Sandy Parochial Church Council
cinemas: equipment auctioned by Peacocks 97–8; in Bedford 46
civil engineering equipment auctioned by Peacocks 102n.13
Clapham Lodge Estate 189, 324
clocks auctioned by Peacocks 35, 80
clothing: regulations on second-hand goods 99; shops in Bedford 45–6; *see also* uniforms
cobbler's shop auctioned by Peacocks 297; *see also* shops
coins auctioned by Peacocks 41
collectables auctioned by Peacocks 24, 60, 111–12
College of Estate Management 30, 30n.17
commission charges 40; introduced by Peacocks 58
Compton's Horse *see* 28th (Bedfordshire) Company, Imperial Yeomanry
convalescent home auctioned by Peacocks 388
corn merchants auctioned by Peacocks 145
Corporation of Bedford *see* Bedford Corporation
Councils *see* Baldock Urban District Council; Bedford Borough Council; Bedford Corporation; Bedfordshire County Council; Biggleswade Rural District Council; Biggleswade Urban District Council; Bromham Parish Council; Hitchin Rural District Council; Sandy Town Council; Sandy Urban District Council; Stevington Parish Council
country houses: auction sales 2–4; auctioned by Peacocks 67, 119, 126, 128, 136, 152, 206, 247, 269, 281, 323, 358; contents auctioned by Peacocks 35; demolition of in Bedfordshire 43, 43n.3, 50; for rent in Bedfordshire 16; for sale in Bedfordshire 16, 89n.21
Court of Protection instruct auction 290, 300, 326, 398
cranes auctioned by Peacocks 98–9, 102; *see also* vehicles
Cranfield Estate 52, 68, 221–4
cricket played by Peacocks 92–3
Crown Estate Commissioners instruct auction 363

Dame Ursula Taylor Charity 28n.13
damp 74
dealers' rings *see* bidding
decorator's yard auctioned by Peacocks 359
department stores in Bedford 45; *see also* shops
dinners for Peacocks' staff 94–6
Diocese of St Alban's instruct action 343
domestic staff shortages 43
drapers' shops auctioned by Peacocks 128, 161; *see also* shops
dry rot 74–5
duties *see* taxation

earth closets 14, 50, 155, 201, 206, 252, 283, 289, 291, 307
East of England Show 95

eau-de-Cologne auctioned by Peacocks 99
education *see* schools; Harpur Trust
eggs: auctioned by Peacocks 20, 26, 103; 'candeling' 104; collected for Dr Barnado's 29n.14; packing stations 103–4; quality marks 103; shortages 103; *see also* food
electrical goods auctioned by Peacocks 24, 59, 98, 112
electricity supply in Bedford 15, 15n.30
ephemera auctioned by Peacocks 112
estate agency: boards used by Peacocks 90–1; estate agents in Bedford 17, 30–1, 47; services offered by Peacocks 12, 42, 52, 56; *see also* Bedford and District Estate Agents' Association
Estates Gazette 7
Eyeworth Charity instruct auction 362

farms: accounts dealt with by Peacocks 27; auctioned by Peacocks 69, 119, 123, 124, 125, 135, 139, 142, 144, 151, 152, 154, 160, 170, 176, 179, 181, 182, 185, 191, 198, 199, 207, 208, 209, 219, 220, 224, 227, 228, 236, 237, 238, 249, 265, 272, 281, 283, 291, 303, 305, 309, 310, 312, 313, 316, 318, 320, 323, 324, 325, 326, 327, 330, 332, 333, 334, 335, 336, 337, 345, 346, 348, 357, 358, 359, 360, 362, 364, 375, 385, 386, 391, 392, 398, 404, 406, 408, 418; 'brusseling' 33; deadstock sales by Peacocks 36, 112, 190; livestock sales by Peacocks 36, 190; plans of 33; stocktaking valuations by Peacocks 32; *see also* agriculture; poultry; smallholdings
Fen Reeves: officers 64; common right auctioned by Peacocks 209
ferrets: auctioned by Peacocks 21; owned by Harry Peacock 23, 32
Festival of Britain 1951 boat procession in Bedford 93–4
fire at James Turner & Sons 34
fire engines auctioned by Peacocks 98
First World War: British Farmers' Red Cross Sales 19, 19n.58, 21n.5; effect on auction sales 8, 38; effect on property market in Bedfordshire 42–3, 76–7; requisitioning in Bedford 18, 18n.56, 76–7, 77n.4; surplus military equipment auctioned by Peacocks 19, 19n.63; *see also* Rent Restrictions Acts
fishing plot auctioned by Peacocks 264
fishmonger's shop auctioned by Peacocks 172; *see also* shops
flats: auctioned by Peacocks 159, 213, 219, 220, 233, 244, 247, 255, 258, 260, 262, 264, 266, 299, 301, 315, 319, 329, 338, 344, 349, 353, 377, 382, 413, 416; conversions in houses 49; rented in Bedford 48, 79; *see also* houses
food: effect of imported foods 26, 103; increased demand for 4–5; increased supply of 26; rationing 8; *see also* eggs; fruit; vegetables
Francis Coles Charitable Foundation instruct auction 69
Francklin Estate 68–9, 227–8
fruit: auctioned by Peacocks 26; trees auctioned by Peacocks 35, 236; *see also* nutteries; orchards
furniture: auction sales 2; auctioned by Peacocks 20, 23–4, 35, 37–9, 111–12; fashions in 39; shops in Bedford 34, 46, 55, 105; storage by Peacocks 105; *see also* houses

garages auctioned by Peacocks 142, 164, 269, 278, 288, 323, 332, 335, 343, 360, 414; *see also* petrol station
garden land auctioned by Peacocks 118, 130, 139, 142, 150, 162, 170, 181, 182, 184, 185, 187, 195, 198, 200, 202, 204, 206, 207, 210, 215, 216, 217, 218, 220, 221, 224, 229, 232, 234, 236, 240, 246, 249, 250, 257, 280, 292, 307, 311, 312, 316, 335, 370, 395; *see also* land
gas supply in Bedfordshire 14, 14n.23
glass auctioned by Peacocks 112
granaries auctioned by Peacocks 142, 163
grasskeeping auctioned by Peacocks 323
gravel deposits auctioned by Peacocks 151, 163, 182, 316, 330, 350
grocers: 263; shops auctioned by Peacocks 67, 294; shops in Bedford 46, 101; *see also* shops
guinea pigs auctioned by Peacocks 21–2
guns: auctioned by Peacocks 112; sighting telescopes auctioned by Peacocks 97

hairdressing premises auctioned by Peacocks 314
Harpur Trust 14–17, 20, 27; *see also* schools
Harrold Park Estate 69n.22, 152
haulage contractors' yard auctioned by Peacocks 339, 345
Hertfordshire, Bedfordshire and Buckinghamshire Agricultural Valuers Association 95
High Sheriff of Bedfordshire 64, 95
Highland Division 18, 18n.56, 76; *see also* First World War
Hitchin Rural District Council requisitioned property 272, 273, 274
horses: auctioned by Peacocks 19, 20, 36, 84; fairs 5; *see also* Bedfordshire Light Horse Breeding Society; Bedfordshire Shire Horse Society
horticultural land auctioned by Peacocks 352, 356; *see also* land
hotels: auction venues 68–9; auctioned by Peacocks 411
house longhorn beetle 75
houses: auction sales 65, 70; auction sales by Peacocks 65–7, 116–419 *passim*; clearances 40; contents auctioned by Peacocks 35, 35n.35, 40, 69, 155, 158, 163, 164, 165, 168, 171, 175, 179, 180, 187, 199, 203, 206, 209, 215, 218, 225, 229, 230, 236, 240, 244, 247, 256, 257, 262, 278, 290, 294, 296, 298, 300, 305, 308, 310, 326; heating 14–15, 49, 81; lighting 14–15, 49, 80; outside effects auctioned by Peacocks 172; prices in Bedford

14–15, 49, 49n.18–22, 51, 51n.29, 85; rented in Bedford 13–15, 48, 76, 78–80; rented in villages 14, 80–1; sales in Bedford 47–9; surveys of 73–5; water supply 14, 49, 80, 81; unfit for habitation in Bedford 47, 47n.11; upper class accommodation in Bedford 14–15; working class accommodation in Bedford 14; *see also* country houses; flats; housing development; property market
housing development: in Bedford 13, 47–8, 48n.13–16, 51, 51n.27–8; in Harrold 50
huts auctioned by Peacocks 102

Illustrated Property Register *see* Peacocks
immigration effect on Peacocks 22
industrial land auctioned by Peacocks 392; *see also* land
Instruction Books *see* Peacocks
ironmongers in Bedford 17, 46; *see also* shops

jeeps auctioned by Peacocks 98; *see also* vehicles
jewellery: auctioned by Peacocks 111–12; shops in Bedford 17; *see also* shops

Kimbolton Estate 70, 378–80

land: agents 6; auction sales 7–8; auctioned by Peacocks 117–419 *passim*; boundary disputes undertaken by Peacocks 72–3; surveys 72; *see also* accommodation land; agricultural land; allotments; amenity land; arable land; building land; garden land; grasskeeping; horticultural land; industrial land; market garden land; meadows; paddocks; pastures; spinney; Town and Country Planning Act 1947; water meadow; woodlands
laundries: auctioned by Peacocks 146; in Bedford 67, 119, 142
livestock: auction sales 5–8; auctioned by F. W. Western & Co. 63; *see also* cattle; ferrets; guinea pigs; horses; pigs; poultry; rabbits; sheep
Livestock Auctioneers Pool Committee 8
London College tenant 122

machinery auctioned by Peacocks 102n.13
manors: Blunham 119; Colworth, Lordship of 335
maps auctioned by Peacocks 112; *see also* Ordnance Survey
marina auctioned by Peacocks 401, 402, 403
market garden land auctioned by Peacocks 123, 208, 288, 298, 308, 319, 324, 341, 344, 346, 355, 356, 358, 359, 360, 363, 364, 365, 368, 369, 386; *see also* land
meadows auctioned by Peacocks 218, 305, 402; *see also* accommodation land; land; paddocks; pasture
Medland Estate 118
memorabilia auctioned by Peacocks 112
Mid Bedfordshire District Council instruct auction 363, 378, 391, 397
Midland Counties Agricultural Valuers Association 95
mills auctioned by Peacocks 66, 117, 163, 264, 326, 365
mining equipment auctioned by Peacocks 102n.13
Ministry of Agriculture, Fisheries and Food instruct auction 313, 362
Ministry of Defence 8; instruct auction 335, 357, 366
Ministry of Food 103
Ministry of Health: instruct auction 329; requisitioned property 248, 258
Ministry of Supply instruct auction 97
Ministry of Transport instruct auction 297
Ministry of Works requisitioned property 228
moats in Bedfordshire 67, 124, 135, 140, 187
motorcycles: auctioned by Peacocks 24, 98; shop in Bedford 53; *see also* shops; vehicles
motors (electric) auctioned by Peacocks 97–8
music shop auctioned by Peacocks 230; *see also* shops

National Fire Service tenant 220
newspapers: in Bedford 17, 86, 88; use by auction houses 7; use by estate agents 85–6; *see also Bedford and District Circular (The)*; *Bedfordshire Journal (The)*; *Bedfordshire Mercury (The)*; *Bedfordshire Standard (The)*; *Bedfordshire Times (The); Bedfordshire Times and Independent (The)*; *Times (The)*
night club contents auctioned by Peacocks 36
Norris Estate 118
nurseries auctioned by Peacocks 153, 157, 254, 280, 281, 302, 311, 364, 384, 402; in Bedford 48, 48n.15
nutteries auctioned by Peacocks 67, 123, 124; *see also* fruit; orchards

Oakley Hunt: administration of 29; instruct auction 237
OBE awarded to Robert Peacock 95
offices auctioned by Peacocks 116, 254, 323, 338, 340, 349, 351, 354, 370, 380; *see also* business premises
Old English Fair 1936 in Bedford 93
optical equipment auctioned by Peacocks 98
orchards auctioned by Peacocks 67, 119, 123, 132, 158, 172, 195, 199, 209, 236, 250, 259, 269, 290, 292, 300, 394, 418; see also fruit; nutteries
Ordnance Survey maps of Bedfordshire 33
osier beds auctioned by Peacocks 160, 162

paddocks auctioned by Peacocks 120, 123, 125, 138, 148, 149, 154, 158, 163, 170, 172, 188, 204, 209, 231, 240, 248, 253, 257, 265, 284, 317, 367, 376, 381, 418; *see also* accommodation land; land; meadows; pasture
Panacea Society 10, 111
parachutes auctioned by Peacocks 98

valuation services offered by Peacocks 40
valuers' associations: served by Robert Peacock 95; served by Dudley Peacock 95
vegetables auctioned by Peacocks 26; *see also* food
vehicles: auctioned by Peacocks 20, 36, 84, 97–8, 101–2, 112, Plate 10; depot auctioned by Peacocks 345; parts auctioned by Peacocks 102; *see also* aircraft; airships; amphibious vehicles; bicycles; cars; cranes; jeeps; motorcycles; petrol tankers; prime movers; road rollers; tank transporters; trailers; trains; trucks

War Department: requisitioned property 133, 227, 233; *see also* Ministry of Defence
warehouses auctioned by Peacocks 124
water meadow auctioned by Peacocks 175; *see also* land; meadows
water supply in Bedfordshire 14, 14n.22, 50; *see also* standpipes, wells
wells 14, 50, 118, 120, 133, 154, 155, 161, 166, 206, 283; *see also* artesian well; standpipes; water supply
wet rot 74
Whitbread Estate 11, 11n.2
Wilden Charity 11
windmills auctioned by Peacocks 199, 210
wine auctioned by Peacocks 35–6
Wingfield Estate 11, 11n.2
woodlands auctioned by Peacocks 141, 191, 199, 207, 220, 343, 347, 355, 357; *see also* land
woodworm 74
workshops auctioned by Peacocks 152, 159, 193, 200, 215, 234, 240, 245, 338, 339, 360, 364, 370, 379; *see also* business premises
Wyman Estate 156